新국제법판례
· 120선 ·

정인섭 · 이재민 · 정서용

박영사

머 리 말

이 책은 2008년 초판 이후 2016년 제4 개정판까지 발행한 「국제법 판례 100선」의 후속편이다. 기존 책자의 제목은 판례 100선이었지만 이미 초판부터 100건이 넘는 판례를 수록하고 있었는데, 이번 신판에서도 분량이 조금 더 늘자 이 기회에 제목을 「신국제법 판례 120선」으로 현실화했다. 20개 장 분류와 내용 구성방식은 기존 100선의 경우와 동일하다. 지난 제4판과 비교할 때 17건의 판례가 추가되고, 9건이 삭제되었다. 유지된 판례의 경우도 영문 발췌문의 부분적 변경이나 해설 원고의 수정이 적지 않았다. 신간의 형식을 취하고 있으나, 실질적으로는 제5 개정판에 해당하는 셈이다.

법학의 학습과정에서 판례의 중요성은 아무리 강조해도 지나침이 없으며, 국제법 분야 역시 예외가 아니다. 중앙집권적 입법기관이 없는 국제법 분야는 법의 발견, 해석, 적용 과정에서 판례가 한층 더 중요한 역할을 한다. 판례 학습 없이는 진정한 국제법의 공부가 불가능하다고 말해도 과언이 아니다. 이 책자는 국내에서 국제법 강의와 학습에 조금이라도 도움이 되려는 취지에서 시작되었다. 2008년 「국제법 판례 100선」 초판을 발간했을 때는 이 책자가 이렇게 독자의 호응을 받고, 긴 수명을 가지리라고는 솔직히 예상 못했다. 독자의 호응에 힘입어 10년이 넘도록 개정과 보완을 계속할 수 있었다.

신간의 형식으로 제작되었기에 이 책자가 만들어진 경과를 잠시 소개한다. 이 책의 초판은 서울대학교 정인섭, 고려대학교 정서용, 한양대학교 이재민(현 서울대학교) 3인의 협업으로 만들어졌다. 국제법 판례는 내용 요지의 암기만으로는 제대로 된 학습이 불가능하고, 판결문의 번역은 엄청난 수고에 비해 이를 통한 법리 이해에는 한계가 있다. 이에 고심 끝에 판결문의 주요 내용은 영문으로 발췌하고, 기본적인 내용은 우리말로 설명하는 현재와 같은 체제를 고안해 냈다. 총 20개장으로 구성된 책자의 2008년 초판과 2010년 제2판은 정인섭이 10개장, 정서용이 6개장, 이재민이 4개장의 집필을 담당했다. 2012년 간행된 제3판부터는 정서용이 개정작업에 참여하지 않고, 그 부분은 정인섭이 이어받아 정인섭이 16개장, 이재민이 4개장의 개편을 담당했다. 이번 120선 책자 역시 정인섭이 15개장, 이재민이 5개장의 집필과 개정을 담당했다. 이재민이 담당한 부분은 제8장 국가의 대외기관, 제13장 국제환경법, 제16장 국제형사법, 제17장 국제경제법, 제19장 국제사회의 평화와 안전보장이며, 나머지 부분은 정인섭이 전담했다. 내용에 관해서는 해당 필자가 최종적인 책임을 진다. 이 책자에 수록된 120건 정도의 국제법 판례를 학습하면 통상적인 국제법 교과서에 공통적으로 등장하는 주요 판례는 대부분 커버될 것으로 기대한다.

　　필자들로서는 좀 더 알찬 내용의 국제법 판례집을 내려고 노력하고 있지만, 독자의 눈에는 어떻게 비추어질지 늘 걱정이 앞선다. 아직도 미흡한 부분이 적지 않으리라 생각하지만, 독자 여러 분의 많은 성원을 바란다. 아울러 내용상 수정이 필요한 부분이나 오탈자가 발견되면 후일의 개정을 위해 각 담당필자에게 연락을 요망한다.

　　이번에 제작과정에서는 박영사 김선민 이사의 노고가 특히 컸다. 구 판례 100선을 제작하던 출판 프로그램을 이번에 변경하게 되어 특히 작업량이 많았는데, 국영문 혼합의 어려운 편집을 깔끔히 마무리해 주었다. 아울러 박영사의 여러 관계자들의 도움 없이는 이 작업이 쉽게 마무리 되지 못했을 것이다. 모든 담당자들에게 감사한다. 코로나로 인한 미증유의 사태를 모두 잘 극복하기를 희망한다.

2020년 9월 1일

집필자를 대표하여

정인섭

차 례

제 1 장

국제법의 법원

1. 북해대륙붕 사건(1969)
— 관습국제법의 성립요건

North Sea Continental Shelf.
Federal Republic of Germany/Denmark; Federal Republic of Germany/Netherlands, 1969 ICJ Reports 3.

☑ 사 안

이 사건은 독일과 네덜란드 및 독일과 덴마크 사이의 대륙붕 경계획정에 관한 분쟁이다. 네덜란드, 독일, 덴마크는 유럽대륙에서 나란히 북해를 면하고 있는 인접국들이다. 네덜란드와 덴마크의 해안선은 북해를 향해 돌출적인 형상을 띠고 있으나, 독일의 해안선은 오목하게 안으로 굽어 있다(본서 p. 8 지도 참조). 이와 같은 해안선의 형태로 인해 등거리선 원칙을 적용하면 독일은 해안선의 길이나 육지영토의 크기에 비하여 대륙붕 경계획정에서 크게 불리했다.

1958년 제1차 UN 해양법회의 결과 채택된 「대륙붕 협약」 제6조는 당사국간 합의가 없는 경우 다른 특별한 사정이 없다면 경계선은 중간선·등거리선에 의한다고 규정하고 있었다. 이 협약의 당사국인 네덜란드와 덴마크는 독일과의 대륙붕 경계가 등거리선에 의해 획정되어야 한다고 주장했다. 반면 협약 비당사국인 독일은 이에 반대하며, 정당하고 형평한 배분원칙을 주장했다. 네덜란드와 덴마크는 등거리선 원칙이 관습국제법에 해당하므로 독일도 이에 구속된다고 반박했다. 결국 3국은 협상 끝에 ICJ에 북해 대륙붕의 경계선 획정시 적용될 수 있는 국제법 원칙을 제시해 달라는 소송을 제기하기로 합의했다. 재판과정에서는 등거리선 원칙이 대륙붕 경계획정에 관한 관습국제법에 해당하느냐 여부가 주요 쟁점으로 제기되었다.

☑ 쟁 점

판습국세법의 성립 요건.

☑ 판 결

조약의 특정조항이 관습국제법화되었다고 판단되기 위하여는 ⅰ) 해당 조항이 근본적으로 규범창출적 성격을 지녀야 하며, ⅱ) 이에 의해 이해관계가 특별히 영향받는 국가를 포함하는 매우 폭넓은 그리고 대표적인 국가의 참여가 있어야 하며, ⅲ) 국가의 관행이 광범위하고 실질적으로 일관되어야 하며, ⅳ) 그러한 관행이 법적 의무라는 판단 하에서 실행되었어야 한다.

판 결 문

70. The Court must now proceed to the last stage in the argument put forward on behalf of Denmark and the Netherlands. This is to the effect that even if there was at the date of the Geneva Convention no rule of customary international law in favour of the equidistance principle, and no such rule was crystallized in Article 6 of the Convention, nevertheless such a rule has come into being since the Convention, partly because of its own impact, partly on the basis of subsequent State practice,—and that this rule, being now a rule of customary international law binding on all States, including therefore the Federal Republic, should be declared applicable to the delimitation of the boundaries between the Parties' respective continental shelf areas in the North Sea.

71. In so far as this contention is based on the view that Article 6 of the Convention has had the influence, and has produced the effect, described, it clearly involves treating that Article as a norm-creating provision which has constituted the foundation of, or has generated a rule which, while only conventional or contractual in its origin, has since passed into the general *corpus* of international law, and is now accepted as such by the *opinio juris*, so as to have become binding even for countries which have never, and do not, become parties to the Convention. There is no doubt that this process is a perfectly possible one and does from time to time occur: it constitutes indeed one of the recognized methods by which new rules of customary international law may be formed. At the same time this result is not lightly to be regarded as having been attained.

72. It would in the first place be necessary that the provision concerned should, at all events potentially, be of a fundamentally norm-creating character such as could be regarded as forming the basis of a general rule of law. Considered *in abstracto* the equidistance principle might be said to fulfil this requirement. Yet in the particular form in which it is embodied in Article 6 of the Geneva Convention, and having regard to the relationship of that Article to other provisions of the Convention, this must be open to some doubt. In the first place, Article 6 is so framed as to put second the obligation to make use of the equidistance method, causing it to come after a primary obligation to effect delimitation by agreement. Such a primary obligation constitutes an unusual preface to what is claimed to be a potential general rule of law. Without attempting to enter into, still less pronounce upon any question of *jus cogens*, it is well understood that, in practice, rules of international law can, by agreement, be derogated from in particular cases, or as between particular parties,—but this is not normally the subject of any express provision, as it is in Article 6 of the Geneva Convention. Secondly the part played by the notion of special circumstances relative to the principle of equidistance as embodied in Article 6, and the very considerable, still unresolved controversies as to the exact meaning and scope of this notion, must raise further doubts as to the potentially norm-creating character of the rule. Finally, the faculty of making reservations to Article 6, while it might not of itself prevent the equidistance principle being eventually received as general law, does add considerably to the difficulty of regarding this result as having been brought about (or being potentially possible) on the basis of the Convention: for so long as this faculty continues to exist, and is not the subject of any revision brought about in consequence of a request made under Article 13 of the Convention—of which there is at present no official indication—it is the Convention itself which would, for the reasons already indicated, seem to deny to the provisions of Article 6 the same norm-creating character as, for instance, Articles 1 and 2 possess.

73. With respect to the other elements usually regarded as necessary before a conventional rule can be considered to have become a general rule of international law, it might be that, even without the passage of any considerable period of time, a very widespread and representative participation in the convention might suffice of itself, provided it included that of States whose interests were specially affected. In the present case however, the Court notes that, even if allowance is made for the existence of a number of States to whom participation in the Geneva Convention is not open, or which, by reason for instance of being land-locked States, would have no interest in becoming parties to it, the number of ratifications and accessions so far secured is, though respectable, hardly sufficient. That non-ratification may sometimes be due to factors other than active disapproval of the convention concerned can hardly constitute a basis on which positive acceptance of its principles can be implied: the reasons are speculative, but the facts remain.

74. As regards the time element, the Court notes that it is over ten years since the Convention was signed, but that it is even now less than five since it came into force in June 1964, and that when the present proceedings were brought it was less than three years, while less than one had elapsed at the time when the respective negotiations between the Federal Republic and the other two Parties for a complete delimitation broke down on the question of the application of the equidistance principle. Although the passage of only a short period of time is not necessarily, or of itself, a bar to the formation of a new rule of customary international law on the basis of what was originally a purely conventional rule, an indispensable requirement would be that within the period in question, short though it might be, State practice, including that of States whose interests are specially affected, should have been both extensive and virtually uniform in the sense of the provision invoked; and should moreover have occurred in such a way as to show a general recognition that a rule of law or legal obligation is involved.

75. The Court must now consider whether State practice in the matter of continental shelf delimitation has, subsequent to the Geneva Convention, been of such a kind as to satisfy this requirement. Leaving aside cases which, for various reasons, the Court does not consider to be reliable guides as precedents, such as delimitations effected between the present Parties themselves, or not relating to international boundaries, some fifteen cases have been cited in the course of the present proceedings, occurring mostly since the signature of the 1958 Geneva Convention, in which continental shelf boundaries have been delimited according to the equidistance principle—in the majority of the cases by agreement, in a few others unilaterally—or else the delimitation was foreshadowed but has not yet been carried out. Amongst these fifteen are the four North Sea delimitations United Kingdom/ Norway-Denmark-Netherlands, and Norway/ Denmark already mentioned in paragraph 4 of this Judgment. But even if these various cases constituted more than a very small proportion of those potentially calling for delimitation in the world as a whole, the Court would not think it necessary to enumerate or evaluate them separately, since there are, *a priori*, several grounds which deprive them of

weight as precedents in the present context.

76. To begin with, over half the States concerned, whether acting unilaterally or conjointly, were or shortly became parties to the Geneva Convention, and were therefore presumably, so far as they were concerned, acting actually or potentially in the application of the Convention. From their action no inference could legitimately be drawn as to the existence of a rule of customary international law in favour of the equidistance principle. As regards those States, on the other hand, which were not, and have not become parties to the Convention, the basis of their action can only be problematical and must remain entirely speculative. Clearly, they were not applying the Convention. But from that no inference could justifiably be drawn that they believed themselves to be applying a mandatory rule of customary international law. There is not a shred of evidence that they did and, as has been seen (paragraphs 22 and 23), there is no lack of other reasons for using the equidistance method, so that acting, or agreeing to act in a certain way, does not of itself demonstrate anything of a juridical nature.

77. The essential point in this connection—and it seems necessary to stress it —is that even if these instances of action by non-parties to the Convention were much more numerous than they in fact are, they would not, even in the aggregate, suffice in themselves to constitute the *opinio juris*; for, in order to achieve this result, two conditions must be fulfilled. Not only must the acts concerned amount to a settled practice, but they must also be such, or be carried out in such a way, as to be evidence of a belief that this practice is rendered obligatory by the existence of a rule of law requiring it. The need for such a belief, i.e., the existence of a subjective element, is implicit in the very notion of the *opinio juris sive necessitatis*. The States concerned must therefore feel that they are conforming to what amounts to a legal obligation. The frequency, or even habitual character of the acts is not in itself enough. There are many international acts, e.g., in the field of ceremonial and protocol, which are performed almost invariably, but which are motivated only by considerations of courtesy, convenience or tradition, and not by any sense of legal duty. […]

81. The Court accordingly concludes that if the Geneva Convention was not in its origins or inception declaratory of a mandatory rule of customary international law enjoining the use of the equidistance principle for the delimitation of continental shelf areas between adjacent States, neither has its subsequent effect been constitutive of such a rule; and that State practice up-to-date has equally been insufficient for the purpose.

☑ 해 설

이 판결은 대륙붕 경계획정을 주 사안으로 하고 있으나, 학계에서는 관습국제법의 성립요건을 설명해 주는 전형적인 판례로 많이 활용된다. 즉 이 판결이 설명하고 있는 관습국제법의 성립과정은 국제법학계의 일반적 이해와 일치하며, 여기서 제시된 판단기준은 다른 사례에서도 관습국제법의 성립 여부 결정에 유용하게 이용될 수 있다.

독일은 북해에 면한 해안이 오목하게 들어간 형상이라 등거리선·중간선 원칙에 따라 해양경계를 획정하면 지도의 A−B−E−D−C를 이은 비교적 좁은 대륙붕만을 확보할 수 있고, 육지는 서로 떨어진 네덜란드와 덴마크의 대륙붕이 E−F 선에서 접하게 된다. 이에 독일은 등거리선·중간선 원칙의 적용에 반대했다.

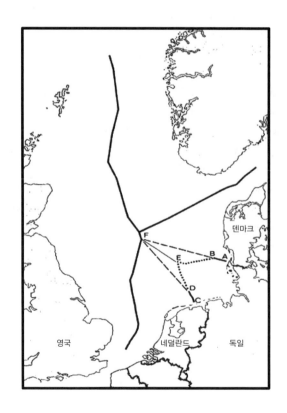

이 사건의 당사국들은 ICJ에 대하여 3국간 대륙붕의 구체적인 경계를 획정해 달라고 요청하지는 않았으며, 단지 경계획정에 적용될 법원칙만을 제시해 달라고 요청했다.

ICJ는 1958년 제네바 대륙붕 협약에 규정된 등거리선 원칙의 법적 성격을 면밀히 검토한 끝에 이 원칙이 관습국제법에 해당하지 않는다고 판단했다. 재판부는 인접국간 대륙붕에 관하여는 형평의 원칙에 입각한 당사국간 합의에 기해 경계가 획정되어야 한다고 제시했다. 또한 대륙붕은 육지의 자연적 연장이어야 하며, 타국의 자연적 연장을 침해하지 말아야 한다고 보았다. 이어 형평의 원칙을 달성하기 위해서는 경계획정시 해안선의 일반적 형상, 특별한 사정의 존재 여부, 대륙붕의 외형적 및 지질학적 구조와 천연자원의 존재, 연안선의 길이 등이 고려되어야 한다고 제시했다.

이러한 판단은 독일측에 유리한 결과가 되었다. 후일 3국은 대륙붕 경계에 관한 협상을 재개해 등거리선 원칙을 적용한 결과보다는 독일측 대륙붕이 대폭 확대된 경계획정에 합의했다. 즉 독일의 대륙붕은 F지점까지 도달해 영국의 대륙붕과 직접 면하고, 네덜란드와 덴마크의 대륙붕은 서로 분리되었다.

이 판결문을 면밀히 검토하면 ICJ는 관습국제법을 확인하기 위하여 각국의 실행을 먼저 검토하고 이어서 그러한 실행이 법적 확신을 수반하고 있는가를 판단하고 있음을 발견하게 된다. 그러나 아래의 Military and Para-military Activities in and against Nicaragua(Merits)(1986 ICJ Reports 14) 판결에서 ICJ는 무력 불행사와 불간섭의무 원칙에 대한 법적 확신을 먼저 확인하고, 이러한 인식이 관행에 의해 확인되어야 한다고 판단한 점에서 관습국제법의 성립요건을 검토하는 순서에서 차이를 보이고 있다.

184. The Court notes that there is in fact evidence, to be examined below, of a considerable degree of agreement between the Parties as to the content of the customary international law relating to the non-use of force and non-intervention. This concurrence of their views does not however dispense the Court from having itself to ascertain what rules of customary international law are applicable. The mere fact that States declare their recognition of certain rules is not sufficient for the Court to consider these as being part of customary international law, and as applicable as such to those States. Bound as it is by Article 38 of its Statute to apply, *inter alia*, international custom 'as evidence of a general practice accepted as law', the Court may not disregard the essential role played by general practice. Where two States agree to incorporate a particular rule in a treaty, their agreement suffices to make that rule a legal one, binding upon them; but in the field of customary international law, the shared view of the Parties as to the content of what they regard as the rule is not enough. The Court must satisfy itself that the existence of the rule in the *opinio juris* of States is confirmed by practice. [⋯]

186. It is not to be expected that in the practice of States the application of the rules in question should have been perfect, in the sense that States should have refrained, with complete consistency, from the use of force or from intervention in each other's internal affairs. The Court does not consider that, for a rule to be established as customary, the corresponding practice must be in absolutely rigorous conformity with the rule. In order to deduce the existence of customary rules, the Court deems it sufficient that the conduct of States should, in general, be consistent with such rules, and that instances of State conduct inconsistent with a given rule should generally have been treated as breaches of that rule, not as indications of the recognition of a new rule. If a State acts in a way *prima facie* incompatible with a recognized rule, but defends its conduct by appealing to exceptions or justifications contained within the rule itself, then whether or not the State's conduct is in fact justifiable on that basis, the significance of that attitude is to confirm rather than to weaken the rule.

▶ 참고문헌 ────────────────────────────

- 전순신, 북해대륙붕 사건, 동아법학 7집(1988), p. 173.
- 최홍배, ICJ의 북해대륙붕사건에 대한 판례연구, 해사법연구 12권 1호(2000), p. 187.
- E. Grisel, The Lateral Boundaries of the Continental Shelf and the Judgement of the International Court of Justice in the North Sea Continental Shelf Cases, AJIL Vol. 64(1970), p. 562.

2. 인도령 통행권 사건(1960)
― 지역 관습국제법

Case concerning Right of Passage over Indian Territory(Merits).
Portugal v. India, 1960 ICJ Reports 6.

☑ 사   안

포르투갈은 16세기 초부터 인도로 진출하여 남부 연안 Goa, Daman, Diu 지역과 내륙 위요지인 Dadra, Nagar-Aveli를 식민지로 지배하고 있었다. 포르투갈은 Daman 등의 연안 도시로부터 내륙 위요지를 출입하기 위해서는 영국령 지역을 반드시 통과해야만 했다. 식민기간 중 포르투갈은 이들 지역을 관행적으로 통과해 왔다.

1947년 인도가 영국으로부터 독립한 이후에도 포르투갈은 이 지역을 식민지로 고수하며, 인도의 반환 요구에 응하지 않았다. 인도는 포르투갈에 대한 압박책으로 1953년부터 위 지역 상호간의 육로통행을 제한했다. 1954년 7월에는 인도의 민족주의 단체들이 Dadra와 Nagar-Aveli를 점령했다. 포르투갈은 Dadra에는 군대를, Nagar-Aveli에는 진상 파악을 위한 관리를 파견하기 위해 이들 지역으로 접근할 수 있는 인접 인도 영토의 통과를 요구했으나, 인도는 포르투갈측의 통행을 금지시켰다. 포르투갈은 자국 영역에 접근하는 데 필요한 인도 영토를 통행할 권리가 있다고 주장하며, 이 사건을 ICJ로 제소했다. 재판과정에서 인도-포르투갈 2개국 사이에서도 지역 관습국제법이 성립될 수 있는가 여부가 쟁점의 하나로 제기되었다.

☑ 쟁   점

포르투갈은 인도내 자국령을 연결하기 위해 인접 인도령을 통과할 권리가 있는가?—지역관습법의 성립 여부.

☑ 판 결

2개국 간에도 지역 관습국제법이 성립할 수 있으며, 포르투갈의 민간인, 공무원, 일반 물품이 이 지역 인도령을 통과할 수 있는 관습국제법상의 권리가 확립되어 있다.

판 결 문

(p. 39-) For the purpose of determining whether Portugal has established the right of passage claimed by it, the Court must have regard to what happened during the British and post-British periods. During these periods, there had developed between the Portuguese and the territorial sovereign with regard to passage to the enclaves a practice upon which Portugal relies for the purpose of establishing the right of passage claimed by it.

With regard to Portugal's claim of a right of passage as formulated by it on the basis of local custom, it is objected on behalf of India that no local custom could be established between only two States. It is difficult to see why the number of States between which a local custom may be established on the basis of long practice must necessarily be larger than two. The Court sees no reason why long continued practice between two States accepted by them as regulating their relations should not form the basis of mutual rights and obligations between the two States.

As already stated, Portugal claims a right of passage to the extent necessary for the exercise of its sovereignty over the enclaves, without any immunity and subject to the regulation and control of India. In the course of the written and oral proceedings, the existence of the right was discussed with reference to the different categories making up the right, namely private persons, civil officials, goods in general, armed forces, armed police, and arms and ammunition. The Court will proceed to examine whether such a right as is claimed by Portugal is established on the basis of the practice that prevailed between the Parties during the British and post-British periods in respect of each of these categories.

It is common ground between the Parties that the passage of private persons and civil officials was not subject to any restrictions, beyond routine control, during these periods. There is nothing on the record to indicate the contrary.

Goods in general, that is to say, all merchandise other than arms and ammunition, also passed freely between Daman and the enclaves during the periods in question, subject only, at certain times, to customs regulations and such regulation and control as were necessitated by considerations of security or revenue. The general prohibition of the transit of goods during the Second World War and prohibitions imposed upon the transit of salt and, on certain occasions, upon that of liquor and materials for the distillation of liquor, were specific measures necessitated by the considerations just referred to. The scope and purpose of each prohibition were clearly defined. In all other cases the passage of goods was free. No authorization or licence was required.

The Court, therefore, concludes that, with regard to private persons, civil officials and goods in general there existed during the British and post-British periods a constant and uniform practice allowing free passage between Daman and the enclaves. This practice having continued over a period extending beyond a century and a quarter unaffected by the change of regime in respect of the intervening territory which occurred when India became independent, the Court is, in view of all the circumstances of the case, satisfied that that practice was accepted as law by the Parties and has given rise to a right and a correlative obligation.

The Court therefore holds that Portugal had in 1954 a right of passage over intervening Indian territory between coastal Daman and the enclaves and between the enclaves, in respect of private persons, civil officials and goods in general, to the extent necessary, as claimed by Portugal, for the exercise of its sovereignty over the enclaves, and subject to the regulation and control of India. [···]

Where therefore the Court finds a practice clearly established between two States which was accepted by the Parties as governing the relations between them, the Court must attribute decisive effect to that practice for the purpose of determining their specific rights and obligations. Such a particular practice must prevail over any general rules.

☑ 해   설

ICJ는 판결에서 2개국간에도 지역 관습국제법이 성립할 수 있으며, 그 성립요건은 일반 관습국제법의 경우와 동일하다고 판시했다. 구체적으로 영국 식민지 시절과 인도 독립 이후까지 1세기를 훨씬 넘는 장기간의 관행을 바탕으로 포르투갈의 민간인과 일반물자는 인도령을 통행할 법적 권리가 확립되어 있다고 판단했다(재판관 11 : 4의 판결). 다만 군인, 경찰, 군수물자의 이 지역 통과에 관하여는 과거에도 사전허가제가 적용되었으므로 포르투갈의 주장과는 달리 통행권이 관습법상의 권리로 확립되지 못했다고 판단했다 (8 : 7의 판결). 그러나 결론에서는 9 : 6의 판결로 당시 문제의 지역은 인도의 민족주의적 단체들에 의해 점거되는 등 긴장관계가 벌어진 특수한 상황이었으므로 인도가 민간인이나 일반 물자에 대해 포르투갈 측의 통행을 제한한 조치가 국제법 위반은 아니었다고 판단했다.

한편 Quintana 판사는 포르투갈의 통행권을 입증할 결정적 근거는 없으며, 포르투갈측 주장의 인정은 유엔 헌장 시대에도 식민지제도의 존속을 함의한다며 반대의견을 첨부했다.

이 판결 외에도 지역관습법의 존재를 긍정한 대표적인 판례로는 비호권 사건(Colombian－Peruvian Asylum case (Colombia/Peru), 1950 ICJ Reports 266, p. 276)이 있다(본서 p. 227 이하 참조). 다만 이 판결에서 ICJ는 콜롬비아가 주장한 것과 같은 지역관습법은 성립되지 않았거나 최소한 페루에 대하여는 주장할 수 없다고 판단했다. 한편 Dispute regarding Navigational and Relagted Rights, Costa Rica v. Nicaragua, 2009 ICJ Reports 213, para. 141－144에서도 지역관습법의 존재가 인정되었다.

한편 인도는 1961년 12월 자국내 포르투갈령을 무력을 통해 모두 회복했다. 이에 불복하던 포르투갈은 1974년에야 고아에 대한 인도의 주권을 인정했다.

▶ 참고문헌 ─────────────────────────────────

- F. Krenz, International Enclaves and Rights of Passage(1961).
- E. Lauterphact, International Court of Justice, Case concerning Right of Passage over Indian Territory, ICLQ Vol. 7(1958), p. 593.

3. 프랑스 핵실험 사건(1974)
— 일방적 행위의 구속력

Nuclear Tests Case.
Australia v. France, 1974 ICJ Reports 253.

☑ 사 　 안

프랑스는 1960년대 후반부터 프랑스령 남태평양 수역에서 대기권 내 핵실험을 실시했다. 인접 오스트레일리아와 뉴질랜드는 이에 강력히 항의하며, 프랑스의 대기권 내 핵실험을 중단하라고 요구했다. 외교협상이 제대로 진척되지 않자, 결국 오스트레일리아와 뉴질랜드는 남태평양 수역에서의 프랑스의 핵실험이 국제법 위반임을 선언하고, 프랑스는 향후 더 이상의 핵실험을 실시하지 말라고 명령해 달라는 소송을 ICJ에 각각 제소했다. 아울러 최종판결 이전에 프랑스가 더 이상의 핵실험을 실시하지 말라는 잠정조치를 내려달라고 요청했다. 반면 프랑스는 이 사건에 대한 ICJ의 관할권 성립을 부인하며, 일체의 소송 절차에 참여하지 않았다. 그러면서도 프랑스의 대통령과 국방장관 등은 1974년까지 계획된 핵실험만 실시하면 더 이상의 대기권 내 실험을 수행하지 않겠다고 여러 차례 발표했다. 아래는 오스트레일리아의 제소에 대한 판결문에서 발췌한 부분이다.

☑ 쟁 　 점

국가의 일방적 선언의 법적 구속력 여부.

☑ 판 　 결

일방적 선언이라도 이를 준수할 의도하에서 발표되었다면 당사국은 이에 법적으로 구속되며, 그 같은 의도는 당사국 행위의 내용을 통해 확인될 수 있다.

판 결 문

43. It is well recognized that declarations made by way of unilateral acts, concerning legal or factual situations, may have the effect of creating legal obligations. Declarations of this kind may be, and often are, very specific. When it is the intention of the State making the declaration that it should become bound according to its terms, that intention confers on the declaration the character of a legal undertaking, the State being thenceforth legally required to follow a course of conduct consistent with the declaration. An undertaking of this kind, if given publicly, and with an intent to be bound, even though not made within the context of international negotiations, is binding. In these circumstances, nothing in the nature of a *quid pro quo*[1] nor any subsequent acceptance of the declaration, nor even any reply or reaction from other States, is required for the declaration to take effect, since such a requirement would be inconsistent with the strictly unilateral nature of the juridical act by which the pronouncement by the State was made.

44. Of course, not all unilateral acts imply obligation; but a State may choose to take up a certain position in relation to a particular matter with the intention of being bound—the intention is to be ascertained by interpretation of the act. When States make statements by which their freedom of action is to be limited, a restrictive interpretation is called for.

45. With regard to the question of form, it should be observed that this is not a domain in which international law imposes any special or strict requirements. Whether a statement is made orally or in writing makes no essential difference, for such statements made in particular circumstances may create commitments in international law, which does not require that they should be couched in written form. Thus the question of form is not decisive. [⋯]

46. One of the basic principles governing the creation and performance of legal obligations, whatever their source, is the principle of good faith. Trust and confidence are inherent in international co-operation, in particular in an age when this co-operation in many fields is becoming increasingly essential. Just as the very

---

1) give and take — 필자 주.

rule of *pacta sunt servanda*[2] in the law of treaties is based on good faith, so also is the binding character of an international obligation assumed by unilateral declaration. Thus interested States may take cognizance of unilateral declarations and place confidence in them, and are entitled to require that the obligation thus created be respected. [···]

49. Of the statements by the French Government now before the Court, the most essential are clearly those made by the President of the Republic. There can be no doubt, in view of his functions, that his public communications or statements, oral or written, as Head of State, are in international relations acts of the French State. His statements, and those of members of the French Government acting under his authority, up to the last statement made by the Minister of Defence (of 11 October 1974), constitute a whole. Thus, in whatever form these statements were expressed, they must be held to constitute an engagement of the State, having regard to their intention and to the circumstances in which they were made.

50. The unilateral statements of the French authorities were made outside the Court, publicly and *erga omnes*, even though the first of them was communicated to the Government of Australia. As was observed above, to have legal effect, there was no need for these statements to be addressed to a particular State, nor was acceptance by any other State required. The general nature and characteristics of these statements are decisive for the evaluation of the legal implications, and it is to the interpretation of the statements that the Court must now proceed. The Court is entitled to presume, at the outset, that these statements were not made *in vacuo*,[3] but in relation to the tests which constitute the very object of the present proceedings, although France has not appeared in the case.

51. In announcing that the 1974 series of atmospheric tests would be the last, the French Government conveyed to the world at large, including the Applicant, its intention effectively to terminate these tests. It was bound to assume that other States might take note of these statements and rely on their being effective. The validity of these statements and their legal consequences must be considered within the general framework of the security of international intercourse, and the confidence and trust which are so essential in the relations among States. It is from the actual substance of these statements, and from the circumstances attending their making, that the legal implications of the unilateral act must be deduced. The objects of these statements are clear and they were addressed to the international

---

2) 약속은 지켜져야 한다 — 필자 주.

3) in isolation — 필자 주.

community as a whole, and the Court holds that they constitute an undertaking possessing legal effect. The Court considers that the President of the Republic, in deciding upon the effective cessation of atmospheric tests, gave an undertaking to the international community to which his words were addressed. It is true that the French Government has consistently maintained, for example in a Note dated 7 February 1973 from the French Ambassador in Canberra to the Prime Minister and Minister for Foreign Affairs of Australia, that it 'has the conviction that its nuclear experiments have not violated any rule of international law', nor did France recognize that it was bound by any rule of international law to terminate its tests, but this does not affect the legal consequences of the statements examined above. The Court finds that the unilateral undertaking resulting from these statements cannot be interpreted as having been made in implicit reliance on an arbitrary power of reconsideration. The Court finds further that the French Government has undertaken an obligation the precise nature and limits of which must be understood in accordance with the actual terms in which they have been publicly expressed.

☑ 해   설

사건을 접수한 ICJ는 일단 오스트레일리아와 뉴질랜드가 요청한 잠정조치의 필요성을 인정했으나, 이후 당사자간에는 더 이상의 분쟁이 존재하지 않아 판결을 내릴 필요가 없다고 판단하고 사건을 종결했다. 즉 프랑스 정부가 더 이상의 대기권 핵실험을 하지 않기로 했기 때문에, 원고측 청구의 목적이 달성되었다고 보았다.

이 판결에서 재판부는 일방적 행위로 발표된 선언도 법적 의무를 창출할 수 있다는 사실은 널리 인정되어 있다고 전제했다. 다만 국가의 모든 일방적 행위가 법적 효과를 가져오는 것은 아님을 인정했다. 그러나 이 사건에서는 프랑스의 대통령과 국방장관이 대기권 핵실험을 중단할 의사를 국제사회를 상대로 공개적으로 명확히 밝혔으므로 이는 프랑스라는 국가의 법적 약속을 구성한다고 해석했다. 또한 일방적 선언이 구속력을 갖기 위해 그 표시형식은 문제되지 않으며, 이해관계국의 수락이 요구되지도 않는다고 보았다. 프랑스가 전세계를 상대로 더 이상의 대기권 핵실험을 하지 않겠다고 공언했으며, 이는 프랑스에 대하여도 법적 구속력을 지니므로, 재판부는 이 사건의 당사국간에는 더 이상의 분쟁이 존재하지 않는다고 판단했다. 뉴질랜드는 프랑스를 별도로 제소했기 때문에 이에 대한 판결문은 1974 ICJ Reports 457(New Zealand v. France)에 수록되어 있다.

이 판결 이전에는 국제법상 일방적 행위의 구속력 여부가 별다른 주목을 받지 못했었다는 점에서 재판부가 전제한 바와 같이 일방적 행위도 국제법상 구속력을 가질 수 있다는 사실이 과연 널리 인정되고 있었는지는 의심스럽다. 그리고 재판부의 판단대로 프랑스가 과연 더 이상의 핵실험을 하지 않겠다는 확고한 의도를 갖고 있었는지도 명확하지 않다. 핵실험을 조만간 중단하겠다는 프랑스의 발표는 대부분 일정한 조건이 만족되면(if) 중단하겠다는 식이었지 무조건 중단하겠다는 엄격한 약속과는 거리가 있었기 때문이다.

사실 이 사건은 재판부를 정치적으로 어려운 처지로 몰아넣을 수 있었다. 어떤 나라도 인접지역에서의 핵실험으로 인한 방사능 피해를 수인해야한다는 의무는 없을 것이다. 그렇다고 하여 재판부가 대기권 핵실험은 국제법상 금지되었다는 결론을 쉽게 내리기도 어려웠다. 그 직전까지 미국·소련·중국 등이 여러 차례 핵실험을 실시해 왔다는 사실은 잘 알려져 있었기 때문이다. 안보리 상임이사국에 대한 패소판결이 결국은 이행되지 않을 것임을 잘 알고 있는 재판부는 이러한 이론적 난점들을 외면하고 일종의 우회로를 찾은 셈이었다. 재판부는 프랑스에 패소의 불명예를 지우지 않으면서 프랑스가 곧 핵실험을 중지하지 않을 수 없게 만들어 호주와 뉴질랜드도 크게 반발하지 않게 만들었다. J. Klabbers는 재판부의 목적이 훌륭하게 달성되었다고 평가했다.[4]

이 판결은 약 20년 후 다시 주목을 받았다. 1995년 프랑스는 8차례의 핵실험을 남태평양 지역에서 실시할 계획임을 발표했다. 뉴질랜드는 1974년 판결(para. 63)을 근거로 1974년 사건을 ICJ가 재개할 것을 청구했다. 이에는 오스트레일리아, 사모아, 솔로몬 제도, 마샬 제도, 마이크로네시아 연방 등이 소송참가를 신청했다. 그러나 ICJ는 1974년 판결은 대기권 핵실험에 관한 사건이었던 데 반해, 프랑스가 새로이 실시하기로 발표한 것은 지하핵실험이라는 이유에서 뉴질랜드의 재판 재개 요청을 각하했다(1995 ICJ Reports 288).

---

4) J. Klabbers, International Law 2nd ed.(Cambridge UP, 2017), p. 39.

일방적 행위의 구속력이란 측면에서 이 판결은 ICJ의 Frontier Dispute 사건(Burkina Faso/Mali)과 대비된다. 이 경우 ICJ는 언론사와의 인터뷰를 통하여 밝힌 말리 대통령의 발언에 대해 법적 구속력을 인정하지 않았다. 프랑스 핵실험 사건과 달리 이 사건은 양자적 성격을 지니었으므로 상호 합의가 통상적인 의사표시의 방법이라고 보았기 때문이었다(1986 ICJ Reports 554, 573-574).

한편 UN 국제법위원회는 법적 구속력을 유발하는 일방적 선언과 관련하여 2006년 제58차 회기에서 "법적 의무를 창출하는 국가의 일방적 선언에 관한 적용원칙"(Guiding principles applicable to unilateral declarations of States capable of creating legal obligations)을 채택하여 총회로 보고한 바 있다(Yearbook of the International Law Commission 2006 Vol. Ⅱ, Part Two에 수록). 그 요지는 다음과 같다. 즉 일방적 선언은 공개적으로 발표되고 이를 준수할 의지가 표명된 경우에만 법적 구속력을 창출할 수 있다. 또한 권한이 있는 자에 의해 발표되어야 하며, 특히 국가원수·정부수반·외교장관은 그 직책상 당연히 법적 구속력 있는 일방적 선언을 발표할 수 있는 자로 인정된다(제4항). 선언의 내용은 명백하고 구체적인 용어로 발표되어야 한다. 의무의 내용을 해석할 때는 선언의 문언에 가장 비중을 두고, 의무의 범위에 관해 의심이 발생하는 경우 의무는 엄격하게 해석되어야 한다(제7항). 구속력을 갖는 일방적 선언은 서면은 물론 구두로도 발표가 가능하며, 국제공동체 전체에 대하여 발표될 수도 있고, 제한된 국가나 실체(entity)를 대상으로 발표될 수도 있다. 그리고 일단 발표된 일방적 선언은 자의적으로 취소될 수 없다. 이같은 내용은 본 Nuclear Test 사건 판결과 기조를 같이 하고 있다.

➡ 참고문헌 ──────────────────────────────

- 전순신, 핵실험에 관한 사건, 인권과 정의 1989년 12월호, p. 97.
- 나인균, 국제법의 법원으로서 일방적 행위, 성균관법학 제13권 제1호(2001), p. 63.
- 김석현, 국가의 일방적 행위의 법적 지위: UN 국제법위원회의 작업을 중심으로, 국제법평론 제23호(2006년 4월), p. 107.
- 김정건·이재곤, 국가에 의한 일방적 선언의 국제법적 효과에 관한 연구, 연세논총 제24호(1988. 3), p. 213.
- T. Frank, Word−Made Law, The Decision of the ICJ in the Nuclear Tests Cases, AJIL Vol. 69(1975), p. 612.
- R. MacDonald & B. Hough, The Nuclear Test Cases Revisited, Indian Journal of International Law Vol. 18(1978), p. 322.

4. 텍사코 석유 국유화 사건(1977)
─ 유엔 총회 결의의 효력

Award on the Merits in Dispute between Texaco Overseas Petroleum Company/California Asiatic Oil Company and the Government of the Libyan Arab Republic(Compensation for Nationalized Property).
Texaco Overseas Petroleum *et al.* v. Libyan Arab Republic. International Arbitral Award(by Rene-Jean Dupuy).[1]

☑ 사 안

리비아는 1955년부터 1966년 사이 외국계 회사인 Texaco Overseas Petroleum 및 California Asiatic Oil과 석유개발을 위한 14건의 양허계약을 체결했다. 1973년과 1974년 리비아는 이들 외국계 석유회사를 국유화했다. 이들 석유회사는 국유화가 원래의 양허계약 위반임을 주장하며 계약상의 중재조항에 따라 ICJ 소장에게 단독 중재재판관을 임명해 달라고 요청했다. ICJ 소장은 Rene-Jean Dupuy 교수를 단독 중재재판관으로 임명했으나, 리비아는 국유화가 주권행사라는 이유에서 중재의 대상이 될 수 없다고 주장하며 중재절차에 불참했다. 중재재판관은 리비아가 제기한 쟁점까지 고려한 끝에 양허계약이 리비아 정부에게도 구속력을 가지며 리비아 정부의 국유화 조치는 양허계약 위반이라고 판정했다. 판단 과정에서 리비아측이 제기한 유엔 총회 결의의 법적 효과가 정밀하게 분석되었다.

---

1) International Legal Materials Vol. 17(1978), p. 1에 수록된 비공식 번역문임. 공식 언어인 불어본은 Journal du droit international Vol. 104, No. 2(April-May-June, 1977) 수록.

☑ 쟁   점

유엔 총회 결의의 법적 효력.

☑ 판   결

총회 결의의 법적 효력은 일반적으로 정의하기 어렵고, 결의의 유형과
채택되던 상황, 결의의 내용에 관한 분석 등을 바탕으로 판단해야 한다.

판 결 문

83. [⋯] Refusal to recognize any legal validity of United Nations Resolutions
must, however, be qualified according to the various texts enacted by the United
Nations. These are very different and have varying legal value, but it is impossible
to deny that the United Nations' activities have had a significant influence on the
content of contemporary international law. In appraising the legal validity of the
above-mentioned Resolutions, this Tribunal will take account of the criteria usually
taken into consideration, *i.e.*, the examination of voting conditions and the analysis
of the provisions concerned.

84. (1) With respect to the first point, Resolution 1803 (XVII) of 14 December
1962[2] was passed by the General Assembly by 87 votes to 2, with 12 abstentions.
It is particularly important to note that the majority voted for this text, including
many States of the Third World, but also several Western developed countries with
market economies, including the most important one, the United States. The
principles stated in this Resolution were therefore assented to by a great many
States representing not only all geographical areas but also all economic systems.

From this point of view, this Tribunal notes that the affirmative vote of several
developed countries with a market economy was made possible in particular by the
inclusion in the Resolution of two references to international law, and one passage
relating to the importance of international cooperation for economic development.
[⋯]

The reference to international law, in particular in the field of nationalization,
was therefore an essential factor in the support given by several Western countries
to Resolution 1803(XVII).

---

2) "천연자원에 관한 영구주권 선언"(Permanent Sovereignty over Natural Resources).

85. On the contrary, it appears to this Tribunal that the conditions under which Resolutions 3171(XXVIII),[3] 3201(S-VI) and 3281(XXIX) (Charter of the Economic Rights and Duties of States) were notably different:

- Resolution 3171(XXVIII) was adopted by a recorded vote of 108 votes to 1, with 16 abstentions, but this Tribunal notes that a separate vote was requested with respect to the paragraph in the operative part mentioned in the Libyan Government's Memorandum whereby the General Assembly stated that the application of the principle according to which nationalizations effected by States as the expression of their sovereignty implied that it is within the right of each State to determine the amount of possible compensation and the means of their payment, and that any dispute which might arise should be settled in conformity with the national law of each State instituting measures of this kind. As a consequence of a roll-call, this paragraph was adopted by 86 votes to 11 [⋯] with 28 abstentions [⋯].

This specific paragraph concerning nationalizations, disregarding the role of international law, not only was not consented to by the most important Western countries, but caused a number of the developing countries to abstain. [⋯]

- The conditions under which Resolution 3281 (XXIX), proclaiming the Charter of Economic Rights and Duties of States, was adopted also show unambiguously that there was no general consensus of the States with respect to the most important provisions and in particular those concerning nationalization. Having been the subject matter of a roll-call vote, the Charter was adopted by 118 votes to 6, with 10 abstentions. The analysis of votes on specific sections of the Charter is most significant insofar as the present case is concerned. From this point of view, paragraph 2 (c) of Article 2 of the Charter, which limits consideration of the characteristics of compensation to the State and does not refer to international law, was voted by 104 to 16, with 6 abstentions, all of the industrialized countries with market economies having abstained or having voted against it.

86. [⋯] In fact, while it is now possible to recognize that resolutions of the United Nations have a certain legal value differs considerably, depending on the type of resolution and the conditions attached to its adoption and its provisions. [⋯]

As this Tribunal has already indicated, the legal value of the resolutions which are relevant to the present case can be determined on the basis of circumstances under which they were adopted and by analysis of the principles which they state:

---

3) "천연자원에 관한 영구주권 선언"(Permanent Sovereignty over Natural Resources).

- With respect to the first point, the absence of any binding force of the resolutions of the General Assembly of the United Nations implies that such resolutions must be accepted by the members of the United Nations in order to be legally binding. In this respect, the Tribunal notes that only Resolution 1803(XVII) of 14 December 1962 was supported by a majority of Member States representing all of the various groups. By contrast, the other Resolutions mentioned above, and in particular those referred to in the Libyan Memorandum, were supported by a majority of States but not by any of the developed countries with market economies which carry on the largest part of international trade.

87. (2) With respect to the second point, to wit the appraisal of the legal value on the basis of the principles stated, it appears essential to this Tribunal to distinguish between those provisions stating the existence of a right on which the generality of the States has expressed agreement and those provisions introducing new principles which were rejected by certain representative groups of States and having nothing more than a *de lege ferenda*[4] value only in the eyes of the States which have adopted them; as far as the others are concerned, the rejection of these same principles implies that they consider them as being *contra legem*.[5] With respect to the former, which proclaim rules recognized by the community of nations, they do not create a custom but confirm one by formulating it and specifying its scope, thereby making it possible to determine whether or not one is confronted with a legal rule. As has been noted by Ambassador Castaneda, "[such resolutions] do not create the law; they have a declaratory nature of noting what does exist" (*129 R.C.A.D.I. 204 (1970)*, at 315).

On the basis of the circumstances of adoption mentioned above and by expressing an *opinio juris communis*, Resolution 1803(XVII) seems to this Tribunal to reflect the state of customary law existing in this field. Indeed, on the occasion of the vote on a resolution finding the existence of a customary rule, the States concerned clearly express their views. The consensus by a majority of States belonging to the various representative groups indicates without the slightest doubt universal recognition of the rules therein incorporated, *i.e.*, with respect to nationalization and compensation the use of the rules in force in the nationalizing State, but all this in conformity with international law.

88. While Resolution 1803(XVII) appears to a large extent as the expression of a real general will, this is not at all the case with respect to the other Resolutions

---

4) (현행법이 아닌) 있어야 할 법 — 필자 주.

5) against law — 필자 주.

mentioned above, which has been demonstrated previously by analysis of the circumstances of adoption. In particular, as regards the Charter of Economic Rights and Duties of States, several factors contribute to denying legal value to those provisions of the document which are of interest in the instant case.

- In the first place, Article 2 of this Charter must be analyzed as a political rather than as a legal declaration concerned with the ideological strategy of development and, as such, supported only by non-industrialized States.

- In the second place, this Tribunal notes that in the draft submitted by the Group of 77 to the Second Commission (U.N. Doc A/C.2/L. 1386 (1974), at 2), the General Assembly was invited to adopt the Charter "as a first measure of codification and progressive development" within the field of the international law of development. However, because of the opposition of several States, this description was deleted from the text submitted to the vote of the Assembly. […]

The absence of any connection between the procedure of compensation and international law and the subjection of this procedure solely to municipal law cannot be regarded by this Tribunal except as a *de lege ferenda* formulation, which even appears *contra legem* in the eyes of many developed countries. Similarly, several developing countries, although having voted favorably on the Charter of Economic Rights and Duties of States as a whole, in explaining their votes regretted the absence of any reference to international law.

☑ 해   설

리비아는 천연자원에 대한 영구주권을 선언한 유엔총회 결의들이 천연자원을 국유화할 주권적 권리를 확인하고 있으므로 국유화와 관련된 모든 분쟁은 해당국의 국내법에 따라 해결되어야 한다고 주장했다. 중재재판관은 이 사건의 경우 양허계약 제28조에 따라 우선적으로 국제법과 일치하는 리비아 국내법에 따라 규율되며, 그러한 일치가 존재하지 않는 경우 법의 일반원칙에 따라 판단되어야 한다고 해석했다. 일단 중재재판관은 국유화의 권리는 확립된 국제법상의 원칙이며, 본 사건의 양허계약 자체도 국유화를 금지하는 조항은 갖고 있지 않음을 인정했다. 그러나 그는 양허계약이 국제법에 의해 규율될 경우 해당국가는 국유화 조치를 통해 계약을 일방적으로 파기할 수 없다고 보았다. 이에 중재재판관은 국유화 이전으로의 원상회복을 명했다.

이러한 판단과정에서 천연자원에 대한 주권국가의 권리를 규정한 UN 총회 결의의 효력이 분석되었다. 국제법에 따른 국유화를 규정하고 있는 총회 결의 제1803호(1962)는 제3세계 국가들뿐만 아니라 미국을 포함한 여러 산업화 국가들도 찬성함으로써, 지리적으로나 경제 체제상으로 폭 넓은 국가들의 지지를 받았다는 점에서 그 내용이 관습국제법에 해당한다고 평가되었다. 반면 국내법에 따른 국유화를 규정하고 있는 총회 결의 제3171호(1973)나 제3281호(1974)는 채택 과정에서도 여러 반대가 제기되었고, 특히 시장경제체제 국가들의 찬성 없이 채택되었다는 점에서 관습국제법의 성격을 지니지 못한다고 판단되었다.

이 판결은 1962년 채택된 총회 결의 제1803호(천연자원에 관한 영구주권선언)과 1974년의 총회 결의 제3281호(국가의 경제적 권리의무에 관한 헌장)의 법적 구속력을 각각 어떻게 구분하여 분석했는가를 보여 주고 있다는 점에서 국제기구에서 채택된 결의의 법적 가치를 판단하는 데 좋은 길잡이가 되고 있다.

판결은 원상회복을 명했지만 실제로는 리비아가 금전배상을 지불함으로써 사건은 일단락 되었다. 주권국가가 일단 국유화를 단행했다면 비록 수년 후 그 행위가 국제법 위반으로 판정되어 원상회복의 의무를 부여받을지라도 이의 실현을 기대하기는 어려울 것이다. 이러한 현실이 ILC의 국제위법행위에 대한 국가책임 초안(2001) 제35조에 원상회복이 그에 따른 이익에 비해 현저히 불균형적인 부담을 수반하는 경우에는 원상회복이 요구되지 아니한다는 규정이 마련된 배경이기도 하다.

➼ 참고문헌 ─────────────────────────────

- 김종수, 국유화사건 중재판단: 최근의 국제판례 연구의 일례 : 리비아 국유화를 중심으로, (전남대) 사회과학논총 제10집(1982), p. 367.
- D. Bowett, Libyan Nationalization of American Oil Companies's Assets, Cambridge Law Journal, Vol. 37(1978), p. 5.
- A. Varma, Petroleum Concessions in International Arbitration, Texaco Overseas Petroleum Company v. Libyan Arab Republic, Columbia Journal of

Transnational Law, Vol. 18(1979), p. 259.

- G. Kerwin, The Role of United Nations General Assembly Resolutions in Determining Principles of International Law in United States Courts, Duke Law Journal, Vol. 1983, No. 4, p. 883.
- J. Cantegreil, "The Audacity of the Texaco/Calasiatic Award: René−Jean Dupuy and the Internationalization of Foreign Investment Law", The European Journal of International Law, Vol. 22, no. 2(2011), p. 452.

제 2 장

국제법과 국내법의 관계

1. 유엔 본부협정 해석에 관한 분쟁(1988)
— 국내법에 대한 국제법의 우위

Application of the Obligation to Arbitrate under Section 21 of the United Nations Headquarters Agreement of 26 June 1947. Advisory Opinion, 1988 ICJ Reports 12.

☑ 사　　안

팔레스타인 해방기구(Palestine Liberation Organization: PLO)는 1974년 이래 유엔 총회의 옵저버 자격을 인정받았고 뉴욕에 대표부 사무실도 설치했다. 한편 미국 의회는 1987년 테러방지법을 제정했다(1988년 3월 발효). 미국 법무장관은 PLO가 미국과 동맹국의 이익 그리고 국제법을 위협하는 테러단체로서 바로 이 법의 규제대상에 해당한다고 판단하고, 이에 따라 뉴욕의 PLO 사무소를 폐쇄시키겠다고 발표했다. 유엔은 이러한 미국의 입장이 1947년 유엔과 미국이 체결한 본부협정에 위반된다고 항의했고, 유엔 주재 미국 대표부도 PLO 사무소 폐쇄는 본부협정 위반임을 인정했다. 테러방지법의 발효가 임박하자 유엔은 이 문제를 본부협정 제21조에 규정된 바와 같이 중재재판에 회부하자고 제의했으나, 미국은 응하지 않았다. 이에 유엔 총회는 미국이 본부협정 제21조에 따른 중재재판에 응할 의무가 있는가에 관하여 ICJ에 권고적 의견을 요청했다.

☑ 쟁　　점

(1) PLO 대표부 폐쇄와 관련하여 유엔과 미국간에는 본부협정이 상정하고 있는 분쟁이 존재하는가 여부.

(2) 국내법상의 의무와 조약상의 의무가 충돌하는 경우의 우선 순위.

☑ 판   결

(1) 유엔과 미국간에는 본부협정 제21조에 규정된 분쟁이 존재하며, 미국은 유엔이 요청한 중재재판에 응할 의무가 있다.

(2) 국제법이 국내법에 우월하다는 것은 국제법상의 기본원칙이다.

판 결 문

55. […] In the present case, the Court regards it as similarly beyond any doubt that the dispute between the United Nations and the United States is one "not settled by negotiation" within the meaning of section 21, paragraph (a), of the Headquarters Agreement.

56. Nor was any "other agreed mode of settlement" of their dispute contemplated by the United Nations and the United States. In this connection the Court should observe that current proceedings brought by the United States Attorney General before the United States courts cannot be an "agreed mode of settlement" within the meaning of section 21 of the Headquarters Agreement. The purpose of these proceedings is to enforce the Anti-Terrorism Act of 1987; it is not directed to settling the dispute, concerning the application of the Headquarters Agreement, which has come into existence between the United Nations and the United States. Furthermore, the United Nations has never agreed to settlement of the dispute in the American courts; it has taken care to make it clear that it wishes to be admitted only as *amicus curiae* before the District Court for the Southern District of New York.

57. The Court must therefore conclude that the United States is bound to respect the obligation to have recourse to arbitration under section 21 of the Headquarters Agreement. The fact remains however that, as the Court has already observed, the United States has declared (letter from the Permanent Representative, 11 March 1988) that its measures against the PLO Observer Mission were taken "irrespective of any obligations the United States may have under the [Head-quarters] Agreement." If it were necessary to interpret that statement as intended to refer not only to the substantive obligations laid down in, for example, sections 11, 12 and 13, but also to the obligation to arbitrate provided for in section 21, this conclusion would remain intact. It would be sufficient to recall the fundamental principle of international law that international law prevails over domestic law. This principle was endorsed by judicial decision as long ago as the arbitral award of 14 September 1872 in the *Alabama* case between Great Britain and the United States, and has frequently been recalled since, for example in the case concerning the *Greco-Bulgarian* "*Communities*" in which the Permanent Court of International Justice laid it down that "it is a generally accepted principle of international law that in the relations between Powers who are contracting Parties to a treaty, the provisions of municipal law cannot prevail over those of the treaty" (*P.C.I.J., Series B, No. 17*, p. 32).

☑ 해　　설

ICJ는 권고적 의견에서 PLO 대표부 사무실을 둘러싼 논란으로 유엔과 미국간에는 본부협정 제21조가 예정하고 있는 분쟁이 존재하며, 따라서 미국은 중재재판에 응할 의무가 있다고 판단했다. 다만 미국의 테러방지법 제정과 시행이 본부협정상의 의무를 위반한 것이냐에 대하여는 판단하지 않았는데, 이는 본부협정 제21조에 규정된 중재재판을 통해 결정될 문제라고 보았다. 이 과정에서 ICJ는 위 판결문에 나타난 바와 같이 분명한 어조로 국제재판에서 국내법에 대한 국제법의 우위를 단언했다.

한편 미국 법무장관은 본부협정상의 의무와 상관없이 국내법에 따라 폐쇄절차를 진행하겠다고 발표하고, 법이 발효하자 곧 바로 뉴욕지구 연방법원에 PLO 대표부 사무실 폐쇄소송을 제기했다. 그러나 뉴욕 연방법원은 PLO 대표부의 지위는 미국이 체결한 본부협정에 의해 보호되며, 미국 의회가 테러방지법의 제정을 통해 이러한 조약상의 의무를 배제시키고 PLO 대표부 사무소를 폐쇄시키려는 의도는 없었다고 판단해 법무장관의 신청을 기각했다(695 F.Supp. 1456(1988)). 이후 미국 법무부도 이 판결을 수락하고 더 이상 PLO 사무소의 폐쇄를 시도하지 않아 사건은 일단락되었다.

➡ 참고문헌 ————————————————————————————

- T. Fitschen, Closing the PLO Observer Mission to the United Nations in New York: The Decisions of International Court of Justice and the U.S. District Court, Southern District of New York, German Yearbook of International Law Vol. 31(1988), p. 595.
- T. Maluwa, Treaty Interpretation and the Exercise of Prudential Discretions of the PLO Mission Case, Netherlands International Law Review Vol. 37(1990), p. 330.
- W. Reisman, An International Farce: The Sad Case of the PLO Mission, Yale Journal of International Law Vol. 14(1989), p. 412.

2. 아마두 사디오 디알로 사건(2010)
─ 국제재판소에서의 국내법 해석

Ahamadou Sadio Diallo(Merits).
Republic of Guinea v. Democratic Republic of the Congo.
2010 ICJ Reports 639.

☑ 사 안

Diallo는 기니 국민으로 1964년부터 콩고에 정착하여 사업에 종사했다. 그는 사업 수행과정에서 콩고 당국과의 마찰이 발생해 1988년 체포되었다가 석방되었다. Diallo는 공공질서, 특히 경제적·재정적 분야의 질서를 훼손했다는 혐의로 1995년 11월 다시 체포·구금되었다가 결국 1996년 1월 31일 콩고로부터 추방당했다. 이에 기니 정부는 Diallo가 콩고에 의해 불법적으로 구금되었다가 모든 재산을 박탈당하고 추방되었다고 주장하며 이 사건을 ICJ에 제소했다.

재판과정에서 기니측은 콩고 당국의 Diallo 추방이 「시민적 및 정치적 권리에 관한 국제규약」 제13조와 「아프리카 인권헌장」 제12조 4항의 위반이라고 주장했다. 즉 이들 조항은 외국인의 추방이 "법률"에 따른 결정에 의할 것을 규정하고 있는데, Diallo의 추방시 콩고 법률에 합당한 절차가 적용되지 않았다고 주장했다. 또한 기니측은 콩고의 Diallo 체포·구금이 위 규약 제9조와 아프리카 인권헌장 제6조를 위반이라고 주장했다. 이에 Diallo의 추방이 과연 콩고 법률에 따라 진행되었는가를 판단하기 위해 ICJ가 콩고 법률을 해석할 필요가 있었다.

☑ 쟁 점

국제재판소는 특정 국가의 국내법 해석시 그 국가에서의 법해석을 존중해야 하는가?

☑ 판   결

국제재판소는 국내법을 해석함에 있어서 해당 국가 당국(특히 최고재판소)의 입장을 존중한다. 단 명백히 잘못된 해석이라면 그러하지 아니한다.

판 결 문

69. According to Guinea, the decision to expel Mr. Diallo first breached Article 13 of the Covenant and Article 12, paragraph 4, of the African Charter because it was not taken in accordance with Congolese domestic law, for three reasons: it should have been signed by the President of the Republic and not by the Prime Minister; it should have been preceded by consultation of the National Immigration Board; and it should have indicated the grounds for the expulsion, which it failed to do.

70. The Court is not convinced by the first of these arguments. It is true that Article 15 of the Zairean Legislative Order of 12 September 1983 concerning immigration control, in the version in force at the time, conferred on the President of the Republic, and not the Prime Minister, the power to expel an alien. However, the DRC explains that since the entry into force of the Constitutional Act of 9 April 1994, the powers conferred by particular legislative provisions on the President of the Republic are deemed to have been transferred to the Prime Minister—even though such provisions have not been formally amended—under Article 80 (2) of the new Constitution, which provides that "the Prime Minister shall exercise regulatory power by means of decrees deliberated upon in the Council of Ministers."

The Court recalls that it is for each State, in the first instance, to interpret its own domestic law. The Court does not, in principle, have the power to substitute its own interpretation for that of the national authorities, especially when that interpretation is given by the highest national courts (*see*, for this latter case, *Serbian Loans, Judgment No.14, 1929, P.C.I.J., Series A, No.20*, p. 46 *and Brazilian Loans, Judgment No.15, 1929, P.C.I.J., Series A, No.21*, p. 124). Exceptionally, where a State puts forward a manifestly incorrect interpretation of its domestic law, particularly for the purpose of gaining an advantage in a pending case, it is for the Court to adopt what it finds to be the proper interpretation.

71. That is not the situation here. The DRC's interpretation of its Constitution, from which it follows that Article 80 (2) produces certain effects on the laws already in force on the date when that Constitution was adopted, does not seem manifestly incorrect. It has not been contested that this interpretation corresponded, at the time in question, to the general practice of the constitutional authorities. The DRC has included in the case file, in this connection, a number of other expulsion decrees issued at the same time and all signed by the Prime Minister. Consequently, although it would be possible in theory to discuss the validity of that interpretation, it is certainly not for the Court to adopt a different interpretation of Congolese domestic law for the purposes of the decision of this case. It therefore cannot be concluded that the decree expelling Mr. Diallo was not issued "in accordance with law"by virtue of the fact that it was signed by the Prime Minister.

72. However, the Court is of the opinion that this decree did not comply with the provisions of Congolese law for two other reasons.

First, it was not preceded by consultation of the National Immigration Board, whose opinion is required by Article 16 of the above-mentioned Legislative Order concerning immigration control before any expulsion measure is taken against an alien holding a residence permit. The DRC has not contested either that Mr. Diallo's situation placed him within the scope of this provision, or that consultation of the Board was neglected. This omission is confirmed by the absence in the decree of a citation mentioning the Board's opinion, whereas all the other expulsion decrees included in the case file specifically cite such an opinion, in accordance with Article 16 of the Legislative Order, moreover, which concludes by stipulating that the decision "shall mention the fact that the Board was consulted."

Second, the expulsion decree should have been "reasoned" pursuant to Article 15 of the 1983 Legislative Order; in other words, it should have indicated the grounds for the decision taken. The fact is that the general, stereotyped reasoning included in the decree cannot in any way be regarded as meeting the requirements of the legislation. The decree confines itself to stating that the "presence and conduct [of Mr. Diallo] have breached Zairean public order, especially in the economic, financial and monetary areas, and continue to do so." The first part of this sentence simply paraphrases the legal basis for any expulsion measure according to Congolese law, since Article 15 of the 1983 Legislative Order permits the expulsion of any alien "who, by his presence or conduct, breaches orthreatens to breach the peace or public order."As for the second part, while it represents an addition, this is so vague that it is impossible to know on the basis of which activities the presence of Mr. Diallo was deemed to be a threat to public order (in the same sense, *mutatis mutandis, see Certain Questions of Mutual Assistance in Criminal Matters (Djibouti v. France), Judgment, I.C.J. Reports 2008*, p. 231, para. 152). The formulation used by the author of the decree therefore amounts to an absence of reasoning for the expulsion measure.

73. The Court thus concludes that in two important respects, concerning procedural guarantees conferred on aliens by Congolese law and aimed at protecting the persons in question against the risk of arbitrary treatment, the expulsion of Mr. Diallo was not decided" in accordance with law."

Consequently, regardless of whether that expulsion was justified on the merits, a question to which the Court will return later in this Judgment, the disputed measure violated Article 13 of the Covenant and Article 12, paragraph 4, of the African Charter.

☑ 해   설

ICJ는 Diallo의 추방과정에서 콩고의 국내법도 제대로 준수되지 못해 법률에 근거한 결정이 될 수 없었고, 결과적으로 국제조약도 위반되었다고 결론내렸다. 이어 재판부는 콩고가 불법적인 구금과 추방으로 인한 손해에 적절한 배상을 해야 한다고 판단하고, 6개월 내에 배상문제를 합의하지 못한다면 재판소가 결정한다고 판시했다. 6개월 시한인 2011년 5월 30일이 별다른 합의 없이 도과되자 ICJ는 2012년 6월 19일 콩고에 대해 미화 95,000달러의 배상을 명했다.

국제재판소는 분쟁 당사국의 국내법을 어떻게 취급하는가? PCIJ는 아래 Certain German Interests in Polish Upper Silesia 판결에서 국제재판시 각국의 국내법은 구속력을 지닌 법이 아닌 단순한 사실로 취급된다는 점을 명확히 한 바 있다.

"From the standpoint of International Law and of the Court which is its organ, municipal laws are merely facts which express the will and constitute the activities of States, in the same manner as do legal decisions or administrative measures."(1926 PCIJ Reports Series A No. 7, p. 19)

그러나 Brazilian Loan 사건에서는 이러한 입장을 약간 조정했다. 국내법의 내용은 사실의 문제에 속하기는 하나, 이는 특별한 성격의 사실로서 국제재판소는 국내법을 해당국 법원과 같은 방법으로 해석·적용할 것을 제시했다.

"Once the Court has arrived at the conclusion that it is necessary to apply the municipal law of a particular country, there seems no doubt that it must seek to apply it as it would be applied in that country. It would not be applying the municipal law of a country if it were to apply it in a manner different from that in which that law would be applied in the country in which it is in force. It follows that the Court must pay the utmost regard to the decisions of the municipal courts of a country, for it is with the aid of their jurisprudence that it will be enabled to decide what are the rules which, in actual fact, are applied in the country the law of which is recognize as applicable in a given case."(1929 PCIJ Reports Series A No. 21, 93, p. 124)

다만 문제는 국제재판소가 어떻게 각국의 국내법의 내용을 확인할 수 있느냐는 점이다. 국내법의 내용이 상대적으로 널리 알려진 주요 국가의 경우에는 가능할지 몰라도 모든 국가에 관하여 이를 기대하기는 어렵다. 특히 국내법의 내용을 해당국이 제시하는 증거를 통해 파악하게 된다면 이는 국제재판에서의 공평성 확보라는 측면에서 바람직하지 않다.

한편 ICJ는 Barcelona Traction, Light and Power Company Limited Case(2nd Phase)(Belgium v. Spain, 1970 ICJ Reports 3)에서 국제재판에서도 국내법상 개념을 활용할 필요성이 있음을 또 다른 측면에서 제시했다.

50. [···] the Court must, as already indicated, start from the fact that the present case essentially involves factors derived from municipal law — the distinction and the community between the company and the shareholder — which the Parties, however widely their interpretations may differ, each take as the point of departure of their reasoning. If the Court were to decide the case in disregard of the relevant institutions of municipal law it would, without justification, invite serious legal difficulties. It would lose touch with reality, for there are no corresponding institutions of international law to which the Court could resort. Thus the Court has, as indicated, not only to take cognizance of municipal law but also to refer to it.[1]

즉 비록 주식회사라는 제도는 국제법상의 개념이 아닌 국내법상의 제도에 불과할지라도 국제재판소가 이 내용을 무시하고 판결을 하면 현실과 괴리된 결과가 야기될 수밖에 없으므로 ICJ는 국제재판에서도 이의 활용이 불가피하다고 판단했다.

➡ 참고문헌 ─────────────────────────────────

- A. Vermeer—Kunzli, The Subject Matters: The ICJ and Human Rights, Rights of Shareholders, and the Diallo Case, Leiden Journal of International Law, Vol. 24 (2011), p. 607.
- G. Ulfstein, Awarding Compensation in a Fragmented Legal System: The Diallo Case, Journal of International Dispute Settlement Vol. 4(2013), p. 477.

────────────────────

1) 이 판결 다른 부분의 내용은 본서 p. 167 이하 참조.

1. 빠께뜨 아바나 사건(1900)
— 국제관습법의 국내적 효력

The Paquete Habana.
Supreme Court of the U.S., 175 U.S. 677(1900).

☑ 사   안

스페인 식민지 쿠바 아바나항에 정박 중인 미국 군함 메인호가 원인 모를 폭발사고에 의해 침몰하자, 1898년 4월 미국은 스페인에 선전포고를 하고 쿠바 인근 해상에 봉쇄령을 내렸다. 이 사실을 모르던 스페인 선적의 소형어선 Lola호와 Paquete Habana호가 미국 해군에 의해 나포되었다. 이들 선박과 화물은 플로리다 법원에 의해 공매처분이 결정되었다. 이에 대해 선박 소유자는 비무장의 연안어선은 전시포획에서 면제된다고 주장하며, 선박과 화물의 피해에 대한 배상을 청구했다. 이 사건에서 쟁점 중의 하나는 비무장 연안어선은 전시포획에서 면제되는 관습국제법이 성립되어 있는가와 이러한 관습국제법이 미국 법원에서 직접 재판의 근거가 될 수 있는가 여부였다.

☑ 쟁   점

미국 법원에서의 관습국제법의 효력.

☑ 판   결

관습국제법은 미국법의 일부이며, 미국 법원은 이를 직접 근거로 판결을 내릴 수 있다.

판 결 문

(p. 686-) We are then brought to the consideration of the question whether, upon the facts appearing in these records, the fishing smacks were subject to capture by the armed vessels of the United States during the recent war with Spain.

By an ancient usage among civilized nations, beginning centuries ago, and gradually ripening into a rule of international law, coast fishing vessels, pursuing their vocation of catching and bringing in fresh fish, have been recognized as exempt, with their cargoes and crews, from capture as prize of war. [⋯][1]

International law is part of our law, and must be ascertained and administered by the courts of justice of appropriate jurisdiction as often as questions of right depending upon it are duly presented for their determination. For this purpose, where there is no treaty and no controlling executive or legislative act or judicial decision, resort must be had to the customs and usages of civilized nations, and, as evidence of these, to the works of jurists and commentators who by years of labor, research, and experience have made themselves peculiarly well acquainted with the subjects of which they treat. Such works are resorted to by judicial tribunals, not for the speculations of their authors concerning what the law ought to be, but for trustworthy evidence of what the law really is. [⋯][2]

This review of the precedents and authorities on the subject appears to us abundantly to demonstrate that at the present day, by the general consent of the civilized nations of the world, and independently of any express treaty or other public act, it is an established rule of international law, founded on considerations of humanity to a poor and industrious order of men, and of the mutual convenience of belligerent states, that coast fishing vessels, with their implements and supplies, cargoes and crews, unarmed and honestly pursuing their peaceful calling of catching and bringing in fresh fish, are exempt from capture as prize of war.

The exemption, of course, does not apply to coast fishermen or their vessels if

---

1) 이어 재판부는 연안어선에 대한 전시포획 면제에 관하여 다양한 국제선례를 설명했다.
2) 이어서 재판부는 연안어선에 대한 전시포획 면제를 지지하는 다양한 학자들의 견해를 소개했다. 또한 미국 정부가 국제법을 위반해 연안어선을 나포하라는 지시를 한 바 없으며, 국제법에 따라 전쟁을 수행함이 미국의 정책이라고 평가했다.

employed for a warlike purpose, or in such a way as to give aid or information to the enemy; nor when military or naval operations create a necessity to which all private interests must give way.

Nor has the exemption been extended to ships or vessels employed on the high sea in taking whales or seals or cod or other fish which are not brought fresh to market, but are salted or otherwise cured and made a regular article of commerce.

This rule of international law is one which prize courts administering the law of nations are bound to take judicial notice of, and to give effect to, in the absence of any treaty or other public act of their own government in relation to the matter.

☑ 해   설

이 판결문에서 international law라고 칭하는 부분은 내용상 관습국제법을 의미한다. 미국은 Common Law의 전통에 따라 영국과 같이 관습국제법은 당연히 미국법의 일부이며, 미국 법원은 이를 근거로 바로 판결을 내릴 수 있다는 입장을 취하고 있다. 다만 연방 제정법은 관습국제법에 대해 우월한 효력을 지닌다. 이 판결은 미국 법원이 관습국제법을 어떻게 확인하는가와 국제관습법은 미국법의 일부로 편입되어 있음을 보여주는 비교적 이른 시기의 대표적 사례이다. 결국 이 판결에서 미국 연방대법원은 미국 정부가 국제법을 위반했으므로 선주에게 나포로 인한 손해를 배상하라고 결정했다.

이후 1907년 제2차 헤이그 평화회의는 Convention (XI) relative to certain Restrictions with regard to the Exercise of the Right of Capture in Naval War을 채택하고 이 판결의 취지와 같은 다음 조항을 두었다.

"Art.3: Vessels used exclusively for fishing, along the coast or small boats employed in local trade are exempt from capture, as well as their appliances, rigging, tackle, and cargo.

They cease to be exempt as soon as they take any part whatever in hostilities.

The Contracting Powers agree not to take advantage of the harmless character of the said vessels in order to use them for military purposes while preserving their peaceful appearance."

다만 현대전의 특성상 연안어선이 전시포획에서 면제된다는 관습국제법
이 아직도 유지되고 있는지에 대하여는 오늘날 의문이 제기되고 있다.3)

▶ 참고문헌 ───

- S. Stucky, The Paquete Habana: A Case History in the Development of International Law, University of Baltimore Law Review Vol. 15(1985), p. 1.
- J. Paust, Paquete Habana and the President: Rediscovering the Brief for the United States, Virginia Journal of International Law Vol. 34(1994), p. 981.

---

3) 김정건, 신판 국제법(박영사, 2004), pp. 100−101.

2. 세이 후지이 사건(1952)
― 조약의 국내적 효력

Sei Fujii v. State of California.
Supreme Court of California, U.S., 38 Cal. 2d 718(1952).

☑ 사 안

미국 캘리포니아주의 1920년 외국인토지법은 미국 시민권을 취득할 자격이 봉쇄된 외국인은 캘리포니아에서 토지를 취득할 수 없다고 규정하고 있었다. 이 법은 원래 아시아계 이민자의 토지취득을 제한하려는 목적에서 제정되었으나, 이 사건이 문제될 무렵에는 일본인이 주 대상이었다. 사건의 원고는 캘리포니아에서 토지를 구입했다가 이 법 위반으로 몰수를 당했다. 그는 이 법조항이 일종의 인종차별입법이며, 이 같은 캘리포니아 법은 인권과 기본적 자유의 존중을 규정한 유엔 헌장 위반으로 무효화되었다고 주장했다. 왜냐하면 1945년 미국이 유엔 헌장을 비준함으로써 이에 위반되는 주법인 캘리포니아 법은 실효되었다는 것이었다. 이 사건에서의 쟁점은 유엔 헌장의 해당 조항에 의해 문제의 캘리포니아 주법이 바로 무효로 되었는가 여부였다.

☑ 쟁 점

유엔 헌장상의 인권존중에 관한 조항이 미국에서 자기집행력을 갖는가 여부.

☑ 판 결

유엔 헌장상의 인권조항은 비자기집행적이므로, 이와 충돌되는 미국 국내법을 바로 무효화시키지 못한다.

판 결 문

(p. 718-) It is first contended that the land law has been invalidated and superseded by the provisions of the United Nations Charter pledging the member nations to promote the observance of human rights and fundamental freedoms without distinction as to race. Plaintiff relies on statements in the preamble and in Articles 1, 55 and 56 of the Charter, 59 Stat. 1035.

It is not disputed that the charter is a treaty, and our federal Constitution provides that treaties made under the authority of the United States are part of the supreme law of the land and that the judges in every state are bound thereby. U.S.Const., art. VI. A treaty, however, does not automatically supersede local laws which are inconsistent with it unless the treaty provisions are self-executing. In the words of Chief Justice Marshall: A treaty is 'to be regarded in courts of justice as equivalent to an act of the Legislature, whenever it operates of itself, without the aid of any legislative provision. But when the terms of the stipulation import a contract when either of the parties engages to perform a particular act, the treaty addresses itself to the political, not the judicial department; and the Legislature must execute the contract, before it can become a rule for the court.' Foster v. Neilson, 1829, 2 Pet. 253, 314, 7 L.Ed. 415.

In determining whether a treaty is self-executing courts look to the intent of the signatory parties as manifested by the language of the instrument, and, if the instrument is uncertain, recourse may be had to the circumstances surrounding its execution. […]

In order for a treaty provision to be operative without the aid of implementing legislation and to have the force and effect of a statute, it must appear that the framers of the treaty intended to prescribe a rule that, standing alone, would be enforceable in the courts. […]

It is clear that the provisions of the preamble and of Article 1 of the charter which are claimed to be in conflict with the alien land law are not self-executing. They state general purposes and objectives of the United Nations Organization and do not purport to impose legal obligations on the individual member nations or to create rights in private persons. It is equally clear that none of the other provisions relied on by plaintiff is self-executing. Article 55 declares that the United Nations 'shall promote: ⋯ universal respect for, and observance of, human rights and fundamental freedoms for all without distinction as to race, sex, language, or religion,' and in Article 56, the member nations 'pledge themselves to take joint and separate action in cooperation with the Organization for the achievement of the purposes set forth in Article 55.' Although the member nations have obligated themselves to cooperate with the international organization in promoting respect for, and observance of, human rights, it is plain that it was contemplated that future legislative action by the several nations would be required to accomplish the declared objectives, and there is nothing to indicate that these provisions were intended to become rules of law for the courts of this country upon the ratification of the charter.

The language used in Articles 55 and 56 is not the type customarily employed in treaties which have been held to be self-executing and to create rights and duties in individuals. For example, the treaty involved in Clark v. Allen, 331 U.S. 503, 507-508, 67 S.Ct. 1431, 1434, 91 L.Ed. 1633, relating to the rights of a national of one country to inherit real property located in another country, specifically provided that 'such national shall be allowed a term of three years in which to sell the (property) ⋯ and withdraw the proceeds ⋯' free from any discriminatory taxation. [⋯] In Nielsen v. Johnson, 279 U.S. 47, 50, 49 S.Ct. 223, 73 L.Ed. 607, the provision treated as being self-executing was equally definite. There each of the signatory parties agreed that 'no higher or other duties, charges, or taxes of any kind, shall be levied' by one country on removal of property therefrom by citizens of the other country 'than are or shall be payable in each state, upon the same, when removed by a citizen or subject of such state respectively.' In other instances treaty provisions were enforced without implementing legislation where they prescribed in detail the rules governing rights and obligations of individuals or specifically provided that citizens of one nation shall have the same rights while in the other country as are enjoyed by that country's own citizens. [⋯] It is significant to note that when the framers of the charter intended to make certain provisions effective without the aid of implementing legislation they employed language which is clear and definite and manifests that intention. [⋯][1]

The provisions in the charter pledging cooperation in promoting observance of fundamental freedoms lack the mandatory quality and definiteness which would

---

1) 재판부는 예를 들어 유엔 헌장 제104조와 제105조 같은 경우 자기집행적 조항이라고 판단했다.

indicate an intent to create justiciable rights in private persons immediately upon ratification. Instead, they are framed as a promise of future action by the member nations. Secretary of State Stettinius, Chairman of the United States delegation at the San Francisco Conference where the charter was drafted, stated in his report to President Truman that Article 56 'pledges the various countries to cooperate with the organization by joint and separate action in the achievement of the economic and social objectives of the organization without infringing upon their right to order their national affairs according to their own best ability, in their own way, and in accordance with their own political and economic institutions and processes.' […]

The humane and enlightened objectives of the United Nations Charter are, of course, entitled to respectful consideration by the courts and Legislatures of every member nation, since that document expresses the universal desire of thinking men for peace and for equality of rights and opportunities. The charter represents a moral commitment of foremost importance, and we must not permit the spirit of our pledge to be compromised or disparaged in either our domestic or foreign affairs. We are satisfied, however, that the charter provisions relied on by plaintiff were not intended to supersede existing domestic legislation, and we cannot hold that they operate to invalidate the alien land law.

☑ 해   설

이 사건의 재판부는 원고가 지적한 유엔 헌장의 해당조항은 자기집행력을 갖지 못하므로 이를 근거로 캘리포니아 주법이 바로 무효화되지는 않는다고 판시했다. 다만 문제의 캘리포니아 주법은 미국 연방헌법 수정 제14조 평등보호조항에 위반되어 무효라고 판단했다. 이 판결은 주법원의 판결에 불과하므로 이론상 전국적인 선례로 기능할 수 없지만, 후일 미국 내에서 유엔 헌장상의 인권조항을 비자기집행적이라고 해석하는 경향의 향도적 역할을 했다. 연방대법원은 이 점에 대하여 명확한 입장을 밝힌 바 없다.

미국 사법부는 건국 초기부터 국내적 효력과 관련해서 조약을 의회의 입법적 조력이 없이도 법원이 직접 적용할 수 있는 자기집행적 조약(self-executing treaty)과 의회의 이행입법이 있어야만 집행이 가능한 비자기집행적 조약(nonself-executing treaty)으로 구분해 왔다. 조약은 미국의 최고법의 하나로서 일반적으로 연방법률과 동등한 효력을 지니지만, 비자기집행적 조약은 그 자체만으로는 모순되는 기존의 연방법률이나 주법률에 대해 우월적 집행력을 발휘하지 못한다고 보았다. 실제 자기집행적 조약과 비자기집행적 조약의 구분이 항상 용이하지는 않으나, 건국 초기에 비해 미국의 사법부는 비자기집행적 조약의 범위를 지속적으로 확대시키는 경향을 보여 왔다. 미국 사법부가 발전시켜 온 조약의 자기집행성 여부는 미국 헌법의 해석과정에서 제기된 문제이나, 여기서 제기되는 쟁점은 한국 등 조약의 국내적 시행에 관하여 수용이론을 취하고 있는 모든 국가에서도 동일하게 제기될 수 있는 문제이다.

➡ **참고문헌**

- C. Vázquez, The Four Doctrine of Self－Executing Treaties, AJIL vol. 89(1995), p. 695.
- J. Paust, Self－Executing Treaties, AJIL vol. 82(1988), p. 760.
- Thomas Buergenthal, Modern Constitutions and Human Rights Treaties, Columbia Journal of Transnational Law Vol. 36(1997), p. 211.
- Richard Lillich, Invoking International Human Rights Law in Domestic Courts, University of Cincinnati Law Review Vol. 54(1985), p. 367.
- B. Schluter, The Domestic Legal Status of Human Rights Clauses of the United Nations Charter, California Law Review Vol. 61(1973), p. 110.
- Quincy Wright, National Court and Human Rights—The Fujii Case, AJIL Vol. 45(1951), p. 51.
- 류성진, 헌법재판에서 국제인권조약의 원용가능성: 미국, 남아프리카 공화국, 우리나라의 사례를 중심으로, 아주법학 제7권 제1호(2013), p. 20.

3. 트렌드텍스 무역회사 사건(1977)
─ 관습국제법의 국내적 효력

Trendtex Trading Corporation v. Central Bank of Nigeria.
Court of Appeal, U.K., 1977 Q.B. 529.

☑ 사　　안

이 사건의 원고는 스위스 회사이고, 피고는 나이지리아 국립 중앙은행
이다. 1975년 나이지리아 중앙은행은 원고에게 신용장을 발급한 바 있는데,
후일 나이지리아 정부는 정치적 이유에서 신용장의 이행을 거부하라고 중앙
은행에게 지시했다. 영국 법원에서의 제소에 대해 피고측은 국가기관으로서
의 주권면제를 주장했고, 원고측은 제한적 주권면제론에 입각한 상사거래상
의 예외를 주장했다. 결국 재판부는 제한적 주권면제론에 입각한 판결을 내
렸다. 재판과정에서 절대적 주권면제론에 입각한 영국 법원에서의 과거 판례
가 이 사건에 대해 선례구속력을 갖느냐가 문제되었다.

☑ 쟁　　점

⑴ 영국 법원에서의 관습국제법의 효력.

⑵ 영국 법원에서 관습국제법에 근거해 내려진 판결에 대해서도 선례구
속성의 원칙이 인정되는가 여부.

☑ 판　　결

⑴ 관습국제법은 자동적으로 영국법의 일부로 편입되고, 영국 법원에서
재판의 근거가 된다.

⑵ 관습국제법에 관하여는 선례구속성의 원칙이 적용되지 않으며, 영국

법원은 항상 재판 당시의 관습국제법에 입각한 판결을 내려야 한다.

판 결 문

(p. 553-) (Lord Denning Mr.) [⋯] A fundamental question arises for decision. What is the place of international law in our English law? One school of thought holds to the doctrine of incorporation. It says that the rules of international law are incorporated into English law automatically and considered to be part of English law unless they are in conflict with an Act of Parliament. The other school of thought holds to the doctrine of transformation. It says that the rules of international law are not to be considered as part of English law except in so far as they have been already adopted and made part of our law by the decisions of the judges, or by Act of Parliament, or long established custom. The difference is vital when you are faced with a change in the rules of international law. Under the doctrine of incorporation, when the rules of international law change, our English law changes with them. But, under the doctrine of transformation, the English law does not change. It is bound by precedent. It is bound down to those rules of international law which have been accepted and adopted in the past. It cannot develop as international law develops.

(i) The doctrine of incorporation. The doctrine of incorporation goes back to 1737 in Buvot v. Barbut (1736) [⋯] in which Lord Talbot L.C. (who was highly esteemed) made a declaration which was taken down by young William Murray (who was of counsel in the case) and adopted by him in 1764 when he was Lord Mansfield C.J. in Triquet v. Beth (1764) 3 Burr. 1478: "Lord Talbot declared a clear opinion—'That the law of nations in its full extent was part of the law of England, ... that the law of nations was to be collected from the practice of different nations and the authority of writers.' Accordingly, he argued and determined from such instances, and the authorities of Grotius, Barbeyrac, Bynkershoek, Wicquefort, etc., there being no English writer of eminence on the subject."

That doctrine was accepted, not only by Lord Mansfield himself, but also by Sir William Blackstone, and other great names, too numerous to mention. In 1853 Lord Lyndhurst in the House of Lords, with the concurrence of all his colleagues there, declared that ... "the law of nations, according to the decision of our greatest judges, is part of the law of England": [⋯]

(ii) The doctrine of transformation. The doctrine of transformation only goes back to 1876 in the judgment of Cockburn C.J. in Reg. v. Keyn (1876) 2 Ex.D. 63, 202-203: "For writers on international law, however valuable their labours may be in elucidating and ascertaining the principles and rules of law, cannot make the law. To be binding, the law must have received the assent of the nations who are to be bound by it. ... Nor, in my opinion, would the clearest proof of unanimous assent on the part of other nations be sufficient to authorise the tribunals of this country to apply, without an Act of Parliament, what would practically amount to a new law. In so doing, we should be unjustifiably usurping the province of the legislature." To this I may add the saying of Lord Atkin in Chung Chi Cheung v. The King [1939] A.C. 160, 167-168: "So far, at any rate, as the courts of this country are concerned, international law has no validity save in so far as its principles are accepted and adopted by our own domestic law."

And I myself accepted this without question in Reg. v. Secretary of State for the Home Department, Ex parte Thakrar [1974] Q.B. 684, 701.

(ⅲ) Which is correct? As between these two schools of thought, I now believe that the doctrine of incorporation is correct. Otherwise I do not see that our courts could ever recognise a change in the rules of international law. It is certain that international law does change. I would use of international law the words which Galileo used of the earth: "But it does move." International law does change: and the courts have applied the changes without the aid of any Act of Parliament. Thus, when the rules of international law were changed (by the force of public opinion) so as to condemn slavery, the English courts were justified in applying the modern rules of international law: [⋯] Again, the extent of territorial waters varies from time to time according to the rule of international law current at the time, and the courts will apply it accordingly: [⋯] The bounds of sovereign immunity have changed greatly in the last 30 years. The changes have been recognised in many countries, and the courts—of our country and of theirs—have given effect to them, without any legislation for the purpose, notably in the decision of the Privy Council in The Philippine Admiral [1977] A.C. 373.

(ⅳ) Conclusion on this point. Seeing that the rules of international law have changed—and do change—and that the courts have given effect to the changes without any Act of Parliament, it follows to my mind inexorably that the rules of international law, as existing from time to time, do form part of our English law. It follows, too, that a decision of this court—as to what was the ruling of international law 50 or 60 years ago—is not binding on this court today. International law knows no rule of *stare decisis*. If this court today is satisfied that the rule of international law on a subject has changed from what it was 50 or 60 years ago, it can give effect to that change—and apply the change in our English law—without waiting for the House of Lords to do it."

☑ 해   설

영국에서는 비교적 이른 시기부터 관습국제법은 Common Law의 일부이며, 따라서 영국 법원은 관습국제법을 직접 근거로 하여 재판할 수 있다는 원칙이 인정되었다. 다만 관습국제법은 의회 제정법에 우선할 수 없다. 한편 관습국제법에 입각해서 내려진 판결에 관하여도 영국법상의 선례구속성 원칙이 적용되는가? 과거 영국 법원은 이를 긍정했다. 그렇다면 문제는 일단 영국에서 관습국제법에 입각한 판례가 성립되면, 영국에서 구현되는 관습국제법은 국제사회의 변화와 상관없이 과거의 법으로 고정된다는 불합리한 결과를 야기한다. 이는 의회 제정법에 의하여만 교정될 수 있다. 이에 근래에 내려진 본 판결은 관습국제법이 있는 그대로 수시로 영국법의 일부를 구성한다는 입장을 제시한 점에서 중요한 판결이다.

영국 법원이 관습국제법을 적용함에 있어서의 현실적 어려움의 하나는 판사가 관습국제법의 존재를 어떻게 확인할 수 있느냐이다. 어느 나라나 법률가들은 주로 국내법만을 다루며 국제법에 관한 전문지식이 부족하다. 그러다 보니 영국의 판사들 역시 관습국제법의 증거를 영국법 속에 이미 구현된 내용에서 찾는 경향을 보이고 있다. 이러한 결과는 영국 법원이 관습국제법의 적용에 관하여 마치 변형이론으로 경사된 것과 같은 외관을 만들기도 했다.

제한적 주권면제론에 입각한 이 판결이 내려진 이듬해 영국은 이를 국내 입법화했고(the State Immunity Act of 1978), 1979년에는 주권면제에 관한 1972년 유럽협약(the European Convention on State Immunity of 1972)도 비준했다.

한편 관습국제법이 영국법의 일부라면 관습국제법상의 범죄도 자동적으로 영국 법원에서 형사처벌의 대상이 되는가? 본래 Common 상 통상적인 형사범죄는 법원의 판례법을 통해 발전했다. 그러나 형사범죄에 관한 한 이 제 영국에서는 의회만이 새로운 범죄를 창설할 수 있는 반면, Common Law 를 통하여는 새로운 범죄가 성립되지 않는다. 다음 판결문은 영국 법원에서 침략범죄가 관습국제법을 근거로 처벌될 수 있는가에 관한 논의를 담고 있다. 결론은 이제 이를 처벌하기 위한 의회 제정법이 없다면 불가능하다는 것이다.

> **28.** The lack of any statutory incorporation is not, however, a neutral factor, for two main reasons. The first is that there now exists no power in the courts to create new criminal offenses, as decided by a unanimous House in R v Knuller (Publishing, Printing and Promotions) Ltd [1973] AC 435. While old common law offenses survive until abolished or superseded by statute, new ones are not created. Statute is now the sole source of new criminal offenses. The second reason is that when it is sought to give domestic effect to crimes established in customary international law, the practice is to legislate. [⋯]
>
> **29.** These reasons, taken together, are very strong grounds for rejecting the appellants contention, since they reflect what has become an important democratic principle in this country: that it is for those representing the people of the country in Parliament, not the executive and not the judges, to decide what conduct should be treated as lying so far outside the bounds of what is acceptable in our society as to attract criminal penalties. One would need very compelling reasons for departing from that principle. (Regina v. Jones (Margaret) and Others. [2006] UKHL 16; [2007] 1 AC 136, House of Lords, U.K.)

▶ 참고문헌 ────────────────────────────────

- R. Higgins, Recent Development in the Law of Sovereign Immunity in the United Kingdom, AJIL Vol. 71(1977), p. 423.
- B. S. Markesinis, The Changing Law of Sovereign Immunity, Cambridge Law Journal Vol. 36(1977), p. 211.
- R. C. A. White, State Immunity and International Law in English Courts, ICLQ Vol. 26(1977), p. 674.

4. 조약을 근거로 한 형사처벌의 가중(1998)

헌법재판소 1998년 11월 26일 선고, 97헌바65 결정.
헌법재판소 판례집 제10권 2집(1998), 685쪽 이하.

☑ 사　안

이 사건 위헌심판 청구인은 중국산 참깨를 밀수하다가 적발되어 관세포탈 등의 혐의로 유죄판결을 받게 되었다. 이 사건에 대한 적용법률인 (구)특가법 제6조 제2항에 따르면 포탈 관세액이 1억원 이상인 때에는 무기 또는 10년 이상의 징역, 포탈 관세액이 2천만원 이상 1억원 미만일 때에는 5년 이상의 유기징역에 처하게 되어 있었다. 한국이 세계무역기구(WTO) 설립조약에 가입함에 따라 참깨의 최소 시장접근물량분(최초 3%에서 점차 5%로 증대)에 대하여는 기존 관세율 40%가 그대로 적용되나, 이를 제외한 일반 수입관세율은 700%로 대폭 인상되었다(단 매년 7%씩 인하). 이에 청구인의 참깨 밀수에 대하여는 686%의 관세율이 적용되어 관세 포탈액이 1억원을 넘게 되었고, 이는 특가법상의 10년 이상 징역형에 해당했다. 청구인은 관련 관세법 등의 개정 없이 새로운 조약 체결로 인하여 자신에 대한 형량이 증가되는 결과가 초래되었으므로 이는 죄형법정주의에 위반된다고 주장했다.

☑ 쟁　점

한국에서 관련 국내법의 개정 없이 조약만을 근거로 형사처벌이 가중될 수 있는가 여부.

☑ 판　결

헌법에 의하여 체결·공포된 조약은 국내법과 같은 효력을 지니므로 이

를 근거로 한 가중처벌도 일반 국내법을 근거로 한 가중처벌과 동일한 효력
을 지닌다.

판 결 문

　청구인은 관세법위반죄를 범한 자에 대한 처벌을 가중하려면 관세법이
나 특가법을 개정하여야 함에도 불구하고 단지 조약에 의하여 관세법위반자
의 처벌을 가중하는 것은 중대한 기본권의 침해이며 죄형법정주의에 어긋나
는 것이라고 주장한다.

　그러나 헌법 제12조 후문 후단은 "누구든지 … 법률과 적법한 절차에
의하지 아니하고는 처벌·보안처분 또는 강제노역을 받지 아니한다"고 규정
하여 법률과 적법절차에 의한 형사처벌을 규정하고 있고, 헌법 제13조 제1
항 전단은 "모든 국민은 행위시의 법률에 의하여 범죄를 구성하지 아니하는
행위로 소추되지 아니하며"라고 규정하여 행위시의 법률에 의하지 아니한
형사처벌의 금지를 규정하고 있으며, 헌법 제6조 제1항은 "헌법에 의하여 체
결·공포된 조약과 일반적으로 승인된 국제법규는 국내법과 같은 효력을 가
진다"고 규정하여 적법하게 체결되어 공포된 조약은 국내법과 같은 효력을
가진다고 규정하고 있다. 마라케쉬협정도 적법하게 체결되어 공포된 조약이
므로 국내법과 같은 효력을 갖는 것이어서 그로 인하여 새로운 범죄를 구성
하거나 범죄자에 대한 처벌이 가중된다고 하더라도 이것은 국내법에 의하여
형사처벌을 가중한 것과 같은 효력을 갖게 되는 것이다. 따라서 마라케쉬협
정에 의하여 관세법위반자의 처벌이 가중된다고 하더라도 이를 들어 법률에
의하지 아니한 형사처벌이라거나 행위시의 법률에 의하지 아니한 형사처벌
이라고 할 수 없으므로, 마라케쉬협정에 의하여 가중된 처벌을 하게 된 구특
가법 제6조 제2항 제1호나 농안법 제10조의 3이 죄형법정주의에 어긋나거나
청구인의 기본적 인권과 신체의 자유를 침해하는 것이라고 할 수 없다.

　☑ 해　　설
　이 판결은 우리 법원이 헌법 제6조 제1항을 근거로 조약을 직접 적용하

여 재판을 할 수 있음을 보여준 예의 하나이다. 국내 법원에서 조약의 직접 적용의 다른 예로는 헌법재판소 2001년 9월 27일 선고, 2000헌바20 결정; 대법원 1986년 7월 22일 선고, 82다카1372 판결; 대법원 2002년 10월 22일 선고, 2002다32523, 32530 판결; 대법원 2004년 7월 22일 선고, 2001다67164 판결; 대법원 2005년 9월 9일 선고, 2004추10 판결; 대법원 2006년 4월 28일 선고, 2005다30184 판결; 대법원 2008년 12월 24일 선고, 2004추72 판결; 대법원 2016년 3월 24일 선고, 2013다81514 판결 등 사례가 적지 않다. 특히 항공운송상 발생한 사고에 관하여는 과거 국내법이 제정된 바 없어 이에 관한 조약을 직접 적용해 내려진 판결이 많았다. 보다 상세는 정인섭, 한국법원에서의 국제법 판례(박영사, 2018), p. 4 이하 수록내용 참조.

➡ 참고문헌 ─────────────────────────────

• 정인섭, 조약의 국내법적 효력에 관한 한국 판례와 학설의 검토, 서울국제법연구 제22권 1호(2015. 6), p. 27.

5. 관습국제법의 국내적 적용 (2013)

서울고등법원 2013년 4월 18일 선고, 2012나63832 판결.
법원도서관 종합법률정보.

☑ 사 안

CCCS(회사)는 홍콩에 등록된 법인으로 우리은행 홍콩지점에 예금계좌를 개설하고 있었다. 이 회사는 한국에도 사무소를 두고 외항 화물운송업을 했다. 이 회사가 한국에서 국세를 체납하고 있다고 판단한 국세청은 우리은행 홍콩지점에 예치된 이 회사 예금에 대해 압류를 결정하고 이를 우리은행 본점과 홍콩지점에 통보했다. 이에 우리은행 홍콩지점은 회사의 예금인출을 허용하지 않았다. 회사는 홍콩법원에 우리은행 홍콩법인을 상대로 예금인출을 허용해 달라는 명령을 청구하는 소를 제기했고, 홍콩법원은 이를 허용했다. 이에 따라 우리은행 홍콩지점은 회사의 예금을 전액 지불했다. 그러자 대한민국은 우리은행을 상대로 압류금 청구소송을 제기했다.

피고(우리은행)측은 이 사건 예금채권이 대한민국 영역 외의 재산으로 국세징수법에 의한 압류대상이 아니고, 홍콩정부의 협조나 동의를 구하지 아니한 채 국내 소재 재산과 마찬가지로 이 사건 압류통지서를 우편 송달했으므로 피고 홍콩지점에 대한 압류는 효력이 없다는 점 등을 주장했다.

☑ 쟁 점

집행관할권의 허용 한계

☑ 판 결

집행관할권은 자국 영토에 한정되어 미침이 원칙이며, 상대국의 동의

등이 없이 외국소재 재산에 강제집행권 행사는 허용되지 않음이 관습국제법
이다.

판 결 문

"일반적으로 승인된 국제법규는 국내법과 같은 효력을 가지고(헌법 제6조
제1항), 특정 국가의 집행관할권은 자국의 영토 등에 한정되어 미치며, 외국
에 있는 재산에 관하여 강제집행권을 행사하기 위하여는 조약 또는 상대국
의 동의가 있거나 외국판결의 승인 등의 절차를 거쳐야 하고, 그러한 절차를
생략한 채 상대국의 허락 없이 곧바로 외국 소재 재산에 관하여 주권을 전
제로 하는 강제집행권을 행사하는 것은 허용되지 않는 것이 일반적으로 승
인된 국제관습법이라 할 것이다. 한편 원고 스스로 과세관청 내부에 있어서
세법의 해석기준 및 집행기준을 시달한 국세징수법 기본통칙에 의하더라도
압류의 대상이 되는 재산은 국세징수법의 효력이 미치는 지역 내에 있는 재
산이어야 한다고 밝히고 있다. 이러한 점을 종합하면, 원고의 국세체납처분
권은 대한민국의 영토 등에 있는 재산에 한하여 미치는 것으로 봄이 타당하
다. […]

이상의 이유로 피고 홍콩지점과 예금거래계약을 체결하고 돈을 예치한
사람은 그 예금이 홍콩지역 내에 존재하는 것으로 인식하고 거래할 것으로
보이는 점 등을 종합하면, 이 사건 피고 홍콩지점에 대한 예금채권의 소재지
는 대한민국 영토 내가 아닌 홍콩이라고 봄이 상당하다. 결국 이 사건 피고
홍콩지점에 대한 예금채권의 압류는 국세체납처분권이 미치지 아니하는 지
역에 소재한 재산에 대한 것이어서 효력이 없다고 할 것이다."

☑ 해   설

헌법 제6조 1항은 "헌법에 의하여 체결·공포된 조약과 일반적으로 승
인된 국제법규는 국내법과 같은 효력을 지닌다"고 규정하고 있고, 이중 "일
반적으로 승인된 국제법규"는 관습국제법을 가리킨다. 그간 한국의 사법부는
관습국제법이 별도의 국내적 입법조치 없이도 직접 적용될 수 있다고 보아

왔다. 이 판례 역시 집행관할권 행사의 속지주의 원칙을 관습국제법이라고 전제하고, 국세체납처분권은 대한민국의 영토 등에 있는 재산에만 미친다고 해석했다. 이 판결은 대법원 2014년 11월 27일 선고, 2013다205198 판결에 의해 상고 기각 확정되었는데, 대법원 판결에서는 관습국제법에 관한 언급은 없었다.

그간 국내 법원에서 가장 빈번하게 적용되었던 유형의 관습국제법은 주권면제법리였다. 이 분야에 대해서는 별도의 국내법률 없이 관습국제법의 형식으로 주권면제가 적용되었다(본서 제5장 3번 판결(p. 143) 참조). 관습국제법의 국내적용과 관련된 판결로는 정인섭, 한국법원에서의 국제법 판례(박영사, 2018), pp. 15−20 및 pp. 44−64 수록 판례 참조.

➠ 참고문헌 ─────────────────────────────

- 이창, 국내은행 해외지점 계좌관련 예금채권에 대한 체납처분: 서울고등법원 2013. 4. 18. 선고 2012나63832 판결을 중심으로, 홍익법학 제15권 제1호 (2014).
- 정인섭, 헌법 제6조 1항상 "일반적으로 승인된 국제법규"의 국내 적용 실행, 서울국제법연구 제23권 1호(2016. 6), p. 49.

제 3 장

국가의 독립과 승인

1. 코소보 독립선언의 합법성(2010)
— 국가의 영토적 일체성 원칙의 침해 여부

Accordance with International Law of the Unilateral Declaration
of Independence in respect of Kosovo.
Advisory Opinion, 2010 ICJ Reports 403.

☑ 사   안

구 유고연방의 붕괴 후 수립된 세르비아 내의 한 지역인 코소보는 알바
니아계 주민이 주축을 이루었다. 이들이 독립 움직임을 보이자 세르비아계에
의한 학살이 발생했고, NATO의 개입으로 이 지역은 UN과 EU의 관리 하에
자치를 실시했다. 코소보는 주민투표를 거쳐 2008년 2월 17일 독립을 선언
했다. 서구 국가들은 이를 승인했으나, 세르비아, 러시아 등은 독립 선언이
위법하다고 주장하며 이를 승인하지 않았다. 2008년 UN 총회는 코소보 자치
정부의 독립 선언이 국제법에 합치되는가에 관해 ICJ 권고적 의견을 구하기
로 하였다("Is the unilateral declaration of independence by the Provisional
Institutions of Self-Government of Kosovo in accordance with international law?").
판단과정에서 쟁점 중 하나는 민족자결권의 성격과 일방적 독립 선언이 기
존 국가의 영토적 일체성을 침해하느냐 여부였다.

☑ 쟁   점

기존 국가내 일부지역의 일방적 독립선언은 국제법 위반인가?

☑ 판   결

일방적 독립을 금지하는 국제법 원칙은 없다. 기존의 영토적 일체성 존
중의 원칙은 국가 사이에 적용되는 원칙이므로 코소보 독립 선언이 일반 국

제법 위반이라고 할 수 없다.

판 결 문

78. The Court now turns to the substance of the request submitted by the General Assembly. The Court recalls that it has been asked by the General Assembly to assess the accordance of the declaration of independence of 17 February 2008 with "international law"(resolution 63/3 of the General Assembly, 8 October 2008). The Court will first turn its attention to certain questions concerning the lawfulness of declarations of independence under general international law, [⋯]

79. During the eighteenth, nineteenth and early twentieth centuries, there were numerous instances of declarations of independence, often strenuously opposed by the State from which independence was being declared. Sometimes a declaration resulted in the creation of a new State, at others it did not. In no case, however, does the practice of States as a whole suggest that the act of promulgating the declaration was regarded as contrary to international law. On the contrary, State practice during this period points clearly to the conclusion that international law contained no prohibition of declarations of independence. During the second half of the twentieth century, the international law of self-determination developed in such a way as to create a right to independence for the peoples of non-self-governing territories and peoples subject to alien subjugation, domination and exploitation ([⋯]). A great many new States have come into existence as a result of the exercise of this right. [⋯]

80. Several participants in the proceedings before the Court have contended that a prohibition of unilateral declarations of independence is implicit in the principle of territorial integrity.

The Court recalls that the principle of territorial integrity is an important part of the international legal order and is enshrined in the Charter of the United Nations, in particular in Article 2, paragraph 4, which provides that:

> "All Members shall refrain in their international relations from the threat or use of force against the territorial integrity or political independence of any State, or in any other manner inconsistent with the Purposes of the United Nations."

In General Assembly resolution 2625(XXV), entitled "Declaration on Principles of International Law concerning Friendly Relations and Co-operation among States in Accordance with the Charter of the United Nations," which reflects customary international law ([···]), the General Assembly reiterated "[t]he principle that States shall refrain in their international relations from the threat or use of force against the territorial integrity or political independence of any State." This resolution then enumerated various obligations incumbent upon States to refrain from violating the territorial integrity of other sovereign States. In the same vein, the Final Act of the Helsinki Conference on Security and Cooperation in Europe of 1 August 1975(the Helsinki Conference) stipulated that "[t]he participating States will respect the territorial integrity of each of the participating States"(Art. IV). Thus, the scope of the principle of territorial integrity is confined to the sphere of relations between States.

81. Several participants have invoked resolutions of the Security Council condemning particular declarations of independence: *see, inter alia*, Security Council resolutions 216(1965) and 217(1965), concerning Southern Rhodesia; Security Council resolution 541(1983), concerning northern Cyprus; and Security Council resolution 787(1992), concerning the Republika Srpska.

The Court notes, however, that in all of those instances the Security Council was making a determination as regards the concrete situation existing at the time that those declarations of independence were made; the illegality attached to the declarations of independence thus stemmed not from the unilateral character of these declarations as such, but from the fact that they were, or would have been, connected with the unlawful use of force or other egregious violations of norms of general international law, in particular those of a peremptory character(*jus cogens*). In the context of Kosovo, the Security Council has never taken this position. The exceptional character of the resolutions enumerated above appears to the Court to confirm that no general prohibition against unilateral declarations of independence may be inferred from the practice of the Security Council. [···]

84. For the reasons already given, the Court considers that general inter-national law contains no applicable prohibition of declarations of independence. Accordingly, it concludes that the declaration of independence of 17 February 2008 did not violate general international law.

Dissenting Opinion of Judge Koroma:

20. [⋯] the Court, in considering the question put before it by the General Assembly, had to apply the rules and principles of general international law. In this regard, it must first be emphasized that it is a misconception to say, as the majority opinion does, that international law does not authorize or prohibit the unilateral declaration of independence. That statement only makes sense when made in the abstract about declarations of independence in general ([⋯]), not with regard to a specific unilateral declaration of independence which took place in a specific factual and legal context against which its accordance with international law can be judged. The question put before the Court is specific and well defined. It is not a hypothetical question. It is a legal question requiring a legal response. Since the Court, according to its Statute, is under an obligation to apply the rules and principles of international law even when rendering advisory opinions, it should have applied them in this case. Had it done so — instead of avoiding the question by reference to a general statement that international law does not authorize or prohibit declarations of independence, which does not answer the question posed by the General Assembly — it would have had to conclude, as discussed below, that the unilateral declaration of independence by the Provisional Institutions of Self-Government of Kosovo amounted to secession and was not in accordance with international law. A unilateral secession of a territory from an existing State without its consent, as in this case under consideration, is a matter of international law.

21. The truth is that international law upholds the territorial integrity of a State. One of the fundamental principles of contemporary international law is that of respect for the sovereignty and territorial integrity of States. This principle entails an obligation to respect the definition, delineation and territorial integrity of an existing State. According to the principle, a State exercises sovereignty within and over its territorial domain. The principle of respect for territorial integrity is enshrined in the Charter of the United Nations and other international instruments. [⋯]

The unilateral declaration of independence involves a claim to a territory which is part of the Federal Republic of Yugoslavia(Serbia). Attempting to dismember or amputate part of the territory of a State, in this case the Federal Republic of Yugoslavia (Serbia), by dint of the unilateral declaration of independence of 17 February 2008, is neither in conformity with international law nor with the principles of the Charter of the United Nations, nor with resolution 1244(1999).

The principle of respect for territorial integrity is also reflected in the Declaration on Principles of International Law concerning Friendly Relations and Co-operation among States in accordance with the Charter of the United Nations, according to which:

> "any attempt aimed at the partial or total disruption of the national unity and *territorial integrity of a State or country or at its political independence* is incompatible with the purposes and principles of the Charter" ([⋯]).

The Declaration further stipulates that "[t]he territorial integrity and political independence of the State are inviolable."

22. Not even the principles of equal rights and self-determination of peoples as precepts of international law allow for the dismemberment of an existing State without its consent. According to the above-mentioned Declaration, "[e]very State shall refrain from *any action* aimed at the partial or total disruption of the national unity and territorial integrity of any other State or country." The Declaration further emphasizes that

> "Nothing in the foregoing paragraphs shall be construed as authorizing or encouraging any action which would dismember or impair, totally or in part, the territorial integrity or political unity of sovereign and independent States." ([⋯])

The Declaration thus leaves no doubt that the principles of the sovereignty and territorial integrity of States prevail over the principle of self-determination. [⋯]

25. It is for these reasons that the Court should have found that the unilateral declaration of independence of 17 February 2008 by the Provisional Institutions of Self-Government of Kosovo is not in accordance with international law.

☑ 해 설

이 결정은 ICJ가 담당했던 가장 정치적 사건 중의 하나였다. 이 결정에서 ICJ의 다수의견은 코소보가 독립 선언으로 국제법상의 국가성을 획득했는가라는 점은 판단하지 않고, 한 국가 내에서의 일방적 독립선언에 대한 국제법상 일반적 금지는 없다고만 답했다. 사실 이는 질문의 핵심을 비켜간 답이었다. 이에 다수의견에 대하여는 적지 않은 이견도 제시되었다.

Simma 판사는 금지규범이 없으므로 국제법상 허용된다는 PCIJ의 Lotus 판결에서의 논리를 ICJ가 이 사건에서 반복하는 태도는 구태의연하다고 비판했다(Declaration of Judge Simma, para. 3).

Koroma 판사 외에 Yusuf 판사도 코소보의 일방적 분리독립 선언 자체의 합법성 여부를 판단하지 않고, ICJ가 단순히 일반론으로서만 일방적 독립선언이 국제법상 금지되지 않아 국제법 위반은 아니라고 판단한다면 모든 형태의 분리주의 운동을 정당화시키는 결과가 되어 국제평화와 안전을 위협하고 국제사회에 혼란을 야기하게 될 것이라고 비판했다(Separate Opinion of Judge Yusuf, para. 6).

➤ 참고문헌
- 이성덕, 코소보의 일방적 독립선언의 국제법상 허용 가능성에 관한 ICJ 권고적 의견에 대한 검토, 중앙법학 12집 4호(2010), p. 243.
- 박정원, 코소보 독립과 현대국제법: 자결권 행사의 어려움에 특히 주목하며, 국제법학회논총 56권 2호(2011), p. 89.
- 김석현, 대외적 자결권에 관한 국제법 상황: 피압박 소수자 집단의 일방적 분리독립권을 중심으로, 국제법평론 제46호(2017), p. 1.

2. 퀘벡주 분리 독립(1998)
— 민족자결권과 분리 독립

Reference re Secession of Quebec.
Supreme Court of Canada, [1998] 2 Supreme Court Reports
217.

☑ 사   안

캐나다 퀘벡주에서 분리주의운동이 고조되자 연방정부는 연방대법원에게 ① 캐나다 헌법상 퀘벡주 의회나 정부가 일방적으로 분리를 결정할 수 있는가? ② 국제법은 퀘벡주 의회나 정부에 일방적 분리를 할 권한을 부여하고 있는가 등에 관한 자문의견을 요청했다(reference jurisdiction). 캐나다 연방대법원은 한 국가 내 일정 집단이 민족자결(self−determination)을 근거로 일방적 분리·독립을 할 수 있는 상황에 대한 판단기준을 제시했다. 즉 일방적 분리를 할 권한은 국제법상 일반적으로 인정되지도 부인되지도 않고 있으나, 다음과 같은 특별한 상황에서는 이러한 권한이 인정될 수 있다. 즉 1) 식민지의 분리 독립 2) 외세지배로부터의 분리 독립 3) 한 국가 내에서 자결권의 실현을 실질적으로 봉쇄당하고 있는 집단의 분리 독립. 이 사안에서 연방대법원은 퀘벡주의 상황이 그 어느 경우에도 해당되지 않는다고 판단해 퀘벡주의 분리·독립권을 부인했다.

☑ 쟁   점

한 국가 내 일정 집단은 민족자결의 실현을 위해 일방적으로 분리 독립할 권한이 있는가?

☑ 판　　결

국제법상 민족자결의 실현을 통한 분리 독립은 ① 식민지 독립 ② 외세 지배로부터 독립 ③ 피차별 집단의 분리 독립의 경우에만 가능하다.

판 결 문

112. International law contains neither a right of unilateral secession nor the explicit denial of such a right, although such a denial is, to some extent, implicit in the exceptional circumstances required for secession to be permitted under the right of a people to self-determination, *e.g.*, the right of secession that arises in the exceptional situation of an oppressed or colonial people, discussed below. As will be seen, international law places great importance on the territorial integrity of nation states and, by and large, leaves the creation of a new state to be determined by the domestic law of the existing state of which the seceding entity presently forms a part. [⋯]

113. While international law generally regulates the conduct of nation states, it does, in some specific circumstances, also recognize the "rights" of entities other than nation states - such as the right of a people to self-determination.

114. The existence of the right of a people to self-determination is now so widely recognized in international conventions that the principle has acquired a status beyond "convention" and is considered a general principle of international law. [⋯]

122. As will be seen, international law expects that the right to self-determination will be exercised by peoples within the framework of existing sovereign states and consistently with the maintenance of the territorial integrity of those states. Where this is not possible, in the exceptional circumstances discussed below, a right of secession may arise. [⋯]

131. Accordingly, the general state of international law with respect to the right to self-determination is that the right operates within the overriding protection granted to the territorial integrity of "parent" states. However, [⋯] there are certain defined contexts within which the right to the self-determination of peoples does allow that right to be exercised "externally", which, in the context of this Reference, would potentially mean secession: [⋯]

132. The right of colonial peoples to exercise their right to self-determination by breaking away from the "imperial" power is now undisputed, but is irrelevant to this Reference.

133. The other clear case where a right to external self-determination accrues is where a people is subject to alien subjugation, domination or exploitation outside a colonial context. [⋯]

134. A number of commentators have further asserted that the right to self-determination may ground a right to unilateral secession in a third circumstance. Although this third circumstance has been described in several ways, the underlying proposition is that, when a people is blocked from the meaningful exercise of its right to self-determination internally, it is entitled, as a last resort, to exercise it by secession. The Vienna Declaration requirement that governments represent "the whole people belonging to the territory without distinction of any kind" adds credence to the assertion that such a complete blockage may potentially give rise to a right of secession.

135. Clearly, such a circumstance parallels the other two recognized situations in that the ability of a people to exercise its right to self-determination internally is somehow being totally frustrated. While it remains unclear whether this third proposition actually reflects an established international law standard, it is unnecessary for present purposes to make that determination. Even assuming that the third circumstance is sufficient to create a right to unilateral secession under international law, the current Quebec context cannot be said to approach such a threshold. [⋯][1)]

138. In summary, the international law right to self-determination only generates, at best, a right to external self-determination in situations of former colonies; where a people is oppressed, as for example under foreign military occupation; or where a definable group is denied meaningful access to government to pursue their political, economic, social and cultural development. In all three situations, the people in question are entitled to a right to external self-determination because they have been denied the ability to exert internally their right to self-determination. Such exceptional circumstances are manifestly inapplicable to Quebec under existing conditions. Accordingly, neither the population of the province of Quebec, even if characterized in terms of "people" or "peoples", nor its

---

1) 그 근거로 직전 50년 중 40년간 퀘벡인이 캐나다 총리를 역임했으며, 이 판결 당시에도 총리와 대법원장, 육군 참모총장 등이 퀘벡인이었던 점 등을 예로 들며, 캐나다의 정치·경제 생활에서 퀘벡인이 억압받지 않고 있음을 지적했다.

representative institutions, the National Assembly, the legislature or government of Quebec, possess a right, under international law, to secede unilaterally from Canada.

☑ 해   설

민족자결은 식민지 독립과정에서는 중요한 역할을 했다. 이제 민족자결이 국제법상 기본 원칙이라는 점에는 이견이 없으나, 이를 실현할 민족(people)의 개념에 대해서는 아직도 국제법상 완전한 합의가 존재하지 않는다. 한 국가의 영토보존 역시 중요한 국제법 원칙이므로 한 국가로부터의 분리 독립은 기존 국가의 국내법에 따라 결정될 문제이기도 하다. 다만 몇 가지 예외적인 상황에서는 민족자결의 실현을 위한 일방적 분리 독립도 가능할 것이다.

캐나다 연방대법원은 앞서 설명한 바와 같이 1) 식민지의 분리 독립 2) 외세지배로부터의 분리 독립 3) 한 국가 내에서 자결권의 실현을 실질적으로 봉쇄당하고 있는 집단의 분리 독립의 경우는 일방적 분리가 국제법상 허용된다고 판단했다(단 3번째 유형에 대해서는 이견이 있음을 인정). 이 판결은 캐나다 국내법원의 판단이지만, 국제법적으로 의미 있는 판단기준을 제공해 주고 있다.

▶ 참고문헌

- 김석현, 대외적 자결권에 대한 국제법 상황: 피압박 소수자 집단의 일방적 분리 독립권을 중심으로, 국제법평론 2017 – I (2017), p. 1.
- 이종훈, 캐나다 퀘벡주주 분리독립 투표의 법적 근거(국회도서관, 1995).

3. 티노코 사건(1923)
― 승인의 의의

Tinoco Arbitration.
U.K./Costa Rica, 1 R.I.A.A. 369.

☑ 사 안

1917년 1월 코스타리카의 Tinoco는 군사 쿠데타를 일으켜 Gonzalez 정부를 전복시키었다. Tinoco는 이어 신 헌법을 제정하고 선거를 통해 계속 집권하였다. Tinoco 정부는 집권시절 Amory사에게 석유 채굴권을 부여했는데 이 권리는 후일 다른 영국계 회사로 넘어갔고, 캐나다 은행에 대한 부채도 있었다. 당시 영국은 Tinoco 정부를 법적으로 승인하지 않았다.

1919년 Tinoco가 퇴임하자 코스타리카의 신 정부는 1871년 제정된 구 헌법을 복원시키고, Tinoco 집권 시절 체결된 계약을 무효화시키는 법률을 제정했다. 영국 정부는 위 계약의 존속을 신정부에 요청했으나, 신정부는 Tinoco 정부의 행위에 대하여는 책임을 질 수 없다고 응답했다. 결국 이 사건은 미국 대법원장이던 W. Taft 판사의 단독 중재재판에 회부되었다. 재판과정에서 코스타리카의 신 정부는 헌법을 위반한 쿠데타로 집권한 Tinoco 정부는 합법적인 정부가 아니었으며, Tinoco 정부를 승인하지 않았던 영국은 이 정부가 부여한 권리를 청구할 수 없으므로, 자신도 구 정부의 책임을 승계할 의무가 없다고 주장했다.

☑ 쟁 점

미승인 정부의 국제법적 지위.

☑ 판   결

정부의 사실상 존재 여부는 국제법적 기준에 의해 객관적으로 판단되어야 하며, 승인의 부여 여부를 통해 결정되지 않는다.

판 결 문

I must hold that from the evidence that the Tinoco government was an actual sovereign government.

But it is urged that many leading Powers refused to recognize the Tinoco government, and that recognition by other nations is the chief and best evidence of the birth, existence and continuity of succession of a government.

Undoubtedly recognition by other Powers is an important evidential factor n establishing proof of the existence of a government in the society of nations. What are the facts as to this? The Tinoco government was recognized by Bolivia on May 17, 1917 [⋯][1]

Probably because of the leadership of the United States in respect to a matter of this kind, her then Allies in the war, Great Britain, France and Italy, declined to recognize the Tinoco government. Costa Rica was, therefore, not permitted to sign the Treaty of Peace at Versailles, although the Tinoco government had declared war against Germany. [⋯]

The non-recognition by other nations of a government claiming to be a national personality, is usually appropriate evidence that it has not attained the independence and control entitling it by international law to be classed as such. But when recognition *vel non*[2] of a government is by such nations determined by inquiry, not into its *de facto* sovereignty and complete governmental control, but into its illegitimacy or irregularity of origin, their non-recognition loses something of evidential weight on the issue with which those applying the rules of international law are alone concerned. What is true of the non-recognition of the United States in its bearing upon the existence of a *de facto* government under Tinoco for thirty months is probably in a measure true of the non-recognition by her Allies in the European War. Such non-recognition for any reason, however,

---

1) 이어서 다양한 국가가 Tinoco 정부를 승인한 사실을 지적하고 있다.
2) or not — 필자 주.

cannot outweigh the evidence disclosed by this record before me as to the *de facto* character of Tinoco's government, according to the standard set by international law.

Second. It is ably and earnestly argued on behalf of Costa Rica that the Tinoco government cannot be considered a *de facto* government, because it was not established and maintained in accord with the constitution of Costa Rica of 1871. To hold that a government which establishes itself and maintains a peaceful administration, with the acquiescence of the people for a substantial period of time, does not become a *de facto* government unless it conforms to a previous constitution would be to hold that within the rules of international law a revolution contrary to the fundamental law of the existing government cannot establish a new government. This cannot be, and is not, true. The change by revolution upsets the rule of the authorities in power under the then existing fundamental law, and sets aside the fundamental law in so far as the change of rule makes it necessary. To speak of a revolution creating a *de facto* government, which conforms to the limitations of the old constitution is to use a contradiction in terms. The same government continues internationally, but not the internal law of its being. The issue is not whether the new government assumes power or conducts its administration under constitutional limitations established by the people during the incumbency of the government it has overthrown. The question is, has it really established itself in such a way that all within its influence recognize its control, and that there is no opposing force assuming to be a government in its place? Is it discharging its functions as a government usually does, respected within its own jurisdiction?

☑ 해   설

이 사건에서 중재재판관은 Tinoco 정부가 코스타리카를 실효적으로 통치했으므로 영국 등 타국이 승인하지 않았다는 사실과 관계 없이 유효한 정부였다고 판단했다. 즉 승인 여부는 정부의 존재에 대한 유력한 증거이기는 하나, 통상 승인의 거부는 여러 가지 외교적 이유에서 비롯되므로 정부의 사실상 존재 여부는 국제법상의 기준에 의하여 객관적으로 판단되어야 한다고 보았다. 즉 이는 승인에 관한 양대 이론 중 선언적 효과설에 입각한 결론이었다. 따라서 중재재판관은 Tinoco 정부의 실체를 인정하고, 이어 코스타리카 신정부가 무효화시킨 구 정부의 계약사항에 대해 실질내용을 검토했다. 캐나다 은행에 대한 부채에 대하여는 영국 정부의 주장을 인정했으나, 석유 채굴권에 관한 계약은 당초 코스타리카 국내법상의 요건도 갖추지 못했으므로 무효라고 판단했다. 1933년 체결된 Montevidedo 협약 제3조는 이 판결의 입장과 마찬가지로 국가의 존재 여부는 타국의 승인과는 무관하다고 규정했다. OAS 헌장 제9조 역시 마찬가지의 규정을 갖고 있다.

➼ 참고문헌 ─────────────────────────────

- J. Brierly, Arbitration between Great Britain and Costa Rica, BYIL Vol. 6(1925), p. 199.
- A. Yianni & D. Tinkler, Is There a Recognized Legal Doctrine of Odious Debts?, North Carolina Journal of International Law and Commercial Regulation Vol. 32(2007), p. 749.
- 배재식, 티노코 중재재판(판결), (서울대학교) 법학 2호(1960), p. 93.

4. 소말리아 대 우드하우스 드레이크 카레이 사건 (1993) ― 미승인 정부의 법인격

Republic of Somalia v. Woodhouse Drake & Carey(Suisse) S.A. and Others.
Queen's Bench, U.K., [1993] Q.B. 54.

☑ 사   안

1991년 1월 소말리아 정부는 외국계 회사를 통하여 쌀을 수입하고 이를 자국 모가디슈항에서 인도받기로 한 계약을 체결하고 대금을 지불했다. 그러나 소말리아는 내전으로 인하여 극심한 혼돈에 빠졌다. 1991년 7월 지부티에서 개최된 국제회의는 Mahdi를 대표로 하는 소말리아 임시정부를 수립하기로 합의했으나, 정파간 분쟁과 소요는 계속되었고 임시정부는 소말리아를 실질적으로 통제할 능력이 없었다. 결국 모가디슈항에 도착한 쌀은 하역과 인도가 불가능한 상태였다. 선주는 이 사건 처리를 영국 법원에 요청했고, 법원은 곡물을 처분하여 운송비를 충당하고 남은 대금은 법원에 예치하도록 명령했다. 원래의 선하증권은 축출된 소말리아 구 정부가 임명한 주유엔대사가 보관하고 있었으나, 소말리아 임시정부는 자신이 잔여대금을 받을 권리가 있다고 주장했다. 재판부는 소말리아 임시정부가 소말리아의 대표로서 남은 대금의 합법적 소유자가 될 수 있는가를 검토했다.

☑ 쟁   점

(1) 영국법원에서 미승인 정부의 법적 지위 ― 소송수행능력의 보유 여부.
(2) 특정 정부가 해당 국가를 대표하는 정부로서 인정받기 위한 요건.

☑ 판 결

(1) 미승인 정부는 영국법원에서 소송수행능력을 갖지 못한다.

(2) 특정 정부가 자국을 대표하는 정부인가를 판단하기 위하여는 1) 합헌적 정부인가? 2) 자국 영토에 대한 행정적 통제권의 정도·성격·안정성, 3) 영국정부와 관계를 맺고 있는지? 있다면 그 관계의 성격은? 4) 특수한 경우에는 국제사회가 이를 해당 국가의 정부로 승인하고 있는지 여부 등을 고려해야 한다.

판 결 문

(p. 62-) The policy of the United Kingdom is now not to confer recognition on governments as opposed to on states. The new policy of Her Majesty's Government was stated in two Parliamentary answers in April and May 1980 […]:

"We have conducted a re-examination of British policy and practice concerning the recognition of governments. This has included a comparison with the practice of our partners and allies. On the basis of this review, we have decided that we shall no longer accord recognition to governments. The British Government recognises states in accordance with common international doctrine.

"Where an unconstitutional change of regime takes place in a recognised state, governments of other states must necessarily consider what dealings, if any, they should have with the new regime, and whether and to what extent it qualifies to be treated as the government of the state concerned. Many of our partners and allies take the position that they do not recognise governments and that therefore no question of recognition arises in such cases. By contrast, the policy of successive British Governments has been that we should make and announce a decision formally 'recognising' the new government.

"This practice has sometimes been misunderstood, and, despite explanations to the contrary, our 'recognition' interpreted as implying approval. For example, in circumstances where there may be legitimate public concern about the violation of human rights by the new regime, or the manner in which it achieved power, it has not sufficed to say that the announcement of 'recognition' is simply a neutral formality.

"We have therefore concluded that there are practical advantages in following the policy of many other countries in not according recognition to governments. Like them, we shall continue to decide the nature of our dealings with regimes which come to power unconstitutionally in the light of our assessment of whether they are able of themselves to exercise effective control of the territory of the State concerned, and seem likely to continue to do so.

"In future cases where a new regime comes to power unconstitutionally our attitude on the question of whether it qualifies to be treated as a government, will be left to be inferred from the nature of the dealings, if any, which we may have with it, and in particular on whether we are dealing with it on a normal government to government basis.

The position in English law before 1980 is conveniently set out in Halsbury's Laws of England, 4th ed., vol. 18 (1977), p. 735, para. 1431:

"A foreign government which has not been recognised by the United Kingdom Government as either *de jure* or *de facto* government has no *locus standi* in the English courts. Thus it cannot institute an action in the courts ... The English courts will not give effect to the acts of an unrecognised government ..."

Thus, recognition by Her Majesty's Government was the decisive matter and the courts had no role save to inquire of the executive whether or not it had recognised the government in question. [⋯]

If recognition by Her Majesty's Government is no longer the criterion of the *locus standi* of a foreign "government" in the English courts and the possession of a legal persona in English law, what criteria is the court to apply? The answers do confirm one applicable criterion, namely, whether the relevant regime is able of itself to "exercise effective control of the territory of the state concerned" and is "likely to continue to do so;" and the statement as to what is to be the evidence of the attitude of Her Majesty's Government provides another - to be inferred from the nature of the dealings, if any, that Her Majesty's Government has with it and whether they are on a normal government to government basis. The nonexistence of such dealings cannot however be conclusive because their absence may be explained by some extraneous consideration, for example, lack of occasion, the attitude of the regime to human rights, its relationship to another state. As the answers themselves acknowledge, the conduct of governments in their relations with each other may be affected by considerations of policy as well as by considerations of legal characterisation. The courts of this country are now only concerned with the latter consideration. How much weight in this connection the courts should give to the attitude of Her Majesty's Government was one of the issues before me. [⋯]

Accordingly, if the question before the court is to be decided on the basis of the attitude adopted by Her Majesty's Government, an order cannot be made in favour of the interim government or Crossman Block. The basis for its attitude is clearly not any disapproval of an established regime but rather that there is no regime which has control, let alone any administrative control which has the requisite element of stable continuity. [⋯]

Accordingly, the factors to be taken into account in deciding whether a government exists as the government of a state are: (a) whether it is the constitutional government of the state; (b) the degree, nature and stability of administrative control, if any, that it of itself exercises over the territory of the state; (c) whether Her Majesty's Government has any dealings with it and if so what is the nature of those dealings; and (d) in marginal cases, the extent of international recognition that it has as the government of the state.

On the evidence before the court the interim government certainly does not qualify having regard to any of the three important factors. Accordingly the court must conclude that Crossman Block does not at present have the authority of the Republic of Somalia to receive and deal with the property of the Republic. The instructions and authority they have received from the interim government are not instructions and authority from the Government of the Republic. I direct that no part of the sum in court should be paid out to Crossman Block without a further order of the court.

☑ 해   설

영국정부로부터 승인을 받지 못한 외국정부는 영국법원에서 소송능력을 가지 못한다는 것이 영국법원의 입장이다. 과거에는 특정 외국정부가 영국정부로부터 승인을 받았는가 여부는 정부에 직접 문의하면 대답이 나왔고, 법원은 이러한 정부의 입장을 존중했다. 그러나 1980년 이후 영국정부는 외국정부의 승인 여부에 대하여 명시적 의사표시를 하지 않기로 했다. 정부 승인에 관한 이 같은 외교정책은 미국정부 등 국제사회에서의 새로운 추세를 따른 것이다. 따라서 특정 외국정부가 자국을 대표하는 진정한 정부로서 영국법원에서 소송능력을 갖는가 여부를 담당 법원이 직접 판단해야만 했다. 소말리아 내전 격화 이후 설립된 임시정부가 소말리아를 대표하는 성부 인가 여부를 판단하기 위해 재판부는 영국정부의 태도, 소말리아의 실상, 국제사회의 움직임 등 여러 가지 요소를 고려했다. 그 결과 문제의 소말리아 임시정부는 자국을 실질적으로 통제하는 정부가 못 되며, 따라서 소말리아정부로서의 권리를 가질 수 없다고 판단했다. 판결문은 특정 정부가 자국을 합법적으로 대표하는가를 판단하기 위한 4가지 고려사항을 제시하고 있다.

한 가지 유의해야 할 사항은 미승인 외국정부에 대해 자국 법원에서 소송능력을 부여할 것인가 여부는 각국의 재량이라는 점이다. 미승인 외국정부에게 자국 법원에서 소송능력을 부인하는 것이 국제법 위반으로 간주되지 않을 뿐이며, 국제법이 미승인 외국정부에게는 국내법원에서의 소송능력을 부인하라고 요구하고 있지는 않다. 한편 소말리아에서는 2012년 가을 반군 거점이 거의 소탕되어 20여년 만에 의회가 새로이 구성되고 정부도 출범하는 등 국기기능을 부분적으로 회복하고 있으나, 아직 완전한 안정화는 이루지 못하고 있다.

반면 개인의 私權에 관하여는 미승인 정부의 행위에 대하여도 법적 효력을 인정하고, 미승인국의 법률도 준거법으로 수락되는 경향이다. 다음은 이와 관련된 ICJ의 판단이다.

> However, non-recognition should not result in depriving the people of Namibia of any advantages derived from international co-operation. In particular, the illegality or invalidity of acts performed by the Government of South Africa on behalf of or concerning Namibia after the termination of the Mandate cannot be extended to such acts as the registration of births, deaths and marriages(*ICJ Advisory Opinion on Namibia, 1971 ICJ Reports 16*, para. 125).

한편 위와 같은 입장과 달리 영국 정부는 리비아의 가다피 정부가 완전 붕괴하기 이전인 2011년 7월 27일 리비아 과도위원회를 리비아의 유일한 정부(the sole governmental authority in Libya)로 승인하며, 기존 가다피 정부가 임명한 외교관은 더 이상 리비아 정부의 대표로 인정하지 않는다고 발표했다. 이후 리비아 대사관 명의로 영국 은행에 예치된 예금을 과도위원회의 지시

에 따라 지출할 수 있느냐가 문제된 사건에서 영국 법원은 외교문제에 관한
한 행정부와 사법부는 한 목소리를 내야 한다며 영국 정부의 승인통지에 결
정적 권위를 인정했다(British Arab Commercial Bank Plc. v. The National Transi-
tional Council of the State of Libya [2011] England and Wales High Court 2274
(Commercial), para. 25).

▶ 참고문헌 ─────────────────────────────

- S. Talmon, Recognition of Governments: An Analysis of the New British
  Policy and Practice, BYIL Vol. 63(1992), p. 231.
- C. Warbrick, Recognition of Governments, The Modern Law Review, vol.
  56, No. 1(1993), p. 92.

5. 셀라시에 망명정부의 지위(1939)
— 승인의 소급효

Haile Selassie v. Cable and Wireless LTD(No.2).
Court of Appeal, U.K., [1939] Ch. 182.

☑ 사　　안

피고 회사는 에티오피아 정부와 시설물 공사계약을 체결했는데, 계약의
이행지체로 인해 일정한 금액을 에티오피아 국고로 반환할 책임을 지게 되
었다. 이 무렵 이탈리아가 에티오피아를 침공해 정복했고(1936. 5), 에티오피
아의 셀라시에 황제는 망명정부를 수립했다. 망명정부는 영국법원에 피고회
사를 상대로 위 금액의 지불을 청구했다. 소제기 당시 영국은 셀라시에 망명
정부를 에티오피아의 법률상 정부로 승인하고 있었고, 이탈리아 정부를 에티
오피아의 사실상의 정부로만 승인하고 있었다. 1심 법원은 셀라시에 망명정
부가 에티오피아의 합법적 정부로서 위 금액에 대한 청구인이 될 자격이 있
다고 판시했다. 피고회사가 항소했는데, 1심 판결 이후 영국정부는 이탈리아
왕을 에티오피아의 대표로 법률상 승인을 했다(1938. 11). 그렇다면 이제는
누가 합법적 권리자이냐가 문제되었다.

☑ 쟁　　점

승인의 소급효—새로이 법률상 승인을 받은 정부는 승인받기 이전에 발
생한 구 정부의 권리에 관하여도 승계를 주장할 수 있는가 여부.

☑ 판　　결

법률상 승인을 받은 신 정부는 사실상 승인만을 받았던 시절까지 소급

하여 구 정부의 권리를 승계한다.

판 결 문

(p. 195-) This is an appeal from a judgment of Bennett J. in an action by the late Emperor of Abyssinia against Cable and Wireless Limited. The claim in the action was for an account of all dealings between the plaintiff and the defendant company under a certain agreement, and payment of the amount found due. The agreement in question was an agreement between the competent Minister of the then Government of Ethiopia and the defendant company in relation to the establishment of a wireless station at Addis Ababa, the capital city of Abyssinia. Under that agreement certain sums admittedly became due from the defendant company. The dispute between the parties turned on the fact that the defendants asserted that the plaintiff had no title to sue for those moneys.

Bennett J. decided in favour of the plaintiff. At the date of the trial the evidence available which was before the learned Judge, so far as it relates to the essential question raised in this appeal, showed that the annexation of Ethiopia by His Majesty the King of Italy had not yet been recognized by His Majesty's Government, but that His Majesty's Government recognized the plaintiff as the *de jure* Emperor of Ethiopia, and that His Majesty's Government recognized the Italian Government as the Government *de facto* of virtually the whole of Ethiopia, and such recognition had existed since the second half of December, 1936, that is to say, since a date earlier than the date of the issue of the writ, which was issued on January 4, 1937. Bennett J. held that the events which had taken place in Ethiopia and the other matters which were established before him were not sufficient to divest the plaintiff as still *de jure* Emperor of Ethiopia, of the right to recover the debt in suit in this country. From that judgment this appeal is brought.

The appeal stood in the list for hearing on November 3 last, and it was called to our attention by Mr. Wynn Parry that, on the day before, an announcement had been made by the Prime Minister in the House of Commons from which it appeared that in the course of a few days, or at any rate a very short time, it was the intention of His Majesty's Government to recognize His Majesty the King of Italy as Emperor of Abyssinia, that is to say, that his position would be recognized *de jure* and no longer merely *de facto*. It was obvious from that announcement that, if it were carried into effect, the situation of this action would be profoundly affected, because circumstances would then be brought to the knowledge of the Court which would have a very important bearing upon the position of the plaintiff and his rights in respect of the debt in question in the action. [⋯]

What has happened is this. As appears from a certificate signed by the direction of His Majesty's Principal Secretary of State for Foreign Affairs, dated November 30, 1938, His Majesty's Government no longer recognizes His Majesty Haile Selassie as *de jure* Emperor of Ethiopia; His Majesty's Government now recognizes His Majesty the King of Italy as *de jure* Emperor of Ethiopia. From that certificate two things emerge as the result of the recognition thereby evidenced. It is not disputed that in the Courts of this country His Majesty the King of Italy as Emperor of Abyssinia is entitled by succession to the public property of the State of Abyssinia, and the late Emperor of Abyssinia's title thereto is no longer recognized as existent.

Further, it is not disputed that that right of succession is to be dated back at any rate to the date when the *de facto* recognition, recognition of the King of Italy as the *de facto* Sovereign of Abyssinia, took place. That was in December, 1936. Accordingly the appeal comes before us upon a footing quite different to that upon which the action stood when it was before Bennett J. We now have the position that in the eye of the law of this country the right to sue in respect of what was held by Bennett J. to be (and no dispute is raised with regard to it) part of the public State property, must be treated in the Courts of this country as having become vested in His Majesty the King of Italy as from a date, at the latest, in December, 1936, that is to say, before the date of the issue of the writ in this action. Now that being so, the title of the plaintiff to sue is necessarily displaced. When the matter was before Bennett J., the *de jure* recognition not having taken place, the question that he had to deal with was whether the effect of the *de facto* conquest of Abyssinia and the recognition *de facto* of the Italian Government's position in Abyssinia, operated to divest the plaintiff of his title to sue. Whether that decision was right or whether it was wrong is a question we are not called upon to answer, but what is admittedly the case is that if Bennett J. had had before him the state of affairs which we have before us, his decision would have been the other way. [⋯]

That being so, the order of the Court will be that the appeal be allowed, that the action be dismissed, but that the order as to costs made by Bennett J. shall not be disturbed, and there will be no costs of the appeal.

☑ 해 설

이 판결에서는 승인의 효과의 소급효를 인정하여, 구 정부 시절 성립된 권리도 신 정부에 귀속된다고 판단했다. 한편 Luther v. Sagor 사건([1921] 3 K.B. 532)에서도 영국 법원은 일단 부여된 승인은 해당 정부가 수립된 시점까지 소급효를 갖는다고 판단했다. 이는 공산혁명 후 수립된 소련 정부의 법령의 효력과 관련된 사건이었다. 재판부는 영국이 소련정부를 승인했으면, 승인받기 이전에 실시된 소련정부의 조치에 대하여도 법적 효력이 인정되어야 한다고 판단했다.

한편 과거 영국법원은 어느 정부가 법률상의 정부로서의 법적 자격을 갖추었는지에 대한 판단은 순전히 영국정부가 해당 정부를 승인하고 있는가 여부를 그대로 존중했다. 본문상의 판결도 그러한 입장에서 내려졌다. 그러나 1980년 이후 영국정부는 외국 정부에 대한 승인 여부에 관하여 의견을 밝히지 않으며, 누가 법률상의 대표자인가도 법원이 판단하고 있음은 앞의 Republic of Somalia v. Woodhouse Drake & Carey(Suisse) S.A. and Others, Queen's Bench Division([1993] Q.B. 54)에서 본 바와 같다.

➡ 참고문헌 ─────────────────────────────

- Q. Wright, The British Courts and Ethiopian Recognition, AJIL Vol. 31 (1937), p. 683.

6. 남북한의 유엔 가입과 상호 국가승인 여부 (1997)

헌법재판소 1997년 1월 16일 선고, 89헌마240 결정.
헌법재판소판례집 제9권 1집(1997), 74쪽 이하.

☑ 사 안

1989년 3월 문익환 목사가 정부 당국과의 아무런 협의 없이 북한을 방문하고 귀환하자 국가보안법 등 위반으로 구속 재판을 받았다. 그는 최종적으로 대법원에서 징역 7년에 자격정지 7년형을 선고받았다. 재판과정에서 피고측은 북한을 반국가단체로 전제하고 있는 국가보안법의 위헌성을 주장했다. 헌법재판소의 위헌소원 판단과정에서는 특히 사건 발생 이후인 1991년 9월 남·북한이 유엔에 동시 가입했고, 1991년 12월 남북 기본합의서가 서명되어 1992년 2월 발효된 사실이 북한의 법적 지위에 관하여 어떠한 법적 의미를 갖는가가 검토되었다.

☑ 쟁 점

⑴ 남·북한의 유엔 동시가입에 따른 상호간 국가승인 여부.
⑵ 1991년 서명된 남북기본합의서의 법적 성격.

☑ 판 결

⑴ 유엔 동시가입은 가맹국 상호간의 국가승인의 효과를 발생시키지 않는다.
⑵ 남북기본합의서는 한민족 내부의 특수관계를 전제로 하는 남북한 당국간의 합의로서 일종의 공동성명 또는 신사협정에 준하는 성격을 가진다.

판 결 문

1991. 9. 남·북한이 유엔(U.N.)에 동시가입하였다. 그러나 이는 "유엔헌장"이라는 다변조약에의 가입을 의미하는 것으로서 유엔헌장 제4조 제1항의 해석상 신규가맹국이 "유엔(U.N.)"이라는 국제기구에 의하여 국가로 승인받는 효과가 발생하는 것은 별론으로 하고, 그것만으로 곧 다른 가맹국과의 관계에 있어서도 당연히 상호간에 국가승인이 있었다고는 볼 수 없다는 것이 현실 국제정치상의 관례이고 국제법상의 통설적인 입장이다.

또 1991. 12. 13. 남·북한의 정부당국자가 소위 남북합의서 "(남북 사이의 화해와 불가침 및 교류·협력에 관한 합의서")에 서명하였고 1992. 2. 19. 이 합의서가 발효되었다. 그러나 이 합의서는 남북관계를 "나라와 나라 사이의 관계가 아닌 통일을 지향하는 과정에서 잠정적으로 형성되는 특수관계"(전문참조)임을 전제로 하여 이루어진 합의문서인바, 이는 한민족공동체 내부의 특수관계를 바탕으로 한 당국간의 합의로서 남북당국의 성의 있는 이행을 상호 약속하는 일종의 공동성명 또는 신사협정에 준하는 성격을 가짐에 불과하다. 따라서 남북합의서의 채택·발효 후에도 북한이 여전히 적화통일의 목표를 버리지 않고 각종 도발을 자행하고 있으며 남·북한의 정치·군사적 대결이나 긴장관계가 조금도 해소되지 않고 있음이 엄연한 현실인 이상, 북한의 반국가단체성이나 국가보안법의 필요성에 관하여는 아무런 상황변화가 있었다고 할 수 없다.

또 1990. 8. 1. 법률 제4239호로 "남북교류협력에관한법률"이 공포·시행된 바 있다. 이 법률은 남·북한간의 상호교류와 협력을 촉진하기 위하여 필요한 사항을 규정할 목적으로 제정된 것인데(제1조) 남·북한간의 왕래·교역·협력사업 및 통신역무의 제공 등 남북교류와 협력을 목적으로 하는 행위에 관하여는 정당하다고 인정되는 범위 안에서 다른 법률에 우선하여 이 법을 적용하도록 되어 있어(제3조) 이 요건을 충족하지 아니하는 경우에는 이 법률의 적용은 배제된다고 할 것이므로 국가보안법이 이 법률과 상충되는 것이라고는 볼 수 없다. 요컨대, 위 두 법률은 상호 그 입법목적과 규제 대상을 달리하고 있는 것이므로 남북교류협력에관한법률 등이 공포·시행되었다 하여 국가보안법의 필요성이 소멸되었다거나 북한의 반국가단체성이 소멸되었다고는 할 수 없다(헌법재판소 1993년 7월 29일 선고, 92헌바48 결정 참조).

그러므로 북한이 남·북한의 유엔동시가입, 소위 남북합의서의 채택·발효 및 남북교류협력에관한법률 등의 시행 후에도 대남적화노선을 고수하면서 우리 자유민주주의체제의 전복을 획책하고 지금도 각종 도발을 계속하고 있음이 엄연한 현실인 점에 비추어, 국가의 존립·안전과 국민의 생존 및 자유를 수호하기 위하여 국가보안법의 해석·적용상 북한을 반국가단체로 보고 이에 동조하는 반국가활동을 규제하는 것 자체가 헌법이 규정하는 국제평화주의나 평화통일의 원칙에 위반된다고 할 수 없다.

☑ 해   설

유엔 동시가입이 남북한 상호승인과는 무관하다는 취지의 다른 판결로는 헌법재판소 1996년 10월 4일 선고, 95헌가2 결정; 동 1997년 1월 16일 선고, 92헌바6·26, 93헌바34·35·36(병합) 결정과 대법원 2008년 4월 17일 선고, 2003도758 판결 등이 있다.

제 4 장

─ ─ ─ ─ ─

국가의 관할권의 행사

1. 로터스호 사건(1927)
― 관할권 행사의 일반원칙

Lotus Case.
France/Turkey, PCIJ Series A No.9(1927).

☑ 사   안

1926년 8월 2일 지중해 공해상에서 프랑스 선박 Lotus호와 터키 선박 Boz―Kourt호가 충돌하여 터키 선박이 침몰하고 터키인 8명이 사망했다. Lotus호가 터키항에 도착하자 터키 사법당국은 프랑스인 당직사관 Demons를 과실치사 혐의로 체포해 기소했다. 터키 법원에서 그는 유죄를 선고받았다. 프랑스는 이에 항의하며, 자국 법원이 이 사건을 재판해야 한다고 주장했다. 결국 양국 정부는 프랑스인에 대한 터키 법원의 형사관할권의 행사가 국제법, 특히 로잔느 조약 제15조(터키와 체약국간의 관할권 문제는 국제법에 따라 결정된다)에 위반되는가에 대한 판단을 PCIJ에 회부하기로 합의했다. 프랑스는 공해상에서의 프랑스인의 행위에 대해 터키 법원이 형사관할권을 행사하려면 국제법상의 허용근거를 제시해야 한다고 주장한 반면, 터키측은 특별히 국제법 원칙에 위배되지 않는 한 자국 내에서의 관할권 행사에 지장이 없다고 반박했다.

☑ 쟁   점

공해상의 자국 선박에 피해를 준 외국선박의 사고책임자에 대한 피해국 법원의 재판관할권.

☑ 판   결

피해국의 그 같은 관할권 행사를 금지하는 국제법은 없으므로 재판이 가능하다.

판 결 문

(p. 18-) International law governs relations between independent States. The rules of law binding upon States therefore emanate from their own free will as expressed in conventions or by usages generally accepted as expressing principles of law and established in order to regulate the relations between these coexisting independent communities or with a view to the achievement of common aims. Restrictions upon the independence of States cannot therefore be presumed.

Now the first and foremost restriction imposed by international law upon a State is that—failing the existence of a permissive rule to the contrary—it may not exercise its power in any form in the territory of another State. In this sense jurisdiction is certainly territorial; it cannot be exercised by a State outside its territory except by virtue of a permissive rule derived from international custom or from a convention.

It does not, however, follow that international law prohibits a State from exercising jurisdiction in its own territory, in respect of any case which relates to acts which have taken place abroad, and in which it cannot rely on some permissive rule of international law. Such a view would only be tenable if international law contained a general prohibition to States to extend the application of their laws and the jurisdiction of their courts to persons, property and acts outside their territory, and if, as an exception to this general prohibition, it allowed States to do so in certain specific cases. But this is certainly not the case under international law as it stands at present. Far from laying down a general prohibition to the effect that States may not extend the application of their laws and the jurisdiction of their courts to persons, property and acts outside their territory, it leaves them in this respect a wide measure of discretion, which is only limited in certain cases by prohibitive rules; as regards other cases, every State remains free to adopt the principles which it regards as best and most suitable. [···]

In these circumstances all that can be required of a State is that it should not overstep the limits which international law places upon its jurisdiction; within these limits, its title to exercise jurisdiction rests in its sovereignty. [···]

Though it is true that in all systems of law the principle of the territorial character of criminal law is fundamental, it is equally true that all or nearly all these systems of law extend their action to offences committed outside the territory of the State which adopts them, and they do so in ways which vary from State to State. The territoriality of criminal law, therefore, is not an absolute principle of international law and by no means coincides with territorial sovereignty. [···]

Consequently, once it is admitted that the effects of the offence were produced on the Turkish vessel, it becomes impossible to hold that there is a rule of international law which prohibits Turkey from prosecuting Lieutenant Demons because of the fact that the author of the offence was on board the French ship. Since, as has already been observed, the special agreement does not deal with the provision of Turkish law under which the prosecution was instituted, but only with the question whether the prosecution should be regarded as contrary to the principles of international law, there is no reason preventing the Court from confining itself to observing that, in this case, a prosecution may also be justified from the point of view of the so-called territorial principle.

It is certainly true that apart from certain special cases which are defined by international law—vessels on the high seas are subject to no authority except that of the State whose flag they fly. In virtue of the principle of the freedom of the seas, that is to say, the absence of any territorial sovereignty upon the high seas, no State may exercise any kind of jurisdiction over foreign vessels upon them. [···]

But it by no means follows that a State can never in its own territory exercise jurisdiction over acts which have occurred on board a foreign ship on the high seas. A corollary of the principle of the freedom of the seas is that a ship on the high seas is assimilated to the territory of the State the flag of which it flies, for, just as in its own territory, that State exercises its authority, upon it, and no other State may do so. All that can be said is that by virtue of the principle of the freedom of the seas, a ship is placed in the same position as national territory; but there is nothing to support the claim according to which the rights of the State under whose flag the vessel sails may go farther than the rights which it exercises within its territory properly so called. It follows that what occurs on board a vessel on the high seas must be regarded as if it occurred on the territory of the State whose flag the ship flies. If, therefore, a guilty act committed on the high seas produces its effects on a vessel flying another flag or in foreign territory, the same principles must be applied as if the territories of two different States were concerned, and the conclusion must therefore be drawn that there is no rule of international law prohibiting the State to which the ship on which the effects of the offence have taken place belongs, from regarding the offence as having been committed in its territory and prosecuting, accordingly, the delinquent.

This conclusion could only be overcome if it were shown that there was a rule of customary international law which, going further than the principle stated above, established the exclusive jurisdiction of the State whose flag was flown. The French Government has endeavoured to prove the existence of such a rule, having recourse for this purpose to the teachings of publicists, to decisions of municipal and international tribunals, and especially to conventions which, whilst creating exceptions to the principle of the freedom of the seas by permitting the war and police vessels of a State to exercise a more or less extensive control over the merchant vessels of another State, reserve jurisdiction to the courts of the country whose flag is flown by the vessel proceeded against.

In the Court's opinion, the existence of such a rule has not been conclusively proved. [⋯]

The conclusion at which the Court has therefore arrived is that there is no rule of international law in regard to collision cases to the effect that criminal proceedings are exclusively within the jurisdiction of the State whose flag is flown. [⋯]

The offence for which Lieutenant Demons appears to have been prosecuted was an—act of negligence or imprudence—having its origin on board the Lotus, whilst its effects made themselves felt on board the Boz-Kourt. These two elements are, legally, entirely inseparable, so much so that their separation renders the offence non-existent. Neither the exclusive jurisdiction of either State, nor the limitations of the jurisdiction of each to the occurrences which took place on the respective ships would appear calculated to satisfy the requirements of justice and effectively to protect the interests of the two States. It is only natural that each should be able to exercise jurisdiction and to do so in respect of the incident as a whole. It is therefore a case of concurrent jurisdiction.

☑ 해   설

이 사건의 처음 표결 결과는 6:6 가부 동수였기 때문에 Max Huber 재판장의 결정 투표권(casting vote) 행사를 통해 터키 법원의 관할권 행사가 국제법 위반이 아니라고 결론내렸다. 이 사건의 다수의견은 공해상 터키 선박에 대한 피해를 곧 터키 영토에서의 피해와 동일시했다. 프랑스측은 공해상에서 발생한 사건에 대한 관할권 행사를 허용하는 국제법상의 근거를 터키가 제시해야 한다고 주장했으나, 재판부는 터키의 그러한 관할권 행사를 금지하는 국제법의 존재는 입증되지 않는다고 판단했다. 결론적으로 공해상 프랑스 선박에서 기인한 행위에 의해 터키 선박에서 발생한 사고에 대하여는 양국 모두가 관할권을 행사할 수 있다고 보았다.

이는 법이란 독립 주권국가의 자유의지에서 비롯되며, 주권국가의 행동에 대한 제한은 특별한 근거가 있어야 한다는 전통적 법실증주의적 사고를 반영하고 있다. 즉 국제법이 특별히 금지하고 있지 않은 한, 주권국가의 어떠한 행동도 허용된다는 논리였다. 다수 의견이 피해자 국적주의(passive nationality rule)에 입각한 관할권 행사의 적절성에 대해서는 판단하지 않았지만, 반대표를 던진 판사들은 모두 그에 입각한 관할권 행사에 반대했다.

이 판결 이후 공해상 선박충돌사건에 대한 형사관할권을 누가 행사하는 편이 정책적으로 적절한가에 대한 국제적 논란이 일었다. 국제형사법에 관한 1940년 몬테비데오 조약을 비롯하여 국제사회의 추세는 기국에게만 형사관할권을 인정하자는 입장이었다. 1982년 유엔 해양법협약 제97조 역시 이 판결의 결과와는 반대로 공해상 선박충돌사건에 관한 형사관할권은 기국에 있다고 규정하고 있으며, EEZ에서도 동일한 규칙이 적용된다(협약 제58조 2항). 이러한 입장이 현재의 관습국제법을 표시한다고 판단된다.

2010년 3월 26일 밤 해군 천안함이 피격, 침몰했다. 인근에서 조업하던 어선 98 금양호가 실종자 수색작업에 참여했다가 귀항하던 4월 2일 밤 서해 대청도 서쪽 약 30해리의 한국측 EEZ에서 캄보디아 화물선 타이요호와 충돌·침몰했다. 이 사고로 선원 9명이 전원 사망·실종되었다. 한국 해경은 이 캄보디아 화물선을 추적·나포하여 대청도로 예인했으나, 해양법 협약에 따라 EEZ에서의 사고에 대해서도 한국이 형사관할권을 행사할 수 없다고 판단하고 사건을 캄보디아로 이첩했다.

국내에서 유사한 사건이 더 발생했다. 그중 2015년 1월 16일 부산 앞바다 EEZ 내를 항해 중이던 라이베리아 선적의 헤밍웨이호가 선원(필리핀 국적) 들의 부주의로 한국 소형 선박 건양호와 충돌했는데 이들은 구조에 나서지 않고 그대로 항해한 사건이 있었다. 이 사고로 건양호는 침몰했고, 선원 2명 이 실종되었다. 한국 검찰은 해양법 협약 제97조는 과실에 의한 사고에만 적 용되며, 충돌 후 구조를 하지 않고 도주한 고의범에 대해서는 한국 법원이 재판권을 행사할 수 있다고 판단하고 헤밍웨이호 선원을 기소했다. 그러나 법원은 도주범죄도 결국 선박 충돌에 의한 항행사고의 일부라고 보아 해양 법 협약에 따라 선박 기국과 선원 국적국만이 형사재판권을 행사할 수 있다 고 판단해 이 부분의 공소를 기각했다(부산지방법원 2015. 6. 12. 선고, 2015고합 52 판결 및 부산고등법원 2015. 12. 16. 선고, 2015노384 판결(확정)).

➡ 참고문헌 ───────────────────────────────

• W. Beckett, Criminal Jurisdiction over Foreigners, The Franconia and the Lotus, BYIL Vol. 8(1927), p. 108.
• G. Berge, The Case of the S. S. Lotus, Michigan Law Review Vol. 26(1928), p. 362.
• J. Brierly, The Lotus Case, Law Quarterly Review Vol. 44(1928), p. 154.
• A. Fachiri, The Case of the S. S. Lotus, BYIL Vol. 9(1928), p. 131.
• 김석현, The Lotus Case 연구, 단국대학교 대학원 학술논총 제6편(1982).

2. 아이히만 사건(1961)
— 보편주의 및 보호주의

Attorney-General of the Government of Israel v. Eichmann
District Court of Jerusalem, Israel. Criminal Case No.40/61.
(https://www.asser.nl/upload/documents/DomCLIC/Docs/NLP/
Israel/Eichmann_Judgement_11-12-1961.pdf)

☑ 사　　안

아이히만(Eichmann)은 나치 시대에 유대인 학살업무를 실행한 주요 인물 중의 하나였다. 제2차 대전 종료 후 그는 알젠틴으로 도주해 숨어 살았다. 후일 그의 소재를 파악한 이스라엘 비밀요원에 의해 1960년 아이히만은 알젠틴으로부터 이스라엘로 납치되었다. 그는 이스라엘 법정에서 1950년 제정된 '나치 및 나치 협력자 처벌법'에 따라 전쟁범죄, 인도에 반하는 죄 등 모두 15개 죄목으로 기소되었다. 재판과정에서 아이히만은 자신은 이스라엘로 불법적으로 납치되어 왔다는 점, 소급입법에 의한 기소라는 점, 범행시 존재하지도 않았던 국가에서의 재판이라는 점 등을 이유로 이스라엘 법원의 재판 관할권 행사를 부인했다.

☑ 쟁　　점

⑴ 이스라엘 건국 이전인 나치 시절 유럽에서 행하여진 아이히만의 행위에 관한 이스라엘 법원의 형사재판 관할권 성립 여부.

⑵ 해외에서 불법납치를 통해 신병을 확보한 범인에 대한 재판관할권.

☑ 판　결

(1) 아이히만의 행위는 국제법상의 범죄로서 그에 대하여는 어떠한 국가도 재판 관할권을 행사할 수 있으며, 특히 이스라엘은 유대인 학살의 피해 당사자로서 재판 관할권을 행사할 수 있다.

(2) 외국으로부터의 불법납치문제는 외교 당국이 처리할 문제이며, 이스라엘 법원은 범인 확보방법과는 관계 없이 국내법에 따른 재판을 할 수 있다.

판 결 문1)

8. Learned Counsel [⋯] contends -

(a) that the Israeli Law, by inflicting punishment for acts committed outside the boundaries of the state and before its establishment, against persons who were not Israeli citizens, and by a person who acted in the course of duty on behalf of a foreign country ("Act of State") conflicts with international law and exceeds the powers of the Israeli legislator;

(b) that the prosecution of the Accused in Israel upon his abduction from a foreign country conflicts with international law and exceeds the jurisdiction of the Court. [⋯]

10. The first contention of Counsel that Israel Law is in conflict with international law, and that therefore it cannot vest jurisdiction in this Court, raises the preliminary question as to the validity of international law in Israel and as to whether, in the event of a conflict between it and the laws of the land, it is to be preferred to the laws of the land. [⋯]

Our jurisdiction to try this case is based on the Nazis and Nazi Collaborators (Punishment) Law, a statutory law the provisions of which are unequivocal. The Court has to give effect to the law of the Knesset, and we cannot entertain the contention that this law conflicts with the principles of international law. For this reason alone, Counsel's first contention must be rejected.

11. But we have also perused the sources of international law, [⋯] and have failed to find any foundation for the contention that Israeli law is in conflict with the principles of international law. On the contrary, we have reached the conclusion

---

1) 비공식 번역임 — 필자 주.

that the Law in question conforms to the best traditions of the law of nations. [⋯]

12. The abhorrent crimes defined in this Law are crimes not under Israeli law alone. These crimes which offended the whole of mankind and shocked the conscience of nations are grave offences against the law of nations itself ("*delicta juris gentium*"). Therefore, so far from international law negating or limiting the jurisdiction of countries with respect to such crimes, in the absence of an International Court, the international law is in need of the judicial and legislative authorities of every country, to give effect to its penal injunctions and to bring criminals to trial. The jurisdiction to try crimes under international law is universal. [⋯]

30. [⋯] The State of Israel's "right to punish" the Accused derives, in our view, from two cumulative sources: a universal source (pertaining to the whole of mankind) which vests the right to prosecute and punish crimes of this order in every state within the family of nations; and a specific or national source which gives the victim nation the right to try any who assault its existence.

This second foundation of penal jurisdiction conforms, according to the acknowledged terminology, to the protective principle. [⋯]

31. [⋯] Learned Counsel summed up his pleadings against the jurisdiction of the Israel legislator by stressing ([⋯]) that under international law there must be a connection between the state and the person who committed the crime, and that, in the absence of an "acknowledged linking point," it was *ultra vires* for the state to inflict punishment for foreign offences. [⋯]

33. [⋯] The "linking point" between Israel and the Accused (and for that matter between Israel and any person accused of a crime against the Jewish People under this law) is striking in the "crime against the Jewish People," a crime that postulates an intention to exterminate the Jewish People in whole or in part. Indeed, even without such specific definition—and it must be noted that the draft law only defined "crimes against humanity" and "war crimes" (Bills of the Year 5710 No. 36, p. 119)—there was a subsisting "linking point," since most of the Nazi crimes of this kind were perpetrated against the Jewish People; but viewed in the light of the definition of "crime against the Jewish People," as defined in the Law, constitutes in effect an attempt to exterminate the Jewish People, or a partial extermination of the Jewish People. If there is an effective link (and not necessarily identity) between the State of Israel and the Jewish People, then a crime intended to exterminate the Jewish People has an obvious connection with the State of Israel.

34. The connection between the State of Israel and the Jewish People needs no explanation. The State of Israel was established and recognized as the State of the Jews. [···] It would appear that there is no need for any further proof of the obvious connection between the Jewish People and the State of Israel: This is the sovereign state of the Jewish People. [···]

36. Counsel contended that the protective principle cannot apply to this case because that principle is designed to protect only an existing state, its security and its interests, while the State of Israel had not existed at the time of the commission of the crime. He further submitted that the same contention applies to the principle of "passive personality" which stemmed from the protective principle, and of which some states have made use for the protection of their citizens abroad through their penal legislation. Counsel pointed out that, in view of the absence of a sovereign Jewish State at the time of the Holocaust, the victims of the Nazis were not, at the time they were murdered, citizens of the State of Israel.

In our view, learned Counsel errs when he examines the protective principle in this retroactive Law according to the time of the commission of the crimes, as is the case in an ordinary law. This Law was enacted in 1950 with a view to its application to a specified period which had terminated five years before its enactment. The protected interest of the State recognized by the protective principle is, in this case, the interest existing at the time of the enactment of the Law, and we have already dwelt on the importance of the moral and protective task which this Law is designed to achieve in the State of Israel. [···]

38. [···] The right of the injured group to punish offenders derives directly, as Grotius explained ([···]) from the crime committed against them by the offender, and it was only want of sovereignty that denied them the power to try and punish the offender. If the injured group or people thereafter reaches political sovereignty in any territory, it may make use of such sovereignty for the enforcement of its natural right to punish the offender who injured it.

[···] The State of Israel, the sovereign State of the Jewish People, performs through its legislation the task of carrying into effect the right of the Jewish People to punish the criminals who killed its sons with intent to put an end to the survival of this people. We are convinced that this power conforms to existing principles of the law of nations. [···]

40. The second contention of learned Counsel for the Defence was that the trial in Israel of the Accused, following upon his capture in a foreign land, is in conflict with international law and takes away the jurisdiction of the Court. Counsel pleaded that the Accused, who had resided in Argentina under an assumed name, was kidnapped on 11 May 1960 by the agents of the State of Israel, and was forcibly brought to Israel. He requested that two witnesses be heard in proof of his contention that the kidnappers of the Accused acted on orders they received from the Government of Israel or its representatives, a contention to which learned Counsel attached considerable importance, in an effort to prove that he was brought to Israel's area of jurisdiction in violation of international law. He summed up his contentions by submitting that the Court ought not to lend its support to an illegal act of the State, and that in these circumstances the Court has no jurisdiction to try the Accused.

On the other hand, the learned Attorney General pleaded that the jurisdiction of the Court was based upon the Nazis and Nazi Collaborators (Punishment) Law which applied to the Accused and to the acts attributed to him in the indictment; that it is the duty of the Court to do no other than try such crimes; and that in accordance with established judicial precedents in England, the United States and Israel, the Court is not to enter into the circumstances of the arrest of the Accused and of his transference to the area of jurisdiction of the State, these questions having no bearing on the jurisdiction of the Court to try the Accused for the offences for which he is being prosecuted, but only on the foreign relations of the State. [⋯]

41. It is an established rule of law that a person standing trial for an offence against the laws of a state may not oppose his being tried by reason of the illegality of his arrest, or of the means whereby he was brought to the area of jurisdiction of the state. The courts in England, the United States and Israel have ruled continuously that the circumstances of the arrest and the mode of bringing of the accused into the area of the state have no relevance to his trial, and they consistently refused in all cases to enter into an examination of these circumstances. [⋯]

☑ 해 설

아이히만 재판은 납치를 통한 나치 전범자의 신병확보라는 극적 요소까지 덧붙여져 세계의 주목을 끌었던 사건이다. 사실 이스라엘과 알젠틴은 납치 2일 전 범죄인인도조약에 서명했었다. 위 판결문은 지방법원 판결이나 그는 최종심에서도 사형이 확정되어 1962년 5월 31일 교수형에 처해졌다.

아이히만측의 항변에 대해 재판부는 아이히만의 행위가 국제법상의 범죄이므로 보편주의에 입각한 관할권 성립을 인정했고, 아울러 유대인과 이스라엘간의 밀접한 관련성에 입각해 보호주의에 입각한 관할권 성립도 인정했다. 반면 소급법에 의한 처벌이라든가 불법납치에 의한 신병확보라는 이유로 이스라엘의 관할권을 부인하는 항변은 수락되지 않았다. 기타 아이히만측은 유대인에 대한 박해가 상부의 지시에 의한 어쩔 수 없는 행위였다고 주장하고, 또 자신이 직접 살해 등을 수행한 것은 아니라는 주장도 했으나, 재판부에 의해 받아들여지지 않았다. 재판부는 이러한 성격의 사건의 경우 직접 살해행위를 한 사람으로부터 "멀리 떨어져 있을수록 그 책임이 커진다"며 상급자 책임의 엄중함을 지적했다.

한편 알젠틴 정부는 이스라엘 정부요원의 아이히만의 납치행위문제를 안전보장이사회에 제기하며, 아이히만의 원상회복과 책임자 처벌을 요구했다. 안보리는 1960년 6월 23일자 결의 제138호를 통해 이스라엘의 행위가 국제평화와 안전을 위협하는 것으로서, 알젠틴에 대해 배상을 하라고 결정했으나, 아이히만을 돌려보내라고 요구하지는 않았다. 오히려 아이히만의 범죄는 적절한 재판에 회부되어야 함을 인정했다. 양국 정부는 별도 협상을 통해 이 사건을 외교적으로 마무리 했다.

▶ 참고문헌 ───────────────────────────────

- Fawcett, The Eichmann Case, BYIL Vol. 38(1962), p. 181.
- H. Silving, In re Eichmann: A Dilemma of Law and Morality, AJIL Vol. 55(1961), p. 307.
- Papadatos, The Eichmann Trial(1964).

3. Yunis 사건(1988)
― 보편주의 및 피해자 국적주의

U.S. v. Fawaz Yunis.
D.C. District Court U.S., 681 F.Supp. 896(1988).

☑ 사   안

레바논인 Yunis 등은 1985년 요르단 항공 소속의 베이루트발 비행기를 레바논 상공에서 납치했다. 항공기에는 미국인 승객 2명이 타고 있었다. 납치범들은 아랍연맹 회의가 개최되는 튀니지로 가기를 원했으나, 튀니지 당국은 착륙을 허용하지 않았다. 결국 이들은 베이루트로 돌아와 인질을 풀어주고 항공기를 폭파시킨 다음 도주했다. 1987년 9월 미국 정보당국은 Yunis를 공해상으로 유인해 체포한 후 미국으로 이송해 기소했다. Yunis가 자신에 대한 미국 재판소의 관할권 성립을 부인하자, 재판부는 보편주의와 피해자 국적주의를 근거로 한 관할권의 성립 여부를 검토했다.

☑ 쟁   점
(1) 항공기 납치행위에 대하여 보편관할권에 입각한 관할권 행사 가능성.
(2) 형사관할권 행사의 근거로서의 피해자 국적주의.

☑ 판   결
(1) 항공기 납치행위는 보편관할권의 행사가 인정되는 극악한 범죄이다.
(2) 심각한 범죄에 대하여는 피해자 국적주의에 입각한 관할권 행사도 허용된다.

판 결 문

(p. 899) The Universal and the Passive Personal principle appear to offer potential bases for asserting jurisdiction over the hostage-taking and aircraft piracy charges against Yunis. However, his counsel argues that the Universal principle is not applicable because neither hostage-taking nor aircraft piracy are heinous crimes encompassed by the doctrine. He urges further, that the United States does not recognize Passive Personal as a legitimate source of jurisdiction. The government flatly disagrees and maintains that jurisdiction is appropriate under both.

1. Universal Principle

The Universal principle recognizes that certain offenses are so heinous and so widely condemned that "any state if it captures the offender may prosecute and punish that person on behalf of the world community regardless of the nationality of the offender or victim or where the crime was committed. [···] The crucial question for purposes of defendant's motion is how crimes are classified as "heinous" and whether aircraft piracy and hostage taking fit into this category.

Those crimes that are condemned by the world community and subject to prosecution under the Universal principle are often a matter of international conventions or treaties. *See Demjanjuk v. Petrovsky*, 776 F.2d. 571, 582 (6th Cir.1985) (Treaty against genocide signed by a significant number of states made that crime heinous; therefore, Israel had proper jurisdiction over Nazi war criminal under the Universal principle).

Both offenses are the subject of international agreements. A majority of states in the world community including Lebanon, have signed three treaties condemning aircraft piracy: The Tokyo Convention, The Hague Convention, and The Montreal Convention. The Hague and Montreal Conventions explicitly rely on the principle of Universal jurisdiction in mandating that all states "take such measures as may be necessary to establish its jurisdiction over the offences ... where the alleged offender is present in its territory." Hague Convention Art. 4 <section> 2; Montreal Convention Art. 5 <section> 2. Further, those treaties direct that all "contracting states ... of which the alleged offender is found, ... shall, be obliged, *without exception whatsoever and whether or not the offense was committed in its territory, to submit the case to its competent authorities for the purpose of prosecution.*" Hague Convention Art. 7; Montreal Convention Art. 7. (emphasis added) These two provisions together demonstrate the international community's strong commitment to punish aircraft hijackers irrespective of where the hijacking occurred.

The global community has also joined together and adopted the International Convention for the Taking of Hostages an agreement which condemns and criminalizes the offense of hostage taking. Like the conventions denouncing aircraft piracy, this treaty requires signatory states to prosecute any alleged offenders "present in its territory."

In light of the global efforts to punish aircraft piracy and hostage taking, international legal scholars unanimously agree that these crimes fit within the category of heinous crimes for purposes of asserting universal jurisdiction. [⋯] In The Restatement (Revised) of Foreign Relations Law of the United States, a source heavily relied upon by the defendant, aircraft hijacking is specifically identified as a universal crime over which all states should exercise jurisdiction. [⋯]

Therefore, under recognized principles of international law, and the law of this Circuit, there is clear authority to assert jurisdiction over Yunis for the offenses of aircraft piracy and hostage taking.

2. Passive Personal Principle

This principle authorizes states to assert jurisdiction over offenses committed against their citizens abroad. It recognizes that each state has a legitimate interest in protecting the safety of its citizens when they journey outside national boundaries. Because American nationals were on board the Jordanian aircraft, the government contends that the Court may exercise jurisdiction over Yunis under this principle. Defendant argues that this theory of jurisdiction is neither recognized by the international community nor the United States and is an insufficient basis for sustaining jurisdiction over Yunis.

Although many international legal scholars agree that the principle is the most controversial of the five sources of jurisdiction, they also agree that the international community recognizes its legitimacy. Most accept that "the extraterritorial reach of a law premised upon the ... principle would not be in doubt as a matter of international law." Paust, *Jurisdiction and Nonimmunity, 23 Va.J. of Int'l Law*, 191, 203 (1983). More importantly, the international community explicitly approved of the principle as a basis for asserting jurisdiction over hostage takers. As noted above, [⋯] the Hostage Taking Convention set forth certain mandatory sources of jurisdiction. But it also gave each signatory country discretion to exercise extraterritorial jurisdiction when the offense was committed "with respect to a hostage who is a national of that state if that state considers it appropriate." Art. 5(a)(d). Therefore, even if there are doubts regarding the international community's acceptance, there can be no doubt concerning the application of this principle to the offense of hostage taking, an offense for which Yunis is charged. [⋯]

Defendant's counsel correctly notes that the Passive Personal principle traditionally has been an anathema to United States lawmakers. But his reliance on the Restatement (Revised) of Foreign Relations Laws for the claim that the United States can never invoke the principle is misplaced. In the past, the United States has protested any assertion of such jurisdiction for fear that it could lead to indefinite criminal liability for its own citizens. This objection was based on the belief that foreigners visiting the United States should comply with our laws and should not be permitted to carry their laws with them. Otherwise Americans would face criminal prosecutions for actions unknown to them as illegal. However, in the most recent draft of the Restatement, the authors noted that the theory "has been increasingly accepted when applied to terrorist and other organized attacks on a state's nationals by reason of their nationality, or to assassinations of a state's ambassadors, or government officials." Restatement (Revised) <section> 402, comment g (Tent. Draft No. 6). [⋯] The authors retreated from their wholesale rejection of the principle, recognizing that perpetrators of crimes unanimously condemned by members of the international community, should be aware of the illegality of their actions. Therefore, qualified application of the doctrine to serious and universally condemned crimes will not raise the specter of unlimited and unexpected criminal liability.

☑ 해   설

아직 국제법은 국가관할권 행사의 범위와 한계에 관한 명확한 기준을 확립하고 있지는 못하다. 대체로 형사재판 관할권의 행사를 중심으로 기본적인 원칙만을 제시하고 있을 뿐이다. 국가의 관할권 행사는 이를 행사하고자 하는 국가와 이의 영향을 받는 국가간의 이해관계를 조화시키는 가운데 행사된다. 대체로 속지주의, 속인주의, 보호주의, 피해자 국적주의, 보편주의 등에 근거한 관할권의 행사가 주장된다. 이 중 속지주의와 속인주의에 입각한 관할권은 이를 행사하고자 하는 국가의 이해가 타국의 이해를 압도하므로 이의 행사에 대하여는 타국의 이의가 별달리 제기되지 아니한다. 그러나 기타의 근거에 입각한 관할권 행사에 대하여는 국가간 이견이 노출되기도 한다.

이 사건의 재판부는 항공기 납치범에 대해 보편주의와 피해자 국적주의에 근거한 미국 법원의 관할권을 인정하고 있다. 그러나 판결문에서도 지적된 바와 같이 미국은 전통적으로 피해자 국적주의에 입각한 관할권 행사에 반대하는 입장이었다. 이 원칙에 입각한 처벌법규를 가진 국가가 적지 않으나, 실제 이에 근거한 처벌이 활발한 것은 아니었고, 그렇다고 하여 국적국의 반대가 격렬하지도 않았다. 근래에는 미국도 자국인이 테러행위 등 국제적 성격의 범죄의 피해자가 된 경우 이 원칙에 근거한 관할권을 인정하는 입법을 하여 왔다(예를 들어 Omnibus Diplomatic Security and Antiterrorism Act 18 U.S.C. 2332 이하). 그러나 미국인이 범죄 피해자자 된 모든 사건에 대하여 형사관할권의 행사를 시도하지는 않는다. 본 판결의 입장은 이후 U.S. Court of Appeals, D.C. Circuit(1991)에 의하여 재확인되었다(288 U.S. App. D.C. 129, 924 F.2nd 1086).

➡ **참고문헌**

- A. Abramovsky, Extraterritorial Jurisdiction: The United States Unwarranted Attempt to Alter, Yale Journal of International Law Vol. 15(1990), p. 121.
- M. H. Drake, United States v. Yunis: The D.C. Circuit's Dubious Approval of U.S. Long−Arm, Northwestern University Law Review Vol. 87(1993), p. 697.
- A. W. Wegner, Extraterritorial Jurisdiction under International Law: The Yunis Decision as a Model for the Prosecution of Terrorists in U.S. Courts, Law and Policy in International Business Vol. 22(1991), p. 409.

1. 납치한 범죄인에 대한 재판권 행사(1991)

State v. Ebrahim.
Supreme Court of South Africa(Appellate Division).
2 SA 553(S. Afr. App. Div.).

☑ 사   안

이 사건의 피고인은 남아프리카공화국 국민으로 흑인민권운동 조직에서 활동하다가 투옥되어 장기간 수형생활을 했다. 석방 후 주거지를 제한한 판사의 명령을 무시하고, 1980년 인접 스와질랜드로 도피했다. 1986년 그는 남아프리카공화국 경찰 또는 기관원으로 판단되는 사람들에 의해 납치되어 남아공 법원에 반역혐의로 기소되었다. 스와질랜드는 자국 영토에서 벌어진 남아공의 납치행위에 대하여 국제법 위반의 항의를 제기하지는 않았다. 하급심은 피고인에 대한 재판관할권을 인정했는데, 최고법원은 아래와 같이 이를 번복했다.

☑ 쟁   점

국제법을 위반하고 납치를 통해 확보한 범죄인에 대하여 재판권을 행사할 수 있는가?

☑ 판   결

국제법 위반의 불법납치를 통해 확보된 범죄인에 대하여는 재판관할권을 행사할 수 없다.

판 결 문

The following facts are undisputed. The appellant is a South African citizen by birth. In 1962 he became a member of ... the military wing of the African National Congress(ANC). In 1964 he was convicted of several acts of sabotage and sentenced to 15 years imprisonment. He served his sentence on Robben Island and was released in 1979. Thereafter he was restricted by executive order to the magistrate's district of Pinetown in Natal. In 1980 he fled to Swaziland while the restriction order was still in force. [⋯]

In December 1986 the appellant was forcibly abducted from his house in Swaziland by two black men who informed him that they were members of the South African Police. He was bound, blindfolded and gagged and taken across the border into South Africa. Once across the border he was met by a group of armed white men who drove him by car to Pretoria. They questioned him about the activities of the ANC from which he inferred they were members of the security police. This opinion was endorsed by the fact they were permitted to pass through an army road blockade without search or questioning. In Pretoria the leader of his abductors made radio contact with an unidentified person. He was then transferred to another vehicle. [⋯]

There was no suggestion made in the application that the government of Swaziland protested to the South African government over appellant's abduction. [⋯]

In the light of the above denials by the police it must be accepted that the South African Police were not involved in any way in the abduction. It is, however, highly likely that the abductors were agents of the South African state. All the circumstances surrounding the abduction point very strongly to an involvement of the state in the abduction. [⋯] When action is authorized and executed at such a lower level, the state is involved and responsible for the consequences, even if such action is not permitted by the highest state authority. This applies also to the conduct of the security agencies of the administration. The abduction of the appellant was clearly the work of one or other of these agencies, excluding the police. [⋯]

Several fundamental legal principles are contained in these rules, namely the protection and promotion of human rights, good inter state relations and a healthy administration of justice. The individual must be protected against illegal detention and abduction, the bounds of jurisdiction must not be exceeded, sovereignty must be respected, the legal process must be fair to those affected and abuse of law must be avoided in order to protect and promote the integrity of the administration of justice. This applies equally to the state. When the state is a party to a dispute, as for example in criminal cases, it must come to court with "clean hands." When the state itself is involved in an abduction across international borders, as in the present case, its hands are not clean.

Principles of this kind testify to a healthy legal system of high standard. Signs of this development appear increasingly in the municipal law of other countries. […]

It follows that, according to our common law, the trial court had no jurisdiction to hear the case against the appellant. Consequently his conviction and sentence cannot stand.

☑ 해   설

재판부는 형사사건을 기소하려면 국가도 "깨끗한 손"으로 법정에 와야 되는데, 국가 자신이 국경을 넘는 납치에 관여했다면 그의 손은 깨끗하지 않다고 판단했다. 사실 이 판결은 흑백차별로 악명이 높던 남아프리카공화국이 백인통치가 종식되고 흑인 다수통치가 실현되는 과도기적 기간에 내려졌다. 즉 27년간 수감되었던 만델라가 1990년 2월 석방되었고, 1994년 5월 대통령으로 선출되었다. Ebrahim은 이 판결 이후 납치피해에 대해 손해배상을 받았다.

한편 이 판결은 미국 연방대법원의 U.S. v. Alvarez-Machain 판결(504 U.S. 655(1992))과 대비된다. 그 내용은 다음과 같다. 1985년 미국 정부의 한 마약단속반원이 멕시코에서 납치되어 고문 끝에 살해되었다. 후일 고문행위에 조력한 멕시코인 의사인 Alvarez-Machain가 미국 당국의 사주를 받은 자들에 의해 멕시코로부터 미국으로 납치되었다. 그는 미국 정부의 요원을 납치해 고문한 혐의로 미국 연방법원에 기소되었다. 멕시코 정부는 납치라는 미국의 주권침해 행위에 항의하며 그의 석방을 요구했다. 미국에서의 1심과 2심 재판부는 그를 납치한 행위는 미국-멕시코 범죄인인도조약의 위반이므로 미국 법원은 그에 대해 관할권을 행사할 수 없다고 판시했다. 그러나 연방대법원은 조약에 국제적 납치를 금하는 명문의 조항이 없다는 이유 등으로 재판 관할권 성립을 인정했다.

> The Treaty says nothing about the obligations of the United States and Mexico to refrain from forcible abductions of people from the territory of the other nation, or the consequences under the Treaty if such an abduction occurs. [⋯]
>
> Respondent and his amici may be correct that respondent's abduction was "shocking," [⋯] and that it may be in violation of general international law principles. Mexico has protested the abduction of respondent through diplomatic notes, [⋯] and the decision of whether respondent should be returned to Mexico, as a matter outside of the Treaty, is a matter for the Executive Branch. We conclude, however, that respondent's abduction was not in violation of the Extradition Treaty between the United States and Mexico, [⋯]. The fact of respondent's forcible abduction does not therefore prohibit his trial in a court in the United States for violations of the criminal laws of the United States.

이러한 미국 법원의 입장은 국제적으로 많은 논란을 일으켰다.[1] 이 사건 이전에 범죄인인도조약을 체결하면서 상대국의 주권을 침해하는 불법납치를 통한 범죄인 확보는 금지된다는 조항을 삽입할 필요가 있다고 생각한 국가는 아마 없었을 것이다.

한편 아래의 영국 상원의 판결은 국가간 합의 하에 범죄인이 인도되었어도 국내 범죄인인도법 상의 절차가 무시되어 피고가 강제로 이송되었다면 영국 법원은 그에 대해 재판관할권을 행사할 수 없다고 선언했다. 그 사안은 다음과 같다.

뉴질랜드인 Bennett은 영국에서의 사기범죄 용의자로서 남아공에서 발견되었다. 영국 경찰은 일단 그의 범죄인인도를 청구하지 않기로 했다. 남아

---

1) 과거 미국 연방대법원은 Ker v. Illinois, 119 U.S. 436(1886)과 Frisbie v. Collins, 342 U.S. 519(1952) 판결에서 적법절차를 무시한 방법으로 피고의 신병을 확보한 경우라도 법원이 그에 대해 유죄판결을 내릴 수 있다는 입장을 취한 바 있다(Ker-Frisbie Doctrine). 미국인 Ker는 페루에서 미국으로 납치되어 재판에 회부되었고, Collins는 미국내 다른 주에서 미시간주로 납치된 사례였다.

공 당국은 Bennett을 체포한 후 대만을 경유해 뉴질랜드로 추방하기로 결정했다. 그런데 그는 대만에서 남아공 경찰에 의해 다시 체포되어 남아공으로 송환되었다. 이어 그는 영국행 비행기에 강제로 탑승당했다. 이 과정에서 넝국의 범죄인인도법(1989) 상의 절차는 무시되었다. 당시 영국과 남아공 사이에는 범죄인인도조약이 체결되어 있지 않았는데, 영국에서 기소된 Bennett은 자신이 영국과 남아공 경찰간의 공모하에 범죄인인도법상의 절차가 무시된 일종의 불법납치를 통해 법정에 서게 되었다고 주장했다. Bennett는 영국법원은 자신에 대하여 형사재판권을 행사할 수 없다고 주장했으나, 하급심은 그가 영국 법정에 서게 된 경위에 대하여는 조사할 권한이 없다며 받아들이지 않았다. 그러나 당시 영국의 최고심인 상원은 범죄인인도 절차는 단지 범죄인을 확보하기 위한 절차일 뿐만 아니라, 피인도자의 인권을 보호하는 절차이기도 하다는 이유에서 재판권 행사를 거부했다. 이 사안은 국제법을 위반한 불법납치가 아니고, 단지 영국 국내법인 범죄인인도법상의 절차를 위반하여 강제로 이송된 사건일 뿐이었다.

> Extradition procedures are designed not only to ensure that criminals are returned from one country to another but also to protect the rights of those who are accused of crimes by the requesting country. Thus sufficient evidence has to be produced to show *a prima facie* case against the accused and the rule of speciality protects the accused from being tried for any crime other than that for which he was extradited. If a practice developed in which the police or prosecuting authorities of this country ignored extradition procedures and secured the return of an accused by a mere request to police colleagues in another country they would be flouting the extradition procedures and depriving the accused of the safeguards built into the extradition process for his benefit. [···]
>
> The courts, of course, have no power to apply direct discipline to the police or the prosecuting authorities, but they can refuse to allow them to take advantage of abuse of power by regarding their behaviour as an abuse of process and thus preventing a prosecution.
>
> In my view your Lordships should now declare that where process of law is available to return an accused to this country through extradition procedures

our courts will refuse to try him if he has been forcibly brought within our jurisdiction in disregard of those procedures by a process to which our own police, prosecuting or other executive authorities have been a knowing party. (Regina v. Horseferry Road Magistrates Court Ex p. Bennett(No.1)(1993). House of Lords. [1994] 1 A.C. 42; [1993] 3 W.L.R. 90)

이 같은 남아공과 영국 법원의 엄격한 태도는 앞서 아이히만 사건에서 납치의 경위에 대하여는 논하지 않은 이스라엘 법원의 태도와 비교된다. 아이히만 사건과 이들 사건과의 성격상의 차이가 있다면 아이히만의 행위는 국제법상의 보편관할권이 인정되는 국제범죄로서 세계 어느 국가에 의하여도 처벌이 가능한 범죄라는 점일 것이다.

한편 국내에서는 독일에서의 조사와 이송과정이 문제되었던 동백림 사건 김종길 및 윤이상에 대한 판결부분에서 대법원은 "수사기관에서 피고인에게 대한 범죄사실을 수사하기 위해 서독으로부터 피고인을 한국으로 연행함에 있어, 서독 정부의 승인을 받지 아니한 사실이 있다고 하여서 그 점이 판결의 결과에 영향을 미친 헌법위반이 된다고 할 수 없다"고 판단했다(대법원 1968. 7. 30. 선고 68도754 판결).

➡ 참고문헌 ─────────────────────────────

- 유선봉, 해외납치행위의 국제법적 고찰, 광운비교법학 제1호(2000), p. 57.
- 서은아, 타국에서 범죄인을 강제납치하여 자국법원으로 소환할 경우 이에 대한 국제법적 유효성 문제, (한양대) 국제소송법무 제1호(2010), p. 163.

2. 전직 대통령에 대한 고문방지협약의 적용(2012)
─ 기소 또는 인도 의무의 성격

Questions Relating to the Obligation to Prosecute or Extradite.
Belgium v. Senegal, 2012 ICJ Reports 422.

☑ 사   안

고문방지협약 제7조 1항은 협약상의 범죄를 저지른 자가 자국 관할 내에 있을 경우 그 국가는 혐의자를 기소하든가 다른 국가로 범죄인인도를 할 것을 규정하고 있다. 이른바 "기소 또는 인도" 의무이다. 세네갈은 1987년 이 협약의 발효 시부터, 벨기에는 1999년부터 협약의 당사국이었다.

1982년부터 1990년간 차드 대통령이던 Hissène Habré는 재직 당시 수많은 고문, 전쟁범죄 및 인도에 반하는 범죄를 저지른 혐의를 받고 있었다. 그는 실각 이후 세네갈로 망명해 계속 거주했다. 차드 출신 자국민의 고발에 근거해 벨기에는 2006년부터 세네갈에게 Habré를 인도해 달라고 요청했다. 그러나 세네갈은 인도요청에 응하지 않았고, Habré를 기소하기 위한 국내절차도 진행하지 않았다. 벨기에는 2009년 세네갈이 Habré에 대한 형사절차를 개시할 의무가 있으며, 불이행시 그를 재판에 회부하기 위해 자국으로 범죄인인도할 의무가 있음을 선언해 달라는 청구를 ICJ에 제출했다.

재판과정에서 "기소 또는 인도"의무의 법적 성격이 여러 측면에서 논의되었다. 세네갈은 협약상의 의무 자체를 부인하지 않았으나, 벨기에의 인도요청에 대해서는 다음과 같은 반론을 제시했다. ① 벨기에가 범죄인인도를 요청한 근거가 된 사건의 피해자들은 사건 발생시 벨기에 국민이 아니었다. ② 많은 고문행위는 벨기에는 물론 세네갈에 대해 협약이 발효하기 이전에 발생했다. ③ 기소를 위해 상당한 재정적 부담이 발생하며, 국내법상의 장애가 있어서 아직 협약상의 의무를 다하시 못하고 있다.

☑ 쟁   점

(1) 고문방지협약 상의 의무 이행을 요구할 수 있는 국가의 자격.

(2) 협약이 적용되는 고문행위와 이에 대한 당사국의 "기소 또는 인도" 의무의 발생시점.

(3) "기소 또는 인도"의무의 이행시한.

☑ 판   결

(1) 협약의 모든 당사국은 혐의자가 소재하는 당사국에게 "기소 또는 인도" 의무의 이행을 요구할 수 있다.

(2) "기소 또는 인도" 의무는 협약의 당사국이 된 이후의 행위에 대해서만 적용된다.

(3) 협약의 당사국은 합리적 기간 내에 지체 없이 "기소 또는 인도" 의무를 이행해야 한다.

판 결 문

68. As stated in its Preamble, the object and purpose of the Convention is "to make more effective the struggle against torture ... throughout the world". The States parties to the Convention have a common interest to ensure, in view of their shared values, that acts of torture are prevented and that, if they occur, their authors do not enjoy impunity. The obligations of a State party to conduct a preliminary inquiry into the facts and to submit the case to its competent authorities for prosecution are triggered by the presence of the alleged offender in its territory, regardless of the nationality of the offender or the victims, or of the place where the alleged offences occurred. All the other States parties have a common interest in compliance with these obligations by the State in whose territory the alleged offender is present. That common interest implies that the obligations in question are owed by any State party to all the other States parties to the Convention. All the States parties "have a legal interest" in the protection of the rights involved [⋯]. These obligations may be defined as "obligations *erga omnes* *partes*" in the sense that each State party has an interest in compliance with them in any given case. [⋯]

69. The common interest in compliance with the relevant obligations under the Convention against Torture implies the entitlement of each State party to the Convention to make a claim concerning the cessation of an alleged breach by another State party. If a special interest were required for that purpose, in many cases no State would be in the position to make such a claim. It follows that any State party to the Convention may invoke the responsibility of another State party with a view to ascertaining the alleged failure to comply with its obligations *erga omnes partes*, such as those under Article 6, paragraph 2, and Article 7, paragraph 1, of the Convention, and to bring that failure to an end.

70. For these reasons, the Court concludes that Belgium, as a State party to the Convention against Torture, has standing to invoke the responsibility of Senegal for the alleged breaches of its obligations under Article 6, paragraph 2, and Article 7, paragraph 1, of the Convention in the present proceedings. Therefore, the claims of Belgium based on these provisions are admissible. [⋯]

91. The obligation to prosecute provided for in Article 7, paragraph 1, is normally implemented in the context of the Convention against Torture after the State has performed the other obligations provided for in the preceding articles, which require it to adopt adequate legislation to enable it to criminalize torture, give its courts universal jurisdiction in the matter and make an inquiry into the facts. These obligations, taken as a whole, may be regarded as elements of a single conventional mechanism aimed at preventing suspects from escaping the consequences of their criminal responsibility, if proven. [⋯]

94. The Court considers that Article 7, paragraph 1, requires the State concerned to submit the case to its competent authorities for the purpose of prosecution, irrespective of the existence of a prior request for the extradition of the suspect. That is why Article 6, paragraph 2, obliges the State to make a preliminary inquiry immediately from the time that the suspect is present in its territory. The obligation to submit the case to the competent authorities, under Article 7, paragraph 1, may or may not result in the institution of proceedings, in the light of the evidence before them, relating to the charges against the suspect.

95. However, if the State in whose territory the suspect is present has received a request for extradition in any of the cases envisaged in the provisions of the Convention, it can relieve itself of its obligation to prosecute by acceding to that

request. It follows that the choice between extradition or submission for prosecution, pursuant to the Convention, does not mean that the two alternatives are to
be given the same weight. Extradition is an option offered to the State by the
Convention, whereas prosecution is an international obligation under the Convention, the violation of which is a wrongful act engaging the responsibility of the
State. [⋯]

99. In the Court's opinion, the prohibition of torture is part of customary
international law and it has become a peremptory norm (*jus cogens*). [⋯]

100. However, the obligation to prosecute the alleged perpetrators of acts of
torture under the Convention applies only to facts having occurred after its entry
into force for the State concerned. [⋯]

The Court notes that nothing in the Convention against Torture reveals an
intention to require a State party to criminalize, under Article 4, acts of torture that
took place prior to its entry into force for that State, or to establish its jurisdiction
over such acts in accordance with Article 5. Consequently, in the view of the Court,
the obligation to prosecute, under Article 7, paragraph 1, of the Convention does
not apply to such acts. [⋯]

102. The Court concludes that Senegal's obligation to prosecute pursuant to
Article 7, paragraph 1, of the Convention does not apply to acts alleged to have
been committed before the Convention entered into force for Senegal on 26 June
1987. The Court would recall, however, that the complaints against Mr. Habre
include a number of serious offences allegedly committed after that date (*see*
paragraphs 17, 19-21 and 32 above). Consequently, Senegal is under an obligation to
submit the allegations concerning those acts to its competent authorities for the
purpose of prosecution. Although Senegal is not required under the Convention to
institute proceedings concerning acts that were committed before 26 June 1987,
nothing in that instrument prevents it from doing so. [⋯]

104. The Court considers that Belgium has been entitled, with effect from 25
July 1999, the date when it became party to the Convention, to request the Court
to rule on Senegal's compliance with its obligation under Article 7, paragraph 1. In
the present case, the Court notes that Belgium invokes Senegal's responsibility for
the latter's conduct starting in the year 2000, when a complaint was filed against
Mr. Habre in Senegal [⋯]

112. The Court is of the opinion that the financial difficulties raised by
Senegal cannot justify the fact that it failed to initiate proceedings against Mr.

Habre. For its part, Senegal itself states that it has never sought to use the issue of financial support to justify any failure to comply with an obligation incumbent upon it. Moreover, the referral of the matter to the African Union, as recognized by Senegal itself, cannot justify the latter's delays in complying with its obligations under the Convention. The diligence with which the authorities of the forum State must conduct the proceedings is also intended to guarantee the suspect fair treatment at all stages of the proceedings (Article 7, paragraph 3, of the Convention).

113. The Court observes that, under Article 27 of the Vienna Convention on the Law of Treaties, which reflects customary law, Senegal cannot justify its breach of the obligation provided for in Article 7, paragraph 1, of the Convention against Torture by invoking provisions of its internal law, in particular by invoking the decisions as to lack of jurisdiction rendered by its courts in 2000 and 2001, or the fact that it did not adopt the necessary legislation pursuant to Article 5, paragraph 2, of that Convention until 2007.

114. While Article 7, paragraph 1, of the Convention does not contain any indication as to the time frame for performance of the obligation for which it provides, it is necessarily implicit in the text that it must be implemented within a reasonable time, in a manner compatible with the object and purpose of the Convention.

115. The Court considers that the obligation on a State to prosecute, provided for in Article 7, paragraph 1, of the Convention, is intended to allow the fulfilment of the Convention's object and purpose, which is "to make more effective the struggle against torture"(Preamble to the Convention). It is for that reason that proceedings should be undertaken without delay. [⋯]

117. The Court finds that the obligation provided for in Article 7, paragraph 1, required Senegal to take all measures necessary for its implementation as soon as possible, in particular once the first complaint had been filed against Mr. Habre in 2000. Having failed to do so, Senegal has breached and remains in breach of its obligations under Article 7, paragraph 1, of the Convention.

☑ 해   설

ICJ는 고문방지협약의 당사국은 가해자나 피해자의 국적이나 사건 발생 장소와 관계없이 혐의자를 조사하여 기소에 회부할 의무를 지며, 이는 협약의 모든 당사국들에 대한 일종의 대세적 의무라고 해석했다(para. 68). 따라서 문제의 사건과 특별한 이해관계가 없는 협약 당사국도 다른 당사국에게 협약 의무의 이행을 요구할 수 있다며 벨기에의 원고 적격을 인정했다(paras. 69-70). 또한 협약 당사국은 타국의 인도요청 여부와 관계없이 고문혐의자를 기소를 위한 절차를 취할 의무가 있으며(para. 94), 인도보다는 기소회부가 1차적 의무라고 보았다(para. 95).

이어 "기소 또는 인도"의 시적 범위에 대해 ICJ는 다음과 같이 판단했다. 고문금지 자체는 국제법상 강행규범에 해당하지만, 협약상의 기소 의무는 소급 적용되지 않으므로 세네갈은 협약의 당사국이 된 1987년 이후의 고문행위에 대해서만 이 같은 의무를 진다고 보았다(para. 102). 한편 Habré의 범죄행위는 벨기에가 1999년에 고문방지협약에 가입하기 이전에 발생했다. 그러나 ICJ는 세네갈의 경우 협약의 당사국이 된 1987년부터 "기소 또는 인도의무"를 지게 되므로, 벨기에는 자국이 협약의 당사국이 된 1999년 이후 세네갈이 협약을 위반하고 있는가에 관해 ICJ에 판정을 요구할 수 있다고 판단했다(para. 104). 또한 세네갈은 재정적 어려움이나 국내법상의 이유로 협약 의무 불이행을 변명할 수 없으며(paras. 112-113), 협약에 기소 또는 인도 의무의 이행시한이 구체적으로 규정되어 있지 않지만 세네갈은 합리적인 시간 내에 지체 없이 이를 이행해야 한다고 판단했다(paras. 114-115).

이 판결은 고문자나 피해자가 청구국과 별다른 관련이 없고, 청구국이 협약에 가입하기 이전에 고문이 발생했을지라도 현재 혐의자가 소재한 당사국에게 협약상의 기소 또는 인도 의무의 이행을 요청할 수 있다고 판단했다는 점에서 고문방지협약의 이행 가능성을 폭넓게 확보하는 효과를 가져왔다.

한편 국제적 압력 끝에 세네갈은 Habré의 재판을 위해 African Union이 임명하는 특별재판소를 자국에 설치하기로 수락했다. 2016년 5월 Extra-ordinary African Chambers는 Habré에게 종신형을 선고했다. 이는 전직 국가원수가 심각한 인권침해행위를 이유로 타국 소재 법정에서 유죄판결을 받은 첫 번째 사례였다.

➡️ 참고문헌 ──────────────────────────

• 김재우, 고문범죄 혐의 전직 국가원수의 신병처리에 관한 ICJ 판결 분석: 벨기에 대 세네갈, 2012. 7. 20 판결, 국제법 동향과 실무 12권 3·4호(2013), p. 164.

3. 정치범 불인도(2013)

서울고등법원 2013년 1월 3일자, 2012토1 결정(확정).
각급법원(제1, 2심) 판결공보 제114호(2013. 2. 10),
173쪽 이하.

☑ **사　　안**

중국 국적의 리우치앙(劉强)은 외조모가 한국 출신의 일본군 강제종군 위안부 피해자였으며, 조부도 중국의 항일투쟁 전투에서 사망했다. 이에 그는 평소 일본의 구 군국주의에 대한 강한 적개심을 갖고 있었다. 리우치앙은 2011년 12월 일본 야스쿠니 신사 신문 기둥에 방화를 시도했으나 별다른 피해를 주지는 못했다. 그는 이 사건 직후 한국으로 와서 주한 일본국 대사관에 화염병을 던진 바도 있다. 리우치앙은 이로 인해 한국법원에서 현존 건조물방화 미수죄 등으로 징역 10월형을 받아 복역했다. 일본은 한국 정부에 대해 리우치앙의 범죄인인도를 요청했다. 리우치앙측은 일본에서의 그의 행위가 정치적 범죄에 해당한다며 인도불가를 주장했다.

☑ **쟁　　점**

정치범 불인도의 대상 여부의 판단 기준.

☑ **판　　결**

범행의 동기, 목적, 대상의 성격, 수단의 적합성, 범행행위의 성격, 결과의 중대성 등을 종합하여 일반범죄로서의 성격과 정치적 성격 중 어느 편이 더 중심인가를 판단한다.

판 결 문

"징치직 범죄의 개념 및 유형, 정치범 불인도 원칙의 발전과정 및 최근의 경향 등을 고려해 볼 때, 어떠한 범죄, 특히 상대적 정치범죄가 정치적 범죄인지 여부에 관한 판단에 있어서는, ① 범행 동기가 개인적인 이익 취득이 아니라 정치적 조직이나 기구가 추구하는 목적에 찬성하거나 반대하는 것인지, ② 범행 목적이 한 국가의 정치체제를 전복 또는 파괴하려는 것이거나, 그 국가의 대내외 주요 정책을 변화시키도록 압력이나 영향을 가하려는 것인지, ③ 범행 대상의 성격은 어떠하며, 나아가 이는 무엇을 상징하는 것인지, ④ 범죄인이 추구하는 정치적 목적을 실현하는데 범행이 상당히 기여할 수 있는 수단으로서 유기적 관련성이 있는지, ⑤ 범행의 법적·사실적 성격은 어떠한지, ⑥ 범행의 잔학성, 즉 사람의 생명·신체·자유에 반하는 중대한 폭력행위를 수반하는지 및 결과의 중대성에 비추어 범행으로 말미암은 법익침해와 정치적 목적 사이의 균형이 유지되고 있는지 등 범죄인에게 유리하거나 불리한 주관적·객관적 사정을 정치범 불인도 원칙의 취지에 비추어 합목적적, 합리적으로 고찰하여 종합적으로 형량하고, 여기에다가 범행목적과 배경에 따라서는 범죄인 인도 청구국과 피청구국 간의 역사적 배경, 역사적 사실에 대한 인식의 차이 및 입장의 대립과 같은 정치적 상황 등도 고려하여, 상대적 정치범죄 내에 존재하는 일반범죄로서의 성격과 정치적 성격 중 어느 것이 더 주된 것인지를 판단하여 결정하여야 할 것이다. [⋯]

차. 이 사건 인도 대상 범죄가 정치적 범죄인지 여부

1) 유의할 판단요소

먼저 이 사건 인도대상 범죄는 오로지 해당 국가의 정치질서를 반대하거나 해당 국가의 권력관계나 기구를 침해하는 행위가 아니라 일반범죄의 성격도 가지고 있음이 분명하므로 이를 절대적 정치범죄라고는 할 수 없다.

그렇다면 이 사건 인도대상 범죄가 상대적 정치범죄라고 할 수 있는지가 쟁점이라고 할 것인데, 이하에서는 앞서 본 정치적 범죄의 판단기준에서 제시한 판단요소별로 살피기로 한다.

다만 유의할 점은, 지금까지의 정치적 범죄에 관한 논의가 한 국가의 질서를 침해하거나 정치형태의 변경을 목적으로 하는 행위에 상대적으로 중점이 두어져 있었다면, 20세기 후반에 들어와 동서냉전의 종식과 함께 이데올로기 대립이 상대적으로 약화된 반면, 개별 국가 간 역사적·민족적 조건하에서 빚어지는 갈등과 대립 및 각국의 경제적 이해관계에 얽힌 분화가 심화된 시대적 상황을 고려할 때, 한 국가가 취하고 있는 대내외 주요 정책을 반대하여 이를 변화시키도록 영향을 가하는 것을 목적으로 하는 행위도 오늘날 정치적 범죄에 관한 논의의 중요한 쟁점으로 부상하였다는 것이다.

이 사건과 연결지어 보면, 종래 상대적 정치범죄에 관하여 국제적인 판례와 학설에서 일반적으로 제시되거나 논의된 개념은 최근 동북아시아에서 논란이 되고 있는 일본군위안부 등 과거의 역사적 사실을 둘러싼 현저한 역사 인식의 차이 및 그와 관련된 대내외 정책을 둘러싼 견해의 대립과 같은 정치적 상황을 고려한 것이 아님을 주목할 필요가 있다.

이러한 관점에서 볼 때, 이 사건 범행이 위와 같은 동북아시아 특유의 정치적 상황과 그에 관련된 청구국의 대내외 정책에 대하여 영향을 미치려는 시도인지 여부가 정치적 범죄인지 여부를 논함에 있어서 중요한 판단요소 중의 하나로 고려할 필요가 있다. […]

나) 범행 동기와 목적의 성격

앞에서 살펴본 일본군위안부의 역사적 의미와 배경, 야스쿠니 신사의 성격 및 내력과 범죄인의 가족력, 이 사건 범행을 전후한 정치상황, 범죄인이 이 사건 범행 직후 대한민국으로 와서 외할머니, 외증조할아버지의 연고지를 찾아다닌 정황, 범죄인이 주한 일본대사관 현존건조물방화미수 사건에서 한 진술과 이 법정에서 한 진술의 내용 및 일관성에다가, 범죄인의 이 사건 범행은 개인적인 이익을 목적으로 한 것이 아니라 청구국 정부의 일본군위안부 등 과거의 역사적 사실에 관한 인식 및 그와 관련된 정책 변화를 촉구하고 그에 관한 메시지를 전달하며 국내외 여론을 환기하기 위한 수단으로 보이는 점, 범죄인은 이 사건 범행 일시를 정함에 있어서 자신의 정치적인 목적에 부합하도록 상징적인 의미를 부여하였고, 그 후에 있었던 주한 일본대사관 현존건조물방화미수 범행의 경우도 마찬가지로 자신의 정치적 목적에 부합하는 의미 있는 일자를 선택한 점, 범죄인은 이 사건 범행의 준비

도구 및 '사죄'라고 적힌 셔츠를 입은 자신의 모습과 범행의 실행 과정을 촬영하였고, 청구국의 수사기관에 의하여 실체가 밝혀지기 전에 스스로 자신의 범행 사실과 그 목적을 언론이나 인터넷 등을 통해 외부에 널리 알리려고 하였던 점, 범죄인은 청구국에서의 이 사건 범행뿐만 아니라 대한민국에서도 주한 일본대사관에 화염병을 던지는 등 청구국의 과거의 역사적 사실에 대한 인식 및 그와 관련된 정책에 항의하는 일련의 행동을 하였는데, 이는 곧 동일한 범행 동기의 발현이라고 볼 수 있고, 범죄인의 인식으로는 일본대사관이라는 공적인 기관과 야스쿠니 신사를 동일한 범주에서 파악하고 있었다고 볼 수 있는 점, 청구국 내에서도 일본군위안부 등의 문제와 정부각료의 야스쿠니 신사 참배를 둘러싸고 정치적 의견 대립이 있는 점, 유엔 등 국제기구와 미국을 비롯한 제3국에서도 청구국 정부에 대하여 일본군 위안부에 대하여 사과하고 역사적인 책임을 져야 한다는 등의 취지를 담은 결의를 한 점 등을 고려하면, 이 사건 범행은 범죄인이 개인적 이익을 취하기 위해서가 아니라 청구국이 과거 군국주의 체제 하에서 침략전쟁을 일으켜 그 과정에서 주변 각국에 일본군위안부나 대량 학살 등 여러 가지 피해를 주고도 이러한 과거의 역사적 사실을 부정하거나 이에 대하여 진정으로 사과하지 않고 오히려 야스쿠니 신사 참배 등을 통하여 전범이나 과거 군국주의 체제를 미화하려는 태도에 분노하여 저지른 것으로서, 그 범행 목적은 범죄인 자신의 정치적 신념 및 과거의 역사적 사실 인식과 반대의 입장에 있는 청구국 정부의 정책을 변화시키거나 이에 영향을 미치기 위하여 압력을 가하고자 하는 것이다. 따라서 이는 정치적 범죄에서 말하는 정치적인 목적에 해당한다고 할 것이다.

다) 범행 대상의 성격 및 범행과 목적 사이의 관계

다만 정치적인 목적으로 범한 범죄라고 하여 모두 정치적 범죄가 된다고 할 수는 없다. 이는 앞서 살핀 바와 같이 주관적·객관적 평가요소들을 종합적으로 형량하여 일반범죄로서의 성격과 정치적 성격 중 어느 것이 더 주된 것인지를 판단하여 결정하여야 하는 문제이기 때문이다.

그러한 관점에서 이 사건 범행 대상의 성격을 살펴보면, 야스쿠니 신사의 제2차 세계대전 종전 전의 지위와 역할, 현재도 A급 전범이 합사되어 있는 점, 제2차 세계대전 종전 후에도 청구국 내에서 야스쿠니 신사를 국가의 관리하에 두려는 시도가 계속되었던 점, 이러한 야스쿠니 신사에 주변국들의 반발에도 청구국 정부각료 등 정치인들이 계속하여 참배해 왔던 점 및 지금까지의 정치 상황에 비추어 볼 때, 야스쿠니 신사가 법률상으로는 사적인 종교시설이라고 할 것이나 사실상 국가시설에 상응하는 정치적 상징성이 있다고 평가할 수 있다. 범죄인 역시 야스쿠니 신사를 단순한 사적 종교시설이 아니라 과거 침략전쟁을 정당화하는 정치질서의 상징으로 간주하고 이 사건 범행을 실행하였던 것이 분명하며, 대한민국과 중국 등 청구국의 주변국들도 청구국 정부각료들의 야스쿠니 신사 참배 때마다 강하게 항의하며 반발하였음에 비추어 볼 때, 야스쿠니 신사가 국가시설에 상응하는 정치적 상징성이 있다고 보는 견해는 범죄인 개인의 독단적인 견해가 아니라 대한민국을 비롯한 주변국에서 폭넓은 공감대를 형성하고 있다고 인정된다.

다음으로 범행과 목적 사이의 관계에 관하여 본다. 지금까지 주한 일본 대사관 앞에서 1,000회 넘게 청구국 정부의 일본군위안부에 대한 정책 변화를 촉구하는 시위가 있었으나 청구국에서 별다른 반응이 없었기에 이 사건 범행에 이르게 되었다는 취지의 범죄인의 진술과, 실제로 이 사건 범행 후 범죄인의 동기와 목적이 언론 등을 통하여 널리 퍼지게 되고 청구국을 비롯한 주변 각국의 관심의 초점이 됨에 따라 과거에 청구국의 침략을 받았던 주변국이 청구국 정부의 일본군위안부 등 과거의 역사적 사실에 대한 인식과 그와 관련된 정책 및 우경화 추세에 대하여 공분을 느끼고 있음을 청구국 정부와 국민이 인식하게 된 점 및 앞서 본 야스쿠니 신사의 성격과 유래에 비추어 볼 때, 범죄인이 이 사건 방화 대상으로 야스쿠니 신사를 택함으로써 자신이 추구하였던 정치적 목적을 상당히 달성한 것으로 보인다. 따라서 이 사건 범행은 그 정치적 목적과 유기적인 관련성이 있다고 인정할 수 있다.

라) 범행의 성격과 의도된 목적과의 균형

이 사건 범행은 우리 형법 제167조 제1항의 일반물건에의 방화죄에 해당하는 것으로서 공공의 위험이 발생되어야 처벌할 수 있는 구체적 위험범에 해당한다.

앞서 살펴본 바와 같이 이 사건 범행 대상인 신문이 건조물이 아닌 일반 물건으로서 방화 당시는 인적이 드문 새벽녘이었고 야스쿠니 신사는 보안 경비가 삼엄하여 화재가 발생하더라도 즉시 진화될 수 있는 인적, 물적 설비가 갖추어져 있는 것으로 보이고 실제로도 이 사건 방화 직후 바로 야스쿠니 신사 경비원에 의하여 즉시 발견되어 바로 소화되기에 이른 점, 이 사건 방화로 인한 피해는 물적인 피해뿐이고 그 피해 또한 크지 않은 것으로 보이는 점, 비록 이 사건 신문이 전소하여 주위 건조물에 연소된다고 하더라도 이 사건 신문의 규모에 비추어 실제로 이 사건 신문이 전소하기에 걸릴 시간은 적지 않으리라 보이고 그 후 주위 건조물에 연소되기까지도 상당한 시간이 걸릴 것으로 예상되는데 앞서 본 보안 경계의 정도에 비추어 그 전에 화재가 진압될 가능성이 큰 점, 청구국 수사기관도 수사 초기에는 이 사건 범행을 기물손괴 피의사건으로 의율하기도 했던 점, 이 사건 신문과 중앙문 원기둥 지주의 크기 및 규모와 실제 불에 탄 면적, 범행 당시 이번에는 흔적만 남기기로 하겠다는 범죄인의 의도, 이 사건 신문과 주위 건조물 사이의 거리 등에 비추어 볼 때, 비록 이 사건 방화로 일부 재산 피해가 생겼고 주위 건조물에의 연소 가능성 및 그로 말미암은 공공의 위험이 발생되었다고 하더라도, 그 재산 피해, 연소 가능성 및 공공의 위험의 정도는 그리 크지 않은 것으로 보인다.

따라서 이 사건 범행을 불특정 다수인의 생명·신체를 침해·위협하거나 이에 대한 위험을 야기한 범죄로서 범죄인이 추구하는 정치적 목적과의 균형을 상실한 잔학한 행위로 평가할 수는 없다.

마) 정치범 불인도 원칙의 취지와의 관계

앞서 본 정치범 불인도 원칙의 취지와 관련하여 이 사건을 살펴본다. 대한민국(범죄인의 국적국인 중국도 마찬가지 입장이다)과 청구국 사이에 그동안 일본군위안부 등 과거의 역사적 사실에 대한 인식 및 그와 관련된 정책과 정부각료의 야스쿠니 신사 참배에 대한 인식 및 그에 관한 대응 등에서 정치적으로 서로 다른 견해의 대립이 있었고, 청구국 내에서도 정치적 견해의 대립이 존재하였다.

범죄인의 이 사건 범행 동기와 목적에 비추어보면 일본군위안부 문제

등 과거의 역사적 사실과 야스쿠니 신사 참배에 대한 인식 및 그와 관련된 청구국의 정책에 대한 범죄인의 견해는 대한민국의 헌법이념과 유엔 등의 국제기구나 대다수 문명국가들이 지향하는 보편적 가치와 궤를 같이하는 것으로 인정된다.

이러한 면에서 볼 때 범죄인을 청구국에 인도하는 것은 대한민국의 정치적 질서와 헌법이념 나아가 대다수 문명국가의 보편적 가치를 부인하는 것이 되어 앞에서 본 정치범 불인도 원칙의 취지에도 맞지 않는다. 더욱이 청구국 내에서도 앞에서와 같은 견해 차이와 견해의 대립이 있는 이상 정치범을 인도하는 것은 청구국 내 정치문제에 간섭하는 것으로 비칠 수도 있어 국제관계상 바람직하지 않다.

바) 소 결 론

이상과 같이 ① 범죄인의 범행 동기가 청구국 정부의 일본군위안부 등 과거의 역사적 사실에 관한 인식 및 그와 관련된 정책에 대한 분노에 기인한 것으로서, 범죄인에게 이 사건 범행으로 개인적인 이익을 취득하려는 동기를 찾아볼 수 없으며, ② 범행 목적이 범죄인 자신의 정치적 신념 및 일본군위안부 등 과거의 역사적 사실에 대한 견해와 반대의 입장에 있는 청구국 정부의 정책을 변화시키거나 이에 영향을 미치기 위하여 압력을 가하고자 하는 것이고, 범죄인의 정치적 신념 및 일본군위안부 등 과거의 역사적 사실에 대한 견해가 범죄인 개인의 독단적인 견해라고 할 수 없으며, 대한민국과 범죄자의 국적국인 중국뿐만 아니라 국제사회에서도 폭넓은 공감대를 형성하고 동의를 얻고 있는 견해와 일치하고, ③ 이 사건 범행의 대상인 야스쿠니 신사가 법률상 종교단체의 재산이기는 하나, 위 신사에 과거 청구국의 대외 침략전쟁을 주도하여 유죄판결을 받은 전범들이 합사되어 있고, 주변국들의 반발에도 청구국 정부각료들이나 정치인들이 참배를 계속하고 있는 등 국가시설에 상응하는 정치적 상징성이 있는 것으로 평가되며, ④ 이 사건 범행은 정치적인 대의를 위하여 행해진 것으로서, 범행 대상인 야스쿠니 신사와 직접적인 범행 동기가 된 일본군위안부 문제의 역사적 의미 및 배경에다가 이 사건 범행 후 청구국을 비롯한 각 국가에서 범죄인의 주장에 관심을 두게 되고 논의가 촉발된 정황에 비추어, 범죄인이 추구하고자 하는 정치적 목적을 달성하는데 이 사건 범행이 상당히 기여한 것으로 보이므로 범행과 정치적 목적 사이에 유기적 관련성이 인정되고, ⑤ 이 사건 범행의 법적 성격은 일반물건에의 방화이나, 범행 동기와 시간대, 범행 대상의 규모와 비교한 소손 면적의 정도, 연소 가능성 등을 고려할 때 실제적으로는 오히려 손괴에 가까운 것으로서 방화로 말미암은 공공의 위험성의 정도가 그리 크다고 볼 수 없으며, ⑥ 이 사건 범행으로 인한 인명 피해가 전혀 없고 물적 피해도 크다고 할 수 없어 이를 중대하고 심각하며 잔학한 반인륜적 범죄로 단정하기 어려우므로 이 사건 범행으로 야기된 위험이 목적과의 균형을 상실했다고 보기도 어렵다.

　　이러한 사정들과 범죄인 불인도원칙의 취지, 범죄인 인도 청구국인 일본국과 피청구국인 대한민국, 나아가 범죄인의 국적국인 중국 간의 역사적 배경, 과거의 역사적 사실에 대한 인식의 차이 및 입장의 대립과 같은 정치적 상황, 유엔을 비롯한 국제기구와 대다수 문명국가들이 추구하는 보편적 가치 등을 종합하여 보면, 이 사건 인도 대상 범죄는 청구국의 일본군위안부 등 과거의 역사적 사실에 대한 인식에 항의하고 그와 관련된 대내외 정책에 영향을 줄 목적으로 행해진 일반물건에의 방화 범죄로서 일반범죄로서의 성격보다 그 정치적 성격이 더 주된 상태에 있는 상대적 정치범죄라 할 수 있고, 이는 이 사건 조약 제3조 다.목 본문 소정의 '정치적 범죄'에 해당한다."

　　☑ 해　　설

　　한국의 범죄인인도법은 "인도범죄가 정치적 성격을 지닌 범죄이거나 그와 관련된 범죄인 경우에는 범죄인을 인도하여서는 아니된다"고 규정하고 있다(제8조). 한국이 외국과 체결한 범조인인도조약에도 예외없이 정치범 불인도 조항을 포함하고 있다. 한국 법원에서 정치범이란 이유로 외국의 범죄인 인도 요청이 실제 거절된 사례는 2건 있었다. 이 사건 외에 2006년 한국을 방문 중인 베트남 출신 미국 거주자 우엔 후 창을 폭탄테러 미수 혐의로 인도해 달라는 베트남 정부의 요청에 대하여 법원이 정치범 불인도 조항을 적용하여 인도를 금지한 바 있다(서울고등법원 2006년 7월 27일 선고, 2006토1 결정).

2004년부터 2019년 사이 서울고등법원에 범죄인인도 심사청구가 제기된 사건은 모두 55건이었는데, 그 중 49건에 대해 인도허가 결정이 내려졌다. 기타 인도거절 5건, 각하 1건(동아일보 2020. 4. 27. A31).

➥ 참고문헌 ────────────────────────────────

- 최태현, 한국 법원에서의 정치범 불인도 원칙의 적용, 서울국제법연구 20권 1호 (2013), p. 1.

주권면제

1. 스쿠너 익스체인지 사건(1812)
— 절대적 주권면제

Schooner Exchange v. McFaddon & Others.
Supreme Court of the U.S., 11 U.S. 116(1812).

☑ 사　　안

미국인 McFaddon 등이 소유한 Schooner Exchange호는 1810년 나폴레옹칙령 위반혐의로 대서양 공해상에서 프랑스에 나포되어 몰수되었다. 후일 프랑스는 이 배를 Balaou호로 명명하고 해군에 편입해 운행했다. 이 선박이 프랑스 해군선의 자격으로 수리를 위해 미국 필라델피아항에 입항하자 원소유주는 자신이 이 배의 정당한 소유자임을 주장하는 소송을 제기했다. 당시 미국 법무부는 이 배가 미국과 평화관계에 있는 프랑스의 군함으로서 미국 법원의 관할권으로부터 면제되므로 원고의 청구를 각하하라는 의견서를 제출했다. 1심에서는 원고의 소유권을 부인했으나, 2심에서는 원고의 소유권을 인정했다. 다음은 연방대법원의 판결이다.

☑ 쟁　　점

미국에 입항한 외국의 군함에 대한 미국 법원의 관할권 행사 가능성.

☑ 판　　결

미국과 우호관계에 있는 외국의 군함은 미국 법원의 관할권으로부터 면제된다.

(p. 136) The jurisdiction of the nation within its own territory is necessarily exclusive and absolute. [···]

This full and absolute territorial jurisdiction being alike the attribute of every sovereign, and being incapable of conferring extra-territorial power, would not seem to contemplate foreign sovereigns nor their sovereign rights as its objects. One sovereign being in no respect amenable to another; and being bound by obligations of the highest character not to degrade the dignity of his nation, by placing himself or its sovereign rights within the jurisdiction of another, can be supposed to enter a foreign territory only under an express license, or in the confidence that the immunities belonging to his independent sovereign station, though not expressly stipulated, are reserved by implication, and will be extended to him.

This perfect equality and absolute independence of sovereigns, and this common interest impelling them to mutual intercourse, and an interchange of good offices with each other, have given rise to a class of cases in which every sovereign is understood to wave the exercise of a part of that complete exclusive territorial jurisdiction, which has been stated to be the attribute of every nation.

1st. One of these is admitted to be the exemption of the person of the sovereign from arrest or detention within a foreign territory. [···]

2d. A second case, standing on the same principles with the first, is the immunity which all civilized nations allow to foreign ministers. [···]

3d. A third case in which a sovereign is understood to cede a portion of his territorial jurisdiction is, where he allows the troops of a foreign prince to pass through his dominions. [···]

When private individuals of one nation spread themselves through another as business or caprice may direct, mingling indiscriminately with the inhabitants of that other, or when merchant vessels enter for the purposes of trade, it would be obviously inconvenient and dangerous to society, and would subject the laws to continual infraction, and the government to degradation, if such individuals or merchants did not owe temporary and local allegiance, and were not amenable to the jurisdiction of the country. [···]

But in all respects different is the situation of a public armed ship. She constitutes a part of the military force of her nation; acts under the immediate and direct command of the sovereign; is employed by him in national objects. He has many and powerful motives for preventing those objects from being defeated by the interference of a foreign state. Such interference cannot take place without affecting his power and his dignity. The implied license therefore under which such vessel enters a friendly port, may reasonably be construed, and it seems to the Court, ought to be construed, as containing an exemption from the jurisdiction of the sovereign, within whose territory she claims the rites of hospitality. [⋯]

Upon these principles, by the unanimous consent of nations, a foreigner is amenable to the laws of the place; but certainly in practice, nations have not yet asserted their jurisdiction over the public armed ships of a foreign sovereign entering a port open for their reception. [⋯]

Without indicating any opinion on this question, it may safely be affirmed, that there is a manifest distinction between the private property of the person who happens to be a prince, and that military force which supports the sovereign power, and maintains the dignity and the independence of a nation. A prince, by acquiring private property in a foreign country, may possibly be considered as subjecting that property to the territorial jurisdiction; he may be considered as so far laying down the prince, and assuming the character of a private individual; but this he cannot be presumed to do with respect to any portion of that armed force, which upholds his crown, and the nation he is entrusted to govern. [⋯]

It seems then to the Court, to be a principle of public law, that national ships of war, entering the port of a friendly power open for their reception, are to be considered as exempted by the consent of that power from its jurisdiction. If the preceding reasoning be correct, the Exchange, being a public armed ship, in the service of a foreign sovereign, with whom the government of the United States is at peace, and having entered an American port open for her reception, on the terms on which ships of war are generally permitted to enter the ports of a friendly power, must be considered as having come into the American territory, under an implied promise, that while necessarily within it, and demeaning herself in a friendly manner, she should be exempt from the jurisdiction of the country.

☑ 해　설

국제법상 주권면제에 관한 이론은 각국의 국내판례를 통해 발전했고, 본 판결은 주권면제에 관한 초기의 대표적 판결로 자주 인용된다. 이 사건에 서 미국의 마샬 대법원장은 국가간의 평등, 독립, 존엄성 존중을 주권면제의 근거로 제시했다. 그 밖에도 대등자는 대등자에 대해 관할권을 행사할 수 없다(*Par in parem non babet imperium*)는 법언도 종종 근거로 인용된다. 당시에는 외국 주권자에 대해 국내 법원은 어떠한 경우에도 관할권을 행사하지 않는 것을 원칙으로 했기 때문에 이를 절대적 주권면제(absolute sovereign immunity)라고 불렀다.

19세기식 자유방임주의적 사조에 따르면 국가란 공적 기능을 행사하는 존재이고, 무역 등의 상업적 활동은 사적 영역이라고 생각했다. 따라서 국가의 공적 기능을 타국 법원의 개입으로부터 보호하기 위하여는 국가 스스로가 원하지 않는 한 국가는 타국 법원의 관할권에 복종하지 않는다는 주권면제론이 지지를 받았다. 외교사절에 대한 관할권 면제는 국제사회에서 일찍부터 인정되고 있었는데, 그렇다면 국가 자신은 그 이상의 면제를 향유한다고 보는 것이 논리적으로도 일관되었다.

한편 이 판결이 내려질 무렵 미국과 영국과의 관계가 극도로 악화되어 1812년 미 - 영 전쟁이 발발했기 때문에, 미국 정부로서는 프랑스와의 동맹 관계가 정치적으로 매우 중요했다는 국제정치적 배경도 무시할 수 없었을 것이다.

➡ 참고문헌 —————————————————————————

• L. M. Caplan, The Constitution and Jurisdiction over Foreign States: The 1996 Amendment to the Foreign Sovereign Immunities Act in Perspective, Virginia Journal of International Law Vol. 41(2001), p. 369.

2. I Congreso호 사건(1981)
― 제한적 주권면제의 적용

House of Lords, U.K., [1981] 3 WLR 328.

☑ 사   안

쿠바의 국영무역회사인 Cubazucar는 1973년 칠레 회사와 설탕 판매계약을 맺었다. 계약상의 첫 번째 선적은 쿠바 국영무역회사 Mambisa가 운행하는 쿠바 국유선박 Play Larga호에 의해 운송되었다. Cubazucar와 Mambisa는 법적으로 쿠바정부와 관계없는 독립된 회사였다. 칠레의 Valparaiso항에서 설탕을 하역 중 아엔데 사회주의 정부가 군사 쿠테타에 의해 전복되었다. 그러자 쿠바 정부의 지시에 따른 Mambisa사의 명령으로 Play Larga호는 약 4/5의 설탕을 하역하지 않고 칠레를 떠났다. 계약상의 두 번째 선적은 Mambisa가 Cubazucar를 위해 용선한 Marbles Islands호에 의해 운송되고 있었다. 아엔데 정부가 실각하자 공해상을 항해 중이던 이 선박은 역시 쿠바 정부의 지시에 따른 Mambisa사의 명령으로 북베트남으로 갔다. 그 사이 쿠바 정부가 이 선박을 구입해 국유선박이 되었다. 이 화물은 쿠바 정부의 지시에 따라 북 베트남에게 기증되었다. 원래 두 선박 화물의 칠레측 소유자의 청구에 의해 쿠바 국유 선박 I Congreso호가 영국 수역에서 나포되었다. 이 사건에서 선박 소유주인 쿠바 정부는 주권면제를 주장해 1심에서는 이 주장이 수락되었다. 아래는 최고법원인 상원의 판결이다.

☑ 쟁   점

제한적 주권면제의 적용 ― 상업적 활동의 판단기준

☑ 판　　결

주권면제의 부여 여부는 행위가 성립된 전반적 맥락을 고려하되 기본적
으로는 행위의 목적 아니 성격을 기준으로 판단한다.

판 결 문

On the basis of these cases I have no doubt that the "restrictive" doctrine
should be applied to the present case, [⋯]

The relevant exception, or limitation, which has been engrafted upon the
principle of immunity of states, under the so called "restrictive theory," arises from
the willingness of states to enter into commercial, or other private law, transactions
with individuals. It appears to have two main foundations: (a) It is necessary in the
interest of justice to individuals having such transactions with states to allow them
to bring such transactions before the courts. (b) To require a state to answer a
claim based upon such transactions does not involve a challenge to or inquiry into
any act of sovereignty or governmental act of that state. It is, in accepted phrases,
neither a threat to the dignity of that state, nor any interference with its sovereign
functions. [⋯]

When therefore a claim is brought against a state ([⋯]) and state immunity is
claimed, it is necessary to consider what is the relevant act which forms the basis
of the claim: is this, under the old terminology, an act *"jure gestionis"* or is it an act
"jure imperii": is it ([⋯]) a "private act" or is it a "sovereign or public act," a
private act meaning in this context an act of a private law character such as a
private citizen might have entered into? [⋯].

In many cases the process of deciding upon the character of the relevant act
presents no difficulty. In The Philippine Admiral [1977] A.C. 373, once it was
accepted that the contract for goods, the obligation to repay disbursements, and the
charterparty, were of a trading or commercial character, the breach of these
obligations was clearly within the same area, none the less because committed by a
state. [⋯] The purpose for which the breach was committed could not alter its
clear character. [⋯]

In other situations it may not be easy to decide whether the act complained of
is within the area of non-immune activity or is an act of sovereignty wholly outside
it.

The activities of states cannot always be compartmentalised into trading or governmental activities; and what is one to make of a case where a state has, and in the relevant circumstances, clearly displayed, both a commercial interest and a sovereign or governmental interest? [⋯]:

Under the "restrictive" theory the court has first to characterise the activity into which the defendant state has entered. Having done this, and (assumedly) found it to be of a commercial, or private law, character, it may take the view that contractual breaches, or torts, *prima facie* fall within the same sphere of activity. [⋯]

The conclusion which emerges is that in considering, under the "restrictive" theory whether state immunity should be granted or not, the court must consider the whole context in which the claim against the state is made, with a view to deciding whether the relevant act(s) upon which the claim is based, should, in that context, be considered as fairly within an area of activity, trading or commercial, or otherwise of a private law character, in which the state has chosen to engage, or whether the relevant act(s) should be considered as having been done outside that area, and within the sphere of governmental or sovereign activity. [⋯]

Application to the facts

(a) Playa Larga.

[⋯] The question is whether the acts which gave rise to an alleged cause of action were done in the context of the trading relationship, or were done by the government of the Republic of Cuba acting wholly outside the trading relationship and in exercise of the power of the state. [⋯] I do not think that there is any doubt that the decision not to complete unloading at Valparaiso, or to discharge at Callao, was a political decision taken by the government of the Republic of Cuba for political and non-commercial reasons. [⋯]

Does this call for characterisation of the act of the Republic of Cuba in withdrawing Playa Larga and denying the cargo to its purchasers as done "*jure imperii*"? In my opinion it does not. Everything done by the Republic of Cuba in relation to Playa Larga could have been done, and, so far as evidence goes, was done, as owners of the ship: it had not exercised, and had no need to exercise, sovereign powers. It acted, as any owner of the ship would act, through Mambisa, the managing operators. It invoked no governmental authority. [⋯]

It may well be that those instructions would not have been issued, as they were, if the owner of Playa Larga had been anyone but a state: it is almost certainly the case that there was no commercial reason for the decision. But these consequences follow inevitably from the entry of states into the trading field. If immunity were to be granted the moment that any decision taken by the trading state were shown to be not commercially, but politically, inspired, the "restrictive" theory would almost cease to have any content and trading relations as to state-owned ships would become impossible. It is precisely to protect private traders against politically inspired breaches, or wrongs, that the restrictive theory allows states to be brought before a municipal court. It may be too stark to say of a state "once a trader always a trader": but, in order to withdraw its action from the sphere of acts done *jure gestionis*, a state must be able to point to some act clearly done *jure imperii*. Though, with much hesitation, I feel obliged to differ on this issue from the conclusion of the learned judge, I respectfully think that he well put this ultimate test [1978] Q.B. 500, 528:

"... it is not just that the purpose or motive of the act is to serve the purposes of the state, but that the act is of its own character a governmental act, as opposed to an act which any private citizen can perform."

As to the Playa Larga, therefore, I [···] would allow the appeal.

☑ 해 설

Playa Larga호 화물과 관련해 재판부는 만장일치로 칠레측에 대한 쿠바회사의 설탕 판매 계약의 불이행 결정은 정부로서의 주권행사라기보다 선주로서의 권한행사라고 판단했다. 물론 재판부도 설탕 판매계약 파기의 근본원인은 쿠바정부의 정치적 판단이었음을 인정했다. 그런데 정치적 이유에서 계약을 파기한 행위에 대해 주권면제를 인정하면 제한적 주권면제론은 설자리가 없을 것이라고 해석했다. 즉 제한적 주권면제의 적용 여부는 청구가 제기된 전체적 맥락에서 판단하되, 행위의 목적이나 동기보다는 문제의 행위가 성격상 정부 행위인지 여부에 의해 판단해야 한다는 입장이었다. 한 가지 유의할 점은 주권면제의 적용 여부를 판단함에 있어서는 단순히 판매계약의 성격뿐만 아니라, 계약 파기의 성격도 검토해야 한다고 보았다. 따라서 당초 판매계약 자체는 상업적 성격의 행위였을지라도, 계약 파기가 주권적 행위였다면 주권면제가 인정될 수 있다고 보았다. 이 사건에서 제시된 판단기준은 영국 법원의 현재의 입장으로 이해된다.

3. 제한적 주권면제의 적용(1998)

대법원 1998년 12월 17일 선고, 97다39216 판결.
대법원판례집 제46권 2집(1998), 335쪽 이하.

☑ 사 안

이 사건의 원고는 주한미군 제2사단 기지 내 햄버거 가게 종업원이었다. 그는 정당한 이유 없이 해고되었다고 주장하며 미합중국을 상대로 해고무효의 확인과 해고기간중의 임금지급을 청구하는 소송을 국내법원에 제출했다. 피고인 미국측은 주권면제의 법리를 근거로 한국법원은 이 사건에 대한 재판관할권이 없다고 주장했다. 제1심과 제2심 법원은 모두 미국측의 주장을 받아들여 원고의 청구를 각하했다. 대법원은 이 사건에서 주권면제의 법리는 인정하나 오늘날의 관습국제법에 비추어 제한적 주권면제론이 적용될 사안인가 여부를 하급심에서 검토하지 않았다는 이유로 사건을 다시 하급심으로 돌려보내는 결정을 했다. 이 판결은 제한적 주권면제론을 지지한 대법원의 첫 판결이다.

☑ 쟁 점
제한적 주권면제론의 적용 여부

☑ 판 결
외국의 주권적 활동에 부당한 간섭이 될 우려가 없는 경우, 외국의 사법적 행위에 대해 외국을 피고로 국내 법원이 재판권을 행사할 수 있다.

판 결 문

1. 원심판결 이유에 의하면, 원심은 원고가 미합중국 산하의 비세출자금 기관인 '육군 및 공군 교역처'(The United States Army and Air Force Exchange Service)에 고용되어 미군 2사단 소재 캠프 케이시(Camp Cacey)에서 근무하다 가 1992. 11. 8. 정당한 이유 없이 해고되었다고 주장하면서 미합중국을 피 고로 하여 위 해고의 무효확인과 위 해고된 날로부터 원고를 복직시킬 때까 지의 임금의 지급을 구함에 대하여, 원래 국가는 국제법과 국제관례상 다른 국가의 재판권에 복종하지 않게 되어 있으므로 특히 조약에 의하여 예외로 된 경우나 스스로 외교상 특권을 포기하는 경우를 제외하고는 외국을 피고 로 하여 우리 나라의 법원이 재판권을 행사할 수는 없다고 할 것인데, 미합 중국이 우리 나라 법원의 재판권에 복종하기로 하는 내용의 조약이 있다거 나 미합중국이 위와 같은 외교상의 특권을 포기하였다고 인정할 만한 아무 런 증거가 없으므로, 이 사건 소는 우리 나라의 법원에 재판권이 없어 부적 법하다고 판단하였다.

2. 국제관습법에 의하면 국가의 주권적 행위는 다른 국가의 재판권으로 부터 면제되는 것이 원칙이라 할 것이나, 국가의 사법적(私法的) 행위까지 다 른 국가의 재판권으로부터 면제된다는 것이 오늘날의 국제법이나 국제관례 라고 할 수 없다. 따라서 우리 나라의 영토 내에서 행하여진 외국의 사법적 행위가 주권적 활동에 속하는 것이거나 이와 밀접한 관련이 있어서 이에 대 한 재판권의 행사가 외국의 주권적 활동에 대한 부당한 간섭이 될 우려가 있다는 등의 특별한 사정이 없는 한, 외국의 사법적 행위에 대하여는 당해 국가를 피고로 하여 우리 나라의 법원이 재판권을 행사할 수 있다고 할 것 이다. 이와 견해를 달리한 대법원 1975년 5월 23일자 74마281 결정은 이를 변경하기로 한다.

따라서 원심으로서는 원고가 근무한 미합중국 산하 기관인 '육군 및 공 군 교역처'의 임무 및 활동 내용, 원고의 지위 및 담당업무의 내용, 미합중국 의 주권적 활동과 원고의 업무의 관련성 정도 등 제반 사정을 종합적으로 고려하여 이 사건 고용계약 및 해고행위의 법적 성질 및 주권적 활동과의 관련성 등을 살펴본 다음에 이를 바탕으로 이 사건 고용계약 및 해고행위에 대하여 우리 나라의 법원이 재판권을 행사할 수 있는지 여부를 판단하였어야 할 것이다. 그럼에도 불구하고 이 사건 고용계약 및 해고행위의 법적 성질 등을 제대로 살펴보지 아니한 채 그 판시와 같은 이유만으로 재판권이 없다고 단정하여 이 사건 소가 부적법하다고 판단한 원심판결에는 외국에 대한 재판권의 행사에 관한 법리를 오해하고 심리를 다하지 아니한 위법이 있다고 할 것이다. 상고이유 중 이 점을 지적하는 부분은 이유 있다.

3. 그러므로 원심판결을 파기하고, 사건을 다시 심리·판단케 하기 위하여 원심법원에 환송하기로 관여 대법관의 의견이 일치되어 주문과 같이 판결한다.

☑ 해   설

주권면제와 관련해 이 판결 이전 대법원 1975년 5월 23일 선고, 74마281 결정과 서울민사지방법원 1985년 9월 25일 선고, 84가합5303 판결(확정)은 외국은 어떠한 경우에도 국내법원의 재판관할권에 복종하지 않는다는 절대적 주권면제론에 입각하고 있었다. 한편 이 판결 이전 서울민사지방법원 1994년 6월 22일 선고, 90가합4223 판결과 이의 항소심 서울고등법원 1995년 5월 19일 선고, 94나274350 판결은 국내에서 최초의 제한적 주권면제론에 입각한 판결이었다. 단 이 사건의 상고심에서는 주권면제 부분이 다투어지지 않아 대법원의 입장이 밝혀질 기회가 없었다. 대법원의 절대적 주권면제에서 제한적 주권면제로의 판례 변경은 본 판결을 통해 이루어졌다.

한편 본 사건은 대법원에 의해 하급심으로 파기 환송되었으나 원고는 서울지방법원 2002년 4월 12일 선고, 99가합101097 판결에서 다시 패소했다. 그는 서울고등법원에 항소했으나, 최종적으로는 서울고등법원 2004년 1월 13일의 화해권고 결정에 의해 사건이 종결되었다.

주권면제 관련 다른 국내 판결들은 정인섭, 한국법원에서의 국제법 판례(박영사, 2018), p. 44 이하 수록분 및 정인섭편, 우리 법원에서의 국제법 관련판결, 서울국제법연구 제26권 2호(2019), p. 350 이하 참조.

한편 유엔 국제법위원회(ILC)에 의하여 작성되고 2004년 유엔 총회에서 채택된 Convention on the Juridical Immunity of States and Their Property 는 주권면제가 인정되지 않는 상업활동을 다음과 같이 정의하고 있다.

"제2조 제1항 c호
(i) 상품의 매매 또는 용역의 공급을 위한 모든 상업적 계약 또는 거래.
(ii) 차관 또는 거래에 관한 모든 보증 또는 배상의 의무를 포함하여 차관 또는 재정적 성격의 그 밖의 거래를 위한 모든 계약.
(iii) 그 밖의 상업적, 산업상, 무역상 또는 전문적 성격의 모든 계약 또는 거래, 다만 고용계약은 포함하지 않는다.

제2항 계약 또는 거래가 제1항(c)에서의 "상업적 거래"인지 여부를 결정함에 있어서는 주로 계약 또는 거래의 성격을 참조해야 하지만, 그 계약 또는 거래의 당사자들이 합의했거나 법정지국의 관행상 그 목적이 계약 또는 거래의 비상업적 성격을 결정하는 데 관련되어 있다면 목적 또한 고려되어야 한다."

➠ 참고문헌 ─────────────────────────

• 유남석, 외국의 사법적 행위에 대한 재판권, 국민과 사법: 윤관 대법원장퇴임기념(박영사, 1999), p. 635.
• 석광현, 외국국가에 대한 민사재판권의 행사와 주권면제, 법조 49권 12호(2000. 12), p. 290.
• 김태천, 외국 국가의 재판권면제: 그 법적 근거와 범위에 관하여, 저스티스 34권 3호(2001. 6), p. 276.
• 최태현, 한국에 있어서의 제한적 주권면제론의 수용, 국제판례연구 제2집(2001), p. 239.

4. 피노체트 사건(1999)
— 전직 국가원수의 면제권

Regina v. Bow Street Metropolitan Stipendiary Magistrate
And Others, Ex Parte Pinochet Ugarte(No.3).
House of Lords, U.K., [2000] 1 A.C. 147.

☑ 사 안

이 사건은 1998년 10월 칠레의 전 국가원수 피노체트가 영국에 일시 체류중 스페인 판사가 그의 범죄인 인도를 요청하는 체포영장을 발부함으로써 시작되었다. 피노체트가 국가원수 재직시 스페인인을 포함한 수많은 사람들을 납치, 고문, 살해했다는 혐의였으며, 이에 근거해 스페인 정부는 영국 정부에 대해 피노체트의 범죄인 인도를 요청했다. 영국 법원의 심리에서 피노체트는 자신의 국가원수 시절의 공적 행위라며 면제를 주장했다. 전직 국가원수인 피노체트가 영국 법원의 관할권으로부터 면제되느냐가 재판의 쟁점의 하나로 부각되었다.

☑ 쟁 점

전직 국가원수의 재직시 고문행위에 대한 주권면제의 인정 가능성.

☑ 판 결

고문행위는 국가원수로서의 공적 기능에 해당하지 않으므로 전직 국가원수는 재직시의 고문에 관해 면제를 향유할 수 없다.

판 결 문

(p. 201-) (Lord Browne-Wilkinson) State Immunity

It is a basic principle of international law that one sovereign state (the forum state) does not adjudicate on the conduct of a foreign state. The foreign state is entitled to procedural immunity from the processes of the forum state. This immunity extends to both criminal and civil liability. State immunity probably grew from the historical immunity of the person of the monarch. In any event, such personal immunity of the head of state persists to the present day: the head of state is entitled to the same immunity as the state itself. The diplomatic representative of the foreign state in the forum state is also afforded the same immunity in recognition of the dignity of the state which he represents. This immunity enjoyed by a head of state in power and an ambassador in post is a complete immunity attaching to the person of the head of state or ambassador and rendering him immune from all actions or prosecutions whether or not they relate to matters done for the benefit of the state. Such immunity is said to be granted *ratione personae*. [···][1]

In my judgment at common law a former head of state enjoys similar immunities, *ratione materiae*, once he ceases to be head of state. He too loses immunity *ratione personae* on ceasing to be head of state: [···]

As ex-head of state he cannot be sued in respect of acts performed whilst head of state in his public capacity: Hatch v. Baez (1876) 7 Hun 596. Thus, at common law, the position of the former ambassador and the former head of state appears to be much the same: both enjoy immunity for acts done in performance of their respective functions whilst in office. [···]

The question then which has to be answered is whether the alleged organisation of state torture by Senator Pinochet (if proved) would constitute an act committed by Senator Pinochet as part of his official functions as head of state. [···]

Can it be said that the commission of a crime which is an international crime against humanity and *jus cogens* is an act done in an official capacity on behalf of the state? I believe there to be strong ground for saying that the implementation of torture as defined by the Torture Convention cannot be a state function. [···]

---

1) 이어서 외교사절의 경우 외교사절로서의 역할을 마치면 더 이상 특권과 면제가 인정되지 않지만, 재임중 행한 공적 행위에 관하여는 계속 면제를 향유한다는 점을 지적했다.

I have doubts whether, before the coming into force of the Torture Convention, the existence of the international crime of torture as *jus cogens* was enough to justify the conclusion that the organisation of state torture could not rank for immunity purposes as performance of an official function. At that stage there was no international tribunal to punish torture and no general jurisdiction to permit or require its punishment in domestic courts. Not until there was some form of universal jurisdiction for the punishment of the crime of torture could it really be talked about as a fully constituted international crime. But in my judgment the Torture Convention did provide what was missing: a worldwide universal jurisdiction. Further, it required all member states to ban and outlaw torture: article 2. How can it be for international law purposes an official function to do something which international law itself prohibits and criminalises?

Thirdly, an essential feature of the international crime of torture is that it must be committed "by or with the acquiesence of a public official or other person acting in an official capacity." As a result all defendants in torture cases will be state officials. Yet, if the former head of state has immunity, the man most responsible will escape liability while his inferiors (the chiefs of police, junior army officers) who carried out his orders will be liable. I find it impossible to accept that this was the intention.

Finally, and to my mind decisively, if the implementation of a torture regime is a public function giving rise to immunity *ratione materiae*, this produces bizarre results. Immunity *ratione materiae* applies not only to ex-heads of state and ex-ambassadors but to all state officials who have been involved in carrying out the functions of the state. Such immunity is necessary in order to prevent state immunity being circumvented by prosecuting or suing the official who, for example, actually carried out the torture when a claim against the head of state would be precluded by the doctrine of immunity. If that applied to the present case, and if the implementation of the torture regime is to be treated as official business sufficient to found an immunity for the former head of state, it must also be official business sufficient to justify immunity for his inferiors who actually did the torturing. Under the Convention the international crime of torture can only be committed by an official or someone in an official capacity. They would all be entitled to immunity. It would follow that there can be no case outside Chile in which a successful prosecution for torture can be brought unless the State of Chile is prepared to waive its right to its officials' immunity. Therefore the whole

elaborate structure of universal jurisdiction over torture committed by officials is
rendered abortive and one of the main objectives of the Torture Convention—to
provide a system under which there is no safe haven for torturers—will have been
frustrated. In my judgment all these factors together demonstrate that the notion of
continued immunity for ex-heads of state is inconsistent with the provisions of the
Torture Convention.

For these reasons in my judgment if, as alleged, Senator Pinochet organised
and authorised torture after 8 December 1988, he was not acting in any capacity
which gives rise to immunity *ratione materiae* because such actions were contrary to
international law, Chile had agreed to outlaw such conduct and Chile had agreed
with the other parties to the Torture Convention that all signatory states should
have jurisdiction to try official torture (as defined in the Convention) even if such
torture were committed in Chile.

☑ 해   설

스페인의 범죄인 인도 청구에 대하여 1998년 11월 25일 영국 상원(당시
최고법원)은 3 : 2의 결정으로 피노체트에게 면제권은 인정되지 않으며, 체포
역시 적법하다고 판단했다. 이 심리 과정에 Amnesty International(AI)이
intervener로 참여가 허용되었는데, 재판부의 일원인 Hoffman 판사가 AI의
활동에 참여했었고 그의 부인도 AI에 근무했다는 사실이 뒤늦게 밝혀졌다.
이에 피노체트 측에서 Hoffman 판사의 편견을 우려하며 재판의 공정성에
의문을 제기했고, 결과적으로 원 판결이 취소되었다(1999. 1. 15.). 이는 영국
사법사상 전례 없는 일로서 5인 재판부가 새로이 구성되어 다시 재판을 진
행했다. 이에 1999년 3월 24일 피노체트 사건에 대한 3번째 판단인 본 결정
이 다시 내려졌으며, 이 때 영국 상원은 6 : 1로써 피노체트를 스페인으로 인
도하라고 결정했다. 당시 칠레 정부측은 칠레 국민은 자신이 처벌해야 한다
며, 피노체트를 칠레로 송환하라고 요구했다.

이 사건은 판결문에서도 지적하고 있듯이 국내법원이 전직 국가원수에
대하여 국제범죄 혐의를 이유로 면제권을 부인한 첫 번째 사례였다. 재판부
는 이 사건의 쟁점을 크게 2가지로 보았다.

첫째, 피노체트의 행위는 스페인으로의 범죄인 인도 대상이 되는 범죄

인가? 이에 대해 재판부는 1988년 영국이 고문방지협약에 가입했고, 이 협약이 금하는 고문을 국내법상으로도 범죄로 규정한 이후의 전세계 어느 곳에서 발생한 고문이라도 영국법상의 범죄화되었으므로 그 이후의 고문행위에 대하여는 국외범일지라도 영국 법원에서의 처벌이 가능하다고 판단했다. 따라서 인도대상에 포함된다고 판단했다.

둘째, 피노체트와 같은 전직 국가원수는 영국 법원의 형사재판권으로 어느 정도의 면제권을 향유하느냐? 재판부는 우선 전직 국가원수의 면제는 공적 행위의 범위 내에서만 인정될 수 있다고 전제했다. 그런데 칠레와 영국, 스페인은 모두 고문방지협약의 당사국이며, 고문은 바로 국제법이 금하는 범죄로서 공적 행위가 될 수 없으므로 피노체트의 고문행위에 대하여는 면제가 인정될 수 없다고 판단했다. 결론적으로 재판부는 피노체트를 스페인으로 범죄인인도를 허용하는 결정을 했다.

그러나 2000년 1월 영국 정부는 피노체트의 건강이 재판을 감내할 만한 상태가 아니라는 이유에서 스페인으로 인도하지 않기로 결정했고, 같은 해 3월 2일 피노체트는 석방되어 칠레로 귀국했다. 2000년 피노체트는 칠레 법원에 기소되었으나, 건강상의 이유로 재판이 바로 진행되지는 않았다. 2004년 칠레 법원은 88세의 피노체트가 재판에 회부될 수 있을 만한 건강상태라고 보아 그에 대한 재판을 시작했다. 피노체트는 재판이 끝나기 전 자택연금 중이던 2006년 12월 10일 사망했다.

▶▶ 참고문헌 ─────────────────────────────

• 이만희, 피노체트와 국제범죄인인도, 법조 2000년 7월호, p. 220.
• 최태현, 피노체트 사건에 대한 국제법적 평가, 국제법학회논총 48권 1호 (2003), p. 271.
• C. A. Bradley and J. L. Goldsmith, Pinochet and International Human Rights Litigation, Michigan Law Review Vol. 97(1999), p. 2129.
• M. Byers, The Law and Politics of the Pinochet case, Duke Journal of Comparative and International Law Vol. 10(2000), p. 415.
• C. Chinkin, International Decisions, AJIL Vol. 93(1999), p. 703.
• O'Neill, A New Customary Law of Head of State Immunity?: Hirohito and

Pinochet, Stanford Journal of International Law Vol. 38(2002), p. 289.
- R. Wedgwood, International Criminal Law and Augusto Pinochet, Virginia Journal of International Law Vol. 40(2000), p. 829.

5. 페리니 사건(2012)
― 주권면제와 강행규범 위반

Jurisdictional Immunities of the State.
Germany v. Italy(Greece Intervening), 2012 ICJ Reports 99.

☑ 사   안

이탈리아인 Ferrini는 제2차 대전 중인 1944년 8월 독일군에 의해 체포되어 독일로 강제이송된 후 종전 시까지 강제노역에 종사했다. 이에 대해 아무런 보상도 받지 못한 Ferrini는 1998년 이탈리아 법원에 독일을 상대로 보상청구소송을 제기했으나, 하급심에서는 주권면제를 이유로 청구가 받아들여지지 않았다. 그러나 2004년 이탈리아의 최고심인 Court of Cassation은 국제범죄에 해당하는 행위에 관하여는 주권면제를 인정할 필요가 없다며 이탈리아 법원이 이 사건에 대하여 재판관할권을 행사할 수 있다고 판시했다. 이후 사건을 환송받은 하급심은 독일에게 배상의무를 선고했다. 이어 이탈리아에서는 독일을 상대로 약 250건의 유사한 성격의 보상청구소송이 제출되었으며, 여러 건의 재판에서 동일한 입장이 확인되었다. 한편 그리스에서도 독일을 상대로 유사한 판결이 내려진 바 있다. 이에 독일은 이탈리아의 행위가 국제법 위반이라며 사건을 ICJ에 제소했다.

재판과정에서 이탈리아는 문제의 독일군 행위가 전쟁범죄와 인도에 반하는 죄에 해당하는 심각한 국제법 위반행위이며, 또한 이는 국제법상 강행규범 위반행위이므로 이탈리아 법원은 주권면제를 부인하고 독일국에 대한 재판관할권을 행사할 수 있다고 주장했다. 즉 강행규범은 이와 모순되는 다른 국제법상의 규칙에 우선하는 효력을 지니므로 강행규범 위반행위로 발생한 민사배상 청구권의 실현을 주권면제의 법리가 봉쇄시킬 수 없다는 입장이었다. 반면 독일은 제2차 대전중 자국의 행위가 국제법 위반임을 부인하지 않았으나, 이탈리아 법정에서 이 사건에 관해 여전히 주권면제를 향유할 권리를 주장했다.

☑ 쟁   점

문제된 국가 행위가 강행규범의 위반인 소송에서는 국가가 주권면제를 향유할 수 없는가?

☑ 판   결

국내법원이 타국에 대해 재판관할권을 행사할 수 있느냐를 결정하는 주권면제의 법칙은 성격상 절차사항으로 이는 문제된 행위가 실체법적으로 위법한가 여부와는 관계가 없다. 따라서 주권면제의 법리는 강행규범의 내용과 서로 충돌의 여지가 없고, 문제의 행위가 강행규범 위반이냐 여부는 주권면제의 적용 여부에 영향을 미치지 않는다.

판 결 문

92. The Court now turns to the second strand in Italy's argument, which emphasizes the *jus cogens* status of the rules which were violated by Germany during the period 1943-1945. This strand of the argument rests on the premise that there is a conflict between *jus cogens* rules forming part of the law of armed conflict and according immunity to Germany. Since *jus cogens* rules always prevail over any inconsistent rule of international law, whether contained in a treaty or in customary international law, so the argument runs, and since the rule which accords one State immunity before the courts of another does not have the status of *jus cogens*, the rule of immunity must give way.

93. This argument therefore depends upon the existence of a conflict between a rule, or rules, of *jus cogens*, and the rule of customary law which requires one State to accord immunity to another. In the opinion of the Court, however, no such conflict exists. Assuming for this purpose that the rules of the law of armed conflict which prohibit the murder of civilians in occupied territory, the deportation of civilian inhabitants to slave labour and the deportation of prisoners of war to slave labour are rules of *jus cogens*, there is no conflict between those rules and the rules on State immunity. The two sets of rules address different matters. The rules of State immunity are procedural in character and are confined to determining whether or not the courts of one State may exercise jurisdiction in respect of another State. They do not bear upon the question whether or not the conduct in respect of which the proceedings are brought was lawful or unlawful. [···] For the same reason, recognizing the immunity of a foreign State in accordance with customary international law does not amount to recognizing as lawful a situation created by the breach of a *jus cogens* rule, or rendering aid and assistance in maintaining that situation, and so cannot contravene the principle in Article 41 of the International Law Commission's Articles on State Responsibility.

94. In the present case, the violation of the rules prohibiting murder, deportation and slave labour took place in the period 1943-1945. The illegality of these acts is openly acknowledged by all concerned. The application of rules of State immunity to determine whether or not the Italian courts have jurisdiction to hear claims arising out of those violations cannot involve any conflict with the rules which were violated. Nor is the argument strengthened by focusing upon the duty of the wrongdoing State to make reparation, rather than upon the original wrongful act. The duty to make reparation is a rule which exists independently of those rules which concern the means by which it is to be effected. The law of State immunity concerns only the latter; a decision that a foreign State is immune no more conflicts with the duty to make reparation than it does with the rule prohibiting the original wrongful act. Moreover, against the background of a century of practice in which almost every peace treaty or post-war settlement has involved either a decision not to require the payment of reparations or the use of lump sum settlements and set-offs, it is difficult to see that international law contains a rule requiring the payment of full compensation to each and every individual victim as a rule accepted by the international community of States as a whole as one from which no derogation is permitted.

95. To the extent that it is argued that no rule which is not of the status of *jus cogens* may be applied if to do so would hinder the enforcement of a *jus cogens* rule, even in the absence of a direct conflict, the Court sees no basis for such a proposition. A *jus cogens* rule is one from which no derogation is permitted but the rules which determine the scope and extent of jurisdiction and when that jurisdiction may be exercised do not derogate from those substantive rules which possess *jus cogens* status, nor is there anything inherent in the concept of *jus cogens* which would require their modification or would displace their application. The Court has taken that approach in two cases, notwithstanding that the effect was that a means by which a *jus cogens* rule might be enforced was rendered unavailable. In Armed Activities, it held that the fact that a rule has the status of *jus cogens* does not confer upon the Court a jurisdiction which it would not otherwise possess (*Armed Activities on the Territory of the Congo(New Application: 2002) (Democratic Republic of the Congo v. Rwanda), Jurisdiction and Admissibility, Judgment, I.C.J. Reports 2006*, p. 32, para. 64, and p. 52, para. 125). In Arrest Warrant, the Court held, albeit without express reference to the concept of *jus cogens*, that the fact that a Minister for Foreign Affairs was accused of criminal violations of rules which undoubtedly possess the character of *jus cogens* did not deprive the Democratic Republic of the Congo of the entitlement which it possessed as a matter of customary international law to demand immunity on his behalf (*Arrest Warrant of 11 April 2000 (Democratic Republic of the Congo v. Belgium), Judgment, I.C.J. Reports 2002*, p. 24, para. 58, and p. 33, para. 78). The Court considers that the same reasoning is applicable to the application of the customary international law regarding the immunity of one State from proceedings in the courts of another. [⋯][1]

97. Accordingly, the Court concludes that even on the assumption that the proceedings in the Italian courts involved violations of *jus cogens* rules, the applicability of the customary international law on State immunity was not affected.

☑ 해　설

ICJ는 외국을 피고로 하는 소송이 제기된 국내법원의 경우 사건의 본안 내용을 검토하기 앞서 우선 자신이 그 사건에 관해 관할권을 행사할 권한이 있는가를 먼저 검토해야 하므로, 주권면제는 성격상 사전적으로 결정되어야 할 사항으로 보았다(para. 82). 또한 주권면제는 이것이 인정되면 외국의 행위가 실체법적으로 위법한가 여부와 상관없이 국내법원이 더 이상 재판을 진행할 수 없다는 절차적 성격의 문제에 불과하다고 보았다(para. 93). 따라서 주권면제의 인정이 강행규범 위반의 결과를 합법적인 것으로 인정하느냐 여부와는 상관없는 문제라고 판단했다. 즉 절차적 성격의 주권면제의 법리와

---

1) 이어 재판부는 강행규범 위반을 이유로 주권면제 법리의 적용을 배제하자는 주장이 거부되었던 각국 국내재판의 사례들을 들으며, 오직 본 판결의 출발점인 Ferrini 사건에 대한 이탈리아 법원 판결만이 이를 수락했다고 지적했다(para. 96).

실체적 성격의 강행규범 위반 여부는 서로 적용의 차원이 다르므로 상호 모순되거나 충돌될 여지가 없다고 판결내렸다. 본 판결에서는 12:3이란 비교적 큰 표차로 독일의 주권면제 주장이 지지되었다.

한편 국제법상 합법적인 상거래 행위에 관해서도 현재 국가가 주권면제의 보호를 받을 수 없음에도 불구하고, 국제법상 강행규범을 위반한 국가의 위법행위 내지 범죄행위에 대해서는 주권면제가 인정되는 결과에 대해 비판이 가해지기도 한다. 또한 국제범죄에 해당하는 심각한 국제법 위반행위를 저지른 국가기관 개인에 대하여는 국제법상의 형사처벌이 실현되는 반면, 그 같은 범행을 지시한 국가를 상대로 한 피해자의 민사배상 청구권은 주권면제로 인해 봉쇄된다는 사실 역시 모순적인 결과로 보인다. 이에 심각한 국제법 위반행위와 관련된 소송에서는 주권면제를 인정하지 말아야 한다는 주장이 국내재판 등에서 여러 차례 제기되었다.

대표적인 사건의 하나가 영국과 유럽인권재판소에서의 Al Adsani 판결이었다. Al Adsani는 영국과 쿠웨이트 2중 국적자인데 쿠웨이트 체류시 국가원수의 친척(the Sheikh)의 지시로 쿠웨이트 정부에 의해 피납되어 고문을 받았다고 주장했다. 그는 런던으로 귀환하여 당시에 받은 신체적·정신적 상처의 치료를 받았으나, 런던에서도 쿠웨이트 대사 등에 의해 협박을 받았다고 주장했다. 그는 영국 법원에 문제의 국가원수 친척과 쿠웨이트 정부를 상대로 손해배상을 청구하는 민사소송을 제기했다. 쿠웨이트 정부를 상대로 한 소송에서 쿠웨이트 정부가 주권면제를 주장하자 영국 법원은 이를 인정했다. 그러자 Al Adsani는 영국법원이 고문과 같은 강행규범 위반행위에 대하여도 주권면제의 법리를 적용함으로써 유럽인권협약 제6조에 따른 공정한 재판을 받을 권리를 침해당했다고 주장하며, 이 사건을 유럽인권재판소에 제소했다.

9 : 8이라는 간발의 차이로 내려진 유럽인권재판소의 다수의견은 고문의 금지가 국제법상의 강행규범임을 인정했으나, 이 사건은 피노체트 사건과 같은 형사사건과 달리 법정지 외에 벌어진 고문과 관련된 민사소송으로 이에 관해 주권면제를 부인하는 국제법상의 법리가 확립된 바 없다고 판단해 원고 패소판결을 내렸다.

"**61.** While the Court accepts, on the basis of these authorities, that the prohibition of torture has achieved the status of a peremptory norm in international law, it observes that the present case concerns not, as in *Furundzija* and *Pinochet*, the criminal liability of an individual for alleged acts of torture, but the immunity of a State in a civil suit for damages in respect of acts of torture within the territory of that State. Notwithstanding the special character of the prohibition of torture in international law, the Court is unable to discern in the international instruments, judicial authorities or other materials before it any firm basis for concluding that, as a matter of international law, a State no longer enjoys immunity from civil suit in the courts of another State where acts of torture are alleged."(Al Adsani v. U.K., ECHR (2001), 34 E.H.R.R.273)

한편 이 판결의 소수의견은 고문금지를 강행규범으로 인정하면 이는 여타의 조약이나 관습국제법보다 우월한 효력이 인정되므로 주권면제의 법리도 이에 양보해야 한다고 주장했다. Ferrari Broavo 판사는 소수의견에서 다음과 같이 탄식했다. "What a pity! [⋯] the Court has unfortunately missed a very good opportunity to deliver a courageous judgement."

이후에도 유럽인권재판소는 Stichting Mothers of Srebrenica and Others v. Netherlands, Application No. 65542/12(2013) 판결에서 "International law does not support the position that a civil claim should override immunity from suit for the sole reason that it is based on an allegation of a particularly grave violation of a norm international law, even a norm of *jus cogens*."라고 판단했다(para. 158). 또한 Jones and Others v. U.K., Application Nos. 34356/06 & 40528/06(2014) 판결에서도 같은 취지의 판결을 내렸다.

사실 UN 주권면제협약에도 국가의 심각한 국제법 위반행위에 대하여는 주권면제의 적용을 배제시킨다는 내용은 포함되어 있지 않다. ICJ가 지적한 바와 같이 주권면제는 국내법원이 주권국가를 자신의 관할권에 복종하도록 강제할 수 없다는 절차적 개념인 것은 사실이다. 그러나 주권면제가 국가 사이의 관계에서 개별 국가의 기능을 보호하기 위한 개념이라면, 강행규범은 개별 국가의 재량의 범위를 넘어서는 국제사회의 근본적인 공통 가치를 보호하기 위한 개념이다. 강행규범이란 어떠한 경우에도 이탈이 허용되지 않는 규범인데 이를 위반한 국가의 책임을 추궁하는 과정에서 주권면제가 어떻게 이탈의 결과를 용인하는 방패가 될 수 있는지에 대한 논란은 계속될 것으로 보인다. 한편 주권면제의 인정이 국가의 법적 책임의 성립 자체를 부인하는 것은 아니므로, 국내법정이 아닌 다른 법정은 국가의 국제법 위반행위에 대해 관할권을 행사할 가능성이 있음은 물론이다.

한편 이탈리아에서는 이 판결과 관련된 위헌소송이 다시 제기되어 헌법재판소는 2014년 UN 헌장 제94조(ICJ 판결 준수의무) 이행과 관련해서 전쟁범죄와 인도에 반하는 죄에 관한 외국의 행위에 대해 이탈리아 법원의 관할권을 부인하는 범위에서는 위헌이라고 판정했다.[2] 이는 Ferrini와 유사한 사건의 피해자들의 이탈리아 국내법원 제소가 여전히 가능함을 의미한다. 그러나 독일을 상대로 한 판결의 결과가 실제 집행에는 이르지 않는 것으로 알려지고 있다. 그리스 법원에서도 독일을 상대로 한 소송에서 주권면제는 부인되었으나, 최종적인 집행에는 이르지 못했다.

➡ 참고문헌 ────────────
- 이성덕, 강행규범과 국가면제: 2012년 ICJ 관할권 면제 사건을 중심으로, 중앙법학 14권 4호(2012), p. 205.

---

[2] Corte Constituzionale Sentenza 238/2014.

제 6 장

－ － － － －

국가책임

1. 호르죠 공장 사건(1928)
— 국가책임에 있어서 물적 손해배상의 기준

Case concerning the Factory at Chorzów.
Germany v. Poland, PCIJ Report Series A No. 17.

☑ 사　　안

　　1915년 독일 정부는 상부 실레지아의 호르죠에 질산염 공장을 건설하려는 계약을 독일의 민간회사와 체결했다. 이 계약은 1941년까지 적용되도록 예정되어 있었다. 1919년 독일 정부와 회사는 베를린에서 이 계획을 구체화하는 일련의 계약을 체결했다. 그러나 독일이 제1차 대전에서 패전함에 따라 상부 실레지아 지역은 폴란드로 할양되었다. 독일과 폴란드는 국제연맹의 주선하에 1922년 할양지인 상부 실레지아에서의 독일인 이익보호에 관한 제네바 협약을 체결했다. 한편 폴란드는 제1차 대전의 휴전이 성립한 1918년 11월 이후 성립된 재산권에 관한 모든 거래를 무효로 하는 법률을 제정했다. 그리고 자국에 할양된 지역내 독일재산을 국유화하여 호르죠 공장도 국유화되었다. 독일은 이 같은 폴란드의 조치가 1922년 제네바협약 위반이라고 주장했고, 이후 양국은 일련의 국제재판을 진행했다. 일단 PCIJ는 폴란드의 공장 수용이 조약 위반이라고 판정했다. 손해배상에 관한 양국간의 교섭이 결렬되자, 독일은 다시 제소했다. 결과적으로 이 판결은 상부 실레지아에서의 독일인 이익보호에 관한 PCIJ의 5번째 판결이다.

☑ 쟁　　점

국가책임법상 물적 손해 배상에 관한 기준.

☑ 판　　결

원상회복이 불가능하면 수용 당시의 모든 가치 및 일실이익에 대해서도 금전배상이 이뤄져야 한다.

판 결 문

(p. 27-) The Court in fact declared itself competent to pass upon the claim for reparation because it regarded reparation as the corollary of the violation of the obligations resulting from an engagement between States. [⋯]

It is a principle of international law that the reparation of a wrong may consist in an indemnity corresponding to the damage which the nationals of the injured State have suffered as a result of the act which is contrary to international law. [⋯] The rules of law governing the reparation are the rules of international law in force between the two States concerned, and not the law governing relations between the State which has committed a wrongful act and the individual who has suffered damage. Rights or interests of an individual the violation of which rights causes damage are always in a different plane to rights belonging to a State, which rights may also be infringed by the same act. The damage suffered by an individual is never therefore identical in kind with that which will be suffered by a State; it can only afford a convenient scale for the calculation of the reparation due to the State. [⋯]

As regards the first point, the Court observes that it is a principle of international law, and even a general conception of law, that any breach of an engagement involves an obligation to make reparation. In Judgment No. 8, when deciding on the jurisdiction derived by it from Article 23 of the Geneva Convention, the Court has already said that reparation is the indispensable complement of a failure to apply a convention, and there is no necessity for this to be stated in the convention itself. The existence of the principle establishing the obligation to make reparation, as an element of positive international law, has moreover never been disputed in the course of the proceedings in the various cases concerning the Chorzów factory. [⋯]

The essential principle contained in the actual notion of an illegal act—a principle which seems to be established by international practice and in particular by the decisions of arbitral tribunals—is that reparation must, as far as possible, wipe out all the consequences of the illegal act and reestablish the situation which would, in all probability, have existed if that act had not been committed. Restitution in kind, or, if this is not possible, payment of a sum corresponding to the value which a restitution in kind would bear; the award, if need be, of damages for loss sustained which would not be covered by restitution in kind or payment in place of it—such are the principles which should serve to determine the amount of compensation due for an act contrary to international law.

This conclusion particularly applies as regards the Geneva Convention, the object of which is to provide for the maintenance of economic life in Upper Silesia on the basis of respect for the *status quo*. The dispossession of an industrial undertaking—the expropriation of which is prohibited by the Geneva Convention— then involves the obligation to restore the undertaking and, if this be not possible, to pay its value at the time of the indemnification, which value is designed to take the place of restitution which has become impossible. To this obligation, in virtue of the general principles of international law, must be added that of compensating loss sustained as the result of the seizure. The impossibility, on which the parties are agreed, of restoring the Chorzów factory could therefore have no other effect but that of substituting payment of the value of the undertaking for restitution; it would not be in conformity either with the principles of law or with the wish of the parties to infer from that agreement that the question of compensation must henceforth be dealt with as though an expropriation properly socalled was involved.

☑ 해   설

이 판결에서 PCIJ는 수용 당시로 원상회복이 불가능하면 일실이익까지 모두 배상하라고 판시하고 있다. 또한 조약 의무의 위반이 있으면 배상의 수반은 국제법의 원칙이며 법의 기본 개념이라고 전제하여, 조약상 배상의무가 규정되어 있지 않아도 위법행위를 한 국가는 배상책임이 있다고 판단했다. 이 판결 이후 해당 회사와 폴란드는 배상에 관한 합의에 도달했으며, 계류중인 모든 소송을 취하하기로 합의했다. 1929년 5월 PCIJ는 사건의 종결을 선언했다.

이와 관련해 국가책임에 관한 국제법위원회 초안 제34조도 아울러 기억할 필요가 있다. 여기서는 국제불법행위에 대한 배상은 전액 배상이 되어야 하며, 그 형태는 원상회복, 배상 혹은 만족(satisfaction)의 형태로 이뤄지는데 2가지 이상의 방법을 혼용할 수도 있다고 규정하고 있다.

Article 34
Forms of reparation

Full reparation for the injury caused by the internationally wrongful act shall take the form of restitution, compensation and satisfaction, either singly or in combination, in accordance with the provisions of this chapter.

➧ 참고문헌 ─────────────────────────────

- John Fischer Williams, International Law and the Property of Aliens, BYIL Vol. 9(1928), p. 1.
- F. A. Mann, The Consequences of an International Wrong in International and National Law, BYIL Vol. 48(1976−1977), p. 1.
- Rüdiger Wolfrum, Reparation for Internationally Wrongful Acts, Encyclopedia of Public International Law Vol. 10(1987), p. 352.

2. 바르셀로나 전력회사 사건(1970)
― 국가 책임의 추궁 자격

Case Concerning the Barcelona Traction, Light and Power
Company, Limited.(2nd Phase).
Belgium v. Spain, 1970 ICJ Report 4.

☑ 사　　안

바르셀로나 전력회사는 스페인에서 전력 공급 사업을 하기 위한 목적으로 1911년 캐나다에서 설립되었다. 캐나다 회사였지만 이 회사의 대주주는 벨기에인들이었다. 1936년 스페인의 내란으로 그 동안 이 회사가 페세타화 및 파운드화로 지불하던 사채이자 지불에 문제가 생겼다. 스페인 정부가 내란을 이유로 외화이전을 금지했기 때문이었다. 이에 스페인 사채권자는 바르셀로나 전력회사의 파산을 신청하자 법원은 이 회사의 파산을 선고했다. 처음에는 캐나다가 바르셀로나 전력회사를 위하여 사태 해결을 위한 외교교섭에 나섰지만 후에 포기했다. 그러자 대주주(88%)의 국적국인 벨기에가 주주의 이익을 보호하기 위해 1958년 사건을 ICJ에 제소했다. 이후 양국은 협상을 통해 분쟁을 해결하기로 합의했으나, 협상에 진전이 없자 벨기에 정부는 1962년 다시 이 사건을 ICJ에 제소했다.

☑ 쟁　　점

주주의 국적국이 다른 나라 국적의 회사의 피해에 관해 외교적 보호권을 행사할 수 있는가?

☑ 판　　결

회사의 국적국만이 회사를 위하여 국제청구를 제기할 수 있으며, 주주의 국적국은 이에 해당하지 않는다.

판 결 문

38. In this field international law is called upon to recognize institutions of municipal law that have an important and extensive role in the international field. This does not necessarily imply drawing any analogy between its own institutions and those of municipal law, nor does it amount to making rules of international law dependent upon categories of municipal law. All it means is that international law has had to recognise the corporate entity as an institution created by States in a domain essentially within their domestic jurisdiction. This in turn requires that, whenever legal issues arise concerning the rights of States with regard to the treatment of companies and shareholders, as to which rights international law has not established its own rules, it has to refer to the relevant rules of municipal law. Consequently, in view of the relevance to the present case of the rights of the corporate entity and its shareholders under municipal law, the Court must devote attention to the nature and interrelation of those rights. [⋯]

41. Municipal law determines the legal situation not only of such limited liability companies, but also of those persons who hold shares in them. Separated from the company by numerous barriers, the shareholder cannot be identified with it. The concept and structure of the company are founded on and determined by a firm distinction between the separate entity of the company and that of the shareholder, each with a distinct set of rights. The separation of property rights as between company and shareholder is an important manifestation of this distinction. So long as the company is in existence, the shareholder has no right to the corporate assets. [⋯]

44. Notwithstanding the separate corporate personality, a wrong done to the company frequently causes prejudice to its shareholders. But, the mere fact that damage is sustained by both company and shareholder does not imply that both are entitled to claim compensation. Thus, no legal conclusion can be drawn from the fact that the same event caused damage simultaneously affecting several natural or juristic persons. [⋯] Thus, whenever a shareholder's interests are harmed by an act done to the company, it is to the latter that he must look to institute appropriate action; for although two separate entities may have suffered from the same wrong, it is only one entity whose rights have been infringed. [⋯]

47. The situation is different if the act complained of is aimed at the direct rights of the shareholder as such. It is well known that there are rights which municipal law confers upon the latter distinct from those of the company, including the right to any declared dividend, the right to attend and vote at general meetings, the right to share in the residual assets of the company on liquidation. Whenever one of his direct rights is infringed, the shareholder has an independent right of action. On this there is no disagreement between the Parties. But, a distinction must be drawn between a direct infringement of the shareholder's rights and difficulties or financial losses to which he may be exposed as the result of the situation of the company. [⋯]

96. The court considers that the adoption of the theory of diplomatic protection of shareholders as such, by opening the door to competing diplomatic claims, could create an atmosphere of confusion and insecurity in international economic relations. The danger would be all the greater inasmuch as the shares of companies whose activity is international are widely scattered and frequently change hands. It might perhaps be claimed that, if the right of protection belonging to the national States of the shareholders were considered as only secondary to that of the national States of the company, there would be less danger of difficulties of the kind contemplated. However, the Court must state that the essence of a secondary right is that it only comes into existence at the time when the original right ceases to exist. As the right of protection vested in the national State of the Company cannot be regarded as extinguished because it is not exercised, it is not possible to accept the proposition that in case of its non-exercise the national States of the shareholders have a right of protection secondary to that of the national State of the company. Furthermore, study of factual situations in which this theory might possibly be applied gives rise to the following observations.

97. The situations in which foreign shareholders in a company wish to have recourse to diplomatic protection by their own national State may vary. It may happen that the national State of the company simply refuses to grant it its diplomatic protection, or that it begins to exercise it (as in the present case) but does not pursue its action to the end. It may also happen that the national State of the company and the State which has committed a violation of international law with regard to the company arrive as a settlement of the matter, by agreeing on compensation for the company, but that the foreign shareholders find the compensation insufficient. Now, as a matter of principle, it would be difficult to draw a distinction between these three cases so far as the protection of foreign shareholders by their national State is concerned, since in each case they may have suffered real damage. Furthermore, the national State of the company is perfectly free to decide how far it is appropriate for it to protect the company, [···]

99. It should also be observed that the promoters of a company whose operations will be international must take into account the fact that States have, with regard to their nationals, a discretionary power to grant diplomatic protection or to refuse it. When establishing a company in a foreign country, its promoters are normally impelled by particular considerations; it is often a question of tax or other advantages offered by the host State. It does not seem to be in any way inequitable that the advantages thus obtained should be balanced by the risks arising from the fact that the protection of the company and hence of its shareholders is thus entrusted to a State other than the national State of the shareholders.

100. In the present case, it is clear from what has been said above that Barcelona Traction was never reduced to a position of impotence such that it could not have approached its national State, Canada, to ask for its diplomatic protection, and that, as far as appeared to the Court, there was nothing to prevent Canada from continuing to grant its diplomatic protection to Barcelona Traction if it had considered that it should do so.

101. For the above reasons, the Court is not of the opinion that, in the particular circumstances of the present case, *jus standi*[1] is conferred on the Belgian Government by considerations of equity.

☑ 해   설

이 판결은 원칙적으로 대주주 국적국의 원고적격을 부정함으로써 회사와 개인의 경우에 외교적 보호권을 행사하기 위한 기본 바탕이 되는 국적결정에 있어서 진정한 관련성에 대해서 다른 입장을 취하고 있는 것으로 분석할 수 있다. 즉 회사의 경우에는 대주주가 회사의 운영과 소유에 큰 영향력을 행사하고 있더라도 이것이 회사의 국적을 결정하는 데는 고려될 수 없다는 것이다. 다만 판결은 예외적으로 불법행위가 주주에 대해서 행하여지고 있고, 회사가 더 이상 존재하지 않거나 회사의 국적국이 소송을 수행할 능력이 없는 경우에는 예외적으로 대주주의 국적국이 청구를 제기할 수 있음을

---

1) right of standing — 필자 주.

인정하고 있다.

본 판결의 내용은 이후 국제법 위원회의 「외교적 보호에 관한 규정 초
안」(Draft Articles on Diplomatic Protection)(2006)에도 반영되고 있다. 이 초안
제11조는 원칙적으로 대주주의 국적국은 회사가 입은 피해에 관하여 외교적
보호권을 행사할 수 없다고 규정하고 있다. 다만 회사의 주주의 권리에 대한
직접침해가 발생했거나(제12조), 발생한 피해와 관계없이 회사가 국적국 법에
따라서 소멸했거나, 피해 발생시 피해 발생에 대해서 책임이 있는 국가의 국
적을 회사가 보유하고 이것이 그 국가에서 사업을 하기 위한 전제조건으로
요구되는 경우(제11조 (a), (b))에는 주주의 국적국이 외교적 보호권을 행사할
수 있음을 인정하고 있다.

> 제11조(주주의 보호): 기업의 주주의 국적국은 회사가 피해를 입은 경우
> 그 주주를 위해 외교적 보호를 행사할 권한을 갖지 않는다. 단 다음의 경우
> 에는 그렇지 아니한다.
> (a) 그 피해와 관계없는 이유로 회사가 설립지 국가의 법에 따라서 소멸
> 한 경우: 또는
> (b) 피해 발생시 피해에 책임이 있는 국가의 국적을 보유하고 있고, 그
> 국가에서의 설립이 그곳에서의 사업 수행을 위한 전제조건으로 요구되는
> 경우.
> 제12조(주주에 대한 직접적 침해): 국가의 국제위법행위가 주주의 권리
> 에 대한 직접적인 침해를 초래한 경우, 회사의 국적국과는 별개로 그러한 주
> 주의 국적국은 자국민을 위해 외교적 보호를 행사할 권한이 있다.

한편 Ahamadou Sadio Diallo case(Preliminary Objection)(Republic of
Guinea v. Democratic Republic of the Congo, 2007)에서도 ICJ는 주주로서의 권
리침해에 관하여는 주주의 국적국이 외교적 보호를 행할 수 있지만, 주주와
다른 국적을 가진 회사의 권리를 침해한 부분에 대하여는 주주의 국적국이
외교적 보호를 할 수 없다고 판단했다(이 사건 사안은 본서 p. 35 참조).

▶ 참고문헌 ─────────────────────────

- R. Higgins, Aspects of the Case Concerning the Barcelona Traction, Light and Power Company, Ltd., Virginia Journal of International Law Vol. 11(1971), p. 325.
- H. W. Briggs, Barcelona Traction, The Jus Sta of Belgium, AJIL Vol. 65(1971), p. 327.
- L. C. Calfisch, The Protection of Corporate Investments Abroad in the Light of the Barcelona Traction Case, ZaöRV, Vol. 31(1971), p. 162.
- Economic Internationalism vs. National Parochialism, Barcelona Trasction, Law and Policy in International Business Vol. 3(1971).
- R. B. Lilich, Two Perspectives on Barcelona Traction Case, AJIL Vol. 65(1971), p. 327.
- B. H. Weston, Constructive Takings under International Law, A Modest Foray into Problems of 'Creeping Expropriation,' Virginia Journal of International Law, Vol. 16(1975), p. 103.

3. 레인보우 워리어호 사건(1990)
— 불가항력에 의한 위법성 조각

Rainbow Warrior Case.[1]
New Zealand / France, Special Arbitration Tribunal,
20 RIAA 215.

☑ 사   안

1985년 프랑스의 남태평양상에서의 핵실험에 항의하기 위해 현지를 방문중 뉴질랜드 항구에 정박하고 있던 환경단체 그린피스 소속의 Rainbow Warrior호가 프랑스 비밀요원에 의해 폭파되었다. 이로 인해 배는 침몰되고, 네덜란드인 1명이 사망했다. 프랑스 요원 2명은 뉴질랜드 당국에 의해 체포되어 10년형을 선고받았다.

뉴질랜드와 프랑스는 이 사건을 UN 사무총장의 중재에 회부하기로 결정했다. 그 결과 프랑스는 뉴질랜드에 미화 700만 불의 배상금을 지불하는 한편, 체포된 요원은 프랑스령 폴리네시아 Hao섬 군기지에 3년간 구금하기로 합의하고 프랑스가 신병을 인수했다. 이들은 뉴질랜드의 동의 없이 섬을 떠나는 것이 금지되었다. 그러나 2년도 채 못 되어 프랑스는 그 중 한 명은 신병치료라는 이유에서, 다른 한 명은 임신했다는 이유로 뉴질랜드의 동의없이 모두 본국으로 이송했다. 이에 뉴질랜드가 프랑스의 협정 위반을 주장해 이 사건은 Jiménez de Aréchaga를 위원장으로 하는 3인 중재재판부에 회부되었다. 쟁점 중의 하나는 프랑스로의 이송이 불가항력적인 것이었냐 점이었다.

---

1) 정식 명칭: Case concerning the difference between New Zealand and France concerning the interpretation or application of two agreements concluded on 9 July 1986 between the two States and which related to the problems arising from the *Rainbow Warrior* Affair.

☑ 쟁   점

의료적 조치 및 임신을 이유로 합의를 위반하고 대상자를 본국으로 송
환한 프랑스의 행위가 과연 불가항력에 의한 조치로 인정될 수 있는가 여부.

☑ 판   결

급박한 의료처치의 필요는 국제법상 불가항력으로 인정받기 위한 절대
적이고 중대한 불가능에 해당하지 않는다. 의료처지 이후에도 수감자를 다시
섬으로 복귀시키지 않은 프랑스의 행위는 협약 위반이다.

판 결 문

76. Under the title "Circumstances Precluding Wrongfulness" the International
Law Commission proposed in Articles 29 to 35 a set of rules which include three
provisions, on *force majeure* and fortuitous event (Article 31), distress (Article 32),
and state of necessity (Article 33), which may be relevant to the decision on this
case. [⋯]

As to *force majeure*, it was invoked in the French note of 14 December 1987,
where, referring to the removal of Major Mafart, the French authorities stated that
"in this case of *force majeure*" ([⋯]), they "are compelled to proceed without
further delay with the repatriation of the French officer for health reasons."

77. Article 31(1) of the ILC draft reads:

> The wrongfulness of an act of a State not in conformity with an
> international obligation of that State is precluded if the act was due to an
> irresistible force or to an unforseen external event beyond its control which
> made it materially impossible for the State to act in conformity with that
> obligation or to know that its conduct was not in conformity with that
> obligation.

In the light of this provision, there are several reasons for excluding the
applicability of the excuse of *force majeure* in this case. As pointed out in the report
of the International Law Commission, Article 31 refers to "a situation facing the
subject taking the action, which leads it, as it were, *despite itself*, to act in a manner

not in conformity with the requirements of an international obligation incumbent on it" (Ybk, ILC, 1979, Vol. II, para. 2, p. 122, emphasis in the original). *force majeure* is "generally invoked to justify *involuntary*, or at least unintentional conduct," it referes "to an irresistible force or an unforeseen external event against which it has no remedy and which makes it 'materially impossible' for it to act in conformity with the obligation," since "no person is required to do the impossible." (*Ibid.*, p. 123, para. 4)

The report of the International Law Commission insists on the strict meaning of Article 31, in the following terms:

> the wording of paragraph 1 emphasizes, by the use of the adjective "irresistible" qualifying the word "force," that there must, in the case in point, be a constraint which the State was unable to avoid or to oppose by its own means ... The event must be an act which occurs and produces its effect without the State being able to do anything which might rectify the event or might avert its consequences. The adverb "materially" proceeding the word "impossible" is intended to show that, for the purposes of the article, it would not suffice for the "irresistible force" or the "unforeseen external event" to have made it very *difficult* for the State to act in conformity with the obligation ... the Commission has sought to emphasize that the State must not have had any option in that regard (Ybk, cit., p. 133, para. 40, emphasis in the original).

In conclusion, New Zealand is right in asserting that the excuse of *force majeure* is not of relevance in this case because the test of its applicability is of absolute and material impossibility, and because a circumstance rendering performance more difficult or burdensome does not consititute a case of *force majeure*. Consequently, this excuse is of no relevance in the present case. [⋯]

122. There is a long established practice of States and international Courts and Tribunals of using satisfaction as a remedy or form of reparation (in the wide sense) for the breach of an international obligation. This practice relates particularly to the case of moral or legal damage done directly to the State, especially as opposed to the case of damage to persons involving international responsibilities. [⋯]

123. [⋯] For the foregoing reasons the Tribunal:

- declares that the condemnation of the French Republic for its breaches of its treaty obligations to New Zealand, made public by the decision of the Tribunal,

constitutes in the circumstances appropriate satisfaction for the legal and moral
damage caused to New Zealand.

☑ 해   설

재판부는 프랑스의 불가항력의 주장을 받아들이지 않고, 프랑스가 합의
를 위반했다고 판단했다. 즉 재판부는 불가항력의 원용에 엄격한 요건을 부
여함으로써 주장의 남용을 막으려 했다. 프랑스의 의무위반 행위에 대하여는
배상요구가 가능하다고 보았으나, 뉴질랜드가 이에 대한 특별한 배상을 청구
하지는 않았기 때문에 프랑스의 배상을 명령하지는 않았다. 재판부는 뉴질랜
드에 대한 프랑스의 의무위반을 공표함으로써 뉴질랜드에 대한 법적, 도덕적
피해에 대한 적절한 만족(satisfaction)을 구성한다고 보았다. 다만 문제의 요
원을 원래의 기지에 재수감하라는 뉴질랜드의 요구는 당초 합의된 3년이 이
미 지났다는 이유에서 받아들여지지 않았다. 이어 재판부는 양국 국민의 우
호증진을 위한 재단설립을 권고하고, 프랑스가 우선 미화 200만 불을 출연
하라고 요청했다.

판결문은 중간에 당시 제시되고 있던 ILC 초안 제31조를 인용하고 있는
데, 이와 사실상 동일한 내용이 국가책임에 관한 ILC 최종초안(2001) 제23조
로 성안되었다.

제23조 불가항력

1. 행위가 불가항력, 즉 그 상황에서의 의무이행을 실질적으로 불가능하
게 만드는 국가의 통제를 넘어서는 저항할 수 없는 힘 또는 예상하지 못한
사건의 발생에 기인한 경우에는 국제의무와 합치되지 않는 국가행위의 위법
성이 조각된다.

2. 제1항은 다음의 경우에는 적용되지 아니한다:

(a) 불가항력의 상황이 이를 원용하는 국가의 행위에만 의하거나 또는
다른 요소와 결합된 행위에서 기인하는 경우; 또는

(b) 당해 국가가 그 같은 상황발생의 위험을 수락한 경우.

이 선박의 선적국은 영국이었으나, 영국은 프랑스에 대해 특별한 책임
을 추궁하지 않았다. 네덜란드인 사망자의 가족과 보험회사는 프랑스 정부와
직접 배상협상을 진행해 타결을 보았다. 그린피스와 프랑스 간에는 배상협상

이 타결되지 않아 나중에 중재에 회부되었으며, 그 결과 프랑스는 810만 불을 지불하라는 결정이 내려졌다. 침몰한 레인보우 워리어호는 그린피스 회원들의 모금을 통해 1987년 555톤급의 동력범선으로 재건조되었다.

후일 밝혀진 바로는 당시 프랑스의 미테랑 대통령의 직접 지시로 이 사건이 벌어졌으며, 체포되었던 두 요원은 모두 진급을 했다고 한다.

➼ 참고문헌 ─────────────────────────────

• J. Scott Davidson, The Rainbow Warrior Arbitration concerning the Treatment of the French Agents Mafart and Prieur, ICLQ Vol. 40, No. 2, p. 446.

4. 이란·미국간 책임의 귀속에 관한 분쟁(1987)
― 국가책임의 귀속 기준

Yeager v. Iran.
Iran-U.S. Claims Tribunal, 17 Iran-U.S.C.T.R. 92(1987).

☑ 사　　안

미국적을 소지하고 있는 원고는 이란에 소재하고 있는 BHI라는 미국계 회사에서 근무를 하고 있었다. 이란의 혁명 정부가 정권을 장악한 직후인 1979년 2월 13일 혁명수비대가 원고의 아파트로 와서 단 30분 동안 짐을 꾸릴 시간을 준 후에 테헤란 시내의 호텔로 데리고 가서 며칠 동안 감금을 하였다. 그 후 원고는 가까스로 이란을 빠져나올 수 있었다. 그는 사실상 추방되었다고 주장했다. 사건이 발생한 당시 이들 단체는 이란 정부의 공식 조직이 아니었으나, 얼마 후(1979년 5월) 정부로부터 혁명수비대라는 명칭으로 공식 인정을 받았다. 원고는 이란 혁명수비대의 행위에 따른 책임이 이란 정부에 귀속된다고 주장했다.

☑ 쟁　　점

국내법에 의해 공식으로 인정되지 않은 집단의 행위로 인한 책임을 국가에 귀속시킬 수 있는지 여부.

☑ 판　　결

정상적인 정부가 존재하지 않는 상황에서는 정부 권한 일부를 행사하는 개인이나 집단의 행위를 국가의 행위로 볼 수 있다.

39. [⋯] Many of Ayatollah Khomeini's supporters were organized in local revolutionary committees, so-called Komitehs, which [⋯] served as local security forces in the immediate aftermath of the revolution. It is reported that they made arrests, confiscated property, and took people to prison. [⋯] While there were complaints about a lack of discipline among the numerous Komitehs, Ayatollah Khomeini stood behind them [⋯] Soon after the Revolution, the Komitehs [⋯] obtained a firm position within the State structure and were eventually conferred a permanent place in the State budget

40. In May 1979, the Komitehs were officially recognized by decree under the name Revolutionary Guard. [⋯] On the basis of the evidence submitted and public sources available the Tribunal is convinced, therefore, that the names "Revolutionary Komitehs" and "Revolutionary Guards" were interchangeably used to describe the same group of revolutionaries generally loyal to the new government. [⋯]

42. The question then arises whether the acts at issue are attributable to Iran under international law. While there is some doubt as to whether revolutionary "Komitehs" or "Guards" can be considered "organs" of the Government of Iran, since they were not formally recognized during the period relevant to this Case, attributability of acts to the State is not limited to acts of organs formally recognized under internal law. Otherwise a State could avoid responsibility under international law merely by invoking its internal law. It is generally accepted in international law that a State is also responsible for acts of persons, if it is established that those persons were in fact acting on behalf of the State. See ILC-Draft Article 8(a). An act is attributable even if a person or group of persons was in fact merely exercising elements of governmental authority in the absence of the official authorities and in circumstances which justified the exercise of those elements of authority. See ILC-Draft Article 8(b).

43. The Tribunal finds sufficient evidence in the record to establish a presumption that revolutionary "Komitehs" or "Guards" after 11 February 1979 were acting in fact on behalf of the new Government, or at least exercised elements of governmental authority in the absence of official authorities, in operations of which the new Government must have had knowledge and to which it did not specifically object. Under those circumstances, and for the kind of measures involved here, the Respondent has the burden of coming forward with evidence showing that members of "Komitehs" or "Guards" were in fact not acting on its behalf, or were not exercising elements of government authority, or that it would not control them.

☑ 해   설

재판부는 혁명정부 등장과 같이 정상적인 정부가 기능하지 못하는 경우 정부 기능을 행사하는 개인이나 집단의 행위에 대해 국가가 책임을 진다고 판정했다. 판결문에서 지적하고 있는 ILC 초안 제8조는 국가책임에 관한 2001년 ILC 최종초안 제9조로 반영되었다.

제9조(공공당국의 부재 또는 마비 상태에서 수행된 행위)

공공당국의 부재(不在) 또는 마비 상태로서 정부권한의 행사가 요구되는 상황에서 개인 또는 집단이 사실상 그러한 권한을 행사하였다면, 그 행위는 국제법상 국가의 행위로 간주된다.

즉, 공권력의 행사가 요구되는 상황이나 공공당국의 부재나 마비로 인하여 개인이나 집단이 사실상의 공권력을 행사하였다면, 이는 비록 형식상 사인의 행위라고 할지라도 국가의 행위로 간주된다. 만일 이러한 단체들의 행동이 단지 국내에서 이들의 합법성 내지 정부 권한 행사를 인정할 수 있는 법적 근거가 없다는 이유로 국제법상의 책임이 인정되지 않는다면, 정상적인 정부가 존재하지 않는 많은 경우에는 국가의 책임을 회피함으로써 국제법의 실효성을 잃게 되는 결과가 초래될 것이기 때문이다.

➡ 참고문헌

• Note, Dayna L. Kaufman, Don't Do What I Say, Do What I Mean: Assessing a State's Responsibility for the Exploits of Individuals Acting in Conformity with a Statement from a Head of State, Fordham Law Review Vol. 70(2002), p. 2603.

5. 갑치코보-나지마로스 사건(1997)
― 긴급피난, 대응조치, 사정변경원칙 등의 적용요건

Case Concerning the Gabčíkovo-Nagymaros Project.
Hungary/Slovakia, 1997 ICJ Reports 7.

☑ 사   안

헝가리와 (구)체코슬로바키아는 1977년 다뉴브강의 홍수방지, 항행조건 개선, 수력발전 등을 목적으로 댐을 건설하고 수로를 변경하는 종합개발계획에 합의했다(부타페스트 협정). 이에 따르면 체코슬로바키아의 Gabčíkovo에 발전용량 720 MW의 댐을 건설해 주발전을 맡고, 이보다 약 100km 정도 하류인 헝가리의 Nagymaros에 158 MW 용량의 댐을 건설해 수량을 조절하기로 하였다. 양국은 동등한 투자와 동등한 수익에 합의했는데, 건설사업의 상당부분이 체코슬로바키아 지역에 진행될 예정이었기 때문에 헝가리가 체코슬로바키아 지역에서의 건설에도 참여하기로 합의했다.

1981년 헝가리는 재정적인 이유로 사업추진의 속도조절을 요청했다. 그런데 1984년부터 헝가리에서는 이 사업이 부다페스트의 용수공급에 악영향을 미친다는 이유로 반대하는 운동이 조직화되었다. 동구 공산체제가 무너지자 헝가리에서는 이 사업이 구체제의 산물이라는 반감이 높아졌고, 드디어 1989년 헝가리는 환경피해의 우려를 명분으로 내세우며 자국내 Nagymaros 댐 건설을 일방적으로 중단하기로 결정했다. 그러나 체코슬로바키아측의 사업은 이미 거의 완성단계였다. 결국 체코슬로바키아는 1992년 자국 영역 내로 다뉴브강의 유로를 변경해 댐을 건설하도록 하는 방향으로 사업의 일부를 변경시키고, 일부는 축소하는 형태의 대안을 마련해(이른바 C안) 이 사업을 계속 추진하기로 했다. 그러자 헝가리는 수로변경이 자국에 악영향을 미친다고 반대하며, 체코슬로바키아의 조치를 조약의 중대한 위반이라고 간주해 1977년 협정 자체의 종료를 선언했다. 그러나 상류국인 체코슬로바키아는 C안을 그대로 추진했고, 다뉴브강의 수로를 자국으로 돌려 1992년 말부터는 댐에 담수를 시작했다. 1993년 체코슬로바키아가 체코와 슬로바키아로 분리되자 슬로바키아와 헝가리는 이 사건을 ICJ에 회부하기로 합의했다.

이 사건에서는 국가책임법, 조약법, 국가승계법, 국제환경법 등 다양한 분야의 쟁점이 검토되었다. 다음 판결문은 그중 국가책임법과 조약법상의 쟁점 일부를 검토한 내용이다.

☑ 쟁   점

⑴ 헝가리의 1977년 협정 종료(또는 정지) 조치는 긴급피난(necessity)으로 인정되어 위법성이 조각되는가?

⑵ 헝가리의 댐건설 중단으로 인한 슬로바키아의 새로운 C안의 실시는 국제법상의 대응조치(counter measure)로서 정당화될 수 있는가?

⑶ 1977년 협정을 이행할 대상이 상실되었고 헝가리가 처한 재정적 어려움으로 인해 이 협정은 후발적 이행불능에 빠졌다고 할 수 있는가? 또한 경제적 환경의 변화, 환경영향에 관한 지식과 국제환경법의 발전 등의 사정변경을 근거로 헝가리는 1977년 협정의 종료를 주장할 수 있는가?

☑ 판   결

⑴ 그 행위가 중대하고 급박한 위험으로부터 국가의 본질적 이익을 보호하기 위한 유일한 방법인 경우 긴급피난으로서 위법성이 조각되는데, 이 사건의 헝가리에 대하여는 그 같은 급박한 위험이 아직 존재하지 않는다.

⑵ 상대국의 위법행위에 대한 대응조치는 상응하는 범위 내에서 이루어져야 하는데, 슬로바키아의 조치(C안)는 비례성의 원칙을 초과한 것으로 위법하다.

⑶ 이 사건에서는 조약의 종료를 정당화할 정도의 후발적 이행불능 사태나 사정변경이 존재하지 않으므로, 헝가리는 1977년 조약의 종료를 주장할 수 없다.

49. The Court will now consider the question of whether there was, in 1989, a state of necessity which would have permitted Hungary, without incurring international responsibility, to suspend and abandon works that it was committed to perform in accordance with the 1977 Treaty and related instruments.

50. In the present case, the Parties are in agreement in considering that the existence of a state of necessity must be evaluated in the light of the criteria laid down by the International Law Commission in Article 33 of the Draft Articles on the International Responsibility of States that it adopted on first reading.[1) [⋯]

In its Commentary, the Commission defined the "state of necessity" as being

> "the situation of a State whose sole means of safeguarding an essential interest threatened by a grave and imminent peril is to adopt conduct not in conformity with what is required of it by an international obligation to another State" ([⋯]).

It concluded that "the notion of state of necessity is ⋯ deeply rooted in general legal thinking" ([⋯]).

51. The Court considers, first of all, that the state of necessity is a ground recognized by customary international law for precluding the wrongfulness of an act not in conformity with an international obligation. It observes moreover that such ground for precluding wrongfulness can only be accepted on an exceptional basis. The International Law Commission was of the same opinion when it explained that it had opted for a negative form of words [⋯].

Thus, according to the Commission, the state of necessity can only be invoked under certain strictly defined conditions which must be cumulatively satisfied; and the State concerned is not the sole judge of whether those conditions have been met.

52. In the present case, the following basic conditions set forth in Draft Article 33 are relevant: it must have been occasioned by an "essential interest" of the State which is the author of the act conflicting with one of its international obligations; that interest must have been threatened by a "grave and imminent peril"; the act being challenged must have been the "only means" of safeguarding that interest;

---

1) 당시 긴급피난에 관한 ILC 초안 제33조의 내용은 2001년 발표된 최종초안 제25조와 실질적으로 동일했다.

that act must not have "seriously impair[ed] an essential interest" of the State towards which the obligation existed; and the State which is the author of that act must not have "contributed to the occurrence of the state of necessity". Those conditions reflect customary international law.

The Court will now endeavour to ascertain whether those conditions had been met at the time of the suspension and abandonment, by Hungary, of the works that it was to carry out in accordance with the 1977 Treaty.[2]

54. […] It could moreover hardly be otherwise. when the "peril" constituting the state of necessity has at the same time to be "grave" and "imminent". "Imminence" is synonymous with "immediacy" or "proximity" and goes far beyond the concept of "possibility." As the International Law Commission emphasized in its commentary, the "extremely grave and imminent" peril must "have been a threat to the interest at the actual time"([…]). That does not exclude, in the view of the Court, that a "peril" appearing in the long term might be held to be "imminent" as soon as it is established, at the relevant point in time, that the realization of that peril, however far off it might be, is not thereby any less certain and inevitable.

The Hungarian argument on the state of necessity could not convince the Court unless it was at least proven that a real, "grave" and "imminent" "peril" existed in 1989 and that the measures taken by Hungary were the only possible response to it. […]

55. […] The Court notes that the dangers ascribed to the upstream reservoir were mostly of a long-term nature and, above all, that they remained uncertain. Even though the Joint Contractual Plan envisaged that the Gabcikovo power plant would "mainly operate in peak-load time and continuously during high water," the final rules of operation had not yet been determined([…]); however, any dangers associated with the putting into service of the Nagymaros portion of the Project would have been closely linked to the extent to which it was operated in peak mode and to the modalities of such operation. It follows that, even if it could have been established — which, in the Court's appreciation of the evidence before it, was not the case — that the reservoir would ultimately have constituted a "grave peril" for the environment in the area, one would be bound to conclude that the peril was not "imminent" at the time at which Hungary suspended and then abandoned the

---

2) 이어 재판부는 이 사업에 따른 환경영향에 대한 헝가리의 관심이 essential interest에 관련된다는 것은 인정했으나(para. 53), 헝가리의 주장이 긴급피난으로 정당화되기 위하여는 a grave and imminent peril에 대하여 국가의 essential interest를 보호하기 위한 유일한 수단인가를 검토하여야 한다고 판단했다(para. 54).

works relating to the dam. [⋯]

57. The Court concludes from the foregoing that, with respect to both Nagymaros and Gabčíkovo, the perils invoked by Hungary, without prejudging their possible gravity, were not sufficiently established in 1989, nor were they "imminent"; and that Hungary had available to it at that time means of responding to these perceived perils other than the suspension and abandonment of works with which it had been entrusted. [⋯]

The Court infers from all these elements that, in the present case, even if it had been established that there was, in 1989, a state of necessity linked to the performance of the 1977 Treaty, Hungary would not have been permitted to rely upon that state of necessity in order to justify its failure to comply with its treaty obligations, as it had helped, by act or omission to bring it about. [⋯]

82. Although it did not invoke the plea of countermeasures as a primary argument, since it did not consider Variant C to be unlawful, Slovakia stated that "Variant C could be presented as a justified countermeasure to Hungary's illegal acts."

The Court has concluded, in paragraph 78 above, that Czechoslovakia committed an internationally wrongful act in putting Variant C into operation. Thus, it now has to determine whether such wrongfulness may be precluded on the ground that the measure so adopted was in response to Hungary's prior failure to comply with its obligations under international law.

83. In order to be justifiable, a countermeasure must meet certain conditions [⋯].

In the first place it must be taken in response to a previous international wrongful act of another State and must be directed against that State. Although not primarily presented as a countermeasure, it is clear that Variant C was a response to Hungary's suspension and abandonment of works and that it was directed against that State; and it is equally clear, in the Court's view, that Hungary's actions were internationally wrongful.

84. Secondly, the injured State must have called upon the State committing the wrongful act to discontinue its wrongful conduct or to make reparation for it. It is clear from the facts of the case, as recalled above by the Court ([⋯]), that Czechoslovakia requested Hungary to resume the performance of its treaty obligations on many occasions.

85. In the view of the Court, an important consideration is that the effects of a countermeasure must be commensurate with the injury suffered, taking account of the rights in question. [⋯]

The Court considers that Czechoslovakia, by unilaterally assuming control of a shared resource, and thereby depriving Hungary of its right to an equitable and reasonable share of the natural resources of the Danube — with the continuing effects of the diversion of these waters on the ecology of the riparian area of the Szigetkoz — failed to respect the proportionality which is required by international law. [⋯]

87. The Court thus considers that the diversion of the Danube carried out by Czechoslovakia was not a lawful countermeasure because it was not proportionate. [⋯]

101. The Court will now turn to the first ground advanced by Hungary, that of the state of necessity. In this respect, the Court will merely observe that, even if a state of necessity is found to exist, it is not a ground for the termination of a treaty. It may only be invoked to exonerate from its responsibility a State which has failed to implement a treaty. Even if found justified, it does not terminate a Treaty; the Treaty may be ineffective as long as the condition of necessity continues to exist; it may in fact be dormant, but — unless the parties by mutual agreement terminate the Treaty — it continues to exist. As soon as the state of necessity ceases to exist, the duty to comply with treaty obligations revives.

102. Hungary also relied on the principle of the impossibility of performance as reflected in Article 61 of the Vienna Convention on the Law of Treaties. Hungary's interpretation of the wording of Article 61 is, however, not in conformity with the terms of that Article, nor with the intentions of the Diplomatic Conference which adopted the Convention. Article 61, paragraph 1, requires the "permanent disappearance or destruction of an object indispensable for the execution" of the treaty to justify the termination of a treaty on grounds of impossibility of performance. During the conference, a proposal was made to extend the scope of the article by including in it cases such as the impossibility to make certain payments because of serious financial difficulties([⋯]). Although it was recognized that such situations could lead to a preclusion of the wrongfulness of non-performance by a party of its treaty obligations, the participating States were not prepared to consider such situations to be a ground for terminating or suspending a treaty, and preferred to limit themselves to a narrower concept.

103. Hungary contended that the essential object of the Treaty — an economic joint investment which was consistent with environmental protection and which was operated by the two contracting parties jointly — had permanently disappeared and that the Treaty had thus become impossible to perform. It is not necessary for the Court to determine whether the term "object" in Article 61 can also be understood to embrace a legal régime as in any event, even if that were the case, it would have to conclude that in this instance that régime had not definitively ceased to exist. The 1977 Treaty — and in particular its Articles 15, 19 and 20 — actually made available to the parties the necessary means to proceed at any time, by negotiation, to the required readjustments between economic imperatives and ecological imperatives. The Court would add that, if the joint exploitation of the investment was no longer possible, this was originally because Hungary did not carry out most of the works for which it was responsible under the 1977 Treaty; Article 61, paragraph 2, of the Vienna Convention expressly provides that impossibility of performance may not be invoked for the termination of a treaty by a party to that treaty when it results from that party's own breach of an obligation flowing from that treaty.

104. Hungary further argued that it was entitled to invoke a number of events which, cumulatively, would have constituted a fundamental change of circumstances. In this respect it specified profound changes of a political nature, the Project's diminishing economic viability, the progress of environmental knowledge and the development of new norms and prescriptions of international environmental law [⋯].

The prevailing political situation was certainly relevant for the conclusion of the 1977 Treaty. But the Court will recall that the Treaty provided for a joint investment programme for the production of energy, the control of floods and the improvement of navigation on the Danube. In the Court's view, the prevalent political conditions were thus not so closely linked to the object and purpose of the Treaty that they constituted an essential basis of the consent of the parties and, in changing, radically altered the extent of the obligations still to be performed. The same holds good for the economic system in force at the time of the conclusion of the 1977 Treaty. Besides, even though the estimated profitability of the Project might have appeared less in 1992 than in 1977, it does not appear from the record before the Court that it was bound to diminish to such an extent that the treaty obligations of the parties would have been radically transformed as a result.

The Court does not consider that new developments in the state of environmental knowledge and of environmental law can be said to have been completely unforeseen. What is more, the formulation of Articles 15, 19 and 20, designed to accommodate change, made it possible for the parties to take account of such developments and to apply them when implementing those treaty provisions.

The changed circumstances advanced by Hungary are, in the Court's view, not of such a nature, either individually or collectively, that their effect would radically transform the extent of the obligations still to be performed in order to accomplish the Project. A fundamental change of circumstances must have been unforeseen; the existence of the circumstances at the time of the Treaty's conclusion must have constituted an essential basis of the consent of the parties to be bound by the Treaty.

☑ 해   설

재판부는 헝가리가 일방적으로 1977년 부다페스트 협정의 종료(또는 중단)를 선언할 수 없고, 이 조약은 여전히 유효하다고 판단해 헝가리가 협정을 위반했다고 결정했다. 한편 슬로바키아는 헝가리의 일방적 건설 중단에 대해 나름의 대안을 마련할 권리는 있으나, C안과 같이 다뉴브강의 수량을 일방적으로 자국으로 돌릴 수는 없으며, 따라서 슬로바키아의 행위 역시 위법하다고 판단했다. 이에 양국에게 신의성실하게 협상해 1977년 협정의 목적을 달성하도록 하라고 요청했다. 이 사건에서는 ICJ 사상 처음으로 재판부의 현장검증이 이루어지기도 했다.

한편 1996년부터 슬로바키아는 C안에 따라 건설된 발전소에서 전력을 생산하기 시작했고, 우려했던 환경대란은 발생하지 않았다. 이 발전소는 당시 슬로바키아 전력의 1할 이상을 생산했다.

판결 후 헝가리와 슬로바키아는 다시 협상을 벌인 끝에 1998년 헝가리가 자국내 댐 등을 건설하기로 합의했다. 슬로바키아는 즉시 새 합의를 승인했다. 그러나 합의 직후 헝가리에서는 정권 교체가 있었고, 신 정부는 이 합의도 이행할 수 없다고 선언했다. 슬로바키아 정부는 이러한 사태 발전에 따라 ICJ에 새로운 판결을 내려달라고 요청했다.

그러나 슬로바키아가 2017년 6월 30일 ICJ에 이 사건의 종료를 요청했고, 헝가리도 이에 동의해 ICJ는 2017년 7월 18일 양국에 재판절차가 종료되었음을 통지했다.

➡ 참고문헌 ────────────────────────────────

- 강병근, ICJ의 1997년 Gabčíkovo – Nagymaros Project 사건, 한림법학 Forum 7호(1998), p. 223.
- 이재곤·배상오, Gabčíkovo – Nagymaros 공동개발사업 사건, (충남대) 법학연구 9권 1호(1998), p. 35.
- 정진석, Gabčíkovo – Nagymaros Project 사건과 조약법, 서울국제법연구 10권 2호(2003), p. 23.
- 김기순, Gabčíkovo – Nagymaros Project 사건에 대한 국제환경법적 고찰, 중앙법학 9집 4호(2007), p. 289.
- Botchway, F. N. Botchway, The Gabčíkovo – Nagymaros case: A step forward for environmental considerations in the joint development of transboundary resources?, European Environmental Law Review Vol. 8(3), p. 76.
- Stephen Stec, Do Two Wrongs Make a Right? Adjudicating Sustainable Development in the Danube Dam Case, Golden Gate University Law Review Vol. 29(1999), p. 33.

6. 일제 징용 피해자의 대일 청구권 (2012 및 2018)

대법원 2012년 5월 24일 선고, 2009다68620 판결.
법원도서관 종합법률정보(미공간).

☑ 사　　안

이 사건 원고들은 일제 강점기 한반도에서 태어나 1941년 또는 1943년 구 일본제철사에 노무자로 동원되어 근무하다가 광복 후 귀환했다. 이들은 구 일본제철이 일본국과 함께 자신들을 기망이나 강제에 의해 동원하여 강제노동에 종사시킨 일련의 행위가 불법행위였다고 주장하며 구 일본제철의 후신인 현재의 신일본제철을 상대로 당시의 미불임금과 불법행위에 대한 손해배상을 청구했다. 이에 앞서 원고 일부는 같은 내용의 소송을 일본 재판소에 제기했으나 2003년 10월 9일 일본 최고재판소에서 원소 패소가 확정되었다. 국내 재판인 서울고등법원 2009년 7월 16일 선고, 2008나49129 판결에서도 원고들이 패소했다. 그러나 대법원은 본 판결에서 원심을 파기하고 원고의 손해배상청구권을 인정했다. 이 사건은 형식상 사인과 사기업 간의 소송이나 핵심 쟁점은 1965년 한일 청구권 협정의 적용범위에 관한 다툼이다. 국내적으로 이 재판은 대법원 2018년 10월 30일 선고, 2013다61381 판결에 의해 최종적으로 마무리되었다.

☑ 쟁　　점

한일 청구권 협정의 체결로 일제 징용 피해자인 개인의 대일청구권은 해결되었는가?

☑ 판　결

한일 청구권 협정에도 불구하고, 징용 피해자인 개인은 여전히 손해배상 청구권을 행사할 수 있다.

판 결 문

"대한민국 정부는 원고들이 이 사건 소송을 제기하기 직전 청구권협정과 관련한 일부 문서를 공개한 후, 이 사건 소송이 제기된 후인 2005. 8. 26. '한일회담 문서공개 후속대책 관련 민관공동위원회'(이하 '민관공동위원회'라고 한다)를 개최하고, "청구권협정은 일본의 식민지배 배상을 청구하기 위한 협상이 아니라 샌프란시스코 조약 제4조에 근거하여 한일 양국 간의 재정적·민사적 채권·채무관계를 해결하기 위한 것이었으며, 일본군 위안부 문제 등 일본정부와 군대 등 일본 국가권력이 관여한 반인도적 불법행위에 대해서는 청구권협정으로 해결된 것으로 볼 수 없고 일본정부의 법적 책임이 남아 있으며, 사할린동포 문제와 원폭피해자 문제도 청구권협정 대상에 포함되지 않았다."는 취지의 공식의견을 표명하였다. […]

(2) 청구권협정은 일본의 식민지배 배상을 청구하기 위한 협상이 아니라 샌프란시스코 조약 제4조에 근거하여 한일 양국 간의 재정적·민사적 채권·채무관계를 정치적 합의에 의하여 해결하기 위한 것으로서, 청구권협정 제1조에 의해 일본 정부가 대한민국 정부에 지급한 경제협력자금은 제2조에 의한 권리문제의 해결과 법적 대가관계가 있다고 보이지 않는 점, 청구권협정의 협상과정에서 일본 정부는 식민지배의 불법성을 인정하지 않은 채, 강제동원피해의 법적 배상을 원천적으로 부인하였고, 이에 따라 한일 양국의 정부는 일제의 한반도 지배의 성격에 관하여 합의에 이르지 못하였는데, 이러한 상황에서 일본의 국가권력이 관여한 반인도적 불법행위나 식민지배와 직결된 불법행위로 인한 손해배상청구권이 청구권협정의 적용대상에 포함되었다고 보기는 어려운 점 등에 비추어 보면, 위 원고들의 손해배상청구권에 대하여는 청구권협정으로 개인청구권이 소멸하지 아니하였음은 물론이고,

대한민국의 외교적 보호권도 포기되지 아니하였다고 봄이 상당하다.

　나아가 국가가 조약을 체결하여 외교적 보호권을 포기함에 그치지 않고 국가와는 별개의 법인격을 가진 국민 개인의 동의 없이 국민의 개인청구권을 직접적으로 소멸시킬 수 있다고 보는 것은 근대법의 원리와 상충되는 점, 국가가 조약을 통하여 국민의 개인청구권을 소멸시키는 것이 국제법상 허용될 수 있다고 하더라도 국가와 국민 개인이 별개의 법적 주체임을 고려하면 조약에 명확한 근거가 없는 한 조약 체결로 국가의 외교적 보호권 이외에 국민의 개인청구권까지 소멸하였다고 볼 수는 없을 것인데, 청구권협정에는 개인청구권의 소멸에 관하여 한일 양국 정부의 의사의 합치가 있었다고 볼 만큼 충분한 근거가 없는 점, 일본이 청구권협정 직후 일본국 내에서 대한민국 국민의 일본국 및 그 국민에 대한 권리를 소멸시키는 내용의 재산권조치법을 제정·시행한 조치는 청구권협정만으로 대한민국 국민 개인의 청구권이 소멸하지 않음을 전제로 할 때 비로소 이해될 수 있는 점 등을 고려해 보면, 위 원고들의 청구권이 청구권협정의 적용대상에 포함된다고 하더라도 그 개인청구권 자체는 청구권협정만으로 당연히 소멸한다고 볼 수는 없고, 다만 청구권협정으로 그 청구권에 관한 대한민국의 외교적 보호권이 포기됨으로써 일본의 국내 조치로 해당 청구권이 일본국 내에서 소멸하여도 대한민국이 이를 외교적으로 보호할 수단을 상실하게 될 뿐이다.

　(3) 따라서 위 원고들의 피고에 대한 불법행위로 인한 손해배상청구권은 청구권협정으로 소멸하지 아니하였으므로, 위 원고들은 피고에 대하여 이러한 청구권을 행사할 수 있다. [⋯]

　그러므로 원심판결을 파기하고(원고들은 각 국제법 위반과 국내법 위반을 이 사건 손해배상청구의 원인으로 주장하였는데, 원심은 이를 별개의 소송물로 본 듯한 판시를 하였으나, 이는 별개의 소송물이라기보다는 불법행위에 기한 손해배상청구에 있어서의 공격방법을 달리한 것에 지나지 않는다고 봄이 상당하므로 원심판결 전부를 파기한다), 사건을 다시 심리·판단하도록 원심법원에 환송하기로 하여 관여 대법관의 일치된 의견으로 주문과 같이 판결한다.

(2) 대법원 2018년 10월 30일 선고, 2013다61381 판결.

출처: 판례공보 2018(하), 2317쪽 이하.

[위 (1) 판결이 국내외적으로 큰 논란을 야기한 사실은 잘 알려져 있다. 원 판결이 파기 환송된 후 서울고등법원 2013. 7. 10. 선고 2012나44947 판결은 대법원의 취지에 따라 일본 기업의 배상책임을 인정했다. 이는 다시 대법원에 상고되었다. 대법원은 장기간 숙고 끝에 본 판결을 통해 일본 기업의 배상책임을 확정했다. 다수의견은 일본의 반인도적 강제동원에 대한 손해배상 청구권은 한일 청구권협정에 포함되지 않는다고 판단했다. 3명의 대법관은 별개의견을 통해 피해자의 손해배상 청구권은 한일 청구권협정에 포함된 내용이나, 협정을 통해 국가는 단지 외교적 보호권만을 포기했으며, 개인 청구권은 여전히 행사할 수 있다고 판단했다. 2명의 반대의견은 개인의 모든 청구권도 한일 청구권협정에 포함되었으며 이를 국내 소송으로 요구할 수 없다고 판단했다. 사회적 파장이 큰 판결인 만큼 다소 길게 발췌한다.]

"사정을 종합하여 보면, 원고들이 주장하는 피고에 대한 손해배상청구권은 청구권협정의 적용대상에 포함된다고 볼 수 없다. 그 이유는 다음과 같다.

(1) 우선 이 사건에서 문제되는 원고들의 손해배상청구권은, 일본 정부의 한반도에 대한 불법적인 식민지배 및 침략전쟁의 수행과 직결된 일본 기업의 반인도적인 불법행위를 전제로 하는 강제동원 피해자의 일본 기업에 대한 위자료청구권([…])이라는 점을 분명히 해두어야 한다. 원고들은 피고를 상대로 미지급 임금이나 보상금을 청구하고 있는 것이 아니고, 위와 같은 위자료를 청구하고 있는 것이다. […]

구 일본제철의 원고들에 대한 행위는 당시 일본 정부의 한반도에 대한 불법적인 식민지배 및 침략전쟁의 수행과 직결된 반인도적인 불법행위에 해당하고, 이러한 불법행위로 인하여 원고들이 정신적 고통을 입었음은 경험칙상 명백하다.

(2) 앞서 본 청구권협정의 체결 경과와 그 전후사정, 특히 아래와 같은 사정들에 의하면, 청구권협정은 일본의 불법적 식민지배에 대한 배상을 청구

하기 위한 협상이 아니라 기본적으로 샌프란시스코 조약 제4조에 근거하여 한일 양국 간의 재정적·민사적 채권·채무관계를 정치적 합의에 의하여 해결하기 위한 것이었다고 보인다. […]

④ 이후 실제로 체결된 청구권 협정문이나 그 부속서 어디에도 일본 식민지배의 불법성을 언급하는 내용은 전혀 없다. […]

⑤ 2005년 민관공동위원회도 '청구권협정은 기본적으로 일본의 식민지배 배상을 청구하기 위한 것이 아니라 샌프란시스코 조약 제4조에 근거하여 한일 양국 간 재정적·민사적 채권·채무관계를 해결하기 위한 것이다'라고 공식의견을 밝혔다. […]

(4) 청구권협정의 협상과정에서 일본 정부는 식민지배의 불법성을 인정하지 않은 채, 강제동원 피해의 법적 배상을 원천적으로 부인하고, 이에 따라 한일 양국의 정부는 일제의 한반도 지배의 성격에 관하여 합의에 이르지 못하다. 이러한 상황에서 강제동원 위자료청구권이 청구권협정의 적용대상에 포함되었다고 보기는 어렵다. 청구권협정의 일방 당사자인 일본 정부가 불법행위의 존재 및 그에 대한 배상책임의 존재를 부인하는 마당에, 피해자 측인 대한민국 정부가 스스로 강제동원 위자료 청구권까지도 포함된 내용으로 청구권협정을 체결하다고 보이지는 않기 때문이다. […]

다. 환송 후 원심이 이와 같은 취지에서, 강제동원 위자료청구권은 청구권협정의 적용대상에 포함되지 않는다고 판단한 것은 정당하다. 거기에 상고이유 주장과 같이 청구권협정의 적용대상과 효력에 관한 법리를 오해하는 등의 위법이 없다. 한편 피고는 이 부분 상고이유에서, 강제동원 위자료청구권이 청구권협정의 적용 대상에 포함된다는 전제하에, 청구권협정으로 포기된 권리가 국가의 외교적 보호권에 한정되어서만 포기된 것이 아니라 개인 청구권 자체가 포기(소멸)된 것이라는 취지의 주장도 하고 있으나, 이 부분은 환송 후 원심의 가정적 판단에 관한 것으로서 더 나아가 살펴 볼 필요 없이 받아들일 수 없다."

대법관 김소영, 이동원, 노정희의 별개의견:
"청구권협정의 해석상 원고들의 손해배상청구권은 청구권협정의 적용대

상에 포함된다고 보아야 한다. 다만 원고들 개인의 청구권 자체는 청구권협
정으로 당연히 소멸한다고 볼 수 없고, 청구권협정으로 그 청구권에 관한 대
한민국의 외교적 보호권만이 포기된 것에 불과하다. 따라서 원고들은 여전히
대한민국에서 피고를 상대로 소로써 권리를 행사할 수 있다. [⋯]

　　(2) [청구권협정 전문과 제2조의 내용을 적시하고—필자 주] 청구권협
정과 같은 날 체결된 청구권협정에 대한 합의의사록(Ⅰ)은 위 제2조에 관하
여 "동조 1.에서 말 하는 완전히 그리고 최종적으로 해결된 것으로 되는 청
구권협정상 청구권에 관한 문제에는 한일회담에서 한국측으로부터 제출된
'한국의 대일청구요강'(소위 8개 항목)의 범위에 속하는 모든 청구가 포함되어
있고, 따라서 동 대일청구요강에 관하여는 어떠한 주장도 할 수 없게 됨을
확인하였다."라고 정하는데, 8개 항목 중 제5항에는 '피징용 한국인의 미수
금, 보상금 및 기타 청구권(이하 '피징용 청구권'이라 한다)의 변제청구'가 포함
되어 있다. 이러한 청구권협정 등의 문언에 의하면, 대한민국과 일본 양국은
국가와 국가 사이의 청구권에 대해서 뿐만 아니라 일방 국민의 상대국 및
그 국민에 대한 청구권까지도 협정의 대상으로 삼았음이 명백하고, 청구권협
정에 대한 합의의사록(Ⅰ)은 청구권협정상 청구권의 대상에 피징용 청구권
도 포함됨을 분명히 하고 있다. [⋯] 이러한 청구권협정의 체결에 이르기까
지의 경위 등에 비추어 보면, 청구권협정상 청구권의 대상에 포함된 피징용
청구권은 강제동원 피해자의 손해배상청구권까지도 포함한 것으로서, 청구
권협정 제1조에서 정한 경제협력자금은 실질적으로 이러한 손해배상청구권
까지 포함한 제2조에서 정한 권리관계의 해결에 대한 대가 내지 보상으로서
의 성질을 그 안에 포함하고 있다고 보이고, 양국도 청구권협정 체결 당시
그와 같이 인식하였다고 봄이 타당하다. [⋯]

　　(5) 그뿐 아니라 대한민국은 청구권협정에 의해 지급되는 자금을 사용
하기 위한 기본적 사항을 정하기 위하여 청구권자금법 및 청구권신고법 등
을 제정·시행하여, 일본에 의하여 노무자로 징용되었다가 1945. 8. 15. 이전
에 사망한 자의 청구권을 청구권협정에 따라 보상하는 민간청구권에 포함시
켜 그 피징용 사망자에 대한 신고 및 보상 절차를 마쳤다. 이는 강제동원 피
해자의 손해배상청구권이 청구권협정의 적용 대상에 포함되어 있음을 전제

로 한 것으로 보인다. 그리고 청구권협정 관련 일부 문서가 공개된 후 구성된 민관공동위원회도 2005. 8. 26. 청구권협정의 법적 효력에 관하여 공식의견을 표명하는데, 일본국 위안부 문제 능 일본 성부와 군내 등 일본 국가권력이 관여한 반인도적 불법행위에 대해서는 청구권협정으로 해결되었다고 볼 수 없다고 하면서도, 강제동원 피해자의 손해배상청구권에 관하여는 '청구권협정을 통하여 일본으로부터 받은 무상 3억 달러에는 강제동원 피해보상 문제 해결 성격의 자금 등이 포괄적으로 감안되었다'고 보았다. 나아가 대한민국은 2007. 12. 10. 청구권자금법 등에 의하여 이루어진 강제동원 피해자에 대한 보상이 불충분하다는 반성적인 고려에서 2007년 희생자지원법을 제정·시행하여, 1938. 4. 1.부터 1945. 8. 15.까지 사이에 일제에 의하여 노무자 등으로 국외로 강제동원된 희생자·부상자·생환자 등에 대하여 위로금을 지급하고, 강제동원되어 노무를 제공하였으나 일본기업 등으로부터 지급받지 못한 미수금을 대한민국 통화로 환산하여 지급하였다. 이와 같이 대한민국은 청구권협정에 강제동원 피해자의 손해배상청구권이 포함되어 있음을 전제로 하여, 청구권협정 체결 이래 장기간 그에 따른 보상 등의 후속 조치를 취하였음을 알 수 있다.

(6) 이상의 내용, 즉 청구권협정 및 그에 관한 양해문서 등의 문언, 청구권협정의 체결 경위나 체결 당시 추단되는 당사자의 의사, 청구권협정의 체결에 따른 후속 조치 등의 여러 사정들을 종합하여 보면, 강제동원 피해자의 손해배상청구권은 청구권 협정의 적용대상에 포함된다고 봄이 타당하다. […]

다. 그러나 […] '원고들의 개인청구권 자체는 청구권협정만으로 당연히 소멸한다고 볼 수 없고, 다만 청구권협정으로 그 청구권에 관한 대한민국의 외교적 보호권이 포기됨으로써 일본의 국내 조치로 해당 청구권이 일본 내에서 소멸하여도 대한민국이 이를 외교적으로 보호할 수단을 상실하게 될 뿐이다'라는 환송 후 원심의 가정적 판단은 아래와 같은 이유에서 이를 수긍할 수 있다.

(1) 청구권협정에는 개인청구권 소멸에 관하여 한일 양국 정부의 의사 합치가 있었다고 볼만큼 충분하고 명확한 근거가 없다.

과거 주권국가가 외국과 교섭을 하여 자국국민의 재산이나 이익에 관한 사항을 일괄적으로 해결하는 이른바 일괄처리협정(lump sum agreements)이 국제분쟁의 해결·예방을 위한 방식의 하나로 채택되어 왔던 것으로 보이기는 한다. 그런데 이러한 협정을 통해 국가가 '외교적 보호권(diplomatic protection),' 즉 '자국민이 외국에서 위법·부당한 취급을 받은 경우 그의 국적국이 외교절차 등을 통하여 외국 정부를 상대로 자국민에 대한 적당한 보호 또는 구제를 요구할 수 있는 국제법상의 권리'를 포기하는 것에서 더 나아가, 개인의 청구권까지도 완전히 소멸시킬 수 있다고 보려면, 적어도 해당 조약에 이에 관한 명확한 근거가 필요하다고 보아야 한다. 국가와 개인이 별개의 법적 주체라는 근대법의 원리는 국제법상으로도 받아들여지고 있는데, 권리의 '포기'를 인정하려면 그 권리자의 의사를 엄격히 해석하여야 한다는 법률 행위 해석의 일반원칙에 의할 때, 개인의 권리를 국가가 나서서 대신 포기하려는 경우에는 이를 더욱 엄격하게 보아야 하기 때문이다.

그런데 청구권협정은 그 문언상 개인청구권 자체의 포기나 소멸에 관하여는 아무런 규정도 두고 있지 않다. […]

청구권협정 체결을 위한 협상 과정에서 일본은 청구권협정에 따라 제공될 자금과 청구권 간의 법률적 대가관계를 일관되게 부인하고, 청구권협정을 통해 개인청구권이 소멸되는 것이 아니라 국가의 외교적 보호권만이 소멸된다는 입장을 견지하였다. 이에 대한민국과 일본 양국은 청구권협정 체결 당시 향후 제공될 자금의 성격에 대하여 합의에 이르지 못한 채 청구권협정을 체결한 것으로 보인다. 따라서 청구권협정에서 사용된 '해결된 것이 된다'거나 주체 등을 분명히 하지 아니한 채 '어떠한 주장도 할 수 없는 것으로 한다'는 등의 문언은 의도적으로 사용된 것으로 보아야 하고, 이를 개인청구권의 포기나 소멸, 권리행사제한이 포함된 것으로 쉽게 판단하여서는 아니 된다.

이러한 사정 등에 비추어 보면, 청구권협정에서 양국 정부의 의사는 개인청구권은 포기되지 아니함을 전제로 정부 간에만 청구권 문제가 해결된 것으로 하자는 것, 즉 외교적 보호권에 한정하여 포기하자는 것이었다고 봄이 타당하다. […]

라. 결국 원고들의 피고에 대한 손해배상청구권이 청구권협정의 적용대상에 포함되지 않는다고 한 다수의견의 입장에는 동의할 수 없지만, 청구권협정에도 불구하고 원고들이 피고를 상대로 강제동원 피해에 대한 손해배상청구권을 행사할 수 있다고 본 환송 후 원심의 결론은 타당하다."

대법관 권순일, 조재연의 반대의견:

"청구권협정 제2조, 청구권협정에 대한 합의의사록(Ⅰ) 등의 문언, 문맥 및 청구권협정의 대상과 목적 등에 비추어 청구권협정 제2조를 그 문언에 부여되는 통상적 의미에 따라 해석하면, 제2조 1.에서 '완전히 그리고 최종적으로 해결된 것'은 대한민국 및 대한민국 국민의 일본 및 일본 국민에 대한 모든 청구권과 일본 및 일본 국민의 대한민국 및 대한민국 국민에 대한 모든 청구권에 관한 문제임이 분명하고, 제2조 3.에서 모든 청구권에 관하여 '어떠한 주장도 할 수 없는 것으로 한다'라고 규정하고 있는 이상, '완전히 그리고 최종적으로 해결된 것이 된다'라는 문언의 의미는 양 체약국은 물론 그 국민도 더 이상 청구권을 행사할 수 없게 되었다는 뜻으로 보아야 한다.

(4) 국제법상 국가의 외교적 보호권(diplomatic protection)이란, 외국에서 자국민이 위법·부당한 취급을 받았으나 현지 기관을 통한 적절한 권리구제가 이루어지지 않을 경우에 최종적으로 그의 국적국이 외교절차나 국제적 사법절차를 통하여 외국 정부를 상대로 자국민에 대한 적당한 보호 또는 구제를 요구할 수 있는 권리이다. 외교적 보호권의 행사 주체는 피해자 개인이 아니라 그의 국적국이며, 외교적 보호권은 국가 사이의 권리의무에 관한 문제일 뿐 국민 개인의 청구권 유무에 직접 영향을 미치지 아니한다. 그런데 앞서 살펴본 것처럼, 청구권협정 제2조는 대한민국 국민과 일본 국민의 상대방 국가 및 그 국민에 대한 청구권까지 대상으로 하고 있음이 분명하므로 청구권협정을 국민 개인의 청구권과는 관계없이 양 체약국이 서로에 대한 외교적 보호권만을 포기하는 내용의 조약이라 해석하기 어렵다. 또한 청구권협정 제2조 1.에서 규정한 '완전히 그리고 최종적으로 해결된 것'이라는 문언은 청구권에 관한 문제가 체약국 사이에서는 물론 그 국민들 사이에서도 완전하고도 최종적으로 해결되었다는 뜻으로 해석하는 것이 그 문언의 통상적

의미에 부합하고, 단지 체약국 사이에서 서로 외교적 보호권을 행사하지 않기로 한다는 의미로 읽히지 않는다. […]

　⑤ 청구권협정 체결 후 대한민국은 청구권자금법, 청구권신고법, 청구권보상법, 2007년 및 2010년 희생자지원법 등을 제정하여 강제징용 피해자에 대한 보상금을 지급하였다. 2010년 희생자지원법에 따라 설치된 '대일항쟁기 강제동원 피해조사 및 국외강제동원희생자 등 지원위원회'의 결정(전신인 '태평양전쟁 전후 국외 강제동원 희생자 지원위원회'의 결정을 포함한다)을 통하여 2016년 9월경까지 지급된 위로금 등의 내역을 살펴보면, 사망·행방불명 위로금 3,601억 원, 부상장해 위로금 1,022억 원, 미수금지원금 522억 원, 의료지원금 1인당 연 80만 원 등 5,500억 원 가량이 된다. 이러한 사실을 종합하여 보면, 청구권협정 당시 대한민국은 청구권협정으로 강제 징용 피해자의 개인청구권도 소멸되거나 적어도 그 행사가 제한된다는 입장을 취하였음을 알 수 있다. 그러므로 청구권협정 당시 양국의 진정한 의사가 외교적 보호권만을 포기한다는 데에 일치하고 있었던 것도 아니다.

　(6) 한편 국제법상 전후 배상문제 등과 관련하여 주권국가가 외국과 교섭을 하여 자국국민의 재산이나 이익에 관한 사항을 국가간 조약을 통하여 일괄적으로 해결하는 이른바 '일괄처리협정(lump sum agreements)'은 국제분쟁의 해결·예방을 위한 방식의 하나로서, 청구권협정 체결 당시 국제관습법상 일반적으로 인정되던 조약 형식이다. 일괄처리협정은 국가가 개인의 청구권 등을 포함한 보상 문제를 일괄 타결하는 방식이므로, 그 당연한 전제로 일괄처리협정에 의하여 국가가 상대국으로부터 보상이나 배상을 받았다면 그에 따라 자국민 개인의 청구권은 소멸되는 것으로 처리되고, 이때 그 자금이 실제로 피해국민에 대한 보상 용도로 사용되지 아니하다고 하더라도 마찬가지이다[…]. 청구권협정에 관하여도 대한민국은 일본으로부터 강제동원 피해자의 손해배상청구권을 포함한 대일청구요강 8개 항목에 관하여 일괄보상을 받고, 청구권자금을 피해자 개인에게 보상의 방법으로 직접 분배하거나 또는 국민경제의 발전을 위한 기반시설 재건 등에 사용함으로써 이른바 '간접적으로' 보상하는 방식을 채택하였다. 이러한 사정에 비추어 볼 때, 청구권협정은 대한민국 및 그 국민의 청구권 등에 대한 보상을 일괄적으로 해결하

기 위한 조약으로서 청구권협정 당시 국제적으로 통용되던 일괄처리협정에 해당한다고 볼 수 있다. 이 점에서도 청구권협정이 국민 개인의 청구권과는 관계없이 단지 양 체약국이 국가의 외교적 보호권만을 포기하기로 하는 합의를 담은 조약이라고 해석하기는 어렵다. […]

(3) 앞서 본 것처럼 대한민국은 청구권협정 체결 후 청구권보상법, 2007년 및 2010년 희생자지원법 등을 제정하여 강제징용 피해자들에게 보상금을 지급하였다. 이는 청구권협정에 따라 대한민국 국민이 소송으로 청구권을 행사하는 것이 제한된 결과 대한민국이 이를 보상할 목적으로 입법조치를 한 것이다. '외교적 보호권 한정포기설'에 따르면 대한민국이 위와 같은 보상 조치를 취할 이유를 찾기 어렵다. […]

청구권협정이 헌법이나 국제법에 위반하여 무효라고 볼 것이 아니라면 그 내용이 좋든 싫든 그 문언과 내용에 따라 지켜야 하는 것이다. […]

마. 결국, 대한민국 국민이 일본 또는 일본 국민에 대하여 가지는 개인 청구권은 청구권협정에 의하여 바로 소멸되거나 포기되었다고 할 수는 없지만 소송으로 이를 행사하는 것은 제한되게 되었으므로, 원고들이 일본 국민인 피고를 상대로 국내에서 강제동원으로 인한 손해배상청구권을 소로써 행사하는 것 역시 제한된다고 보는 것이 옳다."

☑ 해　설

이 사건에서는 원고들의 손해배상 청구권과 관련하여 다양한 법적 쟁점이 다루어졌다. 즉 ① 일본 회사를 상대로 한 소송에서 한국 법원이 재판관할권을 행사함이 적절한가? ② 이미 원고 패소로 확정된 일본 최고재판소 판결의 효력이 한국에서 승인될 수 있는가? ③ 구 일본제철사는 종전 이후 해산·분할되었는데 이 사건의 피고인 현 신일본제철과 법적으로 동일한 회사라고 평가할 수 있는가? ④ 한일 청구권협정에 의해 원고의 손해배상청구권은 이미 소멸되었는가? ⑤ 원고의 손해배상 청구권은 이미 소멸시효가 완성되었는가? 대법원은 이 모든 쟁점에 관하여 원고에게 유리한 판단을 내리고, 원고는 여전히 손해배상 청구권을 행사할 수 있다고 판단했다. 일본 정부는 이 판결에 강력히 반발하며, 청구권협정에 규정된 바와 같이 중재 회부를 요청했으나, 한국 정부가 이에 응하지 않고 있다.

한편 제2차 대전 후 전후처리에 있어서 대부분의 경우 국가 대 국가의 협상을 통해 일괄보상협정이 체결되고 개인의 권리는 이를 통해 소멸된 것으로 처리되었다. 결과적으로 대부분의 개인 피해자들은 실제 피해규모에 비하여 극히 적은 보상액으로 만족할 수밖에 없었다. 위 판결의 설시를 전제로 한다면 국가간의 외교적 타결 이후에도 그 결과에 만족하지 못하는 개인은 여전히 자국에서 소송을 할 수 있으므로 상대국의 입장에서는 외교교섭 자체를 응할 필요가 없다고 생각할지 모른다. 그렇다면 개인으로서는 Vattel의 이론에 입각한 외교적 보호권 제도가 정립되기 이전 자력구제의 시대로 돌아가는 결과가 되지 않는가?

독일과 이탈리아 간의 유사한 성격의 사건에서 ICJ는 다음과 같이 설시했다.

> "Where the State receiving funds as part of what was intended as a comprehensive settlement in the aftermath of an armed conflict has elected to use those funds to rebuild its national economy and infrastructure, rather than distributing them to individual victims amongst its nationals, it is difficult to see why the fact that those individuals had not received a share in the money should be a reason for entitling them to claim against the State that had transferred money to their State of nationality."(Jurisdictional Immunities of the State, Germany v. Italy(Greece Intervening), 2012 ICJ Reports, para. 102)

➡ 참고문헌

- 박배근, 일제강제징용 피해자의 법적 구제에 관한 국제법적 쟁점과 향후 전망: 2012년 대법원 판결을 중심으로, (한양대) 법학논총 30권 3호(2013), p. 47.
- 오승진, 외교문제에 대한 최근 판례의 분석: 헌재와 대법원의 강제징용 및 위안부 피해자 관련 최근 판례를 중심으로, 서울국제법연구 20권 2호(2013), p. 1.
- 남효순·석광현·이근관·이동진·천경훈, 일제강점기 강제징용사건 판결의 종합적 연구(박영사, 2015).

제 7 장

─ ─ ─ ─ ─

조 약 법

1. 카타르·바레인간 해양경계 및 영토분쟁(1994)
— 조약의 의의

Case Concerning Maritime Delimitation and Territorial
Questions between Qatar and Bahrain(Jurisdiction and Admissibility).
Qatar v. Bahrain, 1994 ICJ Reports 112.

☑ 사   안

이 사건은 카타르와 바레인간의 도서 및 해양 경계에 관한 다툼에서 비롯되었다. 양국 외무장관 사이에 1990년 12월 서명된 공문에 따르면 이 사건을 우선 사우디아라비아 국왕의 주선에 맡기되 1991년 5월 말까지 해결되지 않으면 최종적으로는 ICJ에 회부하기로 합의했다. 정해진 시한 내에 분쟁이 해결되지 않자 카타르는 이 사건을 ICJ에 제소했다. 반면 바레인측은 1990년 12월의 합의공문이 조약으로서의 법적 성격을 지니지 못한 단순한 회의기록에 불과하다며, 이를 근거로 한 카타르의 제소에 대해 ICJ의 관할권을 부인하는 선결적 항변을 제출했다. 아래 관할권 성립 여부에 관한 판결에서 무엇이 국제법상 조약인가에 대한 판단이 있었다.

☑ 쟁   점

1990년 12월 25일자 카타르·바레인간 합의공문은 법적 구속력이 있는 조약에 해당하는가 여부.

☑ 판   결

위의 문서는 양국 정부가 수락한 약속을 기록한 문서로서 국제법상 조약에 해당한다.

판 결 문

17. [···] The King of Saudi Arabia then sent the Amirs of Qatar and Bahrain letters in identical terms dated 19 December 1987, in which he put forward new proposals. Those proposals were accepted by letters from the two Heads of State, dated respectively 21 and 26 December 1987. The Saudi proposals thus adopted included four points. [···]

21. The Court will first enquire into the nature of the texts upon which Qatar relies before turning to an analysis of the content of those texts.

22. The Parties agree that the exchanges of letters of December 1987 constitute an international agreement with binding force in their mutual relations. Bahrain however maintains that the Minutes of 25 December 1990 were no more than a simple record of negotiations, similar in nature to the Minutes of the Tripartite Committee; that accordingly they did not rank as an international agreement and could not, therefore, serve as a basis for the jurisdiction of the Court.

23. The Court would observe, in the first place, that international agreements may take a number of forms and be given a diversity of names. Article 2, paragraph (1) (a), of the Vienna Convention on the Law of Treaties of 23 May 1969 [···]

Furthermore, as the Court said, in a case concerning a joint communique:

> "... it knows of no rule of international law which might preclude a joint communique from constituting an international agreement to submit a dispute to arbitration or judicial settlement" (*Aegean Sea Continental Shelf, Judgment, I.C.J. Reports 1978*, p. 39, para. 96).

In order to ascertain whether an agreement of that kind has been concluded, "the Court must have regard above all to its actual terms and to the particular circumstances in which it was drawn up" (*ibid.*).

24. The 1990 Minutes refer to the consultations between the two Foreign Ministers of Bahrain and Qatar, in the presence of the Foreign Minister of Saudi Arabia, and state what had been "agreed" between the Parties. In paragraph 1 the commitments previously entered into are reaffirmed (which includes, at the least, the agreement constituted by the exchanges of letters of December 1987). In paragraph 2, the Minutes provide for the good offices of the King of Saudi Arabia to continue until May 1991, and exclude the submission of the dispute to the Court prior thereto. The circumstances are addressed under which the dispute may subsequently be submitted to the Court. Qatar's acceptance of the Bahraini formula is placed on record. The Minutes provide that the Saudi good offices are to continue while the case is pending before the Court, and go on to say that, if a compromise agreement is reached during that time, the case is to be withdrawn.

25. Thus the 1990 Minutes include a reaffirmation of obligations previously entered into; they entrust King Fahd with the task of attempting to find a solution to the dispute during a period of six months; and, lastly, they address the circumstances under which the Court could be seised after May 1991.

Accordingly, and contrary to the contentions of Bahrain, the Minutes are not a simple record of a meeting, similar to those drawn up within the framework of the Tripartite Committee; they do not merely give an account of discussions and summarize points of agreement and disagreement. They enumerate the commitments to which the Parties have consented. They thus create rights and obligations in international law for the Parties. They constitute an international agreement.

26. Bahrain however maintains that the signatories of the Minutes never intended to conclude an agreement of this kind. It submitted a statement made by the Foreign Minister of Bahrain and dated 21 May 1992, in which he states that "at no time did I consider that in signing the Minutes I was committing Bahrain to a legally binding agreement." He goes on to say that, according to the Constitution of Bahrain, "treaties 'concerning the territory of the State' can come into effect only after their positive enactment as a law". The Minister indicates that he would therefore not have been permitted to sign an international agreement taking effect at the time of the signature. He was aware of that situation, and was prepared to subscribe to a statement recording a political understanding, but not to sign a legally binding agreement.

27. The Court does not find it necessary to consider what might have been the intentions of the Foreign Minister of Bahrain or, for that matter, those of the Foreign Minister of Qatar. The two Ministers signed a text recording commitments accepted by their Governments, some of which were to be given immediate application. Having signed such a text, the Foreign Minister of Bahrain is not in a position subsequently to say that he intended to subscribe only to a "statement recording a political understanding," and not to an international agreement.

28. Bahrain however bases its contention, that no international agreement was concluded, also upon another argument. It maintains that the subsequent conduct of the Parties showed that they never considered the 1990 Minutes to be an agreement of this kind; and that not only was this the position of Bahrain, but it was also that of Qatar. Bahrain points out that Qatar waited until June 1991 before it applied to the United Nations Secretariat to register the Minutes of December 1990 under Article 102 of the Charter; and moreover that Bahrain objected to such registration. Bahrain also observes that, contrary to what is laid down in Article 17 of the Pact of the League of Arab States, Qatar did not file the 1990 Minutes with the General Secretariat of the League; nor did it follow the procedures required by its own Constitution for the conclusion of treaties. This conduct showed that Qatar, like Bahrain, never considered the 1990 Minutes to be an international agreement.

29. The Court would observe that an international agreement or treaty that has not been registered with the Secretariat of the United Nations may not, according to the provisions of Article 102 of the Charter, be invoked by the parties before any organ of the United Nations. Non-registration or late registration, on the other hand, does not have any consequence for the actual validity of the agreement, which remains no less binding upon the parties. The Court therefore cannot infer from the fact that Qatar did not apply for registration of the 1990 Minutes until six months after they were signed that Qatar considered, in December 1990, that those Minutes did not constitute an international agreement. The same conclusion follows as regards the non-registration of the text with the General Secretariat of the Arab League. Nor is there anything in the material before the Court which would justify deducing from any disregard by Qatar of its constitutional rules relating to the conclusion of treaties that it did not intend to conclude, and did not consider that it had concluded, an instrument of that kind; nor could any such intention, even if shown to exist, prevail over the actual terms of the instrument in question. Accordingly Bahrain's argument on these points also cannot be accepted.

30. The Court concludes that the Minutes of 25 December 1990, like the exchanges of letters of December 1987, constitute an international agreement creating rights and obligations for the Parties.

☑ 해 설

재판과정에서 카타르는 1990년 합의공문이 분쟁을 ICJ로 회부하기로 한 명백한 약속이라고 주장했다. 반면 바레인측은 1990년 자국 외무장관은 해당문서를 정치적 양해사항의 기록으로만 이해하고 서명했으며, 조약으로 의도하고 서명하지 않았다고 주장했다. 특히 바레인 헌법상 영토에 관한 조약은 반드시 입법을 통해 실현될 수 있으므로, 외무장관은 서명만으로 영토에 관한 조약을 발효시킬 권한 자체가 없어 1990년 합의를 조약으로 의도할 수 없었다고 주장했다. 카타르 또한 이 문서의 유엔 등록을 해태, 지연하는 등 당사국의 추후 태도 역시 이를 조약으로 간주하지 않았다고 주장했다.

그러나 ICJ는 당시 바레인 외무장관의 의도가 무엇이었든 간에 1990년 12월의 합의공문의 내용은 단순히 양국간 합의 사항의 논의기록이나 요약이 아니며, 당사국의 약속을 표창하므로 국제법상의 권리의무의 근거가 될 수 있다고 판단했다. 또한 문서의 유엔 등록 여부를 기준으로 조약임을 판단할 수는 없다고 보았다. 결국 1990년 12월 합의공문을 근거로 관할권의 성립을 인정한 ICJ는 2001년 3월 16일 이 사건 본안에 대한 판결을 내렸다(2001 ICJ Reports 40).

한편 이 판결에서 Oda 판사는 정황상 3국 외무장관은 문제의 회의록이 조약이라는 생각을 전혀 하지 않고 서명했으며, 특히 바레인 외교장관은 결코 자신이 조약에 서명한다고 생각하지 않았으므로 이 문서는 법적 구속력을 지닐 수 없다는 소수의견을 제시했다(Dissenting Opinion of Judge Oda, para. 16). 즉 이 판결의 다수의견은 객관적으로 표출된 의도를 중시했고, Oda 판사는 주관적 의도를 중시한 것이다.

이 재판에서는 1990년 합의문서가 조약이냐 여부가 중요한 쟁점이었지만, 위 본문(para. 17)에 지적된 1987년 합의가 조약에 해당하느냐도 검토되었다. 1987년 12월 19일 사우디아리비아 왕은 카타르와 바레인 군주에게 동일한 내용으로 분쟁해결에 관한 제안을 했다. 카타르 군주는 12월 21일, 바레인 군주는 12월 26일 각각 제안을 수락한다는 답신을 사우디아라비아 왕에게 보냈다. 소송과정에서 카타르와 바레인측은 모두 1987년 12월 주고 받은 내용이 양국 관계에 구속력을 갖는 합의에 해당한다고 인정했고(para. 22), 재판부도 이를 조약으로 판단했다(para. 30). Oda 판사는 카타르와 바레인 간에는 직접적인 문서 교환이 없었는데, 각기 당사자가 다른 문서가 하나의 조약을 구성할 수 있냐고 의문을 제기하며, 1987년 합의도 조약이 아니라고 주장했다(dissenting opinion, paras. 10 – 12).

한편 유사한 사례로서 에게해 분쟁과 관련하여 그리스와 터키 양국 수상이 1975년 5월 31일 브뤼셀에서 발표한 공동성명의 법적 성격에 관한 논란이 있다. 이 성명을 근거로 그리스가 사건을 ICJ에 일방적으로 제소하자, 터키는 관할권 성립을 부인했다. ICJ는 Aegean Sea Continental Shelf (Jurisdiction) 판결(1978)에서 문제의 공동성명은 양국이 회담을 마친 후의 기자회견 중 발표된 것으로 서명이나 가서명되지 않았고, 제반 정황상 성명의 내용이 양국간 분쟁에 관하여 ICJ의 관할권을 수락하는 약속을 구성한다고 보기 어렵다고 판단해 재판소의 관할권 성립을 부인했다.

▶ 참고문헌 ─────────────────────────────

- 이기범, 국제사법재판소(ICJ)의 카타르와 바레인 간의 해양경계 및 영토문제에 관한 사건 판결 분석 및 시사점 고찰, 국제법평론 2007 - Ⅱ, p. 187.
- J. McHugo, The Judgments of the International Court of Justice in the Jurisdiction and Admissibility Phase of Qatar v. Bahrain, Netherlands Yearbook of International Law Vol. 28(1997), p. 171.
- S. Rosenne, The Qatar/Bahrain Case, Leiden Journal of International Law Vol. 8(1995), p. 161.

2. 제노사이드 방지협약과 유보(1951)
— 조약의 유보

Reservations to the Convention on the Prevention and
Punishment of the Crime of Genocide.
Advisory Opinion, 1951 ICJ Reports 15.

☑ 사　안

1948년 유엔 총회에서 채택된 제노사이드 방지협약에는 유보의 허용 여부에 관한 별다른 언급이 없었다. 1950년 10월 14일 협약 발효에 필요한 20개국을 넘은 비준이 있었으나, 일부 국가는 유보를 첨부하여 비준했다. 이같이 유보 첨부를 수락한 국가도 있고, 이에 반대하는 국가도 있자, 유엔 총회는 다자조약에 대한 일부 국가의 유보를 법적으로 어떻게 평가할 것인가에 관하여 ICJ에 권고적 의견을 요청했다(총회 결의 제478호(V)(1950. 11. 16)).

☑ 쟁　점

(1) 특정 국가가 유보 첨부를 조건으로 조약의 당사국이 되려 할 때, 다른 당사국 일부의 반대가 있어도 유보 첨부국이 조약 당사국이 될 수 있는가 여부.

(2) 유보 첨부국과 유보에 대한 반대국간 또는 그 유보를 수락한 국가간의 법적 관계.

☑ 판　결

(1) 유보에 대해 일부 당사국은 반대하고 다른 당사국들은 반대하지 않는 경우, 유보내용이 조약의 대상 및 목적(object and purpose)과 양립 가능하면 유보 첨부국은 조약의 당사국이 될 수 있다.

(2) 유보의 내용이 조약의 대상 및 목적과 양립 불가능하다고 생각하는 당사국은 유보 첨부국을 당사국으로 간주하지 않을 수 있다. 반대로 양립 가능하다고 수락하는 국가는 유보 첨부국을 조약의 당사국으로 간주할 수 있으며, 유보 조항을 제외한 조약 내용이 양국간에 적용된다.

판 결 문

(p. 21-) Question I is framed in the following terms:

'Can the reserving State be regarded as being a party to the Convention while still maintaining its reservation if the reservation is objected to by one or more of the parties to the Convention but not by others?' [⋯]

It is well established that in its treaty relations a State cannot be bound without its consent, and that consequently no reservation can be effective against any State without its agreement thereto. It is also a generally recognized principle that a multilateral convention is the result of an agreement freely concluded upon its clauses and that consequently none of the contracting parties is entitled to frustrate or impair, by means of unilateral decisions or particular agreements, the purpose and *raison d'etre* of the convention. To this principle was linked the notion of the integrity of the convention as adopted, a notion which in its traditional concept involved the proposition that no reservation was valid unless it was accepted by all the contracting parties without exception, as would have been the case if it had been stated during the negotiations. [⋯]

It must also be pointed out that although the Genocide Convention was finally approved unanimously, it is nevertheless the result of a series of majority votes. The majority principle, while facilitating the conclusion of multilateral conventions, may also make it necessary for certain States to make reservations. This observation is confirmed by the great number of reservations which have been made of recent years to multilateral conventions.

In this state of international practice, it could certainly not be inferred from the absence of an article providing for reservations in a multilateral convention that the contracting States are prohibited from making certain reservations. Account should also be taken of the fact that the absence of such an article or even the decision not to insert such an article can be explained by the desire not to invite a multiplicity of reservations. The character of a multilateral convention, its purpose, provisions, mode of preparation and adoption, are factors which must be considered in determining, in the absence of any express provision on the subject, the possibility of making reservations, as well as their validity and effect. [···]

It must now determine what kind of reservations may be made and what kind of objections may be taken to them.

The solution of these problems must be found in the special characteristics of the Genocide Convention. The origins and character of that Convention, the objects pursued by the General Assembly and the contracting parties, the relations which exist between the provisions of the Convention, *inter se*, and between those provisions and these objects, furnish elements of interpretation of the will of the General Assembly and the parties. The origins of the Convention show that it was the intention of the United Nations to condemn and punish genocide as 'a crime under international law' involving a denial of the right of existence of entire human groups, a denial which shocks the conscience of mankind and results in great losses to humanity, and which is contrary to moral law and to the spirit and aims of the United Nations (Resolution 96 (I) of the General Assembly, December 11th 1946). The first consequence arising from this conception is that the principles underlying the Convention are principles which are recognized by civilized nations as binding on States, even without any conventional obligation. A second consequence is the universal character both of the condemnation of genocide and of the co-operation required 'in order to liberate mankind from such an odious scourge' (Preamble to the Convention). The Genocide Convention was therefore intended by the General Assembly and by the contracting parties to be definitely universal in scope. It was in fact approved on December 9th, 1948, by a resolution which was unanimously adopted by fifty-six States.

The objects of such a convention must also be considered. The Convention was manifestly adopted for a purely humanitarian and civilizing purpose. It is indeed difficult to imagine a convention that might have this dual character to a greater degree, since its object on the one hand is to safeguard the very existence of certain human groups and on the other to confirm and endorse the most elementary principles of morality. In such a convention the contracting States do not have any interests of their own; they merely have, one and all, a common interest, namely, the accomplishment of those high purposes which are the *raison d'etre* of the convention. Consequently, in a convention of this type one cannot speak of individual advantages or disadvantages to States, or of the maintenance of a perfect contractual balance between rights and duties. The high ideals which inspired the Convention provide, by virtue of the common will of the parties, the foundation and measure of all its provisions.

The foregoing considerations, when applied to the question of reservations, and more particularly to the effects of objections to reservations, lead to the following conclusions.

The object and purpose of the Genocide Convention imply that it was the intention of the General Assembly and of the States which adopted it that as many States as possible should participate. The complete exclusion from the Convention of one or more States would not only restrict the scope of its application, but would detract from the authority of the moral and humanitarian principles which are its basis. It is inconceivable that the contracting parties readily contemplated that an objection to a minor reservation should produce such a result. But even less could the contracting parties have intended to sacrifice the very object of the Convention in favour of a vain desire to secure as many participants as possible. The object and purpose of the Convention thus limit both the freedom of making reservations and that of objecting to them. It follows that it is the compatibility of a reservation with the object and purpose of the Convention that must furnish the criterion for the attitude of a State in making the reservation on accession as well as for the appraisal by a State in objecting to the reservation. Such is the rule of conduct which must guide every State in the appraisal which it must make, individually and from its own standpoint, of the admissibility of any reservation. [⋯]

Having replied to Question I, the Court will now examine Question Ⅱ, which is framed as follows:

'If the answer to Question I is in the affirmative, what is the effect of the reservation as between the reserving State and:

(a) the parties which object to the reservation?

(b) those which accept it?'

The considerations which form the basis of the Court's reply to Question I are to a large extent equally applicable here. As has been pointed out above, each State which is a party to the Convention is entitled to appraise the validity of the reservation, and it exercises this right individually and from its own standpoint. As no State can be bound by a reservation to which it has not consented, it necessarily follows that each State objecting to it will or will not, on the basis of its individual appraisal within the limits of the criterion of the object and purpose stated above, consider the reserving State to be a party to the Convention. In the ordinary course of events, such a decision will only affect the relationship between the State making the reservation and the objecting State; on the other hand, as will be pointed out later, such a decision might aim at the complete exclusion from the Convention in a case where it was expressed by the adoption of a position on the jurisdictional plane.

The disadvantages which result from this possible divergence of views—which an article concerning the making of reservations could have obviated—are real; they are mitigated by the common duty of the contracting States to be guided in their judgment by the compatibility or incompatibility of the reservation with the object and purpose of the Convention. It must clearly be assumed that the contracting States are desirous of preserving intact at least what is essential to the object of the Convention; should this desire be absent, it is quite clear that the Convention itself would be impaired both in its principle and in its application.

It may be that the divergence of views between parties as to the admissibility of a reservation will not in fact have any consequences. On the other hand, it may be that certain parties who consider that the assent given by other parties to a reservation is incompatible with the purpose of the Convention, will decide to adopt a position on the jurisdictional plane in respect of this divergence and to settle the dispute which thus arises either by special agreement or by the procedure laid down in Article IX of the Convention.

Finally, it may be that a State, whilst not claiming that a reservation is incompatible with the object and purpose of the Convention, will nevertheless object to it, but that an understanding between that State and the reserving State will have the effect that the Convention will enter into force between them, except for the clauses affected by the reservation. [···]

On Question I :

by seven votes to five,

that a State which has made and maintained a reservation which has been objected to by one or more of the parties to the Convention but not by others, can be regarded as being a party to the Convention if the reservation is compatible with the object and purpose of the Convention; otherwise, that State cannot be regarded as being a party to the Convention.

On Question Ⅱ:

by seven votes to five,

(a) that if a party to the Convention objects to a reservation which it considers to be incompatible with the object and purpose of the Convention, it can in fact consider that the reserving State is not a party to the Convention;

(b) that if, on the other hand, a party accepts the reservation as being compatible with the object and purpose of the Convention, it can in fact consider that the reserving State is a party to the Convention;

☑ 해   설

다자조약의 유보에 관한 한 20세기 전반부까지는 대체로 다른 당사국 전원일치의 동의가 있어야만 유보부 가입이 허용되었다. 유보 첨부에 대해 다른 당사국의 반대가 있으면, 유보국은 유보를 철회하든가 조약 가입을 포기해야 했다. 이는 국제연맹시절 만장일치에 의해 조약이 채택되던 것과 논리적으로 일치했다.

본 권고적 의견은 그 같은 국제사회의 관행에 획기적 전환을 가져온 계기가 되었다. 즉 이 사건에서 ICJ는 제노사이드 방지협약이 특히 순수한 인도주의적이고 문명적 목적을 가지며, 가능한 한 폭 넓은 참여가 요청되는 조약임을 유의했다. 이에 조약의 대상 및 목적과 양립가능하면 일부 당사국의 반대가 있더라도 유보부 가입이 가능하다는 의견을 제시했다.

당시 학계에서는 ICJ의 이 같은 견해가 조약의 통일성을 저해하고 다자조약을 여러 개의 양자조약으로 분해시키는 결과를 가져올 것이라고 비판하기도 했다. 또한 조약의 대상 및 목적과의 양립 가능성이라는 본질적으로 모호하고 주관적 성격의 개념을 판단기준으로 제시함으로써 다자조약 운영에 혼선을 초래할 것이라고 우려하기도 했다.

그러나 제2차 대전 이후 국제사회의 변화는 ICJ의 입장이 궁극적으로 수락되는 결과를 가져 왔다. 국제사회의 양적 및 질적 확대는 과거와 같은 만장일치 원칙의 고수를 비현실적으로 만들었다. 또한 국제사회에서의 다자조약의 확산을 위하여는 유보에 대한 어느 정도 유연한 입장의 도입이 불가피하였다. ICJ의 이 권고적 의견은 1951년 당시에는 7 : 5라는 근소한 차이로 내려진 결정이었지만,[1] 이후 조약법 발전의 새로운 방향타를 제시했다.

결국 1969년 비엔나 조약법 협약 제19조 역시 본 권고적 의견의 연장선 상에서 유보에 대한 광범위한 자유를 인정했다. ICJ는 인권조약이라는 특수성을 근거로 유보에 대한 새로운 접근을 시도했으나, 비엔나 조약법 협약은 이를 모든 조약으로 확대시킨 것이다. 당초 대상 및 목적과의 양립 가능성이라는 개념의 모호성이 우려되기도 했으나, 실제 현실에 있어서는 그다지 큰 문제를 야기하지 않았다. 다자조약의 체결시 참여국들은 매우 철저하고 신중한 준비를 통해 유보의 필요성을 사전에 봉쇄시키려고 노력하고 있으며, 중요한 조약은 대체로 유보의 가능성에 관한 명문의 조항을 둠으로써 혼선을 미연에 방지하고 있기 때문이다.

➥ 참고문헌 ────────────────────────────

• 유광혁, 조약의 유보와 양립성의 원칙: 집단살해방지협약의 유보에 관한 ICJ 권고적 의견을 중심으로, 국제소송법무 6호(2013), p. 27.
• C. Fenwick, Reservation to Multilateral Conventions: The Report of the International Law Commission, AJIL Vol. 46(1955), p. 120.
• G. Fitzmaurice, Reservations to Multilateral Conventions, ICLQ Vol. 2(1953), p. 1.
• J. K. Koh, Reservations to Multilateral Treaties: How International Legal Doctrine Reflects World Vision, Harvard International Law Journal Vol. 23(1982), p. 71.

---

1) Guerrero, McNair, Read, Mo 판사는 공동 반대의견에서 유보 수락에는 만장일치의 동의가 필요함이 기존의 국제법 규칙임과 동시에 UN의 관행임을 강조했다.

3. Belilos 사건(1988)
— 무효인 유보

Belilos v. Switzerland.
European Court Human Rights, 10 ECRR 466.

☑ 사　안

이 사건의 원고는 스위스에서 금지된 시위에 참석했다는 이유로 경찰청으로부터 벌금형을 통고받았다. 그녀는 경찰청이 유죄를 결정할 권한은 없다며, 법원에 이를 무효화해 달라고 청구했으나 기각 당했다. 이에 그녀는 스위스에서 유럽인권협약 제6조 1항이 규정하고 있는 독립적으로 공정한 법원에 의한 재판을 받지 못했다고 주장하며, 1983년 이 사건을 유럽인권위원회에 통보했다. 위원회는 이를 유럽인권재판소에 회부했다.[1] 이에 대해 스위스정부는 협약 비준시 제6조상의 의무 내용을 수정하는 해석선언을 첨부했음을 지적하며, 이에 따르면 이 사건 청구는 각하되어야 한다고 주장했다. 재판소는 해석선언이라는 명칭에도 불구하고 유보의 법적 효과가 발생할 수 있는가? 스위스의 유보내용이 허용될 수 있는 것인가 등을 검토했다.

☑ 쟁　점

(1) 해석선언은 그 내용에 따라 유보로 취급될 수 있는지 여부.

(2) 허용될 수 없는 유보를 첨부한 경우의 법적 효과.

☑ 판　결

(1) 해석선언의 내용이 유보에 해당하면 그 명칭에도 불구하고 유보로

---

1) 1998년 유럽인권협약 제11의정서가 발효됨에 따라 유럽인권위원회를 거쳐야 하는 구 제도는 폐지되었고, 현재는 개인이 유럽인권재판소에 직접 제소할 수 있다.

취급된다.

(2) 허용될 수 없는 유보는 무효이므로 당사국은 유보 없이 가입한 것으로 취급된다.

판 결 문2)

49. The question whether a declaration described as "interpretative" must be regarded as a "reservation" is a difficult one, particularly—in the instant case— because the Swiss Government have made both "reservations" and "interpretative declarations" in the same instrument of ratification. More generally, the Court recognises the great importance, rightly emphasised by the Government, of the legal rules applicable to reservations and interpretative declarations made by States Parties to the Convention. Only reservations are mentioned in the Convention, but several States have also (or only) made interpretative declarations, without always making a clear distinction between the two.

In order to establish the legal character of such a declaration, one must look behind the title given to it and seek to determine the substantive content. In the present case, it appears that Switzerland meant to remove certain categories of proceedings from the ambit of Article 6 (1) and to secure itself against an interpretation of that Article which it considered to be too broad. However, the Court must see to it that the obligations arising under the Convention are not subject to restrictions which would not satisfy the requirements of Article 64 as regards reservations. Accordingly, it will examine the validity of the interpretative declaration in question, as in the case of a reservation, in the context of this provision. [···]

52. Before the Commission the applicant conceded that the interpretative declaration was not a reservation of a general character, but before the Court she submitted the opposite. She now maintained that the declaration sought to remove all civil and criminal cases from the judiciary and transfer them to the executive, in disregard of a principle that was vital to any democratic society, namely the separation of powers. As "ultimate control by the judiciary" was a pretence if it did not cover the facts, such a system, she claimed, had the effect of excluding the

---

2) 유럽인권협약 개정에 의하여 조문번호가 변경되었으나, 이 판결문에서는 원래 표시된 구 번호를 그대로 사용한다.

guarantee of a fair trial, which was a cardinal rule of the Convention. Switzerland's declaration accordingly did not satisfy the basic requirements of Article 64, which expressly prohibited reservations of a general character and prohibited by implication those which were incompatible with the Convention. [⋯]

54. [⋯] However, the Commission continued, the words "ultimate control by the judiciary" were ambiguous and imprecise. They created great uncertainty as to the effects of the declaration concerned on the application of paragraphs 2 and 3 of Article 6 (art. 6-2, art. 6-3), particularly as regards decisions in criminal matters by administrative authorities. In the Commission's view, the declaration appeared to have the consequence that anyone "charged with a criminal offence" was almost entirely deprived of the protection of the Convention, although there was nothing to show that this had been Switzerland's intention. At least in respect of criminal proceedings, therefore, the declaration had general, unlimited scope.

55. The Court has reached the same conclusion. By "reservation of a general character" in Article 64 is meant in particular a reservation couched in terms that are too vague or broad for it to be possible to determine their exact meaning and scope. While the preparatory work and the Government's explanations clearly show what the respondent State's concern was at the time of ratification, they cannot obscure the objective reality of the actual wording of the declaration. The words "ultimate control by the judiciary over the acts or decisions of the public authorities relating to [civil] rights or obligations or the determination of [a criminal] charge" do not make it possible for the scope of the undertaking by Switzerland to be ascertained exactly, in particular as to which categories of dispute are included and as to whether or not the "ultimate control by the judiciary" takes in the facts of the case. They can therefore be interpreted in different ways, whereas Article 64 (1) requires precision and clarity. In short, they fall foul of the rule that reservations must not be of a general character. [⋯]3)

60. In short, the declaration in question does not satisfy two of the requirements of Article 64 of the Convention, with the result that it must be held to be invalid. At the same time, it is beyond doubt that Switzerland is, and regards itself as, bound by the Convention irrespective of the validity of the declaration. Moreover, the Swiss Government recognised the Court's competence to determine the latter issue, which they argued before it. The Government's preliminary

---

3) 이어서 재판소는 유럽인권협약 제64조 2항은 유보를 하는 경우 관련법령에 대한 간략한 설명을 첨부하라고 요구하고 있는데 스위스는 아무런 설명을 첨가하지 않았다는 점에서 유보와 관련된 의무를 다하지 못했음을 지적했다.

objection must therefore be rejected.

☑ 해   설

당초 스위스는 유럽인권협약 가입시 다음의 내용을 해석선언으로 첨부
했다.

> "The Swiss Federal Council considers that the guarantee of fair trial in
> Article 6 paragraph 1 of the Convention, in the determination of civil rights
> and obligations or any criminal charge against the person in question, is
> intended solely to ensure ultimate control by the judiciary over the acts or
> decisions of the public authorities relating to such rights or obligations or the
> determination of such a charge."

해석선언이란 표현이나 명칭에 관계없이 국가나 국제기구가 조약의 조
항의 의미나 범위를 구체화하거나 분명히 하기 위해 첨부하는 일방적 선언
으로, 조약상의 의무를 제한하려는 행위가 아니라는 점에서 유보와 구별
된다.

이 판결에서 쟁점이 된 유럽인권협약 제64조는 협약 개정으로 현재는
제57조로 번호가 변경되었으나, 내용은 그대로이다. 그 제1항은 "어떠한 국
가도 이 협약의 서명 또는 비준서 기탁시 자국 영역에서 당시 적용중인 국
내법이 이 협약의 규정과 일치하지 않는 한도 내에서 해당 조항에 대한 유
보를 할 수 있다. 본조에 의한 일반적 성격의 유보는 허용되지 아니한다"는
내용이다.

이 사건 재판부는 스위스의 해석선언이 법적으로는 유보에 해당하며,
그 내용이 협약상 허용될 수 없는 일반적 성격의 유보에 해당하므로 무효라
고 판단했다. 왜냐하면 스위스의 선언에 따르게 되면 형사 피고인들은 유럽
인권협약의 보호를 거의 받을 수 없게 될 것이라고 평가했기 때문이었다. 그
렇다면 스위스는 유보없는 가입을 한 당사국으로서의 의무를 부담한다고 판
단하였다. 스위스는 자신의 비준서 기탁시의 해석선언에 대해 사무국이나 타
당사국들이 아무런 이의도 제기하지 않았음을 지적했으나, 재판부는 이 점이
판단에 별 영향을 미치지 않는다고 보았다.

한편 유럽인권재판소는 Loizidou v. Turkey(Preliminary Objection)에서도 금지된 유보에 관하여 동일한 평가를 했다(1995). 또한 시민적 및 정치적 권리에 관한 국제규약의 Human Rights Committee도 R. Kennedy v. Trinidad and Tobago 사건(CCPR/C/67/D/845/1999)에서 무효인 유보를 첨부한 국가는 유보없이 가입한 것과 같이 취급해야 한다고 판단했다. 또한 Committee는 General Comment No. 24(1994)를 통해 동일한 입장을 밝힌 바 있었다.4)

그러나 유보사항이 당사국에게는 근본적으로 중요한 내용으로서 조약비준과 분리될 수 없다고 생각하는데도 불구하고 유보가 무효로 판정된다면 그 법적 효과는 어떻게 될 것인가? 이 경우에도 유보없는 가입으로 취급할 수 있는가? 이 경우에는 당사국의 가입 의사 자체가 없었다고 보아야 하지 않은가 등의 의문이 제기될 수 있다. 다만 이 사건에서 스위스는 제6조에 대한 해석선언이 수락되지 않는다면 유럽인권협약 전체의 적용을 거부하겠다는 의사를 표시하지는 않았다.

무효인 유보의 효력은 국제법위원회(ILC)가 2011년 채택한 「조약 유보에 관한 실행지침」(Guide to Practice on Reservation to Treaties)에서도 분석되었다. ILC는 허용 불가능한 유보를 첨부한 국가가 조약의 당사국인지 여부는 1차적으로 유보 첨부국의 의사에 따르자고 제안했다. 무효인 유보를 첨부한 국가는 일단 유보 없는 가입으로 간주하나, 그 국가는 유보의 이익 없이는 조약의 당사국이 되지 않겠다는 의사를 추후 언제라도 표시할 수 있다고 제시했다. 즉 유보를 포기하고 유보 없는 당사국이 될 것인지 또는 유보 없이는 조약의 당사국이 되지 않을 것인지를 해당국가의 의사에 맡기자는 입장이다. 다만 인권조약과 같이 조약기구가 특정국의 유보를 무효라고 선언한 경우 그 국가가 조약의 당사국으로 남을 의사가 없다면 1년 이내에 탈퇴표시를 하라고 요구했다(para. 4.5.3). 이 같은 내용은 당사국의 의사를 가급적 존중하자는 입장이다.

무효인 유보를 첨부한 국가로서는 그 유보가 조약 가입의 본질적 조건

---

4) "The normal consequence of an unacceptable reservation is not that the Covenant will not be in effect at all for a reserving party. Rather, such a reservation will generally be severable, in the sense that the Covenant will be operative for the reserving party without benefit of the reservation." para. 18.

일 수도 있고, 아닐 수도 있다. ILC의 실행지침은 이러한 양 측면을 모두 포용하려는 의도이다. 결국 무효인 유보를 첨부한 국가의 법적 지위에는 아직도 명확하지 못하다.

ICJ는 아직까지 무효인 유보의 효력 문제를 정면으로 다룬 예가 없다.

➡ **참고문헌** ─────────────────────────────

- 이주윤, 인권조약에 대한 유보의 효력, 국제법학회논총 51권 3호(2006), p. 119.
- H. Bourguignon, The Belilos Case, Virginia Journal of International Law Vol. 29(1989), p. 347.
- S. Marks, Reservations Unhinged: The Belilos Case before the ECHR, ICLQ Vol. 39(1990), p. 300.
- W. Schabas, Invalid Reservations to the International Covenant on Civil and Political Rihgts: Is the United States still a Party?, Brooklin Journal of International law Vol. 21(1995), p. 277.

1. 산 후안 강 항행에 관한 권리 분쟁(2009)
— 문언의 통상적 의미의 변화

Dispute regarding Navigational and Related Rights.
Costa Rica v. Nicaragua, 2009 ICJ Reports 213.

☑ 사   안

산 후안 강은 코스타리카와 니카라구아 간의 국경하천이다. 양국간 1858년 조약은 이 강에 대한 니카라구아의 주권을 인정하는 대신 코스타리카에게는 강 하류지역에서 교역을 목적으로(con objetos de comercio) 한 영구 자유항행권을 인정했다(제6조). 양국간에 강 이용에 관한 분쟁이 발생하여 1998년 니카라구아는 코스타리카 경찰의 강 통행을 금지하고, 이 강을 유람하는 코스타리카측 관광객에게 1인당 미화 25달러를 부과했다. 1858년 조약 제6조의 의미에 관해 니카라구아는 1858년 조약의 체결 당시 "교역(commerce)"이란 상품의 구입이나 판매를 의미했으며, 여객 수송과 같은 서비스 제공은 포함되지 않았고 특히 관광객 수송과 같은 개념은 없었다고 주장했다. 따라서 "교역"을 조약 체결 당시의 의미로 해석해야 한다고 주장했다 (para. 58). 이에 반해 코스타리카는 교역을 여객이나 관광객 수송도 포함되는 개념으로 해석해야 한다고 주장했다.

☑ 쟁   점

문언의 통상적 의미를 해석하는 시점.

☑ 판   결

문언은 체결시의 의미에 따라 해석함이 원칙이나, 경우에 따라서 시대의 흐름에 따른 의미의 변화를 포용해야 한다. 특히 대상이 일반적인 용어이고, 장기간의 적용이 예정된 조약의 경우 시간의 경과에 따라 그 의미가 변할 수 있다는 점이 전제된다.

판 결 문

63. […] It is true that the terms used in a treaty must be interpreted in light of what is determined to have been the parties' common intention, which is, by definition, contemporaneous with the treaty's conclusion. That may lead a court seised of a dispute, or the parties themselves, when they seek to determine the meaning of a treaty for purposes of good-faith compliance with it, to ascertain the meaning a term had when the treaty was drafted, since doing so can shed light on the parties' common intention. […]

64. This does not however signify that, where a term's meaning is no longer the same as it was at the date of conclusion, no account should ever be taken of its meaning at the time when the treaty is to be interpreted for purposes of applying it.

On the one hand, the subsequent practice of the parties, within the meaning of Article 31 (3) (b) of the Vienna Convention, can result in a departure from the original intent on the basis of a tacit agreement between the parties. On the other hand, there are situations in which the parties' intent upon conclusion of the treaty was, or may be presumed to have been, to give the terms used—or some of them—a meaning or content capable of evolving, not one fixed once and for all, so as to make allowance for, among other things, developments in international law. In such instances it is indeed in order to respect the parties' common intention at the time the treaty was concluded, not to depart from it, that account should be taken of the meaning acquired by the terms in question upon each occasion on which the treaty is to be applied. […]

66. […] It is founded on the idea that, where the parties have used generic terms in a treaty, the parties necessarily having been aware that the meaning of the terms was likely to evolve over time, and where the treaty has been entered into for a very long period or is "of continuing duration," the parties must be presumed, as a general rule, to have intended those terms to have an evolving meaning.

67. This is so in the present case in respect of the term "comercio" as used in

Article VI of the 1858 Treaty. First, this is a generic term, referring to a class of activity. Second, the 1858 Treaty was entered into for an unlimited duration; from the outset it was intended to create a legal régime characterized by its perpetuity.

68. This last observation is buttressed by the object itself of the Treaty, which was to achieve a permanent settlement between the parties of their territorial disputes. The territorial rules laid down in treaties of this type are, by nature, particularly marked in their permanence, [⋯]

69. This is true as well of the right of free navigation guaranteed to Costa Rica by Article VI. This right, described as "perpetual," is so closely linked with the territorial settlement defined by the Treaty—to such an extent that it can be considered an integral part of it—that it is characterized by the same permanence as the territorial régime stricto sensu itself.

70. The Court concludes from the foregoing that the terms by which the extent of Costa Rica's right of free navigation has been defined, including in particular the term "comercio," must be understood to have the meaning they bear on each occasion on which the Treaty is to be applied, and not necessarily their original meaning. Thus, even assuming that the notion of "commerce" does not have the same meaning today as it did in the mid-nineteenth century, it is the present meaning which must be accepted for purposes of applying the Treaty.

71. Accordingly, the Court finds that the right of free navigation in question applies to the transport of persons as well as the transport of goods, as the activity of transporting persons can be commercial in nature nowadays. This is the case if the carrier engages in the activity for profit-making purposes. A decisive consideration in this respect is whether a price (other than a token price) is paid to the carrier—the boat operator—by the passengers or on their behalf. If so, then the carrier's activity is commercial in nature and the navigation in question must be regarded as "for the purposes of commerce" within the meaning of Article VI. The Court sees no persuasive reason to exclude the transport of tourists from this category, subject to fulfilment of the same condition.

☑ 해 설

재판과정에서 니카라구아측은 "con objetos de"를 "with goods" 또는 "with articles"로 해석해야 한다고 주장하고, 코스타리카측은 이를 "for the purpose of"로 해석해야 한다고 주장했는데, 재판부는 코스타리카측의 해석을 지지했다. 이어 재판부는 코스타리카측이 상업적 목적으로 산 후앙 강을 자유롭게 항행할 수 있으며, 운송자에게 대가를 지불하고 탑승한 여객이나 관광객 수송활동은 성격상 상업적이라고 판단했다. 즉 일반적 용어인 "comercio"의 해석에 있어서 원래의 의미에 고정되지 말고, 조약이 적용되는 상황에 따라 그 의미를 파악해야 한다고 해석했다. 이에 이 강을 항행하는 코스타리카측 선박의 사람들은 니카라구아의 비자나 관광카드를 취득할 필요가 없다고 판정했다. 그러나 코스타리카측이 경찰기능을 행사하기 위해 이 강을 항행할 권리는 없다고 판단했다. 이는 상업적 목적에 해당하지 않기 때문이다.

　산 후앙 강의 이용에 관한 양국간의 분쟁은 오랜 역사를 갖고 있으나, 최근 태평양과 대서양을 연결하는 제2의 운하 건설이 이 지역으로 예정됨에 따라 강의 이용에 관한 분쟁이 고조되었다. 또한 산 후앙 강 하구의 Calero 섬의 영유권에 관해서도 양국 분쟁이 발생해 이 사건 역시 ICJ에 회부되었는데 2015년 12월 16일 이 섬은 코스타리카령으로 판결이 내려졌다.

5. 프레비히어 사원 사건(1962) — 착오

Case Concerning the Temple of Preah Vihear.
Cambodia v. Thailand, 1962 ICJ Report 6.

☑ 사   안

프레비히어 사원은 태국과 캄보디아 국경지대에 위치하고 있다. 본 사건은 이 사원과 주변 지역의 영유권에 관한 분쟁이다. 1904년과 1907년 태국(구 샴)과 프랑스(당시 캄보디아의 보호국)는 이 일대의 양국 국경을 분수령에 따라 정하기로 하는 조약을 체결하고, 구체적인 경계는 양국 혼성위원회에서 획정하기로 합의했다. 후일 태국은 프랑스측에 자세한 국경지도의 제작을 의뢰하기로 하여, 프랑스측이 제작한 지도가 1908년 태국에게 전달되었다. 프레비히어 지역은 실제 분수령을 기준으로 할 때는 태국측에 속하나, 이 지도상에는 캄보디아령으로 표기되었다. 당시 태국은 별다른 이의 없이 이 지도를 수령하고 국내적으로 활용했다. 한편 혼성위원회는 이 지도를 최종적으로 승인하는 절차는 취하지 못한 상태에서 활동을 종료했다. 1934년 이 지역을 탐사한 태국 당국은 지도상의 국경이 분수령과 일치하지 않고 사원 지역을 프랑스가 관리하고 있음을 발견했으나, 당시는 별다른 이의를 제기하지 않았다. 제2차 대전 후 태국은 문제의 지역에 일방적으로 경비병을 파견, 주둔시키었다. 1953년 독립한 캄보디아는 태국군의 철수와 이 지역이 자국령임을 확인해 달라는 소송을 ICJ에 제기했다. ICJ에서 태국은 문제의 지도가 혼성위원회의 작업결과가 아니므로 구속력이 없고, 지도는 분수령을 따르지 않았다는 점에서 중대한 오류를 포함하고 있다고 주장했다. 만약 태국이 이 지도를 수락했다고 할지라도 지도상의 국경선이 분수령과 일치한다고 생각한 착오에서 비롯되었다고 주장했다. 아래 판결문은 태국측의 착오 주장에 대한 재판부의 판단이다.

☑ 쟁   점

국경지도에 관한 착오 주장의 수락 가능성.

☑ 판   결

문제의 지역은 지도상 명백하게 캄보디아령으로 표시되어 있으므로 지
도가 만들어진 정황이나 이를 수락한 태국 관리의 지위, 이후의 태국의 대응
등을 고려할 때 뒤늦은 착오의 항변은 수락될 수 없다.

판 결 문

(p. 23-) It has been contended on behalf of Thailand that this communication
of the maps by the French authorities was, so to speak, *ex parte*,[1) and that no
formal acknowledgment of it was either requested of, or given by, Thailand. In fact,
as will be seen presently, an acknowledgment by conduct was undoubtedly made in
a very definite way; but even if it were otherwise, it is clear that the circumstances
were such as called for some reaction, within a reasonable period, on the part of
the Siamese authorities, if they wished to disagree with the map or had any serious
question to raise in regard to it. They did not do so, either then or for many years,
and thereby must be held to have acquiesced. [···]

The Court moreover considers that there is no legal foundation for the
consequence it is attempted to deduce from the fact that no one in Thailand at that
time may have known of the importance of the Temple or have been troubling
about it. Frontier rectifications cannot in law be claimed on the ground that a
frontier area has turned out to have an importance not known or suspected when
the frontier was established.

It follows from the preceding findings that the Siamese authorities in due
course received the Annex I map and that they accepted it. Now, however, it is
contended on behalf of Thailand, so far as the disputed area of Preah Vihear is
concerned, that an error was committed, an error of which the Siamese authorities
were unaware at the time when they accepted the map.

---

1) 일방적인 — 필자 주.

It is an established rule of law that the plea of error cannot be allowed as an element vitiating consent if the party advancing it contributed by its own conduct to the error, or could have avoided it, or if the circumstances were such as to put that party on notice of a possible error. The Court considers that the character and qualifications of the persons who saw the Annex I map on the Siamese side would alone make it difficult for Thailand to plead error in law. These persons included the members of the very Commission of Delimitation within whose competence this sector of the frontier had lain. But even apart from this, the Court thinks that there were other circumstances relating to the Annex I map which make the plea of error difficult to receive.

An inspection indicates that the map itself drew such pointed attention to the Preah Vihear region that no interested person, nor anyone charged with the duty of scrutinizing it, could have failed to see what the map was purporting to do in respect of that region. If, as Thailand has argued, the geographical configuration of the place is such as to make it obvious to anyone who has been there that the watershed must lie along the line of the escarpment (a fact which, if true, must have been no less evident in 1908), then the map made it quite plain that the Annex I line did not follow the escarpment in this region since it was plainly drawn appreciably to the north of the whole Preah Vihear promontory. Nobody looking at the map could be under any misapprehension about that.

Next, the map marked Preah Vihear itself quite clearly as lying on the Cambodian side of the line, using for the Temple a symbol which seems to indicate a rough plan of the building and its stairways.

It would thus seem that, to anyone who considered that the line of the watershed at Preah Vihear ought to follow the line of the escarpment, or whose duty it was to scrutinize the map, there was everything in the Annex I map to put him upon enquiry. Furthermore, as has already been pointed out, the Siamese Government knew or must be presumed to have known, through the Siamese members of the Mixed Commission, that the Annex I map had never been formally adopted by the Commission. The Siamese authorities knew it was the work of French topographical officers to whom they had themselves entrusted the work of producing the maps. They accepted it without any independent investigation, and cannot therefore now plead any error vitiating the reality of their consent. The Court concludes therefore that the plea of error has not been made out.

☑ 해   설

현지 지형상 프레비히어 사원 지역은 캄보디아에 속하기 어려운 것이 사실이다. 분수령을 기준으로 할 때 태국쪽에 위치하고 있었으며, 이 소송이 제기될 무렵까지 일반인은 태국령을 통해서만 프레비히어 사원으로 갈 수 있었다.

그러나 ICJ는 1962년 6월에 내린 판결에서 태국이 문제의 지도를 접수한 1908년에 이 내용을 수락했는가에 대하여는 의문이 있다 할지라도, 이후의 사태경과를 보면 태국이 뒤늦게 지도를 수락할 수 없다고 주장하는 것은 용인되지 않는다고 결론내렸다. 즉 태국은 지도를 접수하고도 별다른 이의 없이 이를 광범위하게 배포, 활용했으며, 1930년 이 지역을 방문한 태국 왕자가 프랑스 관리의 환영을 받았는데도 별다른 이의를 제기하지 않았다. 만약 태국이 문제의 지도에 동의하지 않았다면 합리적 기간 내에 대응을 했어야 하는데 그러하지 못했다. 따라서 태국은 조약이 부여한 '안정된 국경이라는 이익'을 지난 50년간 향유하고도 이제 와서 그 합의의 당사자임을 부인할 수 없다고 판시했다. 이에 ICJ는 태국에게 프레비히어 사원과 인접 캄보디아령(its vicinity on Cambodian territory)에서 군대를 철수시키고, 이 사원에서 반출시킨 고미술품을 캄보디아로 반환하라고 요구했다. 후일 태국은 이 판결을 이행했고, 캄보디아 정부는 태국인의 경우 비자 없이 사원을 방문할 수 있도록 허용했다.

그러나 프레비히어 사원을 둘러싼 양국간의 갈등은 계속되었다. 특히 사원 인접지역이 어느 범위를 의미하는지가 명확하지 않아 분쟁이 발생하고, 양국간에는 여러 차례 무력충돌도 발생했다. 이에 2011년 5월 캄보디아는 1962년 ICJ 판결의 사원 인접지역이 어디까지를 의미하는가를 재판소가 다시 해석해 달라는 청구를 제기했다. 2013년 11월 ICJ는 프레비히어 사원이 위치한 봉우리 지역 전체가 캄보디아에 속한다고 해석하며, 이 지역에서 태국관헌과 군대의 철수를 요구하는 판결을 내렸다. 그러나 1962년 판결과 2013년 판결 모두 양국간 구체적 국경을 획정하는 내용은 아니라는 점에서 분쟁의 불씨가 완전히 해소되지는 않았다.

과거 국제관계에서 착오로 인한 합의무효를 주장하였던 사례의 상당수는 지도와 관련된 주장이었다. 이 판결에서 재판부가 착오의 효력에 관해 보여준 태도는 후일 비엔나 조약법 협약 제48조 성안의 바탕이 되었다. 국제재판에서 착오로 인한 조약의 무효주장이 수락된 예는 찾기 어렵다.

➡ 참고문헌 ─────────────────────────────────

• P. C. Chan, Acquiescence, Estoppel in International Boundaries: Temple of Preah Vihear Revisited, Chinese Journal of International Law Vol. 3(2004), p. 421.

• D. Johnson, The Case concerning the Temple of Preah Vihear, ICLQ Vol. 11(1962), p. 1183.

• G. Weissberg, Maps as Evidence in International Boundary Disputes, AJIL Vol. 57(1963), p. 781.

6. 카메룬-나이지리아 경계획정 사건(2002)
― 국내법 위반 조약의 효력

Land and Maritime Boundary between Cameroon and Nigeria.
Cameroon v. Nigeria, 2002 ICJ Reports 303.

☑ 사　　안

이 사건은 나이지리아와 카메룬 간의 국경 및 해양경계 분쟁이다. 그 중 해양경계와 관련해 카메룬은 일정 수역의 경우 과거의 몇몇 조약과 함께 1975년 6월 양국 정상이 서명한 Maroua 선언에 의해 경계가 확정되었다고 주장했다. 반면 나이지리아는 해당 부분에 대한 경계획정이 존재한다는 사실을 부인하는 한편, 특히 Maroua 선언은 법적 구속력이 없는 합의에 불과하다고 반박했다. 나이지리아 측 주장 중에는 이 선언이 나이지리아 헌법상 요구되는 최고군사위원회의 승인을 받지 못해 조약으로 성립되지 않았다는 내용이 포함되어 있다. 즉 국가는 대외관계에 관한 인접국의 국내법상의 변화를 유의하고 있어야 하므로 카메룬은 나이지리아 국가원수의 조약체결권에 대한 제약을 알았거나 알았어야 했으며, 국가원수간의 합의는 추후 별도의 승인절차가 필요하다는 점은 이미 카메룬에 통보되었고, 이 같은 국가원수의 조약체결권의 한계는 카메룬에게도 객관적으로 명백한 상태였다는 주장이었다.

☑ 쟁　　점

조약 체결권에 관한 국내법상의 제한.

☑ 판　　결

국가원수의 조약 체결권에 대한 제한은 적절히 공지되지 않는 한 명백하다고 할 수 없으며, 인접국이 이와 관련된 타국의 국내법상 제한을 알아야 할 의무는 없다.

258. Nigeria likewise regards the Maroua Declaration as lacking legal validity, since it "was not ratified by the Supreme Military Council" after being signed by the Nigerian Head of State. It states that under the Nigerian constitution in force at the relevant time—June 1975—executive acts were in general to be carried out by the Supreme Military Council or subject to its approval. It notes that States are normally expected to follow legislative and constitutional developments in neighbouring States which have an impact upon the inter-State relations of those States, and that few limits can be more important than those affecting the treaty-making power. It adds that on 23 August 1974, nine months before the Maroua Declaration, the then Head of State of Nigeria had written to the then Head of State of Cameroon, explaining, with reference to a meeting with the latter in August 1972 at Garoua, that "the proposals of the experts based on the documents they prepared on the 4th April 1971 were not acceptable to the Nigerian Government," and that the views and recommendations of the joint commission "must be subject to the agreement of the two Governments." Nigeria contends that this shows that any arrangements that might be agreed between the two Heads of State were subject to the subsequent and separate approval of the Nigerian Government.

Nigeria says that Cameroon, according to an objective test based upon the provisions of the Vienna Convention, either knew or, conducting itself in a normally prudent manner, should have known that the Head of State of Nigeria did not have the authority to make legally binding commitments without referring back to the Nigerian Government—at that time the Supreme Military Council—and that it should therefore have been "objectively evident" to Cameroon, within the meaning of Article 46, paragraph 2, of the Vienna Convention on the Law of Treaties that the Head of State of Nigeria did not have unrestricted authority. Nigeria adds that Article 7, paragraph 2, of the Vienna Convention on the Law of Treaties, which provides that Heads of State and Heads of Government "[i]n virtue of their functions and without having to produce full powers ... are considered as representing their State," is solely concerned with the way in which a person's function as a state's representative is established, but does not deal with the extent of that person's powers when exercising that representative function. [⋯]

265. The Court will now address Nigeria's argument that its constitutional rules regarding the conclusion of treaties were not complied with. [⋯] The rules concerning the authority to sign treaties for a State are constitutional rules of fundamental importance. However, a limitation of a Head of State's capacity in this respect is not manifest in the sense of Article 46, paragraph 2, unless at least properly publicized. This is particularly so because Heads of State belong to the group of persons who, in accordance with Article 7, paragraph 2, of the Convention "[i]n virtue of their functions and without having to produce full powers" are considered as representing their State.

The Court cannot accept Nigeria's argument that Article 7, paragraph 2, of the Vienna Convention on the Law of Treaties is solely concerned with the way in which a person's function as a state's representative is established, but does not deal with the extent of that person's powers when exercising that representative function. The Court notes that the commentary of the International Law Commission on Article 7, paragraph 2, expressly states that "Heads of State ⋯ are considered as representing their State for the purpose of performing all acts relating to the conclusion of a treaty" ([⋯]).

266. Nigeria further argues that Cameroon knew, or ought to have known, that the Head of State of Nigeria had no power legally to bind Nigeria without consulting the Nigerian Government. In this regard the Court notes that there is no general legal obligation for States to keep themselves informed of legislative and constitutional developments in other States which are or may become important for the international relations of these States.

In this case the Head of State of Nigeria had in August 1974 stated in his letter to the Head of State of Cameroon that the views of the Joint Commission "must be subject to the agreement of the two Governments." However, in the following paragraph of that same letter, he further indicated: "It has always been my belief that we can, both, together re-examine the situation and reach an appropriate and acceptable decision on the matter." Contrary to Nigeria's contention, the Court considers that these two statements, read together, cannot be regarded as a specific warning to Cameroon that the Nigerian Government would not be bound by any commitment entered into by the Head of State. And in particular they could not be understood as relating to any commitment to be made at Maroua nine months later. The letter in question in fact concerned a meeting to be held at Kano,

Nigeria, from 30 August to 1 September 1974. This letter seems to have been part of a pattern which marked the Parties' boundary negotiations between 1970 and 1975, in which the two Heads of State took the initiative of resolving difficulties in those negotiations through person-to-person agreements, including those at Yaoundé II and Maroua.

267. The Court further observes that in July 1975 the two Parties inserted a correction in the Maroua Declaration, that in so acting they treated the Declaration as valid and applicable, and that Nigeria does not claim to have contested its validity or applicability prior to 1977.

268. In these circumstances the Maroua Declaration, as well as the Yaoundé II Declaration, have to be considered as binding and as establishing a legal obligation on Nigeria.

☑ 해 설

조약체결에 관한 국내법을 위반해 체결된 조약의 효력은 어떻게 취급되는가? 비엔나 협약은 국제법의 우위를 기본원칙으로 하면서도 다음과 같은 약간의 예외를 인정했다. 즉 국내법 위반이 명백하고 또한 근본적으로 중대한 경우에만 조약 동의의 무효를 주장할 수 있다고 규정했다(제46조 1항). 이 조항이 부정형(not … unless)으로 규정되어 있다는 사실은 국내법 위반의 주장이 예외적으로만 인용될 수 있음을 암시한다. 각국 정부는 자신의 대표가 무엇을 하고 있는지 잘 알아야 할 의무가 있다는 점에서도 이 조항은 쉽게 원용되어서는 아니된다. 국내법 위반이 명백하다는 것은 일반적으로 모든 국가에게 객관적으로 분명한 경우를 가리킨다. 중대한 경우라고 할 때의 국내법은 아마도 헌법이나 헌법적 법률 정도를 가리킬 것이다. 그렇다고 하여 헌법을 위반한 모든 경우가 중대한 위반이라고는 하기 어렵다.

국내법 위반 조약의 효력에 관해서는 종전부터 이론적 연구는 많았으나, 실제로 문제된 사례는 드물었고 무효 주장에 성공한 사례는 더욱 찾기 힘들다. 아마도 현실에 있어서 조약 당사국은 국내법 위반을 이유로 조약의 무효를 주장하기보다는 모순되는 국내법을 개정하거나 또는 조약의 개정을 시도할 가능성이 차라리 더 높다. 한편 국내법 위반으로 조약이 무효가 된다 해도 그로 인한 국가책임은 별도로 제기될 수 있다.

7. 나미비아 사건(1971)— 조약의 중대한 위반

Legal Consequences for States of the Continued Presence
of South Africa in Namibia(South West Africa) notwithstanding
Security Council Resolution.
Advisory Opinion, 1971 ICJ Reports 16.

☑ 사   안

나미비아(서남 아프리카)는 국제연맹 시절 남아프리카공화국의 위임통치를 받았다. 제2차 대전 후 국제연맹이 해산되고, 유엔은 새로이 신탁통치제도를 도입했다. 유엔은 위임통치 담당국들에게 새로운 신탁통치제도로의 전환을 요구했으나, 남아공은 이에 응하지 않았다. 남아공은 위임통치에 따른 의무가 국제연맹의 해산과 함께 종료되었으며, 나미비아 지역의 장래는 이 지역을 지배하던 자신이 결정할 권한을 갖는다고 주장했다. 이후 남아공의 나미비아 지배문제는 국제사회에서 지속적인 논란의 대상이 되었으며, 여러 차례 ICJ의 판단대상이 되었다. 유엔 헌장상 신탁통치에 관한 최종적인 권한을 갖는 총회는 1966년 결의 제2145호(XXI)를 통해 국제연맹 시절 부여된 남아공의 위임통치를 종료시키기로 결정했다. 이 같은 총회의 결의에도 불구하고 남아공이 나미비아 지역에 대한 통치권을 이양하지 않자, 안전보장이사회 역시 1970년 결의 제276호를 통해 총회의 결의 내용을 재확인하는 한편, 나미비아 지역에 남아공 당국이 계속 존재하는 것은 위법하다고 선언했다. 남아공이 유엔과의 협조를 계속 거부하자, 안보리는 1970년 이 사태에 대해 ICJ에 권고적 의견을 구하기로 결정했다. 아래 판결문은 남아공과의 위임통치협정을 유엔이 종료시킬 수 있는가에 대한 판단부분이다.

☑ 쟁 점

조약 일방 당사자의 중대한 위반의 효과.

☑ 판 결

조약 일방 당사자의 중대한 위반이 있으면 타방 당사자는 조약을 종료
시킬 수 있다.

판 결 문

90. As indicated earlier, with the entry into force of the Charter of the United Nations a relationship was established between all Members of the United Nations on the one side, and each mandatory Power on the other. The mandatory Powers while retaining their mandates assumed, under Article 80 of the Charter, *vis-à-vis* all United Nations Members, the obligation to keep intact and preserve, until trusteeship agreements were executed, the rights of other States and of the peoples of mandated territories, which resulted from the existing mandate agreements and related instruments [···]

91. One of the fundamental principles governing the international relationship thus established is that a party which disowns or does not fulfil its own obligations cannot be recognized as retaining the rights which it claims to derive from the relationship.

92. The terms of the preamble and operative part of resolution 2145(XXI) leave no doubt as to the character of the resolution. In the preamble the General Assembly declares itself "Convinced that the administration of the Mandated Territory by South Africa has been conducted in a manner contrary" to the two basic international instruments directly imposing obligations upon South Africa, the Mandate and the Charter of the United Nations, as well as to the Universal Declaration of Human Rights. [···]

93. In paragraph 3 of the operative part of the resolution the General Assembly '*Declares* that South Africa has failed to fulfil its obligations in respect of the administration of the Mandated Territory and to ensure the moral and material well-being and security of the indigenous inhabitants of South West Africa and has, in fact, disavowed the Mandate'. In paragraph 4 the decision is reached, as a consequence of the previous declaration 'that the Mandate conferred upon His Britannic Majesty to be exercised on his behalf by the Government of the Union of South Africa is *therefore* terminated ...'. (Emphasis added.) It is this part of the resolution which is relevant in the present proceedings.

94. In examining this action of the General Assembly it is appropriate to have regard to the general principles of international law regulating termination of a treaty relationship on account of breach. For even if the mandate is viewed as having the character of an institution, as is maintained, it depends on those international agreements which created the system and regulated its application. As the Court indicated in 1962 'this Mandate, like practically all other similar Mandates' was 'a special type of instrument composite in nature and instituting a novel international régime. It incorporates a definite agreement ...' (*I.C.J. Reports 1962*, p. 331). The Court stated conclusively in that Judgment that the Mandate '... in fact and in law, is an international agreement having the character of a treaty or convention' (*I.C.J. Reports 1962*, p. 330). The rules laid down by the Vienna Convention on the Law of Treaties concerning termination of a treaty relationship on account of breach (adopted without a dissenting vote) may in many respects be considered as a codification of existing customary law on the subject. In the light of these rules, only a material breach of a treaty justifies termination, such breach being defined as:

(a) a repudiation of the treaty not sanctioned by the present Convention; or

(b) the violation of a provision essential to the accomplishment of the object or purpose of the treaty' (Art. 60, para. 3).

95. General Assembly resolution 2145 (XXI) determines that both forms of material breach had occurred in this case. By stressing that South Africa 'has, in fact, disavowed the Mandate', the General Assembly declared in fact that it had repudiated it. The resolution in question is therefore to be viewed as the exercise of the right to terminate a relationship in case of a deliberate and persistent violation of obligations which destroys the very object and purpose of that relationship.

96. It has been contended that the Covenant of the League of Nations did not confer on the Council of the League power to terminate a mandate for misconduct of the mandatory and that no such power could therefore be exercised by the United Nations, since it could not derive from the League greater powers than the latter itself had. For this objection to prevail it would be necessary to show that the mandates system, as established under the League, excluded the application of the general principle of law that a right of termination on account of breach must be presumed to exist in respect of all treaties, except as regards provisions relating to the protection of the human person contained in treaties of a humanitarian character (as indicated in Art. 60, para. 5, of the Vienna Convention). The silence of a treaty as to the existence of such a right cannot be interpreted as implying the exclusion of a right which has its source outside of the treaty, in general international law, and is dependent on the occurrence of circumstances which are not normally envisaged when a treaty is concluded. [⋯]

101. It has been suggested that, even if the Council of the League had possessed the power of revocation of the Mandate in an extreme case, it could not have been exercised unilaterally but only in co-operation with the mandatory Power. However, revocation could only result from a situation in which the Mandatory had committed a serious breach of the obligations it had undertaken. To contend, on the basis of the principle of unanimity which applied in the League of Nations, that in this case revocation could only take place with the concurrence of the Mandatory, would not only run contrary to the general principle of law governing termination on account of breach, but also postulate an impossibility. For obvious reasons, the consent of the wrongdoer to such a form of termination cannot be required.

☑ 해　　설

　　이 사건과 관련해 ICJ는 유엔 총회의 요청으로 이미 3건의 권고적 의견을 부여한 바 있다(1950 ICJ Reports 128; 1955 ICJ Reports 67; 1956 ICJ Reports 23). 라이베리아와 에티오피아는 재판사건의 형식으로 남아공을 제소했으나, 청구국으로서의 법적 이해관계를 확립하지 못했다는 이유로 청구가 각하되었다(South-West Africa Cases(Second Phase), 1966 ICJ Reports 6).

　　본 권고적 의견에서 ICJ는 「조약법에 관한 비엔나 협약」(1969) 제60조의 내용이 관습국제법에 해당한다고 전제하고, 이에 비추어 남아공의 조약 위반이 위임통치협정을 종료시킬 사유에 해당한다고 판단했다. 1969년 비엔나 협약은 국가간의 조약을 전제로 했으나, 이후 1986년 채택된 「국제기구를 당사자로 하는 조약법에 관한 비엔나 협약」 제60조 역시 같은 내용을 규정하고 있다.

이어 ICJ는 1) 남아공 당국의 나미비아 계속 존속은 위법이므로 즉각 나미비아로부터 철수하고 이에 대한 지배를 종료할 것, 2) 모든 유엔 회원국은 나미비아에서의 남아공의 위법한 존재를 승인하지 말고, 이를 인정하는 것으로 비추어질 어떠한 행동도 삼가라는 의견을 제시했다. 그리고 남아공의 위임통치의 종료 및 나미비아 내 존속의 불법성은 대세적 성격을 지니므로 오든 국가에 대해 대항력을 갖는다고 보았다.

나미비아 사태에 대한 과거 5건의 ICJ 결정은 논리적으로 일관되지 못했다. 그 가장 큰 이유는 아마도 재판소 구성원과 국제정세의 변화에서 비롯되었을 것이다. 또한 남아공의 위임통치를 제도로 보느냐 조약으로 보느냐―어디에 중점을 두느냐에 따라 달라지기도 했다.

최종적으로 나미비아에 대한 남아공의 지배는 1989년 종식되었으며, 나미비아는 1990년 독립했다.

➡ 참고문헌 ─────────────────────────

- N. Hevener, The 1971 South—West Africa Opinion—A New International Judicial Philosophy, ICLQ Vol. 24(1975), p. 791.
- O. Lissitzyn, International Law and Advisory Opinion on Namibia, Columbia Journal of Transnational Law Vol. 11(1972), p. 50.
- A. Rovine, The World Court Opinion on Namibia, Columbia Journal of Transnational Law Vol. 11(1972), p. 203.
- A. Zuijdwijk, The International Court and South West Africa: Latest Phase, Georgia Journal of International Comparative Law Vol. 3(1973), p. 323.

8. 영국·아이슬란드간 어로관할권 사건(1973)
— 사정변경의 원칙

Fisheries Jurisdiction(Jurisdiction of the Court).
U.K. v. Iceland, 1973 ICJ Reports 3.

☑ 사　안

어업에 대한 경제의존도가 높은 아이슬란드는 항시 자국 주변의 배타적 어로수역을 확장하려고 노력했다. 영국과 아이슬란드는 교환공문의 형식으로 1961년 아이슬란드의 12해리 배타적 어업수역을 인정하는 대신 향후 그 이상의 수역확장에 따른 분쟁은 ICJ로 회부하기로 합의했다. 연안국의 해양 관할권 확대 추세에 따라 1972년 아이슬란드가 어업수역을 50해리로 확장하는 법령을 일방적으로 공포하자, 영국과 독일은 이 사건을 ICJ로 제소했다. 아이슬란드는 국제법상 사정변경의 원칙에 따라 1961년 교환공문은 종료되었으며, 따라서 자국은 ICJ의 재판관할권을 인정하지 않겠다고 통보했다. 실제로 아이슬란드는 ICJ에서의 소송절차에 불참했다. 아래 판결문은 선결적 항변에 따른 관할권 존부 판결로서 아이슬란드가 주장한 사정변경 원칙의 적용에 대한 판단부분이다.

☑ 쟁　점

1960년대 이후 어로기술의 발전이 기존 조약상의 분쟁해결조항을 종료시킬 정도의 근본적인 사정의 변경에 해당하는가 여부.

☑ 판　결

국제법상 근본적 사정변경이 조약 종료(중지)의 사유가 될 수도 있으나,

이 사건에서 아이슬란드가 주장하는 변화는 기존 조약상의 분쟁해결 의무조항을 종료시킬 정도로 급격한 사정변경에는 해당하지 않는다.

판 결 문

35. In his letter of 29 May 1972 to the Registrar, the Minister for Foreign Affairs of Iceland refers to "the changed circumstances resulting from the everincreasing exploitation of the fishery resources in the seas surrounding Iceland." [⋯]

36. In these statements the Government of Iceland is basing itself on the principle of termination of a treaty by reason of change of circumstances. International law admits that a fundamental change in the circumstances which determined the parties to accept a treaty, if it has resulted in a radical transformation of the extent of the obligations imposed by it, may, under certain conditions, afford the party affected a ground for invoking the termination or suspension of the treaty. This principle, and the conditions and exceptions to which it is subject, have been embodied in Article 62 of the Vienna Convention on the Law of Treaties, which may in many respects be considered as a codification of existing customary law on the subject of the termination of a treaty relationship on account of change of circumstances.

37. One of the basic requirements embodied in that Article is that the change of circumstances must have been a fundamental one. In this respect the Government of Iceland has, with regard to developments in fishing techniques, referred in an official publication on *Fisheries Jurisdiction in Iceland*, enclosed with the Foreign Minister's letter of 29 May 1972 to the Registrar, to the increased exploitation of the fishery resources in the seas surrounding Iceland and to the danger of still further exploitation because of an increase in the catching capacity of fishing fleets. The Icelandic statements recall the exceptional dependence of that country on its fishing for its existence and economic development. [⋯]

38. The invocation by Iceland of its "vital interests," which were not made the subject of an express reservation to the acceptance of the jurisdictional obligation under the 1961 Exchange of Notes, must be interpreted, in the context of the assertion of changed circumstances, as an indication by Iceland of the reason why it regards as fundamental the changes which in its view have taken place in previously existing fishing techniques. This interpretation would correspond to the traditional view that the changes of circumstances which must be regarded as fundamental or vital are those which imperil the existence or vital development of one of the parties. [...]1)

40. The Court, at the present stage of the proceedings, does not need to pronounce on this question of fact, as to which there appears to be a serious divergence of views between the two Governments. If, as contended by Iceland, there have been any fundamental changes in fishing techniques in the waters around Iceland, those changes might be relevant for the decision on the merits of the dispute, and the Court might need to examine the contention at that stage, together with any other arguments that Iceland might advance in support of the validity of the extension of its fisheries jurisdiction beyond what was agreed to in the 1961 Exchange of Notes. But the alleged changes could not affect in the least the obligation to submit to the Court's jurisdiction, which is the only issue at the present stage of the proceedings. It follows that the apprehended dangers for the vital interests of Iceland, resulting from changes in fishing techniques, cannot constitute a fundamental change with respect to the lapse or subsistence of the compromissory clause establishing the Court's jurisdiction. [...]

43. Moreover, in order that a change of circumstances may give rise to a ground for invoking the termination of a treaty it is also necessary that it should have resulted in a radical transformation of the extent of the obligations still to be performed. The change must have increased the burden of the obligations to be executed to the extent of rendering the performance something essentially different from that originally undertaken. In respect of the obligation with which the Court is here concerned, this condition is wholly unsatisfied; the change of circumstances alleged by Iceland cannot be said to have transformed radically the extent of the jurisdictional obligation which is imposed in the 1961 Exchange of Notes. The compromissory clause enabled either of the parties to submit to the Court any dispute between them relating to an extension of Icelandic fisheries jurisdiction in the waters above its continental shelf beyond the 12-mile limit. The present dispute is exactly of the character anticipated in the compromissory clause of the Exchange of Notes. Not only has the jurisdictional obligation not been radically transformed in its extent; it has remained precisely what it was in 1961.

44. In the United Kingdom Memorial it is asserted that there is a flaw in the

---

1) 이에 대해 영국은 어로기술의 변화와 발전이 아이슬란드가 주장하는 결과를 가져오지 않았으며, 따라서 '근본적이거나 중요한 변화'는 없었다고 주장했다. 특히 1960년대 이래 연간 어획고가 크게 변하지 않았음을 지적했다.

Icelandic contention of change of circumstances: that the doctrine never operates so as to extinguish a treaty automatically or to allow an unchallengeable unilateral denunciation by one party; it only operates to confer a right to call for termination and, if that call is disputed, to submit the dispute to some organ or body with power to determine whether the conditions for the operation of the doctrine are present. In this connection the Applicant alludes to Articles 65 and 66 of the Vienna Convention on the Law of Treaties. Those Articles provide that where the parties to a treaty have failed within 12 months to achieve a settlement of a dispute by the means indicated in Article 33 of the United Nations Charter (which means include reference to judicial settlement) any one of the parties may submit the dispute to the procedure for conciliation provided in the Annex to the Convention.

45. In the present case, the procedural complement to the doctrine of changed circumstances is already provided for in the 1961 Exchange of Notes, which specifically calls upon the parties to have recourse to the Court in the event of a dispute relating to Iceland's extension of fisheries jurisdiction.

☑ 해   설

이 판결은 본안에 대한 결정이 아니라, ICJ의 관할권 성립 여부에 대한 판단이었다. 판결에서 아이슬란드의 사정변경원칙 적용은 수락되지 않았다. 조약법에 관한 비엔나 협약 제62조는 사정변경에 관해 다음과 같이 규정하고 있었는데, 아직 조약으로서 발효되기 이전이었지만 기본적으로는 같은 기준에서 판단되었다.

제62조(사정의 근본적 변경)

① 조약의 체결 당시에 존재한 사정에 관하여 발생하였으며 또한 당사국에 의하여 예견되지 아니한 사정의 근본적 변경은, 다음 경우에 해당되지 아니하는 한, 조약을 종료시키거나 또는 탈퇴하기 위한 사유로서 원용될 수 없다.

(a) 그러한 사정의 존재가 그 조약에 대한 당사국의 기속적 동의의 본질적 기초를 구성하였으며, 또한

(b) 그 조약에 따라 계속 이행되어야 할 의무의 범위를 그 변경의 효과가 급격하게 변환시키는 경우.

② 사정의 근본적 변경은, 다음의 경우에는 조약을 종료시키거나 또는 탈퇴하는 사유로서 원용될 수 없다.

(a) 그 조약이 경계선을 확정하는 경우, 또는

(b) 근본적 변경이 이를 원용하는 당사국에 의한 조약상의 의무나 또는 그 조약의 다른 당사국에 대하여 지고 있는 기타의 국제적 의무의 위반의 결과인 경우.

③ 상기의 제 조항에 따라 당사국이 조약을 종료시키거나 또는 탈퇴하기 위한 사유로서 사정의 근본적 변경을 원용할 수 있는 경우에, 그 당사국은 그 조약의 시행을 정지시키기 위한 사유로서 그 변경을 또한 원용할 수 있다.

ICJ는 어로기술의 발전과 어로채취의 증대가 아이슬란드에게 근본적이거나 사활적 변화를 야기했는지 여부는 본안에서 판단할 문제라고 판단하고, 아이슬란드가 주장하는 사정변경이 1961년 교환공문상의 분쟁해결의무까지 종료시킨다고는 보지 않았다. 즉 당시 제기된 분쟁은 바로 교환공문이 예상한 그러한 사안이라고 평가하여 아이슬란드의 선결적 항변을 배척했다.

이 판결에 이은 1974년의 본안판결(1974 ICJ Reports 3)에서 ICJ는 12해리 이내에서만의 연안국의 우선권을 인정하고, 12해리 이원수역에서는 타국의 기득권이 보호되어야 한다고 강조했다. 그러나 아이슬란드는 1975년 오히려 기왕의 50해리를 더욱 확장하는 200해리 어업수역을 선언했다. 당시 유엔 해양법협약 회의에서는 200해리 배타적 경제수역을 인정하는 방향으로 협상이 진행되고 있었다. 1961년의 합의에 아이슬란드를 묶어 두기에는 현실이 반대방향으로 발전하고 있었다. 결국 아이슬란드 인근의 어로분쟁은 당사국 간 타협으로 마무리되었다.

➡ 참고문헌 ─────────────────────────────

- R. Bilder, The Anglo-Icelandic Fisheries Dispute, Wisconsin Law Review Vol. 37(1973), p. 37.
- R. Churchill, Fisheries Jurisdiction Case, ICLQ Vol. 24(1975), p. 82.
- S. Katz, Issues Arising in the Icelandic Fisheries Case, ICLQ Vol. 22(1973), p. 83.

제 8 장

국가의 대외기관

1. 비호권 사건(1950)
— 외교공관의 불가침과 외교적 비호권

Asylum Case.
Colombia v. Peru, 1950 ICJ Reports 266.

☑ 사　안

1948년 페루의 정치지도자인 Haya de la Torre는 정권 탈취를 목적으로 수도인 리마에서 군사 쿠데타를 시도했다. 그러나 쿠데타는 곧 실패했고 그는 평소에 친분이 있던 주페루 콜롬비아 대사의 도움을 얻고자 리마 주재 콜롬비아 대사관으로 피신했다. 이에 페루 정부는 Haya de la Torre의 인도를 콜롬비아 대사관에 요청했으나 콜롬비아 대사관은 외교적 비호권(right of diplomatic asylum)을 내세워 인도를 거부했다. 콜롬비아는 최소한 남미지역에 적용되는 지역 관습국제법상 각국의 외교공관은 외교적 비호를 부여할 권리가 있기 때문에 페루 주재 콜롬비아 대사관도 Haya de la Torre에 대해 정당하게 외교적 비호를 부여했다고 주장했다. 나아가 콜롬비아가 그의 안전한 국외 이송을 위한 안도권(safe conduct)[1]까지 페루에 요구하자 양국간 분쟁이 발생했다.

☑ 쟁　점

(1) 외교공관에 대한 일반적인 외교적 비호권이 인정되는지 여부.

(2) 특히 이러한 외교적 비호권을 인정하는 조약 또는 남미 지역의 관습국제법이 존재하는지 여부.

---

1) 군사작전지역이나 타국 영역 통과를 허락하는 일종의 안전통행증.

☑ 판 결

(1) 영토적 비호권과는 달리 외교공관에 대한 일반적인 외교적 비호권은 인정되지 않는다.

(2) 또한 외교공관의 외교적 비호권을 인정하는 조약 또는 남미 지역의 관습국제법은 존재하지 않는다. 이 부분에 관한 남미 국가간 상충하는 관행으로 볼 때 남미 지역에 이러한 관습국제법이 존재한다고 볼 수 없다.

판 결 문

(p. 272-) [⋯] On October 3rd, 1948, a military rebellion broke out in Peru. It was suppressed on the same day and investigations were at once opened.

On October 4th, the President of the Republic issued a decree in the recitals of which a political party, the American People's Revolutionary Alliance, was charged with having organized and directed the rebellion. [⋯]

On October 5th, the Minister of the Interior addressed to the Minister for the Navy a "note of denunciation" against the leader of the American People's Revolutionary Alliance, Victor Raul Haya de la Torre, and other members of the party as responsible for the rebellion. [⋯]

(p. 273) On January 3rd, 1949, Haya de la Torre sought asylum in the Colombian Embassy in Lima. On the next day, the Colombian Ambassador sent the following note to the Peruvian Minister for Foreign Affairs and Public Worship:

"I have the honour to inform Your Excellency, in accordance with what is provided in Article 2, paragraph 2 of the Convention on Asylum signed by our two countries in the city of Havana in the year 1928, that Senor Victor Raul Haya de la Torre has been given asylum at the seat of this mission as from 9 p.m. yesterday.

In view of the foregoing, and in view of the desire of this Embassy that Senor Haya de la Torre should leave Peru as early as possible, I request Your Excellency to be good enough to give orders for the requisite safeconduct to be issued, so that Senor Haya de la Torre may leave the country with the usual facilities attaching to the right of diplomatic asylum."

On January 14th, the Ambassador sent to the Minister a further note as follows:

"Pursuant to instructions received from the Chancellery of my country, I have the honour to inform Your Excellency that the Government of Colombia, in accordance with the right conferred upon it by Article 2 of the Convention on Political Asylum signed by our two countries in the city of Montevideo on December 26th, 1933, has qualified Senor Victor Raul Haya de la Torre as a political refugee."

(p. 274) [⋯] The written and oral arguments submitted on behalf of that Government[2] show that its claim must be understood in the sense that Colombia, as the State granting asylum, is competent to qualify the nature of the offence by a unilateral and definitive decision binding on Peru. Colombia has based this submission partly on rules resulting from agreement, partly on an alleged custom.

[⋯]

In the case of diplomatic asylum, the refugee is within the territory of the State where the offence was committed. A decision to grant diplomatic asylum involves a derogation from the (p. 275) sovereignty of that State. It withdraws the offender from the jurisdiction of the territorial State and constitutes an intervention in matters which are exclusively within the competence of that State. Such a derogation from territorial sovereignty cannot be recognized unless its legal basis is established in each particular case.

[⋯]

(p. 276) The Colombian Government has finally invoked "American international law in general." In addition to the rules arising from agreements which have already been considered, it has relied on an alleged regional or local custom peculiar to Latin-American States.

The Party which relies on a custom of this kind must prove that this custom is established in such a manner that it has become binding on the other Party. The Colombian Government must prove that the rule invoked by it is in accordance with a constant and uniform usage practised by the States in question, and that this usage is the expression of a right appertaining to the State granting asylum and a duty incumbent on the territorial State. This follows from Article 38 of the Statute of the Court, which refers to (p. 277) international custom "as evidence of a general practice accepted as law."

---

2) 콜롬비아 정부를 의미함.

[⋯] The facts brought to the knowledge of the Court disclose so much uncertainty and contradiction, so much fluctuation and discrepancy in the exercise of diplomatic asylum and in the official views expressed on various occasions, there has been so much inconsistency in the rapid succession of conventions on asylum, ratified by some States and rejected by others, and the practice has been so much influenced by considerations of political expediency in the various cases, that it is not possible to discern in all this any constant and uniform usage, accepted as law, with regard to the alleged rule of unilateral and definitive qualification of the offence.

The Court cannot therefore find that the Colombian Government has proved the existence of such a custom. But even if it could be supposed that such a custom existed between certain Latin-American States only, it could not be invoked against Peru which, far (p. 278) from having by its attitude adhered to it, has, on the contrary, repudiated it by refraining from ratifying the Montevideo Conventions of 1933 and 1939. [⋯]

For these reasons, the Court has arrived at the conclusion that Colombia, as the State granting asylum, is not competent to qualify the offence by a unilateral and definitive decision, binding on Peru. [⋯]

(p. 283) [⋯] It has not been contended by the Government of Colombia that Haya de la Torre was in such a situation at the time when he sought refuge in the Colombian Embassy at Lima. At that time, three months had elapsed since the military rebellion. This long interval gives the present case a very special character. During those three months, Haya de la Torre had apparently been in hiding in the country, refusing to obey the summons to appear of the legal authorities which was published on November 16th/18th, 1948, and refraining from seeking asylum in the foreign embassies where several of his co-accused had found refuge before these dates. [⋯]

(p. 284) [⋯] In principle, therefore, asylum cannot be opposed to the operation of justice. An exception to this rule can occur only if, in the guise of justice, arbitrary action is substituted for the rule of law. Such would be the case if the administration of justice were corrupted by measures clearly prompted by political aims. Asylum protects the political offender against any measures of a manifestly extra-legal character which a government might take or attempt to take against its political opponents. The word "safety," which in Article 2, paragraph 2, determines the specific effect of asylum granted to political offenders, means that the refugee is protected against arbitrary action by the government, and that he enjoys the benefits of the law. On the other hand, the safety which arises out of asylum cannot be construed as a protection against the regular application of the laws and against the jurisdiction of legally constituted tribunals. Protection thus understood would authorize the diplomatic agent to obstruct the application of the laws of the country whereas it is his duty to respect them; it would in fact become the equivalent of an immunity, which was evidently not within the intentions of the draftsmen of the Havana Convention. [⋯]

☑ 해   설

이 판결의 의의는 과거 외교공관에 대해 치외법권이 인정되던 시절에 존재하던 외교적 비호권 개념이 더 이상 적용되지 않음을 공식적으로 확인한 것이다. 따라서 이제 외교공관은 외교적 비호권을 향유하지 않고 외교공관으로서 불가침권만을 향유한다. 불가침권의 당연한 귀결로 주재국 관헌이 파견국 공관장의 허락 없이 외교공관 영내로 진입할 수 없으므로 마치 외관상으로는 외교적 비호권이 인정되는 것과 유사하다고 할 수 있으나 양자간에는 엄연한 차이가 있다. 치외법권 개념에 기초한 외교적 비호권은 주재국의 입법관할권 자체가 외교공관에는 적용되지 않는 것으로 간주한다. 이에 반해 현재 인정되는 외교공관의 불가침권은 입법관할권의 존재 및 적용은 인정하되 다만 외교관 및 그 공관에 대해 주재국 집행관할권의 적용을 면제하는 것에 불과하다.

외교공관의 불가침권이 적용되는 사례로는 최근 중국 등지에서 해당국에 주재하는 외국 대사관 영역 내로 진입하는 탈북자들의 경우를 들 수 있다. 이들 대사관이 향유하는 외교공관의 불가침권으로 인해 해당국 관헌은 대사관 영내로 진입하여 탈북자를 체포할 수 없다. 결국 해당국과 대사관 파견국간 정치적 타협을 통해 탈북자들은 한국 또는 제3국으로 이송되고 있다. 이 경우 탈북자들이 자신들의 최종 목적지에 도착할 수 있다는 점에서 외관상 마치 이들 대사관들이 치외법권적 지위를 누리고 또 외교적 비호권을 향유하는 것으로 보일 수도 있다. 그러나 이는 외교공관 불가침권 적용의 궁극적 결과물일 뿐이다.

나아가 이 판결은 외교공관의 불가침권을 포함하여 외교관의 특권·면제를 인정하는 근거로 원활한 외교관의 업무활동 보장을 제시하고 있다. 이는 향후 "기능주의"적 입장에 기초한 외교관의 특권·면제 관련 국제법 법리 발전에 중요한 영향을 미친 것으로 평가할 수 있고, 1961년 외교관계에 관한 비엔나 협약의 채택에도 큰 영향을 끼쳤다.

한편, 콜롬비아와 페루간 첨예한 분쟁을 초래한 Torre는 콜롬비아 대사관 영내에서 5년간 은거하다 양국간 정치적 타협으로 파리로 망명함으로써 이 사건은 종결되었다. 이후 Torre는 1962년 페루로 귀국하여 정치활동을 재개했다. 그는 1962년 실시된 대통령 선거에 출마하여 다수득표를 했으나 당선에 필요한 전체 투표자의 1/3의 지지를 얻는 데는 근소한 차이로 실패했다. 1년 뒤 실시된 재선거에서 그는 다시 대통령 후보로 출마했으나 역시 낙선했다. 대통령 선거 낙선에도 불구하고 그의 정당은 계속적인 대중의 지지를 받았으며, Torre는 페루 헌법제정위원회 위원장으로 활동하던 중 1979년 84세의 나이로 사망했다.

▶▶ 참고문헌

- 백충현, 영토적비호에 관한 고찰, 국제법학회논총 제26권 제2호(1982), p. 113.
- J. L. F. van Essen, Some Reflections on the Judgments of the International Court of Justice in the Asylum and Haya de la Torre Cases, International & Comparative Law Quarterly Vol. 1(1952), p. 533.
- A. E. Evans, The Colombian−Peruvian Asylum Case: The Practice of Diplomatic Asylum, American Political Science Review Vol. 46(1952), p. 142.
- G. S. Goodwin−Gill, Asylum(Colombia v. Peru), 1949 and request for interpretation of the judgment of 20 November 1950 in the Asylum Case (Colombia v. Peru), 1950 in Latin America and the International Court of Justice(eds.), Routledge(2017), p. 170.

2. 테헤란 주재 미 외교관 인질 사건(1980)
— 외교관 및 외교공관의 불가침권

United States Diplomatic and Consular Staff in Tehran.
United States of America v. Iran, 1980 ICJ Reports 3.

☑ 사　안

　　1979년 이란 혁명 과정에서 이란 무장 시위대가 테헤란 주재 미국 대사관에 난입해 미국 외교관 및 영사를 1년 이상 인질로 억류한 사건이 발생했다. 1979년 이슬람 최고 지도자인 호메이니를 추종하는 세력이 주도한 반정부 시위로 인해 수십 년 집권 기간 동안 친미 노선을 견지한 이란의 팔레비 국왕은 하야하고 미국으로 망명했다. 미국이 팔레비 국왕의 망명신청을 허용하자 이에 반발한 이란 시위대가 테헤란 주재 미국 대사관에 난입하여 미국 외교관 등 60여 명을 억류한 것이다. 이 과정에서 일부 미대사관 직원은 피살되었다. 이는 외교관의 특권·면제에 대한 극단적인 침해 사례로 볼 수 있다. 이 사건은 수십 년간 집권한 팔레비 왕조에 대한 미국의 지원에 불만을 품은 이란 국민들이 극단적인 방법으로 반미감정을 표출한 것이다. 이란 시위대는 미국이 팔레비 국왕을 즉각 이란으로 송환하고 그간의 내정간섭에 대해 사과하지 않으면 인질들을 석방하지 않겠다는 입장을 견지하며 미국과 대치했다. 대사관을 점거한 것은 민간 시위대였으나 이 과정에서 이란 정부는 시위대의 침입·점거 행위를 묵인 내지 방조했다. 미국은 이러한 이란의 행위가 외교관의 특권·면제 및 외교공관의 불가침권을 침해한다는 점을 주장하며 이란을 ICJ에 제소했다. 그러나 이란은 ICJ재판절차에 참여를 거부했으며 ICJ는 이란의 불참하에 재판을 진행했다.

☑ 쟁 점

(1) 이란 정부는 1961년 외교관계에 관한 비엔나 협약 및 1963년 영사관계에 관한 비엔나 협약의 규정에 따라 자국 주재 미국 외교관을 보호하기 위해 필요한 조치를 취했는지 여부.

(2) 파견국 정부의 지속적인 불법행위에 대한 대응 수단으로 파견국 외교관에 대한 억류가 정당화되는지 여부.

☑ 판 결

(1) 시위대의 대사관 난입과 관련, 미국 정부와 외교관의 지속적인 보호 및 지원 요청에도 불구하고 이란 정부가 적절한 보호 및 지원을 실시하지 않은 것은 부작위에 의한 1961년 비엔나 협약 및 1963년 비엔나 협약에 대한 위반에 해당한다.

(2) 과거 미국의 불법행위로 인해 이러한 사태가 초래되었더라도 이란 정부가 미국 외교관에 대해 취할 수 있는 유일한 합법적인 대응 수단은 기피인물(*persona non grata*)로 선언하여 퇴거를 요청하는 것뿐이다. 따라서 과거 불법행위 혐의를 이유로 한 이란 정부의 미국 외교관 불법 억류는 정당화되지 않는다.

판 결 문

18. During the three hours or more of the assault, repeated calls for help were made from the Embassy to the Iranian Foreign Ministry, and repeated efforts to secure help from the Iranian authorities were also made through direct discussions by the United States Chargé d'affaires,[1] who was at the Foreign Ministry at the time, together with two other members of the mission. From there he made contact with the Prime Minister's Office and with Foreign Ministry officials. A request was also made to the Iranian Chargé d'affaires in Washington for assistance in putting an end to the seizure of the Embassy. Despite these repeated requests, no Iranian security forces were sent in time to provide relief and protection to the Embassy.

---

1) 대사대리.

[···]

22. The persons still held hostage in Iran include, according to the information furnished to the Court by the United States, at least 28 persons having the status, duly recognized by the Government of Iran, of "member of the diplomatic staff" within the meaning of the Vienna Convention on Diplomatic Relations of 1961. [···]

24. Those archives and documents of the United States Embassy which were not destroyed by the staff during the attack on 4 November have been ransacked by the militants. Documents purporting to come from this source have been disseminated by the militants and by the Government-controlled media. [···]

33. It is to be regretted that the Iranian Government has not appeared before the Court in order to put forward its arguments on the questions of law and of fact which arise in the present case; and that, in consequence, the Court has not had the assistance it might have derived from such arguments or from any evidence adduced in support of them. [···]

34. The Iranian Government in its letter of 9 December 1979 drew attention to what it referred to as the "deep rootedness and the essential character of the Islamic Revolution of Iran, a revolution of a whole oppressed nation against its oppressors and their masters." The examination of the "numerous repercussions" of the revolution, it added, is "a matter essentially and directly within the national sovereignty of Iran." However, as the Court pointed out in its Order of 15 December 1979,

> "a dispute which concerns diplomatic and consular premises and the detention of internationally protected persons, and involves the interpretation or application of multilateral conventions codifying the international law governing diplomatic and consular relations, is one which by its very nature falls within international jurisdiction." [···]

In its later letter of 16 March 1980 the Government of Iran confined itself to repeating the observations on this point which it had made in its letter of 9 December 1979, without putting forward any additional arguments or explanations. In these circumstances, the Court finds it sufficient here to recall and confirm its previous statement on the matter in its Order of 15 December 1979.

[···]

58. No suggestion has been made that the militants, when they executed their attack on the Embassy, had any form of official status as recognized "agents" or organs of the Iranian State. Their conduct in mounting the attack, overrunning the Embassy and seizing its inmates as hostages cannot, therefore, be regarded as imputable to that State on that basis. [⋯]

61. The conclusion just reached by the Court, that the initiation of the attack on the United States Embassy on 4 November 1979, and of the attacks on the Consulates at Tabriz and Shiraz the following day, cannot be considered as in itself imputable to the Iranian State does not mean that Iran is, in consequence, free of any responsibility in regard to those attacks; for its own conduct was in conflict with its international obligations. By a number of provisions of the Vienna Conventions of 1961 and 1963, Iran was placed under the most categorical obligations, as a receiving State, to take appropriate steps to ensure the protection of the United States Embassy and Consulates, their staffs, their archives, their means of communication and the freedom of movement of the members of their staffs.

62. Thus, after solemnly proclaiming the inviolability of the premises of a diplomatic mission, Article 22 of the 1961 Convention continues in paragraph 2:

> "*The receiving State is under a special duty to take all appropriate steps to protect the premises of the mission against any* intrusion or damage and to prevent any disturbance of the peace of the mission or impairment of its dignity." (Emphasis added.)

So, too, after proclaiming that the person of a diplomatic agent shall be inviolable, and that he shall not be liable to any form of arrest or detention, Article 29 provides:

> "The receiving State shall treat him with due respect and *shall take all appropriate steps to prevent any attack on his person, freedom or dignity*."(Emphasis added.)

The obligation of a receiving State to protect the inviolability of the archives and documents of a diplomatic mission is laid down in Article 24, which specifically provides that they are to be "inviolable at any time and wherever they may be. Under Article 25 it is required to "accord full facilities for the performance of the functions of the mission," under Article 26 to "ensure to all members of the mission freedom of movement and travel in its territory," and under Article 27 to "permit and protect free communication on the part of the mission for all official purposes." [⋯] In the view of the Court, the obligations of the Iranian Government here in question are not merely contractual obligations established by the Vienna Conventions of 1961 and 1963, but also obligations under general international law.

63. The facts set out in paragraphs 14 to 27 above establish to the satisfaction of the Court that on 4 November 1979 the Iranian Government failed altogether to take any "appropriate steps" to protect the premises, staff and archives of the United States' mission against attack by the militants, and to take any steps either to prevent this attack or to stop it before it reached its completion. [⋯]

64. The total inaction of the Iranian authorities on that date in face of urgent and repeated requests for help contrasts very sharply with its conduct on several other occasions of a similar kind. [⋯]

67. This inaction of the Iranian Government by itself constituted clear and serious violation of Iran's obligations to the United States under the provisions of Article 22, paragraph 2, and Articles 24, 25, 26, 27 and 29 of the 1961 Vienna Convention on Diplomatic Relations, and Articles 5 and 36 of the 1963 Vienna Convention on Consular Relations. [⋯].

76. The Iranian authorities'decision to continue the subjection of the premises of the United States Embassy to occupation by militants and of the Embassy staff to detention as hostages, clearly gave rise to repeated and multiple breaches of the applicable provisions of the Vienna Conventions even more serious than those which arose from their failure to take any steps to prevent the attacks on the inviolability of these premises and staff. [⋯]

85. Thus, it is for the very purpose of providing a remedy for such possible abuses of diplomatic functions that Article 9 of the 1961 Convention on Diplomatic Relations stipulates :

"1. The receiving State may at any time and without having to explain its decision, notify the sending State that the head of the mission or any member of the diplomatic staff of the mission is *persona non grata* or that any other member of the staff of the mission is not acceptable. In any such case, the sending State shall, as appropriate, either recall the person concerned or terminate his functions with the mission. A person may be declared *non grata* or not acceptable before arriving in the territory of the receiving State.

2. If the sending State refuses or fails within a reasonable period to carry out its obligations under paragraph 1 of this Article, the receiving State may refuse to recognize the person concerned as a member of the mission."

[⋯] The way in which Article 9, paragraph 1, takes account of any such difficulty is by providing expressly in its opening sentence that the receiving State may "at any time and without having to explain its decision"notify the sending State that any particular member of its diplomatic mission is *persona non grata*"or "not acceptable" (and similarly Article 23, paragraph 4, of the 1963 Convention provides that "the receiving State is not obliged to give to the sending State reasons for its decision"). Beyond that remedy for dealing with abuses of the diplomatic function by individual members of a mission, a receiving State has in its hands a more radical remedy if abuses of their functions by members of a mission reach serious proportions. This is the power which every receiving State has, at its own discretion, to break off diplomatic relations with a sending State and to call for the immediate closure of the offending mission. [···]

87. [···] The Iranian Government did not, therefore, employ the remedies placed at its disposal by diplomatic law specifically for dealing with activities of the kind of which it now complains. Instead, it allowed a group of militants to attack and occupy the United States Embassy by force, and to seize the diplomatic and consular staff as hostages; instead, it has endorsed that action of those militants and has deliberately maintained their occupation of the Embassy and detention of its staff as a means of coercing the sending State. It has, at the same time, refused altogether to discuss this situation with representatives of the United States. The Court, therefore, can only conclude that Iran did not have recourse to the normal and efficacious means at its disposal, but resorted to coercive action against the United States Embassy and its staff. [···]

☑ 해   설

이 사건의 의의는 외국 대사관의 무단 점거와 외교관의 인질억류 사태를 통해 외교공관의 불가침권을 포함하는 외교관의 특권·면제에 관한 국제법 법리를 확인한 것이다. 특히 ICJ는 이유 여하를 불문하고 자국 주재 외국 외교관에 대한 불만을 표출하는 방법은 해당 외교관을 '기피인물'로 선언하여 퇴거를 요청하는 조치밖에 없음을 확인했다. 정치·외교적 이유로 외교관에 대한 위해 행위를 정당화할 수 없다는 것이다. 또한 주재국 관헌들이 자국 시위대로부터 외교공관을 보호하지 못한 경우 부작위에 의한 국가책임을 부담한다는 점 역시 확인했다. 각국 정부가 자국 소재 외국 외교공관의 보호 및 경비에 최선을 다해야 하는 법적 의무가 여기에 있는 것이다. 이 판결은 주로 1961년 비엔나 협약과 1963년 비엔나 협약에 기초하여 심리가 이루어졌으나 나아가 ICJ가 외교관의 특권·면제를 국제법상 일반원칙의 하나로 파악한 것은 주목할 만하다.

한편 당시 미국의 카터 대통령은 이란 내 미국 인질들을 구출하고자 1980년 4월 24일 미군 특수부대를 투입하여 군사작전을 실시했으나 이들을 수송하던 헬기의 추락으로 구출작전은 실패했다. 미국은 추후 유엔 안전보장이사회에 이 구출작전 관련 내용을 통보하며 이 작전이 주권국가로서 자국이 고유하게 보유하는 자위권 행사의 일환임을 주장했다. 인질로 구금된 52명의 미국 대사관 직원들은 양국간 협상 결과 레이건 행정부 출범 직전인 1981년 1월 20일 모두 석방되었다. 한편, 이 사태로 촉발된 양국간 국교단절과 이란 내 미국 자산에 대한 이란 정부의 수용조치로 인한 재산권 분쟁을 해결하고자 양국은 미국－이란 중재재판소(U.S.－Iran Claims Tribunal)를 설치했다.

2011년에도 테헤란에서는 본 사건을 연상시키는 또 다른 사건이 발생했다. 영국 정부가 핵개발 의혹을 받는 이란에 대한 추가 제재조치로 자국 금융기관과 이란 금융기관간의 모든 거래를 전면 중단하자 이에 반발한 이란 청년들이 2011년 11월 29일 테헤란 주재 영국 대사관을 습격한 것이다. 이란 정부는 이 사건에 유감을 표하며 당국이 즉시 조사에 들어갈 것이라고 밝혔으나, 영국 정부는 런던 주재 이란 대사관을 폐쇄하고 이란 대사를 포함한 모든 외교관에 대해 출국을 명령하는 것으로 대응했다.

이란과 서방국가와의 오랜 갈등은 2015년 7월 14일 이란과 P5＋1(UN 안보리 5개 상임이사국 및 독일)가 이란 핵개발 프로그램 폐기를 위한 최종 합의문인 '포괄적 공동행동계획(Joint Comprehensive Plan of Action: JCPOA)'에 합의함으로써 해소되는 듯 보였다. 이 합의에 따라 2016년 1월 16일 미국과 EU 등은 이란에 대한 경제제재를 해제했고 이란은 국제경제체제로 다시 복귀했으나 이 화해 움직임은 오래 지속되지 못했다. 2017년 1월 20일 미국 트럼프 행정부 출범 이후 양국 관계는 다시 긴장 상태에 빠졌다. 2018년 5월 8일 트럼프 행정부는 '포괄적 공동행동계획'에서 탈퇴하며 이란에 대한 경제제재를 다시 부과함으로써 양국 갈등은 재점화되어 2020년 7월 현재까지 이어지고 있다. 미국의 압박에 맞서 이란은 미국의 경제제재 조치가 양국이 체결한 1955년 영사우호조약을 위반했음을 주장하며 2건에 걸쳐 미국을 ICJ에

제소하여 현재 소송이 진행 중이다.[2]

한편 테헤란 주재 미 외교관 인질 사건에서 미국이 이란을 ICJ에 제소한 관할권의 근거는 비엔나 협약의 선택의정서 제1조로 한국도 이 선택의정서의 당사국이다. 이는 한국에서 이 선택의정서 당사국 소속 대사관의 불가침권 보호 문제와 관련된 법적 분쟁이 혹시라도 발생할 경우 한국이 ICJ에 제소될 수 있음을 의미한다.

➡ 참고문헌 ─────────────────────────────

- 전순신, 테헤란주재 미국외교직원 및 영사관계 직원에 관한 사건, 동아법학 제9호(1989), p. 279.
- L. Gross, The Case Concerning United States Diplomatic and Consular Staff in Tehran: Phase of Provisional Measures, American Journal of International Law Vol. 74(1980), p. 395.
- A. Rafat, The Iran Hostage Crisis and the International Court of Justice: Aspects of the Case Concerning United States Diplomatic and Consular Staff in Tehran, Denver Journal of International Law and Policy Vol. 10(1980), p. 425.
- G. T. McLaughlin and L. A. Teklaff, The Iranian Hostage Agreements: A Legal Analysis, Fordham International Law Journal Vol. 4(1980), p. 223.
- D. P. Houghton, US Foreign Policy and the Iran Hostage Crisis, Cambridge University Press(2001).

─────────────

2) 이 두 건은 2016년 6월 이란이 미국을 제소한 *Certain Iranian Assets* 사건 및 2018년 7월 이란이 미국을 제소한 *Alleged Violations of the 1955 Treaty of Amity Economic Relations, and Consular Rights* 사건이다.

3. 콩고 외교장관 체포영장 발부(2000)
— 외교장관의 대외기관성

Case Concerning the Arrest Warrant of 11 April 2000.
Democratic Republic of the Congo v. Belgium, 2002 ICJ Reports 3.

☑ 사   안

2000년 당시 콩고 외교장관으로 재직 중이던 Abdoulaye Yerodia Ndom-basi는 1998년 8월 일련의 종족 간 차별 조장 발언을 통해 콩고내 종족간 분쟁을 촉발하는 등 콩고 내전 악화에 중요한 역할을 했다. 한편, 벨기에는 과거 자국 식민지였던 아프리카 국가들에서 발생한 전쟁범죄 및 집단학살 등을 방지하기 위한 조치를 제대로 취하지 못했다는 판단 아래 1993년 6월 16일 새로운 국내법을 제정했다. 이 법은 장소와 국적을 불문하고 전쟁범죄, 반인도범죄, 집단학살 등에 대해 벨기에 법원이 관할권을 갖는다고 규정하여 보편주의 관할권을 구체적으로 규정했다. 콩고 내전중 심각한 인권침해를 당한 피해자의 제소로 시작된 이 사건을 담당한 벨기에 판사는 Yerodia의 행위가 새로 도입된 벨기에 국내법을 위반했음을 이유로 2000년 4월 11일 동인에 대한 국제체포영장을 발부했다. 즉, Yerodia에 대해 국제재판소를 통한 처벌이 아닌 벨기에 국내법상 관할권 조항을 통한 국내적 처벌을 시도한 것이다. 벨기에의 체포영장은 콩고 정부에 전달되었고 인터폴에도 통보되었다. Yerodia의 행위는 벨기에 영토에서 발생한 것이 아니며 그가 벨기에 시민권자가 아니었기에 콩고 정부는 이러한 체포영장 발부에 반발했다. 특히 콩고는 자국 외교장관에 대한 국제체포영장의 발부는 관습국제법상 외교장관에 부여되는 특권·면제에 대한 위반임을 주장하며 벨기에를 ICJ에 제소했다.

☑ 쟁   점

(1) 일국의 현직 외교장관에 대한 타국의 형사상 소추가 허용되는지 여부.

(2) 일국 외교장관에 대한 타국의 국제체포영장의 발부가 국제법 위반에 해당하는지 여부.

☑ 판   결

(1) 일국 외교장관이 동 직책 재직중 수행하는 일체의 행위는 공식적 행위, 개인적 행위를 불문하고 관습국제법상 특권·면제의 적용 대상으로 타국 법원의 형사소추로부터 면제된다.

(2) 타국의 현직 외교장관에 대한 국제체포영장 발부와 국제사회 회람은 해당 외교장관의 특권·면제를 침해하기 위한 의도로 시도된 것으로 국제법 을 위반한다.

판 결 문

21. Although the Application of the Congo originally advanced two separate legal grounds ... , the submissions of the Congo in its Memorial and the final submissions which it presented at the end of the oral proceedings refer only to a violation "in regard to the ... Congo of the rule of customary international law concerning the absolute inviolability and immunity from criminal process of incumbent foreign ministers" ...

47. The Congo maintains that, during his or her term of office, a Minister for Foreign Affairs of a sovereign State is entitled to inviolability and to immunity from criminal process being "absolute or complete," that is to say, they are subject to no exception. Accordingly, the Congo contends that no criminal prosecution may be brought against a Minister for Foreign Affairs in a foreign court as long as he or she remains in office, and that any finding of criminal responsibility by a domestic court in a foreign country, or any act of investigation undertaken with a view to bringing him or her to court, would contravene the principle of immunity from jurisdiction. According to the Congo, the basis of such criminal immunity is purely functional, and immunity is accorded under customary international law simply in order to enable the foreign State representative enjoying such immunity to perform his or her functions freely and without let or hindrance. The Congo adds that the immunity thus accorded to Ministers for Foreign Affairs when in office covers *all* their acts, including any committed before they took office, and that it is irrelevant whether the acts done whilst in office may be characterized or not as "official acts."

48. The Congo states further that it does not deny the existence of a principle of international criminal law, deriving from the decisions of the Nuremberg and Tokyo international military tribunals, that the accused's official capacity at the time of the acts cannot, before any court, whether domestic or international, constitute a "ground of exemption from his criminal responsibility or a ground for mitigation of sentence." The Congo then stresses that the fact that an immunity might bar prosecution before a specific court or over a specific period does not mean that the same prosecution cannot be brought, if appropriate, before another court which is not bound by that immunity, or at another time when the immunity need no longer be taken into account. It concludes that immunity does not mean impunity.

49. Belgium maintains for its part that, while Ministers for Foreign Affairs in office generally enjoy an immunity from jurisdiction before the courts of a foreign State, such immunity applies only to acts carried out in the course of their official functions, and cannot protect such persons in respect of private acts or when they are acting otherwise than in the performance of their official functions.

50. Belgium further states that, in the circumstances of the present case, Mr. Yerodia enjoyed no immunity at the time when he is alleged to have committed the acts of which he is accused, and that there is no evidence that he was then acting in any official capacity. It observes that the arrest warrant was issued against Mr. Yerodia personally.

51. The Court would observe at the outset that in international law it is firmly established that, as also diplomatic and consular agents, certain holders of high-ranking office in a State, such as the Head of State, Head of Government and Minister for Foreign Affairs, enjoy immunities from jurisdiction in other States, both civil and criminal. For the purposes of the present case, it is only the immunity from criminal jurisdiction and the inviolability of an incumbent Minister for Foreign Affairs that fall for the Court to consider.

52. A certain number of treaty instruments were cited by the Parties in this regard. These included, first, the Vienna Convention on Diplomatic Relations of 18 April 1961, which states in its preamble that the purpose of diplomatic privileges and immunities is "to ensure the efficient performance of the functions of diplomatic missions as representing States." It provides in Article 32 that only the sending State may waive such immunity. On these points, the Vienna Convention on Diplomatic Relations, to which both the Congo and Belgium are parties, reflects customary international law. The same applies to the corresponding provisions of the Vienna Convention on Consular Relations of 24 April 1963, to which the Congo and Belgium are also parties. [⋯] These conventions provide useful guidance on certain aspects of the question of immunities. They do not, however, contain any provision specifically defining the immunities enjoyed by Ministers for Foreign Affairs. It is consequently on the basis of customary international law that the Court must decide the questions relating to the immunities of such Ministers raised in the present case.

53. In customary international law, the immunities accorded to Ministers for Foreign Affairs are not granted for their personal benefit, but to ensure the effective performance of their functions on behalf of their respective States. [⋯] In the performance of these functions, he or she is frequently required to travel internationally, and thus must be in a position freely to do so whenever the need should arise. He or she must also be in constant communication with the Government, and with its diplomatic missions around the world, and be capable at any time of communicating with representatives of other States. The Court further observes that a Minister for Foreign Affairs, responsible for the conduct of his or her State's relations with all other States, occupies a position such that, like the Head of State or the Head of Government, he or she is recognized under international law as representative of the State solely by virtue of his or her office. [⋯]

54. The Court accordingly concludes that the functions of a Minister for Foreign Affairs are such that, throughout the duration of his or her office, he or she when abroad enjoys full immunity from criminal jurisdiction and inviolability. That immunity and that inviolability protect the individual concerned against any act of authority of another State which would hinder him or her in the performance of his or her duties.

55. In this respect, no distinction can be drawn between acts performed by a Minister for Foreign Affairs in an "official" capacity, and those claimed to have been performed in a "private capacity," or, for that matter, between acts performed before the person concerned assumed office as Minister for Foreign Affairs and acts committed during the period of office. Thus, if a Minister for Foreign Affairs is arrested in another State on a criminal charge, he or she is clearly thereby prevented from exercising the functions of his or her office. The consequences of such impediment to the exercise of those official functions are equally serious, regardless of whether the Minister for Foreign Affairs was, at the time of arrest, present in the territory of the arresting State on an "official" visit or a "private" visit, regardless of whether the arrest relates to acts allegedly performed before the person became the Minister for Foreign Affairs or to acts performed while in office, and regardless of whether the arrest relates to alleged acts performed in an "official" capacity or a "private" capacity. Furthermore, even the mere risk that, by traveling to or transiting another State a Minister for Foreign Affairs might be exposing himself or herself to legal proceedings could deter the Minister from traveling internationally when required to do so for the purposes of the performance of his or her official functions. [⋯]

59. It should further be noted that the rules governing the jurisdiction of national courts must be carefully distinguished from those governing jurisdictional immunities: jurisdiction does not imply absence of immunity, while absence of immunity does not imply jurisdiction. Thus, although various international conventions on the prevention and punishment of certain serious crimes impose on States obligations of prosecution or extradition, thereby requiring them to extend their criminal jurisdiction, such extension of jurisdiction in no way affects immunities under customary international law, including those of Ministers for Foreign Affairs. These remain opposable before the courts of a foreign State, even where those courts exercise such a jurisdiction under these conventions.

60. The Court emphasizes, however, that the *immunity* from jurisdiction enjoyed by incumbent Ministers for Foreign Affairs does not mean that they enjoy *impunity* in respect of any crimes they might have committed, irrespective of their gravity. Immunity from criminal jurisdiction and individual criminal responsibility are quite separate concepts. While jurisdictional immunity is procedural in nature, criminal responsibility is a question of substantive law. Jurisdictional immunity may well bar prosecution for a certain period or for certain offences; it cannot exonerate the person to whom it applies from all criminal responsibility.

61. Accordingly, the immunities enjoyed under international law by an incumbent or former Minister for Foreign Affairs do not represent a bar to criminal prosecution in certain circumstances. First, such persons enjoy no criminal immunity under international law in their own countries, and may thus be tried by those countries' courts in accordance with the relevant rules of domestic law. Secondly, they will cease to enjoy immunity from foreign jurisdiction if the State which they represent or have represented decides to waive that immunity. Thirdly, after a person ceases to hold the office of Minister for Foreign Affairs, he or she will no longer enjoy all of the immunities accorded by international law in other States. Provided that it has jurisdiction under international law, a court of one State may try a former Minister for Foreign Affairs of another State in respect of acts committed prior or subsequent to his or her period of office, as well as in respect of acts committed during that period of office in a private capacity. Fourthly, an incumbent or former Minister for Foreign Affairs may be subject to criminal proceedings before certain international criminal courts, where they have jurisdiction. […]

70. The Court notes that the *issuance*, as such, of the disputed arrest warrant represents an act by the Belgian judicial authorities intended to enable the arrest on Belgian territory of an incumbent Minister for Foreign Affairs on charges of war crimes and crimes against humanity. The fact that the warrant is enforceable is clearly apparent from the order given to "all bailiffs and agents of public authority ... to execute this arrest warrant" and from the assertion in the warrant that "the position of Minister for Foreign Affairs currently held by the accused does not entail immunity from jurisdiction and enforcement." The Court notes that the warrant did admittedly make an exception for the case of an official visit by Mr. Yerodia to Belgium, and that Mr. Yerodia never suffered arrest in Belgium. The Court is bound, however, to find that, given the nature and purpose of the warrant, its mere issue violated the immunity which Mr. Yerodia enjoyed as the Congo's incumbent Minister for Foreign Affairs. The Court accordingly concludes that the issue of the warrant constituted a violation of an obligation of Belgium towards the Congo, in that it failed to respect the immunity of that Minister and, more particularly, infringed the immunity from criminal jurisdiction and the inviolability then enjoyed by him under international law. […]

☑ 해   설

이 판결은 현직 외교장관에 대해서는 범죄의 경중 및 시점과 관계 없이 관습국제법상의 특권 및 면제가 적용되어 타국에서 형사소추의 대상이 되지 않음을 확인하고 있다. 특히 이 판결은 인도에 반한 죄 등 중대한 범죄를 저지른 자에 대해서도 현직 외교장관으로 재직 중인 경우에는 외교관의 특권·면제가 적용됨을 확인한다. 다만, 이 판결에서 이 같은 보호는 재직 중 형사소추로부터의 면제에 국한되며 일체의 형사책임이 면제되는 것은 아님을 강조한 것은 주목을 요한다. 즉 외교관의 특권·면제는 일정 기간 동안 집행관할권으로부터의 면제이지 입법관할권으로부터의 면제를 의미하지는 않음을 확인한 것이다. 그리고 여기서 문제는 타국 외교장관에 대해 일국 법원이 자국 국내법에 근거하여 관할권을 행사했기에 발생한 점을 유념해야 한다. 즉, 관할권에 관한 요건이 충족될 경우 Yerodia 외교장관에 대해 적절한 국제법원(가령, ICC)이 기소, 처벌하고자 하는 경우에는 외교관의 특권·면제법리가 적용되지 않을 것이다. 외교관의 특권·면제는 일국의 수사당국 내지 법원에서만 유의미한 원칙이기 때문이다. 이 판결에서 ICJ가 일국 외교장관의 업무와 역할의 중요성을 거듭 언급한 것은 흥미롭다. 외교장관 직책의 중요성으로 인해 이 직위에 있는 자에 대한 적절한 보호가 필요하다는 것이다. 역시 "기능주의"적 입장에 기초한 법리라고 할 수 있을 것이다. 이 판결과 1933년 PCIJ의 Eastern Greenland Case를 함께 반추해 보면 국제법이 일국의 외교장관에 부여하는 권한과 책임을 잘 알 수 있다. 이 판결에서 ICJ가 관할권으로부터의 면제를 논하며 그 내용이 외교관의 특권·면제를 의미하는지 또는 인적 측면에서의 주권면제(sovereign immunity)를 의미하는지가 분명하게 표시되어 있지는 않다. 어느 면제 원칙을 적용하더라도 결과는 동일할 것이다.

한편 2002년 7월 30일 콩고와 르완다는 내전을 종식시키는 평화협정에 정식 서명했으며, 2002년 12월 16일 콩고 정부와 반군, 민병대, 야당, 시민단체 등 각 정파 대표들은 과도정부를 수립하기로 합의했다. 평화협정 당시 콩고 대통령이었던 Joseph Kabila는 협정에 따라 콩고 과도정부의 대통령이 되었으며, 그는 내각 구성 과정에서 Yerodia를 과도정부의 부통령으로 임명했다. 이에 따라 Yerodia는 콩고 과도정부(2003년~2006년)의 부통령직을 담당했다. 그러나 콩고내 무력충돌은 평화협정 이후에도 계속됐으며 특히 광물자원이 풍부한 동부지역의 무력분쟁은 2008년 하반기 급격히 악화되어 다수의 난민과 인권침해 문제를 야기하였다. 이러한 상황은 2020년 현재에도 지속되고 있다. 안타깝게도 콩고 동부지역 무력분쟁의 평화적 해결은 여전히 난망하다.

한편 2019년 10월 31일 몽골 헌법재판소장은 서울행 대한항공 기내에서 저지른 성추행 등 위법행위와 관련하여 인국 성질에 의해 현행범으로 체포 되었다. 몽골측은 헌법재판소장이 고위급 인사로서 국제법상 면제를 향유한 다고 주장했으나 한국은 헌법재판소장은 국제법상 타국 형사관할권의 면제 를 향유하지 않는다는 입장을 표명했다. 이에 그는 우리나라 법원에 벌금형 으로 약식기소되었고, 벌금 납부 후 몽골로 출국했다. 몽골의 주장은 주로 헌법재판소장의 자국 국내법상 지위에 기초한 내용이었다. 국내법상 지위와 국제법상 대외기관성 및 이에 따라 부여되는 지위는 서로 상이하다는 점을 이 사건은 잘 보여준다.

▶ 참고문헌

- 최태현, 국제법 위반행위에 대한 국가면제의 제한, 국제법학회논총 제51권 제2호(2006), p. 11.
- A. Cassese, When May Senior State Officials Be Tried for International Crimes? Some Comments on the Congo v. Belgium Case, European Journal of International Law Vol. 13(2002), p. 853.
- A. Nelson, Democratic Republic of Congo v. Belgium: The International Court's Consideration of Immunity of Foreign Ministers from Criminal Prosecution in Foreign States, New York Law School Journal of Human Rights Vol. 19(2003), p. 859.
- N. Boister, The ICJ in the Belgian Arrest Warrant Case: Arresting the Development of International Criminal Law, Journal of Conflict and Security Law Vol. 7(2002), p. 293.
- B. Chok, Let the responsible be responsible: Judicial oversight and over-optimism in the Arrest Warrant case and the fall of the head of state immunity doctrine in international and domestic courts, American University International Law Review Vol. 30(2015), p. 489.

4. Avena 사건(2004)
─ 영사통지 의무 발생 시기 및 재심의 의미

Case Concerning Avena and Other Mexican Nationals.
Mexico v. United States of America, 2004 ICJ Reports 12.

☑ 사 안

미국과 멕시코는 지리적으로 인접하여 전통적으로 적지 않은 양국 국민들이 상대국을 방문하거나 상대국에 체류하고 있다. 이러한 현실을 반영하여 양국은 이미 1942년 영사협약을 체결하여 상대방 국가에 체류하는 자국민 보호를 도모했다. 이후 양국은 1963년 영사관계에 관한 비엔나 협약에도 각각 가입했다(멕시코는 1965년 6월 16일, 미국은 1969년 11월 25일 이 협약을 각각 비준). 2001년 독일과 미국간 독일국민에 대한 영사통지 및 영사접견권과 관련하여 진행된 LaGrand 사건[1]을 지켜본 멕시코는 미국 형사사법당국에 체포, 구금 중인 자국민들도 이러한 권리를 제대로 보장받지 못했음을 인지했다. 이에 따라 멕시코는 유사한 문제를 미국측에 본격적으로 제기하기 시작했다. 먼저 멕시코는 미국 주법원 및 연방법원에서 진행되는 자국민에 대한 일련의 형사재판절차에서 이러한 취지의 주장을 전개했다. 그러나 미국 법원이 미국법상 문제가 없다는 취지로 미온적인 반응을 보이자 결국 2004년 멕시코는 미국을 ICJ에 제소하기에 이르렀다. 멕시코는 미국에서 형사재판이 진행 중이거나 또는 유죄 확정 판결 후 수감시설에서 복역 중인 52명의 자국민이 체포 후 영사접견권을 보장받지 못했고 영사통지도 이루어지지 않았으므로 이들에 대한 미국 법원의 유죄판결은 비엔나 협약 제36조 제1항 (b)호 위반이라고 주장했다.

---

1) LaGrand Case. Germany v. The United States of America, 2001 ICJ Reports 466.

☑ 쟁   점

(1) 1963년 영사관계에 관한 비엔니 협약 제36조 제1항 (b)호2)가 규정하고 있는 영사통지와 영사접견권 고지의무의 발생시기.

(2) 1963년 영사관계에 관한 비엔나협약 위반에 따른 "재검토(review and reconsideration)"의 의미.

☑ 판   결

(1) 영사통지 및 영사접견권 고지의무와 관련하여 비엔나 협약 제36조 제1항 (b)호에 규정된 "지체없이(without delay)"의 정확한 의미는 이 협약에 명시되어 있지 않다. 협약의 대상과 목적에 비추어 보아도 "지체없이"가 멕시코 주장처럼 체포 직후 또는 심문 개시 전으로 해석되어야 하는 것은 아니다. 그러나 체포당국이 피체포자가 외국인임을 알았거나 알 수 있었던 경우에는 즉시 고지의무가 발생한다. 따라서 하나의 사건(Salcido 사건, case No. 22)을 제외하고 미국은 멕시코인 구금자에게 영사접견권을 고지하고 멕시코 영사에게 체포사실을 통지해야 하는 비엔나 협약상 의무를 위반했다.

(2) LaGrand 사건에서 영사통지 및 영사접견권 고지의무 위반을 치유하기 위한 재검토의 구체적인 방법은 미국의 선택에 맡긴다고 판시했으나, 이는 재검토 방법의 선택에 있어 무제한의 재량을 인정하는 것은 아니다. 이 과정에서 진행되는 재검토는 비엔나 협약 위반, 특히 협약위반에 따른 형사절차에서 발생한 모든 법적 결과를 고려하여 이루어져야 한다.

판 결 문

15. The present proceedings have been brought by Mexico against the United

---

2) 영사관계에 관한 비엔나 협약 제36조 제1항 (b)호: 파견국의 영사관할구역내에서 파견국의 국민이 체포되는 경우, 재판에 회부되기 전에 구금 또는 유치되는 경우, 또는 기타의 방법으로 구속되는 경우에, 그 국민이 파견국의 영사기관에 통보할 것을 요청하면 접수국의 권한 있는 당국은 지체없이 통보하여야 한다. 체포, 구금, 유치 또는 구속되어 있는 자가 영사기관에 보내는 어떠한 통신도 동 당국에 의하여 지체없이 전달되어야 한다. 동 당국은 관계자에게 본 세항에 따른 그의 권리를 지체없이 통보하여야 한다.

States on the basis of the Vienna Convention, and of the Optional Protocol providing for the jurisdiction of the Court over "disputes arising out of the interpretation or application" of the Convention. Mexico and the United States are, and were at all relevant times, parties to the Vienna Convention and to the Optional Protocol. Mexico claims that the United States has committed breaches of the Vienna Convention in relation to the treatment of a number of Mexican nationals who have been tried, convicted and sentenced to death in criminal proceedings in the United States. The original claim related to 54 such persons, but as a result of subsequent adjustments to its claim made by Mexico, only 52 individual cases are involved, These criminal proceedings have been taking place in nine different States of the United States, namely California (28 cases), Texas (15 cases), Illinois (three cases), Arizona (one case), Arkansas (one case), Nevada (one case), Ohio (one case), Oklahoma (one case) and Oregon (one case), between 1979 and the present. [···]

17. [···] Article 36 relates, according to its title, to "Communication and contact with nationals of the sending State." Paragraph 1 (*b*) of that Article provides that if a national of that State "is arrested or committed to prison or to custody pending trial or is detained in any other manner," and he so requests, the local consular post of the sending State is to be notified. The Article goes on to provide that the "competent authorities of the receiving State" shall "inform the person concerned without delay of his rights" in this respect. Mexico claims that in the present case these provisions were not complied with by the United States authorities in respect of the 52 Mexican nationals the subject of its claims. As a result, the United States has according to Mexico committed breaches of paragraph 1 (*b*). [···]

20. Of the 52 cases referred to in Mexico's final submissions, 49 are currently at different stages of the proceedings before United States judicial authorities at state or federal level, and in three cases, those of Mr. Fierro (case No. 31), Mr. Moreno (case No. 39) and Mr. Torres (case No. 53), judicial remedies within the United States have already been exhausted. [···]

50. The Court has already in its Judgment in the *LaGrand* case described Article 36, paragraph 1, as "an interrelated regime designed to facilitate the implementation of the system of consular protection." [···] It is thus convenient to set out the entirety of that paragraph.

"With a view toward facilitating the exercise of consular functions relating to nationals of the sending State:

(*a*) consular officers shall be free to communicate with nationals of the sending State and to have access to them. Nationals of the sending State shall have the same freedom with respect to communication with and access to consular officers of the sending State;

(*b*) if he so requests, the competent authorities of the receiving State shall, without delay, inform the consular post of the sending State if, within its consular district, a national of that State is arrested or committed to prison or to custody pending trial or is detained in any other manner. Any communication addressed to the consular post by the person arrested, in prison, custody or detention shall be forwarded by the said authorities without delay. The said authorities shall inform the person concerned without delay of his rights under this subparagraph;

(*c*) consular officers shall have the right to visit a national of the sending State who is in prison, custody or detention, to converse and correspond with him and to arrange for his legal representation. They shall also have the right to visit any national of the sending State who is in prison, custody or detention in their district in pursuance of a judgment. Nevertheless, consular officers shall refrain from taking action on behalf of a national who it; in prison, custody or detention if he expressly opposes such action." [⋯]

61. The Court thus now turns to the interpretation of Article 36, paragraph 1 (*b*), having found in paragraph 57 above that it is applicable to the 52 persons listed in paragraph 16. It begins by noting that Article 36, paragraph 1 (*b*), contains three separate but interrelated elements: the right of the individual concerned to be informed without delay of his rights under Article 36, paragraph 1 (*b*); the right of the consular post to be notified without delay of the individual's detention, if he so requests; and the obligation of the receiving State to forward without delay any communication addressed to the consular post by the detained person. [⋯]

63. The Court finds that the duty upon the detaining authorities to give the Article 36, paragraph 1 (*b*), information to the individual arises once it is realized that the person is a foreign national, or once there are grounds to think that the person is probably a foreign national. Precisely when this may occur will vary with circumstances. [⋯]

83. The Court now addresses the question of the proper interpretation of the expression "without delay" in the light of arguments put to it by the Parties. The

Court begins by noting that the precise meaning of "without delay," as it is to be understood in Article 35, paragraph 1 (b), is not defined in the Convention. This phrase therefore requires interpretation according to the customary rules of treaty interpretation reflected in Articles 31 and 32 of the Vienna Convention on the Law of Treaties.

84. [⋯] The Court observes that dictionary definitions, in the various languages of the Vienna Convention, offer diverse meanings of the term "without delay" (and also of "immediately"). It is therefore necessary to look elsewhere for an understanding of this term.

85. As for the object and purpose of the Convention, the Court observes that Article 36 provides for consular officers to be free to communicate with nationals of the sending State, to have access to them, to visit and speak with them and to arrange for their legal representation. It is not envisaged, either in Article 36, paragraph 1, or elsewhere in the Convention, that consular functions entail a consular officer himself or herself acting as the legal representative or more directly engaging in the criminal justice process. Indeed, this is confirmed by the wording of Article 36, paragraph 2, of the Convention. Thus, neither the terms of the Convention as normally understood, nor its object and purpose, suggest that "without delay" is to be understood as "immediately upon arrest and before inter-rogation." [⋯]

87. The Court thus finds that "without delay" is not necessarily to be interpreted as "immediately" upon arrest. It further observes that during the Conference debates on this term, no delegate made any connection with the issue of interrogation. The Court considers that the provision in Article 36, paragraph 1 (*b*), that the receiving Stale authorities "shall inform the person concerned without delay of his rights" cannot be interpreted to signify that the provision of such information must necessarily precede any interrogation, so that the commencement of inter-rogation before the information is given would be a breach of Article 36.

88. Although, by application of the usual rules of interpretation, "without delay" as regards the duty to inform an individual under Article 36, paragraph 1 (*b*), is not to be understood as necessarily meaning "immediately upon arrest," there is nonetheless a duty upon the arresting authorities to give that information to an arrested person as soon as it is realized that the person is a foreign national, or once there are grounds to think that the person is probably a foreign national.

89. With one exception, no information as to entitlement to consular notification was given in any of the cases cited in paragraph 77 within any of the various time periods suggested by the delegates to the Conference on the Vienna Convention, or by the United States itself. Indeed, the information was given either not at all or at periods very significantly removed from the time of arrest, In the case of Mr. Juarez (case No. 10), the defendant was informed of his consular rights 40 hours after his arrest. The Court notes, however, that Mr. Juarez's arrest report stated that he had been born in Mexico; moreover, there had been indications of his Mexican nationality from the time of his initial interrogation by agents of the Federal Bureau of Investigation (FBI) following his arrest. It follows that Mr. Juarez's Mexican nationality was apparent from the outset of his detention by the United States authorities. In these circumstances, in accordance with its interpretation of the expression "without delay," the Court concludes that the United States violated the obligation incumbent upon it under Article 36, paragraph 1 (*b*), to inform Mr. Juarez without delay of his consular rights. The Court notes that the same finding was reached by a California Superior Court, albeit on different grounds.

90. The Court accordingly concludes that, with respect to each of the individuals listed in paragraph 16, with the exception of Mr. Salcido (case No. 22), the United States has violated its obligation under Article 36, paragraph 1 (b), of the Vienna Convention to provide information to the arrested person.

131. In stating in its Judgment in the *LaGrand* case that "the United States of America, *by means of its own choosing*, shall allow the review and reconsideration of the conviction and sentence" ..., the Court acknowledged that the concrete modalities for such review and reconsideration should be left primarily to the United States. It should be underlined, however, that this freedom in the choice of means for such review and reconsideration is not without qualification: ... such review and reconsideration has to be carried out "by taking account of the violation of the rights set forth in the Convention" ..., including in particular, the question of the legal consequences of the violation upon the criminal proceedings that have followed the violation.

☑ 해 설

2001년 LaGrand 사건 이래로 1963년 영사관계에 관한 비엔나 협약이 규정하는 영사통지 및 영사접견권은 새로운 조명을 받고 있으며, 이 분쟁 역시 그러한 배경에서 제기되었다. 따라서 Avena 판결에서는 LaGrand 판결

내용이 자주 원용되는 것을 볼 수 있다. Avena 사건은 전체적으로 LaGrand 사건과 유사한 부분도 많이 있으나 한편으로 영사통지 및 영사접견권 관련 새로운 법리도 아울러 제시하고 있다.

우선 Avena 사건에서 ICJ는 LaGrand 사건에서는 명확하지 않았던 비엔나 협약 제36조 제1항 (b)호에 규정된 영사통지 및 영사접견권 고지의무의 발생시기, 즉 "지체없이"의 의미에 대한 해석을 시도했다. ICJ에 따르면 "지체없이"의 의미는 비엔나 협약 당사국 사법당국이 피의자 체포시 또는 상당한 기간 내에 정기적으로 외국인인지 여부를 질문해야 하며 만약 피의자가 외국인이라는 사실을 알았거나 알 수 있었을 경우 그 고지의무가 즉시 발생한다는 것이다. 또한 ICJ가 제36조 제1항 (b)호에 따른 고지의무가 형사 피의자 체포시 적용되는 소위 미란다(Miranda) 원칙의 고지와 동일한 의미를 가지는 것으로 판단한 부분 역시 눈에 띈다. ICJ 입장에서는 영사통지 및 영사접견권의 고지가 형사사법 절차 측면에서 미란다 고지에 버금가는 중요성을 띠는 것으로 이해하고 있다는 의미로 볼 수도 있기 때문이다.

또한 Avena 사건은 LaGrand 사건에서 처음으로 구제방법으로 인정된 재검토(review and reconsideration)의 의미를 더욱 명확히 했다. ICJ에 따르면 재검토는 실질적인 사법적 재검토를 요구하며 단지 사면절차가 존재한다는 사실만으로는 충분하지 않다는 것이다. 미국은 자신들이 사면절차를 도입하고 있으므로 이 절차를 통해 재검토 의무를 완수했다고 주장했으나 ICJ는 여기서 요구되는 재검토는 실제 판결을 다시 한번 살펴볼 수 있는 실질적 의미의 재검토라고 보았다.

한편 Avena 판결 이후 미국은 비엔나 협약 선택의정서 가입을 철회했고, 일부 사건의 경우(Torres 사건 및 Camargo 사건) Avena 판결에 따른 실질적 재심을 통해 사형이 무기징역으로 감형되기도 했다. 그러나 대부분의 사건들은 Avena 판결의 적용을 받지 못했고 미국 국내법 절차에 따라 진행되어 당사자에 대한 처벌이 이루어졌다. 특히 2008년 Medellin v. Texas 사건의 경우 미국 연방대법원은 미국이 Avena 판결에 따라야 할 국제법상 의무가 있음을 인정하면서도 모든 국제법상 의무가 연방법을 적용해야 하는 미국 법원을 당연히 구속하는 것은 아니라는 판시를 하며 양자를 구별한 이후

Medellin의 재심 청구를 기각한 바 있다.

▶ 참고문헌 ─────────────── ──────────────

• C. Hoppe, Implementation of LaGrand and Avena in Germany and the United States: Exploring a Transatlantic Divide in Search of a Uniform Interpretation of Consular Rights, European Journal of International Law(2007).

• J. Goodman, Avena & Other Mexican Nationals (MEX. V. U.S.): The International Court of Justice Deems U.S. Actions in Fifty-two Death Penalty Cases as Violations of International Law, Tulane Journal of International and Comparative Law(2005).

• D. M. Tranel, The Ruling of the International Court of Justice in Avena And Other Mexican Nationals: Enforcing the Right to Consular Assistance in U.S. Jurisprudence, American University International Law Review(2005).

• R. A. Valencia et al., Avena and the World Court's Death Penalty Jurisdiction in Texas: Addressing the Odd Notion of Texas's Independence from the World, Yale Law and Policy Review Vol. 23, No. 2(2015).

• W. J. Aceves, Consular Notification and the Death Penalty: The ICJ's Judgment in Avena, American Society of International Law, ASIL Insight Vol. 8 Issue 10(2004).

• B. Simma & C. Hoppe, From LaGrand and Avena to Medellin — A Rocky Road toward Implementation, Tulane Journal of International and Comparative Law Vol. 14(2005), p. 7.

제 9 장

국제기구

1. 유엔 가입조건(1948)
— 헌장상 가입조항의 의미

Conditions of Admissions of a State to Membership in the
United Nations.
Advisory Opinion, 1948 ICJ Report 57.

☑ 사 안

유엔 헌장 제4조 1항은 회원국의 가입이 "헌장에 규정된 의무를 수락하고, 이러한 의무를 이행할 능력과 의사가 있다고 기구가 판단하는 그 밖의 평화애호국 모두에게 개방된다"고 규정하고 있다. 회원국으로 승인받기 위하여는 "안전보장이사회의 권고에 따라 총회의 결정"이 있어야 한다(제4조 2항). 그러나 유엔 설립 직후부터 동서 냉전이 격화되자 상임이사국들은 정치적 이해관계에 따라 신규 회원국 신청에 대하여 거부권을 자주 행사했다. 1946년 8월 미국이 8개국 신규 가입을 일괄추천하자고 제의했으나, 소련은 개별심사를 주장했다. 1947년 9월에는 동구권 국가들이 이탈리아, 핀란드, 불가리아, 헝가리, 루마니아 등의 일괄추천을 제안했으나, 이번에는 서방 국가들이 개별심사를 주장했다. 그 결과 1946년과 1947년 15개국이 가입신청을 했으나, 4개국만이 가입할 수 있었다. 회원국 가입에 관한 갈등이 자주 표출되자 1947년 11월 유엔 총회는 헌장 제4조의 해석과 관련하여 ICJ에 대해 아래와 같은 쟁점에 관한 권고적 의견을 구했다.

☑ 쟁 점
⑴ 유엔 헌장 제4조 1항은 유엔 가입과 관련하여 필요충분 조건인가 여부.
⑵ 유엔 가입 신청국에 대한 동의에 다른 국가의 가입을 연계할 수 있는가 여부.

☑ 판 결

(1) 유엔 가입과 관련한 헌장 제4조 1항상 조건은 망라적인 조건이며, 정치적 고려에 의한 추가적인 조건을 부과할 수 없다.

(2) 유엔 헌장 제4조 1항은 가입 신청 개별 국가별로 적용되며 다른 국가의 가입과 연계될 수 없다.

판 결 문

(p. 62-) In framing this answer, it is necessary first to recall the "conditions" required, under paragraph 1 of Article 4, of an applicant for admission. This provision reads as follows:

> "Membership in the United Nations is open to all other peace-loving States which accept the obligations contained in the present Charter and, in the judgment of the Organization, are able and willing to carry out these obligations."

The requisite conditions are five in number: to be admitted to membership in the United Nations, an applicant must (1) be a State; (2) be peace-loving; (3) accept the obligations of the Charter; (4) be able to carry out these obligations; and (5) be willing to do so.

All these conditions are subject to the judgement of the Organization. The judgement of the Organization means the judgement of the two organs mentioned in paragraph 2 of Article 4, and, in the last analysis, that of its Members. The question put is concerned with the individual attitude of each Member called upon to pronounce itself on the question of admission.

Having been asked to determine the character, exhaustive or otherwise, of the conditions stated in Article 4, the Court must in the first place consider the text of that Article. The English and French texts of paragraph 1 of Article 4 have the same meaning, and it is impossible to find any conflict between them. The text of this paragraph, by the enumeration which it contains and the choice of its terms, clearly demonstrates the intention of its authors to establish a legal rule which, while it fixes the conditions of admission, determines also the reasons for which admission may be refused; for the text does not differentiate between these two cases and any attempt to restrict it to one of them would be purely arbitrary.

The terms "Membership in the United Nations is open to all other peaceloving States which..." and *"Peuvent devenir Membres des Nations unies tous autres Etats pacifiques,"* indicate that States which fulfil the conditions states have the qualifications requisite for admission. The natural meaning of the words used leads to the conclusion that these conditions constitute an exhaustive enumeration and are not merely stated by way of guidance or example. The provision would lose its significance and weight, if other conditions, unconnected with those laid down, could be demanded. The conditions states in paragraph 1 of Article 4 must therefore be regarded not merely as the necessary conditions, but also as the conditions which suffice.

Nor can it be argued that the conditions enumerated represent only an indispensable minimum, in the sense that political considerations could be superimposed upon them, and prevent the admission of an applicant which fulfils them. Such an interpretation would be inconsistent with the terms of paragraph 2 of Article 4, which provide for the admission of *"tout Etat remplissant ces conditions"* —"any *such* State." It would lead to conferring upon Members an indefinite and practically unlimited power of discretion in the imposition of new conditions. Such a power would be inconsistent with the very character of paragraph 1 of Article 4 which, by reason of the close connexion which it establishes between membership and the observance of the principles and obligations of the Charter, clearly constitutes a legal regulation of the question of the admission of new States. To warrant an interpretation other than that which ensues from the natural meaning of the words, a decisive reason would be required which has not been established. [⋯]

The second part of the question concerns a demand on the part of a Member making its consent to the admission of an applicant dependent on the admission of other applicants.

Judged on the basis of the rule which the Court adopts in its interpretation of Article 4, such a demand clearly constitutes a new condition, since it is entirely unconnected with those prescribed in Article 4. It is also in an entirely different category from those conditions, since it makes admission dependent, not on the conditions required of applicants, qualifications which are supposed to be fulfilled, but on an extraneous consideration concerning States other than the applicant State.

The provisions of Article 4 necessarily imply that every application for admission should be examined and voted on separately and on its own merits; otherwise it would be impossible to determine whether a particular applicant fulfils the necessary conditions. To subject an affirmative vote for the admission of an applicant State to the condition that other States be admitted with that State would prevent Members from exercising their judgment in each case with complete liberty, within the scope of the prescribed conditions. Such a demand is incompatible with the letter and spirit of Article 4 of the Charter.

☑ 해   설

총회가 권고적 의견을 요청하자, 이에 반대하는 측은 이 문제가 법률적 사안이 아닌 정치적 사안이며, ICJ는 헌장 해석을 할 권한이 없다는 등의 이의를 제기하며 의견을 부여하지 말아야 한다고 주장했다. 그러나 ICJ는 이 요청이 다자조약인 UN 헌장 제4조의 해석문제이므로 권고적 의견 부여 대상이라고 판단했다.

이어 ICJ는 신규 회원국의 가입에 즈음하여 만약 기존 회원국이 헌장 제4조 1항상의 요건 외에 추가적인 조건을 요구할 수 있다면, 이는 헌장이 예정하지 않았던 방법으로 기존 회원국에게 실질적으로 무제한한 재량권을 인정하는 결과가 될 수 있다고 판단했다.

사실 유엔 헌장을 채택하던 샌프란시스코 회의에서의 분위기는 가입에 추가조건을 붙일 수 있다는 분위기였으나,1) 재판부는 가입조건에 관한 한 헌장의 문언이 충분할 정도로 명백하며, 조약문 자체가 분명하면 교섭기록 등에 의지할 필요가 없다고 판단했다(it does not feel that it should deviate from the consistent practice of the Permanent Court of International Justice, according to which there is no occasion to resort to preparatory work if the text of a convention is sufficiently clear in itself. p. 63).

이러한 의견에도 불구하고 동서냉전은 유엔 초기 신규 회원국의 가입을 지극히 어렵게 만들었다. 1945년부터 1955년 사이 31개 신청국 중 9개국만이 가입할 수 있었으며, 특히 1950년부터 1955년 가을까지는 단 1개국도 신규로 가입할 수 없었다. 결국 동서 양진영은 1955년 12월 한국과 베트남 2개

---

1) 이 권고적 의견의 소수의견은 이러한 입장이었다.

의 분단국을 제외한 16개 신청국의 일괄가입에 합의했다. 당시는 안보리에서 표결은 각 국가별로 하나, 총회로는 일괄적으로 추천하기로 했다. 일괄추천 방식은 ICJ가 제시한 의견의 취지와는 맞지 않는다고 할 수 있으나, 회원국의 문호를 널리 개방하는 결과는 헌장의 정신에 합당하다고 평가할 수 있다. 이후에는 보편주의에 입각하여 신생국은 거의 자동으로 유엔에 가입해 왔다.

우리나라는 1949년, 1951년, 1961년 그리고 1975년 가입신청을 했으나 모두 받아들여지지 않았었다. 그 후 동서 화해 분위기에 힘입어서 마침내 1991년 북한과 함께 동시에 유엔 가입이 성사되었다. 남북한이 가입할 때에도 안보리는 한 개의 결의(제702호)를 통하여 총회로 남북한을 일괄추천했다.

➡ 참고문헌 ─────────────────────────

- William W. Bishop, Jr., Conditions of Admission of a State to Membership in the United Nations, AJIL Vol. 42, No. 4, p. 927.

2. 유엔 직원에 대한 손해배상 사건(1949)
― 국제기구의 국제법 주체성

Reparation for Injuries Suffered in the Service of the United Nations.

Advisory Opinion, 1949 ICJ Report 174.

☑ 사　　안

국제연맹 시절 영국의 위임통치 하에 있던 팔레스타인 지역 문제는 제2차 대전 후 유엔으로 회부되었다. 1948년 제1차 중동전 당시 유엔은 휴전교섭을 위하여 스웨덴인 Bernadotte를 조정관으로 파견했다. 그와 프랑스인 1명이 당시 이스라엘의 점령하에 있던 동예루살렘 지역에서 피살되었다. 유엔 사무총장은 피살자와 부상자를 위한 보상금과 치료비를 우선 유엔의 경비로 지불했다. 유엔은 이스라엘이 범죄를 방지하고 범인들을 처벌하는 데 충분한 주의의무를 다하지 않았다고 판단하고, 그에 대한 책임을 묻고자 했다. 이와 관련하여 국제기구인 유엔이 비회원국인 이스라엘을 상대로 직접 배상청구를 할 수 있는지 등의 문제가 제기되었다. 유엔 총회는 1948년 12월 ICJ에 대하여 이 문제에 대한 권고적 의견을 구하기로 했다.

☑ 쟁　　점

(1) 국제기구인 유엔이 국가를 상대로 국제청구를 할 수 있는가 여부.

(2) 유엔의 기능적 보호권과 국적국의 외교적 보호권과의 관계.

☑ 판　　결

(1) 유엔은 국제기구로서 그 임무를 적절히 수행하기 위해서는 국가와 마찬가지로 국제법인격을 갖는 것으로 인정되어야 하며, 이에 따라서 책임이

있는 국가에 대해서 국제청구를 제기할 수 있다.

(2) 국적국의 외교적 보호권과 유엔의 기능적 보호권간에 우선순위가 있지는 않으며, 유엔 공무원이 속한 국가와 유엔은 상호 협의를 통해 해결할 수 있을 것이다.

판 결 문

(p. 178-) But, in the international sphere, has the Organization such a nature as involves the capacity to bring an international claim? In order to answer this question, the Court must first enquire whether the Charter has given the Organization such a position that it possesses, in regard to its Members, rights which it is entitled to ask them to respect. In other words, does the Organization possess international personality? [⋯]

To answer this question, which is not settled by the actual terms of the Charter, we must consider what characteristics it was intended thereby to give to the Organization.

The subjects of law in any legal system are not necessarily identical in their nature or in the extent of their rights, and their nature depends upon the needs of the community. Throughout its history, the development of international law has been influenced by the requirements of international life, and the progressive increase in the collective activities of States has already given rise to instances of action upon the international plane by certain entities which are not States. This development culminated in the establishment in June 1945 of an international organization whose purposes and principles are specified in the Charter of the United Nations. But to achieve these ends the attribution of international personality is indispensable. [⋯]

In the opinion of the Court, the Organization was intended to exercise and enjoy, and is in fact exercising and enjoying, functions and rights which can only be explained on the basis of the possession of a large measure of international personality and the capacity to operate upon an international plane. It is at present the supreme type of international organization, and it could not carry out the intentions of its founders if it was devoid of international personality. It must be acknowledged that its Members, by entrusting certain functions to it, with the attendant duties and responsibilities, have clothed it with the competence required to enable those functions to be effectively discharged.

Accordingly, the Court has come to the conclusion that the Organization is an international person. [···]

The next question is whether the sum of the international rights of the Organization comprises the right to bring the kind of international claim described in the Request for this Opinion. [···][1]

The Charter does not expressly confer upon the Organization the capacity to include, in its claim for reparation, damage caused to the victim or to persons entitled through him. The Court must therefore begin by enquiring whether the provisions of the Charter concerning the functions of the Organization, and the part played by its agents in the performance of those functions, imply for the Organization power to afford its agents the limited protection that would consist in the bringing of a claim on their behalf for reparation for damage suffered in such circumstances. Under international law, the Organization must be deemed to have those powers which, though not expressly provided in the Charter, are conferred upon it by necessary implication as being essential to the performance of its duties. [···]

Having regard to its purposes and functions already referred to, the Organization may find it necessary, and has in fact found it necessary, to entrust its agents with important missions to be performed in disturbed parts of the world. Many missions, from their very nature, involve the agents in unusual dangers to which ordinary persons are not exposed. For the same reason, the injuries suffered by its agents in these circumstances will sometimes have occurred in such a manner that their national State would not be justified in bringing a claim for reparation on the ground of diplomatic protection, or, at any rate, would not feel disposed to do so. Both to ensure the efficient and independent performance of these missions and to afford effective support to its agents, the Organization must provide them with adequate protection. [···]

In order that the agent may perform his duties satisfactorily, he must feel that this protection is assured to him by the Organization, and that he may count on it. To ensure the independence of the agent, and, consequently, the independent action of the Organization itself, it is essential that in performing his duties he need not have to rely on any other protection than that of the Organization. [···]

---

1) 우선 재판부는 유엔이 자신이 입은 손해에 대하여 배상을 받기 위하여 국제청구를 제기할 자격이 있다고 결론내렸다. 이어서 피해자 개인에게 발생한 손해를 배상받기 위하여도 유엔이 국제청구를 제기할 수 있는가를 검토했다.

Upon examination of the character of the functions entrusted to the Organization and of the nature of the missions of its agents, it becomes clear that the capacity of the Organization to exercise a measure of functional protection of its agents arises by necessary intendment out of the Charter. […]

When the victim has a nationality, cases can clearly occur in which the injury suffered by him may engage the interest both of his national State and of the Organization. In such an event, competition between the State's right of diplomatic protection and the Organization's right of functional protection might arise, and this is the only case with which the Court is invited to deal.

In such a case, there is no rule of law which assigns priority to the one or to the other, or which compels either the State or the Organization to refrain from bringing an international claim. The Court sees no reason why the parties concerned should not find solutions inspired by goodwill and common sense, and as between the Organization and its Members it draws attention to their duty to render 'every assistance' provided by Article 2, paragraph 5, of the Charter. […]

The risk of competition between the Organization and the national State can be reduced or eliminated either by a general convention or by agreements entered into in each particular case. There is no doubt that in due course a practice will be developed, and it is worthy of note that already certain States whose nationals have been injured in the performance of missions undertaken for the Organization have shown a reasonable and co-operative disposition to find a practical solution.

☑ 해   설

이 사건은 국제기구의 국제법 주체성과 관련하여 가장 많이 인용되는 사례 중의 하나이다. 2차 세계대전 이후 국제사회에서 국제기구의 역할이 증대되어감에 따라서 주권국가 중심의 국제법 질서에서 변화가 필요했고, 이는 그러한 변화를 인정한 판례라고 할 수 있다.

유엔 헌장에는 기구의 법인격에 관한 규정이 없다. 그러나 이 사건 발생 이전부터 국제기구는 국제사회에서 주권국가들의 행위와 마찬가지로 다양한 행위를 하고 있었고, 국제기구에게 국제법인격을 인정하지 않는다면 국제사회에서 발생하는 문제들을 적절하게 해결할 수 없었을 것이다. 유엔 헌장에 따르면 유엔은 단순히 국가들 간의 행위를 조정하는 단순한 국제기구의 역할을 넘어서 유엔 자체에 많은 기관을 두고 주권 국가와 직접적인 관계를 맺고 역할을 수행하고 있다는 점을 고려하면 유엔에 대해서 법인격을 인정하는 것이 타당하다.

이어 ICJ는 국제기구가 식섭 국세성구를 할 수 있는지를 김도했다. 세만부는 기구 자신에 대한 직접 손해는 물론 직원이 입은 손해에 관해서는 회원국과 비회원국 모두에게 손해배상을 청구할 수 있다고 보았다. 만약 직원의 피해에 대한 청구를 국적국의 보호에만 의존하는 경우 기구 업무의 독립성과 효율성을 달성할 수 없기 때문에, 기구가 독자적으로 직접 보호할 필요가 있다고 판단했다.

다만 국제기구의 법인격을 인정함에 따라서 주권국가 중심의 국제법 질서에서 어려운 문제가 발생할 수도 있는데, 국가의 외교적 보호권과 국제기구의 기능적 보호권이 충돌할 가능성도 그 한 예이다. 이 권고적 의견에서 ICJ는 이 문제에 대해서 양자의 충돌 가능성을 인정하면서 이를 해결하기 위한 가장 바람직한 방안은 해당 국가와 국제기구와 조약이나 협정에 의해서 개별적으로 양자의 충돌 문제를 해결하는 것이라고 설시했다. 당시 ICJ는 향후 이에 관한 관행이 수립되면 이에 따라서 해결할 수 있으리라고 예상했지만 현재까지 이에 대한 명확한 국제법상 기준이 마련되지 않고 있는 것이 현실이다. 이 의견에 대하여 당시 사회주의 국가들은 자국민에 대한 국가의 권위를 훼손할 수 있는 위험한 의견이라고 반발하기도 했다.

이 사건이 발생한 당시에는 사건의 배후에 이스라엘 정부가 있을 것으로 의심되었으나, 체포된 유태인 범인들은 자신들의 독자적 소행이라고 주장했다. 최종적으로 범인들이 형사처벌을 받지는 않았다. 이 권고적 의견이 내려진 직후인 1949년 5월 11일 이스라엘은 유엔에 가입했고, 이듬해 이스라엘은 유엔 사무총장이 요구한 배상금을 지불했다.

한편 ICJ는 다른 권고적 의견에서도 국제기구는 이를 창설한 국가에 의해 협정을 통해 명시적으로 부여된 권한을 보유함이 원칙이나, 국제사회의 현실에서는 기구의 목적을 달성하는데 필요한 묵시적 권한도 행사할 수 있음이 인정된다고 보았다.

"The powers conferred on international organizations are normally the subject of an express statement in their constituent instruments. Nevertheless, the necessities of international life may point to the need for organizations, in order to achieve their objectives, to possess subsidiary powers which are not expressly provided for in the basic instruments which govern their activities. It is generally accepted that international organizations can exercise such powers, known as 'implied' powers." (*Legality of the Use by a State of Nuclear Weapons in Armed Conflict(WHO), Advisory Opinion, 1996 ICJ Reports 66,* para. 25).

➡ 참고문헌 ─────────────────────────────────

- 전순신, 국제연합 근무중 입은 손해배상청구사건, 대한변호사협회지 제149호 (1989년 1월), p. 104.
- Stanford Law Review editorial board, The United Nations and its Agents, Stanford Law Review Vol. 2(1949), p. 193.
- Y. L. Liang, Notes on Legal Questions Concerning the United Nations: Reparation for Injuries Suffered in the Service of the United Nations, AJIL Vol. 43(1949), p. 460.
- F. B. Sloan, Reparation for Injuries to Agents of the United Nations, Nebraska Law Review Vol. 28(1949), p. 401.
- Q. Wright, Responsibility for Injuries to United Nations Officials, AJIL Vol. 43(1949), p. 95.

3. 유엔 가입에 관한 총회의 권한(1950)
─ 유엔 가입요건

Competence of the General Assembly for the Admission
of a State to the United Nations.
Advisory Opinion, 1950 ICJ Report 4.

☑ 사   안

유엔 헌장 제4조 2항에 따르면 총회는 안보리의 권고에 따라서 유엔 회
원국으로의 가입 여부를 결정을 하도록 규정하고 있다. 그런데 동서 냉전시
대에 안보리가 다수결 혹은 상임이사국의 거부권 행사로 회원국 가입 권고
를 총회에 하지 못하는 경우가 발생을 하게 되었다. 이 경우 과연 총회가 안
보리의 권고 없이 독자적으로 유엔 가입 신청국에 대해서 가입 여부를 결정
할 수 있는가가 문제가 되었다. 이에 유엔 총회는 국제사법재판소에 이 문제
에 대한 권고적 의견을 구하기에 이르렀다.

☑ 쟁   점

가입 신청국의 유엔 가입에 대한 안보리의 권고가 없는 경우에도 총회
가 유엔 가입 여부를 결정할 수 있는가 여부.

☑ 판   결

유엔 총회는 안보리의 권고가 있는 경우에만 유엔 회원 가입 신청국의
가입여부를 결정할 수 있다.

판결문

(p. 7-) The Court is, therefore, called upon to determine solely whether the General Assembly can make a decision to admit a State when the Security Council has transmitted no recommendation to it. Article 4, paragraph 2, is as follows:

> "The admission of any such State to membership in the United Nations will be effected by a decision of the General Assembly upon the recommendation of the Security Council."

The Court has no doubt as to the meaning of this text. It requires two things to effect admission: a "recommendation" of the Security Council and a "decision" of the General Assembly. It is in the nature of things that the recommendation should come before the decision. The word "recommendation", and the word "upon" preceding it, imply the idea that the recommendation is the foundation of the decision to admit, and that the latter rests upon the recommendation. Both these acts are indispensable to form the judgement of the Organization to which the previous paragraph of Article 4 refers. The text under consideration means that the General Assembly can only decide to admit upon the recommendation of the Security Council; it determines the respective roles of the two organs whose combined action is required before admission can be effected": in other words, the recommendation of the Security Council is the condition precedent to the decision of the Assembly by which the admission is effected. [⋯]

To hold that the General Assembly has power to admit a State to membership in the absence of a recommendation of the Security Council would be to deprive the Security Council of an important power which has been entrusted to it by the Charter. It would almost nullify the role of the Security Council in the exercise of one of the essential functions of the Organization. It would mean that the Security Council would have merely to study the case, present a report, give advice, and express an opinion. This is not what Article 4, paragraph 2, says. [⋯]

Reference has also been made to a document of the San Francisco Conference, in order to put the possible case of an unfavourable recommendation being voted by the Security Council: such a recommendation has never been made in practice. In the opinion of the Court, Article 4, paragraph 2, envisages a favourable recommendation of the Security Council and that only. An unfavourable recommendation would not correspond to the provisions of Article 4, paragraph 2.

While keeping within the limits of a Request which deals with the scope of the powers of the General Assembly, it is enough for the Court to say that nowhere has the General Assembly received the power to change, to the point of reversing, the meaning of a vote of the Security Council.

In consequence, it is impossible to admit that the General Assembly has the power to attribute to a vote of the Security Council the character of a recommendation when the Council itself considers that no such recommendation has been made.

☑ 해   설

이 사건은 1948년 유엔 헌장 제4조상 유엔 가입조건에 관한 ICJ 권고적 의견과 함께 이해를 하면 도움이 되는 사례이다. 헌장 제4조 1항은 유엔 가입과 관련한 요건이 규정되어 있다면, 제4조 2항은 가입 결정을 위한 절차가 규정되어 있다.

제4조 2항에 따르면 회원 가입에 관한 최종 결정권은 총회에 부여되어 있으나, 가입을 위한 실제 난관은 안보리 추천과정에서의 상임이사국의 거부권이었다. 유엔 설립 초기부터 냉전의 여파로 신규 가입신청에 대해 안보리에서 거부권이 매우 빈번하게 사용되자, 가입 절차와 관련하여 2가지 쟁점이 제기되었다. 첫째, 안보리에서의 신규 회원 가입에 관한 표결에 상임이사국의 거부권이 적용되는가? 둘째, 총회는 안보리의 가입 권고 없이 또는 가입 반대 권고에도 불구하고 신규 회원국의 가입을 승인할 수 있는가? 즉 신규 회원 가입절차에 있어서 안보리의 "권고"란 그 자체 구속력이 없는 조언 정도에 해당하지 않는가? 총회가 최종 판단권이 있는 사항에 대한 안보리의 권고에도 거부권이 적용되는가? 안보리의 권고가 없다거나 부정적 권고가 있어도 총회가 가입 결정을 할 수는 없는가? 이상과 같은 의문이 제기되었다. 어떤 의미에서 이 같은 논란은 총회와 안보리 간의 권한 경쟁이기도 하였다. 이에 1949년 11월 22일 총회는 그 때까지 거부권으로 인해 가입이 성사되지 못하고 있던 한국을 포함한 9개국의 가입 신청을 안보리가 재검토할 것과 이 때 상임이사국은 거부권의 행사를 자제하도록 요청함과 동시에, ICJ에 대하여 안보리의 가입 권고가 없어도 총회가 독자적으로 신규 회원국의 가입

을 결정할 수 있는가에 관해 권고적 의견을 묻기로 결의했다(총회 결의 제296호(IV)).

　이 사건에서 ICJ는 헌장 제4조 2항의 자연적이고 통상적인 의미를 확인하는데 별다른 어려움이 없다고 보았다. 헌장상 안보리와 총회는 어느 편도 상대에 종속된 기관이 아니며, 신규 가입에 관한한 안보리와 총회의 합치된 행동이 필요한데, 이 때 총회의 결정에 앞서 안보리의 권고가 반드시 선행되어야 한다고 해석했다. 즉 "upon recommendation"이란 표현은 안보리의 권고가 총회 결정의 기초이며, 결정이 권고에 근거함을 암시한다고 보았다. ICJ는 이미 지난 수년간 UN의 실행 상으로도 총회는 항상 안보리의 긍정적 권고를 받은 경우에만 신규 가입을 결정해 왔음을 주목했다. 따라서 안보리의 권고 없이도 총회가 신규 가입을 결정할 수 있다는 주장은 헌장이 안보리에 부여한 주요한 권한을 박탈시키는 결과를 야기한다고 보았다. ICJ는 12 : 2의 표결로써 헌장 제4조 2항의 권고는 안보리의 긍정적 권고만을 의미하며, 안보리의 가입 권고 없이 총회가 독자적으로 신규 가입을 결정할 수 없다고 판단했다.

➤ 참고문헌 ────────────────────

- 정인섭, 한국문제를 통한 UN법의 발전, 서울국제법연구 제22권 2호, p. 81.
- Myres S. McDougal & Richard N. Gardner, The Veto and the Charter: An Interpretation for Survival, Yale Law Journal Vol. 60(1951), p. 258.
- Norman Kogan, United Nations—Agent of Collective Security?, Yale Law Journal Vol. 61(1952), p. 1.

4. 아랍통화기금 사건(1991)
— 국제기구의 비회원국에서의 법적 지위

Arab Monetary Fund v. Hashim(No. 3).
House of Lords, U.K., 2. WLR 729, 영국 상원(1991).

☑ 사　안

21개 아랍국가들을 회원국으로 하여 아부다비에 본부를 두고 있는 아랍통화기금(Arab Monetary Fund: A.M.F.)의 전 사무총장 Hashim은 재직 시절 약 5,000만 달러의 공금을 횡령했고, 여러 은행들이 이 돈의 세탁을 도와주었다는 혐의를 받았다. 아랍통화기금은 퇴임후 영국에 거주하던 Hashim과 자금세탁에 조력했던 은행들을 상대로 자금 회수를 위한 손해배상 청구소송 등을 영국 법원에 제기했다. 아랍통화기금의 설립협정(1976)은 기금을 독립적인 사법상의 주체로 규정하고 있으며, 본부 소재국인 아랍에미리트(U.A.E.)는 기금에 대해 독립적인 법인격과 소송 수행능력을 인정하고 있다. 그러나 영국은 아랍통화기금 설립협정의 당사국이 물론 아니었으며, 영국의 국내법(International Organization Act)도 아랍통화기금에 별도의 법인격을 부여한 바 없다. 그러자 피고측은 영국이 당사국이 아닌 조약을 근거로 성립된 국제기구는 영국 법원에서 법인격을 인정받을 수 없으므로, 제소자격도 없다고 주장했다.

☑ 쟁　점

영국이 회원국이 아닌 국제기구의 영국 국내법상의 법인격.

☑ 판　　결

영국이 당사국이 아닌 조약에 의해 설립된 국제기구도 국제예양(comity of nations)에 의해 영국에서의 법인격이 인정될 수 있다.

판 결 문

(p. 161-) In Chaff and Hay Acquisition Committee v. J. A. Hemphill and Sons Pty. Ltd. (1947) 74 C.L.R. 375, a committee of four persons created under a statute of South Australia to acquire property in its collective name and to sue and be sued in its collective name was held by the High Court of Australia not to be a corporation but though unincorporated it was a legal entity in South Australia and as such was entitled to recognition outside the state in accordance with the principle of the comity of nations. McTiernan J. said succinctly, at p. 390: "The courts of one country give recognition, by a comity of nations, to a legal personality created by the law of another country." The courts of the United Kingdom can therefore recognise the fund as a legal personality created by the law of the U.A.E.

It was submitted on behalf of the respondent banks that the fund was created a legal personality not only by the U.A.E. but also by the other 20 states who were parties to the A.M.F. agreement. Therefore, it is said, there are 21 legal personalities and it is not clear whether Dr. Hashim embezzled the money of the U.A.E. fund or the money of a fund established by some other Arab state. My Lords, though the fund was incorporated by 21 states and has multiple incorporation and multiple nationality there is only one fund with its head office in Abu Dhabi, one board of governors, one executive board of directors and one director-general. The domicile and residence of the fund are in the U.A.E. and nowhere else. Dr. Hashim was appointed by the board of governors of the fund as director-general of the fund and stole the money belonging to the fund. It was argued that the fund as incorporated in Iraq, for example, might be different from the fund as incorporated in the U.A.E. and that the Iraqi fund might even sue the U.A.E. fund. But there is only one fund to which each of the member states accorded legal personality. No one can bring an action to recover the money of the fund in any part of the world except the one duly authorised director-general. The articles of agreement which were annexed to the federal decree of the U.A.E. and which thus became part of the law of the

U.A.E. are no different from the memorandum and articles of a limited liability company established under the law of England.

It is beyond dispute that if the fund had been incorporated in the U.A.E. and nowhere else, the fund would have been recognised in this country as a legal personality. If the fund has been incorporated not only in the U.A.E. but also in a number of friendly foreign states recognised by the government of this country, it still has legal personality and is capable of suing in this country.

The evidence by affirmation of Dr. Faquih, the present director-general of the fund, is that the fund holds assets and has incurred liabilities in its own name in every part of the world. The fund has in its own name deposits in the London market which at 30 June 1989 exceeded U.S.$235m. The fund has brought proceedings in different parts of the world. It may safely be assumed that no one except Dr. Hashim and the other respondents has doubted that the fund is a separate corporate entity or has conceived the fanciful notion of the existence of more than one fund.

The deposits of U.S.$235m. must belong to someone entitled to sue for them and recognisable by the English courts. The deposits cannot belong to an unincorporated association composed of Arab states and cannot belong to Arab states jointly and severally consistently with the A.M.F. treaty which is part of U.A.E. law. The deposits do not belong to the individuals who made the deposits in the name of the fund. Deposits do not belong to 21 different funds; they belong to the one and only fund. It would be perverse of the English court to pretend that there is any insuperable difficulty in identifying and recognising the fund which owns the deposits of U.S.$235m. and is entitled to recover from Dr. Hashim the money which he has embezzled.

In 1978 (*see The British Yearbook of International Law 1978*, pp. 346-348) the advice of Her Majesty's Government was sought with regard to the status of:

> "banks and other financial entities set up by a group of foreign sovereign states by a treaty (to which the United Kingdom is not a party), empowering them, expressly or by implication, to engage in banking, financial or other trading activities in member and non-member states and conferring on them, by virtue of the treaty, any related agreements and any necessary implementing legislation, legal personality in one or more states outside the United Kingdom, and, in particular, under the law of one or more member states or the state wherein the entity concerned has its seat or permanent location."

The reply from the Foreign and Commonwealth Office was:

"In these circumstances, and on the assumption that the entity concerned enjoys, under its constitutive instrument or instruments and under the law of one or more member states or the state wherein it has its seat or permanent location, legal personality and capacity to engage in transactions of the type concerned governed by the law of a non-member state, the Foreign and Commonwealth Office, as the branch of the executive responsible for the conduct of foreign relations, would be willing officially to acknowledge that the entity concerned enjoyed such legal personality and capacity, and to state this."

It seems to me that it would be unthinkable for the courts of the United Kingdom applying the principles of comity to reach any other conclusion. It will be observed that the reply of the Foreign and Commonwealth Office stipulates that the international organisation for which recognition is sought must have acquired legal personality and capacity under the laws of one or more member states or the state wherein it has its seat or permanent location. This requirement is necessary because the courts of the United Kingdom cannot enforce treaty rights but they can recognise legal entities created by the laws of one or more sovereign states. A treaty cannot create a corporation but a sovereign state which is party to a treaty can, in pursuance of its obligations accepted under the treaty, create a corporation which will be recognised in the United Kingdom. A member state can create a corporation by signing and ratifying the treaty if in that member state a treaty is self-executing and becomes part of domestic law on signature and ratification. Another member state, such as the U.A.E., can only create legal personality by the legislative process which was adopted in the case of the A.M.F. agreement. In the present case the fund was given legal personality and capacity by the law of the state wherein it has its seat or permanent location. There is every reason why the fund should be recognised as a legal personality by the courts of the United Kingdom and no reason whatsoever why recognition should be withheld.

☑ 해　설

조약의 국내법적 효력에 대해 2원론의 입장을 취하는 영국에서는 의회의 입법이 있어야만 조약내용이 국내적으로 시행될 수 있다. 이를 그대로 적용한다면 국내법화되지 않은 조약을 근거로 설립된 국제기구는 영국에서 법인격을 인정받기 어렵다. 이 사건에 대한 영국 고등법원(Court of Appeal) 판결도 아랍통화기금의 영국 국내법상의 법인격을 부인했다.

그러나 영국 상원(대법원)에서는 보다 실용적인 접근방법을 취해서 아랍통화기금의 법인격을 인정했다. 즉 아랍통화기금은 영국 내에서 아랍에미리트 법에 의해 설립된 일종의 사적 회사법인과 같은 성격을 갖고 있는 것으로서 예양의 원칙에 의해 영국이 승인을 한 국가의 법에 따라 설립된 회사는 영국 내에서도 법인격을 인정해야 한다는 것이다.

영국에서 국제기구가 법인격을 인정받는 방법은 다음과 같다. 첫째, 의회가 입법으로 국제기구 설립조약을 국내법화하는 방안. 둘째, 영국 정부가 명시적으로 국제기구를 승인하는 방안. 셋째, 국내법인 International Organization Act에 근거하여 법인격 있는 기관으로 지정받는 방안. 넷째, 위 판결에서와 같이 외국에서 법인격을 인정받은 기구에 대하여 법원이 예양으로 법인격을 인정하는 방안. 그러나 이러한 방안들의 적용이 항상 명확한 것은 아니다.[1]

유사한 문제는 국내에서도 발생할 수 있다. 한국이 당사국이 아닌 조약을 통해 설립된 국제기구는 국내에서 법인격을 인정받고, 국내 법원에 제소자격이 있는가?

➡ 참고문헌 ─────────────────────

- Geoffrey Marston, The Personality of International Organizations in English Law, Hofstra Law and Policy Symposium Vol. 2(1997), p. 75.

───────────────

1) M. Shaw, International Law 8th ed.(Cambridge University Press, 2017), p. 994.

5. 인권위원회 특별보고관의 면제에 관한 사건

(1999) — 유엔 특별보고관의 법적 지위

Difference Relating to Immunity from Legal Process of A Special Rapporteur of the Commission on Human Rights. Advisory Opinion, 1999 ICJ Report 62.

☑ 사 안

말레이시아의 법률가 Dato Param Cumaraswamy는 1994년 유엔 인권위원회로부터 "법관과 변호사의 독립성"에 관한 주제의 특별보고관으로 임명되었다. 그는 1995년 영국에서 발간되고 말레이시아에서도 판매되는 International Commercial Litigation지와의 인터뷰에서 말레이시아 법원에서의 몇몇 소송에 대하여 논평을 했는데, 이 때 언급된 2개의 말레이시아 회사로부터 명예훼손을 당했다며 총 1억 1200만 달러에 해당하는 손해배상을 청구당했다.

소송이 제기되자 사건을 조사한 유엔측은 Cumaraswamy의 발언이 특별보고관의 자격의 임무 수행중 나온 것이므로 그는 「유엔 특권과 면제에 관한 협약」 제6조 22항에 의하여 소송으로부터 면제를 향유한다고 결론내렸다. 유엔 사무총장은 이러한 입장을 말레이시아 정부에 여러 차례 전달했으나, 말레이시아 정부는 사법부에서의 소송에 관여하지 않겠다고 응답했다. 이에 경제사회이사회는 1998년 8월 이 문제에 관하여 ICJ에 권고적 의견을 묻기로 결의했다. 유엔측은 유엔의 전문가가 면제를 향유하는 범위를 개별국가의 법원이 결정하게 된다면 유엔 직원과 전문가들은 업무내용으로 인하여 언제 자국 법원에 소환될지를 두려워하게 되고, 이는 직원과 전문가들의 업무의 독립성에 악영향을 미친다고 주장했다.

☑ 쟁 점

특별보고관의 인터뷰 행위에 대해서 「유엔 특권과 면세에 관한 협약」 제6조 22항이 적용되는지 여부.1)

☑ 판 결

(1) 유엔에 의해 임명된 전문가의 행동이 협약에 따른 면제의 부여 대상이냐 여부에 관하여는 유엔 사무총장의 판단이 결정적 역할을 한다.

(2) 유엔 사무총장의 판단과 같이 Cumaraswamy의 인터뷰는 특별보고관으로서의 임무수행중의 행위로서 모든 종류의 소송으로부터 면제를 향유한다.

(3) 말레이시아 정부는 이 문제에 관한 유엔 사무총장의 입장과 ICJ의 권고적 의견을 자국의 담당법원에 전달할 의무가 있다.

판 결 문

47. The Court will now consider whether the immunity provided for in Section 22 (b) applies to Mr. Cumaraswamy in the specific circumstances of the case; namely, whether the words used by him in the interview, as published in the article in *International Commercial Litigation* (November issue 1995), were spoken in the course of the performance of his mission, and whether he was therefore immune from legal process with respect to these words. [⋯]

50. In the process of determining whether a particular expert on mission is entitled, in the prevailing circumstances, to the immunity provided for in Section 22 (b), the Secretary-General of the United Nations has a pivotal role to play. The Secretary-General, as the chief administrative officer of the Organization, has the authority and the responsibility to exercise the necessary protection where required. This authority has been recognized by the Court when it stated:

"Upon examination of the character of the functions entrusted to the

---

1) 제22항은 전문가가 임무 수행중 기능적 특권과 면제를 향유하며 특히 "b호: 임무 수행중 구두 또는 서면으로 행한 말과 행동에 대해 모든 종류의 법적 절차로부터의 면제. 그가 더 이상 UN 임무에 종사하지 않더라도 법적 절차로부터의 면제는 지속적으로 부여된다"고 규정하고 있다.

Organization and of the nature of the missions of its agents, it becomes clear that the capacity of the Organization to exercise a measure of functional protection of its agents arises by necessary intendment out of the Charter." (*Reparation for Injuries Suffered in the Service of the United Nations, Advisory Opinion, I. C. J. Reports 1949*, p. 184.)

51. Article VI, Section 23, of the General Convention provides that "[privileges and immunities are granted to experts in the interests of the United Nations and not for the personal benefit of the individuals themselves". In exercising protection of United Nations experts, the Secretary-General is therefore protecting the mission with which the expert is entrusted. In that respect, the Secretary-General has the primary responsibility and authority to protect the interests of the Organization and its agents, including experts on mission. As the Court held:

"In order that the agent may perform his duties satisfactorily, he must feel that this protection is assured to him by the Organization, and that he may count on it. To ensure the independence of the agent, and, consequently, the independent action of the Organization itself, it is essential that in performing his duties he need not have to rely on any other protection than that of the Organization ..." (*Ibid.*, p. 183.)

52. The determination whether an agent of the Organization has acted in the course of the performance of his mission depends upon the facts of a particular case. In the present case, the Secretary-General, or the Legal Counsel of the United Nations on his behalf, has on numerous occasions informed the Government of Malaysia of his finding that Mr. Cumaraswamy had spoken the words quoted in the article in *International Commercial Litigation* in his capacity as Special Rapporteur of the Commission and that he consequently was entitled to immunity from "every kind" of legal process.

53. As is clear from the written and oral pleadings of the United Nations, the Secretary-General was reinforced in this view by the fact that it has become standard practice of Special Rapporteurs of the Commission to have contact with the media. This practice was confirmed by the High Commissioner for Human Rights who, in a letter dated 2 October 1998, included in the dossier, wrote that:

"It is more common than not for Special Rapporteurs to speak to the press about matters pertaining to their investigations, thereby keeping the general public informed of their work".

54. As noted above [⋯], Mr. Cumaraswamy was explicitly referred to several times in the article "Malaysian Justice on Trial" in *International Commercial Litigation* in his capacity as United Nations Special Rapporteur on the Independence of Judges and Lawyers. In his reports to the Commission [⋯], Mr. Cumaraswamy had set out his methods of work, expressed concern about the independence of the Malaysian judiciary, and referred to the civil lawsuits initiated against him. His third report noted that the Legal Counsel of the United Nations had informed the Government of Malaysia that he had spoken in the performance of his mission and was therefore entitled to immunity from legal process.

55. As noted in [⋯], in its various resolutions the Commission took note of the Special Rapporteur's reports and of his methods of work. In 1997, it extended his mandate for another three years [⋯]. The Commission presumably would not have so acted if it had been of the opinion that Mr. Cumaraswamy had gone beyond his mandate and had given the interview to *International Commercial Litigation* outside the course of his functions. Thus the Secretary-General was able to find support for his findings in the Commission's position.

56. The Court is not called upon in the present case to pass upon the aptness of the terms used by the Special Rapporteur or his assessment of the situation. In any event, in view of all the circumstances of this case, elements of which are set out in paragraphs 1 to 15 of the note by the Secretary-General, the Court is of the opinion that the Secretary-General correctly found that Mr. Cumaraswamy, in speaking the words quoted in the article in *International Commercial Litigation*, was acting in the course of the performance of his mission as Special Rapporteur of the Commission. Consequently, Article VI, Section 22 (b), of the General Convention is applicable to him in the present case and affords Mr. Cumaraswamy immunity from legal process of every kind.

57. The Court will now deal with the second part of the Council's question, namely, "the legal obligations of Malaysia in this case."

58. Malaysia maintains that it is premature to deal with the question of its obligations. It is of the view that the obligation to ensure that the requirements of Section 22 of the Convention are met is an obligation of result and not of means to be employed in achieving that result. It further states that Malaysia has complied with its obligation under Section 34 of the General Convention, which provides that

a party to the Convention must be "in a position under its own law to give effect to [its] terms", by enacting the necessary legislation; finally it contends that the Malaysian courts have not yet reached a final decision as to Mr. Cumaraswamy's entitlement to immunity from legal process.

59. The Court wishes to point out that the request for an advisory opinion refers to "the legal obligations of Malaysia in this case." The difference which has arisen between the United Nations and Malaysia originated in the Government of Malaysia not having informed the competent Malaysian judicial authorities of the Secretary-General's finding that Mr. Cumaraswamy had spoken the words at issue in the course of the performance of his mission and was, therefore, entitled to immunity from legal process [···]. It is as from the time of this omission that the question before the Court must be answered.

60. As the Court has observed, the Secretary-General, as the chief administrative officer of the Organization, has the primary responsibility to safeguard the interests of the Organization; to that end, it is up to him to assess whether its agents acted within the scope of their functions and, where he so concludes, to protect these agents, including experts on mission, by asserting their immunity. This means that the Secretary-General has the authority and responsibility to inform the Government of a member State of his finding and, where appropriate, to request it to act accordingly and, in particular, to request it to bring his finding to the knowledge of the local courts if acts of an agent have given or may give rise to court proceedings.

61. When national courts are seised of a case in which the immunity of a United Nations agent is in issue, they should immediately be notified of any finding by the Secretary-General concerning that immunity. That finding, and its documentary expression, creates a presumption which can only be set aside for the most compelling reasons and is thus to be given the greatest weight by national courts. The governmental authorities of a party to the General Convention are therefore under an obligation to convey such information to the national courts concerned, since a proper application of the Convention by them is dependent on such information. Failure to comply with this obligation, among others, could give rise to the institution of proceedings under Article VIII, Section 30, of the General Convention.

62. The Court concludes that the Government of Malaysia had an obligation, under Article 105 of the Charter and under the General Convention, to inform its courts of the position taken by the Secretary-General. [⋯]

65. According to Article VIII, Section 30, of the General Convention, the opinion given by the Court shall be accepted as decisive by the parties to the dispute. Malaysia has acknowledged its obligations under Section 30. Since the Court holds that Mr. Cumaraswamy is an expert on mission who under Section 22 (b) is entitled to immunity from legal process, the Government of Malaysia is obligated to communicate this advisory opinion to the competent Malaysian courts, in order that Malaysia's international obligations be given effect and Mr. Cumaraswamy's immunity be respected.

☑ 해　설

이 사건은 유엔에 의해서 임명된 전문가의 행위가 「유엔 특권과 면제에 관한 협약」의 적용대상이 되는가에 대해 다루었다. 인권 분야의 경우 국내적 민감성으로 인해 특정 문제를 다루기 위한 특별보고관으로 임명된 개인은 여러 정치적 도전에 직면할 수 있다. 특히 특별보고관이 조사 대상국의 국적을 갖고 있는 경우 이들의 직무활동에 대한 특권과 면제가 보장되지 않는다면 적절한 활동을 하기가 사실상 불가능하다.

본 건에서는 특별보고관 Mr. Cumaraswamy는 한 잡지와의 인터뷰 과정에서 말레이시아 법원에서의 소송에 관해 피력한 의견에 대해서 말레이시아 국내법원에서 거액의 배상 소송에 휘말렸는데 그가 「유엔 특권과 면제에 관한 협약」의 적용을 받아 말레이시아 국내 소송절차로부터 면제될 수 있다는 결론에 도달하기 위해 국제사법재판소는 2가지를 고려했다.

먼저 특별보고관이 「유엔 특권과 면제에 관한 협약」의 적용이 되는 전문가인가 여부를 결정함에 있어서 소위 1989년 Mazilu 사건(1989 ICJ Reports 177)을 원용하면서 인권위원회에 의해 임명된 특별보고관은 「유엔 특권과 면제에 관한 협약」의 적용대상이 되는 전문가라고 판단을 했다. 그 후 국제사법재판소는 Mr. Cumaraswamy가 잡지와 인터뷰를 하면서 계속해서 본인의 특별보고관으로서의 직무와 관련되어서 인터뷰를 한다는 사실을 강조했고, 여러 정황으로 보아도 직무행위로서 인터뷰 행위를 인정할 수 있기 때문에 그의 인터뷰 행위는 「유엔 특권과 면제에 관한 협약」의 적용대상이 되는 행위임을 명확히 했다.

다만 ICJ는 소송절차로부터의 면제는 유엔이나 그의 직원의 임무상 행동으로 인하여 발생한 피해의 보상문제와는 별개로 다루어져야 한다고 지적했다. 즉 유엔도 자신의 잘못에 대하여는 법적 책임을 지게 된다. 다만 유엔에 대한 청구가 개별국가의 법정에서 다루어져서는 아니 되며, 이는「특권과 면제에 관한 협약」제8조 29항에 규정된 적절한 분쟁해결절차에 따라야 한다고 강조했다(para. 66).

Cumaraswamy는 1994년부터 2003년까지 특별보고관의 직책을 수행했으며, 그는 2005년 Gruber Prize for Justice를 수상했다.

제10장

국가영역

1. 팔마스 섬 사건(1928)
─ 실효적 지배의 요건

Island of Palmas Arbitration.
Netherlands/U.S.A., 2 R.I.A.A. 829(1949).

☑ 사   안

　팔마스(Palmas)(또는 Miangas) 섬은 오늘날 필리핀 민다나오 섬과 인도네시아 사이에 위치한 소도이다. 1898년 미국─스페인 전쟁의 결과 미국은 스페인으로부터 필리핀을 할양받았는데, 이 섬은 강화조약에 첨부된 필리핀 경계지도상 약 20해리 안쪽에 위치하고 있었다. 1906년 필리핀을 통치하던 미국의 Moro주 지사가 이 섬을 방문했을 때, 네덜란드 국기가 게양되어 있는 사실을 발견하고 본국에 보고했다. 이후 미국과 네덜란드는 약 15년간 이 섬의 영유권에 관한 협상을 했으나 합의를 보지 못하자, 양국은 이 사건을 중재재판에 회부하기로 결정했다. 이 사건은 상설중재재판소를 통해 Max Huber 단독 중재관에 회부되었다.

　미국은 이 섬이 1898년 파리조약을 통한 스페인의 필리핀 할양과 함께 미국령으로 되었다고 주장했다. 즉 1) 스페인은 16세기 발견을 통해 이 섬의 영유권을 취득했으며, 이는 파리조약을 통해 미국으로 할양되었다. 2) 팔마스 섬에 대한 스페인의 영유권은 17세기 이래 스페인과 네덜란드 간 일련의 조약에 의해 확인된 바 있었다. 3) 팔마스 섬은 미국령 필리핀에 더욱 가까우므로 미국령으로 판단되어야 한다고 주장했다.

　반면 네덜란드측은 1677년 동인도회사와 원주민간의 협정 이래 200년 이상 평온하게 이 섬에 대한 주권을 행사해 왔으며, 그간 스페인을 비롯한 어떠한 국가도 이에 이의를 제기하지 않았음을 근거로 이 섬이 자국령이라고 주장했다.

☑ 쟁　섬

발견을 근거로 한 스페인의 권원의 지속 여부.

☑ 판　결

발견만을 근거로 한 권원은 불완전한 권원에 불과하다. 영토취득을 위한 선점은 실효적이어야 하며, 실효성은 권원의 유지에도 요구된다.

판 결 문

(p. 839-) If a dispute arises as to the sovereignty over a portion of territory, it is customary to examine which of the States claiming sovereignty possesses a title—cession, conquest, occupation, etc.—superior to that which the other State might possibly bring forward against it. However, if the contestation is based on the fact that the other Party has actually displayed sovereignty, it cannot be sufficient to establish the title by which territorial sovereignty was validly acquired at a certain moment; it must also be shown that the territorial sovereignty has continued to exist and did exist at the moment which for the decision of the dispute must be considered as critical. This demonstration consists in the actual display of State activities, such as belongs only to the territorial sovereign.

[⋯] It seems therefore natural that an element which is essential for the constitution of sovereignty should not be lacking in its continuation. So true is this, that practice, as well as doctrine, recognizes—though under different legal formulae and with certain differences as to the conditions required—that the continuous and peaceful display of territorial sovereignty (peaceful in relation to other States) is as good as a title. [⋯]

The principle that continuous and peaceful display of the functions of State within a given region is a constituent element of territorial sovereignty is not only based on the conditions of the formation of independent States and their boundaries (as shown by the experience of political history) as well as on an international jurisprudence and doctrine widely accepted; [⋯]

Manifestations of territorial sovereignty assume, it is true, different forms, according to conditions of time and place. Although continuous in principle, sovereignty cannot be exercised in fact at every moment on every point of a territory. The intermittence and discontinuity compatible with the maintenance of the right necessarily differ according as inhabited or uninhabited regions are involved, or regions enclosed within territories in which sovereignty is incontestably displayed or again regions accessible from, for instance, the high seas. It is true that neighbouring States may by convention fix limits to their own sovereignty, even in regions such as the interior of scarcely explored continents where such sovereignty is scarcely manifested, and in this way each may prevent the other from any penetration of its territory. The delimitation of Hinterland may also be mentioned in this connection. [···][1]

It is admitted by both sides that international law underwent profound modifications between the end of the Middle-Ages and the end of the 19th century, as regards the rights of discovery and acquisition of uninhabited regions or regions inhabited by savages or semicivilised peoples. Both Parties are also agreed that a juridical fact must be appreciated in the light of the law contemporary with it, and not of the law in force at the time when a dispute in regard to it arises or falls to be settled. The effect of discovery by Spain is therefore to be determined by the rules of international law in force in the first half of the 16th century or (to take the earliest date) in the first quarter of it, i.e. at the time when the Portuguese or Spaniards made their appearance in the Sea of Celebes.

If the view most favourable to the American arguments is adopted with every reservation as to the soundness of such view that is to say, if we consider as positive law at the period in question the rule that discovery as such, i.e. the mere fact of seeing land, without any act, even symbolical, of taking possession, involved *ipso jure* territorial sovereignty and not merely an "inchoate title", a *jus ad rem*, to be completed eventually by an actual and durable taking of possession within a reasonable time, the question arises whether sovereignty yet existed at the critical date, i.e. the moment of conclusion and coming into force of the Treaty of Paris.

As regards the question which of different legal systems prevailing at successive periods is to be applied in a particular case (the so-called intertemporal law), a distinction must be made between the creation of rights and the existence of rights. The same principle which subjects the act creative of a right to the law in force at

---

1) 이어서 미국측은 스페인이 발견을 통해 팔마스섬에 대한 1차적 권원을 취득했고, 미국은 할양을 통해 이 섬에 대한 권원을 이양받았다고 주장했음을 지적했다.

the time the right arises, demands that the existence of the right, in other words its continued manifestation, shall follow the conditions required by the evolution of law. International law in the 19th century, having regard to the fact that most parts of the globe were under the sovereignty of States members of the community of nations, and that territories without a master had become relatively few, took account of a tendency already existing and especially developed since the middle of the 18th century, and laid down the principle that occupation, to constitute a claim to territorial sovereignty, must be effective, that is, offer certain guarantees to other States and their nationals. It seems therefore incompatible with this rule of positive law that there should be regions which are neither under the effective sovereignty of a State, nor without a master, but which are reserved for the exclusive influence of one State, in virtue solely of a title of acquisition which is no longer recognized by existing law, even if such a title ever conferred territorial sovereignty. For these reasons, discovery alone, without any subsequent act, cannot at the present time suffice to prove sovereignty over the Island of Palmas (or Miangas); [···]

If on the other hand the view is adopted that discovery does not create a definitive title of sovereignty, but only an "inchoate" title, such a title exists, it is true, without external manifestation. However, according to the view that has prevailed at any rate since the 19th century, an inchoate title of discovery must be completed within a reasonable period by the effective occupation of the region claimed to be discovered. This principle must be applied in the present case, for the reasons given above in regard to the rules determining which of successive legal systems is to be applied (the so-called intertemporal law). [···][2]

The Netherlands on the contrary found their claim to sovereignty essentially on the title of peaceful and continuous display of State authority over the island. Since this title would in international law prevail over a title of acquisition of sovereignty not followed by actual display of State authority, it is necessary to ascertain in the first place, whether the contention of the Netherlands is sufficiently established by evidence, and, if so, for what period of time. [···]

The acts of indirect or direct display of Netherlands sovereignty at Palmas (or Miangas), especially in the 18th and early 19th centuries are not numerous, and

---

2) 재판부는 팔마스 섬에서 스페인의 권리 행사가 없었고, 스페인의 불완전한 권원이 1898년까지 존속했다고 할지라도 이는 타국의 지속적이고도 평온한 권한행사에 우선할 수는 없다고 보았다. 이어서 지리적 인접성에 근거한 미국측의 권원주장도 검토했으나 이것만으로는 권원입증이 곤란하다고 판단했다. 그리고 네덜란드가 이 섬에 대한 종속관계 수립을 제3국에 통지할 국제법상의 의무도 없다고 판단했다.

there are considerable gaps in the evidence of continuous display. But apart from the consideration that the manifestations of sovereignty over a small and distant island, inhabited only by natives, cannot be expected to be frequent, it is not necessary that the display of sovereignty should go back to a very far distant period. It may suffice that such display existed in 1898, and had already existed as continuous and peaceful before that date long enough to enable any Power who might have considered herself as possessing sovereignty over the island, or having a claim to sovereignty, to have, according to local conditions, a reasonable possibility for ascertaining the existence of a state of things contrary to her real or alleged rights.

It is not necessary that the display of sovereignty should be established as having begun at a precise epoch; it suffices that it had existed at the critical period preceding the year 1898. It is quite natural that the establishment of sovereignty may be the outcome of a slow evolution, of a progressive intensification of State control. [⋯][3]

The Netherlands title of sovereignty, acquired by continuous and peaceful display of State authority during a long period of time going probably back beyond the year 1700, therefore holds good.

☑ 해　　설

이는 단독 중재재판관에 의한 판결이나 영토주권에 관한 개념 발전에 커다란 기여를 했으며, 후일 국제사회에서의 영토분쟁 해결에 관하여 가장 많은 영향을 끼친 판결 중의 하나이다. 이 판결에서 Huber 재판관은 권원의 성립과 권원의 지속을 별개로 보았다. 따라서 설사 16세기 무렵 스페인이 이 섬을 발견함으로써 권원이 성립되었다고 할지라도, 스페인의 권원이 유지되려면 후일의 국제법 발전에 따른 선점요건을 만족시켜야 한다고 전제했다. 즉 19세기의 국제법에 따르면 발견은 불완전한 권원에 불과하므로, 선점을 통한 권원확립에는 실효적 점유가 필요하다고 보았다. 지난 약 2세기 동안 팔마스 섬에 대하여는 네덜란드 외 다른 나라의 주권행사가 없었으며, 네덜란드의 주권행사에 대한 타국의 항의도 없었다는 점에서 네덜란드의 주권행

---

3) 재판부는 이어 네덜란드가 팔마스 섬을 자국령의 일부로 간주해 왔으며, 17세기 중엽 이래 네덜란드의 평화적인 주권 행사에 비해 스페인 등 다른 국가가 팔마스섬에 대하여 주권행사를 한 증거를 확인하기 어려움을 지적했다.

사는 평화적이면서도 배타적이었으며, 또한 공개적이었다고 평가했다. 따라서 17세기 이래 네덜란드가 이 섬에 대해 지속적이고 평화로운 주권행사를 했다면 네덜란드의 권원이 우선한다고 보았다. 또한 소수의 주민민이 사는 고립된 섬의 경우 제한적인 주권행사만으로도 권원 유지가 가능하며, 단순히 지리적으로 인접했다는 사실만으로는 국제법상의 권원 확립의 근거가 될 수 없다고 판단했다.

이 판결에서 시제법(intertemporal law) 원칙에 관한 Huber 재판관의 언급은 후일 적지 않은 논란을 일으켰다. 그는 특정 사실이나 행위가 행위당시의 국제법에 따라 평가되어야 하며, 한편 일단 취득된 권원도 이후 국제법의 변화에 따라 항시 재검토될 수 있다고 주장했다. 이중 후단의 주장은 국제관계를 끊임없이 불안정하게 만들 수 있다는 비판이 제기되었다.

➡ **참고문헌**
- 김한택, 팔마스섬 사건, 국제해양분쟁사례연구 1(해양법포럼, 2004), p. 58.
- P. Jessup, The Palmas Island Arbitration, AJIL Vol. 22(1928), p. 735.
- D. E. Khan, Max Huber as Arbitrator: The Palmas (Miangas) case and Other Arbitrations, EJIL Vol. 18(2007), p. 145.
- F. Nielsen, The Island of Palmas Arbitration(1928).

2. 동부 그린란드 사건(1933)
— 선점의 요건

Legal Status of Eastern Greenland.
Norway v. Denmark, PCIJ Reports Series A/B No.53.

☑ 사   안

1931년 노르웨이는 그린란드 동부지역을 자국령에 편입시키는 칙령을 발표했다. 노르웨이는 과거 덴마크의 주권은 그린란드 전역이 아니라, 서부지역만을 중심으로 행사되었으며, 그린란드 동부지역은 아직 무주지로 남아 있었다고 주장했다. 이에 대해 덴마크는 1721년 이래 전체 그린란드가 덴마크령이었으므로 노르웨이의 선점대상이 될 수 없으며, 덴마크는 오랜 기간동안 전체 그린란드에 대해 평화적이고 지속적인 주권행사를 하여 왔다고 주장했다. 또한 노르웨이는 이미 조약을 통해 그린란드에 대한 덴마크의 주권을 승인한 바 있으며, 1919년 노르웨이 외무장관은 전 그린란드에 대한 덴마크 영유권에 대해 이의를 제기하지 않겠다는 구두약속을 한 바 있다고 주장했다.

☑ 쟁   점

그린란드와 같은 극지에서의 영유권 확립을 위해 요구되는 실효적 지배의 정도.

☑ 판   결

선점을 통한 영유권 확립을 위하여는 주권자로서의 지배의사와 실제 권한의 행사가 필요하다. 다만 그린란드에 관해서는 거주인구가 없거나 매우 소멸하다는 극지로서의 특성이 고려되어야 한다.

판 결 문

(p. 46-) It must be borne in mind, however, that as the critical date is July 10th, 1931, it is not necessary that sovereignty over Greenland should have existed throughout the period during which the Danish Government maintains that it was in being. Even if the material submitted to the Court might be thought insufficient to establish the existence of that sovereignty during the earlier periods, this would not exclude a finding that it is sufficient to establish a valid title in the period immediately preceding the occupation.

Before proceeding to consider in detail the evidence submitted to the Court, it may be well to state that a claim to sovereignty based not upon some particular act or title such as a treaty of cession but merely upon continued display of authority, involves two elements each of which must be shown to exist: the intention and will to act as sovereign, and some actual exercise or display of such authority.

Another circumstance which must be taken into account by any tribunal which has to adjudicate upon a claim to sovereignty over a particular territory, is the extent to which the sovereignty is also claimed by some other Power. In most of the cases involving claims to territorial sovereignty which have come before an international tribunal, there have been two competing claims to the sovereignty, and the tribunal has had to decide which of the two is the stronger. One of the peculiar features of the present case is that up to 1931 there was no claim by any Power other than Denmark to the sovereignty over Greenland. Indeed, up till 1921, no Power disputed the Danish claim to sovereignty.

It is impossible to read the records of the decisions in cases as to territorial sovereignty without observing that in many cases the tribunal has been satisfied with very little in the way of the actual exercise of sovereign rights, provided that the other State could not make out a superior claim. This is particularly true in the case of claims to sovereignty over areas in thinly populated or unsettled countries. [⋯]

Norway has argued that in the legislative and administrative acts of the XVIIIth century on which Denmark relies as proof of the exercise of her sovereignty, the word "Greenland" is not used in the geographical sense, but means only the colonies or the colonized area on the West coast.

This is a point as to which the burden of proof lies on Norway. The geo-graphical meaning of the word "Greenland," i.e. the name which is habitually used in the maps to denominate the whole island, must be regarded as the ordinary meaning of the word. If it is alleged by one of the Parties that some unusual or exceptional meaning is to be attributed to it, it lies on that Party to establish its contention. In the opinion of the Court, Norway has not succeeded in establishing her contention. It is not sufficient for her to show that in many of these legislative and administrative acts action was only to be taken in the colonies. [···]

The conclusion to which the Court is led is that, bearing in mind the absence of any claim to sovereignty by another Power, and the Arctic and inaccessible character of the uncolonized parts of the country, the King of Denmark and Norway displayed during the period from the founding of the colonies by Hans Egede in 1721 up to 1814 his authority to an extent sufficient to give his country a valid claim to sovereignty, and that his rights over Greenland were not limited to the colonized area. [···][1]

The concessions granted for the erection of telegraph lines and the legislation fixing the limits of territorial waters in 1905 are also manifestations of the exercise of sovereign authority.

In view of the above facts, when taken in conjunction with the legislation she had enacted applicable to Greenland generally, the numerous treaties in which Denmark, with the concurrence of the other contracting Party, provided for the non-application of the treaty to Greenland in general, and the absence of all claim to sovereignty over Greenland by any other Power, Denmark must be regarded as having displayed during this period of 1814 to 1915 her authority over the uncolonized part of the country to a degree sufficient to confer a valid title to the sovereignty.

☑ 해 설

그린란드에 대한 영유권 분쟁은 복잡한 역사적 배경을 갖고 있다. 1261년 노르웨이 왕국이 그린란드에 대한 진출을 시작했는데, 1380년부터 1814년까지 덴마크와 노르웨이는 동일한 군주에 의해 통치되는 연합왕국을 형성

---

[1] 이어서 덴마크는 과거 자신이 체결한 각종 조약에 그린란드에는 적용을 배제한다는 조항을 삽입했던 사실을 지적하며 그린란드에 대한 덴마크의 주권의 증거로 제시했다. 이에 대하여 노르웨이는 조약상에 지적된 그린란드는 덴마크가 실제 식민 한 지역만을 가리킨다고 주장했다.

하고 있었다. 1605년 덴마크 - 노르웨이 연합왕국은 초창기 유럽 정착민이 사라진 그린란드를 재발견했고, 17세기부터 서부 그린란드에 정착지가 건설되기 시작했다. 나폴레옹 전쟁에서 패배한 덴마크 - 노르웨이 왕국은 노르웨이를 스웨덴으로 할양했으나, 애초 노르웨이에 속했던 그린란드, 아이슬란드 등은 할양대상에서 제외됨으로써 분리된 덴마크가 그린란드를 지배하게 되었다. 1905년 노르웨이가 스웨덴으로부터 분리·독립을 한 후, 그린란드 지역을 탐사하고 임시 무선국을 설치하자 덴마크가 항의했다. 제1차 대전 후 덴마크는 그린란드에 대한 주권을 공고화하려는 노력을 계속했고, 노르웨이와의 갈등이 본격화되었다.

이 사건 재판부는 구체적으로 어떠한 근거에 의해 덴마크의 권원이 성립되었는가는 설시하지 않았다. 다만 경쟁적인 권원의 주장이 있는 경우 어느 편 주장이 더 우월한가를 기준으로 판단한다는 입장만을 밝혔다. 재판부는 12대 2의 판결로 1921년 이전에는 그린란드에 대한 덴마크의 주권주장에 대해 어떤 국가도 이의제기를 하지 않았다는 점, 실효적 지배와 관련해서는 문제의 극지지역은 거주인구가 없거나 소밀하다는 지역적 특성이 고려되어야 한다는 점, 덴마크의 여러 국내법령과 조약에 비추어 볼 때 비록 덴마크가 전 그린란드를 세세히 통제하고 있지 못했더라도 그린란드 전체가 덴마크령이라고 결론내렸다. 판단과정에서는 오래된 과거의 증거보다는 비교적 최근의 증거에 결정적 의미를 부여했다.

한편 제1차 대전 직후인 1919년 7월 14일 노르웨이 주재 덴마크 공사는 Ihlen 외무장관을 방문하면서 전 그린란드에 대한 덴마크의 영유권 주장을 노르웨이가 반대하지 않는다면 파리 평화회담시 스피츠베르겐에 대한 노르웨이의 영유권 주장에 덴마크도 반대하지 않겠다는 제안을 하였다. 당시 Ihlen 장관은 생각해 보겠다고만 답하였다. 이후 7월 22일 Ihlen 장관은 덴마크 공사에게 이 문제의 해결에 있어서 노르웨이 정부는 어떠한 어려움도 일으키지 않겠다고 구두로 통보했다. 이후 덴마크는 Ihlen의 발언을 문서로 확인해 줄 것을 노르웨이 정부에 여러 차례 요청했으나, 노르웨이 정부는 이를 거부했다. 덴마크측은 이 발언이 노르웨이에 구속력을 갖는다고 주장했고, 재판부는 7월 22일자 Ihlen 선언에 의해 노르웨이는 전 그린란드에 대한 덴마크의 영유권을 다투지 않을 의무를 지게 되었다고 판단했다.

▶ 참고문헌 ──────────────────────────────

- 이석용, 덴마크－노르웨이간 동부 그린랜드 사건, Strategy 21 7권 2호(2006), p. 82.
- 제성호, 동부 그린란드 사건과 독도영유권 문제, 중앙법학 8집 2호(2006), p. 201.
- C Hyde, The Case concerning the Legal Status of Eastern Greenland, AJIL Vol. 27(1933), p. 732.
- L. Preuss, The Dispute between Denmark and Norway over the Sovereignty of East Greenland, AJIL Vol. 26(1932), p. 469.
- O. Svarrlien, The Eastern Greenland Case in Historical Perspective(1964).

3. 멩끼에·에크레오 섬 사건(1953)
─ 관할권 행사의 증거

The Minquiers and Ecrehos Case.
France/U.K., 1953 ICJ Reports 47.

☑ 사   안

Minquiers 및 Ecrehos 섬은 노르망디 반도 앞 영국령 Channel 군도 소속의 Jersey 섬과 프랑스령 Chausey 섬 부근에 위치한 작은 제도이다. 영국과 프랑스는 각기 고대로부터 이 섬을 지속적으로 영유하고 있었다고 주장했다. 영국은 본래 이 섬이 노르망디공 윌리엄의 소유령으로 노르만의 영국점령을 통해 이들 지역은 영국과 일체화되었고, 이후 프랑스 왕이 대륙에서 노르만 세력을 몰아내려 했으나, 이들 섬을 포함한 Channel 군도는 계속 영국왕의 관할하에 남았다고 주장했다. 반면 프랑스는 노르망디공이 원래 프랑스 왕의 신하의 자격으로 봉토를 보유하고 있었는데, 1202년 프랑스 법원 판결로 그의 모든 토지가 몰수당했기 때문에 이들 섬에 대한 주권은 프랑스로 귀속되었다고 주장했다. 이어 양국은 20세기 초까지 이들 섬에 대하여 자신들이 관할권을 행사한 여러 가지 다양한 역사적 증거를 제출하며, 자국령이 유지되었다고 주장했다.

☑ 쟁   점

영국과 프랑스 양국이 고대로부터의 원시적 권원을 주장한 멩끼에 및 에크레오 섬은 어느 국가 소속인가?

☑ 판　　결

영유권 분쟁에 있어서 오래된 역사적 증거를 통한 간접적 추정보다는 근래 당사국이 관할권을 행사해 온 직접적 증거에 중점을 두고 판단할 때, 이들 섬은 영국령이다.

판 결 문

(p. 56-) These opposite contentions are based on more or less uncertain and controversial views as to what was the true situation in this remote feudal epoch. For the purpose of deciding the present case it is, in the opinion of the Court, not necessary to solve these historical controversies. The Court considers it sufficient to state as its view that even if the Kings of France did have an original feudal title also in respect of the Channel Islands, such a title must have lapsed as a consequence of the events of the year 1204 and following years. Such an alleged original feudal title of the Kings of France in respect of the Channel Islands could today produce no legal effect, unless it had been replaced by another title valid according to the law of the time of replacement. [⋯]

What is of decisive importance, in the opinion of the Court, is not indirect presumptions deduced from events in the Middle Ages, but the evidence which relates directly to the possession of the Ecrehos and Minquiers groups. [⋯]

From the beginning of the nineteenth century the connection between the Ecrehos and Jersey became closer again because of the growing importance of the oyster fishery in the waters surrounding the islets, and Jersey authorities took, during the subsequent period, action in many ways in respect of the islets. Of the manifold facts invoked by the United Kingdom Government, the Court attaches, in particular, probative value to the acts which relate to the exercise of jurisdiction and local administration and to legislation.

In 1826 criminal proceedings were instituted before the Royal Court of Jersey against a Jerseyman for having shot at a person on the Ecrehos. Similar judicial proceedings in Jersey in respect of criminal offences committed on the Ecrehos took place in 1881, 1883, 1891, 1913 and 1921. [⋯] These facts show therefore that Jersey courts have exercised criminal jurisdiction in respect of the Ecrehos during nearly a hundred years.

Evidence produced shows that the law of Jersey has for centuries required the holding of an inquest on corpses found within the Bailiwick where it was not clear that death was due to natural causes. Such inquests on corpses found at the Ecrehos were held in 1859, 1917 and 1948 and are additional evidence of the exercise of jurisdiction in respect of these islets.

Since about 1820, and probably earlier, persons from Jersey have erected and maintained some habitable houses or huts on the islets of the Ecrehos, where they have stayed during the fishing season. Some of these houses or huts have, for the purpose of parochial rates, been included in the records of the Parish of St. Martin in Jersey, which have been kept since 1889, and they have been assessed for the levying of local taxes. Rating schedules for 1889 and 1950 were produced in evidence.

A register of fishing boats for the port of Jersey shows that the fishing boat belonging to a Jersey fisherman, who lived permanently on an islet of the Ecrehos for more than forty years, was entered in that register in 1872, the port or place of the boat being indicated as 'Ecrehos Rocks', and that the licence of that boat was cancelled in 1882. According to a letter of June, 1876, from the Principal Customs Officer of Jersey, an official of that Island visited occasionally the Ecrehos for the purpose of endorsing the licence of that boat.

It is established that contracts of sale relating to real property on the Ecrehos islets have been passed before the competent authorities of Jersey and registered in the public registry of deeds of that island. Examples of such registration of contracts are produced for 1863, 1881, 1884 and some later years.

In 1884, a custom-house was established in the Ecrehos by Jersey customs authorities. The islets have been included by Jersey authorities within the scope of their census enumerations, and in 1901 an official enumerator visited the islets for the purpose of taking the census.

These various facts show that Jersey authorities have in several ways exercised ordinary local administration in respect of the Ecrehos during a long period of time.

By a British Treasury Warrant of 1875, constituting Jersey as a Port of the Channel Islands, the "Ecrehou Rocks" were included within the limits of that port. This legislative Act was a clear manifestation of British sovereignty over the Ecrehos at a time when a dispute as to such sovereignty had not yet arisen. [···]

Of other facts which throw light upon the dispute, it should be mentioned that

Jersey authorities have made periodical official visits to the Ecrehos since 1885, and that they have carried out various works and constructions there, such as a slipway in 1895, a signal post in 1910 and the placing of a mooring buoy in 1939. [⋯]

In the course of the diplomatic exchanges between the two Governments in the beginning of the nineteenth century concerning fisheries off the coast of Cotentin, the French Ambassador in London addressed to the Foreign Office a Note, dated June 12th, 1820, attaching two charts sent from the French Ministry of Marine to the French Ministry of Foreign Affairs purporting to delimit the areas within which the fishermen of each country were entitled to exclusive rights of fishery. In these charts a blue line marking territorial waters was drawn along the coast of the French mainland and round the Chausey Islands, which were indicated as French, and a red line marking territorial waters was drawn round Jersey, Alderney, Sark and the Minquiers, which were indicated as British. No line of territorial waters was drawn round the Ecrehos group, one part of which was included in the red line for Jersey and consequently marked as belonging to Great Britain and the other part apparently treated as *res nullius*.[1] When the French Government in 1876 protested against the British Treasury Warrant of 1875 and challenged British sovereignty over the Ecrehos, it did not itself claim sovereignty, but continued to treat the Ecrehos as *res nullius*. In a letter of March 26th, 1884, from the French Ministry of Foreign Affairs to the French Minister of Marine, it was stated that the British Government had not ceased to claim the Ecrehos as a dependency to the Channel Islands, and it was suggested that French fishermen should be prohibited access to the Ecrehos. It does not appear that any such measure was taken, and subsequently, in a Note to the Foreign Office of December 15th, 1886, the French Government claimed for the first time sovereignty over the Ecrehos '*a la lumiere des nouvelles donnees historiques et geologiques.*'[2]

The Court, being now called upon to appraise the relative strength of the opposing claims to sovereignty over the Ecrehos in the light of the facts considered above, finds that the Ecrehos group in the beginning of the thirteenth century was considered and treated as an integral part of the fief of the Channel Islands which were held by the English King, and that the group continued to be under the dominion of that King, who in the beginning of the fourteenth century exercised jurisdiction in respect thereof. The Court further finds that British authorities during the greater part of the nineteenth century and in the twentieth century have

---

1) 무주지 — 필자 주.
2) "새로운 역사적 및 지질학적 여건에 비추어."

exercised State functions in respect of the group. The French Government, on the other hand, has not produced evidence showing that it has any valid title to the group. In such circumstances it must be concluded that the sovereignty over the Ecrehos belongs to the United Kingdom.[3]

☑ 해 설

영국과 프랑스 양국은 모두 이들 섬에 대해 원시적 권원을 갖고 있다고 주장하며, 이들 섬이 무주지 또는 공유지로서의 지위를 가질 수 있다는 점은 처음부터 배제했다. 고래로부터의 원시적 권원을 주장하기 위해 양국은 중세 이래의 다양한 증거를 제시했으나, 재판부는 설사 프랑스가 봉건적 권원을 보유했었다 할지라도 이는 후일 유효한 권원으로 대체되지 않았으면 법적 효과가 없다고 보았다. 이어 중세의 증거로부터의 간접적 추정은 필요 없고 섬의 영유권에 대한 근래의 직접적 증거만을 중시하겠다고 전제했다. 이에 재판부가 두 섬의 영유권의 소재를 판정함에 있어서 중요하게 사용한 증거는 모두 19세기 이후의 관할권 행사에 관한 사실들이다. 즉 각종 재판권의 행사, 시체검시, 세금징수, 어선등록, 부동산 등기, 세관설치 등의 행정권의 행사, 입법권 행사 등에 관하여 영국이 제시한 증거가 상대적으로 우월하다고 판단해 문제의 섬들이 영국령이라고 판결했다.

이 판결은 분쟁 당사국들이 고래로부터의 원시적 권원을 주장하는 섬에 관한 영유권 다툼이라는 점에서 독도문제와 유사하다는 이유에서 주목을 받았다. 그러나 재판부는 오래된 역사적 증거에 대하여는 법적 효과를 인정하지 않고, 근래의 국가행정권의 행사에 관한 증거만을 중심으로 판결을 내렸다. 또한 특정한 권원에 입각해 영유권의 소재를 결정하지 않고, 양국 주장 중 누가 상대적으로 우월한 증거를 제시하고 있느냐를 기준으로 종합적으로 판단했다. 결국 이 판결 역시 영역에 대한 실효적 지배의 중요성을 재차 강조한 것이다.

한편 이 판결은 1999년 한일 신어업협정을 통해 독도 주변을 포함한 동해에 중간수역을 설치한 것이 한국의 독도 영유권을 훼손하는 것이냐는 논

---

3) 이어서 재판부는 Minquiers 섬에 대하여도 거의 유사한 지방행정권을 영국령 Jersey 당국이 행사해 왔다는 점에 주목해 영국령으로 판단했다.

란과 더불어 다시 한번 국내에서 주목을 받았다. 즉 영국과 프랑스 양국은 1839년 멩끼에 및 에크레오 섬 주변에 공동어업구역을 설정하는 어업협정을 체결한 바 있었는데, 그 제5조는 다음과 같았다.

(5) that the islets and rocks of the Minquiers and Ecrehos groups, being within the common fishery zone as so defined, were, in 1839, subjected by the Parties to a regime of common user for fishery purposes, without the territorial sovereignty over these islets and rocks being otherwise affected by the said Convention;

재판부는 다음과 같이 공동어업수역의 설치가 멩끼에 등의 섬의 영유권 다툼에 영향을 미치지 않는다고 판단했다.

(p. 58-) The Court does not consider it necessary, for the purpose of deciding the present case, to determine whether the waters of the Ecrehos and Minquiers groups are inside or outside the common fishery zone established by Article 3.

Even if it be held that these groups lie within this common fishery zone, the Court cannot admit that such an agreed common fishery zone in these waters would involve a regime of common user of the land territory of the islets and rocks, since the Articles relied on refer to fishery only and not to any kind of user of land territory. Nor can the Court admit that such an agreed common fishery zone should necessarily have the effect of precluding the Parties from relying on subsequent acts involving a manifestation of sovereignty in respect of the islets. The Parties could have established such a common fishery zone, including the waters of the groups, even if these groups had in 1839 been under the undisputed exclusive sovereignty of one of them; and they could equally have acquired or claimed exclusive sovereignty after 1839 and relied upon subsequent acts involving the manifestation of sovereignty, notwithstanding such an agreed common fishery zone, provided of course that the common fishery in this zone would not in any way be impaired thereby.

▶ 참고문헌 ─────────────────────────────

- 이한기, The Minquiers and Ecrehos case 연구, (서울대학교) 법학 제9권 제1호(1967), p. 5.
- 이창위, 영국과 프랑스간 멩끼에 · 에끄레오 도서 사건, Strategy 제7권 제2호(2004), p. 106.
- 황승현, ICJ 망키에 · 에크르오 사건(1953)을 통해서 본 일본의 독도 분쟁 지역화 시사점(국립외교원, 2017).
- Young-Min Youn, Sung-Ho Park & Yun-Cheol Lee, A critical survey of the channel islands dispute between the UK and France : a comparative study of the Minquiers − Ecrehos case and the Dokdo problem, 해사법연구 제21권 제3호(2009), p. 149.
- W. Bishop, Minquiers and Ecrehos Case, AJIL Vol. 48(1954), p. 316.
- Fitzmaurice, The Law and Procedure of the International Court of Justice, 1951 − 1954: Points of Substantive Law Part II BYIL Vol. 32(1955 − 56), p. 20.
- D. Johnson, The Minquiers and Ecrehos Case, ICLQ Vol. 3(1954), p. 189.
- E. C. Wade, The Minquiers and Ecrehos Case, (1954) 40 Transactions of the Grotius Society for the year 1954, Vol. 40(1955), p. 97.

4. 리기탄 및 시파단 섬 영유권 분쟁(2002)
— 영토분쟁과 effectivités

Case Concerning Sovereignity over Pulau Ligitan and Pulau Sipadan.
Indonesia/Malaysia, 2002 ICJ Reports 625.

☑ 사 안

리기탄 섬과 시파단 섬은 말레이지아 남동부 셀레베스 해에 소재한 작은 무인도였다. 인도네시아는 1891년 영국－네덜란드간 「보르네오 경계획정에 관한 협약」 이래 이들 섬이 네덜란드령으로 확인된 바 있으며, 1945년 인도네시아의 독립과 동시에 이들 섬에 대한 영유권을 승계했다고 주장했다. 또한 과거 네덜란드 식민지 시절 이들 지역에 대한 네덜란드 해군 활동 등에 의해 영유권이 확인된 바 있다고 주장했다. 반면 말레이시아는 역사적으로 1878년 영국과 이곳 술탄간의 협정에 의해 영유권이 확인된 바 있고, 이후의 여러 종류의 실효적 지배권 행사를 통해 이들 섬의 영유권을 유지해 왔다고 주장했다. 1969년 양국간 대륙붕 경계획정을 협의하는 과정에서 이 섬에 대한 영유권 분쟁이 표면화되었으며, 당시 양국은 일단 이들 섬의 법적 지위를 현상 동결하기로 합의했다. 이후 80년대 중반 말레이지아가 이 섬을 관광지로 개발하려고 하자 다시 분쟁이 격화되었다. 수년 간의 영유권 협상이 실패로 돌아가자 이 사건은 1998년 당사국 합의하에 ICJ로 회부되었다.

☑ 쟁 점

영토분쟁의 판정기준으로서 *effectivités*의 기능.

☑ 판 결

분쟁 당사국의 주장을 입증할 다른 설성적 권원이 존재하지 않는 경우, *effectivités*를 근거로 영토주권의 소재를 판정할 수 있다.

판 결 문

134. The Court first recalls the statement by the Permanent Court of International Justice in the Legal Status of Eastern Greenland (Denmark v. Norway) case: [⋯]

> "It is impossible to read the records of the decisions in cases as to territorial sovereignty without observing that in many cases the tribunal has been satisfied with very little in the way of the actual exercise of sovereign rights, provided that the other State could not make out a superior claim. This is particularly true in the case of claims to sovereignty over areas in thinly populated or unsettled countries." (*P.C.I.J., Series A/B, No. 53*, pp. 45-46.)

In particular in the case of very small islands which are uninhabited or not permanently inhabited—like Ligitan and Sipadan, which have been of little economic importance (at least until recently)—*effectivités* will indeed generally be scarce. [⋯]

136. The Court finally observes that it can only consider those acts as constituting a relevant display of authority which leave no doubt as to their specific reference to the islands in dispute as such. Regulations or administrative acts of a general nature can therefore be taken as *effectivités* with regard to Ligitan and Sipadan only if it is clear from their terms or their effects that they pertained to these two islands.

137. Turning now to the *effectivités* relied on by Indonesia, the Court will begin by pointing out that none of them is of a legislative or regulatory character. Moreover, the Court cannot ignore the fact that Indonesian Act No. 4 of 8 February 1960, which draws Indonesia's archipelagic baselines, and its accompanying map do not mention or indicate Ligitan and Sipadan as relevant base points or turning points.[1] [⋯]

---

1) 이어서 인도네시아는 분쟁도서 주변 수역에 네덜란드와 인도네시아 해군이 계속적으로 주둔

140. Finally, Indonesia states that the waters around Ligitan and Sipadan have traditionally been used by Indonesian fishermen. The Court observes, however, that activities by private persons cannot be seen as *effectivités* if they do not take place on the basis of official regulations or under governmental authority.

141. The Court concludes that the activities relied upon by Indonesia do not constitute acts *a titre de souverain* reflecting the intention and will to act in that capacity.

142. With regard to the *effectivités* relied upon by Malaysia, the Court first observes that pursuant to the 1930 Convention, the United States relinquished any claim it might have had to Ligitan and Sipadan and that no other State asserted its sovereignty over those islands at that time or objected to their continued administration by the State of North Borneo. [···]

143. As evidence of such effective administration over the islands, Malaysia cites the measures taken by the North Borneo authorities to regulate and control the collecting of turtle eggs on Ligitan and Sipadan, an activity of some economic significance in the area at the time. It refers in particular to the Turtle Preservation Ordinance of 1917, the purpose of which was to limit the capture of turtles and the collection of turtle eggs "within the State [of North Borneo] or the territorial waters thereof". The Court notes that the Ordinance provided in this respect for a licensing system and for the creation of native reserves for the collection of turtle eggs and listed Sipadan among the islands included in one of those reserves.

Malaysia adduces several documents showing that the 1917 Turtle Preservation Ordinance was applied until the 1950s at least. In this regard, it cites, for example, the licence issued on 28 April 1954 by the District Officer of Tawau permitting the capture of turtles pursuant to Section 2 of the Ordinance. The Court observes that this licence covered an area including "the islands of Sipadan, Ligitan, Kapalat, Mabul, Dinawan and Si-Amil."

Further, Malaysia mentions certain cases both before and after 1930 in which it has been shown that administrative authorities settled disputes about the collection of turtle eggs on Sipadan.

144. Malaysia also refers to the fact that in 1933 Sipadan, under Section 28 of the Land Ordinance, 1930, was declared to be "a reserve for the purpose of bird sanctuaries."

하거나, 정찰 활동을 한 사실을 영유권의 증거로 제시했으나, 재판부는 그것만으로는 분쟁 도서가 자국령이라는 결론을 도출할 수는 없다고 판단했다.

145. The Court is of the opinion that both the measures taken to regulate and control the collecting of turtle eggs and the establishment of a bird reserve must be seen as regulatory and administrative assertions of authority over territory which is specified by name.

146. Malaysia further invokes the fact that the authorities of the colony of North Borneo constructed a lighthouse on Sipadan in 1962 and another on Ligitan in 1963, that those lighthouses exist to this day and that they have been maintained by Malaysian authorities since its independence. It contends that the construction and maintenance of such lighthouses is "of a pattern of exercise of State authority appropriate in kind and degree to the character of the places involved." [···]

148. The Court notes that the activities relied upon by Malaysia, both in its own name and as successor State of Great Britain, are modest in number but that they are diverse in character and include legislative, administrative and quasijudicial acts. They cover a considerable period of time and show a pattern revealing an intention to exercise State functions in respect of the two islands in the context of the administration of a wider range of islands.

The Court moreover cannot disregard the fact that at the time when these activities were carried out, neither Indonesia nor its predecessor, the Netherlands, ever expressed its disagreement or protest. In this regard, the Court notes that in 1962 and 1963 the Indonesian authorities did not even remind the authorities of the colony of North Borneo, or Malaysia after its independence, that the construction of the lighthouses at those times had taken place on territory which they considered Indonesian; even if they regarded these lighthouses as merely destined for safe navigation in an area which was of particular importance for navigation in the waters off North Borneo, such behaviour is unusual.

149. Given the circumstances of the case, and in particular in view of the evidence furnished by the Parties, the Court concludes that Malaysia has title to Ligitan and Sipadan on the basis of the *effectivités* referred to above.

☑ 해   설

이 사건에서 말레이시아와 인도네시아는 모두 식민지 시절인 19세기 체결된 조약을 근거로 한 역사적 권원을 주장했으나, 재판부는 이들 조약들이 영유권의 근거가 될 수 없다고 판단했다. 일단 이들 섬이 무주지는 아니라고 전제한 재판부는 이들 지역에 대한 관할권 행사의 증거로서의 *effectivités*를 검토했다. *effectivités*라는 용어는 ICJ 판결에서는 Frontier Dispute(Burkina Faso, Mali, 1986)에서 처음 등장했다. 이의 의미는 1) 권원 취득에 직접 관계되는 주권의 표시(권원 성립의 근거) 또는 2) 이미 성립된 권원을 확인하기 위한 증거로서 고려되는 관할권의 행사나 표시이다(권원의 증거).

Burkinan Faso/Mali 사건 재판부는 *effectivité*의 역할을 다음과 같이 설명했다.

> "**63.** [⋯] Where the act corresponds exactly to law, where effective administration is additional to the *uti possidetis juris*, the only role of *effectivité* is to confirm the exercise of the right derived from a legal title. Where the act does not correspond to the law, where the territory which is the subject of the dispute is effectively administered by a State other than the one possessing the legal title, preference should be given to the holder of the title. In the event that the *effectivité* does not co-exist with any legal title, it must invariably be taken into consideration. Finally, there are cases where the legal title is not capable of showing exactly the territorial expanse to which it relates. The *effectivités* can then play an essential role in showing how the title is interpreted in practice."

인도네시아는 분쟁 도서 주변에서의 해군활동과 전통적으로 자국 어민이 부근 수역에서 어로행위를 했다는 사실을 강조했으나, 재판부는 이러한 주장에 대해 별다른 가치를 인정하지 않았다. 특히 인근 수역에서의 私人의 어로행위는 국가주권 행사의 증거로 인정되지 않는다고 판단했다. 반면 말레이지아는 식민시대부터 이들 섬에서의 바다 거북과 그 알 채취의 제한, 어로 면허의 발급, 조류 보호구역의 지정, 등대의 설치 유지 등, 비록 그 수는 많지 않았어도 입법, 행정 및 준사법적 다양한 조치를 취해 왔다고 보아 이들 섬에 대한 국가기능 행사의지가 표현되었다고 보았다. 결국 재판부는 말레이시아의 영유권을 인정했다. 이 판결 역시 독도 분쟁과의 부분적 유사성으로 인하여 우리의 관심을 끈다.

➡ 참고문헌 ────────────────────────────

- 허숙연, 영역분쟁의 해결기준의 변용─ICJ에 있어서의 effectivités의 흡입에 내하여, 서울국제법연구 11권 1호(2004), p. 231.
- 정민정, 인도네시아와 말레이시아간의 도서분쟁사안 연구: 한일간 독도영유권 사안에의 적용, 서울국제법연구 12권 1호(2005), p. 157.
- 이창위, 말레이시아와 인도네시아의 리기탄·사파단 도서분쟁, 이석용·이창위·김채형, 국제해양법 판례연구(세창출판사, 2015), p. 181.
- D. Caron, Sovereignty over Pulau Ligitan and Pulau Sipadan(Indonesia/Malaysia), AJIL Vol. 97(2003), p. 398.
- J. Merrils, Sovereignty over Pulau Ligitan and Pulau Sipadan(Indonesia/Malaysia), ICLQ Vol. 52(2003), p. 797.

5. 서부 사하라의 법적 지위(1975)
— 무주지의 개념

Western Sahara.
Advisory Opinion, 1975 ICJ Reports 12.

☑ 사   안

아프리카 북서부의 서부 사하라 지역은 1884년 이래 스페인의 식민지였다. 1970년대 중반 인구는 약 75,000명으로 대부분이 유목민이었다. 1966년 유엔 총회는 서부 사하라 지역 원주민의 민족자결을 바탕으로 한 탈식민지화 실현을 목표로 스페인과 인접 모로코, 그리고 모리타니아를 초청했다. 협상과정에서 모로코와 모리타니아는 이 지역의 독립에 반대하며, 스페인 식민지화 이전부터의 역사적 권원을 바탕으로 자국에 귀속되어야 한다고 주장했다. 이러한 주장을 판단하기 위하여 유엔 총회는 1974년 아래와 같은 쟁점에 관하여 ICJ에 권고적 의견을 요청했다.

☑ 쟁   점

(1) 서부 사하라가 스페인의 식민지로 될 당시 국제법상 무주지였는가 여부.

(2) 스페인의 식민지 성립 직전의 모로코 또는 모리타니아와 서부 사하라간의 법적 관계.

☑ 판   결

(1) 사회적 및 정치적 조직을 갖춘 부족이 거주하던 지역은 국제법상 무주지가 아니므로 스페인의 식민지 건설 당시 서부 사하라 지역은 무주지가

아니었다.

⑵ 모로코 및 모리타니아와 서부 사하라 지역간에는 일정한 법적 유대가 존재했으나, 이것이 영토주권관계는 아니었으며 또한 서부 사하라 주민의 민족자결권 행사에 영향을 미치는 성격의 법적 유대도 아니었다.

판 결 문

79. Turning to Question I, the Court observes that the request specifically locates the question in the context of 'the time of colonization by Spain', and it therefore seems clear that the words 'Was Western Sahara ... a territory belonging to no one (*terra nullius*)?' have to be interpreted by reference to the law in force at that period. The expression '*terra nullius*' was a legal term of art employed in connection with 'occupation' as one of the accepted legal methods of acquiring sovereignty over territory. 'Occupation' being legally an original means of peaceably acquiring sovereignty over territory otherwise than by cession or succession, it was a cardinal condition of a valid 'occupation' that the territory should be *terra nullius* —a territory belonging to no-one—at the time of the act alleged to constitute the 'occupation' (cf. *Legal Status of Eastern Greenland, P.C.I.J., Series A/B, No. 53*, pp. 44 f. and 63 f.). In the view of the Court, therefore, a determination that Western Sahara was a '*terra nullius*' at the time of colonization by Spain would be possible only if it were established that at that time the territory belonged to no-one in the sense that it was then open to acquisition through the legal process of 'occupation'.

80. Whatever differences of opinion there may have been among jurists, the State practice of the relevant period indicates that territories inhabited by tribes or peoples having a social and political organization were not regarded as *terrae nullius*. It shows that in the case of such territories the acquisition of sovereignty was not generally considered as effected unilaterally through 'occupation' of terra nullius by original title but through agreements concluded with local rulers. On occasion, it is true, the word 'occupation' was used in a non-technical sense denoting simply acquisition of sovereignty; but that did not signify that the acquisition of sovereignty through such agreements with authorities of the country was regarded as an 'occupation' of a '*terra nullius*' in the proper sense of these terms. On the contrary, such agreements with local rulers, whether or not considered as an actual 'cession' of the territory, were regarded as derivative roots of title, and not original titles obtained by occupation of *terrae nullius*.

81. In the present instance, the information furnished to the Court shows that at the time of colonization Western Sahara was inhabited by peoples which, if nomadic, were socially and politically organized in tribes and under chiefs competent to represent them. It also shows that, in colonizing Western Sahara, Spain did not proceed on the basis that it was establishing its sovereignty over *terrae nullius*. In its Royal Order of 26 December 1884, far from treating the case as one of occupation of *terra nullius*, Spain proclaimed that the King was taking the Rio de Oro under his protection on the basis of agreements which had been entered into with the chiefs of the local tribes: the Order referred expressly to 'the documents which the independent tribes of this part of the coast' had 'signed with the representative of the Sociedad Espanola de Africanistas', [···].

82. [···] It is asked only to state whether Western Sahara (Rio de Oro and Sakiet El Hamra) at the time of colonization by Spain was 'a territory belonging to no one (*terra nullius*)'. As to this question, the Court is satisfied that, for the reasons which it has given, its answer must be in the negative. [···]

84. Question II asks the Court to state 'what were the legal ties between this territory'—that is, Western Sahara—'and the Kingdom of Morocco and the Mauritanian entity'. [···]

91. [···] Morocco, however, invokes *inter alia* the decision of the Permanent Court of International Justice in the Legal Status of Eastern Greenland case (*P.C.I.J., Series A/B, No. 53*). Stressing that during a long period Morocco was the only independent State which existed in the north-west of Africa, it points to the geographical contiguity of Western Sahara to Morocco and the desert character of the territory. In the light of these considerations, it maintains that the historical material suffices to establish Morocco's claim to a title based 'upon continued display of authority' (*loc. cit.*, p. 45) on the same principles as those applied by the Permanent Court in upholding Denmark's claim to possession of the whole of Greenland.

92. This method of formulating Morocco's claims to ties of sovereignty with Western Sahara encounters certain difficulties. As the Permanent Court stated in the case concerning the Legal Status of Eastern Greenland, a claim to sovereignty based upon continued display of authority involves 'two elements each of which must be shown to exist: the intention and will to act as sovereign, and some actual exercise or display of such authority' (*ibid.*, pp. 45 f). True, the Permanent Court recognized that in the case of claims to sovereignty over areas in thinly populated or unsettled countries, 'very little in the way of actual exercise of sovereign rights' (*ibid.*, p. 46) might be sufficient in the absence of a competing claim. But, in the present instance, Western Sahara, if somewhat sparsely populated, was a territory across which socially and politically organized tribes were in constant movement and where armed incidents between these tribes were frequent. In the particular circumstances outlined in paragraphs 87 and 88 above, the paucity of evidence of actual display of authority unambiguously relating to Western Sahara renders it difficult to consider the Moroccan claim as on all fours with that of Denmark in the Eastern Greenland case. Nor is the difficulty cured by introducing the argument of geographical unity or contiguity. In fact, the information before the Court shows that the geographical unity of Western Sahara with Morocco is somewhat debatable, which also militates against giving effect to the concept of contiguity. Even if the geographical contiguity of Western Sahara with Morocco could be taken into account in the present connection, it would only make the paucity of evidence of unambiguous display of authority with respect to Western Sahara more difficult to reconcile with Morocco's claim to immemorial possession.

93. In the view of the Court, however, what must be of decisive importance in determining its answer to Question II is not indirect inferences drawn from events in past history but evidence directly relating to effective display of authority in Western Sahara at the time of its colonization by Spain and in the period immediately preceding that time. [⋯][1]

162. The materials and information presented to the Court show the existence, at the time of Spanish colonization, of legal ties of allegiance between the Sultan of Morocco and some of the tribes living in the territory of Western Sahara. They equally show the existence of rights, including some rights relating to the land, which constituted legal ties between the Mauritanian entity, as understood by the Court, and the territory of Western Sahara. On the other hand, the Court's conclusion is that the materials and information presented to it do not establish any tie of territorial sovereignty between the territory of Western Sahara and the Kingdom of Morocco or the Mauritanian entity. Thus the Court has not found legal

---

1) 이어서 재판부는 모로코 술탄과 사하라 부족간에 개인적 충성관계는 있었을지라도, 이것이 주권과 연관된 정치적 실체로는 존재하지 않았다고 판단했으며, 국제사회가 서부 사하라에 대한 모로코의 주권을 승인했다는 주장도 배척했다. 또한 모리타니아와 서부 사하라 지역간에 지리적, 언어적, 사회적, 문화적 유대가 존재했을지라도 그것이 주권관계는 아니었다고 판단했다.

ties of such a nature as might affect the application of resolution 1514 (XV) in the decolonization of Western Sahara and, in particular, of the principle of self-determination through the free and genuine expression of the will of the peoples of the Territory.

☑ 해　설

영토취득의 권원으로서 선점(occupation)은 매우 서구 중심적 개념이다. 과거 서구세력의 해외 영토 취득은 부족장과 같은 현지 통치자와의 보호협정이나 매매 등의 형식을 취한 경우가 많았다. 그러나 제국주의 시절 다수의 서구학자들—특히 19세기 말 영국학자들은 일정한 주민이 거주하고 있어도 유럽적 기준에 맞는 정치·사회적 조직을 갖추지 못한 지역은 무주지로 간주했다. 따라서 이들 지역은 할양이 아닌 선점의 대상이라고 해석했다. 현지인과의 합의는 국제법적 의미의 조약에 해당하지 않는다고 보아, 제국주의 시절 선점을 국제법상 영토취득의 기본유형으로 만들었다. 그러나 본 사건에서 ICJ는 만장일치로 제국주의 시대의 무주지 개념을 거부하고, 일정한 부족사회가 형성되어 있으면 국제법상 무주지가 아니라고 해석했다.

Mabo v. Queensland, High Court, Australia(1992)도 과거 오스트레일리아가 무주지는 아니었으며 따라서 토지에 대한 원주민의 권리가 계속 존속한다고 판단했다. 다만 이 판결은 국내법원의 판결로 주권의 문제를 다룬 것이 아니고, 원주민의 국내법상 토지 소유권만을 인정한 것이다.

➡ 참고문헌 ─────────────────────────────

- M. Janis, The International Court of Justice: Advisory Opinion on the Western Sahara, Harvard International Law Journal Vol. 17(1976), p. 609.
- B. Okere, The Western Sahara Case, ICLQ Vol. 28(1979), p. 296.
- E. Riedel, Confrontation in Western Sahara in the Light of Justice of 16 October 1975, German Yearbook of International Law Vol. 19(1976), p. 405.

6. 부르키나 파소·말리간 국경분쟁(1986)
— *Uti possidetis* 원칙 및 지도의 증거가치

Case concerning the Frontier Dispute.
Burkina Faso/Republic of Mali, 1986 ICJ Reports 554.

☑ 사 안

과거 프랑스 식민지였던 부르키나 파소와 말리는 1960년 각각 독립했다. 식민지 시절 이 두 국가가 속했던 프랑스령 서아프리카는 여러 개의 식민구역으로 구분을 거듭하며 행정경계가 여러 차례 변경되었고, 오늘날 부르키나 파소와 말리의 경계에 관하여는 명확한 법적 조치가 취해지지 않았다. 이에 독립 이후 양국간에는 국경분쟁이 벌어졌고, 무력충돌도 발생했다. 양국은 약 1,300㎞에 달하는 국경 중에 약 300㎞ 부분에 대하여 이견을 보였다. 결국 양국은 식민시대부터의 경계유지를 기본원칙으로 하는 전제하에 국경 획정문제를 ICJ의 5인 Chamber에 회부하기로 합의했다.

☑ 쟁 점

(1) 식민지 독립시의 국경 획정과 *Uti possidetis*(현상유지) 원칙의 적용.
(2) 영토분쟁에 있어서 지도의 증거가치

☑ 판 결

(1) 국가승계시 기존 국경존중 의무는 국제법상의 일반원칙이다.
(2) 식민지 독립시 *Uti possidetis*(현상유지)의 적용은 일반 원칙에 해당한다.
(3) 일반적으로 지도는 영토 권원에 대한 직접적 증거가 되지 못한다.

판 결 문

20. Since the two Parties have, as noted above, expressly requested the Chamber to resolve their dispute on the basis, in particular, of the 'principle of the intangibility of frontiers inherited from colonization', the Chamber cannot disregard the principle of *uti possidetis juris*, the application of which gives rise to this respect for intangibility of frontiers. Although there is no need, for the purposes of the present case, to show that this is a firmly established principle of international law where decolonization is concerned, the Chamber nonetheless wishes to emphasize its general scope, in view of its exceptional importance for the African continent and for the two Parties. In this connection it should be noted that the principle of *uti possidetis* seems to have been first invoked and applied in Spanish America, inasmuch as this was the continent which first witnessed the phenomenon of decolonization involving the formation of a number of sovereign States on territory formerly belonging to a single metropolitan State. Nevertheless the principle is not a special rule which pertains solely to one specific system of international law. It is a general principle, which is logically connected with the phenomenon of the obtaining of independence, wherever it occurs. Its obvious purpose is to prevent the independence and stability of new States being endangered by fratricidal struggles provoked by the challenging of frontiers following the withdrawal of the administering power.

21. It was for this reason that, as soon as the phenomenon of decolonization characteristic of the situation in Spanish America in the 19th century subsequently appeared in Africa in the 20th century, the principle of *uti possidetis*, in the sense described above, fell to be applied. The fact that the new African States have respected the administrative boundaries and frontiers established by the colonial powers must be seen not as a mere practice contributing to the gradual emergence of a principle of customary international law, limited in its impact to the African continent as it had previously been to Spanish America, but as the application in Africa of a rule of general scope. [···]

23. There are several different aspects to this principle, in its well-known application in Spanish America. The first aspect, emphasized by the Latin genitive *juris*, is found in the pre-eminence accorded to legal title over effective possession as a basis of sovereignty. Its purpose, at the time of the achievement of independence by the former Spanish colonies of America, was to scotch any designs which non-American colonizing powers might have on regions which had been assigned by the former metropolitan State to one division or another, but which were still uninhabited or unexplored. However, there is more to the principle of *uti possidetis* than this particular aspect. The essence of the principle lies in its primary aim of securing respect for the territorial boundaries at the moment when independence is achieved. Such territorial boundaries might be no more than delimitations between different administrative divisions or colonies all subject to the same sovereign. In that case, the application of the principle of *uti possidetis* resulted in administrative boundaries being transformed into international frontiers in the full sense of the term. This is true both of the States which took shape in the regions of South America which were dependent on the Spanish Crown, and of the States Parties to the present case, which took shape within the vast territories of French West Africa. *Uti possidetis*, as a principle which upgraded former administrative delimitations, established during the colonial period, to international frontiers, is therefore a principle of a general kind which is logically connected with this form of decolonization wherever it occurs.

24. The territorial boundaries which have to be respected may also derive from international frontiers which previously divided a colony of one State from a colony of another, or indeed a colonial territory from the territory of an independent State, or one which was under protectorate, but had retained its international personality. There is no doubt that the obligation to respect pre-existing international frontiers in the event of a State succession derives from a general rule of international law, whether or not the rule is expressed in the formula *uti possidetis*. Hence the numerous solemn affirmations of the intangibility of the frontiers existing at the time of the independence of African States, whether made by senior African statesmen or by organs of the Organization of African Unity itself, are evidently declaratory rather than constitutive: they recognize and confirm an existing principle, and do not seek to consecrate a new principle or the extension to Africa of a rule previously applied only in another continent.

25. However, it may be wondered how the time-hallowed principle has been able to withstand the new approaches to international law as expressed in Africa, where the successive attainment of independence and the emergence of new States have been accompanied by a certain questioning of traditional international law. At first sight this principle conflicts outright with another one, the right of peoples to self-determination. In fact, however, the maintenance of the territorial *status quo* in

Africa is often seen as the wisest course, to preserve what has been achieved by peoples who have struggled for their independence, and to avoid a disruption which would deprive the continent of the gains achieved by much sacrifice. The essential requirement of stability in order to survive, to develop and gradually to consolidate their independence in all fields, has induced African States judiciously to consent to the respecting of colonial frontiers, and to take account of it in the interpretation of the principle of self-determination of peoples.

26. Thus the principle of *uti possidetis* has kept its place among the most important legal principles, despite the apparent contradiction which explained its coexistence alongside the new norms. Indeed it was by deliberate choice that African States selected, among all the classic principles, that of *uti possidetis*. This remains an undeniable fact.

54. [···] maps merely constitute information which varies in accuracy from case to case; of themselves, and by virtue solely of their existence, they cannot constitute a territorial title, that is, a document endowed by international law with intrinsic legal force for the purpose of establishing territorial rights. Of course, in some cases maps may acquire such legal force, but where this is so the legal force does not arise solely from their intrinsic merits: it is because such maps fall into the category of physical expressions of the will of the State or States concerned. This is the case, for example, when maps are annexed to an official text of which they form an integral part. Except in this clearly defined case, maps are only extrinsic evidence of varying reliability or unreliability which may be used, along with other evidence of a circumstantial kind, to establish or reconstitute the real facts. [···]

56. [···] Since relatively distant times, judicial decisions have treated maps with a considerable degree of caution: less so in more recent decisions, at least as regards the technical reliability of maps. But even where the guarantees described above are present, maps can still have no greater legal value than that of corroborative evidence endorsing a conclusion at which a court has arrived by other means unconnected with the maps. In consequence, except when the maps are in the category of a physical expression of the will of the State, they cannot in themselves alone be treated as evidence of a frontier, since in that event they would form an irrebuttable presumption, tantamount in fact to legal title. The only value they possess is as evidence of an auxiliary or confirmatory kind, and this also means that they cannot be given the character of a rebuttable or *juris tanturn*[1]) presumption

---

1) legal but rebuttable — 필자 주.

such as to effect a reversal of the onus of proof.

☑ 해   설

이는 흑인 아프리카 국가간의 분쟁으로는 ICJ에 제소된 첫 번째 사건이었다. 재판부는 제시된 모든 증거를 검토한 끝에 분쟁 지역을 8개 구역으로 나누고 일련의 직선으로 경계를 획정했다. 양국은 이 결과를 수용하고 후일 구체적인 국경획정을 위한 3인 전문가 위원회를 구성했다.

이 판결은 탈식민과정에서는 *Uti possidetis*(현상유지) 원칙의 적용이 국제법상의 일반 원칙의 하나라고 자리매김했다. *Uti possidetis*(현상유지) 원칙이 과연 그러한 위치를 차지할 수 있느냐에 대하여는 의문이 제기되기도 하나, 적어도 중남미와 아프리카 국가들이 독립 이후 영토적 일체성을 유지하는 데 큰 기여를 한 점은 부인할 수 없다. 특히 이 원칙은 민족자결 원칙과 충돌될 수 있음에도 불구하고, 재판부가 아프리카 탈 식민과정의 특성상 이의 적용은 불가피하다고 판단했다는 점에서 주목을 끌었다. 즉 아프리카 국가들의 독립과정에서는 민족자결원칙의 강조가 당연하지만, 독립 이후 안정적 국가발전을 달성하고자 하는 입장에서는 구 식민시대의 경계를 수용하지 않았을 때 예상되는 혼란을 경계했다.

이 판결은 고지도의 증거가치에 대해서도 설시를 했다. 즉 지도란 본질적으로 전문증거에 불과하며, 따라서 지도는 영토적 권원을 확립하는 독자적인 증거는 될 수 없다고 판단했다. 다만 국경조약 등에 첨부된 공식지도만은 조약의 일부로서 증명력을 가질 수 있다고 보았다. 지도에 대한 이 같은 평가기준은 Kasikili/Sedudu Island, 1999 ICJ Reports 1045, para. 87; Sovereignty over Pulau Ligitan and Pulau Sipadan, 2002 ICJ Reports 625, para. 88; Case Concerning The Frontier Dispute, Vening/Niger, 2005 ICJ Report 90, para. 44 등에서도 지지되었다.

➡ 참고문헌 ────────────────────────────────

• 박희권, UTI POSSIDETIS 원칙의 연구; 부르키나파소·말리간 국경분쟁에 관한 ICJ 판결을 중심으로, 국제법학회논총 35권 2호(1990), p. 185.

• 이세련, 국제법상 영토분쟁의 해결에 관한 고찰: Uti Possidetis 원칙을 중심으로, (전북대) 법학연구 31집(2010), p. 231.

• M. Leigh, Judicial Decisions: Case Concerning the Frontier Dispute(Burkina Faso/Republic of Mali), AJIL Vol. 81(1987), p. 411.

• G. Nandi, The Case concerning the Frontier Dispute(Burkina Faso/Republic of Mali): Uti Possidetis in an African Perspective, ICLQ Vol. 36(1987), p. 893.

7. 페드라 브랑카 섬 영유권 사건(2008)
― 원시적 권원의 인정

Case concerning Sovereignity over Pedra Branca/Pulau
Batu Puteh, Middle Rocks and South Ledge.
Malaysia/Singapore, 2008 ICJ Reports 12.

☑ 사 안

이는 싱가포르 해협내 3개 소도의 영유권 분쟁에 관한 판결이다. Pedra
Branca(말레이시아 명칭 Pulau Batu Puteh)는 약 8,560㎡의 소도이며, Middle
Rocks는 암초군, South Ledge는 간출지이다. Pedra Branca는 말레이시아로
부터 약 7.7해리, 싱가포르로부터는 24해리의 거리에 위치하고 있으며, ICJ
회부 당시 싱가포르의 등대 관리원이 상주하고 있었다.

말레이시아는 이들 섬이 아주 오래 전부터의 고유 영토라고 주장했다.
반면 싱가포르는 과거 영국에 의한 무주지 선점을 중요한 권원의 하나로 주
장했다. 싱가포르는 Pedra Branca의 영유권을 갖는 국가가 이의 속도인
Middle Rocks와 South Ledge의 영유권도 갖는다고 주장했으나, 말레이시아
는 세 개의 도서가 별개로 취급되어야 한다고 주장했다.

이 판결에서 ICJ는 가장 큰 도서인 Pedra Branca는 싱가포르령, 기타 암
초인 Middle Rocks는 말레이시아령, South Ledge는 추후 결정될 대상이라고
판단했다. 특히 ICJ는 1953년 조호르의 국무장관 대행이 싱가포르 당국에게
보낸 공한에서 자신의 정부는 Pedra Branca 소유권을 주장하지 않겠다고 한
표현을 영유권 포기의 결정적 증거로 취급해 이 섬의 영유권이 싱가포르에
있다고 판단했다. 이와는 별도로 이 판결은 특히 Pedra Branca에 대한 말레
이시아의 원시적 권원을 인정했다는 점에서 주목을 끌었다. 다음은 그에 해
당하는 판결문이다.

☑ 쟁　　점

분쟁도서에 관한 말레이시아의 원시적 권원(original title).

☑ 판　　결

분쟁도서의 영유권에 대하여는 과거 술탄이 고래의 원시적 권원을 갖고 있었으나, 이러한 원시적 권원은 다른 법적 근거에 의해 이전될 수 있다.

판 결 문

52. Regarding the question as to whether "[t]he Sultanate [of Johor] covered all the islands within this large area [of its territory], including all those in the Singapore Straits, such as Pulau Batu Puteh ...," the Court starts by observing that it is not disputed that the Sultanate of Johor, since it came into existence in 1512, established itself as a sovereign State with a certain territorial domain under its sovereignty in this part of southeast Asia. [⋯]

59. Thus from at least the seventeenth century until early in the nineteenth it was acknowledged that the territorial and maritime domain of the Kingdom of Johor comprised a considerable portion of the Malaya Peninsula, straddled the Straits of Singapore and included islands and islets in the area of the Straits. Specifically, this domain included the area where Pedra Branca/Pulau Batu Puteh is located.

60. It now falls to the Court, after having described the general understanding at the relevant time of the extent of Johor, to ascertain whether the original title to Pedra Branca/Pulau Batu Puteh claimed by Malaysia is founded in law.

61. Of significance in the present context is the fact that Pedra Branca/Pulau Batu Puteh had always been known as a navigational hazard in the Straits of Singapore, an important channel for international navigation in east-west trade connecting the Indian Ocean with the South China Sea. It is therefore impossible that the island could have remained unknown or undiscovered by the local community. Pedra Branca/Pulau Batu Puteh evidently was not *terra incognita*.[1] It is thus reasonable to infer that Pedra Branca/Pulau Batu Puteh was viewed as one of the islands lying within the general geographical scope of the Sultanate of Johor.

---

1) 알려지지 않은 땅.

62. Another factor of significance which the Court has to take into consideration in assessing the issue of the original title in the present case is the fact that throughout the entire history of the old Sultanate of Johor, there is no evidence that any competing claim had ever been advanced over the islands in the area of the Straits of Singapore. [···]

66. If this conclusion was valid with reference to the thinly populated and unsettled territory of Eastern Greenland, it should also apply to the present case involving a tiny uninhabited and uninhabitable island, to which no claim of sovereignty had been made by any other Power throughout the years from the early sixteenth century until the middle of the nineteenth century.

67. The Court further recalls that, as expounded in the *Eastern Greenland* case [···], international law is satisfied with varying degrees in the display of State authority, depending on the specific circumstances of each case. Moreover, as pointed out in the *Island of Palmas Case, State* authority should not necessarily be displayed "in fact at every moment on every point of a territory." [···]

68. Having considered the actual historical and geographical context of the present case relating to the old Sultanate of Johor, the Court concludes that as far as the territorial domain of the Sultanate of Johor was concerned, it did cover in principle all the islands and islets within the Straits of Singapore, which lay in the middle of this Kingdom, and did thus include the island of Pedra Branca/Pulau Batu Puteh. This possession of the islands by the old Sultanate of Johor was never challenged by any other Power in the region and can in all the circumstances be seen as satisfying the condition of "continuous and peaceful display of territorial sovereignty (peaceful in relation to other States)" [···].

69. The Court thus concludes that the Sultanate of Johor had original title to Pedra Branca/Pulau Batu Puteh.

70. Malaysia further argues that the title of the Sultanate of Johor to Pedra Branca/Pulau Batu Puteh is confirmed by the ties of loyalty that existed between the Sultanate and the Orang Laut, "the people of the sea". The Orang Laut were engaged in various activities such as fishing and piratical activities in the waters in the Straits of Singapore, including in the area of Pedra Branca/Pulau Batu Puteh. [···]

75. Given the above, the Court finds that the nature and degree of the Sultan of Johor's authority exercised over the Orang Laut who inhabited the islands in the Straits of Singapore, and who made this maritime area their habitat, confirms the ancient original title of the Sultanate of Johor to those islands, including Pedra Branca/Pulau Batu Puteh. [⋯]

117. In the light of the foregoing, the Court concludes that Malaysia has established to the satisfaction of the Court that as of the time when the British started their preparations for the construction of the lighthouse on Pedra Branca/ Pulau Batu Puteh in 1844, this island was under the sovereignty of the Sultan of Johor.

☑ 해　　설

과거 영토분쟁에 관한 대부분의 국제재판에서는 역사적으로 오래된 증거에 대하여는 주목하지 않고, 근래의 실질적인 국가관할권 행사실적만을 주목해 영유권의 판단을 내렸었다. 이러한 국제판례의 경향은 현지 사정의 역사성을 무시하고, 제3세계에 있어서 과거 식민지배 당국의 행동에만 결정적 의미를 부여하는 결과를 가져 왔다. 그러나 이 판결은 비록 결론에 있어서는 Pedra Branca의 싱가포르령을 선언했지만, 역사적 사실을 조사해 이 섬의 원시적 권원(original title)은 원래 말레이시아에 있었다고 판단했다는 점에서 주목할 가치가 있다.

즉 19세기 영국이 Pedra Branca 섬을 무주지 선점했다는 싱가포르측의 주장을 배제하고, 오래 전부터 말레이시아 지역의 술탄이 싱가포르 해협내의 도서에 대해 계속적이고 평화롭게 영유권을 행사하였음을 인정했다. 즉 말레이시아의 원시적 권원을 인정했다. 이어 재판부는 최소한 말레이시아가 1824년 크로포드 조약을 통해 싱가포르 일대를 영국에 할양할 당시까지는 페드라 브랑카에 대한 말레이시아의 영유권이 유지되었다고 인정했으나, 1840년 이후에도 이 같은 권원이 유지되었는지는 불분명하다고 판단했다. 그러나 1953년 페드라 블랑카의 지위에 관한 싱가포르측 질의에 대해 조호르 국무장관 대행이 이 섬의 소유권을 주장하지 않는다는 답신을 보낸 사실에 재판부는 결정적 의미를 부여해 이를 영유권 포기의사로 간주했다(para. 203). 이어 섬 주변에서의 난파선 수색, 방문자에 대한 통제행사, 이 섬에 싱가포르 국기게양, 통신시설 설치, 매립 계획 발표, 지도 발간 등과 같은 일련의 싱가포르의 행위에 말레이시아가 장기간 항의하지 않은 사실도 주목했다

(paras. 273–276). 결론적으로 페드라 블랑카에 관한 말레이시아의 영유권은 싱가포르로 이전되었다고 판단했다.

재판과정에서 싱가포르는 Pedra Branca를 포함해 Middle Rocks와 South Ledge 전부가 일체로서 자국령이라고 주장했다. 재판부는 위와 같은 근거에서 Pedra Branca가 싱가포르령이라고 판단했으나, Middle Rocks에 대하여는 동일한 주권이전의 논리가 적용될 수 없으므로 원래의 소유국인 말레이시아령이라고 선언했고, 간출지인 South Ledge는 해당 수역의 소속국에 속한다고 판단했다.

판결 이후 양국 정부는 공동성명을 통해 이의 이행을 약속하고, 인근 수역에서 사고 발생시 인도적 지원을 제공할 것과 양국 어민들의 전통적 어로행위를 계속 보장하는 데 동의했다.

이후 양국은 판결이행을 위한 합동위원회를 구성하여 협의를 계속했는데, 세부적인 점에서 이견이 계속되었다. 특히 말레이시아는 2017년 2월 2일 영국 정부에 의해 근래 비밀 해제된 과거 문서에 따르면 영국과 싱가포르 당국이 Pedra Branca를 싱가포르의 일부로 간주하지 않았다는 사실이 발견되었다며, 이 같은 사실에 입각해 2008년 판결의 재심을 청구했다. 또한 말레이시아는 2017년 6월 30일 다음 2가지 사항에 관해 원 판결의 의미를 해석해 달라는 청구도 제출했다. ① Pedra Branca 주변의 수역은 말레이시아 영해에 해당한다. ② South Lodge는 말레이시아 영해 내에 위치하며, 그 결과 이 섬에 대한 주권은 말레이시아에 속한다. 그러나 2018년 5월 28일 말레이시아는 당사국간 합의에 따라 이 소송의 종결을 원한다는 입장을 재판소로 제출했고, 그 다음 날 이 사건은 종결 처리되었다.

➡ 참고문헌 ──────────────────────────────

- 김용환, 페드라 블랑카, 미들락스 및 사우스레지의 영유권에 관한 ICJ 판례 분석, 국제법학회논총 53권 2호(2008), p. 11.
- 마르셀로 코헨(김하양 역), 페드라 브랑카 사건에 관한 국제사법재판소 판결에 있어서의 본원적 권원, 영토해양연구 4호(2012), p. 6.
- 이창위, 싱가포르와 말레이시아의 페드라 브랑카 도서분쟁, 이석용·이창위·김채형, 국제해양법 판례연구(세창출판사, 2015), p. 253.

제11장

국가승계

1. 제노사이드 방지협약의 적용(1996)
― 국가의 분리독립과 조약의 승계

Case Concerning the Application of the Convention on the
Prevention and Punishment of the Crime of Genocide
(Preliminary Objections).
Bosnia-Herzegovina v. Yugoslavia, 1996 ICJ Reports 595.

☑ 사   안

　1980년 티토 사후 유고슬라비아는 혼란에 빠져 1991년-1992년 사이 5
개 국가로 분열되었다. 과거 유고사회주의연방(구 유고연방)의 중심을 이루었
던 신 유고연방(세르비아-몬테네그로)은 분리되어 떨어져나간 새 국가 내 세
르비아인들의 반란을 지원했다. 이들은 더 많은 영역을 차지하기 위한 인종
청소, 학살 등 여러 범죄행위를 저질렀다. 특히 구 유고연방에서 분리된 보
스니아-헤르체고비나 내 이슬람교도에 대한 잔학행위는 악명이 높았다.

　구 유고연방은 1950년 「제노사이드 방지협약」을 유보 없이 비준한 바
있다. 신 유고연방은 1992년 4월 27일 자국이 구 유고연방의 계속으로 과거
구 유고연방이 부담하던 모든 국제적 약속을 준수하겠다고 선언하고, 이 내
용을 유엔 사무총장에게 공한으로 통지했다.

　한편 보스니아-헤르체고비나는 1992년 12월 29일 구 유고연방의 일부
였던 자신도 「제노사이드 방지협약」 당사국의 지위를 승계한다는 의사를 유
엔 사무총장에게 통고했다. 이후 1993년 3월 20일 보스니아-헤르체고비나
는 신 유고연방이 1948년 「제노사이드 방지협약」 등을 위반한 잔학행위를
자행했음을 주장하며 이 사건을 ICJ에 제소했다.

　이에 대하여 신 유고연방은 1) 보스니아-헤르체고비나는 「제노사이드
방지협약」의 당사국이 아니다. 2) 설사 보스니아-헤르체고비나가 협약 당

사국이라 할지라도 그는 1992년 12월에 가입 신청을 하여 90일 후에 당사국이 되므로 이 사건 제소일인 1993년 3월 20일에는 아직 당사국이 아니라 제소자격이 없다고 주장하는 선결적 항변을 제술했다. 선설석 항변에 내한 핀단과정에서 보스니아－헤르체고비나가 구 유고연방의 「제노사이드 방지협약」 당사국 지위를 승계하여 이 협약의 당사국이 되었는가가 검토되었다.

☑ 쟁 점
구 유고연방의 일부였던 보스니아－헤르체고비나는 조약에 관한 국가승계를 통해 「제노사이드 방지협약」의 당사국이 되었는지 여부.

☑ 판 결
보스니아－헤르체고비나는 국가승계를 통해 「제노사이드 방지협약」의 당사국이 되었다.

판 결 문

18. For its part, on 29 December 1992, Bosnia-Herzegovina transmitted to the Secretary-General of the United Nations, as depositary of the Genocide Convention, a Notice of Succession in the following terms:

> "the Government of the Republic of Bosnia and Herzegovina, having considered the Convention on the Prevention and Punishment of the Crime of Genocide, of December 9, 1948, to which the former Socialist Federal Republic of Yugoslavia was a party, wishes to succeed to the same and undertakes faithfully to perform and carry out all the stipulations therein contained with effect from March 6, 1992, the date on which the Republic of Bosnia and Herzegovina became independent."

On 18 March 1993, the Secretary-General communicated the following Depositary Notification to the parties to the Genocide Convention:

> "On 29 December 1992, the notification of succession by the Government of Bosnia and Herzegovina to the above-mentioned Convention was deposited

with the Secretary-General, with effect from 6 March 1992, the date on which Bosnia and Herzegovina assumed responsibility for its international relations."

19. Yugoslavia has contested the validity and legal effect of the Notice of 29 December 1992, contending that, by its acts relating to its accession to independence, the Republic of Bosnia-Herzegovina had flagrantly violated the duties stemming from the "principle of equal rights and self-determination of peoples." According to Yugoslavia, Bosnia-Herzegovina was not, for this reason, qualified to become a party to the convention. Yugoslavia subsequently reiterated this objection in the third preliminary objection which it raised in this case.

The Court notes that Bosnia-Herzegovina became a Member of the United Nations following the decisions adopted on 22 May 1992 by the Security Council and the General Assembly, bodies competent under the Charter. Article XI of the Genocide Convention opens it to "any Member of the United Nations"; from the time of its admission to the Organization, Bosnia-Herzegovina could thus become a party to the Convention. Hence the circumstances of its accession to independence are of little consequence.

20. It is clear from the foregoing that Bosnia-Herzegovina could become a party to the Convention through the mechanism of State succession. Moreover, the Secretary-General of the United Nations considered that this had been the case, and the Court took note of this in its Order of 8 April 1993 (*I.C.J. Reports 1993*, p. 16, para. 25).

21. The Parties to the dispute differed as to the legal consequences to be drawn from the occurrence of a State succession in the present case. In this context, Bosnia-Herzegovina has, among other things, contended that the Genocide Convention falls within the category of instruments for the protection of human rights, and that consequently, the rule of "automatic succession" necessarily applies. Bosnia-Herzegovina concluded therefrom that it became a party to the Convention with effect from its accession to independence. Yugoslavia disputed any "automatic succession" of Bosnia-Herzegovina to the Genocide Convention on this or any other basis. [⋯]

23. Without prejudice as to whether or not the principle of "automatic succession" applies in the case of certain types of international treaties or conventions, the Court does not consider it necessary, in order to decide on its jurisdiction in this case, to make a determination on the legal issues concerning State succession in respect to treaties which have been raised by the Parties.

Whether Bosnia-Herzegovina automatically became party to the Genocide Convention on the date of its accession to independence on 6 March 1992, or whether
It became a party as a result — retroactive or not—of its Notice of Succession of 29
December 1992, at all events it was a party to it on the date of the filing of its
Application on 20 March 1993. These matters might, at the most, possess a certain
relevance with respect to the determination of the scope *ratione temporis* of the
jurisdiction of the Court, a point which the Court will consider later (paragraph 34
below).

24. Yugoslavia has also contended, in its sixth preliminary objection, that, if
the Notice given by Bosnia-Herzegovina on 29 December 1992 had to be interpreted
as constituting an instrument of accession within the meaning of Article XI of the
Genocide Convention, it could only have become effective, pursuant to Article XIII
of the Convention, on the 90th day following its deposit, that is, 29 March 1993.

Since the Court has concluded that Bosnia-Herzegovina could become a party
to the Genocide Convention as a result of a succession, the question of the
application of Articles XI and XIII of the Convention does not arise. However, the
Court would recall that, as it noted in its Order of 8 April 1993, even if
Bosnia-Herzegovina were to be treated as having acceded to the Genocide
Convention, which would mean that the Application could be said to be premature
by nine days when filed on 20 March 1993, during the time elapsed since then,
Bosnia-Herzegovina could, on its own initiative, have remedied the procedural defect
by filing a new Application. It therefore matters little that the Application had been
filed some days too early. As will be indicated in the following paragraphs, the
Court is not bound to attach the same degree of importance to considerations of
form as they might possess in domestic law. [⋯]

34. Having reached the conclusion that it has jurisdiction in the present case,
both *ratione personae* and *ratione materiae* on the basis of Article IX of the Genocide
Convention, it remains for the Court to specify the scope of that jurisdiction *ratione
temporis*. In its sixth and seventh preliminary objections, Yugoslavia, basing its
contention on the principle of the non-retroactivity of legal acts, has indeed asserted
as a subsidiary argument that, even though the Court might have jurisdiction on
the basis of the Convention, it could only deal with events subsequent to the
different dates on which the Convention might have become applicable as between
the Parties. In this regard, the Court will confine itself to the observation that the
Genocide Convention—and in particular Article IX—does not contain any clause the

object or effect of which is to limit in such manner the scope of its jurisdiction *ratione temporis*, and nor did the Parties themselves make any reservation to that end, either to the Convention or on the occasion of the signature of the Dayton-Paris Agreement. The Court thus finds that it has jurisdiction in this case to give effect to the Genocide Convention with regard to the relevant facts which have occurred since the beginning of the conflict which took place in Bosnia and Herzegovina. This finding is, moreover, in accordance with the object and purpose of the Convention as defined by the Court in 1951 and referred to above ([⋯]). As a result, the Court considers that it must reject Yugoslavia's sixth and seventh preliminary objections.

☑ 해   설

변론과정에서 보스니아-헤르체고비나는 인권조약인 「제노사이드 방지 협약」에 관하여는 이른바 자동승계원칙(rule of automatic succession)이 적용되어, 자국은 독립과 동시에 자동적으로 「제노사이드 방지 협약」의 당사국이 되었다고 주장했다. 반면 신 유고 연방은 자동승계원칙을 부인했다. 재판부는 관할권 결정에 있어서는 보스니아-헤르체고비나가 인권조약의 자동승계 원칙에 의해 당사국이 되었는지, 1992년 12월 승계통고에 의해 당사국이 되었는지는 구별할 필요가 없다며 이에 대한 견해는 밝히지 않았다. 한편 S. Weeramantry 판사는 이 판결에 대한 다음의 개별의견에서 인권조약의 자동 승계를 지지했다.

(p. 649-) If the contention is sound that there is no principle of automatic succession to human rights and humanitarian treaties, the strange situation would result of the people within a State, who enjoy the full benefit of a human rights treaty, such as the International Covenant on Civil and Political Rights, and have enjoyed it for many years, being suddenly deprived of it as though these are special privileges that can be given or withdrawn at the whim or fancy of governments. Populations once protected cease to be protected, may be protected again, and may again cease to be protected, depending on the vagaries of political events. Such a legal position seems to be altogether untenable, especially at this stage in the development of human rights. [⋯]

All of the foregoing reasons combine to create what seems to me to be a principle of contemporary international law that there is automatic State succession to so vital a human rights convention as the Genocide Convention. [⋯]

Without automatic succession to such a Convention, we would have a situation where the worldwide system of human rights protections continually generates gaps in the most vital part of its framework, which open up and close, depending on the break up of the old political authorities and the emergence of the new. The international legal system cannot condone a principle by which the subjects of these States live in a state of continuing uncertainty regarding the most fundamental of their human rights protections. Such a view would grievously tear the seamless fabric of international human rights protections, endanger peace, and lead the law astray from the Purposes and Principles of the United Nations, which all nations, new and old, are committed to pursue.

이 사건에 대한 ICJ의 본안판결은 2007년 2월 26일 내려졌다(본서 p. 514 참조).

이 사건과는 별도로 Human Rights Committee는 General Comment 26(1997)에서 「시민적 및 정치적 권리에 관한 국제규약」의 경우 규약상의 권리는 당사국 영토에 거주하는 사람들의 것으로서, 일단 규약상의 권리에 관한 보호가 부여된 다음에는 이후의 국가의 분열이나 승계, 당사국 정부의 변경 등과 관계 없이 해당지역 거주자들은 계속 규약상의 권리의 보호를 받는다고 발표했다(Para. 4). 즉 기왕의 규약을 승계국이 폐기하거나 탈퇴할 수 없다는 판단이었다.

구유고 국제형사재판소는 2001년의 한 판결에서 국제인도법조약의 자동승계를 지지하는 결정을 내린 바 있고,[1] 유럽 인권재판소도 인권조약상의 기본적 권리는 주민들의 권리로서 국가승계의 영향을 받지 않고 계속 적용된다는 판결을 내린 바 있다.[2] 그러나 소련방 해산 이후 분리·독립한 국가

---

1) Čelebići case, Prosecutor v. Delacic et al., 2001 ICTY Case No. IT−96−21−A), para. 111: "It may be now considered in international law that there is automatic State succession to multilateral humanitarian treaties in the broad sense, *i.e.*, treaties of universal character which express fundamental human rights."
2) Bijelic v. Montenegro and Serbia, ECHR Application No.11890/05(2009), para. 69.

들은 기존 인권조약의 자동승계를 인정하기보다 대체로 이들 조약에 신규 가입하는 절차를 밟았다. 20세기 말 이후 대부분의 국가승계과정에서 인권조약은 자동승계되기보다 해당 국가의 개별적 결정에 따라 처리되었다.[3] 인권조약의 자동승계 여부에 관한 국제법은 아직 불분명하다.

한편 신 유고연방은 2006년 몬테네그로가 분리 독립을 한 후 세르비아로 국호를 변경했다.

➡ 참고문헌 —————————————————————————

- P. H. F. Bekker and P. C. Szasz, International Decisions, AJIL Vol. 91(1997), p. 121.
- C. Gray, ICJ: Recent Cases, ICLQ Vol. 46(1997), p. 688.
- P. Williams, The Treaty Obligations of the Successor States of the Former Soviet Union, Yugoslavia, and Czechoslovakia: Do They Continue in Force?, Denver Journal of International Law and Policy(1994), p. 1.

---

3) 박소민, 인권조약의 자동승계에 관한 고찰(2017, 서울대학교 석사논문), pp. 130-154 참조.

2. 리비아·차드간 국경분쟁(1994)
— 국가승계와 국경조약

Case concerning the Territorial Dispute.
Libya/Chad, 1994 ICJ Reports 6.

☑ 사　　안

　　리비아는 1951년 독립 시부터 인접 차드(당시 프랑스령)와의 국경지역인 Aouzou 일대가 자신의 영토라고 주장했다. 토착민들의 땅이 오스만 터키령으로 되었고, 1912년 리비아를 점령한 이탈리아령이 되었다가, 1951년 리비아 독립시 이 지역의 영유권이 리비아로 승계되었다는 주장이었다.

　　리비아는 1955년 Aouzou를 포함한 차드의 지배국인 프랑스와 20년을 유효기간으로 하는 우호선린조약을 체결한 바 있다. 1972년 리비아와 우호관계에 있던 차드 정부는 Aouzou 지역을 리비아로 이양하기로 했다가, 1975년 차드의 신 정부는 다시 반환을 요구했다. 이후 리비아는 차드 내 반군을 지원했고, 프랑스의 지원을 받는 차드와 전쟁도 벌였으나 리비아군이 패퇴했다. 1989년 휴전이 성립된 이후 리비아와 차드는 이 분쟁을 ICJ로 회부하기로 합의했다.

　　재판에서 리비아는 Aouzou 지역에는 원래 양국간 국경이 존재하지 않았다고 주장한 반면, 차드는 기존의 국경에 따라 분쟁을 해결해 달라고 요청했다. 재판과정에서는 1955년 조약이 리비아-차드간 경계를 획정하고 있었는가? 만약 있었다면 원 조약의 유효기간이 도과된 이후에도 조약에 따른 국경선이 계속 유효한가 등이 문제되었다.

☑ 쟁　점

⑴ 구 식민지 지배국이 체결한 국경조약이 독립 이후에도 유효한가 여부.

⑵ 기존 조약의 유효기간이 도과된 경우 그 조약에 따른 국경획정의 효력도 상실되는가 여부.

☑ 판　결

⑴ 구 식민지 지배국이 체결한 국경조약은 이후 독립국에도 승계된다.

⑵ 일단 합의된 국경은 원 조약의 유효기간이 경과했어도 항구성을 지닌다.

판 결 문

72. Article 11 of the 1955 Treaty provides that:

"The present Treaty is concluded for a period of 20 years.

The High Contracting Parties shall be able at all times to enter into consultations with a view to its revision.

Such consultations shall be compulsory at the end of the ten-year period following its entry into force.

The present Treaty can be terminated by either Party 20 years after its entry into force, or at any later time, provided that one year's notice is given to the other Party."

These provisions notwithstanding, the Treaty must, in the view of the Court, be taken to have determined a permanent frontier. There is nothing in the 1955 Treaty to indicate that the boundary agreed was to be provisional or temporary; on the contrary it bears all the hallmarks of finality. The establishment of this boundary is a fact which, from the outset, has had a legal life of its own, independently of the fate of the 1955 Treaty. Once agreed, the boundary stands, for any other approach would vitiate the fundamental principle of the stability of boundaries, the importance of which has been repeatedly emphasized by the Court (*Temple of Preah Vihear, I.C.J. Reports 1962, p. 34; Aegean Sea Continental Shelf, I.C.J. Reports 1978, p. 36*).

73. A boundary established by treaty thus achieves a permanence which the treaty itself does not necessarily enjoy. The treaty can cease to be in force without in any way affecting the continuance of the boundary. In this instance the Parties have not exercised their option to terminate the Treaty, but whether or not the option be exercised, the boundary remains. This is not to say that two States may not by mutual agreement vary the border between them; such a result can of course be achieved by mutual consent, but when a boundary has been the subject of agreement, the continued existence of that boundary is not dependent upon the continuing life of the treaty under which the boundary is agreed. [⋯]

75. It will be evident from the preceding discussion that the dispute before the Court, whether described as a territorial dispute or a boundary dispute, is conclusively determined by a Treaty to which Libya is an original party and Chad a party in succession to France. The Court's conclusion that the Treaty contains an agreed boundary renders it unnecessary to consider the history of the "Borderlands" claimed by Libya on the basis of title inherited from the indigenous people, the Senoussi Order, the Ottoman Empire and Italy. Moreover, in this case, it is Libya, an original party to the Treaty, rather than a successor State, that contests its resolution of the territorial or boundary question. Hence there is no need for the Court to explore matters which have been discussed at length before it such as the principle of *uti possidetis* and the applicability of the Declaration adopted by the Organization of African Unity at Cairo in 1964. [⋯]

77. For these reasons,

THE COURT,

By 16 votes to 1,

(1) Finds that the boundary between the Great Socialist People's Libyan Arab Jamahiriya and the Republic of Chad is defined by the Treaty of Friendship and Good Neighbourliness concluded on 10 August 1955 between the French Republic and the United Kingdom of Libya.

☑ 해　설

이 사건의 발단은 1955년 리비아－프랑스 우호선린조약 제3조가 양측 국경은 19세기 말부터 20세기 초 무렵 프랑스, 영국, 이탈리아, 오스만터키 등의 국가들 간에 체결된 다양한 협정 속에 획정된 국경을 인정하기로 한다고 규정한데서 비롯되었다. 리비아는 이들 협정 속에 Aouzou 지역에 대한 국경은 포함되지 않았다고 주장한 반면, 차드측은 이들 협정이 문제의 지역에 대한 국경을 설정하고 있다고 주장했다. 이에 리비아는 기존 경계가 존재하지 않았다는 전제 하에 국경을 획정해 줄 것을 요청한 반면, 차드는 기존 경계가 존재한다는 전제 하에 이를 확인해 달라고 요청했다. 재판부는 1955년 우호선린조약에 이 지역 국경이 포함되어 있다고 판단하고 재판을 진행했다. 위 판결문 발췌는 국가승계가 국경조약에 미치는 영향에 관한 설시를 중심으로 하고 있다.

국가승계시 국제사회의 가장 큰 관심은 기존조약에 대한 영향이었다. 종래부터 국가승계의 유형과 기존조약의 성격에 따라 국가승계의 법적 효과가 달라진다고 이해했다. 그러나 국경조약만은 국가승계의 유형과 상관 없이 계속성의 원칙이 적용되어 구속력을 유지한다는 데 큰 이견이 없었다. 조약의 「국가승계에 관한 1978년 비엔나 협약」 제11조도 기존조약에 의한 국경과 국경제도에 대하여는 국가승계가 영향을 미치지 못한다고 규정했으며, 이점이 반영된 국제판례도 여러 건이 있었다.

Article 11 (Boundary regimes)

A succession of States does not as such affect:

(a) a boundary established by a treaty; or

(b) obligations and rights established by a treaty and relating to the regime of a boundary.

다음의 헝가리와 슬로바키아간 Gabčíkovo-Nagymaros Project 판결 (1997 ICJ Reports 7)은 이러한 법리를 보다 분명히 제시하고 있다.

123. [⋯] In its Commentary on the Draft Articles on Succession of States in respect of Treaties, adopted at its twenty-sixth session, the International Law Commission identified "treaties of a territorial character" as having been regarded both in traditional doctrine and in modern opinion as unaffected by a succession of States ([⋯]). The draft text of Article 12, which reflects this principle, was subsequently adopted unchanged in the 1978 Vienna Convention. The Court considers that Article 12 reflects a rule of customary international law; it notes that neither of the Parties disputed this. Moreover, the Commission indicated that "treaties concerning water rights or navigation on rivers are commonly regarded as candidates for inclusion in the category of territorial treaties" ([⋯]). The Court observes that Article 12, in providing only, without reference to the treaty itself, that rights and obligations of a territorial character established by a treaty are unaffected by a succession of States, appears to lend support to the position of Hungary rather than of Slovakia. However the Court concludes that this formulation was devised rather to take account of the fact that, in many cases, treaties which had established boundaries or territorial regimes were no longer in force ([⋯]). Those that remained in force would nonetheless bind a successor State.

Taking all these factors into account, the Court finds that the content of the 1977 Treaty indicates that it must be regarded as establishing a territorial regime within the meaning of Article 12 of the 1978 Vienna Convention. It created rights and obligations "attaching to" the parts of the Danube to which it relates; thus the Treaty itself cannot be affected by a succession of States. The Court therefore concludes that the 1977 Treaty became binding upon Slovakia on 1 January 1993.

같은 법리는 이후 ICJ의 Territorial and Maritime Dispute(Preliminary Objections), Nicaragua v. Colombia, 2007 ICJ Reports 832, para. 89; The Dispute regarding Navigational and Related Rights, Costa Rica v. Nicaragua, 2009 ICJ Reports 213, para. 68에서도 그대로 반복되었다.

1994년 이 판결이 내려지자 프랑스의 중재 하에 리비아는 점령중이던 Aouzou 지역을 차드에게 반환했다.

➠ 참고문헌 ─────────────────────────────────

- C. Arguello─Gomez, Some Procedural and Substantive Aspects of the Libya/Chad Case, Leiden Hournal of International Law Vol. 9(1996), p. 167.
- M. Ricciardi, Title to the Aouzou Strip: a Legal and Historical Analysis, Yale Journal of International Law Vol. 17(1994), p. 442.

3. 구 유고연방의 해외재산 분배(1996)
― 국가승계와 국유재산의 분배

Republic of Croatia *et al.* v. Girocredit Bank A.G. Der Sparkassen.

Oberster Gerichtshof, Austria, 4 Ob 2304/96v(1996).[1]

☑ 사 안

유고사회주의연방(구 유고연방) 중앙은행은 이 사건 피고은행과 계약을 체결하고 일정한 자산을 오스트리아에 투자했다. 1991년~1992년 사이 구 유고연방이 5개국으로 해체되자 해외에 소재한 국유재산의 처리방법이 문제되었다.[2] 구 유고연방의 중심세력이던 세르비아계가 수립한 신 유고연방의 중앙은행은 자신이 오스트리아 은행에 투자된 재산의 단독 승계자라고 주장했다. 반면 구 유고연방 해체 후 독립한 크로아티아와 마세도니아 등은 이 재산에 대한 지분을 주장했다. 오스트리아 대법원(Oberster Gerichtshof)에서는 신 유고연방이 구 유고의 단독 승계국인가? 신 유고연방의 중앙은행은 구 유고연방 중앙은행의 해외재산의 단독 승계자인가 등이 문제되었다.

☑ 쟁 점

구 유고사회주의연방 해체의 법적 성격과 이의 해외재산의 처리방향.

☑ 판 결

구 유고사회주의연방은 해체를 통해 소멸하고 5개 승계국으로 대체되었

---

1) 이 판결문은 International Legal Materials Vol. 36, 1520(1997)에 번역 수록된 것을 이용한다.

2) 이후 구 유고연방의 구성국은 더욱 여러 국으로 분열되었으며, 신 유고연방은 2006년 국호를 세르비아로 변경했다.

다. 해외재산은 5개 승계국이 공동으로 소유하게 되었으므로 합의를 통하여 처리되어야 한다.

판 결 문

The National Bank of the Socialist Federal Republic of Yugoslavia (hereinafter SFRY) had concluded banking contracts with the Defendant, on the basis of which funds were invested upon interest in Austria and assets were deposited.

The SFRY has been dissolved by "*dismembratio*."[3] The successor States of Croatia, Macedonia, Slovenia, Bosnia-Herzegovina and the Federal Republic of Yugoslavia have so far not reached any agreement on the distribution of the assets and liabilities of the SFRY. The National Bank of the Federal Republic of Yugoslavia, founded in 1993, claims to be the sole lawful successor to the former National Bank of the SFRY. [⋯]

It is in this sense that Art. 8 of the 1983 "Vienna Convention on Succession of States in Respect of State Property, Archives and Debts", prepared by the International Law Commission, defines "State property of the predecessor State" as property and rights which, at the date of the succession of States, were, according to the internal law of the predecessor State, owned by that State. The purpose of this codification was to formulate existing customary international law [⋯]

All these provisions taken together show that the assets of the National Bank of the SFRY—although it enjoyed legal personality as a "socialized company"— formed part of State property of the SFRY according to international law, which in the case of a "*dismembratio*" has to be distributed among the successor States.[4] [⋯]

While the Federal Republic of Yugoslavia considers itself to be the sole successor State to the SFRY and identical with it, the international community unanimously views the disintegration of the SFRY as a case of "*dismembratio*". In international law this means the complete dissolution of the predecessor State and replacement by several successor States [⋯].

The opinion of the international community is expressed in the following documents:

In Security Council Resolution 757 (1992) it was stated that the claim of the successor States of Serbia and Montenegro to continue automatically the member-

---

3) dismemberment; separation — 필자 주.
4) 이에 앞서 재판부는 구 유고연방 중앙은행이 정치적 독립성은 없는 기관이라고 판단했다.

ship of the former SFRY in the United Nations was not recognized.

In Security Council Resolution 777 (1992) the view was expressed that the SFRY had ceased to exist, that there was no identity of the Federal Republic of Yugoslavia, consisting of Serbia and Montenegro, with the former State of the SFRY. The Federal Republic of Yugoslavia could not participate in the General Assembly of the United Nations and would have first to apply for membership.

Pursuant to a recommendation of the Security Council, the General Assembly of the United Nations decided in a Resolution of 22 September 1992 that the Federal Republic of Yugoslavia should apply for membership and could not participate in the work of the General Assembly.

The Arbitration Commission set up by the Members of the European Community and chaired by Badinter also dealt with the question of State succession and in its Opinions No. 1, 8 and 10 (1992) held the view that the SFRY had been dissolved and had ceased to exist, that the Federal Republic of Yugoslavia was one of the successor States and not the sole legal successor. This view was also supported in a declaration of the European Political Cooperation of 20 July 1992 as well as the EU Declaration of 9 April 1996 on the Recognition of the Federal Republic of Yugoslavia as a successor State.

On the basis of this, Austria recognized the Federal Republic of Yugoslavia as one of the successor States of the SFRY and as an independent and sovereign Member of the community of States (Note of the Federal Minister for Foreign Affairs of the Republic of Austria of 17 April 1996, presented to the Federal Republic of Yugoslavia on 25 April 1996; [⋯]).

In terms of international law, the disintegration of the SFRY therefore is to be regarded as a case of "*dismembratio.*" The SFRY as a subject of international law has ceased to exist, its State territory has been divided among five successor States, which have in the meantime been recognized by Austria.

Under customary international law, in the case of "*dismembratio*" State property is to be distributed according to the international principle of "equity" [⋯]. In such a case Art. 18 of the "Vienna Convention on Succession of States in Respect of State Property, Archives and Debts" of 1983 prepared by the International Law Commission provides for the passing of movable State property to the successor States in "equitable proportions." Thus, the successor States have an international law title to distribution recognized by the community of States.

Resolution 1022 of the General Assembly of the United Nations, leaving it to the Member States to release funds and assets frozen pursuant to Security Council Resolutions 757 and 820, specifically points out in operative paragraph 6 that these funds and assets had to be released without prejudice to claims of the successor States to such property. Moreover, operative paragraph 5 provides (this being binding on Members) that property being subject to legal action shall remain frozen until released in accordance with applicable law.

Also the EU Arbitration Commission chaired by Badinter states in its Opinion No. 9 that State property of the SFRY located in third countries must be distributed equitably among the successor States in accordance with an agreement to be reached among them. [⋯]

As a result of the disintegration of the SFRY by "*dismembratio*" the legal personalities of that State and its National Bank ceased to exist. The property attributable to the State (of the SFRY) is to be distributed among the successor States in accordance with international agreements still to be concluded. As far as funds and assets deposited with Austrian banks are concerned, surrendering the joint property to only one of the successor States—ignoring the claims of the other members of such a community—would even more amount to the recognition of an expropriation without compensation in the State of the actual administrative seat, as the Federal Republic of Yugoslavia claims to be the sole successor State to the SFRY, if not identical with it. As the confiscation of property, being contrary to ordre public, does not extend to property located in Austria of a legal person the extinction of which has to be recognized in Austria under <section> 12 of the [Austrian] Federal Statute on Private International Law [⋯], such property constitutes a "*communio incidens*," i.e. a joint-ownership community of all successor States [⋯]. Each member of this community thus has only a joint-ownership claim vis-a-vis the Defendant, which would be—illegally—infringed upon by any unilateral acts of disposal by one of them. Hence, each member of this community has a private law claim to the maintenance of the *status quo*, thus also a legal claim against the Defendant to desist from any disposal of such property as long as the successor States do not jointly dispose of such funds and assets."(원문의 각주 생략)

☑ 해 설

이후 2001년 구 유고 구성 공화국들은 해외재산 분배에 합의했다. 즉 신 유고연방(세르비아, 몬테네그로) 38%, 크로아티아 23%, 슬로베니아 16%, 보스니아-헤르체고비나 15.5%, 마케도니아 7.5%로 분배하기로 했다. 대상 재산에는 고정 및 유동산, 재외공관, 해외 예치금 등이 포함되었다.

➡ 참고문헌 ─────────────────────────────

- 김도형, 구유고연방의 해체와 1993년 국가재산, 국가문서 및 국가채무의 국가 승계에 관한 비엔나협약, 서울국제법연구 제9권 2호(2002), p. 193.
- K. Buhler, Casenote: Two Recent Austrian Supreme Court Decisions on State Succession from an International Law Perspective, Austrian Review of International and European Law Vol. 2(1997), p. 213.

4. 일제와 대한민국간의 국유재산 승계(1966)

대법원 1966년 9월 6일 선고, 65다868 판결.
대법원판례집 제14권 3집(민사)(1966), 1쪽 이하.

☑ 사　안

일제의 식민지배를 받던 한국은 3년간의 미군정을 거쳐 1948년 대한민국 정부를 수립했다. 일제가 한반도에서 소유, 관리하던 공공재산은 미군정의 관리를 거쳐 「대한민국 정부와 미합중국 정부간 재정 및 재산에 관한 최초협정」을 통하여 모두 한국 정부로 이양되었다. 이 사건은 일제시 조선총독부 소유의 토지를 매입했으나 미처 소유권 등기를 하기 전에 종전을 맞은 경우, 매입자는 광복 후 대한민국 정부를 상대로 소유권 이전등기를 청구할 수 있는가에 관한 다툼이었다.

☑ 쟁　점

구 조선총독부 소유의 재산권은 광복 후 대한민국 정부로 승계되었는가 여부.

☑ 판　결

구 조선총독부 소유 국유재산은 그에 부속된 권리의무와 함께 대한민국 정부의 국유재산으로 당연 승계되었다.

판 결 문

1945. 8. 9. 이전에 조선총독부 소관으로 있던 국유재산은, 대한민국 정

부수립과 동시에 당연히 대한민국의 국유가 되는 것이고, 또 국유재산과 관련하여 일본정부가, 한국인에게 부담하는 계약상 의무도 대한민국 정부수립과 동시에, 대한민국이 이를 승계한다고 할 것이다.

그리고 대한민국 정부와 미국 정부간에 체결된 재정 및 재산에 관한 최초협정이 국유재산을 그 제5조에 규정한 귀속재산에 포함시키지 않고, 제1조에 따로히 규정한 점으로 보아도, 미군정법령 제33호에 의하여 미군정청이 1945. 9. 25.자로 소유권을 취득한 재산중에는 위와 같은 국유재산은 포함되지 않았다고 해석하는 것이 타당하므로, 본건 계쟁재산은 이른바 귀속재산이 아니며, 1948. 7. 28.자 군정장관지령의 적용을 받지 않는 것이라고 할 것이다.

그러므로, 본건 임야에 관하여 원고 주장과 같은 양여사실을 인정할 수 있다고 하면, 피고는 특별한 다른 사정이 없는 한, 그 양여계약에 의하여 원고에게 소유권 이전등기절차를 이행할 의무가 있다고 할 것이다.

원심은 결국 1945. 8. 9. 이전에 조선총독부 소관으로 있던 국유재산의 귀속에 관한 법리를 오해한 잘못이 있다고 할 것이다.

☑ 해   설

제2차 대전 후 미군정 당국은 군정법령 제33호(1945년 12월 6일 공포)를 통해 1945년 8월 9일자를 기준으로 일본 정부나 그 기관 또는 일본인 및 회사, 단체 등이 소유하거나 관리하던 일체의 재산에 대한 소유권을 미군정청이 취득한다고 발표했다. 이에 따라 미군정청이 소유하던 각종 재산권의 대부분은 1948년 「대한민국 정부와 미합중국 정부간 재정 및 재산에 관한 최초협정」을 통해 한국 정부로 이양되었다. 이 사건에서의 쟁점은 구 조선총독부 소유의 재산도 군정법령 제33조를 통해 귀속재산으로 되었다가 대한민국 정부로 소유권이 이양되었는가 여부였다.

이와 동일 취지의 판결로 대법원 1966년 9월 20일 선고, 65다1355 판결; 대법원 1969년 8월 19일 선고, 69다797 판결; 대법원 1981년 9월 8일 선고, 81다61·62 판결; 대법원 1989년 8월 8일 선고, 88다카25496 판결; 대법원 1994년 2월 8일 선고, 93다54040 판결 등이 있다.

➡ 참고문헌 ─────────────────────────────────

- 정용인, 대법원 판례를 중심으로 한 일본인 재산의 귀속에 관한 법령연구, 사법 연구자료 2집(법원행정처, 1975), p. 173.

5. 광복 이후 일제 법령의 효력(1960)

대법원 1960년 9월 15일 선고, 58다492(4291민상492) 판결.
대법원판례집 제8권(민사)(1960), 136쪽 이하.

☑ **사   안**

일제시 제정된 사찰령에 따르면 각 사찰은 조선총독의 허가 없이는 사찰재산을 처분할 수 없었으며, 이를 위반한 처분행위는 무효라고 규정하고 있었다. 이 사건은 광복후 주무장관의 허가 없이 사찰재산을 담보로 제공하였다가 경매에 처해진 경우 그 법적 효력을 인정하여 경락자에게 소유권 이전등기를 할 수 있느냐에 관한 다툼이었다.

☑ **쟁   점**

일제가 제정한 법령이 대한민국 정부 수립 이후에도 효력을 지속하는지 여부.

☑ **판   결**

일제 제정의 법령이라도 제헌헌법 제100조에 의하여 그 내용이 헌법에 위배되지 않는 한 계속 효력을 가진다.

판 결 문

위선 대한민국이 독립된 후 사찰령의 존폐에 관하여 논의가 있는 듯 하나 비록 사찰령이 일제 당시 제령의 형식으로 제정 실시된 것이라 할지라도 대한민국 독립 후 차를 폐지하는 법령이 시행된 바 없고 일방 우령(右令)은 일제의 식민지였든 한반도 소재의 사찰이나 한민족의 종교활동을 탄압하거나 반대로 사찰에 대하여 특권을 부여하는 취지가 아니고 단지 사찰에 의안 종교활동을 보호하려는 행정목적과 사찰재산이 형성된 역사적인 유래에 감하여 사찰행정의 원칙적인 규범과 사찰재산의 관리처분에 관한 준칙을 규정한 것인바, 우 기의 입법 취지는 대한민국 헌법의 정신에 저촉된다고는 인정되지 않으므로 사찰령은 우 헌법의 공표실시 후에도 의연 존속한다고 할 것이다.

☑ 해 설

1948년 8월 15일 대한민국 정부 수립 당시 5.10 선거에 의하여 구성된 국회가 제정한 법률은 헌법, 국회법, 정부조직법 등 극소수에 불과했다. 그러면 정부수립 초기 국내의 법질서는 무엇으로 규율될 수 있었는가? 제헌헌법은 "현행법령은 이 헌법에 위배되지 않는 한 계속 효력을 가진다"라는 조항을 두어 이에 대처했다(제100조). 이는 대한민국 수립 초기의 법적 공백을 메우기 위한 불가피한 조치였다. 외세통치로부터 벗어나 새로이 주권국가를 성립시킨 경우 기존법령의 잠정적 승계를 인정했던 예는 외국에서도 쉽게 찾을 수 있다.

당시 "현행법령"에 해당하는 것으로는 (1) 미군정 법령 (2) 군정 종료 당시까지 유효하던 일제 법령 (3) 군정 종료 당시까지 유효하던 조선시대의 법령 등이었다. 제헌헌법 제100조에 따라 우리 법질서의 일부로 수용된 구법령은 대체법령 제정작업이 빠르게 진척되지 않아 그 후 무려 13년 이상 국내법 질서의 중요 부분을 차지하였다. 제1공화국 말기까지는 구법령이 우리의 일상생활을 규제하던 법령의 대종을 이루었다. 구법령은 5.16 이후 1961년 7월 15일 공포된 구법령 정리에 관한 특별조치법을 통하여 1962년 1월 20일 모든 효력을 상실했다. 구 법령의 운영과정에서는 헌법에 위배되어 더 이상 효력을 가질 수 없는 법령의 범위, 미군정 법령에 위배되어 효력을 상실한 일제시 법령의 범위, 광복 후 국회 제정 법률에 의해 대체된 법률의 범위 등을 정확히 파악할 수 없어서 적지 않은 혼선이 야기되기도 했다. 이 판결은 일제의 제령이 제1공화국 시절까지 적용되었음을 보여주는 한 예이다.

➠ 참고문헌 ─────────────────────────────

• 정인섭, 대한민국의 수립과 구법령의 승계—제헌헌법 제100조 관련판례의 분석, 국제판례연구 1집(1999, 박영사), p. 261.

제12장

해 양 법

1. 코르푸해협 사건(1949)
— 국제해협에서 군함의 무해통항

Corfu Channel Case(Merits).
U.K. v. Albania. 1949 ICJ Reports 4.

☑ 사　안

1946년 5월 15일 알바니아 본토와 그리스령 코르푸 섬 사이의 해협(폭 3-23km)을 통과하던 영국 군함이 사전 경고도 없이 알바니아로부터 포탄공격을 받았다. 이 사건 직후 영국 정부는 군함도 코르푸 해협에서 무해통항권을 갖는다고 주장한 반면, 알바니아 정부는 외국 선박은 사전허가하에서만 이 해협을 지날 수 있다고 주장했다.

영국은 알바니아의 의사를 확인하기 위해 같은 해 10월 22일 순양함 2척과 구축함 2척으로 구성된 함대를 코르푸 해협으로 다시 파견했다. 이때 알바니아의 영해를 항해 도중 구축함들이 기뢰와 충돌해 큰 피해를 입었다. 승무원도 44명이 사망하고, 42명이 부상을 입었다. 영국은 5월 사건 이후에 알바니아가 국제해협인 코르푸 해협에 계획적으로 기뢰를 부설했다고 의심했다. 한편 알바니아는 당시 인접 그리스와의 긴장관계인 특수상황에서 외국 군함의 자국 영해 통과를 규제할 권한이 있으며, 사전허가 없는 영국 함대의 코르푸 해협 통과는 국제법 위반인 동시에 당시 영국 함대의 통항은 무해통항에도 해당하지 않았다고 주장했다. 이 사건이 발생한 직후인 11월 12-13일 영국은 코르푸 해협에 다시 함대를 파견해 소해작업을 벌인 결과, 22개의 수중기뢰를 제거했다.

영국은 10월 22일자 사고의 책임을 묻기 위해 알바니아를 ICJ에 제소하였다. 이 사건의 쟁점은 크게 2가지였다. 첫째, 1946년 10월 22일 코르푸 해협 알바니아 영해 내에서 발생한 폭발사고에 대해 알바니아가 국제법상의 책임이 있는가? 둘째, 1946년 10월 22일 및 11일 12 13일 일바니아 넝해에서의 영국의 행위는 알바니아의 주권을 침해한 행위인가?

☑ 쟁 점

군함은 국제해협에서 무해통항권을 갖는가?

☑ 판 결

(1) 자국 영해에 기뢰가 부설되었음을 알았거나 알 수 있었음에도 불구하고, 이를 공표하지 않았다면 연안국은 그로 인한 피해에 대하여 책임이 있다.

(2) 국제항로로 이용되는 국제해협의 경우 평시에는 군함도 무해통항권을 갖는다.

판 결 문

(p. 12-) By the first part of the Special Agreement, the following question is submitted to the Court :

> "(1) Is Albania responsible under international law for the explosions which occurred on the 22nd October 1946 in Albanian waters and for the damage and loss of human life which resulted from them and is there any duty to pay compensation?" [⋯]

(p. 22) From all the facts and observations mentioned above, the Court draws the conclusion that the laying of the minefield which caused the explosions on October 22nd, 1946, could not have been accomplished without the knowledge of the Albanian Government. The obligations resulting for Albania from this knowledge are not disputed between the Parties. Counsel for the Albanian Government expressly recognized that [translation] if Albania had been informed of the operation before the incidents of October 22nd, and in tune to warn the British vessels and shipping in general of the existence of mines in the Corfu Channel, her responsibility would be involved ...".

The obligations incumbent upon the Albanian authorities consisted in notifying, for the benefit of shipping in general, the existence of a minefield in Albanian territorial waters and in warning the approaching British warships of the imminent danger to which the minefield exposed them. Such obligations are based, not on the Hague Convention of 1907, No.VIII, which is applicable in time of war, but on certain general and well-recognized principles, namely: elementary considerations of humanity, even more exacting in peace than in war the principle of the freedom of maritime communication and every State's obligation not to allow knowingly its territory to be used for acts contrary to the rights of other States.

In fact, Albania neither notified the existence of the minefield, nor warned the British warships of the danger they were approaching. [⋯]

In fact, nothing was attempted by the Albanian authorities to prevent the disaster. These grave omissions involve the international responsibility of Albania.

The Court therefore reaches the conclusion that Albania is responsible under international law for the explosions which occurred on October 22nd, 1946, in Albanian waters, and for the damage and loss of human life which resulted from them, and that there is a duty upon Albania to pay compensation to the United Kingdom. [⋯]

(p. 28-) The Court will now consider the Albanian contention that the United Kingdom Government violated Albanian sovereignty by sending the warships through this Strait without the previous authorization of the Albanian Government. It is, in the opinion of the Court, generally recognized and in accordance with international custom that States in time of peace have a right to send their warships through straits used for international navigation between two parts of the high seas without the previous authorization of a coastal State, provided that the passage is *innocent*. Unless otherwise prescribed in an international convention, there is no right for a coastal State to prohibit such passage through straits in time of peace.

The Albanian Government does not dispute that the North Corfu Channel is a strait in the geographical sense but it denies that this Channel belongs to the class of international highways through which a right of passage exists, on the grounds that it is only of secondary importance and not even a necessary route between two parts of the high seas, and that it is used almost exclusively for local traffic to and from the ports of Corfu and Saranda.

It may be asked whether the test is to be found in the volume of traffic passing through the Strait or in its greater or lesser importance for international navigation. But in the opinion of the Court the decisive criterion is rather its geographical situation as connecting two parts of the high seas and the fact of its being used for international navigation. Nor can it be decisive that this Strait is not a necessary route between two parts of the high seas, but only an alternative passage between the Egean and the Adriatic Seas. It has nevertheless been a useful route for international maritime traffic. In this respect, the agent of the United Kingdom Government gave the Court the following information relating to the period from April 1st, 1936, to December 31st, 1937: "The following is the total number of ships putting in at the Port of Corfu after passing through or just before passing through the Channel. During the period of one year nine months, the total number of ships was 2,884. The flags of the ships are Greek, Italian, Roumanian, Yugoslav, French, Albanian and British. Clearly, very small vessels are included, as the entries for Albanian vessels are high, and of course one vessel may make several journeys, but 2,884 ships for a period of one year nine months is quite a large figure. These figures relate to vessels visited by the Customs at Corfu and so do not include the large number of vessels which went through the Strait without calling at Corfu at all." [⋯]

One fact of particular importance is that the North Corfu Channel constitutes a frontier between Albania and Greece, that a part of it is wholly within the territorial waters of these States, and that the Strait is of special importance to Greece by reason of the traffic to and from the port of Corfu.

Having regard to these various considerations, the Court has arrived at the conclusion that the North Corfu Channel should be considered as belonging to the class of international highways through which passage cannot be prohibited by a coastal State in time of peace.

On the other hand, it is a fact that the two coastal States did not maintain normal relations, that Greece had made territorial claims precisely with regard to a part of Albanian territory bordering on the Channel, that Greece had declared that she considered herself technically in a state of war with Albania, and that Albania, invoking the danger of Greek incursions, had considered it necessary to take certain measures of vigilance in this region. The Court is of opinion that Albania, in view of these exceptional circumstances, would have been justified in issuing regulations in respect of the passage of warships through the Strait, but not in prohibiting such passage or in subjecting it to the requirement of special authorization.

For these reasons the Court is unable to accept the Albanian contention that the Government of the United Kingdom has violated Albanian sovereignty by sending the warships through the Strait without having obtained the previous authorization of the Albanian Government.

☑ 해   설

이 판결은 유엔 체제에서 ICJ가 설립된 이후 첫 번째 재판사건이었다. 당초 영국은 이 사건을 안전보장이사회에 회부했다. 당시 알바니아는 아직 유엔 회원국은 아니었으나 안보리에서의 토의에 참여하며 자신은 안보리의 권고를 전적으로 수용할 것임을 천명했다(1947년 1월 24일 전문). 안보리는 1947년 4월 9일 이 분쟁을 ICJ에 회부하라고 권고하는 결의를 채택했고, 5월 22일 영국은 이를 ICJ에 제소했다.

알바니아는 1947년 7월 2일자로 ICJ에 보낸 서한에서 영국이 자국과의 합의없이 일방적으로 이 사건을 ICJ에 제소할 권한은 없으나, 그러한 영국의 행동에도 불구하고 자국은 안보리의 권고를 수락하며 법정에 출두할 용의가 있다고 통지했다. 그러나 서면심리 중인 1947년 12월 9일 알바니아는 ICJ가 자국 사건에 대하여 관할권을 행사할 수 없다고 주장하는 선결적 항변을 제출했다.

ICJ는 관할권에 관한 알바니아의 선결적 항변을 먼저 판단했다. 재판부는 알바니아의 1947년 1월 24일자 안보리에 대한 전문과 1947년 7월 2일자 ICJ에 대한 서한의 내용상 알바니아는 이미 ICJ의 관할권을 수락했으며, 일단 성립된 관할권은 추후 부정할 수 없다며 선결적 항변을 기각했다(1948년 3월 25일). 이어 ICJ는 본안소송을 진행했다.

본안판결에서 ICJ는 누가 코르푸 해협에 기뢰를 설치했는가를 확정할 수는 없으나, 적어도 1946년 10월 22일 사건 당시 알바니아는 자국 영해 내의 기뢰의 존재를 알 수 있었다고 판단했다. 그럼에도 불구하고 이를 통항중인 영국 군함에 경고하지 않은 알바니아의 부작위는 인도주의에 대한 기본적 고려와 해상교통의 자유 및 자국의 영토가 고의로 타국의 권리를 침해하도록 사용되는 것을 허용하지 말아야 할 의무를 위반했다고 평가했다.

이어서 ICJ는 평시에는 군함도 국제해협에서 무해통항권을 가지며, 문제

의 해협이 국제통항에 필수적 항로인가 여부는 중요하지 않다고 보았다. 알
바니아는 1946년 10월 22일 영국 함대의 통과는 무해통항이 아니었다고 주
장했으나, 재판부는 여러 정황상 그 같은 근거가 없다고 판단했다. 결국 ICJ
는 1946년 10월 22일 무해통항을 하던 영국 군함에 발생한 피해에 대해 알
바니아가 배상책임이 있다고 결론내렸다.

한편 ICJ는 1946년 11월 12-13일 코르푸 해협에서 영국의 소해행위는
알바니아의 주권을 침해한 행위라고 판단했다. 영국은 자신의 행위가 알바니
아의 영토적 일체성이나 정치적 독립성에 대한 어떠한 위협도 아니었으므로
유엔 헌장 제2조 4항에 위반되지 않는다고 주장했으나, ICJ는 영국의 행위가
영토주권 존중 원칙을 침해했다고 판단했다. 다만 이 같은 ICJ의 판정이 그
자체로 알바니아에 대한 만족(satisfaction)을 준다고 평가했다.

이어 ICJ는 1949년 12월 15일 알바니아의 배상금액에 대한 또 하나의
판결을 내렸다. 재판부는 알바니아가 영국에게 84만 3947파운드(미화 약 201
만 달러)의 지불을 명했다. 선결적 항변이 기각되자 이후 알바니아는 이 재판
에 참여하지 않았으며, 배상금의 지불도 거부했다. 한편 연합국은 제2차 대
전중 주축국이 알바니아에서 약탈한 금괴 1574kg을 압수해 런던의 영국은행
에 보관하고 있었는데, 영국은 이 금괴의 반환을 거부했고 이 사건의 최종처
리는 미결로 남았다.

1991년 알바니아의 공산정권이 몰락하자, 영국과 알바니아는 코르푸 해
협 사건에 대해 상호 유감을 표명하고 1991년 5월 29일 외교관계 수립에 합
의했다. 알바니아는 ICJ가 명한 201만 달러의 배상금 지불에 동의하자, 1996
년 영국도 알바니아의 금괴를 반환했다. 2009년 미국과 알바니아 조사팀은
당시 손상된 선체 일부의 잔해를 발견했다고 한다.

이 판결은 후일 1982년 해양법협약에도 영향을 미쳤다. 즉 협약 제24조
2항은 연안국이 자국 영해에서의 통항의 위험에 관하여 공시할 의무가 있다
고 규정하고 있고, 제44조는 연안국이 국제해협이나 그 상공에서의 항행이
나 비행의 위험을 적절히 공표해야 한다고 규정하고 있다.

▶ 참고문헌 ─────────────────────────────────

- 박현석, UN의 분쟁해결제도와 ICJ이 역할: 한국에 대한 코르푸해협 사건의 영향을 중심으로, 국제법평론 2016-I, p. 1.
- E. Leggelt, The Corfu Incident(1974).
- J. M. Jones, Corfu Channel Case, Jurisdiction, Transactions of the Grotius Society for the Year 1949 Vol. 35(1950), p. 91.
- N. H. Shah, Discovered by Intervention, The Right of a State to Seize Evidence Located within the Territory of the Respondent State, AJIL Vol. 53(1959), p. 595.

2. 영국 · 노르웨이 어업 사건(1951)
— 직선기선 설정 요건

Anglo-Norwegian Fisheries Case.
U.K. v. Norway, 1951 ICJ Report 116.

☑ 사   안

영국 어민들은 17세기 초부터 노르웨이 근방에서 어로활동을 자제해 왔으나 20세기에 들어 다시 노르웨이 수역에서 어로 활동을 증대했다. 이에 노르웨이 정부는 1935년 7월 12일 노르웨이의 영해 내에서 어로구역에 관한 국왕칙령을 공포해 직선기선을 사용한 노르웨이 어업한계선을 설정했다. 즉 육지, 도서 및 저조시에 출현하는 간출지를 연결하는 47개의 직선기선을 사용하여 어업구역을 설정했는데 경우에 따라서는 기점이 육지에서 40해리나 떨어진 곳도 있었다. 이에 근거하여 1948년과 1949년 노르웨이 정부는 다수의 영국 어선을 나포했고, 이에 영국과 노르웨이는 이 문제의 해결을 위한 협상을 했으나 성공하지 못했다. 이 사건에서는 노르웨이가 직선기선을 통해 영해 기선을 획정할 수 있느냐가 중요 쟁점의 하나로 부각되었다.

☑ 쟁   점

영해의 기선을 설정하는 데 있어서 직선기선을 사용할 수 있는지 여부.

☑ 판   결

해안선의 일반적인 방향, 본토와 해역과의 관계 및 그 해역에서의 경제적 이해관계 등을 고려하여 연안국은 직선기선을 획정할 수 있다.

판 결 문

(p. 127-) The coastal zone concerned in the dispute is of considerable length. It lies north of latitude 66° 28.8 N., that is to say, north of the Arctic Circle, and it includes the coast of the mainland of Norway and all the islands, islets, rocks and reefs, known by the name of the 'skjaergaard' (literally, rock rampart), together with all Norwegian internal and territorial waters. The coast of the mainland, which, without taking any account of fjords, bays and minor indentations, is over 1,500 kilometres in length, is of a very distinctive configuration. Very broken along its whole length, it constantly opens out into indentations often penetrating for great distances inland: the Porsangerfjord, for instance, penetrates 75 sea miles inland. To the west, the land configuration stretches out into the sea: the large and small islands, mountainous in character, the islets, rocks and reefs, some always above water, others emerging only at low tide, are in truth but an extension of the Norwegian mainland. The number of insular formations, large and small, which make up the 'skjaergaard', is estimated by the Norwegian Government to be one hundred and twenty thousand. From the southern extremity of the disputed area to the North Cape, the 'skjaergaard' lies along the whole of the coast of the mainland; east of the North Cape, the 'skjaergaard' ends, but the coast line continues to be broken by large and deeply indented fjords.

Within the 'skjaergaard', almost every island has its large and its small bays; countless arms of the sea, straits, channels and mere waterways serve as a means of communication for the local population which inhabits the islands as it does the mainland. The coast of the mainland does not constitute, as it does in practically all other countries, a clear dividing line between land and sea. What matters, what really constitutes the Norwegian coast line, is the outer line of the 'skjaergaard.' [···]

Along the coast are situated comparatively shallow banks, veritable underwater terraces which constitute fishing grounds where fish are particularly abundant; these grounds were known to Norwegian fishermen and exploited by them from time immemorial. Since these banks lay within the range of vision, the most desirable fishing grounds were always located and identified by means of the method of alignments ('meds'), at points where two lines drawn between points selected on the coast or on islands intersected.

In these barren regions the inhabitants of the coastal zone derive their livelihood essentially from fishing.

Such are the realities which must be borne in mind in appraising the validity of the United Kingdom contention that the limits of the Norwegian fisheries zone laid down in the 1935 Decree are contrary to international law. [⋯]

The Court has no difficulty in finding that, for the purpose of measuring the breadth of the territorial sea, it is the low-water mark as opposed to the high-water mark, or the mean between the two tides, which has generally been adopted in the practice of States. This criterion is the most favourable to the coastal State and clearly shows the character of territorial waters as appurtenant to the land territory. The Court notes that the Parties agree as to this criterion, but that they differ as to its application. [⋯]

The Court finds itself obliged to decide whether the relevant low-water mark is that of the mainland or of the 'skjaergaard'. Since the mainland is bordered in its western sector by the 'skjaergaard', which constitutes a whole with the mainland, it is the outer line of the 'skjaergaard' which must be taken into account in delimiting the belt of Norwegian territorial waters. This solution is dictated by geographic realities.

Three methods have been contemplated to effect the application of the low-water mark rule. The simplest would appear to be the method of the trace parallele, which consists of drawing the outer limit of the belt of territorial waters by following the coast in all its sinuosities. This method may be applied without difficulty to an ordinary coast, which is not too broken. Where a coast is deeply indented and cut into, as is that of Eastern Finnmark, or where it is bordered by an archipelago such as the 'skjaergaard' along the western sector of the coast here in question, the base-line becomes independent of the low-water mark, and can only be determined by means of a geometrical construction. In such circumstances the line of the low-water mark can no longer be put forward as a rule requiring the coastline to be followed in all its sinuosities. Nor can one characterize as exceptions to the rule the very many derogations which would be necessitated by such a rugged coast: the rule would disappear under the exceptions. Such a coast, viewed as a whole, calls for the application of a different method; that is, the method of base-lines which, within reasonable limits, may depart from the physical line of the coast. [⋯]

The principle that the belt of territorial waters must follow the general direction of the coast makes it possible to fix certain criteria valid for any delimitation of the territorial sea; these criteria will be elucidated later. The Court will confine itself at this stage to noting that, in order to apply this principle, several States have deemed it necessary to follow the straight base-lines method and that they have not encountered objections of principle by other States. This method consists of selecting appropriate points on the low-water mark and drawing straight lines between them. This has been done, not only in the case of welldefined bays, but also in cases of minor curvatures of the coast line where it was solely a question of giving a simpler form to the belt of territorial waters.

It has been contended, on behalf of the United Kingdom, that Norway may draw straight lines only across bays. The Court is unable to share this view. If the belt of territorial waters must follow the outer line of the 'skjaergaard', and if the method of straight base-lines must be admitted in certain cases, there is no valid reason to draw them only across bays, as in Eastern Finnmark, and not also to draw them between islands, islets and rocks, across the sea areas separating them, even when such areas do not fall within the conception of a bay. It is sufficient that they should be situated between the island formations of the 'skjaergaard', *inter fauces terrarum*.[1] [···]

It does not at all follow that, in the absence of rules having the technically precise character alleged by the United Kingdom Government, the delimitation undertaken by the Norwegian Government in 1935 is not subject to certain principles which make it possible to judge as to its validity under international law. The delimitation of sea areas has always an international aspect it cannot be dependent merely upon the will of the coastal State as expressed in its municipal law. Although it is true that the act of delimitation is necessary a unilateral act, because only the coastal State is competent to undertake it, the validity of the delimitation with regard to other States depends upon international law.

In this connection, certain basic considerations inherent in the nature of the territorial sea, bring to light certain criteria which, though not entirely precise, can provide courts with an adequate basis for their decisions, which can be adapted to the diverse facts in question.

Among these considerations, some reference must be made to the close dependence of the territorial sea upon the land domain. It is the land which confers upon the coastal State a right to the waters off its coasts. It follows that while such a State must be allowed the latitude necessary in order to be able to adapt its delimitation to practical needs and local requirements, the drawing of base-lines

---

1) natural entrance points — 필자 주.

must not depart to any appreciable extent from the general direction of the coast.

Another fundamental consideration, of particular importance in this case, is the more or less close relationship existing between certain sea areas and the land formations which divide or surround them. The real question raised in the choice of base-lines is in effect whether certain sea areas lying within these lines are sufficiently closely linked to the land domain to be subject to the regime of internal waters. This idea, which is at the basis of the determination of the rules relating to bays, should be liberally applied in the case of a coast, the geographical configuration of which is as unusual as that of Norway.

Finally, there is one consideration not to be overlooked, the scope of which extends beyond purely geographical factors: that of certain economic interests peculiar to a region, the reality and importance of which are clearly evidenced by a long usage.

Norway puts forward the 1935 Decree as the application of a traditional system of delimitation, a system which she claims to be in complete conformity with international law. [⋯]

From the standpoint of international law, it is now necessary to consider whether the application of the Norwegian system encountered any opposition from foreign States. Norway has been in a position to argue without any contradiction that neither the promulgation of her delimitation Decrees in 1869 and in 1889, nor their application, gave rise to any opposition on the part of foreign States. Since, moreover, these Decrees constitute, as has been shown above, the application of a well-defined and uniform system, it is indeed this system itself which would reap the benefit of general toleration, the basis of an historical consolidation which would make it enforceable as against all States.

The general toleration of foreign States with regard to the Norwegian practice is an unchallenged fact. For a period of more than sixty years the United Kingdom Government itself in no way contested it. [⋯]

The notoriety of the facts, the general toleration of the international community, Great Britain's position in the North Sea, her own interest in the question, and her prolonged abstention would in any case warrant Norway's enforcement of her system against the United Kingdom.

The Court is thus led to conclude that the method of straight lines, established in the Norwegian system, was imposed by the peculiar geography of the Norwegian coast; that even before the dispute arose, this method had been consolidated by a constant and sufficiently long practice, in the face of which the attitude of governments bears witness to the fact that they did not consider it to be contrary to international law.

☑ 해   설

이 판결은 직선기선이 해양법상의 일반적 제도로 인정되는 계기가 되었다. 즉 해안선이 복잡하게 굴곡되거나 해안선 가까이 일련의 섬이 산재한 지역에서는 통상기선을 기준으로 한 경계획정이 쉽지 않다. 이 판결에서 ICJ는 노르웨이와 같이 특별한 지질학적 요인과 함께 경제적 요인을 갖는 경우 직선기선을 설정할 수 있다는 점을 인정했다. 다만 직선기선은 연안국 해안의 일반적 방향성으로부터 현저하게 이탈해서는 아니 된다. 또한 기선의 내측 수역이 내수제도로 인정받기 위하여 육지와 충분히 밀접한 관계를 갖고 있어야 한다. 그리고 그 지역 특유의 경제적 이익이 오랜 관행을 통해 증명되고 있어야 한다. 직선기선의 개념은 1958년 「영해 및 접속수역에 관한 협약」에 반영되었으며, 1982년 「해양법 협약」 제7조도 직선기선을 인정하고 있다.

또한 이 판결은 관습국제법의 성립에 지속적으로 반대한 국가에 대해서는 관습법의 효력이 적용되지 않는다는 점을 적시했다. 판결문은 영국이 만의 입구를 연결하는 기선으로부터 10해리 한계에 대한 관습법의 존재의 입증을 하지 못했는데, 설사 그러한 관습법이 존재한다고 하더라도 노르웨이는 그러한 원칙의 적용에 처음부터 반대하여 왔고, 그것이 지속적이었으므로 해당 관습법은 노르웨이에 적용되지 않는다고 판단했다.

➥ 참고문헌 ─────────────────────────

- 이창위, 영국·노르웨이 어업사건, 아세아연구 94호(1995), p. 163.
- 이창위, 직선기선제도의 제문제에 관한 고찰, Strategy 21 3권 2호(2000), p. 32.
- 김현수, 직선기선의 일반적 기준에 관한 연구, 해사논문집 42집(1999), p. 145.
- Jens Evensen, The Anglo-Norwegian Fisheries Case and Its Legal Consequences, AJIL Vol. 46(1952), p. 609.

- C. H. M. Waldock, The Anglo—Norwegian Fisheries Case, BYIL Vol. 28(1951), p. 114.
- R. O. Wilberforce, Some Aspects of the Anglo—Norwegian Fisheries Case, Transactions of the Grotius Society Vol. 38(1953), p. 151.
- T. Kobayashi, The Anglo—Norwegian Fisheries Case of 1951 and the Changing Law of the Territorial Sea(1965).

3. 리비아·몰타 대륙붕 사건(1985)
— 대륙붕 경계획정 원칙

Case Concerning the Continental Shelf.
Libyan Arab Jamahiriya/Malta, 1985 ICJ Reports 13.

☑ 사　　안

지중해 중앙에 위치한 몰타는 리비아 북방으로 최단거리 183해리 떨어진 주섬인 몰타섬과 몇 개의 부속도서로 구성되어 있다. 몰타는 중간선 원칙에 기해 리비아와의 대륙붕 경계획정을 주장했지만, 육지 영토가 훨씬 크고 해안선 길이도 긴 리비아는 이를 거부했다. 리비아는 해저의 지질학적 및 지형학적 특징을 감안한 육지의 자연연장 개념에 입각하여 대륙붕 경계가 획정되어야 한다고 주장했다. 특히 리비아는 동서 1,700km에 이르는 자국의 긴 해안선과 몰타 인근 수중 해구로 인한 자연연장의 단절이 중요한 고려요소가 되어야 한다고 주장했다. 반면 몰타는 200해리 이내의 범위에서는 자연연장보다도 거리 개념이 우선해야 한다고 주장했다. 양국은 대륙붕 경계에 관해 합의에 이르지 못하자, 1982년 이 사건을 ICJ에 회부하기로 합의했다.

☑ 쟁　　점

거리가 400해리 이내인 대안국(對岸國)간의 형평한 대륙붕 경계획정 방법.

☑ 판　　결

(1) 배타적 경제수역이 관습국제법화되었으므로 200해리 이내의 대륙붕 경계획정에서는 해저지형은 중요하지 않고, 거리 개념이 1차적으로 적용된다.

(2) 공평한 경계획정을 위해서는 1) 잠정적으로 중간선을 그린 다음, 2) 해안선의 길이의 불균형 등 모든 관련사항을 고려하여 잠정적 중간선을 조정하고, 3) 그 결과 양측 해안선 길이의 비율과 할당된 수역의 비율간에 현저한 불공평이 없는가를 검토한다.

판 결 문

34. For Malta, the reference to distance in Article 76 of the 1982 Convention represents a consecration of the 'distance principle'; for Libya, only the reference to natural prolongation corresponds to customary international law. It is in the Court's view incontestable that, apart from those provisions, the institution of the exclusive economic zone, with its rule on entitlement by reason of distance, is shown by the practice of States to have become a part of customary law; in any case, Libya itself seemed to recognize this fact when, at one stage during the negotiation of the Special Agreement, it proposed that the extent of the exclusive economic zone be included in the reference to the Court. Although the institutions of the continental shelf and the exclusive economic zone are different and distinct, the rights which the exclusive economic zone entails over the sea-bed of the zone are defined by reference to the regime laid down for the continental shelf. Although there can be a continental shelf where there is no exclusive economic zone, there cannot be an exclusive economic zone without a corresponding continental shelf. It follows that, for juridical and practical reasons, the distance criterion must now apply to the continental shelf as well as to the exclusive economic zone; and this quite apart from the provision as to distance in paragraph 1 of Article 76. This is not to suggest that the idea of natural prolongation is now superseded by that of distance. What it does mean is that where the continental margin does not extend as far as 200 miles from the shore, natural prolongation, which in spite of its physical origins has throughout its history become more and more a complex and juridical concept, is in part defined by distance from the shore, irrespective of the physical nature of the intervening sea-bed and subsoil. The concepts of natural prolongation and distance are therefore not opposed but complementary; and both remain essential elements in the juridical concept of the continental shelf. As the Court has observed, the legal basis of that which is to be delimited cannot be other than pertinent to the delimitation [···]; the Court is thus unable to accept the Libyan contention that distance from the coast is not a relevant element for the decision of the present case. [⋯]

39. The Court however considers that since the development of the law enables a State to claim that the continental shelf appertaining to it extends up to as far as 200 miles from its coast, whatever the geological characteristics of the corresponding sea-bed and subsoil, there is no reason to ascribe any role to geological or geophysical factors within that distance either in verifying the legal title of the States concerned or in proceeding to a delimitation as between their claims. This is especially clear where verification of the validity of title is concerned, since, at least in so far as those areas are situated at a distance of under 200 miles from the coasts in question, title depends solely on the distance from the coasts of the claimant States of any areas of sea-bed claimed by way of continental shelf, and the geological or geomorphological characteristics of those areas are completely immaterial. It follows that, since the distance between the coasts of the Parties is less that 400 miles, so that no geophysical feature can lie more than 200 miles from each coast, the feature referred to as the 'rift zone' cannot constitute a fundamental discontinuity terminating the southward extension of the Maltese shelf and the northward extension of the Libyan as if it were some natural boundary. [⋯]

61. The Court has little doubt which criterion and method it must employ at the outset in order to achieve a provisional position in the present dispute. The criterion is linked with the law relating to a State's legal title to the continental shelf. As the Court has found above, the law applicable to the present dispute, that is, to claims relating to continental shelves located less than 200 miles from the coasts of the States in question, is based not on geological or geomorphological criteria, but on a criterion of distance from the Coast or, to use the traditional term, on the principle of adjacency as measured by distance. It therefore seems logical to the Court that the choice of the criterion and the method which it is to employ in the first place to arrive at a provisional result should be made in a manner consistent with the concepts underlying the attribution of legal title.

62. [⋯] It is clear that, in these circumstances, the tracing of a median line between those coasts, by way of a provisional step in a process to be continued by other operations, is the most judicious manner of proceeding with a view to the eventual achievement of an equitable result.

63. The median line drawn in this way is thus only provisional. [⋯] Thus, under existing law, it must be demonstrated that the equidistance method leads to an equitable result in the case in question. To achieve this purpose, the result to which the distance criterion leads must be examined in the context of applying equitable principles to the relevant circumstances. [　]

65. In thus establishing, as the first stage in the delimitation process, the median line as the provisional delimitation line, the Court could hardly ignore the fact that the equidistance method has never been regarded, even in a delimitation between opposite coasts, as one to be applied without modification whatever the circumstances. [⋯] It is thus certain that, for the purposes of achieving an equitable result in a situation in which the equidistance line is *prima facie* the appropriate method, all relevant circumstances must be examined, since they may have a weight in the assessment of the equities of the case which it would be proper to take into account and to reflect in an adjustment of the equidistance line. [⋯]

68. [⋯] The coast of Libya from Ras Ajdir to Ras Zarruq, measured following its general direction, is 192 miles long, and the coast of Malta from Ras il-Wardija to Delimara Point, following straight baselines but excluding the islet of Filfla, is 24 miles long. In the view of the Court, this difference is so great as to justify the adjustment of the median line so as to attribute a larger shelf area to Libya; the degree of such adjustment does not depend upon a mathematical operation and remains to be examined.

71. In the light of these circumstances, the Court finds it necessary, in order to ensure the achievement of an equitable solution, that the delimitation line between the areas of continental shelf appertaining respectively to the two Parties, be adjusted so as to lie closer to the coasts of Malta. Within the area with which the Court is concerned, the coasts of the Parties are opposite to each other, and the equidistance line between them lies broadly West to east, so that its adjustment can be satisfactorily and simply achieved by transposing it in an exactly northward direction. [⋯]

73. The position reached by the Court at this stage of its consideration of the case is therefore the following. It takes the median line (ignoring Filfla as a base-point) as the first step of the delimitation. But relevant circumstances indicate that some northward shift of the boundary line is needed in order to produce an equitable result. These are first, the general geographical context in which the islands of Malta appear as a relatively small feature in a semi-enclosed sea ; and secondly, the great disparity in the lengths of the relevant coasts of the two Parties. [⋯][1]

---

1) 재판부는 리비아와 몰타 간의 중간선을 그리고, 다시 리비아와 시실리 간의 중간선을 그렸

75. This does not mean, however, that the Court is debarred from considering the equitableness of the result of the delimitation which it has in contemplation from the viewpoint of the proportional relationship of coasts and continental shelf areas. The Court does not consider that an endeavour to achieve a predetermined arithmetical ratio in the relationship between the relevant coasts and the continental shelf areas generated by them would be in harmony with the principles governing the delimitation operation. The relationship between the lengths of the relevant coasts of the Parties has of course already been taken into account in the determination of the delimitation line; if the Court turns its attention to the extent of the areas of shelf lying on each side of the line, it is possible for it to make a broad assessment of the equitableness of the result, without seeking to define the equities in arithmetical terms. The conclusion to which the Court comes in this respect is that there is certainly no evident disproportion in the areas of shelf attributed to each of the Parties respectively such that it could be said that the requirements of the test of proportionality as an aspect of equity were not satisfied.

76. Having thus completed the task conferred upon it by the Special Agreement of 23 May 1976, the Court will briefly summarize the conclusions reached in the present Judgment. The Court has found that that task is to lay down the principles and rules of international law which should enable the Parties to effect a delimitation of the areas of continental shelf between the two countries in accordance with equitable principles and so as to achieve an equitable result. [⋯]

77. The Court has thus had occasion to note the development which has occurred in the customary law of the continental shelf, and which is reflected in Articles 76 and 83 of the United Nations Convention on the Law of the Sea, concerning the relationship between the concept of the continental shelf as the natural prolongation of the land territory of the coastal State and the factor of distance from the coast. As the Court has explained, in a geographical situation like that with which the present case is concerned, where a single continental shelf falls to be delimited between two opposite States, so that no question arises, as between those States, of delimitation by reference to a continental margin extending beyond 200 miles from the baselines round the coast of either State, the legal concept of natural prolongation does not attribute any relevance to geological or geophysical factors either as basis of entitlement or as criterion for delimitation. Each coastal

---

다. 그리고 양선에 의하여 중복되는 부분에 대하여는 리비아에게 3/4, 몰타에게 1/4의 효과를 인정하는 경계선을 획정했다.

State is entitled to exercise sovereign rights over the continental shelf off its coasts for the purpose of exploring it and exploiting its natural resources(Art. 77 of the Convention) up to a distance of 200 miles from the baselines — subject of course to delimitation with neighbouring States — whatever the geophysical or geological features of the sea-bed within the area comprised between the Coast and the 200-mile limit. The introduction of this criterion of distance has not however had the effect of establishing a principle of "absolute proximity" or of conferring upon the equidistance method of delimitation the status of a general rule, or an obligatory method of delimitation, or of a priority method, to be tested in every case. [⋯] The fact that the Court has found that, in the circumstances of the present case, the drawing of a median line constitutes an appropriate first step in the delimitation process, should not be understood as implying that an equidistance line will be an appropriate beginning in all cases, or even in all cases of delimitation between opposite States.

78. Having drawn the initial median line, the Court has found that that line requires to be adjusted in view of the relevant circumstances of the area, namely the considerable disparity between the lengths of the coasts of the Parties here under consideration, the distance between those coasts, the placing of the basepoints governing any equidistance line, and the general geographical context. Taking these into consideration, and setting as an extreme limit for any northward displacement of the line the notional median line which, on the hypothesis of a delimitation between Italy and Libya on the basis of equidistance, in the area to which the Judgment relates, would deny any effect whatever to Malta, the Court has been able to indicate a method making it possible for the Parties to determine the location of a line which would ensure an equitable result between them. This line gives a result which seems to the Court to meet the requirements of the test of proportionality, and more generally to be equitable, taking into account all relevant circumstances.

☑ 해　　설

이 사건이 제소된 시점은 제3차 유엔 해양법협약이 막 타결된 무렵이었으며, 판결이 내려진 1985년에도 아직 해양법협약이 발효하지 않았다. 재판부는 비록 본 사안이 대륙붕 경계획정에 관한 사건이지만, 배타적 경제수역과 대륙붕 간의 관련성을 감안할 때 배타적 경제수역제도에서의 경계획정원칙이 고려되지 않을 수 없다고 전제했다(para. 33). 이어 거리 기준에 기반한 배타적 경제수역제도가 이미 관습국제법화되었다고 판단했다(para. 34).

리비아는 몰타 인근의 해구에서 양국 대륙붕의 자연적 연장이 단절되었으므로 이 해구가 경계로 되어야 한다고 주장했으나(para. 36), 재판부는 배타적 경제수역이 대륙붕 지역에 대한 권리도 포함하므로 연안으로부터 200해리 이내의 지역에서의 경계획정에 있어서는 지질학적, 지형적 요소에 결정적 의미를 부여할 이유가 없고 거리 기준이 우선 적용되어야 한다고 판단했다(para. 39).

이어서 재판부는 공평한 결과를 얻기 위한 경계획정을 다음과 같이 3단계로 진행했다. 첫째, 양국간 잠정적 중간선을 긋는다. 둘째, 이 지역의 모든 관련요소를 고려하여 형평에 맞게 잠정 중간선을 조정한다. 셋째, 그 결과가 양국간 해안선 길이와 할당면적 간의 비례성 원칙에 비추어 볼 때 현저한 불공평이 없는가를 검토한다. 이 사건에서 리비아의 해안선은 192마일이고, 몰타의 해안선은 24마일이었는데(즉 8 : 1), 이는 중간선의 조정을 정당화할 정도의 커다란 차이라고 판단해(para. 68), 양국간 경계선을 몰타 방향으로 상향 조정했다.

이를 적용하는 과정에서 재판부는 육지의 크기 등 배후지를 고려해야 한다는 리비아의 주장은 국가의 관행이나 학설상 수용할 수 없다고 평가하였다. 또한 경제적 및 안보적 요소를 고려해야 한다는 몰타의 주장 역시 가난한 국가가 더 많은 대륙붕을 가져야 한다는 원칙은 없다며 수용하지 않았다. 그리고 몰타섬 남단 약 5km 지점에 위치한 0.06㎢ 크기의 무인암도 Filfla는 경계획정시 고려하지 않았다. 해양경계획정에 있어서 위와 같은 3단계 접근방법은 이후 ICJ의 기본 입장으로 발전했으며, 국제해양법재판소 역시 같은 방식을 채용하고 있다.

한편 리비아와 몰타의 대륙붕 경계획정으로 영향을 받는다고 생각한 이탈리아는 국제사법재판소 규정 제62조와 규칙 제82조에 따라서 소송참가를 신청했다. 그러나 국제사법재판소는 이탈리아는 분쟁당사국과의 합의 없이 새로운 분쟁을 제기하는 것이며, 단순히 자국의 권리를 인정받기 위한 목적이 아닌 적극적으로 보전(preservation)하려는 의도로서 소송참가 요건을 충족하지 못한다고 판시했다(*Continental Shelf(Libyan Arab Jamahiriya/Malta)*,

Application to Intervene, 1984 ICJ 3).

　　재판소가 이탈리아의 소송참가를 허용하지는 않았지만 이탈리아 문제를 고려하여 판결을 내렸다. 즉 이해관계가 있는 제3국이 설사 소송의 당사자로 참여하고 있지 않더라도 계쟁 사건으로 인한 이해관계를 주장하는 경우 제3국의 입장이 분쟁 당사국 간의 분쟁해결 결과에 반영되어야 한다는 것이다. 이에 따라서 국제사법재판소는 리비아와 몰타가 판단을 요청한 특정 대륙붕 지역의 경계획정에 대해서만 판단을 하고, 그 이외 지역에 대해서는 판단을 유보했다.

➤ 참고문헌 ─────────────────────────────

- 이석용, 리비아와 몰타간 대륙붕 사건, 이석용·이창위·김채형, 국제해양법 판례연구(세창출판사, 2015), p. 11.
- Jonathan I. Charney, Progress in International Maritime Boundary Delimitation Law, AJIL Vol. 88(1994), p. 227.

4. M/V Saiga호 사건(1999)
— 추적권 행사의 요건, 어선에 대한 무력사용의 기준 등

The M/V Saiga(No.2) Case
Saint Vincent and the Grenadines v. Gunea,
International Tribunal for the Law of the Sea(1999).

☑ 사   안

M/V Saiga호는 1997년 10월 27일 서아프리카 기니의 200해리 배타적 경제수역 내에서 어로 중인 3척의 세네갈과 그리스 선박에 연료를 판매했다. 다음 날 기니의 경비정이 사격을 하며 다가와 기니의 배타적 경제수역 외곽에서 Saiga호를 나포했다. Saiga호의 선장은 재판에 회부되었다.

이 배의 선적국인 세인트 빈센트 그레나딘이 국제해양법재판소에 선박과 선원의 석방을 요구하는 잠정조치를 요청하자, 재판소는 1997년 12월 4일 보석금을 납부하는 조건으로 선박과 선원의 석방을 하라고 결정했다. 그러나 선박과 선장은 바로 석방되지 않고, 기니 국내법원에서 유죄판결을 받았다.

이후 이 사건은 세인트 빈센트 그레나딘의 요청으로 중재재판에 회부되었다가, 국제해양법재판소로의 이관이 합의되었다. 본안 재판에서는 다양한 쟁점이 제기되었다. 다음의 판결문은 그 중 특히 기니가 Saiga호를 나포할 권리가 있었는가? 추적권은 정당하게 집행되었는가? 나포시 기니측의 무력사용은 적절했는가 등에 관한 부분이다.

☑ 쟁   점

(1) 연안국은 배타적 경제수역에서 자국 관세법을 외국선박에 적용할 수 있는가?

(2) 추적권 행사의 요건.

(3) 나포를 위한 무력행사의 요건.

☑ 판   결

(1) 배타적 경제수역에서 연안국은 자국의 관세법을 외국 선박에 적용할 수 없다.

(2) 추적은 외국 선박이 정선신호를 보거나 들을 수 있는 거리에서 개시되어야 하며, 도중에 중단되어서는 아니 된다.

(3) 상선의 나포를 위한 무력사용은 일정한 경고조치를 먼저 취하고 다른 적절한 조치가 모두 실패한 후 마지막 수단으로만 사용되어야 한다.

판 결 문

123. Saint Vincent and the Grenadines claims that, in applying its customs laws to the Saiga in its customs radius, which includes parts of the exclusive economic zone, Guinea acted contrary to the Convention. It contends that in the exclusive economic zone Guinea is not entitled to exercise powers which go beyond those provided for in articles 56 and 58 of the Convention. It further asserts that Guinea violated its rights to enjoy the freedom of navigation or other internationally lawful uses of the sea in the exclusive economic zone, since the supply of gas oil by the Saiga falls within the exercise of those rights. […]

126. The Tribunal needs to determine whether the laws applied or the measures taken by Guinea against the Saiga are compatible with the Convention. In other words, the question is whether, under the Convention, there was justification for Guinea to apply its customs laws in the exclusive economic zone within a customs radius extending to a distance of 250 kilometres from the coast.

127. The Tribunal notes that, under the Convention, a coastal State is entitled to apply customs laws and regulations in its territorial sea (articles 2 and 21). […]

In the exclusive economic zone, the coastal State has jurisdiction to apply customs laws and regulations in respect of artificial islands, installations and structures (article 60, paragraph 2). In the view of the Tribunal, the Convention does not empower a coastal State to apply its customs laws in respect of any other parts of the exclusive economic zone not mentioned above. […]

136. The Tribunal, therefore, finds that, by applying its customs laws to a customs radius which includes parts of the exclusive economic zone, Guinea acted in a manner contrary to the Convention. Accordingly, the arrest and detention of the Saiga, the prosecution and conviction of its Master, the confiscation of the cargo and the seizure of the ship were contrary to the Convention. [···]

139. Saint Vincent and the Grenadines contends that, in arresting the Saiga, Guinea did not lawfully exercise the right of hot pursuit under article 111 of the Convention. [···]

140. Saint Vincent and the Grenadines asserts that, even if the Saiga violated the laws and regulations of Guinea as claimed, its arrest on 28 October 1997 did not satisfy the other conditions for hot pursuit under article 111 of the Convention. [···]

146. The Tribunal notes that the conditions for the exercise of the right of hot pursuit under article 111 of the Convention are cumulative; each of them has to be satisfied for the pursuit to be legitimate under the Convention. In this case, the Tribunal finds that several of these conditions were not fulfilled.

147. With regard to the pursuit alleged to have commenced on 27 October 1997, the evidence before the Tribunal indicates that, at the time the Order for the Joint Mission of the Customs and Navy of Guinea was issued, the authorities of Guinea, on the basis of information available to them, could have had no more than a suspicion that a tanker had violated the laws of Guinea in the exclusive economic zone. The Tribunal also notes that, in the circumstances, no visual or auditory signals to stop could have been given to the Saiga. Furthermore, the alleged pursuit was interrupted. According to the evidence given by Guinea, the small patrol boat P35 that was sent out on 26 October 1997 on a northward course to search for the Saiga was recalled when information was received that the Saiga had changed course. This recall constituted a clear interruption of any pursuit, whatever legal basis might have existed for its commencement in the first place.

148. As far as the pursuit alleged to have commenced on 28 October 1998 is concerned, the evidence adduced by Guinea does not support its claim that the necessary auditory or visual signals to stop were given to the Saiga prior to the commencement of the alleged pursuit, as required by article 111, paragraph 4, of the Convention. Although Guinea claims that the small patrol boat(P35) sounded its siren and turned on its blue revolving light signals when it came within visual and hearing range of the Saiga, both the Master who was on the bridge at the time and

Mr. Niasse who was on the deck, categorically denied that any such signals were given. In any case, any signals given at the time claimed by Guinea cannot be said to have been given at the commencement of the alleged pursuit.

149. The Tribunal has already concluded that no laws or regulations of Guinea applicable in accordance with the Convention were violated by the Saiga. It follows that there was no legal basis for the exercise of the right of hot pursuit by Guinea in this case.

150. For these reasons, the Tribunal finds that Guinea stopped and arrested the Saiga on 28 October 1997 in circumstances which did not justify the exercise of the right of hot pursuit in accordance with the Convention. [⋯]

153. Saint Vincent and the Grenadines claims that Guinea used excessive and unreasonable force in stopping and arresting the Saiga. It notes that the Saiga was an unarmed tanker almost fully laden with gas oil, with a maximum speed of 10 knots. It also notes that the authorities of Guinea fired at the ship with live ammunition, using solid shots from large-calibre automatic guns.

154. Guinea denies that the force used in boarding, stopping and arresting the Saiga was either excessive or unreasonable. It contends that the arresting officers had no alternative but to use gunfire because the Saiga refused to stop after repeated radio messages to it to stop and in spite of visual and auditory signals from the patrol boat P35. Guinea maintains that gunfire was used as a last resort, and denies that large-calibre ammunition was used. Guinea places the responsibility for any damage resulting from the use of force on the Master and crew of the ship.

155. In considering the force used by Guinea in the arrest of the Saiga, the Tribunal must take into account the circumstances of the arrest in the context of the applicable rules of international law. Although the Convention does not contain express provisions on the use of force in the arrest of ships, international law, which is applicable by virtue of article 293 of the Convention, requires that the use of force must be avoided as far as possible and, where force is unavoidable, it must not go beyond what is reasonable and necessary in the circumstances. Considerations of humanity must apply in the law of the sea, as they do in other areas of international law.

156. These principles have been followed over the years in law enforcement operations at sea. The normal practice used to stop a ship at sea is first to give an auditory or visual signal to stop, using internationally recognized signals. Where this does not succeed, a variety of actions may be taken, including the firing of shots across the bows of the ship. It is only after the appropriate actions fail that the pursuing vessel may, as a last resort, use force. Even then, appropriate warning must be issued to the ship and all efforts should be made to ensure that life is not endangered ([⋯]). The basic principle concerning the use of force in the arrest of a ship at sea has been reaffirmed by the Agreement for the Implementation of the Provisions of the United Nations Convention on the Law of the Sea of 10 December 1982 Relating to the Conservation and Management of Straddling Fish Stocks and Highly Migratory Fish Stocks. Article 22, paragraph 1(f), of the Agreement states:

> 1. The inspecting State shall ensure that its duly authorized inspectors: ...
> (f) avoid the use of force except when and to the degree necessary to ensure the safety of the inspectors and where the inspectors are obstructed in the execution of their duties. The degree of force used shall not exceed that reasonably required in the circumstances.

157. In the present case, the Tribunal notes that the Saiga was almost fully laden and was low in the water at the time it was approached by the patrol vessel. Its maximum speed was 10 knots. Therefore it could be boarded without much difficulty by the Guinean officers. At one stage in the proceedings Guinea sought to justify the use of gunfire with the claim that the Saiga had attempted to sink the patrol boat. During the hearing, the allegation was modified to the effect that the danger of sinking to the patrol boat was from the wake of the Saiga and not the result of a deliberate attempt by the ship. But whatever the circumstances, there is no excuse for the fact that the officers fired at the ship itself with live ammunition from a fast-moving patrol boat without issuing any of the signals and warnings required by international law and practice.

158. The Guinean officers also used excessive force on board the Saiga. Having boarded the ship without resistance, and although there is no evidence of the use or threat of force from the crew, they fired indiscriminately while on the deck and used gunfire to stop the engine of the ship. In using firearms in this way, the Guinean officers appeared to have attached little or no importance to the safety of the ship and the persons on board. In the process, considerable damage was done to the ship and to vital equipment in the engine and radio rooms. And, more seriously, the indiscriminate use of gunfire caused severe injuries to two of the persons on board.

159. For these reasons, the Tribunal finds that Guinea used excessive force and endangered human life before and after boarding the Saiga, and thereby violated the rights of Saint Vincent and the Grenadines under international law.

☑ 해 설

이 사건은 기니의 경우 어선의 연료에 부과하는 석유세가 주요 수입원의 하나였고, 세인트 빈센트 그레나딘의 경우 편의치적을 통한 선박등록세가 국가의 주요 수입원이었다는 경제적 배경에서 발생한 것이었다.

이 사건에서는 과연 세인트 빈센트 그레나딘이 사이가호의 기국(旗國)인가부터 논란이 되었다. 사이가호의 소유주는 키프러스의 Tabona사였으며, 관리는 스코틀랜드의 Seascot사가 맡고 있었으며, 스위스의 Lemania사가 용선하여 사용하고 있었다. 선장과 승무원은 모두 우크라이나인이었으며, 세네갈인 페인트공 3명이 추가로 고용되어 있었다. 사이가호는 1997년 3월 12일 세인트 빈센트 그레나딘에 잠정등록을 하여 1997년 4월 14일 임시등록증만 발급받았다. 임시등록증의 효력은 1997년 9월 12일에 만료되었고, 나포 이후인 1997년 11월 28일에야 세인트 빈센트 그레나딘의 정식 등록증이 발급되었다. 기니는 나포 시점인 10월 27일에는 사이가호가 일시 무국적 상태였기 때문에 세인트 빈센트 그레나딘이 외교적 보호권을 행사할 수 없다고 주장했다. 이에 대해 재판소는 제반 정황상 사이가호가 세인트 빈센트 그레나딘의 국적을 계속 보유했다고 보아야 한다고 해석하고, 만약 이러한 사정으로 재판소가 이 사건의 처리를 거부함은 정의에 부합하지 않는다고 설시했다(para. 73).

한편 기니는 사이가호와 세인트 빈센트 그레나딘 사이에는 해양법협약 제91조 1항이 요구하고 있는 진정한 유대(genuine link)가 없으므로 세인트 빈센트 그레나딘이 외교적 보호를 행할 수 없다고 주장했다. 이에 대하여 재판소는 그 같은 기니의 주장을 입증할 만한 충분한 증거가 제시되지 못했다고 보아 받아들이지 않았다(para. 87).

이어 기니는 사이가호가 기니에서의 국내적 구제를 완료하지 못했다고 주장했다. 그러나 재판소는 이 사건에서는 세인트 빈센트 그레나딘이 주장하는 청구와 관련해 기니와 자연인/법인간에는 관할권의 연결이 없으므로, 이 사건에는 국내적 구제 완료의 원칙이 적용되지 않는다고 판단했다(para. 100).

기니는 또한 선박 소유자, 화물 소유자, 선장, 기타 선원 등 그 누구도 세인트 빈센트 그레나딘의 국민이 아니므로 세인트 빈센트 그레나딘은 외교적 보호권을 행사할 수 없다고 주장했다. 그러나 재판소는 선박의 특성상 기니의 주장은 수용할 수 없다고 판단했다(para. 106).

한편 세인트 빈센트 그레나딘은 사이가호가 어떠한 기니 법령도 위반하지 않았으며, 기니가 배타적 경제수역에서 자국 관세법을 적용하는 것은 위법하다고 주장했다.

재판소는 기니가 배타적 경제수역에서 사이가호에 자국 관세법 적용이 해양법협약 위반이며, 따라서 사이가호의 나포 및 억류가 협약 위반이라고 판단했다(para. 136).

또한 사이가호는 기니의 배타적 경제수역을 벗어나 나포되었는데, 적절한 정선신호의 발령과 중단 없는 추적이 이루어지지 않아 기니의 추적권 행사에 하자가 있었다고 재판소는 판단했다(para. 148).

마지막으로 재판소는 저속의 비무장 상선인 사이가호에 대해 기니는 경고신호도 없이 과도하게 무력을 행사했다고 판단했다(para. 157 – 158).

결론적으로 재판소는 기니가 세인트 빈센트 그레나딘에 대하여 미화 2,123,357 달러와 이자를 배상하라고 명령했다.

➠ 참고문헌 ──────────────────

• 홍성근, 제2차 엠/브이 사이가호 사건, 외법논집 17집(2004).
• B. Oxman & V. Bantz, The M/V Saiga(No. 2) (Saint Vincent and the Grenadines v. Guinea), Judgment(ITLOS Case No. 2), AJIL Vol. 94, No. 1(2000).

5. 가이아나-수리남 중재판정(2007)
─ 경계 미획정 수역의 법적 지위

Guyana v. Surinam, PCA Case No. 2004-04(2007).

☑ **사** **안**

유엔 해양법협약은 경계 미획정 수역에 관해 합의가 이루어지기 전에는 "이해와 상호협력의 정신으로 실질적 잠정약정을 체결할 수 있도록 모든 노력을 다하며, 과도적인 기간 동안 최종합의에 이르는 것을 위태롭게 하거나 방해하지 아니한다"(제74조 3항 및 제83조 3항)는 조항을 두고 있을 뿐이다.

가이아나와 수리남은 남미의 인접국으로 해양경계획정에 관한 분쟁을 겪고 있다. 양국은 1991년 경계 미획정 수역 이용에 관한 양해각서에 합의하기도 했으나, 양측 협상은 잘 진행되지 않았다. 특히 수리남이 협상에 소극적이었다. 1998년 가이아나는 캐나다 회사 CGX Rosources Inc.(이하 회사)에 분쟁 대륙붕 지역 석유개발에 관한 양허계약을 체결했다. 회사는 1999년부터 탐사를 실시하고, 2000년 시험굴착까지 진행했다. 수리남은 외교경로를 통해 분쟁 지역에서의 가이아나측 석유탐사를 중지하라고 요구하는 한편, 2000년 6월 수리남의 해군이 회사의 석유 탐사선에 강제 승선한 후 석유굴착 장비를 압류했다. 이어 12시간 내 퇴거를 요구하며, 불응하면 예측할 수 없는 책임이 따를 것이라고 위협했다. 이어 가이아나와 양허계약을 맺은 다른 회사에 대해서도 동일한 경고를 보냈다. 수리남의 위협으로 인해 더 이상의 탐사는 진행되지 않았다. 이후 양국은 이 문제를 협상했으나, 별다른 진전이 없자 2004년 2월 가이아나는 해양법협약에 따른 중재재판을 신청했다.

☑ 쟁 점

(1) 잠정약정 체결에 노력할 의무

(2) 경계 미획정 수역에서 합의 없이 가능한 탐사행위의 범위

☑ 판 결

(1) 분쟁 당사국은 결과의 성공과 관계없이 경계 미획정 수역에 관한 잠정약정을 체결하기 위해 모든 노력을 다해야 한다.

(2) 경계 미획정 수역에서는 해양환경에 물리적 변경을 초래하지 않는 범위 내의 일방적 행위만 가능하다.

판 결 문

471. Suriname claims that Guyana violated its duty to make every effort to enter into provisional arrangements as it persistently demanded that Suriname permit CGX to resume exploratory drilling and that Suriname accept Guyana's concessions in the disputed area. Guyana, on its side, claims that Suriname, both before and after the CGX incident, failed to make serious efforts to negotiate provisional arrangements. [⋯]

476. At all times Suriname was under an obligation to make every effort to reach a provisional arrangement. However, this obligation became particularly pressing and relevant when Suriname became aware of Guyana's concession holder's planned exploratory drilling in disputed waters. Instead of attempting to engage Guyana in a spirit of understanding and cooperation as required by the Convention, Suriname opted for a harder stance. Even though Guyana attempted to engage it in a dialogue which may have led to a satisfactory solution for both Parties, Suriname resorted to self-help in threatening the CGX rig, in violation of the Convention. In order to satisfy its obligation to make every effort to reach provisional arrangements, Suriname would have actively had to attempt to bring Guyana to the negotiating table, or, at a minimum, have accepted Guyana's last minute 2 June 2000 invitation and negotiated in good faith. It notably could have insisted on the immediate cessation of CGX's exploratory drilling as a condition to participating in further talks. However, as Suriname did not opt for either of these courses of action, it failed, in the build-up to the CGX incident, in its duties under Articles 74(3) and 83(3) of the Convention.

477. The Tribunal rules that Guyana also violated its obligation to make every effort to enter into provisional arrangements by its conduct leading up to the CGX incident. Guyana had been preparing exploratory drilling for some time before the incident, and should have, in a spirit of cooperation, informed Suriname directly of its plans. Indeed, notification in the press by way of CGX's public announcements was not sufficient for Guyana to meet its obligation under Articles 74(3) and 83(3) of the Convention. Guyana should have sought to engage Suriname in discussions concerning the drilling at a much earlier stage. Its 2 June 2000 invitation to Suriname to discuss the modalities of any drilling operations, although an attempt to defuse a tense situation, was also not sufficient in itself to discharge Guyana's obligation under the Convention. Steps Guyana could have taken consistent with efforts to enter into provisional arrangements include (1) giving Suriname official and detailed notice of the planned activities, (2) seeking cooperation of Suriname in undertaking the activities, (3) offering to share the results of the exploration and giving Suriname an opportunity to observe the activities, and (4) offering to share all the financial benefits received from the exploratory activities.

478. Following the CGX incident in June of 2000, numerous meetings and communications between the Parties took place in which, in the opinion of the Tribunal, they both engaged in good faith negotiations relating to provisional arrangements. Already on 6 June 2000 the Parties expressed their determination to "put in place arrangements to end the current dispute over the oil exploration concessions." Further discussions then took place, including on 13 June 2000 at a meeting of the Joint Technical Committee, as well as on 17-18 June 2000 and 28-30 January 2002. A meeting of the Subcommittee of the Guyana-Suriname Border Commission was held on 31 May 2002, at which modalities for negotiating a provisional arrangement were discussed. Subsequently, two joint meetings of the Suriname and Guyana Border Commissions were held (on 25-26 October 2002 and 10 March 2003). Although they were ultimately unsuccessful in reaching a provisional arrangement, both Parties demonstrated a willingness to negotiate in good faith in relatively extensive meetings and communications. As a result, the Tribunal is satisfied that both Parties respected their obligation relating to pro-visional arrangements after the CGX incident. [⋯]

479. Suriname claims that Guyana violated its obligation to make every effort not to hamper or jeopardise the reaching of a final agreement by allowing its concession holder to undertake exploratory drilling in the disputed waters. With respect to this claim, the Tribunal finds that there is a substantive legal difference between certain oil exploration activities, notably seismic testing, and exploratory drilling.

480. The question that the Tribunal has to address here is whether a party engaging in unilateral exploratory drilling in a disputed area falls short of its obligation to make every effort, in a spirit of understanding and cooperation, not to jeopardise or hamper the reaching of the final agreement on delimitation. As set out above, unilateral acts that cause a physical change to the marine environment will generally be comprised in a class of activities that can be undertaken only jointly or by agreement between the parties. This is due to the fact that these activities may jeopardize or hamper the reaching of a final delimitation agreement as a result of the perceived change to the *status quo* that they would engender. Indeed, such activities could be perceived to, or may genuinely, prejudice the position of the other party in the delimitation dispute, thereby both hampering and jeopardising the reaching of a final agreement.

481. That however is not to say that all exploratory activity should be frozen in a disputed area in the absence of a provisional arrangement. Some exploratory drilling might cause permanent damage to the marine environment. Seismic activity on the other hand should be permissible in a disputed area. In the present case, both Parties authorised concession holders to undertake seismic testing in disputed waters, and these activities did not give rise to objections from either side. In the circumstances at hand, the Tribunal does not consider that unilateral seismic testing is inconsistent with a party's obligation to make every effort not to jeopardise or hamper the reaching of a final agreement. [⋯]

483. Guyana claims Suriname violated its obligations under Article 74(3) and 83(3) to make every effort not to hamper or jeopardise the reaching of a final agreement by its use of a threat of force to respond to Guyana's exploratory drilling.

484. Suriname had a number of peaceful options to address Guyana's authorisation of exploratory drilling. The first, in keeping with its other obligation under Articles 74(3) and 83(3), was to enter into discussions with Guyana regarding provisional arrangements of a practical nature to establish the modalities of oil exploration and potentially of exploitation. In the event of failure of the nego-

tiations, Suriname could have invoked compulsory dispute resolution under Part XV, Section 2 of the Convention. That course of action would also then have given Suriname the possibility to request provisional measures "to preserve [its] rights ... or to prevent serious harm to the marine environment, pending the final decision." The Tribunal finds that Surname's threat of force in a disputed area, while also threatening international peace and security, jeopardised the reaching of a final delimitation agreement.

☑ 해   설

재판부는 가이아나와 수리남 모두 경계 미획정 수역에 관한 잠정약정을 체결하기 위해 충분한 노력을 기울이지 않은 점에서 해양법협약상의 노력의 무를 위반했다고 판단했다. 즉 수리남은 초반 협상에 소극적이었으며 충돌사고 직전의 협상 초청에도 응하지 않았다. 가이아나 역시 회사의 탐사가 실시되기 이전 이를 좀 더 성실하게 수리남에 통지하고 협상했어야 했다고 평가했다. 다만 2000년 6월 충돌 이후 양국은 신의칙에 맞게 협상의사를 표시하고, 이행함으로써 해양법협약 상의 의무를 존중했다고 판단했다.

이어 재판부는 합의가 없더라도 경계 미획정 수역의 모든 탐사가 중지되어야 하는 것은 아니며, 해양환경에 물리적 변경을 야기하지 않는 탐사는 허용된다고 판단했다. 시험굴착은 해양환경에 영구적 변경을 야기할 수 있으나, 예를 들어 지진파 탐사는 최종 경계획정 합의를 방해하지 않는 활동이므로 가능하다고 평가했다. 이에 회사의 시험 굴착은 협약 위반이라고 판정했다.

이어 수리남이 해군함정을 통해 회사의 굴착장비를 압류하고 탐사중단을 위협한 행위는 국제법상 무력 위협 금지에 위반되고, 최종 합의의 성립을 위태롭게 하는 행위라고 판단했다. 즉 수리남은 다른 평화적 수단에 의한 분쟁해결을 도모했어야 했다고 평가했다.

이는 경계 미획정 수역에 관한 해양법협약 제74조 3항과 제83조 3항의 내용을 실질적으로 판단한 첫 번째 국제판결이었다. 다소 막연한 내용의 협약상 잠정약정 체결 의무를 법적 의무로 구체화시켰다는 의의를 지닌다. 경계 미획정 수역이라도 해양환경에 물리적 변경을 야기하지 않는 범위 내의 탐사는 허용된다는 판단은 에게해 대륙붕 사건(1976)에서 ICJ가 터키측의 탐사중지를 요구하는 그리스의 잠정조치 신청의 판단기준으로 "회복 불가능한 침해(irreparable prejudice)"를 제시한 것과 유사한 맥락이다.

이 판결은 한반도 주변 해양경계가 대부분 미획정으로 주변국의 주장이 크게 상충되고 있다는 점에서 주목할 만하다. 특히 회사가 시험굴착을 한 지점은 결과적으로 가이아나의 대륙붕으로 판정되었음에도 불구하고, 이 지역에서의 굴착행위가 협약 위반으로 판단되었다는 점이 주목을 요한다(para. 485).

한편 국제해양법재판소가 Dispute concerning Delimitation of the Maritime Boundary between Ghana and Côte D'Ivoire in the Atlantic Ocean 판결(2017, ITLOS Case NO.23)을 통해 분쟁수역에서 가나의 일방적인 굴착행위에도 불구하고 1) 재판소의 잠정조치 명령 이후 새로운 굴착행위를 하지 않았고, 2) 문제의 수역이 최종적으로 가나의 수역으로 귀속되자, 가나의 협약의무를 인정하지 않았던 판단과 대비되기도 한다. 이러한 차이는 당사국인 코뜨디브와르가 분쟁 수역 아닌 "코뜨디브와르 수역"에서 가나가 일방적으로 수행한 행위가 해양법협약 제83조 위반임을 선언해 줄 것을 청구취지로 요청한 사실에서 기인했다. 즉 가나는 결과적으로 "코뜨디브와르 수역"에서 굴착행위를 하지 않았기 때문이다.

➡ 참고문헌 ────────────────────────────────

- 김민철, 경계 미획정 수역에서 연안국의 권리행사와 분쟁해결(서울대학교 박사학위논문, 2019).
- 이기범, 경계 미획정 수역을 규율하는 국제법적 체제에 관한 비판적 소고, 국제법학회논총 제64권 제3호(2019), p. 127.
- 김현수, 중첩주장수역에서의 관할권 행사, (인하대) 법학연구 제21집 제4호(2018), p. 105.
- 김채형, UN해양법협약상 해양경계획정시 중첩수역의 국제법적 지위, (국민대) 법학논총 제30권 제3호(2018), p. 153.
- 박덕영, 가이아나(Guyana)−수리남(Suriname) 해양경계획정을 위한 중재판정의 주요 법적 쟁점 고찰, 국제법학회논총 제54권 제1호(2009).

6. 흑해 해양경계 획정 사건(2009)
─ 해양경계의 획정 원칙, 작은 섬의 역할

Maritime Delimitation in the Black Sea.
Romania v. Ukraine, 2009 ICJ Reports 61.

☑ 사 안

2004년 9월 루마니아는 ICJ에 우크라이나를 상대로 흑해에서의 대륙붕 및 배타적 경제수역의 경계획정을 위한 소송을 제기했다. 이 사건에 있어서 중요 쟁점 중 하나는 우크라이나의 Serpents' Island(뱀섬)이 해양경계에 어떠한 영향을 미치는가였다. 이 섬은 우크라이나 연안에서 약 20해리 거리에 위치하고 있다. 크기는 0.17㎢이며, 일반 주민은 없이 국가기관의 연구원만 약 100명 정도 체류하고 있었다.

재판과정에서 우크라이나는 뱀섬에 대해 완전한 효과를 부여하고, 이 섬을 기준으로 루마니아와 중간선 원칙에 따른 대륙붕 및 배타적 경제수역의 경계획정을 하자고 주장했다. 반면 루마니아는 이 섬이 해양법협약 제121조 3항 상의 암석(rock)에 해당하므로 오직 영해만을 가질 수 있고, 대륙붕이나 배타적 경제수역은 가질 수 없다고 주장했다.

☑ 쟁 점

인접국간의 해양경계획정 방법, 특히 소도의 역할.

☑ 판 결

(1) 해양경계획정은 이른바 3단계 방법이 적용된다. 즉 1) 잠정적 중간선을 그린 다음, 2) 형평한 결과를 달성하기 위해 잠정적 중간선을 조정해야

할 요인이 있는가를 검토하고, 3) 그 결과 양측 해안선 길이의 비율과 할당된 수역의 비율 간에 현저한 불공평이 없는가를 검토한다.

(2) 본토에서 20해리 떨어진 작은 섬은 우크라이나의 연안을 구성하지 못하며, 해양경계획정시 무시될 수 있다.

판 결 문

115. When called upon to delimit the continental shelf or exclusive economic zones, or to draw a single delimitation line, the Court proceeds in defined stages.

116. These separate stages, broadly explained in the case concerning Continental Shelf (Libyan Arab Jamahiriya/Malta) (*Judgment, I.C.J. Reports 1985*, p. 46, para. 60), have in recent decades been specified with precision. First, the Court will establish a provisional delimitation line, using methods that are geometrically objective and also appropriate for the geography of the area in which the delimitation is to take place. So far as delimitation between adjacent coasts is concerned, an equidistance line will be drawn unless there are compelling reasons that make this unfeasible in the particular case (*see Territorial and Maritime Dispute between Nicaragua and Honduras in the Caribbean Sea (Nicaragua v. Honduras), Judgment, I.C.J. Reports 2007(II)*, p. 745, para. 281). So far as opposite coasts are concerned, the provisional delimitation line will consist of a median line between the two coasts. No legal consequences flow from the use of the terms "median line" and "equidistance line" since the method of delimitation is the same for both.

117. Equidistance and median lines are to be constructed from the most appropriate points on the coasts of the two States concerned, with particular attention being paid to those protuberant coastal points situated nearest to the area to the delimited. The Court considers elsewhere (*see* paragraphs 135-137 below) the extent to which the Court may, when constructing a single-purpose delimitation line, deviate from the base points selected by the Parties for their territorial seas. When construction of a provisional equidistance line between adjacent States is called for, the Court will have in mind considerations relating to both Parties' coastlines when choosing its own base points for this purpose. The line thus adopted is heavily dependent on the physical geography and the most seaward points of the two coasts.

118. In keeping with its settled jurisprudence on maritime delimitation, the first stage of the Court's approach is to establish the provisional equidistance line. At this initial stage of the construction of the provisional equidistance line the Court is not yet concerned with any relevant circumstances that may obtain and the line is plotted on strictly geometrical criteria on the basis of objective data.

119. In the present case the Court will thus begin by drawing a provisional equidistance line between the adjacent coasts of Romania and Ukraine, which will then continue as a median line between their opposite coasts.

120. The course of the final line should result in an equitable solution (Articles 74 and 83 of UNCLOS). Therefore, the Court will at the next, second stage consider whether there are factors calling for the adjustment or shifting of the provisional equidistance line in order to achieve an equitable result [⋯]. The Court has also made clear that when the line to be drawn covers several zones of coincident jurisdictions, "the so-called equitable principles/relevant circumstances method may usefully be applied, as in these maritime zones this method is also suited to achieving an equitable result" [⋯].

121. This is the second part of the delimitation exercise to which the Court will turn, having first established the provisional equidistance line.

122. Finally, and at a third stage, the Court will verify that the line (a provisional equidistance line which may or may not have been adjusted by taking into account the relevant circumstances) does not, as it stands, lead to an inequitable result by reason of any marked disproportion between the ratio of the respective coastal lengths and the ratio between the relevant maritime area of each State by reference to the delimitation line [⋯]. A final check for an equitable outcome entails a confirmation that no great disproportionality of maritime areas is evident by comparison to the ratio of coastal lengths.

This is not to suggest that these respective areas should be proportionate to coastal lengths — as the Court has said "the sharing out of the area is therefore the consequence of the delimitation, not *vice versa*"[1) [⋯].

149. Serpents' Island calls for specific attention in the determination of the provisional equidistance line. [⋯] However, Serpents' Island, lying alone and some 20 nautical miles away from the mainland, is not one of a cluster of fringe islands constituting "the coast" of Ukraine.

To count Serpents' Island as a relevant part of the coast would amount to grafting an extraneous element onto Ukraine's coastline; the consequence would be

---

1) 반대도 마찬가지 — 필자 주.

a judicial refashioning of geography, which neither the law nor practice of maritime delimitation authorizes. The Court is thus of the view that Serpents' Island cannot be taken to form part of Ukraine's coastal configuration([⋯]).

For this reason, the Court considers it inappropriate to select any base points on Serpents' Island for the construction of a provisional equidistance line between the coasts of Romania and Ukraine. Further aspects relevant to Serpents' Island are dealt with at paragraphs 179 to 188 below. [⋯]

155. As the Court indicated above(paragraphs 120-121), once the provisional equidistance line has been drawn, it shall "then [consider] whether there are factors calling for the adjustment or shifting of that line in order to achieve an 'equitable result'"([⋯]). Such factors have usually been referred to in the jurisprudence of the Court, since the North Sea Continental Shelf ([⋯]) cases, as the relevant circumstances. [⋯]

164. Where disparities in the lengths of coasts are particularly marked, the Court may choose to treat that fact of geography as a relevant circumstance that would require some adjustments to the provisional equidistance line to be made. [⋯]

168. In the present case, however the Court sees no such particularly marked disparities between the relevant coasts of Ukraine and Romania that would require it to adjust the provisional equidistance line at this juncture. [⋯]

185. In determining the maritime boundary line, in default of any delimitation agreement within the meaning of UNCLOS Articles 74 and 83, the Court may, should relevant circumstances so suggest, adjust the provisional equidistance line to ensure an equitable result. In this phase, the Court may be called upon to decide whether this line should be adjusted because of the presence of small islands in its vicinity. As the jurisprudence has indicated, the Court may on occasion decide not to take account of very small islands or decide not to give them their full potential entitlement to maritime zones, should such an approach have a disproportionate effect on the delimitation line under consideration. [⋯]

210. The Court now turns to check that the result thus far arrived at, so far as the envisaged delimitation line is concerned, does not lead to any significant disproportionality by reference to the respective coastal lengths and the apportionment of areas that ensue. [⋯]

215. It suffices for this third stage for the Court to note that the ratio of the respective coastal lengths for Romania and Ukraine, measured as described above, is approximately 1:2.8 and the ratio of the relevant area between Romania and Ukraine is approximately 1:2.1.

210. The Court is not of the view that this suggests that the line as constructed, and checked carefully for any relevant circumstances that might have warranted adjustment, requires any alteration.

☑ 해   설

뱀섬은 본래 루마니아령이었으나, 1948년 구 소련에게 양도되었으며, 1991년 구 소련 해체 이후 우크라이나령으로 되었다. 루마니아는 이 섬의 영유권 자체에 대해서는 이의를 제기하지 않았다. 이 섬은 그 크기나 성격으로 미루어 볼 때 독도와 매우 유사한 상황이라, 한국의 주목을 받았던 사건이다.

재판과정에서 우크라이나와 루마니아는 뱀섬의 지위가 해양법협약 제121조 3항의 암석(rock)에 해당하느냐에 관하여 크게 이견을 보였다. 이 판결에서 ICJ는 역시 3단계 방식을 적용했다. 첫째, 본토에서 20해리 거리에 홀로 떨어진 이 섬을 우크라이나 연안을 구성하는 섬으로 보지 않고(para. 149), 일단 이 섬의 존재를 무시하고 등거리선을 통한 양국간의 잠정적 해양경계를 설정했다. 다음 단계로 이 섬의 존재를 포함한 해안선의 길이, 흑해의 성격, 여러 경제활동의 양상, 안보적 상황 등을 종합적으로 고려한 결과 앞서 제시된 잠정 등거리선을 조정할 필요가 없다고 평가했다(paras. 179-188). 마지막으로 루마니아와 우크라이나의 관련 해안선 길이의 비율(1:2.8)과 잠정 등거리선을 통해 양국에 할당된 수역의 비율(1:2.1)을 비교해 보아도 이 잠정선이 형평을 해칠 정도로 현저한 불균형을 초래하지 않는다고 판단했다(paras. 215-216). 결과적으로 뱀섬의 존재는 완전히 무시된 상태에서 양국간 해양경계선이 획정되었다. ICJ는 뱀섬의 존재가 경계획정에 아무런 영향을 미치지 못하므로 이 섬이 과연 제121조 3항의 적용을 받는 암석인지 여부를 굳이 평가할 필요도 없다고 판단했다(para. 187). 그 결과 양측간 이견의 대상이 된 수역 약 8할은 루마니아에 할당되었다.

이 판결과 관련하여 유의할 점은 해양경계획정에 있어서 멀리 떨어져 있는 작은 섬의 역할이다. 근래 배타적 경제수역이나 대륙붕의 경계획정에 관한 국제재판의 실행을 본다면 매우 작은 도서의 존재로 인해 관할수역의

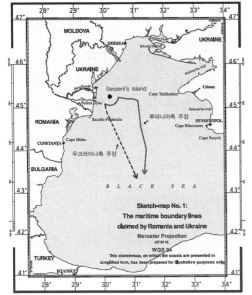

지도 1. 양측 주장의 해양경계

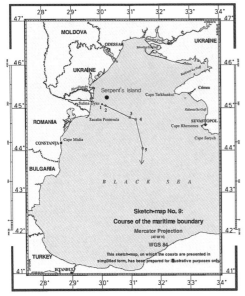

지도 2. 해양 경계획정 결과

범위가 크게 영향을 받는다면 그 섬은 아예 고려에 넣지 않거나 매우 제한적 효과만을 인정하는 경향이 현저하다. 독도는 크기가 0.187㎢로서 울릉도와는 87.4km(47.2해리), 힌반ㄷ(경븟 죽변)와는 216.8km(117.1해리)의 거리에 있다. 이 판결의 법리에 따른다면 설사 독도가 해양법협약상의 녹사의 대륙붕과 배타적 경제수역을 가질 수 있는 섬이라고 할지라도 한일간 동해 배타적 경제수역 경계획정에서는 그 존재가 무시되리라고 예상된다.

➠ 참고문헌 ─────────────────────────────

- 김현수, 루마니아─우크라이나 흑해 해양경계획정 사건에 관한 분석 및 평가, 해사법연구 21권 2호(2009), p. 101.
- 정진석, 흑해 해양경계획정사건(루마니아 v. 우크라이나) 판결의 의의, 서울국제법연구 17권 1호(2010), p. 29.
- 정인섭, 한일간 동해 EEZ 경계획정분쟁에 관한 보도의 국제법적 분석, 저스티스 126호(2011. 10), p. 150.
- 이창위, 루마니아와 우크라이나 사이의 흑해 해양경계 사건, 이석용·이창위·김채형, 국제해양법 판례연구(세창출판사, 2015), p. 277.
- 이석용, 국제사법재판소의 흑해해양경계획정사건 판결에 나타난 특징분석, (서울시립대) 서울법학 제20권 2호(2012), p. 1.

7. 벵골만 해양경계 획정(2012)
— 해양경계 획정시 섬의 효과

Dispute concerning Delimitation of the Maritime
Boundary between Bangladesh and Myanmar in the Bay
of Bengal(Case No. 16).
Bangladesh/Myanmar
International Tribunal for the Law of the Sea(2012).

☑ 사   안

방글라데시와 미얀마는 벵골만의 인접국으로 해양경계 획정에 합의를
보지 못하고 있었다. Naaf 강이 벵골만으로 이르는 양국 국경을 형성하고 있
는데, 이 강 하구로부터 남측 방향 6.5해리 지점에 방글라데시에 속하는 St.
Martin 섬이 위치하고 있다. 넓이 약 8㎢, 인구 약 7,000명의 이 섬은 미얀마
해안에 거의 평행으로 펼쳐져 있어 미얀마의 해안을 가로 막는 형상이다. 양
국은 영해와 배타적 경제수역 및 대륙붕의 경계를 획정함에 있어서 St.
Martin 섬이 어떠한 역할을 할 것인가에 관해 대립했다.

섬을 영유하고 있는 방글라데시는 이 섬이 본토와의 인접성, 많은 상주
인구, 경제적 역할 등을 고려할 때 자국 해안선의 불가분의 일부를 이루므로
완전한 12해리 영해를 가져야 한다고 주장했다(para. 145). 반면 미얀마는 이
섬에 완전한 효과를 준다면 해안선의 일반적 형상에 상당한 왜곡을 초래하
므로 이는 영해경계 획정에 관한 "특별한 사정"에 해당하여 제로 또는 매우
제한적인 효과만이 부여되어야 한다고 주장했다(para. 137). 배타적 경제수역
및 대륙붕의 경계획정에 있어서도 방글라데시는 St. Martin 섬이 무시될 수
없다고 주장했으나, 미얀마는 이 섬이 기점에서 제외되어야 한다고 주장
했다.

☑ 쟁　점

(1) 영해 경계획정 시 인접 도서의 역할.

(2) 배타적 경제수역 및 대륙붕의 경계획정 시 특이한 위치에 있는 도서의 역할.

☑ 판　결

(1) 크기와 인구, 경제활동 등에 있어서 상당한 규모의 섬은 영해 경계획정 시 완전한 효과가 부여된다.

(2) 인접국의 해안선 앞을 가로 막고 있는 형상의 섬은 배타적 경제수역과 대륙붕 경계획정시 왜곡된 효과를 초래하므로 기점에서 무시될 수 있다.

판 결 문

146. The Tribunal will now consider whether St. Martin's Island constitutes a special circumstance for the purposes of the delimitation of the territorial sea between Bangladesh and Myanmar.

147. The Tribunal notes that neither case law nor State practice indicates that there is a general rule concerning the effect to be given to islands in maritime delimitation. It depends on the particular circumstances of each case.

148. The Tribunal also observes that the effect to be given to islands in delimitation may differ, depending on whether the delimitation concerns the territorial sea or other maritime areas beyond it. Both the nature of the rights of the coastal State and their seaward extent may be relevant in this regard.

149. The Tribunal notes that, while St. Martin's Island lies in front of Myanmar's mainland coast, it is located almost as close to Bangladesh's mainland coast as to the coast of Myanmar and it is situated within the 12 nm territorial sea limit from Bangladesh's mainland coast.

150. The Tribunal observes that most of the cases and the State practice referred to by Myanmar concern the delimitation of the exclusive economic zone or the continental shelf, not of the territorial sea, and that they are thus not directly relevant to the delimitation of the territorial sea.

151. While it is not unprecedented in case law for islands to be given less than full effect in the delimitation of the territorial sea, the islands subject to such treatment are usually "insignificant maritime features," such as the island of Qit' at Jaradah, a very small island, uninhabited and without any vegetation, in the case concerning *Maritime Delimitation and Territorial Questions between Qatar and Bahrain* (*Merits, Judgment, I.C.J. Reports 2001*, p. 40, at p. 104, para. 219). In the view of the Tribunal, St. Martin's Island is a significant maritime feature by virtue of its size and population and the extent of economic and other activities.

152. The Tribunal concludes that, in the circumstances of this case, there are no compelling reasons that justify treating St. Martin's Island as a special circumstance for the purposes of article 15 of the Convention or that prevent the Tribunal from giving the island full effect in drawing the delimitation line of the territorial sea between the Parties. [⋯]

164. Having concluded that full effect should be given to St. Martin's Island, the Tribunal decides that the delimitation line should follow an equidistance line up to the point beyond which the territorial seas of the Parties no longer overlap. [⋯]

177. The Tribunal will now turn to the delimitation of the exclusive economic zone and the continental shelf within 200 nm. [⋯]

265. Concerning the question whether St. Martin's Island could serve as the source of a base point, the Tribunal is of the view that, because it is located immediately in front of the mainland on Myanmar's side of the Parties' land boundary terminus in the Naaf River, the selection of a base point on St. Martin's Island would result in a line that blocks the seaward projection from Myanmar's coast. In the view of the Tribunal, this would result in an unwarranted distortion of the delimitation line, and amount to "a judicial refashioning of geography" ([⋯]). For this reason, the Tribunal excludes St. Martin's Island as the source of any base point. [⋯]

316. The Tribunal will now consider whether St. Martin's Island, in the circumstances of this case, should be considered a relevant circumstance warranting an adjustment of the provisional equidistance line.

317. The Tribunal observes that the effect to be given to an island in the delimitation of the maritime boundary in the exclusive economic zone and the continental shelf depends on the geographic realities and the circumstances of the specific case. There is no general rule in this respect. Each case is unique and requires specific treatment, the ultimate goal being to reach a solution that is equitable.

318. St. Martin's Island is an important feature which could be considered a relevant circumstance in the present case. However, because of its location, giving effect to St. Martin's Island in the delimitation of the exclusive economic zone and the continental shelf would result in a line blocking the seaward projection from Myanmar's coast in a manner that would cause an unwarranted distortion of the delimitation line. The distorting effect of an island on an equidistance line may increase substantially as the line moves beyond 12 nm from the coast.

319. For the foregoing reasons, the Tribunal concludes that St. Martin's Island is not a relevant circumstance and, accordingly, decides not to give any effect to it in drawing the delimitation line of the exclusive economic zone and the continental shelf. [···]

☑ 해   설

이 사건에서 방글라데시는 양국간 이미 1974년과 2008년 합의의사록을 통한 경계 합의가 있었다고 주장했으나, 재판부에 의해 받아들여지지 않았다. 또한 약 30년간의 국가실행을 통해 영해 경계선에 관한 묵시적 합의가 성립했다는 방글라데시의 주장도 재판부는 인정하지 않았다.

영해에 관해서는 재판부가 고려되어야 할 역사적 권원이나 다른 특별한 사정이 없다고 보고, St. Martin 섬에 완전한 효과를 인정해 통상적인 등거리선을 기준으로 경계를 획정했다. 이 선은 양국이 1974년 합의의사록에서 고려하던 경계와 거의 일치했다.

배타적 경제수역과 대륙붕의 경계획정에 있어서는 국제해양법재판소 역시 ICJ가 리비아-말타 대륙붕 사건 이래 발전시켜온 이른바 3단계 획정방식을 그대로 따랐다. 즉 ① 양국간 잠정 등거리선의 획정 ② 잠정 등거리선의 조정을 필요로 하는 관련사항이 있다면 조정을 통해 형평한 결과를 도모 ③ 조정된 경계선이 양국 해안선 길이의 비율과 양국에 할당된 해역의 비율 사이에 현저한 불균형을 초래하는지를 검토하는 방식이다(para. 240).

이어 재판부는 St. Martin 섬이 미얀마 해안을 가로 막는 위치에 있으므로 이 상황에서 경계획정에 부당한 왜곡을 야기하게 된다는 이유로 배타적 경제수역과 대륙붕 경계획정에서는 존재를 무시하기로 결정했다.

재판소는 양국 기선으로부터 200해리 너머의 대륙붕에 대해서도 경계를

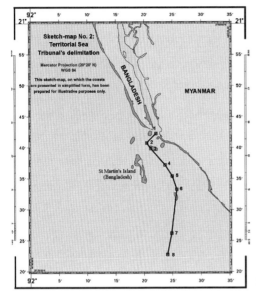

지도 1. 양국간 영해 경계획정선

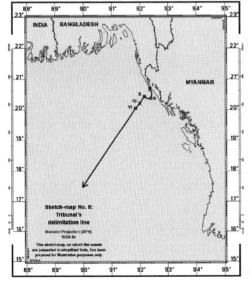

지도 2. 양국간 해양경계선

획정했다. 해양법협약상 200해리 외측 대륙붕의 한계는 대륙붕한계위원회의 권고를 받아 확정하도록 예정되어 있다(제76조 8항). 이 같은 절차를 거치지 않은 상태에서 해양법재판소가 200해리 외측 경계를 획정할 권한이 있느냐는 문제가 제기되었으나, 재판부는 제76조에 의한 외측 경계설정과 제83조에 의한 경계획정은 서로 다른 문제라고 해석하고 자신이 경계획정을 자제할 이유가 없다고 판단했다(para. 394). 이어 200해리까지의 대륙붕 경계획정에 사용한 조정된 등거리선을 그대로 연장하여 경계로 삼았다(para. 462). 이는 200해리를 넘는 대륙붕 경계획정에 관한 최초의 국제재판소 판결이다.

➡ 참고문헌 ─────────────────────────────────

- 이석용, 방글라데시와 미얀마간 벵갈만 해양경계선 획정 분쟁, 이석용·이창위·김채형, 국제해양법 판례연구(세창출판사, 2015), p. 304.
- 이창열, 200해리 이내의 배타적경제수역 및 대륙붕 경계획정 판결에 관한 동향과 함의: 방글라데시와 미얀마 벵골만 해양경계획정 사건을 중심으로, 국제법학회논총 57권 2호(2012), p. 145.
- 백진현, 벵골만 해양경계획정 사건에 대한 회고, 독도연구저널(2013년 여름), p. 4.

8. 남중국해 중재재판(2016)
― 섬의 법적 지위

South China Sea Arbitration.
Philippines v. PR China., PCA No.2013-19(2016).

☑ 사   안

남중국해에 임한 중국, 필리핀, 베트남, 대만, 말레이시아 등은 이 지역 섬의 영유권과 해양경계 획정에 관해 분쟁을 겪고 있었다. 특히 중국은 이른바 9단선을 주장하며, 남중국해 대부분에 대한 자국의 권리를 주장해, 인접국의 반발을 샀다. 이에 필리핀은 남중국해에서 특히 스프래틀리(Spratly) 군도를 중심으로 한 중국과의 분쟁을 유엔 해양법협약 제7부속서상의 중재재판에 회부했다. 중국은 처음부터 이 재판에 참여를 거부했다. 중국의 불참에도 불구하고, 5인 중재재판관에 의해 구성된 재판소는 2015년 10월 필리핀의 청구에 대해 관할권 성립을 선언하고, 재판을 진행했다. 이어 2016년 7월 본안 판결이 내려졌다. 이 판결은 국제재판에서는 처음으로 유엔 해양법협약 제121조가 규정하고 있는 섬(Island)과 암석(rock)의 구체적 구별기준을 제시했다.

☑ 쟁   점

독자의 EEZ와 대륙붕을 가질 수 있는 섬과 그렇지 못한 암석의 구별기준

☑ 판   결

아래 해설 참조

"iv. Conclusions on the Interpretation of Article 121(3)

539. Drawing on the foregoing consideration of the text, context, object and purpose, and drafting history of Article 121(3), the Tribunal reaches the following conclusions with respect to the interpretation of that provision.

540. First, [⋯] the use of the word "rock" does not limit the provision to features composed of solid rock. The geological and geomorphological characteristics of a high-tide feature are not relevant to its classification pursuant to Article 121(3).

541. Second, the status of a feature is to be determined on the basis of its natural capacity, without external additions or modifications intended to increase its capacity to sustain human habitation or an economic life of its own.

542. Third, with respect to "human habitation," the critical factor is the non-transient character of the inhabitation, such that the inhabitants can fairly be said to constitute the natural population of the feature, for whose benefit the resources of the exclusive economic zone were seen to merit protection. The term "human habitation" should be understood to involve the inhabitation of the feature by a stable community of people for whom the feature constitutes a home and on which they can remain. Such a community need not necessarily be large, and in remote atolls a few individuals or family groups could well suffice. Periodic or habitual residence on a feature by a nomadic people could also constitute habitation, and the records of the Third UN Conference record a great deal of sensitivity to the livelihoods of the populations of small island nations. An indigenous population would obviously suffice, but also non-indigenous inhabitation could meet this criterion if the intent of the population was truly to reside in and make their lives on the islands in question.

543. Fourth, the term "economic life of their own" is linked to the require-ment of human habitation, and the two will in most instances go hand in hand. [⋯] The Tribunal considers that the "economic life" in question will ordinarily be the life and livelihoods of the human population inhabiting and making its home on a maritime feature or group of features. Additionally, Article 121(3) makes clear that the economic life in question must pertain to the feature as "of its own." Economic life, therefore, must be oriented around the feature itself and not focused solely on the waters or seabed of the surrounding territorial sea. Economic activity that is entirely dependent on external resources or devoted to using a feature as an object for extractive activities without the involvement of a local population would also fall inherently short with respect to this necessary link to the feature itself. Extractive economic activity to harvest the natural resources of a feature for the benefit of a population elsewhere certainly constitutes the exploitation of resources for economic gain, but it cannot reasonably be considered to constitute the economic life of an island as its own.

544. Fifth, the text of Article 121(3) is disjunctive, such that the ability to sustain either human habitation or an economic life of its own would suffice to entitle a high-tide feature to an exclusive economic zone and continental shelf. However, as a practical matter, the Tribunal considers that a maritime feature will ordinarily only possess an economic life of its own if it is also inhabited by a stable human community. One exception to that view should be noted for the case of populations sustaining themselves through a network of related maritime features. [⋯]

545. Sixth, Article 121(3) is concerned with the capacity of a maritime feature to sustain human habitation or an economic life of its own, not with whether the feature is presently, or has been, inhabited or home to economic life. The capacity of a feature is necessarily an objective criterion. [⋯]

546. Seventh, the capacity of a feature to sustain human habitation or an economic life of its own must be assessed on a case-by-case basis. [⋯] The Tribunal considers that the principal factors that contribute to the natural capacity of a feature can be identified. These would include the presence of water, food, and shelter in sufficient quantities to enable a group of persons to live on the feature for an indeterminate period of time. Such factors would also include considerations that would bear on the conditions for inhabiting and developing an economic life on a feature, including the prevailing climate, the proximity of the feature to other inhabited areas and populations, and the potential for livelihoods on and around the feature. The relative contribution and importance of these factors to the capacity to sustain human habitation and economic life, however, will vary from one feature to another. While minute, barren features may be obviously uninhabitable (and large, heavily populated features obviously capable of sustaining habitation), the Tribunal does not consider that an abstract test of the objective requirements to sustain human habitation or economic life can or should be formulated. This is particularly the case in light of the Tribunal's conclusion that human habitation entails more than the mere survival of humans on a feature and that economic life entails more than the presence of resources. [···]

547. Eighth, the Tribunal considers that the capacity of a feature should be assessed with due regard to the potential for a group of small island features to collectively sustain human habitation and economic life. On the one hand, the requirement in Article 121(3) that the feature itself sustain human habitation or economic life clearly excludes a dependence on external supply. A feature that is only capable of sustaining habitation through the continued delivery of supplies from outside does not meet the requirements of Article 121(3). Nor does economic activity that remains entirely dependent on external resources or that is devoted to using a feature as an object for extractive activities, without the involvement of a local population, constitute a feature's "own" economic life. [···]

548. Ninth, [···] If a feature is entirely barren of vegetation and lacks drinkable water and the foodstuffs necessary even for basic survival, it will be apparent that it also lacks the capacity to sustain human habitation. The opposite conclusion could likewise be reached where the physical characteristics of a large feature make it definitively habitable. The Tribunal considers, however, that evidence of physical conditions is insufficient for features that fall close to the line. It will be difficult, if not impossible, to determine from the physical characteristics of a feature alone where the capacity merely to keep people alive ends and the capacity to sustain settled habitation by a human community begins. [···]

549. In such circumstances, the Tribunal considers that the most reliable evidence of the capacity of a feature will usually be the historical use to which it has been put. [···] If the historical record of a feature indicates that nothing resembling a stable community has ever developed there, the most reasonable conclusion would be that the natural conditions are simply too difficult for such a community to form and that the feature is not capable of sustaining such habitation. In such circumstances, the Tribunal should consider whether there is evidence that human habitation has been prevented or ended by forces that are separate from the intrinsic capacity of the feature. War, pollution, and environmental harm could all lead to the depopulation, for a prolonged period, of a feature that, in its natural state, was capable of sustaining human habitation. In the absence of such intervening forces, however, the Tribunal can reasonably conclude that a feature that has never historically sustained a human community lacks the capacity to sustain human habitation.

550. Conversely, if a feature is presently inhabited or has historically been

inhabited, the Tribunal should consider whether there is evidence to indicate that habitation was only possible through outside support. Trade and links with the outside world do not disqualify a feature to the extent that they go to improving the quality of life of its inhabitants. Where outside support is so significant that it constitutes a necessary condition for the inhabitation of a feature, however, it is no longer the feature itself that sustains human habitation. In this respect, the Tribunal notes that a purely official or military population, serviced from the outside, does not constitute evidence that a feature is capable of sustaining human habitation. Bearing in mind that the purpose of Article 121(3) is to place limits on excessive and unfair claims by States, that purpose would be undermined if a population were installed on a feature that, as such, would not be capable of sustaining human habitation, precisely to stake a claim to the territory and the maritime zones generated by it. The Tribunal notes that, as a result, evidence of human habitation that predates the creation of exclusive economic zones may be more significant than contemporary evidence, if the latter is clouded by an apparent attempt to assert a maritime claim.

551. The same mode of analysis would apply equally to the past or current existence of economic life. The Tribunal would first consider evidence of the use to which the feature has historically been put before considering whether there is evidence to suggest that that historical record does not fully reflect the economic life the feature could have sustained in its natural condition.

☑ 해 설

당초 중국이 이 사건에 대한 재판부의 관할권을 부인하며 불참한 논리는 다음과 같다. 첫째, 필리핀이 회부한 재판의 실질적 쟁점은 영토 귀속에 관한 내용으로 해양법협약의 해석이나 적용과 관련된 분쟁이 아니다. 둘째, 중국은 2006년 8월 협약 제298조에 따라 해양경계획정에 관한 분쟁에 대해서는 협약상의 절차를 배제하는 선언을 한 바 있다. 셋째, 필리핀은 이 문제를 협상을 통해 해결하기로 합의하고도 일방적으로 중재재판에 회부했다.

반면 필리핀은 이 같은 중국측 논리를 우회해 자신의 청구취지가 이 수역 도서의 영유권 귀속이나 해양경계획정을 구하는 것이 아니라고 주장했다. 즉 자신은 중국의 해양관할권 주장과 그에 근거한 활동이 해양법협약에 위반되는지에 관한 판단만을 구하고 있으므로 제298조에 따른 관할권 배제

선언에 저촉되지 않는다고 주장했다. 재판부는 필리핀의 주장을 수락해 재판
을 진행한 것이다.

이 판결은 다양한 쟁점을 다루었으나 한국의 독도문세와도 관련해 득히
관심을 끈 부분은 협약 제121조 3항 독자의 배타적 경제수역(EEZ)과 대륙붕
을 가질 수 없는 암석(rock)의 판단기준을 제시한 점이다. 그 주요 골자는 다
음과 같다. ① "암석(rock)"이란 섬의 한 종류에 불과하며, 지질학상 또는 지
형학상의 기준과는 관계없다. 즉 반드시 바위로 구성된 섬만을 가리키는 의
미가 아니다. ② "인간의 거주"라 함은 일시적 성격이나 단순한 생존이 아닌
안정적인 공동체가 상당기간 주거생활을 이루고 있어야 한다. ③ "독자의 경
제생활"이란 외부 투입에 크게 의존하지 않으면서 주민들이 섬 자체를 바탕
으로 생활하며 주거를 이룰 수 있어야 한다. 지역 주민의 참여 없는 채취활
동만으로는 이에 해당하지 않는다. ④ "인간의 거주"와 "독자의 경제활동"
중 어느 한 요건만 만족하면 그 섬은 자신의 EEZ와 대륙붕을 가질 수 있다.
⑤ 섬이 "인간의 거주"나 "독자의 경제활동"을 만족시킬 수 있는 객관적 조
건을 갖추면 충분하지, 반드시 현재의 인간 거주나 경제활동이 요구되지는
않는다. ⑥ "인간의 거주"나 "독자의 경제활동"의 가능성은 개별적으로 판단
되어야 한다. 충분한 양의 물, 음식, 숙소는 판단을 위한 중요 요소이기는 하
나, 획일적인 판단기준은 제시하기 어렵다. ⑦ 여러 개의 인접 섬이 집단으
로 이러한 조건을 만족시킬 수도 있다.

이러한 기준에 따라 재판부는 필리핀이 문제를 제기한 수역의 Spratly
군도나 Scarborough Shoal의 모든 섬이 협약 제121조 3항에 규정한 "암석"
에 해당하며, 독자적 EEZ와 대륙붕을 가질 수 없다고 판정했다. 그 중 특히
대만이 통제하고 있는 Itu Aba(太平島)는 길이 1.4km, 최대 폭 400m, 면적
0.43㎢로서, 다수의 건물과 활주로, 등대, 병원, 절, 항구시설이 마련되어 있
으며 약간의 농작물도 수확하고 있다. 필리핀이 통제하고 있는 Thitu(中業島)
는 길이 710m, 폭 약 570m, 면적 0.41㎢로, 역시 다수의 건물, 등대, 비포장
활주로가 존재한다. 이들 섬은 면적에서 독도의 2배를 크게 초과하고 인간의
거주요건을 훨씬 더 갖추고 있으나, 모두 "암석"으로 판정되었다.

이 판결은 내용적으로 중국의 완패였다. 중국은 판결의 무효를 주장하

며, 수락을 거부하고 있다.

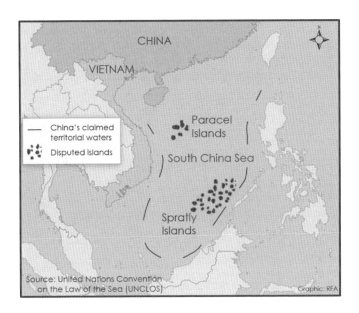

▶▶ 참고문헌 ─────────────────────────────────

- 정진석, 남중국해 중재판정을 통해 본 암석의 정의, (국민대) 법학논총 제29권 제3호(2017), p. 423.
- 김원희, 남중국해 중재사건의 관할권 판정, 서울국제법연구 제23권 1호(2016), p. 79.
- 김원희, 남중국해 중재판정과 독도의 법적 지위에 대한 함의, 해양정책연구 제31권 제2호(2016), p. 55.
- 이석용, 남중국해 중재판정의 국제해양법상 도서제도에 대한 영향, 영토해양연구 제12권(2016), p. 102.
- 박배근, 섬과 암석에 관한 남중국해 중재판정과 한일간 해양경계획정에 대한 함의, 영토해양연구 제15권(2018), p. 76.
- 김태운, 남중국해 바위섬에 관한 상설중재재판소 판정에 따르는 섬으로서 독도, 해사법연구 제28권 제3호(2016), p. 75.
- 김현정, 유엔해양법협약 제121조 3항 해석에 관한 소고 ― 필리핀 ― 중국 남중국해 중재판정의 의의를 중심으로, (단국대) 법학논총 제40권 제3호(2016), p. 225.

제13장

─ ─ ─ ─ ─

국제환경법

1. 트레일 제련소 사건(1941)
— 인접국에 환경피해를 입히지 않을 의무

Trail Smelter Case.
USA v. Canada, 3 RIAA 1905(1941).

☑ 사　　안

캐나다 브리티시 콜롬비아주의 콜롬비아 강변에는 납과 아연을 생산하는 트레일 제련소가 있는데, 제련과정에서 대량의 아황산가스가 배출되었다. 이 제련소는 미국과의 국경에서 불과 18km 정도 떨어져 있어서 여기에서 배출되는 아황산가스는 미국 영역내 특히 인접한 워싱턴주에 심각한 피해를 입혔다. 문제가 심각해지자 이 사건은 1928년 미국－캐나다 국경하천협정에 의해 설립된 국제공동위원회(International Joint Commission)에 회부됐다. 국가들이 조약을 체결하고 그 조약의 해석과 적용과 관련한 분쟁을 다루기 위하여 양국 대표로 구성되는 공동위원회를 구성하는 것은 흔히 목도되는 상황이다. 경우에 따라서는 관련 분야 전문가를 공동위원회에 포함시키기도 한다. 이 위원회는 1932년 심의를 종결하고 1932년 1월 1일까지 발생한 피해에 대해 캐나다가 미국에 35만 달러를 보상하도록 권고했다. 캐나다는 해당 금액을 미국에 지불하였다. 그러나 이후에도 피해는 계속 발생했고, 미국의 항의는 이어지게 되었다. 결국 양국의 법적 주장이 대립하게 되자 1935년 미국과 캐나다는 이 사건을 중재재판에 회부하기로 합의했다.

☑ 쟁　　점

자국 영토 내 행위로 인하여 타국에 피해가 발생하지 않도록 할 의무를 국가가 부담하는지 여부.

☑ 판　정

국제법과 미국 국내법에 따라 어떤 국가도 그 영토의 사용 혹은 사용 허락을 통해 다른 국가 혹은 그러한 다른 국가 내 재산이나 개인에게 피해를 초래할 수 없다.

판 결 문

(p. 1962-) The second question under art. III of the Convention is as follows:

In the event of the answer to the first part of the preceding question being in the affirmative, whether the Trail Smelter should be required to refrain from causing damage in the State of Washington in the future and, if so, to what extent?

Damage has occurred since 1 January 1932 as fully set forth in the previous decision. To that extent, the first part of the preceding question has thus been answered in the affirmative. [⋯]

(p. 1963-) As Professor Eagleton puts in(*Responsibility of States in International Law*, 1928, p. 80): "A State owes at all times a duty to protect other States against injurious acts by individuals from which its jurisdiction." A great number of such general pronouncements by leading authorities concerning the duty of a State to respect other States and their territory have been presented to the Tribunal. These and many others have been carefully examined. International decisions, in various matters, from the Alabama case onwards and also earlier ones, are based on the same general principle and, indeed, this principle, as such, has not been questioned by Canada. But, the real difficulty often arises rather when it comes to determine what, *pro subjecta materie*, is deemed to constitute an injurious act.

A case concerning, as the present one does, territorial relations, decided by the Federal Court of Switzerland between the Cantons of Soleure and Argovia, may serve to illustrate the relativity of the rule. Soleure brought a suit against her sister State to enjoin use of a shooting establishment which endangered her territory. The Court, in granting the injunction, said: "This right(sovereignty) excludes ... not only the usurpation and exercise of sovereign rights (of another State) ... but also an actual encroachment of its inhabitants." As a result of the decision, Argovia made plans for the improvement of the existing installations. These, however, were considered as insufficient protection by Soleure. The Canton of Argovia then moved the Federal Court to decree that the shooting be again permitted after completion of the projected improvements. This motion was granted. "The demand of the Government of Soleure," said the Court, "that all endangerment be absolutely abolished apparently goes too far." The Court found that all risk whatever had not been eliminated, as the region was flat and absolutely safe shooting ranges were only found in mountain valleys; that there was a federal duty for the communes to provide facilities for military target practice and that "no more precautions may be demanded for shooting ranges near the boundaries of two Cantons than are required for shooting ranges in the interior of a Canton." [⋯]

No case of air pollution dealt with by an international tribunal has been brought to the attention of the Tribunal, nor does the Tribunal know of any such case. The nearest analogy is that of water pollution. But, here also, no decision of an international tribunal has been cited or has been found.

(p. 1964-) There are, however, as regards both air pollution and water pollution, certain decisions of the Supreme Court of the United States which may legitimately be taken as a guide in this field of international law, for it is reasonable to follow by analogy, in international cases, precedents established by that court in dealing with controversies between States of the Union or with other controversies concerning the quasi-sovereign rights of such States, where no contrary rule prevails in international law and no reason for rejecting such precedents can be adduced from the limitations of sovereignty inherent in the Constitution of the United States [⋯]

(p. 1965-) The Tribunal, therefore, finds that the above decisions, taken as a whole, constitute an adequate basis for its conclusions, namely that, under the principles of international law, as well as of the law of the United States, no State has the right to use or permit the use of its territory in such a manner as to cause injury by fumes in or to the territory of another or the properties or persons therein, when the case is of serious consequence and the injury is established by clear and convincing evidence.

The decisions of the Supreme Court of the United States which are the basis of these conclusions are decisions in equity and a solution inspired by them, together with the regime hereinafter prescribed, will, in the opinion of the Tribunal, be "just to all parties concerned," as long, at least, as the present conditions in the Columbia River Valley continue to prevail.

Considering the circumstances of the case, the Tribunal holds that the Dominion of Canada is responsible in international law for the conduct of the Trail Smelter. Apart from the undertakings in the Convention, it is, (p. 1966) therefore, the duty of the Government of the Dominion of Canada to see to it that this conduct should be in conformity with the obligation of the Dominion under international law as herein determined.

The Tribunal, therefore, answers Question Number 2 as follows: (2) So long as the present conditions in the Columbia River Valley prevail, the Trail Smelter shall be required to refrain from causing any damage, through fumes, in the State of Washington the damage herein referred to and its extent being such as would be recoverable under the decisions of the Courts of the United States in suits between private individuals. The indemnity for such damage should be fixed in such manner as the Governments, acting under Article IX of the Convention, should agree upon. [···]

☑ 해 설

트레일 제련소 사건은 국제환경법에서 가장 많이 인용되는 판정례 중 하나이다. 전통적으로 주권국가는 자국 영토 내에서 절대적인 주권행사가 가능하다고 생각했다. 요컨대 다른 인접국의 상황에 괘념치 않는다는 뜻이다. 그러나 20세기 들어 경제활동의 규모가 커지고 방식이 다양하게 발전함에 따라 그 결과가 종종 인접국에도 상당한 영향을 미치게 되었다. 이 사건이 발생한 시점에는 국제적 대기오염의 선례가 거의 없었으므로 이 사건을 담당한 중재판정부는 판정을 내림에 있어 국내 판례도 원용하며 결과를 도출했다. 이러한 현상은 역사가 짧은 국제환경법 분야에서 어쩌면 당연한 결과이다. 또한 미국과 캐나다는 서로 비슷한 법률문화, 사회·경제적 배경을 갖고 있으므로 중재판정부 입장에서도 국내법 이론을 다수 인용하며 양국이 수용할 수 있는 결과를 이끌어낼 수 있었던 것으로 추측된다.

국제환경법에서 많이 인용되는 원칙들은 바로 이 판정에서 다뤄진 내용들이다. 중재재판 회부 시 양국은 아래의 4가지 쟁점에 대해 판단을 구했다.

1. 공동위원회를 거쳐 이 문제가 일단락된 1932년 이후에도 트레일 제련소가 미국 워싱턴주에 손해를 입혔는지 그리고 이에 대해 캐나다

가 배상을 해야 하는지 여부

2. 만약 손해를 입혔다면 캐나다는 향후 유사한 손해 발생을 회피하기 위해 노력하여야 하는지 여부 및 그러한 의무의 구체적 범위

3. 제련소가 특별한 조치나 제도를 채택, 유지하도록 확보할 의무를 캐나다가 부담하는지 여부

4. 상기 두 번째, 세 번째 문제에 대해 재판소가 내린 결정에 따라 캐나다가 배상을 해야 하는지 여부

상기 4가지 쟁점 중 중재판정부는 첫 번째 문제에 대해 미국 워싱턴주의 토지(land)에 손해가 발생했음을 확인했다. 이에 따라 1938년 중간판정에서 중재판정부는 1932년부터 1937년까지 기간 동안 발생한 손해에 대해 78,000달러의 손해배상을 결정했다. 그러나 토지 이외 경제적 이익 등 다른 부분에 대해서는 제출된 증거가 불충분하다는 이유로 판단하지 않았다. 그후 1941년 중재판정부는 나머지 3가지 문제에 대해 결론을 도출하였다. 즉, 미래에 손해가 발생하지 않도록 캐나다 정부는 제련소 운영을 적절히 통제하여야 하고, 그렇지 않은 경우에는 추가 손해배상에 관한 결정이 내려질 것이라고 판정했다. 이후 캐나다 정부와 트레일 제련소는 동 판정을 이행했고, 미국 정부는 1949년 11월 워싱턴주 피해 문제를 해결하고 남은 잔액 428,179.51 달러를 캐나다 정부에 반환했다.

트레일 제련소는 이후 여러 차례 회사 소유주와 명칭이 바뀌며, 2020년 7월 현재에는 Teck 에너지그룹에 속한 Trail Operations라는 상호로 여전히 캐나다 브리티시 콜롬비아주에서 아연 및 납 제련업에 종사하고 있다. 캐나다 브리티시 콜롬비아주 환경부 및 미국 환경보호청에 따르면, 이 회사는 트레일 제련소 사건 이후에도 2014년까지 여러 차례 환경유해물질 및 독극물을 인근 강에 유출시키는 등 환경오염을 야기했다고 한다.

트레일 제련소 사건은 '다른 국가에 대해 국경을 초월한 환경오염(transboundary pollution)'을 직·간접적으로 야기한 국가는 이에 대해 법적 책임을 진다는 국제환경법상 기본 원칙을 형성한 점에서 중요한 의의를 가진다. 또한 이 맥락에서 우리나라에도 중요한 시사점을 제시하고 있다. 특히 중국발 미세먼지 문제에 대한 국제법상 책임 문제 논의에 있어 이 판정은 흔히 언

급되고 있다. 나아가 2020년 코로나 바이러스의 세계적 확산에 따른 특정 국가의 책임 문제가 논의되는 과정에서도 이 법리는 여전히 중요한 시사점을 제시하고 있다.

➡ **참고문헌** ─────────────────────────────

- 김석현, 트레일 제련소 사건 연구, (단국대) 법학논총 제22권(1996), p. 216.
- 소병천, 국외 발생 미세먼지 관련 국제법적 분석 및 대응방안, 환경법연구 제39권 제2호(2017), p. 29.
- A. K. Kuhn, The Trail Smelter Arbitration—United States and Canada, AJIL Vol. 32, No. 4(1938), p. 785.
- A. L. Parrish, Trail Smelter Deja Vu: Extraterritoriality, International Environmental Law, and Search for Solutions to Canadian—US Transboundary Water Pollution Disputes, Boston University Law Review Vol. 85(2005), p. 363.
- R. M. Bratspies & R. A. Miller, Transboundary Harm in International Law: Lessons from the Trail Smelter Arbitration, Cambridge University Press (2006).

2. 멕시코산 참치 수입제한(2012)
— Dolphin-safe 라벨의 무역제한 조치 여부

United States — Measures Concerning the Importation, Marketing and Sale of Tuna and Tuna Products.
Mexico v. United States, Report of the Appellate Body, WT/DS381/AB/R(2012).

☑ 사 안

이 분쟁은 미국의 "dolphin — safe" 라벨 부착조치가 WTO 부속협정 중 하나인 GATT 협정과 무역에 대한 기술장벽협정(Agreement on Technical Barriers to Trade, TBT 협정)을 각각 위반하는지 여부를 다루고 있다. 참치는 상어를 주적으로 인식하고 경계하는 습성이 있어 생존을 위해 돌고래 무리와 함께 움직이는 경우가 많다. 돌고래와 상어는 바다에서 가능한 한 서로 마주치지 않으려 하므로 돌고래 근처에 있는 것만으로도 참치는 생존을 도모할 수 있기 때문이다. 이러한 습성을 파악한 어민들은 돌고래가 해수면 위로 뛰어오르는 지역에서 집중적으로 참치를 포획하는 어로방식을 채택했다. 그러나 이 과정에서 상당수의 돌고래들이 참치 포획용 그물에 걸려 죽게 되는 문제가 발생했으며, 이를 방지하기 위해 미국에서는 'save the dolphins'라는 구호 아래 돌고래 보호운동이 광범위하게 전개되었다.

이러한 보호운동의 하나는 돌고래 동시 포획을 방지하는 방식으로 어획된 참치에 대해 "dolphin — safe" 라벨을 참치 통조림에 부착하는 것을 허용하는 것이었다. 이는 소비자들이 해당 참치 통조림이 '돌고래를 보호하는 방법으로 포획된 참치로 제조되었다'는 사실을 알 수 있도록 추가정보를 제공하는 것을 목표로 하였다. 일종의 소비자에게 정보를 제공하는 것을 골자로 한다. 해당 라벨이 부착되지 않았다고 하여 수입 및 판매가 금지되는 것은 아니다. 해당 라벨의 부착여부와 상관없이 미국산 및 해외산 모든 참치 통조림이 동일한 환경에서 판매됐다. 그러나 당시 미국 내에서 돌고래 보호에 대한 관심이 고조되고 있었으므로 소비자늘은 라벨이 부착된 제품을 전반적으로 선호했다. 그런데 돌고래 동시 포획 방지 장치를 부착하는 데에는 적지 않은 비용이 소요되므로 영세어민과 소규모 선박이 주를 이루는 멕시코 선단은 이 장치를 부착하지 않았고, 그 결과 이 라벨을 부착할 수 없었던 멕시코산 참치 통조림은 결국 미국 시장에서 경쟁력을 잃게 되었다. 멕시코는 이러한 미국의 dolphin-safe 라벨 부착 조치가 GATT 제1조 1항과 제3조 4항, 그리고 TBT 협정 제2조 1항, 2항 및 4항을 위반한다고 주장했다. 주로 내국민 대우 위반 관련 조항들이다. 멕시코산을 미국산에 비해 차별대우하였다는 것이다. 패널은 미국의 조치가 이들 조항에 대한 위반에 해당한다고 보았고 이에 대해 상소심이 진행되었다.

☑ 쟁 점

(1) 미국의 dolphin-safe 라벨 부착 조치가 '기술규정'에 해당하는지 여부.

(2) 미국의 조치가 멕시코 상품에 대해 자국 상품에 비해 차별적으로 불리한 대우를 부여하는지 여부.

(3) 미국의 조치가 정당한 목적을 달성하기 위해 필요한 정도 이상으로 무역제한적인지 여부.

☑ 판 정

(1) 미국의 조치는 기술규정에 해당한다. 참치 관련 상품의 생산자, 수출입업자, 유통업자 및 판매자가 돌고래와 관련된 정보를 표시하기 위해서는 반드시 해당 조치를 따라야 하므로 이는 사실상 강제성을 띠는 기술규정에 해당한다.

(2) 미국의 조치는 멕시코 상품을 차별적으로 대우한다. 멕시코산 참치의 대부분이 dolphin-safe 라벨을 부착할 수 없는 반면 미국산 참치 통조림은 이 라벨을 상대적으로 용이하게 부착할 수 있다. 이는 미국 시장 내에서 멕시코산 참치 통조림의 경쟁력(conditions of competition)에 심각한 부정적인

변화(modification)를 초래했다. Dolphin－safe 라벨 부착 여부에 대해 멕시코 어민들에게도 선택의 기회가 있기는 하였으나 산업 구조상 멕시코가 어로 방법을 변경하는 것은 쉽지 않다.

(3) 미국의 조치는 국제교역에 대해 불필요한 장애를 초래하지 않는다. TBT 협정 제2조 2항에서 기술규정이 '정당한 목적수행에 필요한 이상으로 무역을 규제하지 않아야 한다'고 명시한 것을 볼 때, 기술규정으로 인해 어느 정도의 무역제한이 발생할 수 있음은 예상된다. 멕시코 정부가 제시한 대안을 채택할 경우 미국이 달성하고자 하는 목적을 현재와 같이 효율적으로 성취할 수 없는 것으로 판단되고 이에 따라 미국의 조치가 필요한 한도 이상으로 무역상 장애를 초래하는 것으로 볼 수 없다.

판 결 문

190. As already mentioned, we consider that a determination of whether a particular measure constitutes a technical regulation must be made in the light of the features of the measure and the circumstances of the case. [⋯]

199. As noted, a determination of whether a particular measure constitutes a technical regulation must be made in the light of the characteristics of the measure at issue and the circumstances of the case. In this case, we note that the US measure is composed of legislative and regulatory acts of the US federal authorities and includes administrative provisions. In addition, the measure at issue sets out a single and legally mandated definition of a "dolphin-safe" tuna product and disallows the use of other labels on tuna products that do not satisfy this definition. In doing so, the US measure prescribes in a broad and exhaustive manner the conditions that apply for making any assertion on a tuna product as to its "dolphin-safety," regardless of the manner in which that statement is made. As a consequence, the US measure covers the entire field of what "dolphin-safe" means in relation to tuna products. For these reasons, we find that the Panel did not err in characterizing the measure at issue as a "technical regulation" within the meaning of Annex 1.1 to the *TBT Agreement*. [⋯]

230. Earlier in our analysis, we found that the Panel did not err in characterizing the measure at issue as a technical regulation within the meaning of Annex 1.1. We further note that the United States has not appealed the Panel's finding that Mexican tuna products are "like" tuna products of US origin and tuna products originating in any other country within the meaning of Article 2.1 of the *TBT Agreement*. This brings us to the question of whether, in the light of the findings of fact made by the Panel and uncontested facts on the record, it can be concluded that Mexico has established that the US "dolphin-safe" labelling provisions accord "less favourable treatment" to Mexican tuna products than that accorded to tuna products of the United States and tuna products originating in other countries.

231. Our analysis of this issue proceeds in two parts. First, we will assess whether the measure at issue modifies the conditions of competition in the US market to the detriment of Mexican tuna products as compared to US tuna products or tuna products originating in any other Member. Second, we will review whether any detrimental impact reflects discrimination against the Mexican tuna products. [⋯]

235. In our view, the factual findings by the Panel clearly establish that the lack of access to the "dolphin-safe" label of tuna products containing tuna caught by setting on dolphins has a detrimental impact on the competitive opportunities of Mexican tuna products in the US market. [⋯]

237. The relevant question is thus whether the *governmental* intervention "affects the conditions under which like goods, domestic and imported, compete in the market within a Member's territory." In this regard, we recall that it is the measure at issue that establishes the requirements under which a product can be labelled "dolphin-safe" in the United States. [⋯]

239. These findings by the Panel suggest that it is the governmental action in the form of adoption and application of the US "dolphin-safe" labelling provisions that has modified the conditions of competition in the market to the detriment of Mexican tuna products, and that the detrimental impact in this case hence flows from the measure at issue. [⋯] The fact that the detrimental impact on Mexican tuna products may involve some element of private choice does not, in our view, relieve the United States of responsibility under the *TBT Agreement*, where the measure it adopts modifies the conditions of competition to the detriment of Mexican tuna products.

240. In the light of the above, we consider that it is the measure at issue that modifies the competitive conditions in the US market to the detriment of Mexican tuna products. We turn next to the issue of whether this detrimental impact reflects discrimination. […]

296. We see no error in the Panel's assessment. In addition, we note that nowhere in its reasoning did the Panel state that imposing a requirement that an independent observer certify that no dolphins were killed or seriously injured in the course of the fishing operations in which the tuna was caught would be the *only* way for the United States to calibrate its "dolphin-safe" labelling provisions to the risks that the Panel found were posed by fishing techniques other than setting on dolphins. We note, in this regard, that the measure at issue itself contemplates the possibility that only the captain provide such a certification under certain circumstances.

297. In the light of the above, we conclude that the United States has not demonstrated that the difference in labelling conditions for tuna products containing tuna caught by setting on dolphins in the ETP, on the one hand, and for tuna products containing tuna caught by other fishing methods outside the ETP, on the other hand, is "calibrated" to the risks to dolphins arising from different fishing methods in different areas of the ocean. It follows from this that the United States has not demonstrated that the detrimental impact of the US measure on Mexican tuna products stems exclusively from a legitimate regulatory distinction. […]

298. In the light of uncontested facts and factual findings made by the Panel, we consider that Mexico has established a *prima facie* case that the US "dolphin-safe" labelling provisions modify the conditions of competition in the US market to the detriment of Mexican tuna products and are not even-handed in the way in which they address the risks to dolphins arising from different fishing techniques in different areas of the ocean. We consider further that the United States has not met its burden of rebutting this *prima facie* case. Since we are not persuaded that the Panel acted inconsistently with Article 11 of the DSU in reviewing the evidence and arguments before it, we accept the Panel's conclusions that the use of certain tuna fishing methods other than setting on dolphins "outside the ETP may produce and has produced significant levels of dolphin bycatch" and that "the US dolphin-safe provisions do not address observed mortality, and any resulting adverse effects on dolphin populations, for tuna not caught by setting on dolphins or high seas driftnet fishing outside the ETP." Thus, in our view, the United States has not justified as non-discriminatory under Article 2.1 the different requirements that it applies to tuna caught by setting on dolphins inside the ETP and tuna caught by other fishing methods outside the ETP for access to the US "dolphin-safe" label.

The United States has thus not demonstrated that the detrimental impact of the US measure on Mexican tuna products stems exclusively from a legitimate regulatory distinction.

299. For these reasons, we *reverse* the Panel's finding, in paragraphs 7.374 and 8.1(a) of the Panel Report, that the US "dolphin-safe" labelling provisions are not inconsistent with Article 2.1 of the *TBT Agreement*. We *find*, instead, that the US "dolphin-safe" labelling provisions provide "less favourable treatment" to Mexican tuna products than that accorded to tuna products of the United States and tuna products originating in other countries and are therefore inconsistent with Article 2.1 of the *TBT Agreement*. [⋯]

301. We turn next to the United States' appeal of the Panel's finding that the measure at issue is more trade restrictive than necessary to fulfil the legitimate objectives pursued by the United States, and that, therefore, the measure is inconsistent with Article 2.2 of the *TBT Agreement*. The United States alleges that the Panel erred in its application of Article 2.2 of the *TBT Agreement* and failed to make an objective assessment of the matter before it as required pursuant to Article 11 of the DSU. Mexico raises a conditional other appeal with respect to the Panel's finding under Article 2.2 of the *TBT Agreement*.

312. The first sentence of Article 2.2 requires WTO Members to ensure that their technical regulations are not prepared, adopted, or applied with a view to, or with the effect of, creating unnecessary obstacles to international trade. The second sentence explains that "[f]or this purpose, technical regulations shall not be more trade restrictive than necessary to fulfil a legitimate objective, taking account of the risks non-fulfilment would create." [⋯]

314. Accordingly, in adjudicating a claim under Article 2.2 of the *TBT Agreement*, a panel must assess what a Member seeks to achieve by means of a technical regulation. In doing so, it may take into account the texts of statutes, legislative history, and other evidence regarding the structure and operation of the measure. A panel is not bound by a Member's characterization of the objectives it pursues through the measure, but must independently and objectively assess them. Subsequently, the analysis must turn to the question of whether a particular objective is legitimate, pursuant to the parameters set out above.

315. Next, we consider the meaning of the word "fulfil" in the context of the phrase "fulfil a legitimate objective" in Article 2.2 of the *TBT Agreement*. We note, first, that the word "fulfil" is defined as "provide fully with what is wished for".

Read in isolation, the word "fulfil" appears to describe complete achievement of something. But, in Article 2.2, it is used in the phrase "to fulfil a legitimate objective" and, as described above, the word "objective" means "a target, goal, or aim". As we see it, it is inherent in the notion of an "objective" that such a "goal, or aim" may be something that is pursued and achieved to a greater or lesser degree. Accordingly, we consider that the question of whether a technical regulation "fulfils" an objective is concerned with the degree of contribution that the technical regulation makes toward the achievement of the legitimate objective.

316. We see support for this reading of the term "fulfil a legitimate objective" in the sixth recital of the preamble of the *TBT Agreement*, which provides relevant context for the interpretation of Article 2.2. It recognizes that a Member shall not be prevented from taking measures necessary to achieve its legitimate objectives "at the levels it considers appropriate", subject to the requirement that such measures are not applied in a manner that would constitute a means of arbitrary or unjustifiable discrimination between countries where the same conditions prevail or a disguised restriction on international trade, and are otherwise in accordance with the *TBT Agreement*. As we see it, a WTO Member, by preparing, adopting, and applying a measure in order to pursue a legitimate objective, articulates either implicitly or explicitly the level at which it seeks to pursue that particular legitimate objective.

317. A panel adjudicating a claim under Article 2.2 of the *TBT Agreement* must seek to ascertain to what degree, or if at all, the challenged technical regulation, as written and applied, actually contributes to the legitimate objective pursued by the Member. The degree of achievement of a particular objective may be discerned from the design, structure, and operation of the technical regulation, as well as from evidence relating to the application of the measure. As in other situations, such as, for instance, when determining the contribution of a measure to the achievement of a particular objective in the context of Article XX of the GATT 1994, a panel must assess the contribution to the legitimate objective actually achieved by the measure at issue.

318. We turn next to the terms "unnecessary obstacles to international trade" in the first sentence and "not ⋯ more trade-restrictive than necessary" in the second sentence of Article 2.2 of the *TBT Agreement*. [⋯]

322. In sum, we consider that an assessment of whether a technical regulation is "more trade-restrictive than necessary" within the meaning of Article 2.2 of the

TBT Agreement involves an evaluation of a number of factors. A panel should begin by considering factors that include: (i) the degree of contribution made by the measure to the legitimate objective at issue; (ii) the trade-restrictiveness of the measure; and (iii) the nature of the risks at issue and the gravity of consequences that would arise from non-fulfilment of the objective(s) pursued by the Member through the measure. [···]

323. With respect to the burden of proof in showing that a technical regulation is inconsistent with Article 2.2, the complainant must prove its claim that the challenged measure creates an unnecessary obstacle to international trade. In order to make a *prima facie* case, the complainant must present evidence and arguments sufficient to establish that the challenged measure is more trade restrictive than necessary to achieve the contribution it makes to the legitimate objectives, taking account of the risks non-fulfilment would create. [···]

327. With respect to the degree to which the measure at issue contributes to the United States' consumer information objective, we recall the Panel's finding that the measure at issue "can only *partially* ensure that consumers are informed about whether tuna was caught by using a method that adversely affects dolphins." This conclusion is based on the Panel's finding that fishing methods other than setting on dolphins or high-sea driftnet fishing outside the ETP may cause adverse effects on dolphins, and that to the extent tuna caught under such circumstances may be labelled "dolphin-safe" pursuant to the US "dolphinsafe" labelling provisions, consumers may be misled about whether tuna was caught using a technique that does not adversely affect dolphins. [···] Accordingly, the Panel concluded that US "dolphin-safe" labelling provisions "may, at best, only partially fulfil their stated objective of protecting dolphins by ensuring that the US market is not used to encourage fishing fleets to catch tuna in a manner that adversely affects dolphins." [···]

329. In any event, it would appear that, in respect of the conditions for labelling as "dolphin-safe" tuna products containing tuna harvested *outside* the ETP, there is no difference between the measure at issue and the alternative measure identified by Mexico, namely, the coexistence of the US "dolphin-safe" labelling provisions with the AIDCP rules. We recall that the geographic scope of application of the AIDCP rules is limited to the ETP. Thus, the conditions for fishing *outside* the ETP would be identical under the alternative measure proposed by Mexico, since only those set out in the US measure would apply. Therefore, for fishing

activities *outside* the ETP, the degree to which the United States' objectives are achieved under the alternative measure would not be higher or lower than that achieved by the US measure, it would be the same. *Inside* the ETP, however, the measure at issue and the alternative measure set out different requirements. Under the alternative measure identified by Mexico, tuna that is caught by setting on dolphins would be eligible for a "dolphin-safe" label if the prerequisites of the AIDCP label have been complied with. By contrast, the measure at issue prohibits setting on dolphins, and thus tuna harvested in the ETP would only be eligible for a "dolphin-safe" label if it was caught by methods other than setting on dolphins.

330. It would seem, therefore, that the Panel's comparison of the degree to which the alternative measure identified by Mexico contributes to the United States' objectives should have focused on the conditions inside the ETP. In particular, for tuna harvested inside the ETP, the Panel should have examined whether the labelling of tuna products complying with the requirements of the AIDCP label would achieve the United States' objectives to an equivalent degree as the measure at issue. [···]

331. For these reasons, we find that the Panel's comparison and analysis is flawed and cannot stand. Therefore, the Panel erred in concluding, in paragraphs 7.620 and 8.1(b) of the Panel Report, that it has been demonstrated that the measure at issue is more trade restrictive than necessary to fulfil the United States' legitimate objectives, taking account of the risks non-fulfilment would create. Accordingly, we reverse the Panel's findings that the measure at issue is inconsistent with Article 2.2 of the *TBT Agreement*. [···]

333. We have concluded that the Panel erred in finding that it has been demonstrated that the US measure is more trade restrictive than necessary within the meaning of Article 2.2 of the *TBT Agreement*. Having reversed this finding, we do not find it necessary to address the United States' additional claim that the Panel acted inconsistently with its obligations under Article 11 of the DSU. [···]

☑ 해   설

이 분쟁은 GATT 시대에 멕시코산 참치에 대해 내려진 수입제한 조치와 관련하여 전개된 미국·멕시코간 U.S.−Tuna 사건[1]의 연장선상에 있는 것으로 흔히 U.S.−Tuna II로 불린다.

---

1) Panel Report, *United States−Restrictions on imports of Tuna*, GATT DS21/R(1991).

이 판정은 어느 정도 무역제한적 요소를 포함할 수밖에 없는 각국의 환경보호 목적의 다양한 정책과 점차 엄격해지는 듯한 모습을 보이고 있는 WTO 규범 간의 충돌상황을 잘 보여주는 대표적인 판정례 중 하나이다. 일견 미국이 내세우는 정책목표가 정당하다는 점에서 이 분쟁은 미국이 WTO 분쟁해결절차가 자국 주권을 침해한다고 주장하는 주요 논거 중 하나로 지금도 빈번히 언급되고 있다. 이러한 불만이 축적되어 2016년부터 미국이 WTO 상소기구 위원 선임에 반대하고 급기야 2019년 12월 상소기구 운영이 중단되는 사태까지 초래되었다. 2020년 7월 현재 중국 국적의 상소기구 위원 1인만이 남아 최소 3인을 요하는 상소심이 물리적으로 불가능하게 되었고 이러한 상황을 임시적으로라도 타파하고자 EU, 캐나다, 중국 등 16개국은 상소기구를 대신할 별도의 중재절차에 합의하는 상황까지 이르러 WTO 분쟁해결절차는 중대한 위기에 봉착했다.

이 분쟁은 미국의 원산지 표시제도와 관련하여 전개된 U.S.−COOL 분쟁,2) 미국의 향료 첨가 담배 판매 제한 조치와 관련하여 전개된 U.S.−Clove Cigarettes 분쟁,3) 그리고 유럽연합의 물개관련 상품 수입제한 조치와 관련하여 전개된 EC−Seal Products 분쟁4)과 함께 GATT 및 TBT 협정의 내국민 대우 개념을 더욱 발전시키고 정립한 대표적인 판정으로 간주된다. 이들 분쟁들은 대체로 2011−2013년 사이에 전개되어 통상협정상 내국민 대우의 개념을 정리하는 데 중요한 기여를 했다. 본건 멕시코산 참치 수입제한 조치 분쟁에서 WTO 상소기구는 패널 판정을 번복했다. 패널은 미국의 조치가 멕시코산 상품에 대해 차별적 효과를 초래하지는 않았으므로 TBT 협정 제2조 1항 위반이 아니라고 판정한 반면, 상소기구는 이를 번복하고 이 조항에 대한 위반으로 판단했다. 또한 패널은 미국의 조치가 무역에 불필요하게 제한적인 효과를 초래하며 따라서 TBT 협정 제2조 2항 위반이라고 결정한 반면

---

2) Appellate Body Reports, *United States−Certain Country of Origin Labelling(COOL) Requirements*, WT/DS384/AB/R, WT/DS386/AB/R(2012).

3) Appellate Body Reports, *United States−Measures Affecting the Production and Sale of Clove Cigarettes*, WT/DS406/AB/R(2012).

4) Appellate Body Reports, *European Communities−Measures Prohibiting the Importation and Marketing of Seal Products*, WT/DS400/AB/R, WT/DS401/AB/R(2014).

상소기구는 다시 이를 번복하여 그러한 효과가 입증되지 않으므로 이 조항에 대한 위반이 아니라고 확인했다. 결국 미국의 조치가 협정 위반으로 귀결된 점은 동일하나 패널과 상소기구가 정반대의 분석을 행한 것이다. 물론 상소기구 판단이 패널 판단에 앞서지만 과연 그 분석과 논리가 정확한지에 대해서는 중요한 의문을 제기하게 되었다. 지금까지도 미국이 이 판정에 대해 불만을 표출하는 중요한 동인이기도 하다.

상소기구 판정에 따르면 미국 정부는 돌고래보호 소비자정보법(US Dolphin Protection Consumer Information Act)을 통해 돌고래 관련 라벨링 조치를 도입하며 멕시코산 상품 차별이 아닌 단지 소비자들에 대한 추가적 정보 제공을 위한 의도만을 가졌다. 그러나 이러한 정당한 의도에도 불구하고 실제 시장에서 소비자들이 돌고래 보호 라벨링이 부착된 상품을 선호하였고 이러한 선호가 시장에서 멕시코산 참치에 대해 구조적으로 불리한 결과를 초래한 것이 확인되자 상소기구는 내국민 대우 위반으로 결론내리게 되었다. 시장에서의 경쟁조건이 구조적으로 불리한 방식으로 변경되었는지 여부가 내국민 대우 위반의 기준이라는 점은 GATT 협정 제3조의 내국민 대우 위반에서 이미 확립된 법리이며 동일한 원칙은 TBT 협정 제2조 1항 위반 확인에도 마찬가지로 적용되었다. 정부의 조치가 단지 소비자의 선호도와 결합하여 시장에서 특정한 효과를 초래하는 경우에도 내국민 대우 위반 문제가 제기될 수 있다는 것이다. 그러한 효과가 외국의 동종상품이 수입국 시장에서 경쟁하는데 있어 구조적으로 불리한 영향을 초래한다면 여기에 해당한다는 것이다.

상소기구 판정 이후 미국은 2013년 7월 돌고래보호 소비자정보법을 개정하여 판정 내용을 이행하고자 하였으나, 이에 대해 멕시코는 다시 불만을 표출하며 같은 해 11월 이행패널의 설치를 요청했다. 그에 따라 2015년 미국의 이행 조치에 대한 패널과 상소기구의 판정이 다시 이루어졌고, 이들은 미국의 이행 조치 역시 WTO 관련 협정 위반이라고 판단했다. 이에 따라 멕시코는 2016년 3월 미국에 대한 관세양허 또는 WTO 관련 협정의 다른 의무의 적용을 정지할 수 있는 허가(소위 보복허가)를 WTO 분쟁해결기구(Dispute Settlement Body: DSB)에 요청하기에 이르렀다. 이에 대해 미국은 멕시코의 보복 요청 수준에 대해 이의를 제기하여 WTO 분쟁해결양해(Dispute Settlement Understanding: DSU) 제22조 6항상 중재를 요청했다. 이 중재절차에서 중재인은 "멕시코는 미국에 대해 연간 163,230,000달러를 초과하지 않는 수준에서 양허 또는 다른 의무 정지를 할 수 있다"는 판정을 내렸다. 2017년 5월 멕시코는 이 중재 판정에 기초하여 해당 금액에 상응하는 미국에 대한 관세양허 또는 GATT 협정 상 관련 의무의 적용의 정지 허가를 DSB에 요청하였고 DSB는 이를 허가하였다.

이 과정에서 미국은 2016년 3월 23일 돌고래보호 소비자정보법을 이행 분쟁의 상소기구 판정을 고려하여 재개정했으며(이 법은 2018년에도 다시 개정), 이렇게 재개정된 법에 대해 2016년 6월 9일 멕시코는 다시 2차 이행패널 설치를 요청했다. 이 절차에서 제2차 이행패널과 상소기구는 2016년과 2018년에 각각 개정된 미국의 돌고래보호 소비자정보법이 WTO 관련 협정에 합치된다고 판시하였으며, 2019년 1월 11일 이 상소보고서가 채택되어 멕시코는 미국에 대해 더 이상 보복조치를 취할 수 없게 되었다. 이에 따라 이 분쟁은 현재 종결된 상태이다. 이 분쟁을 거치며 미국의 WTO 분쟁해결절차, 특히 상소기구에 대한 불만이 크게 증폭되었다.

➠ 참고문헌 ───────────────────────────

- 김민정, '미국－멕시코 참치분쟁 Ⅱ'에 대한 WTO판결 분석, 국제경제법연구 Vol. 10, No. 2, 한국국제경제법학회(2012), pp. 117－166.
- 안덕근 & 김민정, WTO 무역기술장벽대응체제와 표준정책, 서울대학교출판문화원(2019).
- T. Kelly, Tuna－Dolphin Revisited, 48 J. World Trade 501 (2014).
- L. J. Ankersmit, Future of Environmental Labelling: US － Tuna II and the Scope of the TBT, 39 Legal Issues of Econ. Integration 127 (2012).
- D. D. Murphy, Tuna－Dolphin Wars, 40 J. World Trade 597 (2006).
- E. Baroncini & C. Brunel, A WTO Safe Harbour for the Dolphins: The Second Compliance Proceedings in the US－TUna II (Mexico) case, World Trade Review Vol. 19(2020), p. 196.

3. 일본 포경 사건(2014)
— 국제포경협약상 「과학적 포경」의 의미 등

Case Concerning Whaling in the Antarctic.
Australia v. Japan: New Zealand intervening, 2014 ICJ Reports
226.

☑ 사   안

　호주와 일본은 국제포경규제협약(International Convention for the Regulation of Whaling: "ICRW")의 체약당사국이다. 국제포경위원회(International Whaling Commission: "IWC")는 해당 협약에 근거해 멸종위기 고래 12종에 대한 상업적 포경활동을 금지하고 있다. 다만 이 협약 제8조는 당사국이 일정한 조건에 따라 "과학적 연구를 목적으로(for purposes of scientific research)" 하는 자국민의 포경을 예외적으로 허가할 수 있도록 규정한다. 일본은 해당 조항에 의거, 1987년부터 남극해에서 과학적 연구 목적으로 고래를 포획하는 소위 JARPA(Japanese Whale Research Program under Special Permit in the Antarctic) 프로그램을 도입·운영했다. 일본은 2005년 JARPA를 폐지했으나 그 직후 본질적으로 동일한 JARPA Ⅱ 프로그램을 새로이 도입했다. JARPA Ⅱ는 매년 남극해에서 과학적 연구를 목적으로 약 1,000여 마리의 고래를 포획할 것을 예상하고 있으며 이 프로그램이 바로 이 사건의 대상이다. 그 동안 다양한 경로를 통해 지속적으로 일본의 포경행위 중단을 요구해 온 호주는 JARPA Ⅱ가 과학적 연구를 가장한 불법적인 상업적 포경활동으로 ICRW를 위반했음을 주장하며 2010년 5월 31일 ICJ에 일본을 제소했다.

☑ 쟁   점

(1) ICRW 제8조상의 과학적 포경(scientific whaling)의 구체적인 의미는

무엇인지 여부.

(2) 패소국인 일본은 어떻게 판정을 이행해야 하는지 여부.

☑ 판   결

(1) "과학적 연구를 목적으로 하는(for purposes of scientific research)" 포경의 해석은 "과학적 연구(scientific research)"와 "목적으로 하는(for purposes of)"에 대한 각각의 해석을 요한다. 따라서 JARPA Ⅱ 프로그램이 과학적 연구를 수반하더라도 동시에 과학적 연구를 "목적으로 해야만" 협약 제8조의 적용대상이 된다. JARPA Ⅱ 프로그램은 그 포획규모와 이행방식을 종합적으로 감안할 때 과학적 연구를 목적으로 하는 것으로 볼 수 없다.

(2) 일본 정부는 JARPA Ⅱ 프로그램에 따라 부여된 포경허가를 취소하고, 향후 추가적 승인을 자제해야 한다.

판 결 문

55. The Court notes that Article Ⅷ is an integral part of the Convention. It therefore has to be interpreted in light of the object and purpose of the Convention and taking into account other provisions of the Convention, including the Schedule. However, since Article Ⅷ, paragraph 1, specifies that "the killing, taking, and treating of whales in accordance with the provisions of this Article shall be exempt from the operation of this Convention," whaling conducted under a special permit which meets the conditions of Article Ⅷ is not subject to the obligations under the Schedule concerning the moratorium on the catching of whales for commercial purposes, the prohibition of commercial whaling in the Southern Ocean Sanctuary and the moratorium relating to factory ships. [⋯]

58. [⋯] The Court notes that programmes for purposes of scientific research should foster scientific knowledge; they may pursue an aim other than either conservation or sustainable exploitation of whale stocks. [⋯]

67. When reviewing the grant of a special permit authorizing the killing, taking and treating of whales, the Court will assess, first, whether the programme under which these activities occur involves scientific research. Secondly, the Court will consider if the killing, taking and treating of whales is "for purposes of" scientific research by examining whether, in the use of lethal methods, the programme's design and implementation are reasonable in relation to achieving its stated objectives. [⋯]

69. The Court observes that, in applying the above standard of review, it is not called upon to resolve matters of scientific or whaling policy. The Court is aware that members of the international community hold divergent views about the appropriate policy towards whales and whaling, but it is not for the Court to settle these differences. The Court's task is only to ascertain whether the special permits granted in relation to JARPA II fall within the scope of Article VIII, paragraph 1, of the ICRW. [⋯]

71. In the view of the Court, the two elements of the phrase "for purposes of scientific research" are cumulative. As a result, even if a whaling programme involves scientific research, the killing, taking and treating of whales pursuant to such a programme does not fall within Article VIII unless these activities are "for purposes of" scientific research. [⋯]

77. As to the question whether a testable or defined hypothesis is essential, the Court observes that the experts called by both Parties agreed that scientific research should proceed on the basis of particular questions, which could take the form of a hypothesis, although they disagreed about the level of specificity required of such a hypothesis. In short, the opinions of the experts reveal some degree of agreement, albeit with important nuances, regarding the role of hypotheses in scientific research generally. [⋯]

82. The Court observes that, as a matter of scientific opinion, the experts called by the Parties agreed that lethal methods can have a place in scientific research, while not necessarily agreeing on the conditions for their use. [⋯]

83. Article VIII expressly contemplates the use of lethal methods, and the Court is of the view that Australia and New Zealand overstate the legal significance of the recommendatory resolutions and Guidelines on which they rely. [⋯] The Court however observes that the States parties to the ICRW have a duty to co-operate with the IWC and the Scientific Committee and thus should give due regard to recommendations calling for an assessment of the feasibility of non-lethal alternatives. [⋯]

86. Taking into account these observations, the Court is not persuaded that activities must satisfy the four criteria advanced by Australia in order to constitute "scientific research" in the context of Article VIII. As formulated by Australia, these criteria appear largely to reflect what one of the experts that it called regards as well-conceived scientific research, rather than serving as an interpretation of the term as used in the Convention. Nor does the Court consider it necessary to devise alternative criteria or to offer a general definition of "scientific research."

87. The Court turns next to the second element of the phrase "for purposes of scientific research," namely the meaning of the term "for purposes of."

88. [⋯] In order to ascertain whether a programme's use of lethal methods is for purposes of scientific research, the Court will consider whether the elements of a programme's design and implementation are reasonable in relation to its stated scientific objectives [⋯]. As shown by the arguments of the Parties, such elements may include: decisions regarding the use of lethal methods; the scale of the programme's use of lethal sampling; the methodology used to select sample sizes; a comparison of the target sample sizes and the actual take; the time frame associated with a programme; the programme's scientific output; and the degree to which a programme co-ordinates its activities with related research projects [⋯].

89. The Parties agree that the design and implementation of a programme for purposes of scientific research differ in key respects from commercial whaling. The evidence regarding the programme's design and implementation must be considered in light of this distinction. [⋯]

94. As the Parties and the intervening State accept, Article VIII, paragraph 2, permits the processing and sale of whale meat incidental to the killing of whales pursuant to the grant of a special permit under Article VIII, paragraph 1. In the Court's view, the fact that a programme involves the sale of whale meat and the use of proceeds to fund research is not sufficient, taken alone, to cause a special permit to fall outside Article VIII. Other elements would have to be examined, such as the scale of a programme's use of lethal sampling, which might suggest that the whaling is for purposes other than scientific research. [⋯]

97. The Court observes that a State often seeks to accomplish more than one goal when it pursues a particular policy. Moreover, an objective test of whether a programme is for purposes of scientific research does not turn on the intentions of individual government officials, but rather on whether the design and imple-mentation of a programme are reasonable in relation to achieving the stated research objectives. Accordingly, the Court considers that whether particular government officials may have motivations that go beyond scientific research does not preclude a conclusion that a programme is for purposes of scientific research within the meaning of Article VIII. At the same time, such motivations cannot justify the granting of a special permit for a programme that uses lethal sampling on a larger scale than is reasonable in relation to achieving the programme's stated research objectives. The research objectives alone must be sufficient to justify the programme as designed and implemented. [···]

244. In addition to asking the Court to find that the killing, taking and treating of whales under special permits granted for JARPA II is not for purposes of scientific research within the meaning of Article VIII and that Japan thus has violated three paragraphs of the Schedule, Australia asks the Court to adjudge and declare that Japan shall:

"(a) refrain from authorizing or implementing any special permit whaling which is not for purposes of scientific research within the meaning of Article VIII;

(b) cease with immediate effect the implementation of JARPA II; and

(c) revoke any authorization, permit or licence that allows the implementation of JARPA II."

245. The Court observes that JARPA II is an ongoing programme. Under these circumstances, measures that go beyond declaratory relief are warranted. The Court therefore will order that Japan shall revoke any extant authorization, permit or licence to kill, take or treat whales in relation to JARPA II, and refrain from granting any further permits under Article VIII, paragraph 1, of the Convention, in pursuance of that programme.

246. The Court sees no need to order the additional remedy requested by Australia, which would require Japan to refrain from authorizing or implementing any special permit whaling which is not for purposes of scientific research within the meaning of Article VIII. That obligation already applies to all States parties. It is to be expected that Japan will take account of the reasoning and conclusions contained in this Judgment as it evaluates the possibility of granting any future permits under Article VIII, paragraph 1, of the Convention. [···]

☑ 해   설

이 분쟁은 일본이 최초로 ICJ 분쟁해결절차에 참여한 사안으로 주목을 받았다. 2010년 5월 31일 호주는 일본을 ICJ에 제소하며 관할권의 근거를 ICJ 규정 제36조 제2항[1)]에 따라 제출된 2002년 3월 22일자 호주의 강제관할

권 수락 선언 및 2007년 7월 9일자 일본의 강제관할권 수락 선언2)에서 찾았
다. 이후 2012년 11월 20일 뉴질랜드도 ICJ 규칙 제63조 제2항에 따라 동 소
송을 통해 해석이 이루어질 다자협약(국제포경규제협약)의 당사국임을 수상하
며 제3자 소송참가를 신청하였고 2013년 2월 6일 ICJ는 이를 수락했다. 이
사안에서 뉴질랜드는 호주와 비슷한 입장을 유지하는 국가이며, 뉴질랜드가
동 소송에 참가했기에, ICJ의 판결에 의해 부여된 해석은 뉴질랜드에게도 동일
한 구속력을 가진다.

그간 호주와 일본은 어획활동과 관련하여 FAO, OECD, WTO 등 여러 국
제기구에서 오랜 기간 서로 대립해 오고 있다. 해양생물자원의 보호를 강조
하는 호주 등 일부 국가는 여러 해역에서 활발하게 어획활동을 전개하는 일
본에 대해 항상 우려와 불만을 갖고 있었기 때문이다. 이 분쟁은 이 중 일본
의 포경활동에 국한하여 전개되었다. 포경활동에 대하여는 ICRW라는 국제
협약이 존재하기 때문이다. 이 협약은 체약당사국의 포경활동을 금지하고 있
다. 다만 이 협약 제8조는 이에 대한 한 가지 예외로서 과학적 연구를 목적
으로 하는 포경활동은 허용하고 있다. 일본과 호주의 입장 대립은 바로 이
부분에 관한 것이다. 호주는 일본의 포경활동은 과학적 연구를 목적으로 하
는 것으로 볼 수 없다고 주장하고, 일본은 자신들의 활동이 규모가 클지언정
여전히 과학적 연구를 목적으로 한다고 반박했다. 조약법에 관한 비엔나 협
약 제31조에 따라 이 협약 제8조를 해석한 ICJ는 과학적 연구에 대하여는 특
별한 가이드라인을 제시하지는 않았으나 과학적 연구를 목적으로 하는지 여
부에 대하여는 중요한 지침을 제시했다. 관련 프로그램이 그 규모와 체제에

---

1) 이 조항은 ICJ의 강제관할권 수락에 관한 내용으로 다음과 같이 규정하고 있다. "재판소규정
   의 당사국은 다음 사항에 관한 모든 법률적 분쟁에 대하여 재판소의 관할을, 동일한 의무를
   수락하는 모든 다른 국가와의 관계에 있어서 당연히 또한 특별한 합의 없이도, 강제적인 것으
   로 인정한다는 것을 언제든지 선언할 수 있다."

2) 참고로 일본은 ICJ 강제관할권을 최초로 1958년 9월 15일자로 수락하였다. 그러나 그 이후
   2007년 7월 9일 및 2015년 10월 6일 두 번에 걸쳐 개정한다. 본 사건은 2007년 1차 개정 강
   제관할권 선언에 따라 ICJ 관할권이 인정되었다. 이 당시 개정 선언은 강제관할권 예외를 확대
   하였는데, 1958년 강제관할권 선언상 예외는 당사자 간 합의뿐이었으나, 2007년 개정 강제관
   할권 선언상 예외는 분쟁상대국이 본 분쟁에 대해서만 강제관할권을 수락한 경우 등을 추가하
   였으며, 2015년 강제관할권 선언상 예외에는 바다 생물자원에 대한 연구, 보존, 관리 또는 이
   용과 관련하여 발생하는 모든 분쟁까지 추가하게 된다.

있어 과학적 연구 목적을 달성하기 위해 합리적으로 운용되어야 한다는 것이다. 요컨대 일본의 JARPA Ⅱ 프로그램이 연간 1,000마리에 달하는 고래를 포획하는 것을 목표로 하는 한 제시된 '과학'적 목표를 달성하는 데 비합리적이며, 따라서 과학적 연구를 목적으로 하는 것으로 볼 수 없다는 것이다.

한편 ICJ는 일본의 JARPA Ⅱ 프로그램이 ICRW 제8조에 위반한다는 판결만을 내리고, 향후 일본이 이 조항에 위반하는 포경 프로그램을 도입하는 것을 금지해 달라는 호주의 요청은 거부했다. 전자에 대한 판단만으로 충분하고 모든 체약당사국은 ICRW에 위반하는 조치를 취하지 않을 의무를 원래부터 부담하고 있으므로 이에 대한 별도의 판결은 필요 없다는 것이다. 그러나 JARPA Ⅱ 프로그램에만 국한된 ICJ의 판결은 일본이 이 프로그램을 폐지하고 이와 유사한 새로운 프로그램을 도입할 경우 또 다시 관련 분쟁이 재개될 소지를 내포하고 있었다. 이 판결에 따라 일본은 문제의 JARPA Ⅱ 는 폐지했으나 새로운 프로그램인 NEWREP－A를 2014년 11월 19일 발표했다. 이 프로그램은 남극 해역에서 2015년 여름 밍크고래 333마리 포획을 시작으로, 이후 12년에 걸쳐 약 4,000마리를 포획하는 내용을 담고 있다. 더욱이 2015년 10월 6일 일본 정부는 ICJ에 제출한 제36조 제2항 상 관할권 수락 조건 변경에 관한 서한을 통해 '바다생물자원 관련 분쟁'에 대해서는 ICJ 강제관할권의 예외를 선언한 바, 향후 호주 등 외국정부가 NEWREP－A 에 대해 일본을 ICJ에 다시 제소하는 것은 이제는 힘들 것으로 보인다. 나아가 일본은 2019년 6월 30일자로 IWC에서도 탈퇴함으로써 1986년 이후 33년만에 상업포경을 공식적으로 개시하게 되었다. ICJ 소송을 거쳤지만 이들 국가 간 분쟁이 해결되었다기보다 새로운 차원에서 전개되고 있어 향후 귀추가 주목된다.

한편 이러한 일본의 상업포경 재개에 대해 국제사회는 심각한 우려를 표명하고 있다. 가령 영국, 호주 정부는 일본의 결정에 대해 유감을 표명하며, "모든 종류의 상업 포경에 강력히 반대한다"는 입장을 밝혔다. 우리 정부 또한 심각한 우려를 표명하는 성명을 발표했다. 그린피스 등 비정부간기구(NGO)도 일본의 결정을 비판한 바 있다.

➠ 참고문헌 ─────────────────────────────────

- 이석우, 국제사법재판소의 호주와 일본간 포경사건 분석, 법학연구 Vol. 16, No. 3, 인하대학교법학연구소(2013), pp. 295 – 322.
- D. K. Anton, Antarctic Whaling: Australia's Attempt to Protect Whales in the Southern Ocean, 36 BC. Envtl. Aff. L. Rev. 319 (2009).
- S. E. Rolland, Whaling in the Antarctic (Australia v. Japan: New Zealand Intervening), 108 Am. J. Int'l L. 496 (2014).
- B. Plant, Sovereignty, Science, and Cetaceans: The Whaling in the Antarctic Case, 74 Cambridge L.J. 40 (2015).
- 이재곤, 남극해포경사건(Whaling in Antarctic Case)과 포경활동의 국제적 규제, 법학연구 제46권, 전북대학교 법학연구소(2015), pp. 304 – 326.

4. 니카라과 국경지역 활동 및 코스타리카 도로 건설[2015(본안) 및 2018(손해배상)]
― 환경영향평가의무의 의의 및 환경피해의 배상

- Certain Activities Carried Out by Nicaragua in the Border Area (Costa Rica v. Nicaragua) and Construction of a Road in Costa Rica along the San Juan River(Nicaragua v. Costa Rica), Judgment ICJ Reports 2015, p. 665.
- Certain Activities Carried Out by Nicaragua in the Border Area (Costa Rica v. Nicaragua), Compensation, Judgment, ICJ Reports 2018, p. 15.

☑ 사   안

산 후안(San Juan)강은 니카라과와 코스타리카의 국경을 이루는 국제하천이다. 산 후안강은 하류의 콜로라도 삼각주를 중심으로 북쪽으로 흘러 카리브해로 들어가는 '산 후안강 하부'와 남쪽으로 흘러 카리브해로 들어가는 '콜로라도강' 두 갈래로 나뉜다. 산 후안강 하부와 콜로라도강 사이에 있는 Isla Calero 지역에는 코스타리카에선 Isla Portillos로, 니카라과에선 Harbor Head로 불리는 곳이 있으며, 이곳이 이 사건의 분쟁지역이다. Isla Calero는 1996년 코스타리카 정부에 의해 국제적으로 중요한 습지로 지정되었고, 이에 접한 Refugis de Vida Silvestre Rio San Juan 지역은 2001년 니카라과 정부에 의해 국제적으로 중요한 습지로 지정되었다.

니카라과와 코스타리카 양국은 1858년 국경조약을 체결했다. 동 조약에 따르면 양국간 국경은 산 후안강의 코스타리카 쪽 제방을 따라 Punta del Castilla 끝지점까지 이어지며, 산 후안강의 영유권은 니카라과가 갖지만, 코스타리카는 상업목적의 자유항행권이 부여되었다. 국경조약체결 이후에도 니카라과가 조약의 정당성에 이의를 제기하여 양국은 1886년 미국 클리블랜드 대통령에게 조약의 정당성에 대한 중재를 부탁했다. 1888년 클리블랜드 대통령은 국경조약의 정당성을 인정하고 양국간 국경선은 산 후안강의 Punta del Castilla의 끝지점에서 시작된다고 판정했다.

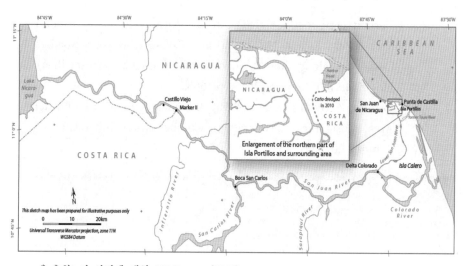

* 출처: 이 사건에 대한 ICJ Report (2015) p. 31.

　　2010년 10월 니카라과는 산 후안강에서 수로 준설작업을 시작하면서 분쟁지역인 Isla Portillos에서도 이 작업을 시작했다. 이에 대해 코스타리카는 니카라과가 인위적으로 Isla Portillos에 있는 코스타리카 영토에 수로를 건설한다고 주장했고, 반면 니카라과는 니카라과 영토에 있는 기존 수로를 준설한 것에 불과하다고 주장하면서 이 지역에 군대와 인력을 파견했다. 2010년 11월 18일 코스타리카는 니카라과의 행위가 국제법 위반이라고 주장하며 ICJ에 제소했다.

　　한편 코스타리카는 니카라과의 분쟁지역에서의 활동에 대응하여 2010년 12월 니카라과와의 국경을 따라 하안도로를 건설했는데 이 도로 중 일부는 산 후안강을 따라 건설되었다. 2011년 2월 코스타리카는 국경지역에서 비상사태를 선언하는 행정명령을 발하고 도로건설 전 시행해야 하는 환경영향평가의무를 면제했다. 2011년 12월 니카라과는 코스타리카의 도로건설이 중

대한 초국경적 피해를 야기하며, 공사 전 환경영향평가 시행결과를 자국에 통보하지 않은 행위는 국제법 위반이라고 주장하며 코스타리카를 ICJ에 역시 제소했다. ICJ는 2013년 4월 양국이 제기한 두 사건을 병합심리하기로 결정했다.

☑ 쟁   점

(1) 니카라과의 산 후안강 준설공사가 국제환경법상 의무 ─ 환경영향평가를 수행할 절차적 의무 및 실체적 의무 ─ 를 위반했는지 여부 및 손해배상.

(2) 코스타리카의 산 후안 강변 도로건설이 국제환경법상 의무 ─ 환경영향평가를 수행할 절차적 의무 및 실체적 의무 ─ 를 위반했는지 여부 및 손해배상.

(3) 환경피해에 대한 구체적인 손해배상 산정 방법 및 손해배상액.

☑ 판   결

(1) 니카라과는 중대한 초국경적 피해(transboundary harm)를 야기하지 않았기에, 국제법상 환경영향평가를 시행해야 할 절차상 의무나 실체적 의무를 위반하지 않았다. 그러나 니카라과의 활동은 코스타리카의 영토 내에서 이루어져 코스타리카의 영토주권을 침해했고, 이로 인한 환경 피해 등의 손해를 배상할 의무가 있다.

(2) 코스타리카는 중대한 초국경적 피해를 야기하여 환경영향평가를 시행해야 할 국제법상 의무를 부담함에도 불구하고 이를 시행하지 않아 이에 대한 절차적 의무를 위반했다. 코스타리카의 행위가 국제법상 의무 위반이라고 선언한 ICJ 판결이 이에 대한 '만족'에 해당한다.

(3) 환경피해에 대한 손해배상의 판단도 국제위법행위에 대한 국제법상 일반규칙에 따르며, 전반적인 평가 방식에 따라 구체적인 손해를 산정한다.

판 결 문

A. ICJ 2015년 판결 (국제법 위반 여부)

III. Issues in the *Costa Rica v. Nicaragua* Case

100. The Court will now turn to Costa Rica's allegations concerning violations by Nicaragua of its obligations under international environmental law in connection with its dredging activities to improve the navigability of the Lower San Juan River. [⋯]

104. As the Court has had occasion to emphasize in its Judgment in the case concerning *Pulp Mills on the River Uruguay (Argentina v. Uruguay)*:

"the principle of prevention, as a customary rule, has its origins in the due diligence that is required of a State in its territory. It is 'every State's obligation not to allow knowingly its territory to be used for acts contrary to the rights of other States' (*Corfu Channel (United Kingdom v. Albania), Merits, Judgment, I.C.J. Reports 1949,* p. 22). A State is thus obliged to use all the means at its disposal in order to avoid activities which take place in its territory, or in any area under its jurisdiction, causing significant damage to the environment of another State." (*Judgment, I.C.J. Reports 2010 (I),* pp. 55-56, para. 101.)

Furthermore, the Court concluded in that case that "it may now be considered a requirement under general international law to undertake an environmental impact assessment where there is a risk that the proposed industrial activity may have a significant adverse impact in a transboundary context, in particular, on a shared resource" (*ibid.,* p. 83, para. 204). Although the Court's statement in the *Pulp Mills* case refers to industrial activities, the underlying principle applies generally to proposed activities which may have a significant adverse impact in a transboundary context. Thus, to fulfil its obligation to exercise due diligence in preventing significant transboundary environmental harm, a State must, before embarking on an activity having the potential adversely to affect the environment of another State, ascertain if there is a risk of significant transboundary harm, which would trigger the requirement to carry out an environmental impact assessment.

Determination of the content of the environmental impact assessment should be made in light of the specific circumstances of each case. As the Court held in the *Pulp Mills* case:

"it is for each State to determine in its domestic legislation or in the authorization process for the project, the specific content of the environmental impact assessment required in each case, having regard to the nature and magnitude of the proposed development and its likely adverse impact on the environment as well as to the need to exercise due diligence in conducting such an assessment" (*I.C.J. Reports 2010 (I)*, p. 83, para. 205).

If the environmental impact assessment confirms that there is a risk of significant transboundary harm, the State planning to undertake the activity is required, in conformity with its due diligence obligation, to notify and consult in good faith with the potentially affected State, where that is necessary to determine the appropriate measures to prevent or mitigate that risk.

105. [⋯] Having examined the evidence in the case file, including the reports submitted and testimony given by experts called by both Parties, the Court finds that the dredging programme planned in 2006 was not such as to give rise to a risk of significant transboundary harm, either with respect to the flow of the Colorado River or to Costa Rica's wetland. In light of the absence of risk of significant transboundary harm, Nicaragua was not required to carry out an environmental impact assessment.

112. In light of the above, the Court concludes that it has not been established that Nicaragua breached any procedural obligations owed to Costa Rica under treaties or the customary international law of the environment. The Court takes note of Nicaragua's commitment, made in the course of the oral proceedings, to carry out a new Environmental Impact Study before any substantial expansion of its current dredging programme. The Court further notes that Nicaragua stated that such a study would include an assessment of the risk of transboundary harm, and that it would notify, and consult with, Costa Rica as part of that process.

113. [⋯] What remains to be examined is whether Nicaragua is responsible for any transboundary harm allegedly caused by its dredging activities which have taken place in areas under Nicaragua's territorial sovereignty, in the Lower San Juan River and on its left bank.

120. The Court therefore concludes that the available evidence does not show that Nicaragua breached its obligations by engaging in dredging activities in the Lower San Juan River.

139. The declaration by the Court that Nicaragua breached the territorial sovereignty of Costa Rica by excavating three caños and establishing a military presence in the disputed territory provides adequate satisfaction for the non-material injury suffered on this account. The same applies to the declaration of the breach of the obligations under the Court's Order of 8 March 2011 on provisional measures. Finally, the declaration of the breach of Costa Rica's rights of navigation in the terms determined above in Section D provides adequate satisfaction for that breach.

142. Costa Rica is entitled to receive compensation for the material damage caused by those breaches of obligations by Nicaragua that have been ascertained by the Court. The relevant material damage and the amount of compensation may be assessed by the Court only in separate proceedings. The Court is of the opinion that the Parties should engage in negotiation in order to reach an agreement on these issues. However, if they fail to reach such an agreement within 12 months of the date of the present Judgment, the Court will, at the request of either Party, determine the amount of compensation on the basis of further written pleadings limited to this issue.

IV. Issues in the Nicaragua v. Costa Rica Case

152. […] the Court will first examine whether Costa Rica was under an obligation to carry out an environmental impact assessment under general international law. If so, the Court will assess whether it was exempted from the said obligation or whether it complied with that obligation by carrying out the Environmental Diagnostic Assessment and other studies.

153. The Court recalls […] that a State's obligation to exercise due diligence in preventing significant transboundary harm requires that State to ascertain whether there is a risk of significant transboundary harm prior to undertaking an activity having the potential adversely to affect the environment of another State. If that is the case, the State concerned must conduct an environmental impact assessment. The obligation in question rests on the State pursuing the activity. Accordingly, in the present case, it fell on Costa Rica, not on Nicaragua, to assess the existence of a risk of significant transboundary harm prior to the construction of the road, on the basis of an objective evaluation of all the relevant circumstances.

154. In the oral proceedings, counsel for Costa Rica stated that a preliminary assessment of the risk posed by the road project was undertaken when the decision to build the road was made. […] The Court observes that to conduct a preliminary assessment of the risk posed by an activity is one of the ways in which a State can ascertain whether the proposed activity carries a risk of significant transboundary harm. However, Costa Rica has not adduced any evidence that it actually carried out such a preliminary assessment.

155. In evaluating whether, as of the end of 2010, the construction of the road posed a risk of significant transboundary harm, the Court will have regard to the nature and magnitude of the project and the context in which it was to be carried out. First, the Court notes that [···] the scale of the road project was substantial. [···] Secondly, the Court notes that, because of the planned location of the road along the San Juan River, any harm caused by the road to the surrounding environment could easily affect the river, and therefore Nicaragua's territory. [···] Thirdly, the geographic conditions of the river basin where the road was to be situated must be taken into account. [···]

156. In conclusion, the Court finds that the construction of the road by Costa Rica carried a risk of significant transboundary harm. Therefore, the threshold for triggering the obligation to evaluate the environmental impact of the road project was met.

157. The Court now turns to the question of whether Costa Rica was exempted from its obligation to evaluate the environmental impact of the road project because of an emergency. First, the Court recalls its holding that "it is for each State to determine in its domestic legislation or in the authorization process for the project, the specific content of the environmental impact assessment required in each case", having regard to various factors (see paragraph 104 above, quoting *Pulp Mills on the River Uruguay (Argentina v. Uruguay), Judgment, I.C.J. Reports 2010 (I)*, p. 83, para. 205). The Court observes that this reference to domestic law does not relate to the question of whether an environmental impact assessment should be undertaken. Thus, the fact that there may be an emergency exemption under Costa Rican law does not affect Costa Rica's obligation under international law to carry out an environmental impact assessment.

158. Secondly, independently of the question whether or not an emergency could exempt a State from its obligation under international law to carry out an environmental impact assessment, or defer the execution of this obligation until the emergency has ceased, the Court considers that, in the circumstances of this case, Costa Rica has not shown the existence of an emergency that justified constructing the road without undertaking an environmental impact assessment. [···]

159. Having thus concluded that, in the circumstances of this case, there was no emergency justifying the immediate construction of the road, the Court does not need to decide whether there is an emergency exemption from the obligation to carry out an environmental impact assessment in cases where there is a risk of significant transboundary harm. It follows that Costa Rica was under an obligation to conduct an environmental impact assessment prior to commencement of the construction works.

160. Turning now to the question of whether Costa Rica complied with its obligation to carry out an environmental impact assessment, the Court notes that Costa Rica produced several studies, including an Environmental Management Plan for the road in April 2012, an Environmental Diagnostic Assessment in November 2013, and a follow-up study thereto in January 2015. These studies assessed the adverse effects that had already been caused by the construction of the road on the environment and suggested steps to prevent or reduce them.

161. In its Judgment in the *Pulp Mills* case, the Court held that the obligation to carry out an environmental impact assessment is a continuous one, and that monitoring of the project's effects on the environment shall be undertaken, where necessary, throughout the life of the project (*I.C.J. Reports 2010 (I)*, pp. 83-84, para. 205). Nevertheless, the obligation to conduct an environmental impact assessment requires an *ex ante* evaluation of the risk of significant transboundary harm, and thus "an environmental impact assessment must be conducted prior to the implementation of a project" (*ibid.*, p. 83, para. 205). In the present case, Costa Rica was under an obligation to carry out such an assessment prior to commencing the construction of the road, to ensure that the design and execution of the project would minimize the risk of significant transboundary harm. In contrast, Costa Rica's Environmental Diagnostic Assessment and its other studies were post hoc assessments of the environmental impact of the stretches of the road that had already been built. These studies did not evaluate the risk of future harm. The Court notes moreover that the Environmental Diagnostic Assessment was carried out approximately three years into the road's construction.

162. For the foregoing reasons, the Court concludes that Costa Rica has not complied with its obligation under general international law to carry out an environmental impact assessment concerning the construction of the road.

173. In conclusion, the Court finds that Costa Rica failed to comply with its obligation to evaluate the environmental impact of the construction of the road. Costa Rica remains under an obligation to prepare an appropriate environmental

impact assessment for any further works on the road or in the area adjoining the San Juan River, should they carry a risk of significant transboundary harm. Costa Rica accepts that it is under such an obligation. There is no reason to suppose that it will not take note of the reasoning and conclusions in this Judgment as it conducts any future development in the area, including further construction works on the road. The Court also notes Nicaragua's commitment, made in the course of the oral proceedings, that it will cooperate with Costa Rica in assessing the impact of such works on the river. In this connection, the Court considers that, if the circumstances so require, Costa Rica will have to consult in good faith with Nicaragua, which is sovereign over the San Juan River, to determine the appropriate measures to prevent significant transboundary harm or minimize the risk thereof.

174. The Court now turns to the examination of the alleged violations by Costa Rica of its substantive obligations under customary international law and the applicable international conventions. In particular, Nicaragua claims that the construction of the road caused damage to the San Juan River, which is under Nicaragua's sovereignty according to the 1858 Treaty. [⋯]

217. [⋯] the Court concludes that Nicaragua has not proved that the construction of the road caused it significant transboundary harm. Therefore, Nicaragua's claim that Costa Rica breached its substantive obligations under customary international law concerning transboundary harm must be dismissed.

224. [⋯] the Court's declaration that Costa Rica violated its obligation to conduct an environmental impact assessment is the appropriate measure of satisfaction for Nicaragua.

228. To conclude, the Court notes that Costa Rica has begun mitigation works in order to reduce the adverse effects of the construction of the road on the environment. It expects that Costa Rica will continue to pursue these efforts in keeping with its due diligence obligation to monitor the effects of the project on the environment. It further reiterates the value of ongoing cooperation between the Parties in the performance of their respective obligations in connection with the San Juan River.

B. ICJ 2018년 판결 (손해배상)

41. The Court has not previously adjudicated a claim for compensation for environmental damage. However, it is consistent with the principles of international law governing the consequences of internationally wrongful acts, including the principle of full reparation, to hold that compensation is due for damage caused to the environment, in and of itself, in addition to expenses incurred by an injured state as a consequence of such damage.

42. The Court is therefore of the view that damage to the environment, and the consequent impairment or loss of the ability of the environment to provide goods and services, is compensable under international law. Such compensation may include indemnification for the impairment or loss of environmental goods and services in the period prior to recovery and payment for the restoration of the damaged environment.

43. Payment for restoration accounts for the fact that natural recovery may not always suffice to return an environment to the state in which it was before the damage occurred. In such instances, active restoration measures may be required in order to return the environment to its prior condition, in so far as that is possible.

52. The Court notes that the valuation methods proposed by the Parties are sometimes used for environmental damage valuation in the practice of national and international bodies, and are not therefore devoid of relevance to the task at hand. However, they are not the only methods used by such bodies for that purpose, nor is their use limited to valuation of damage since they may also be used to carry out cost/benefit analysis of environmental projects and programmes for the purpose of public policy setting (see for example UNEP, "Guidance Manual on Valuation and Accounting of Ecosystem Services for Small Island Developing States" (2014), p. 4). The Court will not therefore choose between them or use either of them exclusively for the purpose of valuation of the damage caused to the protected wetland in Costa Rica. Wherever certain elements of either method offer a reasonable basis for valuation, the Court will nonetheless take them into account. This approach is dictated by two factors: first, international law does not prescribe any specific method of valuation for the purposes of compensation for environmental damage; secondly, it is necessary, in the view of the Court, to take into account the specific circumstances and characteristics of each case.

53. [⋯] In determining the compensation due for environmental damage, the Court will assess, as outlined in paragraph 42, the value to be assigned to the restoration of the damaged environment as well as to the impairment or loss of environmental goods and services prior to recovery.

72. Before assigning a monetary value to the damage to the environmental goods and services caused by Nicaragua's wrongful activities, the Court will

determine the existence and extent of such damage, and whether there exists a direct and certain causal link between such damage and Nicaragua's activities. It will then establish the compensation due.

78. The Court considers [⋯] that it is appropriate to approach the valuation of environmental damage from the perspective of the ecosystem as a whole, by adopting an overall assessment of the impairment or loss of environmental goods and services prior to recovery, rather than attributing values to specific categories of environmental goods and services and estimating recovery periods for each of them.

86. The Court recalls [⋯] that the absence of certainty as to the extent of damage does not necessarily preclude it from awarding an amount that it considers approximately to reflect the value of the impairment or loss of environmental goods and services. In this case, the Court, while retaining some of the elements of the "corrected analysis", considers it reasonable that, for the purposes of its overall valuation, an adjustment be made to the total amount in the "corrected analysis" to account for the shortcomings identified in the preceding paragraph. The Court therefore awards to Costa Rica the sum of US$120,000 for the impairment or loss of the environmental goods and services of the impacted area in the period prior to recovery.

156. The total amount of compensation awarded to Costa Rica is US$378,890.59 to be paid by Nicaragua by 2 April 2018. This amount includes the principal sum of US$358,740.55 and pre-judgment interest on the compensable costs and expenses in the amount of US$20,150.04. Should payment be delayed, post-judgment interest on the total amount will accrue as from 3 April 2018.

☑ 해   설

우선 2015년 ICJ 판결에서 핵심 쟁점은 상대국이 '환경영향평가'를 시행할 국제환경법상 절차적 의무를 위반했는지 여부이다. 원래 국내법상 도입된 환경영향평가는 이제 국제법상 의무로 발전하였으며, 2010년 아르헨티나와 우루과이 간 분쟁인 ICJ의 *Pulp Mills* 판결[1] 등 국제판례는 환경영향평가가 관습국제법상 의무가 되었음을 인정한 바 있다. 이 2015년 판결은 국제환경법상 발전한 환경영향평가의 의의 및 내용을 상세히 판단한 점에서 국제법상 중요한 의의를 가진다.

---

1) Case Concerning Pulp Mills on the River Uruguay(Argentina v. Uruguay), Judgement ICJ Reports 2010, p. 14.

우선 니카라과의 공사와 관련하여, ICJ는 중대한 초국경적 피해를 야기할 위험이 있는 경우 한 국가 내에서 수행될 활동에 관한 환경영향평가를 수행할 국제법상 의무가 있음을 인급하며, 환경영향평가를 시행할 의무 범위에 산업활동만 언급한 *Pulp Mills* 판결을 확장하여 중대한 초국경적 악영향을 미칠 수 있는 활동에 일반적으로 적용된다고 판시했다. 또한 ICJ는 환경영향평가 의무의 내용에 통지 및 협의 의무가 포함된다는 점도 밝혔다. 그러나 ICJ는 본 사건에서 니카라과의 공사가 중대한 초국경적 피해의 위험이 없기에 니카라과는 환경영향평가를 수행할 국제법상 의무가 없다고 결론을 내렸다. 또한 코스타리카가 니카라과의 국제법상 의무 위반을 입증하지 못했다고 판단하여, 결론적으로 니카라과는 국제환경법상 의무를 위반한 것은 아니라고 판시했다.

이외에도 ICJ는 니카라과의 활동은 코스타리카의 영토주권에 대한 침해이기에 니카라과는 코스타리카에 대한 배상의무가 있다고 판시하며, 유형적 손해(material damage)와 비유형적 손해(non-material damage)를 구별하여 배상방식을 판단했다. 즉 ICJ는 코스타리카가 입은 비유형적 손해는 ICJ 판결을 통해 '만족'이라는 방식으로 배상이 되었으나, 유형적 손해는 별도 배상이 필요하다고 판시했다. 하지만 ICJ는 구체적인 유형적 손해 및 보상 정도 등에 대해서는 우선 양국간 합의에 의하고, 합의가 되지 않을 경우 추후 ICJ 제소를 통해 ICJ에서 별도로 판단한다고 판시했다. 이에 따라 이후 2018년도 ICJ 판결이 이루어졌다.

다음으로 코스타리카의 건설 관련 쟁점에서 ICJ는 더욱 상세히 환경영향평가를 다루었다. ICJ는 환경영향평가 의무를 부담하는 중요한 기준은 '중대한' 초국경적 피해를 야기할 위험이 있는지 여부인데, ICJ는 코스타리카의 도로건설은 중대한 초국경적 피해를 야기하여 도로사업에 대한 환경영향평가를 시행해야 할 기준에 합치된다고 결론을 내렸다. 이에 대해 코스타리카는 비상사태의 경우 환경영향평가 의무에서 면제된다고 항변했다. ICJ는 코스타리카의 국내법에 근거하여 비상사태시 환경영향평가 의무를 면제할 수 있다는 사실이 국제법상 요구되는 환경영향평가 수행 의무에 영향을 미치지 않는다고 판단하며, 도로건설 개시 이전에 환경영향평가를 실시할 의무가 있었다고 결론을 내렸다.

ICJ는 코스타리카의 환경영향평가 의무는 사업 시행 전에 이행되어야 한다고 판시했다. 따라서 코스타리카는 건설 개시 전에 환경영향평가를 실시 할 의무가 있었으나 건설 이후 사후적으로 평가를 한 점을 지적하며, 코스타리카가 국제법상 환경영향평가 의무를 준수하지 않았다고 판단했다. 이 외의 국제환경법상 실체적 의무 위반 문제는 입증 부족으로 모두 기각되었다. 손해배상과 관련하여, 환경영향평가에 대한 절차적 의무 위반에 대해서는 ICJ 판결이 손해배상 방식 중 하나인 '만족'이라고 판시하며, 별도의 배상의무는 부과하지 않았다.

2015년 ICJ 판결 이후에도 양국간 손해배상 관련 합의가 이루어지지 않자 코스타리카는 2017년 1월 16일 니카라과의 위법활동에 의해 야기된 환경 피해에 대한 코스타리카의 손해를 해결하고자 ICJ에 니카라과를 다시 제소했다. ICJ는 2018년 2월 2일 판결을 내렸고 이 판결은 초국경적 환경피해로 인해 야기된 손해 배상에 대한 ICJ의 최초 판결이다. 이 사건에서 ICJ는 환경 피해로 인한 배상청구도 국제위법행위를 규율하는 국제법상 기본원칙에 따라 판단함을 확인하고, 환경 피해의 평가와 관련해서 국제법상 정해진 특정한 방법이 없으므로 재판부는 합리적인 방법을 선택 할 수 있다고 설명했다. 손해배상 산정과 관련하여 ICJ는 우선 환경 피해의 존재 및 범위 그리고 환경 피해와 니카라과의 위법활동 간에 직접적이며 확실한 인과관계가 있는지 여부부터 결정한 후 니카라과의 배상액을 확정했다.

여기서 주목할 점은 ICJ가 환경피해 평가시 생태계를 하나로 보는 '전반적 평가방식'을 채택한 점인데, 이는 환경피해를 세부 항목으로 나누고 각 항목별로 평가하는 것과 대조되는 방식이다. 이를 기초로 ICJ는 니카라과의 각 활동이 생태계 전체에 미치는 영향을 전반적으로 평가했다. ICJ는 니카라과의 위법행위를 3가지로 나누고 각 행위별로 코스타리카의 환경에 발생한 손해배상액을 산정하여, 총 보상액을 38만불로 책정했으며, 니카라과는 이 금액을 2018년 4월 2일까지 지불해야 하며, 그렇지 못할 경우 4월 3일부터 연 6%의 이자를 부과한다고 판시했다.

니카라과는 ICJ 판결 이후인 2018년 3월 8일 코스타리카에 판결에서 확정된 금액 및 이자를 모두 지급했으며, 이를 2018년 3월 22일 ICJ 사무국에도 통보했다. 이로써 니카라과는 코스타리카에 대한 손해배상 의무를 모두 이행했다.

상기 일련의 판결은 국제환경법상 주요 쟁점을 전반적으로 다루며 기존 국제환경법상 원칙을 재확인하고 구체화하는 데 일조했다. 특히 최근 중국으로부터 미세먼지 유입 등 우리 주변에서 초국경적 환경피해가 증가하며 이에 대한 국제법상 책임 문제에 대한 관심이 제고되는 상황에서 이러한 국제환경법의 발전과 구체화는 우리에게도 중요한 의미가 있다고 할 수 있다.

➡ 참고문헌 ─────────────────────────────

- 이기범, 국제법상 초국경적 환경영향평가에 관한 소고: 최근 국제재판소 판례 분석을 통한 미해결 쟁점 관련 논의를 중심으로, 국제법학회논총 제64권 제1호 (2019), p. 181.
- 이재곤, 국경지역에서의 니카라과의 활동사건과 코스타리카의 산후안강 하안 도로건설 사건의 국제환경법 쟁점, 법학연구 전북대학교 법학연구소 제52권 (2017), p. 107.
- 정진석, San Juan River 인근에서의 특정 활동과 공사에 관한 사건(코스타리카/ 니카라과, 2015), 법학논총, 국민대학교 법학연구소, 제30권 제3호(2018), p. 461.
- C. Voigt, International Judicial Practice on the Environment: Questions of Legitimacy, Cambridge University Press(2019).
- J. Harrison, Significant International Environmental Law Cases: 2018－2018, Journal of Environmental Law, Vol. 30(2018), p. 527.
- J. Rudall, Certain Activities Carried Out by Nicaragua in the Border Area (Costa Rica v. Nicaragua), American Journal of International Law Vol. 112(2018), p. 288.
- J. Rudall, Compensation for Environmental Damage under International Law, Routledge(2020).
- M. D. Silva, Compensation Awards in International Environmental Law: Two Recent Developments, New York University Journal of International Law and Politics Vol. 50(2018), p. 1417.

제14장

국적과 국민 · 해외동포

1. 튀니지와 모로코에서의 프랑스 국적령 사건(1923)
― 국적문제의 성격

Nationality Decrees in Tunis and Morocco Case.
Advisory Opinion, PCIJ Reports Series B No. 4, 6(1923).

☑ 사　안

프랑스는 1921년 11월 보호령인 튀니지와 모로코에서의 새로운 국적령을 공포했다. 이에 따르면 튀니지나 모로코에서 출생한 자로 부모 중 일방이 튀니지나 모로코에서 태어났던 경우에는 프랑스 국적이 부여되었다. 프랑스 국적자에게는 병역의무가 부과되므로 영국 정부는 이 법으로 인하여 자국민에게도 프랑스 국적과 병역이 부과될 수 있다고 항의했다. 이를 중재재판에 회부하자는 영국의 제의에 프랑스가 응하지 않자, 영국은 이 문제를 국제연맹 이사회로 제기했다. 이사회에서 프랑스는 이 문제가 연맹규약 제15조 8항상의 "국내문제"이므로 연맹이 다룰 수 없다고 항변했다. 연맹 이사회는 이 분쟁이 국제법상 "전적으로 국내관할사항"에 속하느냐 여부에 관해 PCIJ에 권고적 의견을 요청했다.

☑ 쟁　점
(1) 국제법상 국내관할사항의 의미.
(2) 국적문제가 국내관할사항에 해당하는가 여부.

☑ 판　결
(1) 국내관할사항이란 국제법에 의해 규율되지 않고 개별국가가 독자적으로 판단할 수 있는 사항이지만, 어떤 문제가 국내관할사항인가 여부는 상

대적인 문제로서 이는 국제관계의 발전에 따라 가변적이다.

(2) 국적문제는 원칙적으로 국제법의 규제를 받지 않는 분야이다. 단 국가의 재량권 행사도 타국에 대한 의무에 의해 제한받게 되며, 그 경우 국가의 국내관할사항 역시 국제법에 의해 제한된다. 이 사건에서는 보호국이 보호령에서 행사할 수 있는 권한범위가 국제법적 관점에서 검토되어야 하며, 튀니지나 모로코에 관련된 조약의 국제법적 의미가 분석되어야 하므로 프랑스 국적령의 적용문제는 국내관할사항에 속하지 않는다.

판 결 문

(p. 23-) The paragraph to which sub-section (a) of the Council's resolution expressly refers is as follows:

(English text).

"If the dispute between the parties is claimed by one of them, and is found by the Council, to arise out of a matter which by international law is solely within the domestic jurisdiction of that party, the Council shall so report, and shall make no recommendation as to its settlement." [⋯]

Special attention, must be called to the word "*exclusive*" in the French text, to which the word "solely" (within the domestic jurisdiction) corresponds in the English text. The question to be considered is not whether one of the parties to the dispute is or is not competent in law to take or to refrain from taking a particular action, but whether the jurisdiction claimed belongs *solely* to that party.

From one point of view, it might well be said that the jurisdiction of a State is *exclusive* within the limits fixed by international law—using this expression in its wider sense, that is to say, embracing both customary law and general as well as particular treaty law. But a careful scrutiny of paragraph 8 of Article 15 shows that it is not in this sense that exclusive jurisdiction is referred to in that paragraph.

The words "solely within the domestic jurisdiction" seem rather to contemplate certain matters which, though they may very closely concern the interests of more than one State, are not, in principle, regulated by international law. As regards such matters, each State is sole judge.

The question whether a certain matter is or is not solely within the jurisdiction of a State is an essentially relative question; it depends upon the development of international relations. Thus, in the present state of international law, questions of nationality are, in the opinion of the Court, in principle within this reserved domain.

For the purpose of the present opinion, it is enough to observe that it may well happen that, in a matter which, like that of nationality, is not, in principle, regulated by international law, the right of a State to use its discretion is nevertheless restricted by obligations which it may have undertaken towards other States. In such a case, jurisdiction which, in principle, belongs solely to the State, is limited by rules of international law. Article 15, paragraph 8, then ceases to apply as regards those States which are entitled to invoke such rules, and the dispute as to the question whether a State has or has not the right to take certain measures becomes in these circumstances a dispute of an international character and falls outside the scope of the exception contained in this paragraph. To hold that a State has not exclusive jurisdiction does not in any way prejudice the final decision as to whether that State has a right to adopt such measures. [···]

It is certain—and this has been recognised by the Council in the case of the Aaland Islands—that the mere fact that a State brings a dispute before the League of Nations does not suffice to give this dispute an international character calculated to except it from the application of paragraph 8 of Article 15.

It is equally true that the mere fact that one of the parties appeals to engagements of an international character in order to contest the exclusive jurisdiction of the other is not enough to render paragraph 8 inapplicable. But when once it appears that the legal grounds (*titres*) relied on are such as to justify the provisional conclusion that they are of juridical importance for the dispute submitted to the Council, and that the question whether it is competent for one State to take certain measures is subordinated to the formation of an opinion with regard to the validity and construction of these legal grounds (*titres*), the provisions contained in paragraph 8 of Article 15 cease to apply and the matter, ceasing to be one solely within the domestic jurisdiction of the State, enters the domain governed by international law.

☑ 해 설

이 판결에서 PCIJ가 제시한 국내관할사항에 관한 판단기준과 해석은 기본적으로 오늘날까지도 유효하다고 평가된다. 다만 국제연맹 규약 제15조는 "solely" 국내관할사항에 관한 개입 불가를 규정하고 있었던 데 비하여, 유엔 헌장 제2조 7항은 "essentially" 국내관할사항에 관한 개입을 금하고 있다.

이 사건은 권고적 의견이 국가간 분쟁을 해결할 대체수단이 될 수 있음을 보여준 좋은 사례였다. 이 결정 이후 영국과 프랑스는 1921년 11월 이건 튀니지에서 출생한 영국계 주민에게는 프랑스 국적을 강제하지 않기로 하는 양자조약을 체결했다. 다만 모로코에 관하여는 당시 국적문제가 현실적으로 제기되지 않았기 때문에 더 이상의 논란은 일어나지 않았다. 프랑스는 조약 체결 이후 1923년 국적령을 개정했다.

과거 국적은 가장 대표적인 국내관할사항으로 이해되었다. 오늘날에도 국적부여의 기본원칙을 혈통주의에 입각할 것이냐, 출생지주의에 입각할 것이냐는 각국의 재량사항으로 평가된다. 그러나 국제인권법의 발달에 따라 국적문제에 관한 국가의 재량권은 상당히 축소되고 있다. 대표적인 사례로「세계인권선언」제15조는 국적을 개인의 권리의 일종으로 규정하고, 자의적 국적박탈을 금지하고 있다. 오늘날 다른 국적의 취득을 전제로 하지 않는 한 국가에 의한 일방적 국적박탈은 국제법 위반으로 판단된다.

➡️ 참고문헌 ─────────────────────────

• C. N. Gregory, An Important Decision by the Permanent Court of International Justice, AJIL Vol. 17(1923), p. 298.

2. 노테봄 사건(1955)
― 귀화와 진정한 유대

Nottebohm Case.
Liechtenstein v. Guatemala, 1955 ICJ Reports 4.

☑ 사　　안

Nottebohm은 1881년 함부르크에서 출생한 독일인이나 1905년 과테말라로 이주한 이래 그 곳을 생활 근거지로 삼았다. 그는 제2차 대전 발발 직후인 1939년 10월 리히텐슈타인을 방문하고 귀화신청을 하여 4일만에 리히텐슈타인 국적을 취득했다. 그 이전 Nottebohm과 리히텐슈타인간의 관계는 형제 상봉을 위해 몇 차례 방문했던 사실이 전부였다. 그는 1940년 초 리히텐슈타인 여권으로 과테말라로 돌아와 외국인등록상의 국적도 리히텐슈타인으로 바꾸었다. 1941년 과테말라는 연합국의 일원으로 대독 선전포고를 했다. 1943년 10월 과테말라 정부는 미국 정부의 요청에 따라 Nottebohm을 적국인으로 체포했다. 이후 그는 미국으로 이송되어 2년 3개월 동안 억류생활을 했다. 석방 후 Nottebohm은 과테말라로 돌아가려 했으나 입국허가를 받지 못했고, 과테말라 정부는 1949년 자국내 그의 재산을 몰수했다. 1951년 12월 리히텐슈타인은 과테말라를 상대로 자국민인 Nottebohm의 재산을 반환하고 손해배상을 요구하는 소를 ICJ에 제기했다.

☑ 쟁　　점

진정한 유대가 결여된 귀화의 효력을 제3국에게 주장할 수 있는가 여부.

☑ 판 결

과테말라는 진정한 유대가 설비된 비히텐슈디인의 국적 부여를 바탕으로 한 외교적 보호권의 행사를 인정할 의무가 없다.

판 결 문

(p. 21-) The naturalization of Nottebohm was an act performed by Liechtenstein in the exercise of its domestic jurisdiction. The question to be decided is whether that act has the international effect here under consideration. [⋯]

International arbitrators have decided in the same way numerous cases of dual nationality, where the question arose with regard to the exercise of protection. They have given their preference to the real and effective nationality, that which accorded with the facts, that based on stronger factual ties between the person concerned and one of the States whose nationality is involved. Different factors are taken into consideration, and their importance will vary from one case to the next: the habitual residence of the individual concerned is an important factor, but there are other factors such as the centre of his interests, his family ties, his participation in public life, attachment shown by him for a given country and inculcated in his children, etc. [⋯]

The practice of certain States which refrain from exercising protection in favour of a naturalized person when the latter has in fact, by his prolonged absence, severed his links with what is no longer for him anything but his nominal country, manifests the view of these States that, in order to be capable of being invoked against another State, nationality must correspond with the factual situation. [⋯]

The character thus recognized on the international level as pertaining to nationality is in no way inconsistent with the fact that international law leaves it to each State to lay down the rules governing the grant of its own nationality. The reason for this is that the diversity of demographic conditions has thus far made it impossible for any general agreement to be reached on the rules relating to nationality, although the latter by its very nature affects international relations. It has been considered that the best way of making such rules accord with the varying demographic conditions in different countries is to leave the fixing of such rules to the competence of each State. On the other hand, a State cannot claim that the rules it has thus laid down are entitled to recognition by another State unless it has acted in conformity with this general aim of making the legal bond of nationality accord with the individual's genuine connection with the State which assumes the defence of its citizens by means of protection as against other States. [···]

According to the practice of States, to arbitral and judicial decisions and to the opinions of writers, nationality is a legal bond having as its basis a social fact of attachment, a genuine connection of existence, interests and sentiments, together with the existence of reciprocal rights and duties. It may be said to constitute the juridical expression of the fact that the individual upon whom it is conferred, either directly by the law or as the result of an act of the authorities, is in fact more closely connected with the population of the State conferring nationality than with that of any other State. Conferred by a State, it only entitles that State to exercise protection vis-a-vis another State, if it constitutes a translation into juridical terms of the individual's connection with the State which has made him its national. [···]

Since this is the character which nationality must present when it is invoked to furnish the State which has granted it with a title to the exercise of protection and to the institution of international judicial proceedings, the Court must ascertain whether the nationality granted to Nottebohm by means of naturalization is of this character or, in other words, whether the factual connection between Nottebohm and Liechtenstein in the period preceding, contemporaneous with and following his naturalization appears to be sufficiently close, so preponderant in relation to any connection which may have existed between him and any other State, that it is possible to regard the nationality conferred upon him as real and effective, as the exact juridical expression of a social fact of a connection which existed previously or came into existence thereafter.

Naturalization is not a matter to be taken lightly. To seek and to obtain it is not something that happens frequently in the life of a human being. It involves his breaking of a bond of allegiance and his establishment of a new bond of allegiance. It may have far reaching consequences and involve profound changes in the destiny of the individual who obtains it. It concerns him personally, and to consider it only from the point of view of its repercussions with regard to his property would be to misunderstand its profound significance. In order to appraise its international effect, it is impossible to disregard the circumstances in which it was conferred, the serious character which attaches to it, the real and effective, and not merely the verbal preference of the individual seeking it for the country which grants it to him. [···][1]

---

1) 이어서 재판부는 Nottebohm이 과테말라와는 장기간에 걸쳐 수많은 이해관계를 구축한 반

These facts clearly establish, on the one hand, the absence of any bond of attachment between Nottebohm and Liechtenstein and, on the other hand, the existence of a long-standing and close connection between him and Guatemala, a link which his naturalization in no way weakened. That naturalization was not based on any real prior connection with Liechtenstein, nor did it in any way alter the manner of life of the person upon whom it was conferred in exceptional circumstances of speed and accommodation. In both respects, it was lacking in the genuineness requisite to an act of such importance, if it is to be entitled to be respected by a State in the position of Guatemala. It was granted without regard to the concept of nationality adopted in international relations.

Naturalization was asked for not so much for the purpose of obtaining a legal recognition of Nottebohm's membership in fact in the population of Liechtenstein, as it was to enable him to substitute for his status as a national of a belligerent State that of a national of a neutral State, with the sole aim of thus coming within the protection of Liechtenstein but not of becoming wedded to its traditions, its interests, its way of life or of assuming the obligations-other than fiscal obliga-tions-and exercising the rights pertaining to the status thus acquired.

Guatemala is under no obligation to recognize a nationality granted in such circumstances. Liechtenstein consequently is not entitled to extend its protection to Nottebohm vis-a-vis Guatemala and its claim must, for this reason, be held to be inadmissible."

☑ 해   설

이 사건에서 ICJ는 11대 3으로 리히텐슈타인의 청구를 기각했다. 이 판결에서 재판부가 Nottebohm의 리히텐슈타인 귀화의 유효성 자체를 심사한 것은 아니었다. 오직 리히텐슈타인이 Nottebohm을 위하여 과테말라를 상대로 외교적 보호권을 행사할 수 있느냐만을 검토하여, Nottebohm과 리히텐슈타인 간에는 진정한 유대(genuine connection)가 결여되어 있다는 이유에서 부정적인 결론을 내렸다.

이 판결은 특히 국적이 갖는 사회적 의미를 잘 설명하고 있다. 또한 재판부가 제시한 "진정한 유대"의 개념은 국제법 일반에 적지 않을 영향을 미치었었다. 판결 수년 후 채택된 1958년 「공해에 관한 협약」 제5조는 선박과

면, 리히텐슈타인과는 별다른 실질적 유대를 구축하지 못했음을 자세히 설명했다.

기국간의 진정한 유대를 요구했으며, 이러한 입장은 1982년 해양법 협약 제 91조에서도 유지되고 있다.

한편 이 판결에 대하여는 적지 않은 비판과 의문도 제기되었다. 1) Nottebohm은 리히텐슈타인 귀화로 이미 독일 국적을 상실했는데, 그러면 이제 어느 국가가 그를 위한 외교적 보호권을 행사할 수 있는가? 이 판결은 Nottebohm을 국제사회에서 사실상 무국적자로 만든 것이 아닌가? 2) 출생직 후 외국으로 이주해 평생을 현지에서 외국인으로 거주한 자는 형식적 국적 국과 진정한 유대가 있다고 평가될 수 있는가? 3) 진정한 유대론은 국제사회 에서 개인의 보호를 약화시키게 되며, 이는 국적을 개인의 권리의 일종으로 파악하고 국적변경의 자유를 보장하는 국제인권법의 경향과 배치되지 않는 가? 4) 국적에 있어서 진정한 유대의 요구란 이 판결 이전에는 주로 이중국 적자의 실효적 국적을 결정하는 기준으로 사용되던 개념인데, 이를 귀화에도 적용할 수 있는가? 5) 이 입장에 철저하면 개별국가의 귀화 허용이 적절했는 가에 대하여 국제사회에서 자주 이의가 제기될 것인데, 이는 주권국가들이 원하지 않는 방향이 아닌가? 6) Nottebohm이 리히텐슈타인 국적을 취득한 1939년에는 양자간의 유대가 희박했다고 하더라도, 리히텐슈타인이 이 소송 을 제기한 1951년에도 양자간의 유대가 외교적 보호권 행사를 부정할 정도 로 희박했다고 보아야 하는가?

실제 이 판결에는 제2차 대전이라는 정치상황이 상당한 영향을 미치었 다. 1939년 7월 4일 독일 외무부의 공문은 독일의 이익을 위해 일부 국민에 게 외국국적을 취득시키고 향후 다시 독일 국적을 회복시킬 필요성을 지 지한 바 있다. 그리고 Nottebohm은 적극적인 나치당원으로서 미국과 영국 이 블랙리스트에 올려 놓고 있었다는 점도 판결의 배후에서 고려되었을 것이다.

한편 유엔 국제법위원회(ILC)가 2006년 완성한 「외교적 보호에 관한 규 정 초안」(ILC Draft Articles on Diplomatic Protection)은 외교적 보호를 행사할 수 있는 국적국의 정의에서 "진정한 유대"의 필요성을 의도적으로 포함시키 지 않았다. 현대와 같이 경제의 세계화와 인구의 국제이동이 일상화되어 있 는 현실 속에서 Nottebohm 판결과 같은 엄격한 기준이 요구된다면 수많은 사람들을 외교적 보호로부터 배제시키는 결과를 가져오리라는 점을 우려하였기 때문이었다.

Article 4
State of nationality of a natural person

For the purposes of the diplomatic protection of a natural person, a State of nationality means a State whose nationality that person has acquired, in accordance with the law of that State, by birth, descent, naturalization, succession of States, or in any other manner, not inconsistent with international law.

➠ **참고문헌** —————————————————————————

- 서보현, 노테봄사건, 국제법 판례연구(진성사, 1996), p. 219.
- 이진규, 외교적 보호권 행사 시 국가와 국민 간 '진정한 유대'의 필요성에 관한 비판적 고찰, 가천법학 6권 1호(2013), p. 147.
- J. H. Glazer, Affaire Nottebohm, A Critique, Georgetown Law Journal Vol. 44 (1955/56), p. 387.
- Jones, The Nottebohm Case, ICLQ Vol. 5(1956), p. 230.
- J. Kunz, The Nottebohm Judgement, AJIL Vol. 54(1960), p. 536.
- G. Leigh, Nationality and Diplomatic Protection, ICLQ Vol. 20(1971), p. 453.
- P. Weis, Nationality and Statelessness in International Law 2nd ed.(1979).

3. 이란·미국 이중국적자의 지위(1984)
— 이중국적자와 실효적 국적의 원칙

Iran-United States, Case No. A/18.
Iran-U.S. Claims Tribunal, 5 Iran-U.S. C.T.R. 251(1984).

☑ 사   안

이 사건의 쟁점 중 하나는 미국법과 이란법상 각각 자국민으로 간주되는 이중국적자의 청구에 대하여도 재판부가 관할권을 갖느냐 여부였다. 1930년 「국적법 저촉에 관한 헤이그 협약」 제4조는 이중국적자의 국적국 상호간에는 외교적 보호권을 행사할 수 없다고 규정하고 있었다. 이는 과연 이 사건에도 적용되는 국제법 원칙인가? 아니면 이중국적 중 실효적 국적(effective nationality)이 확인될 수 있으면 위와 같은 제한은 적용되지 않느냐 여부가 쟁점의 하나였다.

☑ 쟁   점

피해자가 이중국적자인 경우 그의 국적국 중 일방에 대한 국제청구의 가능 여부.

☑ 판   결

이중국적 중 실효적 국적이 확인될 수 있으면 타방 국적국에 대하여도 국제청구가 가능하다.

판 결 문

Article 4 of the Convention provides: "A State may not afford diplomatic protection to one of its nationals against a State whose nationality such person also possesses."[1] But this provision must be interpreted very cautiously. Not only is it more than 50 years old and found in a treaty to which only 20 States are parties, but great changes have occurred since then in the concept of diplomatic protection, which concept has been expanded. [···] This concept continues to be in a process of transformation, and it is necessary to distinguish between different types of protection, whether consular or claims-related.

Moreover, the negotiating history of Article 4 of the Hague Convention suggests that its application is doubtful in a case, such as the present one, where a dual national, by himself, brings before an international tribunal his own claim against one of the States whose nationality he possesses. Such a proposal was made during the Conference, but it was rejected. [···]

Another reason why the applicability of Article 4 to the claims of dual nationals before this Tribunal is debatable is that it applies by its own terms solely to "diplomatic protection" by a State. While this Tribunal is clearly an international tribunal established by treaty and while some of its cases involve disputes between the two Governments and involve the interpretation and application of public international law, most disputes (including all of those brought by dual nationals) involve a private party on one side and a Government or Government-controlled entity on the other, and many involve primarily issues of municipal law and general principles of law. In such cases it is the rights of the claimant, not of his nation, that are to be determined by the Tribunal. [···]

In this field, there is a considerable number of relevant judicial and arbitral decisions, most of them prior to the Second World War, supplemented and interpreted by the writings of scholars. The writing of at least one scholar, Professor E.B. Borchard, apparently had a considerable effect, not only because of the later writers who have echoed his views which favored the rule of non-responsibility, but also because of his influence on the Hague Conference that adopted the 1930 Convention discussed above. In fact, the precedents on which Borchard relied did not generally support his conclusion, and the Parties in the present case have acknowledged that the law prior to 1930 was uncertain. Iran, however, considers the

---

1) Hague Convention on the Conflict of Nationality Laws(1930) — 필자 주.

conclusion of the 1930 Convention a decisive turning point that crystalized the rule of non-responsibility. The United States, on the other hand, points to the limited number of parties to that Convention and the practice of States, particularly in the conclusion and interpretation of claims settlement agreements since the Second World War. The Tribunal, having had the benefit of extensive written and oral argument of these issues by eminent counsel, does not believe it would be worthwhile for it to recite and comment upon the many precedents cited by the Parties, for the Tribunal is satisfied that, whatever the state of the law prior to 1945, the better rule at the time the Algiers Declarations[2] were concluded and today is the rule of dominant and effective nationality. [···]

While Nottebohm itself did not involve a claim against a State of which Nottebohm was a national, it demonstrated the acceptance and approval by the International Court of Justice of the search for the real and effective nationality based on the facts of a case, instead of an approach relying on more formalistic criteria. The effects of the Nottebohm decision have radiated throughout the international law of nationality.

A few months later, on 10 June 1955, the Italian-United States Conciliation Commission set up by application of the Peace Treaty of 1947, decided in the Mergé Case that the principle "... based on the sovereign equality of States, which excludes diplomatic protection in the case of dual nationality, must yield before the principle of effective nationality whenever such nationality is that of the claiming State." Mergé Case (United States v. Italy) 14 R.I.A.A. 236, 247 (1955).

Support for the principles applied in these cases is shared by some of the most competent international lawyers. [···][3]

This trend toward modification of the Hague Convention rule of non-responsibility by search for the dominant and effective nationality is scarcely surprising as it is consistent with the contemporaneous development of international law to accord legal protections to individuals, even against the State of which they are nationals. [···]

For the reasons stated above, the Tribunal holds that it has jurisdiction over claims against Iran by dual Iran-United States nationals when the dominant and effective nationality of the claimant during the relevant period from the date the claim arose until 19 January 1981 was that of the United States. In determining the

---

2) 1979년 11월 발생한 이란 주재 미국 대사관 점거사건을 해결하기 위하여 알제리의 주선으로 성립된 1981년 1월 19일자 미국─이란간 합의.

3) 재판부는 이어서 Basdevant, Paul de Visscher 등 여러 학자들의 주장을 소개했다.

dominant and effective nationality, the Tribunal will consider all relevant factors, including habitual residence, center of interests, family ties, participation in public life and other evidence of attachment."(원문의 각주 생략)

☑ 해   설

1930년 헤이그 협약 제4조의 적용범위에 대하여는 그간 논란이 있었다. 과거 1912년 이탈리아 대 페루간 Canevaro 사건(P.C.A., 1912)에서는 실효적 국적이 확인될 수 있으면 이중국적국 상호간에도 외교적 보호권 행사가 가능하다고 인정되었다. 본문의 판결문에서도 지적된 1955년 Mergé 사건(Italian–U.S. Conciliation Commission)에서 역시 이중국적 중 하나가 실효적 국적으로 입증되면 이중국적국 상호간에도 외교적 보호권 행사가 가능하다고 판단했다. 다만 그 사건에서는 청구인의 미국 국적이 실효적 국적으로 확인되지 못하여 청구가 받아 들여지지 않았었다.

본 사건은 국가간에 외교적 보호권을 행사한 경우는 아니나, 이중국적자의 경우 국적국간에 외교적 보호권 행사가 가능한가에 대하여도 상세히 논하고 있다. 재판부는 실효적 국적 원칙의 적용을 지지하며, 이중국적자가 일방 국적국을 상대로도 국제청구가 가능함을 인정했다. 재판부는 실효적 국적을 판단하는 요소로서 상거주지, 이해의 중심지, 가족관계, 공적 생활에의 참여 등을 제시했다.

이 사건의 당사자는 원래 이란인이었으나 미국인으로 귀화한 자였다. 당시 이란 법상 외국 국적을 취득한 후 이란 국적을 포기하기 위하여는 이란 국무회의(Council of Ministers)의 허가가 필요했다. 재판부로서는 그 같은 허가를 받지 못했던 당사자가 이란인 자격으로 이란 법정에서 소송을 한다면 공평한 대우를 받을 수 있을지 의구심을 가졌으리라 보인다.

Iran–U.S. Claims Tribunal은 또 다른 사건인 Esphahanina v. Bank Tejarat(2 Iran–U.S. C.T.R. 157 (1983))에서도 이중국적자의 실효적 국적을 확인할 수 있으면 관할권의 성립을 긍정하고 최종적으로 청구를 인용한 바 있다.

한편 ILC의 Draft Articles on Diplomatic Protection(2006) 제7조는 "A State of nationality may not exercise diplomatic protection in respect of a person against a State of which that person is also a national unless the nationality of the former State is predominant, both at the date of injury and at the date of the official presentation of the claim"이라고 규정하여, 기본적으로 본 판결과 같은 입장을 취하고 있다. 여기서 unless라는 부정적인 표현이 사용된 것은 우세한(predominant) 국적에 대한 입증책임이 주장국에 있음을 의미한다.

이중국적자의 경우 실효적 국적을 확인할 수 있으면 그 중 한 국적국을 상대로도 외교적 보호권이 행사될 수 있다는 입장은 국제법이 피해자 개인을 좀더 보호할 수 있다는 점에서 긍정적이다.

➥ 참고문헌 ─────────────────────────

- N. A. Combs, Toward a New Understanding of Abuse of Nationality in Claims before The Iran—United States Claims Tribunal, American Review of International Arbitration Vol. 10(1999), p. 27.
- Note, Claims of Dual Nationals in the Modern Era: The Iran—United States Claims Tribunal, Michigan Law Review Vol. 83(1984), p. 597.

4. 중국적 재중동포의 국적(2006)

헌법재판소 2006년 3월 30일 선고, 2003헌마806 결정.
헌법재판소판례집 제18권 1집 상(2006), 381쪽 이하.

☑ 사   안

이 사건 위헌확인 청구인들은 일제시 한반도에서 출생한 이후 중국으로 이주했다가 중국 공산화 이후 중국국적을 부여받고 계속 중국에 거주하던 자들이다. 이들은 한중 수교 이후 여러 경로로 한국으로 입국한 이래 당초의 체류예정기간을 초과해 국내에 거주하고 있었다. 한국에서 계속 거주하기를 원하는 청구인들은 자신들이 1948년 대한민국 수립과 함께 한국국적을 부여받았고 이후 중국국적을 자진하여 취득한 바 없으므로 한중 이중국적자에 해당한다고 주장했다. 이어 대한민국은 한중 수교 이후 중국동포들이 대한민국 국적을 선택할 수 있는 절차에 관한 법률을 제정하거나 그러한 내용의 조약을 체결할 헌법상 의무가 있음에도 불구하고 아무런 조치를 취하지 않아 헌법상의 의무를 위반했다고 주장했다. 또한 법무부장관이 「중국동포국적업무처리지침」이라는 차별적인 내부규정을 통해 이들의 한국국적 회복의 길을 가로막고 있는 것은 청구인들의 국적선택권, 평등권 등 헌법상 보장된 기본권에 대한 침해라고 주장했다.

☑ 쟁   점

⑴ 일제시 중국으로 이주한 후 중국적으로 생활해 온 재중동포가 아직도 대한민국 국적을 보유하고 있는가 여부.

⑵ 국가는 중국적 동포에게 대한민국 국적 선택을 위한 절차를 마련할 의무가 있는가 여부.

☑ 판   결

⑴ 중국 공산화 이후 중국적으로 생활해 온 재중동포는 중국국적만 보유한 외국인에 해당한다.

⑵ 중국동포와 같은 특수한 상황에 처한 자를 위한 국적선택이나 회복 절차를 마련해야 할 의무가 국가에게 부과되어 있지는 않다.

결 정 문

3. 판   단

가. 국적선택권의 의의 및 중국동포의 법적 지위

⑴ 국적선택권의 의의

근대국가 성립 이전의 영민(領民)은 토지에 종속되어 영주(領主)의 소유물과 같은 처우를 받았다. 근대국가에서도 개인은 출생지 또는 혈통에 기속되고 충성의무를 강요당하는 지위에 있었으므로 국적선택권이 인정될 여지가 없었다. 그러나 천부인권(天賦人權) 사상은 국민주권을 기반으로 하는 자유민주주의 헌법을 낳았고 이 헌법은 인간의 존엄과 가치를 존중하므로, 개인은 자신의 운명에 지대한 영향을 미치는 정치적 공동체인 국가를 선택할 수 있는 권리, 즉 국적선택권을 기본권으로 인식하기에 이르렀다. 세계인권선언(1948. 12. 10.)이 제15조에서 "① 사람은 누구를 막론하고 국적을 가질 권리를 가진다. ② 누구를 막론하고 불법하게 그 국적을 박탈당하지 아니하여야 하며 그 국적변경의 권리가 거부되어서는 아니 된다"는 규정을 둔 것은 이를 뒷받침하는 좋은 예다. 그러나 개인의 국적선택에 대하여는 나라마다 그들의 국내법에서 많은 제약을 두고 있는 것이 현실이므로, 국적은 아직도 자유롭게 선택할 수 있는 권리에는 이르지 못하였다고 할 것이다(헌재 2000. 8. 31. 97헌가12, 판례집 12-2, 167, 175).

그러므로 "이중국적자의 국적선택권"이라는 개념은 별론으로 하더라도, 일반적으로 외국인인 개인이 특정한 국가의 국적을 선택할 권리가 자연권으로서 또는 우리 헌법상 당연히 인정된다고는 할 수 없다고 할 것이다.

⑵ 중국동포의 법적 지위

국적의 선택은 그 개념상 이중국적의 가능성을 전제로 한다. 따라서 과 연 청구인들과 같은 중국동포들이 이미 중국국적을 취득했음에도 불구하고 여전히 대한민국의 국적을 보유하고 있는지 여부를 먼저 살핀다.

㈎ **정부의 입장**　1992년 8월 한중수교가 이루어지기 이전인 1988년 노태우 대통령의 이른바 '7·7선언'을 계기로 1980년대 후반 무렵부터 극소 수이지만 독립유공자 후손을 비롯한 일부 중국동포들의 한국방문 또는 영주 귀국이 이루어지기 시작하였다. 당시는 중국과 정식으로 수교가 이루어지지 않아서 중국국적을 인정할 수 없었던 관계로 한국으로 입국하는 중국동포들 에 대하여는 중국여권이 아닌 우리 정부가 발급한 "여행증명서"로 입국하도 록 하였고, 영주를 목적으로 귀국한 독립유공자 후손들에 대하여 한국국적을 부여함에 있어서는 중국국적을 전제로 한 국적변경절차 대신 한국국적을 계 속 보유하고 있던 자로서 "국적판정"을 하는 등 당시 시대상황에 따라 예외 적 조치를 취하였다. 그러다가 1992년 한중수교에 따라 중국동포를 중국 국 적을 보유한 중국공민으로 보게 되었다. 이와 같이 정부는 출입국관리사무나 국적사무와 관련하여 중국 국적 동포들을 중국 국적만을 보유한 중국인으로 취급하고 있다.

㈏ **대법원과 헌법재판소의 입장**　대법원은 1998. 9. 18. 선고한 98다 25825 손해배상 사건에서 중화인민공화국 흑룡강성에서 거주하다가 국내에 입국한 조선족 김 아무개 씨에 대하여 "일시적으로 국내에 체류한 후 장래 출국할 것이 예정되어 있는 외국인"이라고 판시하였고(공1998하, 2521), 헌법 재판소도 2001. 11. 29. 선고한 소위 '재외동포법'헌법소원 사건에서 중국동 포들은 중국국적의 "외국인"이라는 점을 전제로 판단하였다(헌재 2001. 11. 29. 99헌마494, 판례집 13-2, 714, 723-724).

㈐ **소　결**　이상 살펴본 바와 같이 정부와 대법원 및 헌법재판소 는 중국동포를 중국 국적만을 보유한 "외국인"으로 보고 있다. 그러나 청구 인들은 1997년 전문개정된 국적법 제12조 내지 제14조, 부칙 제5조 등은 출 생이라는 사유 또는 자진하여 이중국적자가 된 자들의 일반적 이중국적 해 소에 관하여 규율하고 있을 뿐이므로, 중국동포와 같이 특수한 국적상황에

있는 자들의 이중국적 해소 또는 대한민국 국적 선택의 요건과 절차에 관한 입법이라고 볼 수 없다고 주장한다. 그러므로 이하에서는 우리 헌법상 중국 동포와 같이 특수한 국적상황에 있는 이들의 이중국적 해소 또는 대한민국 국적 선택의 요건과 절차에 관한 법률의 제정 또는 조약체결의 의무가 인정되는지 여부를 살펴보기로 한다.

나. 입법부작위 부분에 대한 판단

(1) 청구인들의 주장과 같이 대한민국 정부에게 1992년 한중수교 당시 또는 그 이후 이중국적자인 중국동포들이 대한민국 국적을 선택할 수 있는 절차에 관한 법률을 제정하거나(이하 '법률부작위' 부분이라 한다) 또는 중국정부와의 조약을 체결할(이하 '조약부작위' 부분이라 한다) 헌법적 의무가 있는지 여부를 본다.

(가) **법률부작위 부분에 대한 판단**　　[…] 살펴건대, 청구인들과 같은 중국동포들의 현재의 법적 지위는 일반적으로 중국국적을 가진 외국인으로 보고 있고, 가사 중국동포들은 어쩔 수 없이 중국국적을 취득한 것이므로 당시 그들의 중국국적 취득에도 불구하고 대한민국 국적을 상실한 것이 아니라고 보는 경우에도, 1997년 전문개정된 국적법은 국적선택 및 판정제도를 규정하고 있다. 즉, 이중국적자로서 대한민국의 국적을 선택하고자 하는 자는 만 22세가 되기 전까지 외국 국적을 포기한 후 법무부장관에게 대한민국의 국적을 선택한다는 뜻을 신고하여야 하고 그 때까지 국적을 선택하지 아니하는 경우에는 그 기간이 경과한 때에 대한민국의 국적을 상실한다(동법 제12조, 제13조). 다만, 동법 시행 전에 대한민국의 국적과 외국 국적을 함께 가지게 된 자로서 만 20세 이상인 자는 동법의 시행일(1998. 6. 14.)로부터 2년 내에 대한민국 국적 선택의 신고를 하여야 한다(동법 부칙 제5조).

나아가, 법무부장관은 대한민국 국적의 취득 또는 보유 여부가 분명하지 아니한 자에 대하여 이를 심사한 후 판정할 수 있다(동법 제20조). 이와 같은 국적판정제도는 법무부예규인 "국적업무처리지침"에 기하여 중국 및 사할린 동포에 대하여 시행되다가 위와 같이 개정 국적법에서 실정화되어, 이들뿐만 아니라 한반도 및 그 부속도서에서 국외로 이주한 자와 그 비속으로서 출생 이력면에서는 대한민국 혈통으로 추정되면서도 혈통의 연원이나 대한민국 국적 취득경과의 입증이 어려운 사람 모두를 대상으로 한다.

따라서 청구인들의 주장과 같이 중국동포들이 대한민국과 중국의 이중국적을 갖고 있었다면 이들에게도 이러한 국적선택 및 국적변경의 기회가 주어진 것으로 볼 수 있다. 그럼에도 불구하고, 이와는 별도로 헌법 전문의 '대한민국임시정부 법통의 계승' 또는 제2조 제2항의 '재외국민 보호의무' 규정이 중국동포와 같이 특수한 국적상황에 처해 있는 자들의 이중국적 해소 또는 국적선택을 위한 특별법 제정의무를 명시적으로 위임한 것이라고 볼 수 없고, 뿐만 아니라 동 규정 및 그 밖의 헌법규정으로부터 그와 같은 해석을 도출해 낼 수도 없다고 할 것이다. […]

(3) 소　결

이상 살펴본 바와 같이, 헌법 전문이나 제2조 제2항의 규정이 중국동포와 같은 특수한 상황에 처한 자들의 이중국적 해소 또는 대한민국 국적 선택이나 회복에 관한 법률의 제정 혹은 조약의 체결을 명시적으로 위임하고 있지 않고, 이들 규정 또는 헌법의 다른 어떤 규정의 해석으로부터도 국가의 이와 같은 헌법적 의무를 도출해 낼 수 없으므로, 이 사건 헌법소원 중 입법부작위 부분에 대한 심판청구는 부적법하다.

다. 업무처리지침 부분에 대한 판단

(1) 업무처리지침은 2001. 5. 7. 법무부예규 제551호로 개정된 것으로서, 중국동포에 대한 국적업무처리에 필요한 사항을 정함을 목적으로 한다(동 지침 제1조).

동 지침 제3조의 규정에 의하면, 중국동포 중 중국국적자 또는 무국적자는 국적법, 동법시행령, 동법시행규칙 및 동 지침이 정하는 요건을 갖춘 때에 한하여 법무부장관의 "국적회복"허가 또는 "귀화"허가를 받아 대한민국의 국적을 취득할 수 있는데(제1항), 한반도 및 그 부속도서에서 중국으로 이주한 자 및 그 부계혈통 직계비속으로서 중화인민공화국의 수립일인 "1949년 10월 1일"전에 출생한 자는 국적회복허가 대상자이고(제2항 제1호), 1949년 10월 1일 이후에 중국에서 출생한 자는 귀화허가 대상자이다(제2항 제2호). […]

업무처리지침은 법무부장관이 반복적으로 행하는 국적업무에 관한 행정

사무의 통일을 기하고 그 직무집행에 있어서 지침을 정해 주기 위한 사무처리준칙에 불과할 뿐 대외적으로 국민이나 법원을 기속하는 법규적 효력은 없는 것이라고 보아야 하고, 따라서 헌법소원의 대상이 되는 공권력의 행사에 해당하지 아니한다고 할 것이다.

4. 결   론

이상 살펴본 바와 같이 이 사건 심판청구는 모두 부적법하므로 이를 각하하기로 하여 주문과 같이 결정한다. […]

5. 재판관 조대현의 일부 반대의견

[…]

나. 재중동포의 국적

청구인들을 비롯한 재중동포들도 재일동포나 재소련동포 등과 마찬가지로 조선인을 부친으로 하여 출생하는 등 임시조례상의 국적취득의 요건을 충족한다면, 1948. 7. 17. 제헌 헌법 공포와 동시에 대한민국의 국적을 취득하였다고 보아야 한다. 그리고 위와 같이 대한민국 국적을 취득한 재중동포의 자녀들 역시 혈통주의를 취한 우리 국적법에 따라 대한민국의 국적을 취득하였다고 할 것이다. 그리고 재중동포들은 이에 더하여 1949. 10. 1. '56개 민족 대가정'을 표방하는 중화인민공화국의 성립과 더불어 중국국적도 취득하였다고 할 것이다.

우리 국적법은 자진하여 외국 국적을 취득하면 대한민국 국적을 상실한다고 규정하고 있다. 그러나 재중동포들은 일제의 수탈을 피하여, 또는 일제에 항거하기 위하여, 또는 일제의 만주이주정책에 의하여 조국을 떠나 중국에 정착한 뒤, 중국 공산당 정부에 의하여 일방적으로 중국 국민으로 인정된 것이고, 광복 후 분단과 한국전쟁, 냉전시대를 거치면서 장기간 왕래나 연락이 두절되고 대한민국 정부의 보호도 받지 못한 채 현지 주민으로 생활할 수밖에 없었으므로, 그들이 삶을 영위하기 위한 방편으로 중국 국적을 수용하고 장기간 생활하여 왔다든지, 광복 후에 조국으로 귀국하지 않았다든지, 중국 여권을 소지하고 대한민국을 방문하였다는 등의 사정을 내세워 그들이 자진하여 중국 국적을 취득하였다고 단정하기 어렵다고 할 것이다.

한편 1997. 12. 13. 법률 제5431호로 개정되어 1998. 6. 14.부터 시행된 국적법 제12조는 출생 기타 국적법의 규정에 의하여 만 20세가 되기 전에 대한민국의 국적과 외국 국적을 함께 가지게 된 이중국적자에 대하여는 만 22세가 되기 전까지, 만 20세가 된 후에 이중국적자가 된 사람에 대하여는 그때부터 만 2년 내에 하나의 국적을 선택하도록 국적선택의무를 부과한 후 국적선택의무를 이행하지 아니하면 대한민국 국적을 상실한다고 규정하였고, 국적법시행령 제16조는 위 국적법 제12조에서 말하는 '출생 이외의 사유에 의한 이중국적자'의 범위를 규정하였다.

그런데 1948. 7. 17.부터 1949. 9. 30. 사이에 제헌 헌법과 임시조례, 국적법에 따라 대한민국 국적을 취득한 후 1949. 10. 1. 중화인민공화국의 성립으로 중국 국적을 취득한 재중동포(즉 1949. 9. 30. 이전 출생자, 이하 '재중동포 1세대'라 한다)의 경우는 출생에 의하여 이중국적자가 된 것도 아니고 국적법시행령 제16조에서 정하는 사유로 이중국적자가 된 것도 아니어서 국적법상 국적선택의무가 없다고 할 것이므로, 국적선택을 하지 아니하였다는 이유로 대한민국 국적이 상실되지 않는다. 따라서 재중동포 1세대의 경우는 여전히 대한민국과 중국의 이중국적자이다.

그러나 재중동포 1세대의 자녀들(1949. 10. 1. 이후 출생자, 이하 '재중동포 2세대'라 한다)은 출생에 의하여 대한민국의 국적과 중국의 국적을 아울러 취득한 이중국적자로서 국적법상 국적선택의무가 있으므로, 국적법에서 정한 기간 내에 대한민국과 중국 중 하나의 국적을 선택하지 아니하였다면 대한민국 국적을 상실하였다고 할 것이다.

다. 재중동포에 대한 국적 판정 절차의 필요

이와 같이 재중동포 1·2세대의 국적은 그 혈통(조선인을 부친으로 하여 출생하였는지 여부 등), 그 출생시기와 국적선택 여부에 따라 '대한민국과 중국의 이중국적자', '대한민국 국적을 상실한 중국국적자' 또는 '대한민국 국적을 취득한 적이 없는 자'로 나뉠 수 있다. 따라서 재중동포에 대해서는 위와 같은 점을 살펴서 대한민국의 국적의 취득·보유 여부를 판단할 필요가 있다.[1]

---

1) 이어 반대의견은 문제의 업무처리지침이 형식상 폐기되었다고 할지라도 그와 같은 정부의

(원문의 각주는 생략)

☑ 해   설

2003년 하반기 정부가 장기 불법체류 외국인의 추방을 강력히 추진하겠다고 발표하자, 국내 거주 약 5,000명의 중국동포가 이에 대한 대항수단으로 자신들은 여전히 한국국적을 보유하고 있으므로 강제퇴거대상이 아니라고 주장하는 헌법소원을 제출하였다. 이 사안은 광복 후 최초국민 확정기준, 당시 해외거주 동포에 대한 대한민국 국적 부여 여부, 정치적 사유로 장기간 왕래 교류가 불가능하였던 구 공산권 국가 출신 동포들의 현재 국적 등 다양한 법적 쟁점을 내포하고 있다. 헌법재판소는 이 결정에서 그간 재중동포를 당연의 전제로서 중국국적자로만 파악하던 것에서 더 나아가 적극적으로 이들이 한국국적을 갖고 있지 않으며, 설사 이들이 한중 이중국적자였다고 하더라도 이미 국적선택의 기회가 주어졌었다고 판단하였다(서울행정법원 1998년 12월 23일 선고, 98구17882 판결(확정) 참조).2) 그러나 소수의견은 위와 같은 법해석이 지니고 있는 실질적 문제점을 지적하고 있다고 평가된다.

➡ 참고문헌 ─────────────────────────────

• 정대화, 중국동포 국적확인 소송, 공익과 인권 1권 1호(2004), p. 129.
• 정인섭, 우리 국적법상 최초 국민 확정기준에 관한 검토, 국제법학회논총 43권 2호(1998), p. 235.
• 최경옥, 중국동포와 한국국적취득의 문제점: 2003헌마806을 중심으로, 일감법학 제29호(2014), p. 29.

─────────────────

기본방침은 지속되고 있으므로 재중동포를 출생 시기와 관계 없이 무조건 중국국적을 가진 동포로만 취급함으로써 재중동포 중 대한민국 국적을 갖고 있는 사람들의 기본권을 침해했다고 주장했다.

2) 정인섭, 한국법원에서의 국제법 판례(박영사, 2018), p. 363 이하 수록.

5. 사할린 힌인의 대한민국 국적(2014)

서울행정법원 2014년 6월 19일 선고, 2012구합26159 판결.

☑ 사   안

이 사건의 원고는 1954년 러시아 사할린에서 한국계 부모 하에서 출생한 자이다. 그의 부모는 일제시기 사할린으로 이주해 노동에 종사하다가 광복 후 귀국할 수 없어서 현지에서는 계속 무국적자 자격으로 거주했다. 원고 역시 사할린에서 무국적자 자격으로 거주했다. 그 사이 한국의 재외국민등록이나 여권 신청은 없었다. 원고는 자신의 국적이 대한민국임을 확인해 달라는 본소를 제기했다.

☑ 쟁   점

광복 후 사할린에서 출생해 무국적 자격으로 거주해 온 한인 후손의 국적.

☑ 판   결

사할린 거주 한인은 광복 후 한국국적을 부여받았고, 그의 자손 역시 한국인이다.

판결문

"사할린 거주 무국적 한인들은 일제에 의해 동원되어 사할린으로 강제로 이주하게 되었음에도 조국과 고향으로 돌아갈 날만을 기다리며 현재까지도 아무런 국적을 취득하지 않은 상태에서 무국적자로서의 불이익과 불편함을 감수하고 있다. 이와 같은 상황에서 헌법과 국적법에 따라 대한민국 국민에 해당하는 사할린 거주 무국적 한인들이 대한민국 국민임을 확인하고 이를 통해 대한민국 국민으로서의 지위를 누릴 수 있도록 보장하는 것은 헌법 전문, 제2조 제2항, 제10조에서 규정하고 있는 국가의 재외국민 보호의무 및 기본권 보장의무를 이행하는 것으로서 중요한 의미를 가진다.

　나. 이와 같은 관점에서 원고가 대한민국 국민인지에 관하여 본다.

　1) 사할린 거주 한인의 이주 경위와 국적 취득 과정 등에 비추어 보면 사할린에 강제 이주된 한인은 대부분 일제 강점기에 일본에 의하여 강제 동원되지 않았더라면 1948. 7. 17. 제정된 헌법(이하 '제헌헌법'이라 한다)의 공포와 동시에 당연히 대한민국의 국적을 취득하였을 것이다.

　2) 제헌헌법 제3조는 대한민국의 국민되는 요건은 법률로써 정한다고 규정하여 국적법률주의를 천명하고 있었다. 한편 제헌헌법 제정 당시에는 국적법이 제정되어 있지 않았으나 제헌헌법 제100조는 현행법령은 이 헌법에 저촉되지 아니하는 한 효력을 가진다고 규정하여 1948. 12. 20. 법률 제16호로 국적법이 제정되기 전까지는 남조선과도정부법률 제11호 국적에 관한 임시조례(이하 '임시조례'라 한다)에 의하여 국적관련 법률관계가 규율되었다. 임시조례는 제2조에서 조선의 국적을 가지기 위한 요건을 규정하였는데, 그 중 제1호에서 조선인을 부친으로 하여 출생한 자는 조선의 국적을 가진다고 규정하여 혈통주의를 원칙으로 하였고, 이러한 혈통주의는 1948. 12. 20. 법률 제16호로 제정된 국적법(이하 '제정 국적법'이라 한다)에도 이어져 제정 국적법 제2조 제1호는 출생한 당시에 부(父)가 대한민국의 국민인 자는 대한민국의 국민이라고 규정하고 있었다(이 규정 내용은 1997. 12. 13. 법률 제5431호로 개정된 국적법 제2조 제1항 제1호의 내용이 '출생한 당시에 부 또는 모가 대한민국의 국민인 자'로 개정되기 전까지 계속 유지되었다). 한편 임시조례 제2조 제2호는 조선인을 모친으로 하여 출생한 자로서 그 부친을 알 수 없거나 또는 그 부친이 아무 국적도 가지지 않은 때, 제3호는 조선 내에서 출생한 자로서 그 부모를 알 수 없거나 또는 그 부모가 아무 국적도 가지지 않은 때, 제4호는 외국인으로서 조선인과 혼인하여 처가 된 자(다만 혼인 해소에 의하여 외국에 복적한 자는 제외한다), 제5호는 외국인으로서 조선에 귀화한 자(다만 귀화의 요건 급 귀화

인의 권한은 별도로 법률로서 정한다)를 규정하고 있었다.

이와 같은 제헌헌법과 제정 국적법에 따르면 사할린으로 강제 동원된 한인으로서 임시조례 제2조 각 호에 정한 요건에 해당하는 사람은 조선의 국적을 가지고 있다가 제헌헌법의 공포와 동시에 대한민국 국적을 취득한다. 그리고 그 자녀, 특히 조선인을 부친으로 하여 출생한 자는 제헌헌법 공포 전에 출생한 경우 임시조례 제2조 제1호에 의하여 조선의 국적을 취득하였다가 제헌헌법의 공포와 동시에 대한민국의 국적을 취득하고(대법원 1996. 11. 12. 선고 96누1221 판결 등 참조), 제헌헌법 공포 후에 출생한 경우 임시조례 제2조 제1호 또는 제정 국적법 제2조 제1호에 따라 출생과 동시에 대한민국 국적을 취득한다. [···]

위와 같은 사정을 종합하여 보면 원고는 1954. 1. 10. 러시아 사할린주에서 사할린으로 강제 이주된 조선인 김ㅇㅇ와 이ㅇㅇ 사이에서 태어나 현재까지 무국적자로서 사할린에 거주하고 있다고 보는 것이 합리적이다. 그렇다면 김ㅇㅇ와 이ㅇㅇ은 제헌헌법 공포와 동시에 대한민국 국적을 취득하고, 그 사이에서 태어난 원고 역시 1954. 1. 10. 출생과 동시에 제정 국적법 제2조 제1호에 따라 대한민국 국적을 취득한다."

☑ 해   설

일제 기간중 약 43,000명의 조선인이 사할린으로 이주·동원되어 거주하고 있었다. 남한 출신인 사할린 거주 한인들은 한국으로 귀환을 원했다. 종전 후 약 38만명에 이르는 일본인들은 일본으로 귀환했으나, 동원 책임국 일본은 사할린 한인의 귀환은 수용하지 않았다. 소련은 사할린 한인의 북한 국적 취득과 북한 귀환은 허용했으나, 국교가 없는 한국으로의 귀환은 허용하지 않았다. 냉전시대 사할린 한인은 오갈 데 없는 국제미아가 되었다. 상당수의 사할린 한인은 생활의 편의를 위해 소련 또는 북한적을 취득했으나, 일부는 한국 귀환을 기대하며 끝까지 무국적으로 잔류했다. 소련은 한국 국적을 인정하지 않아 이들은 무국적으로만 처우되었다. 1990년 한소 국교가 수립되자 사할린 한인의 한국 왕래가 자유로워졌다. 사할린 한인 1세 일부는 한국으로 영주귀국을 했다. 본 판결은 종전 후 출생자가 한국국적을 확인받기 위해 제기된 것이다. 이 판결은 1심 판결에 대해 국가가 항소하지 않아 그대로 확정되었다.

➡ **참고문헌** ──────────────────────────────

- 윤지영, 무국적 사할린 동포의 대한민국 국적확인, 민주사회를 위한 변론 제104호(2014).
- 정인섭, 재사할린 한인에 관한 법적 제문제, 국제법학회논총 제34권 제2호(1989), p. 165.
- 최연수, 사할린 억류한인의 국적 귀속과 법적 제문제, 한국근현대사연구 제37집(2006), p. 35.
- 이성환, 사할린 한인 문제에 대한 서론적 고찰, 국제학논총 제7집(2002), p. 215.

C. 재외동포법의 적용대상 차별(2001)

헌법재판소 2001년 11월 29일 선고, 99헌마494 결정.
헌법재판소판례집 제13권 2집(2001), 718쪽 이하.

☑ 사   안

한국은 재외동포들의 법적 지위를 강화하기 위한 목적에서 1999년 「재외동포의출입국과법적지위에관한법률」(재외동포법)을 제정했다. 이 법은 한국적의 재외국민은 물론 현재 외국적인 동포에 대하여도 출입국, 국내체류, 취업 등의 경제활동 등 여러 분야에서의 우대를 규정하고 있다. 그런데 이 법은 외국적 동포로서 대한민국 정부 수립 이전에 국외로 이주한 자의 경우 "외국국적 취득 이전에 대한민국 국적을 명시적으로 확인받은 자와 그 직계비속"으로 적용대상을 제한함으로써 중국 등 구공산권에서 거주해 온 동포들을 사실상 적용대상에서 배제시키었다. 과거 공산권에 거주하던 동포들은 한국정부와의 연락이 불가능했으므로 한국적을 확인받을 방법이 없었기 때문이었다. 이에 중국동포인 청구인들은 재외동포법이 과거 대한민국 국적 보유 여부라는 자의적 기준을 통하여 정부 수립 이전 해외이주 동포를 차별하고 있다고 주장하며, 이 법의 위헌확인소송을 제기했다.

☑ 쟁   점

재외동포법이 과거국적주의에 입각해 적용대상을 구분함으로써 구 공산권 출신 외국적 동포를 적용대상에서 사실상 배제시킨 것은 이들에 대한 합리적 이유없는 차별인가 여부.

☑ 판   결

재외동포법은 합리적 이유 없이 정부수립 이전 이주동포를 차별하여 이들의 평등권을 침해했다.

결 정 문

가. 재외동포법의 입법목적과 주요내용

⑴ 재외동포법의 입법목적 중 외국국적동포에 해당하는 부분은 다음과 같다. […] 즉, 지구촌시대 세계경제체제에 부응하여 재외동포에게 모국의 국경문턱을 낮춤으로써 재외동포의 생활권을 광역화 국제화함과 동시에 우리 국민의 의식형태와 활동영역의 국제화 세계화를 촉진하고, 재외동포의 모국에의 출입국 및 체류에 대한 제한과 부동산취득 금융 외국환거래 등에 있어서의 각종 제약을 완화함으로써 모국투자를 촉진하고 경제회생 동참 분위기를 확산시키며, 재외동포들이 요구하는 이중국적을 허용할 경우 나타날 수 있는 병역 납세 외교관계에서의 문제점과 국민적 일체감 저해 등의 부작용을 제거하면서 이중국적 허용요구에 담긴 애로사항을 선별 수용함으로써 모국에 대한 불만을 해소하기 위한 것이다.

⑵ 재외동포법의 주요내용을 보면, 재외동포를 재외국민과 외국국적동포로 구분하여(제2조), 재외국민과 재외동포 체류자격을 가진 외국국적동포의 출입국과 국내에서의 법적 지위에 관하여 적용하되(제3조), 외국국적동포는 재외동포체류자격으로 2년 동안 체류할 수 있고 그 기간의 연장도 가능하며 재입국허가가 없이 자유롭게 출입국할 수 있고(제10조 제1항 내지 제3항), 재외동포 체류자격의 활동범위 안에서 자유롭게 취업 기타 경제활동을 할 수 있으며(제10조 제5항), […] 90일 이상 국내에 체류하는 때에는 의료보험 관계법령이 정하는 바에 의하여 의료보험을 적용받을 수 있도록(제14조) 하는 등 광범한 혜택을 부여하고 있다.

⑶ 한편, 당초 1998. 9. 29. 입법예고된 재외동포법(안)에서는 '외국국적동포'의 정의를 "한민족 혈통을 지닌 자로서 외국국적을 취득한 자 중 대통

령령으로 정하는 자"로 규정하고 있었으나[…], 우리나라 주변 일부국가의
자국내 소수민족(조선족)을 자극할 우려가 있다는 의견을 받아들여 국회통과
과정에서 이 사건 심판대상규정과 같이 수정되었다. […]

다. 이 사건 심판대상규정의 위헌성

[…]

⑵ 차별의 기준과 효과

㈎ 이 사건 심판대상규정이 나누고 있는 입법구분을 보면, 외국국적동
포(재외동포법 제2조 제2호)란 "대한민국 정부수립 이후에 국외로 이주한 자
중 대한민국의 국적을 상실한 자와 그 직계비속(재외동포법시행령 제3조 제1
호), 그리고 대한민국 정부수립 이전에 국외로 이주한 자 중 외국국적 취득
이전에 대한민국의 국적을 명시적으로 확인받은 자와 그 직계비속(재외동포
법시행령 제3조 제2호)"만을 의미하므로, 대한민국 정부수립 이전에 국외로
이주한 자 중에 외국국적 취득 이전에 대한민국의 국적을 명시적으로 확인
받지 않은 자, 즉 대부분의 중국거주동포와 구 소련거주동포 등 정부수립
이전 이주동포는 재외동포법의 위와 같은 혜택을 누리지 못하게 된다. 왜
냐하면, 재외동포법시행령 제3조 제2호에서 말하는 "대한민국의 국적을 명
시적으로 확인받은 자"라 함은 거주국 소재 대한민국 재외공관 또는 대한
민국정부의 위임을 받은 기관·단체에 재외국민등록법(제정 1949. 11. 24. 법
률 제70호, 전문개정 1999. 12. 28. 법률 제6057호)에 의한 등록을 한 자를 말하
는바(재외동포법시행규칙 제2조 제1항), 예컨대 청구인들과 같은 중국동포의
경우 우리나라가 중국과 외교관계를 수립한 것은 1992. 8. 24.이고 중국주재
한국대사관이 개설된 것은 같은 달 28.{대한무역진흥공사(KOTRA) 북경대표부
는 1991. 1. 30. 개설되었다}이므로, 물리적으로 이 요건을 충족시킬 수 없게 되
어 있다. 이와 같은 사정은 구 소련지역에 거주하고 있는 동포들의 경우에도
마찬가지이다{국회법제사법위원회의 재외동포법(안)에 대한 「심사보고서」(1999. 8),
8면 참조}.

㈏ 이 사건 심판대상규정은 재외국민과 함께 재외동포법의 적용을 받는
외국국적동포에 관한 '정의규정'으로서 외국국적동포에 해당하는 자는 앞에
서 본 바와 같은 광범한 혜택을 누릴 수 있게 된다. 즉, 원래 외국국적동포

는 '외국인'이므로 [⋯]1) 재외동포법의 시행으로 일정한 범위에서 그 제한을
완화한 것으로서, 이 사건 심판대상규정이 나누고 있는 입법구분에 의하여
재외동포법이 부여하는 혜택에서 배제된 청구인들과 같은 정부수립 이전 이
주동포는 이러한 기본권 내지 법적 권리의 행사에 있어 차별을 받게 된 것
이다.

⑶ 평등권의 침해 여부

㈎ 평등의 원칙은 입법자에게 본질적으로 같은 것을 자의적으로 다르
게, 본질적으로 다른 것을 자의적으로 같게 취급하는 것을 금하고 있다. 그
러므로 비교의 대상을 이루는 두 개의 사실관계 사이에 서로 상이한 취급을
정당화할 수 있을 정도의 차이가 없음에도 불구하고 두 사실관계를 서로 다
르게 취급한다면, 입법자는 이로써 평등권을 침해하게 된다. [⋯]

앞에서 본 바와 같이 이 사건 심판대상규정은 실질적으로 대부분 미주
지역이나 유럽 등에 거주하는 정부수립 이후 이주동포와 대부분 중국과 구
소련지역에 거주하는 정부수립 이전 이주동포를 구분하여 전자에게는 재외
동포법의 광범위한 혜택을 부여하고 있고, 후자는 이러한 수혜대상에서 제외
하고 있다. 그런데, 정부수립 이후 이주동포와 정부수립 이전 이주동포는 이
미 대한민국을 떠나 그들이 거주하고 있는 외국의 국적을 취득한 우리의 동
포라는 점에서 같고, 다만 대한민국 정부수립 이후에 국외로 이주한 자인가
또는 대한민국 정부수립 이전에 국외로 이주한 자인가 하는 점에서만 다른
것이다. 이와 같은 차이는 정부수립 이후 이주동포와 정부수립 이전 이주동
포가 법적으로 같게 취급되어야 할 동일성을 훼손할 만한 본질적인 성격이
아니다. 즉, 정부수립 이후 이주동포인지 아니면 정부수립 이전 이주동포인
지는 결정적인 기준이 될 수 없는 것이다.

㈏ [⋯] 재외동포법은 그 적용대상에 포함된 정부수립 이후 이주동포에
대하여는 위에서 본 바와 같은 광범위한 혜택을 주어 사실상 이중국적을 허
용한 것과 같은 지위를 부여하고 있으면서도, 같은 동포 중 이 사건 심판대
상규정에 의하여 그 적용범위에서 제외된 정부수립 이전 이주동포는 기본적
으로 다른 일반 외국인과 동일한 취급을 받게 되는 결과가 되었다. 그리하여

---

1) 이어서 국내법상 외국인에게 제한되는 권리를 열거하고 있다.

정부수립 이후 이주동포(주로 재미동포, 그 중에서도 시민권을 취득한 재미동포 1세)의 요망사항은 재외동포법에 의하여 거의 완전히 해결된 반면, 정부수립 이전 이주동포(주로 중국동포 및 구 소련동포)는 재외동포법의 적용대상에서 제외됨으로써 그들이 절실히 필요로 하는 출입국기회와 대한민국 내에서의 취업기회를 차단당하였고, 법무부가 이를 완화한다는 취지에서 마련한 보완대책도 정부수립 이전 이주동포에게 실질적인 도움이 되지 못하고 있다. 재외동포법이 정부수립 이후 이주동포의 요구에 의하여 제정되었다는 연혁적 이유가 그 자체만으로 이와 같은 커다란 차별을 정당화할 정도의 비중을 가진다고 할 수 없을 뿐만 아니라, 정부수립 이전 이주동포에게도 정부수립 이후 이주동포에 못지않거나 더욱 절실한 필요가 있음을 고려하지 않으면 안 된다. 사회경제적 또는 안보적 이유로 거론하는 우려도, 당초 재외동포법의 적용범위에 정부수립 이전 이주동포도 포함시키려 하였다가 제외시킨 입법과정에 비추어 보면 정부수립 이전 이주동포를 재외동포법의 적용범위에 포함하는 것이 어느 정도의 영향을 가져올 것인지에 대한 엄밀한 검증을 거친 것이라고 볼 수 없다.

정부는 재외동포법에서 외국국적동포를 정의하면서 국제관행에 따라 '과거국적주의'를 채택함으로써 정부수립 이전 이주동포가 그 적용대상에서 제외되었다고 전제한 다음 그렇지 아니하고 '혈통주의'에 따라 외국국적동포를 정의하여 입법을 한다면, 국제법원칙 및 국제관행에 반하고, 외교마찰을 초래할 수 있으며, 그 개념이 불명확하여 대상이 무한정 확대될 우려가 있다는 점을 강조한다. 그러나, 외국국적을 취득한 자국동포에게 출입국 등에서 특례를 인정하는 나라로 과거국적주의를 채택하였다는 아일랜드, 그리스, 폴란드 등(국회법제사법위원회의 위「심사보고서」, 8면)의 나라에서의 과거 국적의 의미와 이 사건 심판대상규정이 정하고 있는 대한민국 정부수립(1948년)까지 국적의 과거로의 소급은 그 제한의 정도가 현저하게 다르다는 점이 지적될 수 있다. 또한 외교마찰의 우려라는 사정이 있다 하더라도 외국국적동포에 대한 이 사건 심판대상규정이 충분한 정책 검토 끝에 나온 필요하고 도 적정한 입법이라고 보기는 어렵다. 정부로서는 외국국적동포의 현실적인 애로를 수용하기 위하여 단일특별법을 제정하기보다 제반 상황을 고려한 개별적

인 제한 완화로 실질적으로 대처할 수는 없는지 우선 살펴보았어야 할 것이
다. 나아가, 혈통주의 입법에 문제가 있다면 당초부터 외국국적동포의 법적
지위보다는 외국인 처우의 전반적 개선이라는 시각에서 출발하되, 재외동포
에 대하여는 정착한 현지에서 민족적 정체성을 자각하고 문화적 유대감을
강화시키는 활동을 지원하는 데 초점을 맞추는 것이 바람직할 수도 있다.

(대) 재외동포법의 적용범위에서 정부수립 이전 이주동포가 제외된 것은
당초부터 과거국적주의를 채택하였기 때문이 아님은 앞에서{4. 가. (3)} 본
바와 같고, 사실은 그와 같은 사정 때문에 재외동포법상 외국국적동포에 대
한 정의규정에는 일응 중립적인 과거국적주의를 표방하고 시행령으로, 일제
시대 독립운동을 위하여 또는 일제의 강제징용이나 수탈을 피하기 위해 조
국을 떠날 수밖에 없었던 중국동포나 구 소련동포가 대부분인 대한민국 정
부수립 이전에 이주한 자들에게 외국국적 취득 이전에 대한민국의 국적을
명시적으로 확인받은 사실을 입증하도록 요구함으로써 이들을 재외동포법의
수혜대상에서 제외한 것으로 볼 수밖에 없다. 암울했던 역사적 상황으로 인
하여 어쩔 수 없이 조국을 떠나야 했던 동포들을 돕지는 못할지언정, 오히려
법적으로 차별하는 정책을 취하는 외국의 예를 찾을 수 없다는 점에서, 이
사건에서의 차별은 민족적 입장은 차치하고라도 인도적 견지에서조차 정당
성을 인정받기가 심히 어렵다고 할 것이다. 이 사건 차별로써 달성하고자 하
는 정부의 이익은 그로 인하여 야기되는 같은 동포 사이의 커다란 상처와
분열을 덮기에는 너무나도 미약하다고 하지 않을 수 없는 것이다. […]

(4) 소 결 론

요컨대, 이 사건 심판대상규정이 청구인들과 같은 정부수립 이전 이주
동포를 재외동포법의 적용대상에서 제외하는 차별취급은 그 차별의 기준이
목적의 실현을 위하여 실질적인 관계가 있다고 할 수 없고, 차별의 정도 또
한 적정한 것이라고는 도저히 볼 수 없으므로, 이 사건 심판대상규정은 합리
적 이유 없이 정부수립 이전 이주동포를 차별하는 자의적인 입법이어서 헌
법 제11조의 평등원칙에 위배되고, 이로 인하여 청구인들의 평등권을 침해
하는 것이다.

☑ 해   설

당시 헌법재판소는 재외동포법 제2조 2호의 시행령 제3조에 대한 단순위헌 결정은 갑작스러운 혼란을 야기할 우려가 있다고 판단하여 일단 헌법불합치를 선고하고, 2003년 말까지만 잠정적용을 인정했다. 이 결정 이후 국내에서는 재외동포법의 개정방향에 대해 상당한 논란이 제기되었다. 일각에서는 혈통주의에 입각하여 모든 한민족 동포를 포용하는 방향으로 법이 개정되어야 한다고 주장했다. 그러나 이 법에 대해 원래부터 비판적이었던 측에서는 차제에 재외동포법을 폐기시키고 재외동포에 대한 필요한 지원은 다른 방향에서 모색하자고 주장했다.

한편 법무부는 헌법불합치 결정에 대한 대응방안으로 법 자체는 개정하지 않고, 시행령 이하의 개정만을 통하여도 헌법재판소 결정의 취지를 만족시킬 수 있다고 주장했다. 이에 시행령 제3조를

"법 제2조 제2호에서 "대한민국의 국적을 보유하였던 자 또는 그 직계비속으로서 외국국적을 취득한 자"라 함은 다음 각호의 1에 해당하는 자를 말한다.

1. 대한민국의 국적을 보유하였던 자로서 외국국적을 취득한 자.
2. 부모의 일방 또는 조부모의 일방이 대한민국의 국적을 보유하였던
   자로서 외국국적을 취득한 자"

로 개정하고, 아울러 출입국관리법 시행령 별표 1 재외동포 체류자격(F4) 부분과 동 시행규칙 별표 5도 개정하여 불법체류 다발국가 출신 동포에 대하여는 사증발급 신청시의 소명자료 요건을 엄격화했다. 즉 재외동포의 구분에 있어서 외견상 과거국적주의는 배제했으나, 실제로는 여전히 구 공산권출신 동포에 대한 재외동포 자격 부여에 제한을 가했다. 그러나 헌법재판소의 헌법불합치 결정의 주문이 재외동포법 제2조 2호와 시행령 제3조가 헌법에 합치되지 않는다고 적시하고 있음에도 불구하고, 단지 시행령만을 개정하여 이를 만족시킬 수 있는가라는 의문이 제기되었다. 결국 2004년 2월 국회는 제2조(정의) 2호 규정을

"2. 대한민국의 국적을 보유하였던 자(대한민국정부 수립 이전에 국외로

이주한 동포를 포함한다) 또는 그 直系卑屬으로서 外國國籍을 취득
한 者중 大統領令이 정하는 者(이하 "外國國籍同胞"라 한다)"

로 개정했다. 이후 정부는 현실적으로 문제가 제기되고 있는 중국동포에 대
한 국내 출입국 및 취업 요건을 지속적으로 완화하여 이 문제에 대한 불만
을 감소시키었다. 그러나 재외동포법의 내용이 국제인권규범상의 인종, 민족
등에 근거한 차별금지 원칙에 위반되지 않느냐는 근본적인 문제는 여전히
해결되지 않고 있다.

➡ 참고문헌 —————————————————————————————————————

- 이철우, 재외동포법의 헌법적 평가: 헌법재판소의 결정을 중심으로, 법과사회 22호(2002), p. 253.
- 이철우, 재외동포법을 둘러싼 논쟁의 비판적 검토, 최대권교수 정년기념논문집 헌법과 사회(철학과 현실사, 2003).
- 정인섭, 유럽의 해외동포 지원입법의 검토—한국의 재외동포법 개정논의와 관련하여, 국제법학회논총 48권 2호(2003. 10), p. 189.
- 정인섭, 재외동포법(사람생각, 2002).

제15장

국제인권법

1. Söring 사건(1989)
— 범죄인인도시의 인도적 고려

Söring v. U.K.
1989 European Court of Human Rights, Series A, Vol. 161
(Application No. 14038/88).

☑ 사   안

독일인인 Jens Söring은 미국 버지니아 대학 유학시절 미국인 여자친구의 부모를 살해하고 영국으로 도주했다가 영국에서 체포되었다. 버지니아 법원은 그를 살인혐의로 기소하기로 하고, 미국 정부를 통해 영국에 범죄인인도를 요청했다. 사형제도가 없는 영국은 Söring을 인도해도 사형집행은 하지 않을 것을 미국측에 요구했으나, 확답은 못 받았다. Söring에 대하여는 독일 정부 역시 범죄인인도를 요청했으나, 영국은 여러 정황을 검토한 끝에 미국으로 인도하기로 결정했다. Söring은 범죄인인도를 막기 위해 영국 법원에 인신보호영장을 청구했으나, 기각당했다. 그는 재차 자신을 미국으로 인도하는 것은 「유럽인권협약」위반이라고 주장하며 European Commission of Human Rights에 청원을 제출했고, 이 사건은 최종적으로 유럽인권재판소에 회부되었다. Söring측은 미국 교도소의 열악한 상황을 지적하고 특히 사형대기자가 되면 극도의 스트레스, 심리적 공황상태, 성적 착취의 대상이 될 우려가 있다고 주장했다. 따라서 이러한 곳으로 범죄인인도를 한다면 "고문, 비인도적인 또는 굴욕적인 처우나 처벌"을 금지한 「유럽인권협약」제3조 위반이 된다고 주장했다.

☑ 쟁   점

범죄인인도 조약상의 의무에도 불구하고, 인도 후 「유럽인권협약」이 금하고 있는 비인도적 처우 등을 받을 것이 우려된다면 범죄인인도가 금지되는가 여부.

☑ 판   결

비인도적 처우 등을 받을 것이 실제로 우려되는 국가로의 범죄인인도는 「유럽인권협약」 위반이다.

판 결 문

85. […] What is at issue in the present case is whether Article 3[1] can be applicable when the adverse consequences of extradition are, or may be, suffered outside the jurisdiction of the extraditing State as a result of treatment or punishment administered in the receiving State. […]

87. In interpreting the Convention regard must be had to its special character as a treaty for the collective enforcement of human rights and fundamental freedoms (*see the Ireland v. the United Kingdom judgment of 18 January 1978, Series A no. 25, p. 90, §239*). Thus, the object and purpose of the Convention as an instrument for the protection of individual human beings require that its provisions be interpreted and applied so as to make its safeguards practical and effective […]. In addition, any interpretation of the rights and freedoms guaranteed has to be consistent with "the general spirit of the Convention, an instrument designed to maintain and promote the ideals and values of a democratic society" […].

88. Article 3 makes no provision for exceptions and no derogation from it is permissible under Article 15 in time of war or other national emergency. This absolute prohibition of torture and of inhuman or degrading treatment or punishment under the terms of the Convention shows that Article 3 enshrines one of the fundamental values of the democratic societies making up the Council of Europe. It is also to be found in similar terms in other international instruments such as the 1966 International Covenant on Civil and Political Rights and the 1969 American Convention on Human Rights and is generally recognised as an internationally accepted standard.

The question remains whether the extradition of a fugitive to another State

---

1) 유럽인권협약 제3조 어느 누구도 고문, 비인도적인 또는 굴욕적인 대우나 처벌을 받지 아니한다.

where he would be subjected or be likely to be subjected to torture or to inhuman or degrading treatment or punishment would itself engage the responsibility of a Contracting State under Article 3. That the abhorrence of torture has such implications is recognised in Article 3 of the United Nations Convention Against Torture and Other Cruel, Inhuman or Degrading Treatment or Punishment, which provides that "no State Party shall ... extradite a person where there are substantial grounds for believing that he would be in danger of being subjected to torture". The fact that a specialised treaty should spell out in detail a specific obligation attaching to the prohibition of torture does not mean that an essentially similar obligation is not already inherent in the general terms of Article 3 of the European Convention. It would hardly be compatible with the underlying values of the Convention, that "common heritage of political traditions, ideals, freedom and the rule of law" to which the Preamble refers, were a Contracting State knowingly to surrender a fugitive to another State where there were substantial grounds for believing that he would be in danger of being subjected to torture, however heinous the crime allegedly committed. Extradition in such circumstances, while not explicitly referred to in the brief and general wording of Article 3, would plainly be contrary to the spirit and intendment of the Article, and in the Court's view this inherent obligation not to extradite also extends to cases in which the fugitive would be faced in the receiving State by a real risk of exposure to inhuman or degrading treatment or punishment proscribed by that Article. [···]

90. It is not normally for the Convention institutions to pronounce on the existence or otherwise of potential violations of the Convention. However, where an applicant claims that a decision to extradite him would, if implemented, be contrary to Article 3 by reason of its foreseeable consequences in the requesting country, a departure from this principle is necessary, in view of the serious and irreparable nature of the alleged suffering risked, in order to ensure the effectiveness of the safeguard provided by that Article [···].

91. In sum, the decision by a Contracting State to extradite a fugitive may give rise to an issue under Article 3, and hence engage the responsibility of that State under the Convention, where substantial grounds have been shown for believing that the person concerned, if extradited, faces a real risk of being subjected to torture or to inhuman or degrading treatment or punishment in the requesting country. The establishment of such responsibility inevitably involves an assessment of conditions in the requesting country against the standards of Article 3 of the

Convention. Nonetheless, there is no question of adjudicating on or establishing the responsibility of the receiving country, whether under general international law, under the Convention or otherwise. In so far as any liability under the Convention is or may be incurred, it is liability incurred by the extraditing Contracting State by reason of its having taken action which has as a direct consequence the exposure of an individual to proscribed ill-treatment. […][2]

111. […] However, in the Court's view, having regard to the very long period of time spent on death row in such extreme conditions, with the ever present and mounting anguish of awaiting execution of the death penalty, and to the personal circumstances of the applicant, especially his age and mental state at the time of the offence, the applicant's extradition to the United States would expose him to a real risk of treatment going beyond the threshold set by Article 3. A further consideration of relevance is that in the particular instance the legitimate purpose of extradition could be achieved by another means which would not involve suffering of such exceptional intensity or duration.

Accordingly, the Secretary of State's decision to extradite the applicant to the United States would, if implemented, give rise to a breach of Article 3.

☑ 해   설

이 판결이 내려진 이후 미국 정부는 Söring이 사형판결을 받을 죄목으로는 재판받지 않을 것임을 약속하고 영국으로부터 그를 인도받았다. Söring은 버지니아 법원에서 종신형을 받았으며, 여자친구는 90년 형을 선고받았다. 이 판결의 논리를 확대한다면 「유럽인권협약」 비당사국에게 협약상의 기준 준수를 요구하는 결과가 되며, 또한 타국의 국내사정에 지나치게 관여하게 된다고 비판될 수도 있다.

사형폐지국이 사형존치국으로 사형을 선고받을 수 있는 자를 범죄인인도하는 것이 국제인권조약 위반인가 여부는 다른 인권조약과의 관계에서도 적지 않게 문제되었다. 예를 들어 「시민적 및 정치적 권리에 관한 국제규약」의 Human Rights Committee(HRC)는 Judge v. Canada 사건에서 사형 폐지국인 캐나다가 사형 불집행의 보장 없이 사형집행이 예견될 수 있는 국가인

---

2) 이어서 재판부는 Söring이 미국으로 인도되었을 경우 미국 교도소에서 직면하게 될 여러 상황과 범행시의 연령과 심리상태 등을 다각도로 검토했다.

미국으로 범죄인을 인도하는 것은 규약 제6조 생명권 보호조항의 위배라고 판단했다(*Judge v. Canada*, HRC Communication No.829/98(2003)).

인권규약 자체는 사형을 금지하지 않고 있으므로 미국의 사형 집행은 규약 위반이 아닌데도 불구하고, 캐나다가 그를 미국으로 인도하는 행위만 규약 위반이라는 평가는 비논리적이라는 비판이 가해질 수 있다. 그러나 HRC는 사형의 가능성을 인정하고 있는 규약 제6조 2항은 사형존치국에 대해서만 적용되며, 사형폐지국들에 대해서는 그 적용이 제외된다고 해석했다. 즉 규약 제6조 2항이 사형의 폐지를 연기하거나 사형의 범위를 확대하거나 사형의 도입 또는 재도입을 허용하는 근거가 될 수는 없다고 보았다. 그리고 사형의 재도입금지에는 자국관할권 내에서의 직접적인 사형실시뿐만 아니라, 자국의 관할권 내에 있는 개인을 인도, 추방, 강제 송환 등을 통해 다른 국가에 넘겨주어 사형에 처해질 위험에 직면하게 하는 경우와 같은 간접적인 재도입도 대상이 된다고 보았다. 따라서 사형폐지국이 사형의 대상이 될 범죄인을 사형존치국으로 별다른 보장 없이 인도하는 행위는 규약 위반이라고 판단했다. 적지 않은 조약은 범죄인 인도 이후 사형의 집행이 예상되는 경우 인도금지를 규정하고 있기도 하다. 이러한 Söring 판결은 현대 국제인권법의 발전방향과 일치한다고 평가된다.

한편 Söring은 수감생활 중 영어 및 독일어로 7권의 책과 여러 편의 논문을 집필하였으며, 그 중 "The Convict Christ(2006)"는 2007년 북미 캐토릭 언론협회로부터 Social Concerns 부분 1등상을 수상했다.

➥ 참고문헌 ────────────────────────

• 최태현, 범죄인인도 결정시 인도적 고려, 서울국제법연구 1권 1호(1994), p. 159.
• S. Breitenmoser & G. Wilms, Human Rights v. Extradition: The Söring Case, Michigan Journal of International Law Vol. 11(1990), p. 845.
• C. den Wyngaert, Applying the European Convention on Human Rights to Extradition: Opening Pandora's Box?, ICLQ Vol. 39(1990), p. 757.

2. 양심적 병역거부(2007)

Yeo-Bum Yoon and Myung-Jin Choi v. Republic of Korea Human Rights Committee, Communication Nos. 1321/ 2004, 1322/2004(2007)(CCPR/C/88/D1321-1322/2004).

☑ 사 안

한국인인 신청인들은 여호와의 증인 신도로 종교상의 이유로 병역을 거부하자, 그 결과 각각 1년 6개월의 형을 선고받았다. 이들은 대체복무제의 마련 없이 일률적으로 병역의무를 부과하고 이를 거부하는 자를 처벌하는 한국의 병역법은 「시민적 및 정치적 권리에 관한 국제규약」 제18조 1항이 보장하고 있는 종교와 신념의 자유를 침해한다고 주장하는 개인통보를 Human Rights Committee에 제기했다.

☑ 쟁 점

종교의 자유에 대한 권리는 종교적 신념에 따라 병역을 거부할 권리를 포함하는가 여부.

☑ 결 정

양심적 병역거부 역시 종교의 자유의 일부로 보호받아야 한다.

결정문

8.1 The Human Rights Committee has considered the present communication in the light of all the information made available to it by the parties, as provided in article 5, paragraph 1, of the Optional Protocol.

8.2 The Committee notes the authors' claim that article 18 of the Covenant guaranteeing the right to freedom of conscience and the right to manifest one's religion or belief requires recognition of their religious belief, genuinely held, that submission to compulsory military service is morally and ethically impermissible for them as individuals. It also notes that article 8, paragraph 3, of the Covenant excludes from the scope of "forced or compulsory labour", which is proscribed, "any service of a military character and, in countries where conscientious objection is recognized, any national service required by law of conscientious objectors". It follows that the article 8 of the Covenant itself neither recognizes nor excludes a right of conscientious objection. Thus, the present claim is to be assessed solely in the light of article 18 of the Covenant, the understanding of which evolves as that of any other guarantee of the Covenant over time in view of its text and purpose.

8.3 The Committee recalls its previous jurisprudence on the assessment of a claim of conscientious objection to military service as a protected form of manifestation of religious belief under article 18, paragraph 1. It observes that while the right to manifest one's religion or belief does not as such imply the right to refuse all obligations imposed by law, it provides certain protection, consistent with article 18, paragraph 3, against being forced to act against genuinely-held religious belief. The Committee also recalls its general view expressed in General Comment 22 that to compel a person to use lethal force, although such use would seriously conflict with the requirements of his conscience or religious beliefs, falls within the ambit of article 18. The Committee notes, in the instant case, that the authors' refusal to be drafted for compulsory service was a direct expression of their religious beliefs, which it is uncontested were genuinely held. The authors' conviction and sentence, accordingly, amounts to a restriction on their ability to manifest their religion or belief. Such restriction must be justified by the permissible limits described in paragraph 3 of article 18, that is, that any restriction must be prescribed by law and be necessary to protect public safety, order, health or morals or the fundamental rights and freedoms of others. However, such restriction must not impair the very essence of the right in question.

8.4 The Committee notes that under the laws of the State party there is no procedure for recognition of conscientious objections against military service. The State party argues that this restriction is necessary for public safety, in order to maintain its national defensive capacities and to preserve social cohesion. The Committee takes note of the State party's argument on the particular context of its national security, as well as of its intention to act on the national action plan for conscientious objection devised by the National Human Rights Commission (see paragraph 6.5, *supra*). The Committee also notes, in relation to relevant State practice, that an increasing number of those States parties to the Covenant which have retained compulsory military service have introduced alternatives to compulsory military service, and considers that the State party has failed to show what special disadvantage would be involved for it if the rights of the authors' under article 18 would be fully respected. As to the issue of social cohesion and equitability, the Committee considers that respect on the part of the State for conscientious beliefs and manifestations thereof is itself an important factor in ensuring cohesive and stable pluralism in society. It likewise observes that it is in principle possible, and in practice common, to conceive alternatives to compulsory military service that do not erode the basis of the principle of universal conscription but render equivalent social good and make equivalent demands on the individual, eliminating unfair disparities between those engaged in compulsory military service and those in alternative service. The Committee, therefore, considers that the State party has not demonstrated that in the present case the restriction in question is necessary, within the meaning of article 18, paragraph 3, of the Covenant.

9. The Human Rights Committee, acting under article 5, paragraph 4, of the Optional Protocol to the International Covenant on Civil and Political Rights, concludes that the facts as found by the Committee reveal, in respect of each author violations by the Republic of Korea of article 18, paragraph 1, of the Covenant.

10. In accordance with article 2, paragraph 3 (a), of the Covenant, the State party is under an obligation to provide the authors with an effective remedy, including compensation. The State party is under an obligation to avoid similar violations of the Covenant in the future. (각주 생략)

☑ 해 설

「시민적 및 정치적 권리에 관한 국제규약 선택의정서」 당사국에 대하여 는 규약상의 권리를 침해당했다고 주장하는 피해자가 Human Rights Committee에 개인통보(Individual Communication)를 제기해 구제를 요청할 수 있 다. 단 피해자는 개인통보를 제기하기 전에 국내적 구제절차를 완료하여야 한다. 한국은 1990년 국제인권규약에 가입하면서 선택의정서도 수락하였다. 이 사건은 한국을 상대로 Human Rights Committee가 내린 10번째 결정이다.

과거 한국에서는 매년 약 500-600명 정도가 병역을 거부하여 형사처벌을 받았으며, 그 거의 대부분은 여호와의 증인 신도들이었다. 비교적 최근까지 국내 법원은 병역거부자의 대체복무를 인정하고 있지 않는 현행 병역법이 헌법 제19조의 양심의 자유나 제20조상의 종교의 자유를 침해하지 않는다고 해석했다. 대법원 2004년 7월 15일 선고, 2004도2965 판결; 대법원 2007년 12월 27일 선고, 2007도7941 판결; 대법원 2014년 6월 26일 선고, 2014도4915 판결; 대법원 2014년 7월 24일 선고, 2014도6249 판결; 대법원 2014년 8월 20일 선고, 2014도7228 판결; 대법원 2014년 9월 26일 선고, 2014도9755 판결; 헌법재판소 2004년 8월 26일 선고, 2002헌가1 결정; 헌법재판소 2004년 10월 28일 선고, 2004헌바61, 62, 75(병합) 결정; 헌법재판소 2011년 8월 30일 선고, 2007헌가12 결정; 헌법재판소 2011년 8월 30일 선고, 2008헌가22 결정 등 참조.

그러나 위 결정문에도 나타나 있는 바와 같이 Human Rights Committee는 1993년 발표한 일반논평 22 등을 통하여 양심적 병역거부가 규약 제18조의 보호범위에 속한다고 보는 입장을 취하였다.

이어 Committee는 2010년 3월 23일 한국 정부가 오태양 외 11명의 양심적 병역거부자를 처벌한 것이 규약 위반이라는 결정했으며(Communication No. 1593-1603/2007), 2011년 4월 5일에는 재차 정민규 등 100명의 한국인 양심적 병역거부자의 처벌이 규약 위반이라고 결정했다(Communication No. 1642-1741/2007). 이어 2012년에도 김종남 등 388명이 제기한 사건에서 규약 위반이라는 결정을 다시 내렸다(Communication No. 1786/2008).

이 같은 Committee의 입장은 국내에서 양심적 병역거부의 지지 논거로 활용되었고, 관련 인권규약조항은 국내 법원에서 가장 빈번히 주장되는 조약문이 되기도 했다. 마침내 헌법재판소는 2018. 6. 28. 선고, 2011헌바379 결정을 통해 양심적 병역거부자를 위해 대체복무제를 인정하지 않는 병역법 조항에 대해 헌법 불합치 판정을 내렸다. 이어 대법원도 2018. 11. 1. 선고, 2016도10912 판결을 통해 양심적 병역거부는 병역법 제88조 1항에 규정된 입영에 응하지 않을 정당한 사유의 하나로 인정해 이들 병역거부자에 대해 무죄를 선고했다. 결국 양심적 병역거부자를 수용하기 위해 새로이 「대체역의 편입 및 복무 등에 관한 법률」이 제정되어 2020년부터 시행되게 되었다. 양심적 병역거부 문제는 국제인권법이 국내 법률 해석 변경에 영향을 미친 대표적 사례의 하나가 되었다.

➡ 참고문헌 ─────────────────────────────────

- 안경환·장복희편, 양심적 병역거부(사람생각, 2002).
- 한인섭·이재승편, 양심적 병역거부제와 대체복무제(경인문화사, 2013).
- 정인섭, 시민적 및 정치적 권리에 관한 국제규약과 군장병 인권(서울대학교), 법학 48권 4호(2007), p. 35.
- 장영수, 양심적 병역거부와 병역법 제88조 제1항 등의 합헌성 여부에 대한 검토, 헌법학연구 21권 3호(2015), p. 161.
- 박찬운, 양심적 병역거부: 국제인권법적 현황과 한국의 선택, 저스티스 141호 (2014), p. 5.
- 채형복, 양심적 병역거부: 권리인가, 도피인가: 유럽의 사례를 중심으로, (경북대) 법학논고 40집(2012), p. 1.

3. 법 앞의 평등의 적용 범위(1987)

S. Broeks v. The Netherlands.
Human Rights Committee, Communication No.172/1984(1987)
(CCPR/C/29/D/172/1984).

☑ 사   안

이 사건의 통보인인 S. Broeks는 여성 장애인이다. 그녀는 간호사로 근무하다가 장애를 이유로 해고당했다. 한동안 그녀는 장애수당과 실업수당을 동시에 받았으나, 1976년부터는 기혼 여성의 경우 자신이 부양 의무자임을 증명하지 못하면 실업수당을 지급하지 않도록 실업수당법이 개정되어 그녀는 더 이상 실업수당을 받지 못했다. 그런데 이 법은 기혼 남성에게는 부양 의무자임을 증명하도록 요구하지 않았다. 이에 그녀는 네덜란드의 법이 기혼 남성과 기혼 여성을 차별함으로써「시민적 및 정치적 권리에 관한 규약」제26조 법 앞의 평등을 위반했다고 주장하며, Human Rights Committee에 개인통보를 제출했다. 이 사건에서 네덜란드는「시민적 및 정치적 권리에 관한 규약」제26조는 오직 당해 규약상의 권리에만 적용되며, 통보자의 주장과 같이 사회경제적 권리에 대하여는 적용되지 않는다고 반박했다. 따라서 이 사건은 Human Rights Committee의 심의대상에 포함되지 않는다고 주장했다. 결론적으로 Committee는 규약 제26조의 적용대상은「시민적 및 정치적 권리에 관한 규약」에 규정된 권리에 한정되지 않는다고 전제하고, 네덜란드의 실업수당법은 기혼인 남녀를 비합리적 수준에서 구별하고 있으므로 규약에 위반된다고 결론내렸다.

☑ 쟁　점

「시민적 및 정치적 권리에 관한 규약」 제26조 법 앞의 평등조항의 적용
범위.

☑ 결　정

규약상의 법 앞의 평등조항이 당사국에 대하여 모든 분야에 있어서의
평등한 입법의 의무를 부과하지는 않으나, 일단 제정된 법률은 그 내용과 관
계없이 차별적인 내용을 담아서는 아니 된다는 의무를 부과한다.

결 정 문

12.1. The State party contends that there is considerable overlapping of the
provisions of article 26 with the provisions of article 2 of the International
Covenant on Economic, Social and Cultural Rights. The Committee is of the view
that the International Covenant on Civil and Political Rights would still apply even
if a particular subject-matter is referred to or covered in other international
instruments, for example, the International Convention on the Elimination of All
Forms of Racial Discrimination, the Convention on the Elimination of All Forms of
Discrimination against Women, or, as in the present case, the International
Covenant on Economic, Social and Cultural Rights. Notwithstanding the interrelated
drafting history of the two Covenants, it remains necessary for the Committee to
apply fully the terms of the International Covenant on Civil and Political Rights.
The Committee observes in this connection that the provisions of article 2 of the
International Covenant on Economic, Social and Cultural Rights do not detract
from the full application of article 26 of the International Covenant on Civil and
Political Rights.

12.2. The Committee has also examined the contention of the State party that
article 26 of the International Covenant on Civil and Political Rights cannot be
invoked in respect of a right which is specifically provided for under article 9 of the
International Covenant on Economic, Social and Cultural Rights (social security,
including social insurance). In so doing, the Committee has perused the relevant
travaux preparatoires of the International Covenant on Civil and Political Rights,

namely, the summary records of the discussions that took place in the Commission on Human Rights in 1948, 1949, 1950 and 1952 and in the Third Committee of the General Assembly in 1961, which provide a "supplementary means of interpretation" (art. 32 of the Vienna Convention on the Law of Treaties) (*see* footnote 2). The discussions, at the time of drafting, concerning the question whether the scope of article 26 extended to rights not otherwise guaranteed by the Covenant, were inconclusive and cannot alter the conclusion arrived at by the ordinary means of interpretation referred to in paragraph 12.3 below.

12.3. For the purpose of determining the scope of article 26, the Committee has taken into account the "ordinary meaning" of each element of the article in its context and in the light of its object and purpose (art. 31 of the Vienna Convention on the Law of Treaties). The Committee begins by noting that article 26 does not merely duplicate the guarantees already provided for in article 2. It derives from the principle of equal protection of the law without discrimination, as contained in article 7 of the Universal Declaration of Human Rights, which prohibits discrimination in law or in practice in any field regulated and protected by public authorities. Article 26 is thus concerned with the obligations imposed on States in regard to their legislation and the application thereof.

12.4. Although article 26 requires that legislation should prohibit discrimination, it does not of itself contain any obligation with respect to the matters that may be provided for by legislation. Thus it does not, for example, require any State to enact legislation to provide for social security. However, when such legislation is adopted in the exercise of a State's sovereign power, then such legislation must comply with article 26 of the Covenant.

12.5. The Committee observes in this connection that what is at issue is not whether or not social security should be progressively established in the Netherlands, but whether the legislation providing for social security violates the prohibition against discrimination contained in article 26 of the International Covenant on Civil and Political Rights and the guarantee given therein to all persons regarding equal and effective protection against discrimination.

13. The right to equality before the law and to equal protection of the law without any discrimination does not make all differences of treatment discriminatory. A differentiation based on reasonable and objective criteria does not amount to prohibited discrimination within the meaning of article 26.

14. It therefore remains for the Committee to determine whether the differentiation in Netherlands law at the time in question and as applied to Mrs. Broeks constituted discrimination within the meaning of article 26. The Committee notes that in Netherlands law the provisions of articles 84 and 85 of the Netherlands Civil Code impose equal rights and obligations on both spouses with regard to their joint income. Under section 13, subsection 1 (1), of the Unemployment Benefits Act (WWV), a married woman, in order to receive WWV benefits, had to prove that she was a "breadwinner" a condition that did not apply to married men. Thus a differentiation which appears on one level to be one of status is in fact one of sex, placing married women at a disadvantage compared with married men. Such a differentiation is not reasonable; and this seems to have been effectively acknowledged even by the State party by the enactment of a change in the law on 29 April 1985, with retroactive effect to 23 December 1984. […]

15. The circumstances in which Mrs. Broeks found herself at the material time and the application of the then valid Netherlands law made her a victim of a violation, based on sex, of article 26 of the International Covenant on Civil and Political Rights, because she was denied a social security benefit on an equal footing with men.

16. The Committee notes that the State party had not intended to discriminate against women and further notes with appreciation that the discriminatory provisions in the law applied to Mrs. Broeks have, subsequently, been eliminated. Although the State party has thus taken the necessary measures to put an end to the kind of discrimination suffered by Mrs. Broeks at the time complained of, the Committee is of the view that the State party should offer Mrs. Broeks an appropriate remedy.

☑ 해 설

이 결정은 상당한 파장을 일으켰다. 이는 「시민적 및 정치적 권리에 관한 국제규약 선택의정서」를 근거로 한 개인통보의 대상을 규약이 규정하고 있는 권리 이상으로 확대시키게 된다. 즉 규약상의 권리에 한하지 않고, 당사국의 모든 입법이 객관적이고 합리적인 구별에 해당하는가를 심사받게 된다. 이는 당사국으로서도 아마 예상치 못한 커다란 부담을 의미하게 될 것이다. 이에 이 결정 이후 선택의정서에 가입한 독일과 같은 국가는 「시민적 및 정치적 권리에 관한 국제규약」에 규정된 권리 이외에 대하여 제26조 위반을

주장하는 개인통보는 수락할 수 없다는 유보를 첨부하기도 했다. 이러한 각
국의 반발을 의식해 Human Rights Committee도 제26조와 관련 합리적 구
별의 허용 범위를 상당히 넓게 인정하는 방향으로 해석하고 있다. 즉 사회·
경제적 권리에 관한 제26조 위반 주장에 대하여는 개인통보 수락에 엄격한
태도를 보여 왔다.

4. 구 식민지 출신 군인에 대한 연금차별(1989)

Ibrahima *et al.* v. France.
Human Rights Committee, Communication No. 196/1985
(1989)(CCPR/C/35/D/196/1985).

☑ 사 안

이 사건 청구인들은(총 743명) 1960년 세네갈이 독립하기 전인 프랑스 식민지 시절 프랑스군에 복무했던 세네갈 출신의 제대군인들로 통보 당시는 세네갈 국민들이었다. 과거 이들은 1951년 프랑스 군인연금법에 따라 현재의 국적과 관계 없이 프랑스인과 동일한 액수의 연금을 지급받았다. 그러나 1975년부터는 법개정에 따라 프랑스인보다 훨씬 적은 액수의 연금만을 지급받게 되었다. 아프리카인들은 프랑스인의 대략 1/10 정도의 액수만 받았다. 프랑스측은 이들이 독립으로 인하여 프랑스 국적을 상실했으며, 프랑스와 구식민지간에는 경제상황에 차이가 있으므로 그에 맞게 연금액수가 조정되는 것은 차별이 아니라고 주장했다. 다만 이들이 프랑스인으로 귀화하면 프랑스인과 동일한 연금을 지불받는다. 청구인은 자신들이 「시민적 및 정치적 권리에 관한 국제규약」 제26조 법 앞의 평등 조항에 위배되는 차별을 받았다며 Human Rights Committee에 개인통보를 제출했다.

☑ 쟁 점

구식민지 출신으로 현재는 외국인인 제대군인에게 자국민보다 적은 액수의 연금만을 지급하는 것은 법 앞의 평등에 위배되는가 여부.

☑ 결   정

동일한 조건에서 동일하게 복무했던 자에 대한 대가로서의 군인연금지급에 관하여는 사후적 국적변경이나 거주국의 경제사정 차이가 금액차별을 합리화할 근거가 될 수 없다.

결 정 문

9.3 The main question before the Committee is whether the authors are victims of discrimination within the meaning of article 26 of the Covenant or whether the differences in pension treatment of former members of the French Army, based on whether they are French nationals or not, should be deemed compatible with the Covenant. In determining this question, the Committee has taken into account the following considerations.

9.4 The Committee has noted the authors claim that they have been discriminated against on racial grounds, that is, one of the grounds specifically enumerated in article 26. It finds that there is no evidence to support the allegation that the State party has engaged in racially discriminatory practices vis-à-vis the authors. It remains, however, to be determined whether the situation encountered by the authors falls within the purview of article 26. The Committee recalls that the authors are not generally subject to French jurisdiction, except that they rely on French legislation in relation to the amount of their pension rights. It notes that nationality as such does not figure among the prohibited grounds of discrimination listed in article 26, and that the Covenant does not protect the right to a pension, as such. Under article 26, discrimination in the equal protection of the law is prohibited on any grounds such as race, colour, sex, language, religion, political or other opinion, national or social origin, property, birth or other status. There has been a differentiation by reference to nationality acquired upon independence. In the Committee's opinion, this falls within the reference to "other status" in the second sentence of article 26. The Committee takes into account, as it did in communication No. 182/1984, that "the right to equality before the law and to equal protection of the law without any discrimination does not make all differences of treatment discriminatory. A differentiation based on reasonable and objective criteria does not amount to prohibited discrimination within the meaning of article 26."

9.5 In determining whether the treatment of the authors is based on reasonable and objective criteria, the Committee notes that it was not the question of nationality which determined the granting of pensions to the authors but the services rendered by them in the past. They had served in the French Armed Forces under the same conditions as French citizens; for 14 years subsequent to the independence of Senegal they were treated in the same way as their French counterparts for the purpose of pension rights, although their nationality was not French but Senegalese. A subsequent change in nationality cannot by itself be considered as a sufficient justification for different treatment, since the basis for the grant of the pension was the same service which both they and the soldiers who remained French had provided. Nor can differences in the economic, financial and social conditions as between France and Senegal be invoked as a legitimate justification. If one compared the case of retired soldiers of Senegalese nationality living in Senegal with that of retired soldiers of French nationality in Senegal, it would appear that they enjoy the same economic and social conditions. Yet, their treatment for the purpose of pension entitlements would differ. Finally, the fact that the State party claims that it can no longer carry out checks of identity and family situation, so as to prevent abuses in the administration of pension schemes cannot justify a difference in treatment. In the Committee's opinion, mere administrative inconvenience or the possibility of some abuse of pension rights cannot be invoked to justify unequal treatment. The Committee concludes that the difference in treatment of the authors is not based on reasonable and objective criteria and constitutes discrimination prohibited by the Covenant.

10. The Human Rights Committee, acting under article 5, paragraph 4, of the Optional Protocol to the International Covenant on Civil and Political Rights, is of the view that the events in this case, in so far as they produced effects after 17 May 1984 (the date of entry into force of the Optional Protocol for France), disclose a violation of article 26 of the Covenant.

11. The Committee, accordingly, is of the view that the State party is under an obligation, in accordance with the provisions of article 2 of the Covenant, to take effective measures to remedy the violations suffered by the victims.

☑ 해   설

「시민적 및 정치적 권리에 관한 국제규약」 제26조(법 앞의 평등조항)가 국적에 의한 차별금지를 명문화하고 있지 않아서 당초 통보자들은 이 사건을 인종에 따른 차별이라고 주장했다. 그러나 Human Rights Committee는 비록 규약 제26조에 국적에 의한 차별금지가 명문화되어 있지 않아도, 기타 지위 (other status)라는 개념에 국적도 포함된다고 판단해 프랑스의 조치가 규약 제26조 위반이라고 결정했다. 이 사건에서는 위에 언급된 사항 외에 관할권 성립과 관련된 법적 쟁점을 몇 가지 더 포함하고 있었다. 즉 프랑스는 청구인이 주장한 것은 연금 수령권인데, 이러한 경제적 권리는 규약의 보호대상이 아니라고 주장했다. 이에 대하여 Committee는 규약 당사국이 법률을 제정하는 경우 비차별적 법을 만들어야 한다는 의무는 경제적 권리에 관한 법률에 관하여도 동일하게 적용되므로 이 사건이 관할대상에 포함된다고 판단했다. 또한 프랑스는 자신이 선택의정서를 수락하기 이전에 군인연금법이 개정되었으므로 이 사건은 Committee의 관할대상이 아니라고 주장했다. 이에 대해 Committee는 차별의 효과가 선택의정서 수락 이후에도 계속되고 있으므로 관할대상에 포함된다고 판단했다. 한편 이 결정은 일제시절 일본군에 복무했던 한국인들에 대하여 일본 정부가 연금지급 등 일체의 원호보상을 거부한 사실과도 비교되었다. 일본 역시 인권규약 당사국이나 일본은 선택의정서를 수락하지 않았기 때문에 일본을 상대로 한 개인통보의 제출은 불가능했다.

5. 난민지위 인정의 요건(2012)

대법원 2012년 4월 26일 선고, 2010두27448 판결.
판례공보 2012년 (상), 876쪽.

☑ 사 안

코트디부아르 국적의 이 사건 원고는 단기체류 자격으로 한국에 입국한
지 약 80일만인 2005년 6월 15일 난민인정신청을 했으나, 법무부는 2009년
6월 4일 불허처분을 내렸다. 원고는 자국 대통령과 같은 종족인 Bete족의 일
원으로서 Bouake 지역에서 집권당인 FPI의 여성 코디네이터로서 활동을 하
였다. 정부군과 반군 사이의 내전이 발생하자 수도 아비장(Abidjan)으로 가
FPI 지역 서기관이던 사촌오빠의 집에 기거하면서 정치활동을 했다. 2004년
경 반군으로부터 베테족의 일원으로서 FPI 활동을 했다는 이유로 사촌오빠
가 살해당하고, 원고는 당시 심한 구타를 당한 후 구조되어 간신히 목숨을
유지할 수 있었다. 원고는 다시 코트디부아르로 귀국할 경우 반군으로부터
생명의 위협을 받게 된다고 주장하며 난민지위 인정을 요청했다. 하급심에서
는 원고의 주장이 다소 일관성이 없었고, 신빙성도 부족하며, 코트디브아르
정세도 최근 호전되었다는 근거에서 원고의 청구를 기각했다.

☑ 쟁 점

난민지위 인정의 요건.

☑ 판 결

(1) 박해의 경험에 관한 진술의 내용이 다소 불일치하거나 과장이 있더
라도 난민 신청자의 궁박하고 불안정한 상황을 감안해 전체적으로 평가해야

한다.

(2) 과거의 박해사실이 합리적으로 수긍되는 경우라면 그 출신국의 상황이 현저히 변경되어 박해의 가능성이 명백히 소멸했다고 볼 만한 특별한 사정이 인정되지 아니하는 한, 박해에 관한 충분한 근거 있는 공포가 있다고 보아야 한다.

판 결 문

"1. 출입국관리법 제2조 제3호, 제76조의2 제1항, 난민의 지위에 관한 협약 제1조, 난민의 지위에 관한 의정서 제1조의 규정을 종합하여 보면, 법무부장관은 인종, 종교, 국적, 특정 사회집단의 구성원 신분 또는 정치적 의견을 이유로 박해를 받을 충분한 근거 있는 공포로 인하여 국적국의 보호를 받을 수 없거나 국적국의 보호를 원하지 않는 대한민국 안에 있는 외국인에 대하여 그 신청이 있는 경우 난민협약이 정하는 난민으로 인정하여야 한다.

그리고 위와 같은 난민 인정의 요건인 박해를 받을 '충분한 근거 있는 공포'가 있다는 점은 원칙적으로 난민 인정의 신청을 하는 외국인이 증명하여야 할 것이나, 난민의 특수한 사정에 비추어 그 외국인에게 객관적인 증거에 의하여 주장사실 전체를 증명하도록 요구할 수는 없고, 그 진술에 일관성과 설득력이 있고 입국 경로, 입국 후 난민 신청까지의 기간, 난민 신청 경위, 국적국의 상황, 주관적으로 느끼는 공포의 정도, 신청인이 거주하던 지역의 정치·사회·문화적 환경, 그 지역의 통상인이 같은 상황에서 느끼는 공포의 정도 등에 비추어 전체적인 진술의 신빙성에 의하여 그 주장사실을 인정하는 것이 합리적인 경우라면 그 증명이 있다고 보아야 한다(대법원 2008년 7월 24일 선고, 2007두3930 판결 참조).

한편 박해의 경험에 관한 난민신청인의 진술을 평가할 때 그 진술의 세부내용에서 다소간의 불일치가 발견되거나 일부 과장된 점이 엿보인다고 하여 곧바로 신청인 진술의 전체적 신빙성을 부정하여서는 아니 되고, 그러한 불일치·과장이 진정한 박해의 경험에 따른 정신적 충격이나 난민신청인의 궁박한 처지에 따른 불안정한 심리상태, 시간의 경과에 따른 기억력의 한계,

우리나라와 서로 다른 문화적·역사적 배경에서 유래한 언어감각의 차이 등에서 비롯되었을 가능성도 충분히 염두에 두고 진술의 핵심내용을 중심으로 전체적인 일관성 및 신빙성을 평가하여야 하며, 특히 난민신청인이 여성으로서 심각한 박해의 피해자라고 주장하는 경우에는 그 가능성과 이에 따른 특수성도 진술의 신빙성을 평가하는 과정에서 염두에 두어야 한다. 그리고 만일 위와 같은 평가에 따라 난민신청인이 주장하는 과거의 박해사실이 합리적으로 수긍되는 경우라면 그 출신국의 상황이 현저히 변경되어 박해의 가능성이 명백히 소멸하였다고 볼 만한 특별한 사정이 인정되지 아니하는 한, 난민 인정의 요건인 박해에 관한 충분한 근거 있는 공포가 있다고 보아야 한다.

2. 원심이 인용한 제1심판결은 그 채용 증거에 의하여 원고의 출신국인 코트디부아르의 국가정황에 관한 판시사실을 인정한 다음, 원고가 피고와의 면담과정에서 한 진술과 이 사건 소송에서 한 진술 사이에 그 판시와 같은 불일치가 있음을 들어 원고가 주장하는 박해에 관한 진술의 신빙성을 부정하고, 일부 인정되는 피해사실도 원고의 종족이나 정치적 활동을 이유로 한 것이라고 단정하기 어려우며, 설령 원고의 종족이나 정치적 활동을 이유로 한 피해사실이 인정된다고 하더라도 2007. 3. 4. 평화협정 체결 이후 코트디부아르 국내사정이 호전된 점에 비추어 원고가 다시 귀국할 경우 박해를 받을 충분한 근거가 있는 위험이 존재한다고 보기 어렵다고 판단하여 원고의 청구를 기각하였다.

3. 그러나 이러한 원심 및 제1심의 판단은 수긍하기 어렵다.

원심이 인용한 제1심판결의 이유에 의하면, 제1심은 원고가 피고와 면담조사 당시에는 원고나 그 사촌이라고 주장하는 소외 1이 소외 2 대통령과 인척관계에 있기 때문에 반군의 표적이 되었다고 주장하다가 이 사건 소송에 이르러 대통령과 인척관계에 있는 것은 아니고 같은 종족일 뿐이라고 진술한 점, 또한 원고는 소외 1의 사망시점에 관하여 2005. 6.경 난민 인정신청 당시에는 2004. 11.경이라고 진술하였다가 2006. 3.경 면담조사 당시에는 2003. 3.경 친오빠가 살해되고 나서 한 달 후 소외 1이 살해되었다고 진술하였고 다시 이 사건 소송에 이르러서는 2004. 6.경이라고 진술한 점, 이 사건

소장에는 원고가 1984년경 아비장(Abidjan)에서 FPI(Le Front Populaire Ivoirien)에 입당하여 활동하다가 1985년경 전 남편과 결혼한 후 부아케(Bouake)로 가서 정치적 활동을 하였다는 취지로 기재되어 있으나 공식자료에 의하면 FPI의 창당시점은 그 이후인 1990년경인 것으로 보이고 원고도 1990년경 FPI가 창당하면서 그 모임에 참석하다가 2000년경 FPI에 입당하였다고 진술한 점 등 그 진술에 일관성이 없어 이를 믿기 어렵다는 취지로 판단하였다.

그러나 제1심이 채용한 증거 및 기록에 의하면, 원고는 피고에게 최초 난민 인정을 신청할 때부터 이 사건 소송에 이르기까지 일관되게, 자신은 소외 2 전 대통령과 같은 종족인 베테(Bete)족의 일원으로서 부아케 지역에서 당시 집권당인 FPI의 당원으로 활동하다가 정부군과 반군 사이의 내전이 발생한 이후 달로아(Daloa)를 거쳐 아비장으로 피신하여 그곳에 있는 원고의 사촌오빠이자 FPI 간부인 소외 1의 집에 기거하면서 정치활동을 하였는데, 2004년경 반군의 습격으로 소외 1이 집에서 살해당하고, 원고 역시 도주하다가 반군으로 생각되는 군인들에게 붙잡혀 나중에 의식을 잃을 정도로 심한 폭행을 당하였고, 이후 친분이 있는 목사의 도움으로 병원 치료를 받다가 계속된 반군에 의한 위협을 피하고자 코트디부아르를 떠나 우리나라에 입국하게 되었다고 주장하였음을 알 수 있고, 이러한 주장사실은 제1심이 인정한 코트디부아르의 국가정황에 비추어 충분히 그 발생의 가능성을 합리적으로 수긍할 수 있는 내용이라고 하지 않을 수 없다.

물론 원심 및 제1심이 지적한 바와 같이 원고의 진술내용이 그 세부사항에서 서로 불일치하거나 스스로 제출한 증거와 맞지 않는 부분이 있으나, 그러한 불일치라고 하는 것도 2004년 피습사건의 정확한 발생시기나 원고와 소외 1 혹은 소외 2 대통령과의 관계, FPI 창당일시 및 입당시기 등에 관한 것으로, 원심 및 제1심이 배척하지 아니한 병원진료기록(갑 제7호증)의 기재에 나타난 원고의 피해사실과 그 부위 및 상해의 내용, 이로 인하여 여성인 원고가 겪었을 정신적 충격, 난민신청인으로서 원고가 처한 처지, 시간의 경과에 따른 기억력의 한계, 우리나라와 코트디부아르 사이의 언어감각의 차이, 코트디부아르의 정치상황 등을 감안할 때, 원고 주장사실의 전체적 신빙성을 부정할 정도라고 보기 어렵다.

　　나아가 위와 같은 원고의 피해사실은 비록 내전상황에서 발생하였다고는 하나 그 정도와 심각성에서 단순히 코트디부아르 국민 일반이 겪는 수준의 고통이나 위협에 그친다고 말할 수 없고, 이러한 원고에 대한 공격이 원고가 당시 집권세력인 베테족의 일원으로서 스스로 FPI 활동을 하거나 그 정치세력과 일정한 인적 관계에 있었기 때문이라는 원고의 주장도 충분히 수긍할 수 있다. 그리고 이와 같이 원고에 대한 과거의 박해사실이 인정된다면 제1심판결이 드는 2007. 3. 4. 평화협정의 체결과 같은 잠정적·과도적 조치만으로 코트디부아르에서 원고가 종족이나 정치적 의견을 이유로 박해를 받을 가능성이 명백히 소멸하였다고 단정할 수도 없다.

　　이러한 사정을 종합하여 보면, 원고가 코트디부아르로 송환될 경우 그 종족 또는 정치적 활동을 이유로 박해를 받을 가능성이 있음이 합리적으로 수긍되고 국적국으로부터 충분한 보호를 기대하기도 어렵다고 할 것임에도, 원심은 제1심판결의 이유를 인용하여 그 판시와 같은 사정만으로 원고에게 난민 인정의 요건이 되는 박해를 받을 충분한 근거 있는 위험이 존재하지 않는다고 판단하였으니, 이러한 원심판결에는 난민 인정의 요건으로서 박해 가능성과 그 증명의 방법 및 정도에 관한 법리를 오해하여 판결에 영향을 미친 위법이 있고, 이를 지적하는 상고이유에는 정당한 이유가 있다.

　　4. 그러므로 원심판결을 파기하고, 사건을 다시 심리·판단하도록 원심법원에 환송하기로 하여 관여 대법관의 일치된 의견으로 주문과 같이 판결한다."

　　☑ **해　　설**

　　한국은 1992년 12월 「난민지위협약」과 의정서에 가입하였다. 국내적으로는 2013년 7월부터 독립적인 난민법이 발효 중이다. 2020년 3월 말 기준 한국에서는 모두 67,633명이 난민신청을 하여 그중 1,044명이 난민인정을 받았고, 이와 별도로 2,265명이 인도적 체류허가를 받았다. 국내에서 난민지위 인정신청을 하였다가 법무부에서 불허된 자가 법원에 불허처분의 취소를 요구하는 소송이 매년 수백건에 이르고 있다.

　　난민으로 인정되기 위한 요건의 핵심은 "박해의 우려"이다. 즉 「난민지

위협약」제1조 A의 (2)는 "인종, 종교, 국적 또는 특정 사회집단의 구성원 신분 또는 정치적 의견을 이유로 박해를 받을 우려가 있다는 충분한 이유가 있는 공포로 인하여 그 국적국의 보호를 받을 것을 원하지 아니하는 자"를 중심으로 난민을 정의하고 있다. 대법원 2008년 7월 24일 선고, 2007두3930 판결 이래 한국 법원은 "'박해'라 함은 생명, 신체 또는 자유에 대한 위협을 비롯하여 인간의 본질적인 존엄성에 대한 중대한 침해나 차별을 야기하는 행위"라고 정의하고 있고, "충분한 근거가 있는 공포"에 대해서는 본 판결 본문에 인용된 바와 같이 설명하고 있다.

▶ 참고문헌 ─────────────────────────────

• 정인섭·황필규 편, 난민의 개념과 인정절차(경인문화사, 2011).
• 오승진, 난민여성의 보호 ─ 난민협약상 사회집단의 구성원 개념을 중심으로(단국대학교), 법학논총 33권 1호(2009).
• 안승훈, 2012. 2. 10. 법률 제11298호로 제정·공포된 「난민법」의 몇 가지 쟁점, 행정재판실무연구 Ⅳ(재판자료 125집, 2013), p. 697.
• 김성수, 난민인정 요건인 '박해에 관한 충분한 근거가 있는 공포'의 증명과 관련하여 박해 경험에 관한 난민신청인 진술의 신빙성을 판단하는 방법, 대법원판례해설 제91호(법원도서관, 2012), p. 1006.

제16장
_ _ _ _ _
국제형사법

1. 뉘른베르크 재판(1946)
— 침략전쟁, 평화에 반한 죄, 인도에 반한 죄

Trial of the Major War Criminals before the International Military Tribunal(1947), Volume I, Official Text in the English Language, Judgment(pp. 171-341).

☑ 사   안

2차 대전이 막바지에 이른 1945년 미국, 영국, 소련은 얄타 회담, 포츠담회담 등을 거치며 종전 후 나치 독일 전범의 처리 문제에 관해 협의를 진행했다. 최종적으로 전범들에 대한 국제군사재판을 실시하기로 합의한 이들 승전국들은 1945년 8월 런던협정(London Agreement)을 채택하여 국제군사재판소(International Military Tribunal)를 설치했다. 런던협정에 따라 이 재판소는 2차 대전 중 행해진 나치 독일 소속 개인의 범죄행위에 대하여만 관할권을 보유했다. 따라서 2차 대전 발발 시점인 1939년 9월 1일 이전의 개인의 행위에 대해서는 관할권을 보유하지 않았다. 이들 3개국에 추후 프랑스가 포함되어 최종적으로 4개국 출신의 재판관 8명과 검사 4명으로 구성된 재판소가 독일 뉘른베르크에 설치되었다. 이 재판소는 전쟁 발발 및 전개에 책임이 있는 나치 독일의 핵심 정치·군사 지도자 24명에 대해 1945년 11월부터 재판을 실시했다. 그 결과 유죄 확정판결을 받은 상당수의 독일 전범들은 처형되었다. 이 재판에서는 패전국인 독일에 대해 국가책임을 묻는 전통적 방식이 아니라, 전쟁 발발 및 인권 유린에 책임이 있는 개인에 대한 형사책임이 추궁되었다. 이는 국제법에서 전례를 찾아볼 수 없는 새로운 시도였다. 한편, 동일한 시기에 일본 동경에서도 일본 전범에 대한 유사한 국제형사재판(극동국제군사재판)이 진행되었다.

☑ 쟁   점

(1) 나치 지휘부의 침략행위에 대한 처벌은 범행 당시에 범죄를 구성하지 않는 행위에 대한 소급처벌에 해당하여 허용되서는 안 되는지 여부.

(2) 나치의 정치·군사 지도자들은 독일 정부와 별도로 국제법상 개별적 형사책임을 부담하는지 여부.

(3) 상급자가 내린 명령의 수행은 하급자의 형사책임에 대한 정당화 사유를 제공하는지 여부.

☑ 판   결

(1) 소급처벌 금지라는 형사법의 기본 원칙은 단순한 형식 논리가 아닌 법적 정의(justice)의 차원에서 접근해야 한다. 1928년 켈로그브리앙조약으로 인해 침략전쟁이 국제법에 위반한다는 점은 독일 지도자들도 이미 인식하였으므로 이들에 대한 처벌은 소급처벌에 해당하지 않는다.

(2) 국제법이 국가뿐 아니라 때로는 개인에 대해 권리를 부여하고 의무를 부과한다는 점은 오랫동안 확인되었다. 따라서 독일 정부와 별도로 나치 독일 정치·군사 지도자들도 국제법상 개별적 형사책임을 부담한다.

(3) 상급자가 내린 명령 수행은 하급자의 형사적 책임에 대한 정당화 사유를 제공하지 않는다. 이 문제의 핵심은 해당 하급자가 실질적인 의미에서 범행 참여 여부에 관해 선택권을 보유하고 있었는지 여부이다.

판 결 문

(p. 171) On the 8th August, 1945, the Government of the United Kingdom of Great Britain and Northern Ireland, the Government of the United States of America, the Provisional Government of the French Republic, and the Government of the Union of Soviet Socialist Republics entered into an Agreement establishing this Tribunal for the Trial of War Criminals whose offences have no particular geographical location. [⋯] The Tribunal was invested with power to try and punish persons who had committed Crimes against Peace, War Crimes and Crimes against Humanity as defined in the Charter. [⋯]

(p. 219) The Charter makes the planning or waging of a war of aggression or a war in violation of international treaties a crime, and it is therefore not strictly necessary to consider whether and to what extent aggressive war was a crime before the execution of the London Agreement. But in view of the great importance of the questions of law involved, the Tribunal has heard full argument from the Prosecution and the Defence, and will express its view on the matter.

It was urged on behalf of the defendants that a fundamental principle of all law-international and domestic-is that there can be no punishment of crime without a pre-existing law. "*Nullum crimen sine lege, nulla poena sine lege.*" It was submitted that *ex post facto* punishment is abhorrent to the law of all civilised nations, that no sovereign power had made aggressive war a crime at the time the alleged criminal acts were committed, that no statute had defined aggressive war, that no penalty had been fixed for its commission, and no court had been created to try and punish offenders.

In the first place, it is to be observed that the maxim *nullum crimen sine lege* is not a limitation of sovereignty, but is in general a principle of justice. To assert that it is unjust to punish those who in defiance of treaties and assurances have attacked neighboring states without warning is obviously untrue, for in such circumstances the attacker must know that he is doing wrong, and so far from it being unjust to punish him, it would be unjust if his wrong were allowed to go unpunished. [⋯] On this view of the case alone, it would appear that the maxim has no application to the present facts.

This view is strongly reinforced by a consideration of the state of international law in 1939, so far as aggressive war is concerned. The General Treaty for the Renunciation of War of 27 August, 1928, more generally known as the Pact of Paris or the Kellogg-Briand Pact, was binding on 63 nations, including Germany, Italy and Japan at the outbreak of war in 1939. [⋯]

(p. 221) [⋯] For many years past, however, military tribunals have tried and punished individuals guilty of violating the rules of land warfare laid down by this (Hague) Convention. In the opinion of the Tribunal, those who wage aggressive war are doing that which is equally illegal and of much greater moment than a breach of one of the rules of the Hague Convention. In interpreting the words of the [Paris] Pact, it must be remembered that international law is not the product of an international legislature, and that such international agreements as the Pact of Paris have to deal with general principles of law, and not with administrative matters of procedure. The law of war is to be found not only in treaties, but in the customs and practices of states which gradually obtained universal recognition, and from the general principles of Justice applied by jurists and practiced by military courts. This law is not static, but by continual adaptation follows the needs of a changing world. Indeed, in many cases treaties do no more than express and define for more accurate reference the principles of law already existing. [⋯]

(p. 222) [⋯] All these expressions of opinion, and others that could be cited, so solemnly made, reinforce the construction which the Tribunal placed upon the Pact of Paris, that resort to a war of aggression is not merely illegal, but is criminal. The prohibition of aggressive war demanded by the conscience of the world, finds its expression in the series of pacts and treaties to which the Tribunal has just referred. [⋯]

It was submitted that international law is concerned with the action of sovereign States, and provides no punishment for individuals; and further, that where the act in question is an act of State, those who carry it out are not personally responsible, but are protected by the doctrine of the sovereignty of the State. In the opinion (p. 223) of the Tribunal, both these submissions must be rejected. That international law imposes duties and liabilities upon individuals as well as upon States has long been recognised. [⋯]

The principle of international law, which under certain circumstances protects the representatives of a state, cannot be applied to acts which are condemned as criminal by international law. The authors of these facts cannot shelter themselves behind their official position in order to be freed from punishment in appropriate proceedings. Article 7 of the Charter expressly declares:

> "The official position of Defendants, whether as heads of State, or responsible officials in Government departments, shall not be considered as freeing them from responsibility, or mitigating punishment."

On the other hand, the very essence of the Charter is that individuals have international duties which transcend the national obligations of obedience imposed by the individual State. [⋯]

It was also submitted on behalf of most of these defendants that in doing what they did they were acting under the orders of Hitler, and therefore cannot be held responsible for the acts committed by them in carrying out these orders. The Charter specifically provides in Article 8:

> (p. 224) "The fact that the Defendant acted pursuant to order of his

Government or of a superior shall not free him from responsibility, but may be considered in mitigation of punishment."

The provisions of this article are in conformity with the law of all nations. That a soldier was ordered to kill or torture in violation of the international law of war has never been recognised as a defence to such acts of brutality, though, as the Charter here provides, the order may be urged in mitigation of the punishment. The true test, which is found in varying degrees in the criminal law of most nations, is not the existence of the order, but whether moral choice was in fact possible. [⋯]

(p. 226) [⋯] The evidence relating to War Crimes has been overwhelming, in its volume and its detail. It is impossible for this Judgment adequately to review it, or to record the mass of documentary and oral evidence that has been presented. The truth remains that War Crimes were committed on a vast scale, never before seen in the history of war. They were perpetrated in all the countries occupied (p. 227) by Germany, and on the High Seas, and were attended by every conceivable circumstance of cruelty and horror. [⋯]

(p. 254) [⋯] With regard to Crimes against Humanity, there is no doubt whatever that political opponents were murdered in Germany before the war, and that many of them were kept in concentration camps in circumstances of great horror and cruelty. The policy of terror was certainly carried out on a vast scale, and in many cases was organised and systematic. [⋯] To constitute Crimes against Humanity, the acts relied on before the outbreak of war must have been in execution of, or in connection with, any crime within the jurisdiction of the Tribunal. The Tribunal is of the opinion that revolting and horrible as many of these crimes were, it has not been satisfactorily proved that they were done in execution of, or in connection with, any such crime. The Tribunal therefore cannot make a general declaration that the acts before 1939 were Crimes against Humanity within the meaning of the Charter, but from the beginning of the war in 1939 War Crimes were committed on a vast scale, which were also Crimes against Humanity; and insofar as the inhumane acts charged in the Indictment, and committed after the beginning of the war, did not constitute War Crimes, they were all committed in execution of, or (p. 255) in connection with, the aggressive war, and therefore constituted Crimes against Humanity. [⋯]

☑ 해   설

뉘른베르크 재판은 국제형사법의 발전에 획기적 전기를 제공했다. 뉘른 베르크 원칙을 반영해 UN 국제법위원회(U.N. International Law Commission)는 1950년 "뉘른베르크 재판에서 확인된 국제법 원칙(Principles of International Law Recognized in the Charter of the Nürnberg Tribunal and in the Judgment of the Tribunal)"이라는 보고서를 채택했다. 1948년 집단살해죄의 방지와 처벌에 관한 협약(Convention on the Prevention and Punishment of the Crime Genocide), 세계인권선언(Universal Declaration of Human Rights)을 시작으로 인권보호 및 범죄인 개인의 처벌을 위한 다양한 형태의 국제법 발전의 단초를 제공한 것 도 뉘른베르크 재판이라고 할 수 있다. 또한 비록 1998년에서야 결실을 맺었 지만 ICC에 관한 국제적 논의도 뉘른베르크 재판이 그 시발점이었다. 이 재 판을 계기로 침략범죄(Crime of Aggression), 인도에 반한 죄(Crimes against Humanity), 및 전쟁범죄(War Crimes)의 법적 개념이 새로이 정립되거나 확인 되었다. 특히 이들 범죄에 대한 국제법상 개인의 형사책임 원칙이 확립되어 20세기 후반 국제형사법의 급속한 발전을 위한 초석이 마련되었다. 일부에 서는 재판관과 검사가 모두 연합국 소속 군인 또는 민간인이었다는 점, 동일 한 시기에 행해진 연합국의 전쟁범죄에 대한 처벌은 이루어지지 않았다는 점 등을 들어 당시 재판이 "승자에 의한 사법적 보복(Victor's Justice)"이라는 주장도 제기되었다. 그러나 이러한 주장은 나치 독일의 역사상 유례 없는 잔 학행위와 추후 이 재판의 국제법 발전에 대한 기여로 인해 특별한 주목을 받지는 못했다.

➡ 참고문헌 ────────────────────────────

- 이장희, [한일 역사현안의 국제법적 재조명] 도쿄국제군사재판과 뉘른베르크 국제군사재판에 대한 국제법적 비교 연구, 동북아역사논총 No. 25(2009).
- H. T. King, Jr., The Judgments and Legality of Nuremberg, Yale Journal of International Law Vol. 23(1997), p. 213.
- E. Borgwardt, Re−Examining Nuremberg as a New Deal Institution: Politics,

Culture and the Limits of Laws in Generating Human Rights Norms, Berkeley Journal of International Law Vol. 23(2005), p. 401.

- L. A. Cohen, Application of the Realist and Liberal Perspective to the Implementation of War Crimes Trials: Case Studies of Nuremberg and Bosnia, UCLA Journal of International Law and Foreign Affairs Vol. 2(1997), p. 113.
- M. Lippman, Nuremberg: Forty Five Years Later, Connell Journal of International Law Vol. 7(1991), p. 1.
- D. P. Stewart, The Norms and Challenges of International Criminal Law, American Journal of International Law Vol. 109, No. 1(2015), pp. 214－224.

2. Radislav Krstic 장군에 대한 처벌(2001)
— 집단살해죄의 구성요건 및 입증

The Prosecutor v. Radislav Krstic.
Trial Chamber I, ICTY IT-98-33-T(2001).

☑ 사 안

구 유고슬라비아 지역 내전이 진행중이던 1995년 당시 Radislav Krstic 는 세르비아계 민병대의 하나인 Drina Corps의 사령관 역할을 수행하고 있었다. 1995년 7월 Krstic 장군은 보스니아 헤르체고비나의 Srebrenica에 서 다른 세르비아계 민병대에 의해 자행된 보스니아 회교도 및 크로아티아 인에 대한 집단살해행위에 협력한 혐의로 ICTY 설립규정 제4조에 따라 기소 되었다. 문제의 집단살해는 주로 Mladic 장군이 이끄는 보스니아 내 세르비 아 민병대에 의해 1995년 자행되었다. Krstic는 이 과정에 직접 참여했다기 보다는 암묵적으로 협조 내지 방조했다는 혐의를 받고 있었다. ICTY 검사는 Krstic가 "집단살해 의도(genocidal intent)"를 Mladic의 세르비아 민병대와 공 유했음을 이유로 그를 기소했다. ICTY 1심 재판부는 심리를 거쳐 집단살해 의도 공유와 집단살해에의 협력을 이유로 Krstic에 대해 유죄 판결을 내렸다. 1심 재판과정에서 Krstic에 대해 활용된 증거는 대부분 정황증거였다. 가령 Krstic가 Mladic 장군과 호텔에서 회동·협의한 사실 또는 여타 회합에 참석 한 사실 등의 정황증거에 기초해 그가 Mladic 장군의 집단살해 준비 및 실행 에 대해 인지하고 있었으며 따라서 집단살해 의도를 공유한 것으로 보아야 한다는 것이 1심 판결의 핵심이었다.

☑ 쟁   점

⑴ Drina Corps 사령관 Krstic가 자신의 관할지역내에서 자행된 보스니아 회교도에 대한 집단살해를 인지했고 이에 수동적으로 동조했는지 여부.

⑵ Krstic가 직접 집단살해에 참여하거나 부하들의 집단살해를 방지하지 못해 자기 책임 및 상급자 책임에 따라 형사책임을 부담하는지 여부.

⑶ 상급자가 자기 책임과 상급자 책임에 따른 개인책임을 동시에 부담할 경우 양자간 우선 순위.

☑ 판   결

⑴ 다양한 정황증거는 Krstic가 Drina Corps의 사령관으로서 자신의 관할지역 내에서 자행되던 보스니아 회교도 집단학살을 인지하였고 이에 최소한 수동적으로 동조했음을 입증한다.

⑵ Krstic는 집단살해에 직접 참여하거나 부하들의 집단살해를 방지하지 못해 각각 자기 책임 및 상급자 책임에 따라 개별적 형사책임을 부담한다.

⑶ 자기 책임과 상급자 책임이 동시 존재할 경우 보다 직접적 형사책임을 초래하는 자기 책임이 상급자 책임을 포섭한다.

판 결 문

303. From 5 July 1995, General Krstic was present at the FCP[1]) in Pribicevac in his capacity as Chief of Staff of the Drina Corps. On 9 July 1995, however, he said that General Mladic arrived at the FCP and subsequently assumed command of the operation, thereby sidelining both himself and General Zivanovic [⋯]. It was General Mladic, acting pursuant to a decision issued by President Karadic, who ordered the continuation of the attack to capture Srebrenica. Although he was present as General Mladic victoriously strode through the streets of Srebrenica, General Krstic testified that he was not happy about the unfolding events. [⋯]

305. Although General Krstic was present at two of the three Hotel Fontana meetings convened by General Mladic to discuss the fate of the Bosnian Muslim

---

1) Forward Commanding Post: 전방군사지휘기지.

civilians from Srebrenica, he maintained that he did not speak or have any discussions with General Mladic about these Bosnian Muslim refugees. He resolutely denied that he had any involvement in organising the transfer of the women, children, and the elderly from Potoari, or that he was even present in Potoari while that was happening. [⋯]

307. General Krstic argued that, throughout the period during which the executions took place, he held the position of Chief of Staff of the Drina Corps. According to his version of events, he did not become Commander of the Drina Corps until 20 or 21 July 1995 [which is after the massacre], when General Mladic appointed him to this position during a ceremony at a restaurant in the Han Kram hamlet. [⋯]

309. General Krstic did not contest the fact that the mass executions of Bosnian Muslim men in the Srebrenica enclave had taken place in July 1995, but he maintained that he first found out about these crimes at the end of August, or the beginning of September 1995. [⋯]

328. The conflicting evidence reveals that, from early July 1995, General Krstic began to assume more and more *de facto* responsibility within the Drina Corps. As discussed in further detail below, he was the person primarily directing Krivaja 95 from the Drina Corps Forward Command from 6 July 1995, at least until General Mladic arrived on 9 July 1995. Further, while General Zivanovic attended the first meeting at the Fontana Hotel with General Mladic on 11 July 1995 at 2200 hours, it was General Krstic who attended the second meeting that same evening at 2300 hours and the third meeting the following morning: General Zivanovic was not present. Some witnesses at these meetings came away with the impression that General Krstic was the Drina Corps Commander. [⋯]

330. The Prosecution accepted that General Zivanovic was, in accordance with the decree issued by President Karadzic, "officially on paper" Corps Commander until 15 July 1995. Nonetheless, from the afternoon of 13 July 1995, General Krstic behaved as Commander of the Drina Corps, commencing with the 13 July search order, which he signed in his newly acquired capacity of Corps Commander. There was no confusion on the part of the Drina Corps: it was clearly understood that General Krstic was the Commander from 13 July 1995 and his orders were implemented accordingly. [⋯]

343. The Trial Chamber finds that, as a result of his attendance at the Hotel Fontana meetings on 11 and 12 July 1995, General Krstic was fully appraised of the catastrophic humanitarian situation confronting the Bosnian Muslim refugees in Potoari and that he was put on notice that the survival of the Bosnian Muslim population was in question following the take-over of Srebrenica. [⋯]

362. The Trial Chamber cannot discount the possibility that the executions plan was initially devised by members of the VRS[2] Main Staff without consultation with the Drina Corps Command generally and General Krstic in particular. Nonetheless, the fact remains that the executions were carried out on a massive scale, all within the Drina Corps zone of responsibility. General Krstic was present within the area of the former Srebrenica enclave at least up until the evening of 13 July by which time the first mass executions had already taken place. [⋯]

421. [I]n July 1995, General Krstic found himself squarely in the middle of one of the most heinous wartime acts committed in Europe since the Second World War. The plan to execute the Bosnian Muslim men may not have been of his own making, but it was carried out within the zone of responsibility of the Drina Corps. Furthermore Drina Corps resources were utilised to assist with the executions from 14 July 1995 onwards. By virtue of his position as Drina Corps Commander, from 13 July 1995, General Krstic must have known about this. [⋯]

540. Article 4(2) of the Statute[3] defines genocide as:

any of the following acts committed with intent to destroy, in whole or in part, a national, ethnical, racial or religious group, as such:

(a) killing members of the group;

(b) causing serious bodily or mental harm to members of the group;

(c) deliberately inflicting on the group conditions of life calculated to bring about its physical destruction in whole or in part;

(d) imposing measures intended to prevent births within the group;

(e) forcibly transferring children of the group to another group. [⋯]

542. Article 4 of the Statute[4] characterises genocide by two constitutive elements:

- the *actus reus* of the offence, which consists of one or several of the acts enumerated under Article 4(2);

- the *mens rea* of the offence, which is described as the intent to destroy, in whole or in part, a national, ethnical, racial or religious group, as such. [⋯]

560. The Chamber concludes that the protected group, within the meaning of

---

2) Vojska Republika Srpska: 보스니아 내 세르비아계 민병대의 일파.
3) ICTY규정 제4조 2항을 의미함.
4) ICTY규정 제4조를 의미함.

Article 4 of the Statute, must be defined, in the present case, as the Bosnian Muslims. The Bosnian Muslims of Srebrenica or the Bosnian Muslims of Eastern Bosnia constitute a part of the protected group under Article 4. [···]

598. The Chamber concludes that the intent to kill all the Bosnian Muslim men of military age in Srebrenica constitutes an intent to destroy in part the Bosnian Muslim group within the meaning of Article 4 and therefore must be qualified as a genocide.

599. The Trial Chamber has thus concluded that the Prosecution has proven beyond all reasonable doubt that genocide, crimes against humanity and violations of the laws or customs of war were perpetrated against the Bosnian Muslims, at Srebrenica, in July 1995. The Chamber now proceeds to consider the criminal responsibility of General Krsti for these crimes in accordance with the provisions of Article 7 of the Statute.

600. The Prosecution alleges that General Krstic is criminally responsible for his participation in the crimes charged in the indictment, pursuant to Article 7(1) of the Statute. [···]

603. The Prosecution "also, or alternatively" alleges that General Krstic incurs "command responsibility" for the crimes charged in the Indictment pursuant to Article 7(3) of the Statute. [···]

605. The facts pertaining to the commission of a crime may establish that the requirements for criminal responsibility under both Article 7(1) and Article 7(3) are met. However, the Trial Chamber adheres to the belief that where a commander participates in the commission of a crime *through his subordinates*, by "planning", "instigating" or "ordering" the commission of the crime, any responsibility under Article 7(3) is subsumed under Article 7(1). [···]

610. In light of these facts, the Trial Chamber is of the view that the issue of General Krstic's criminal responsibility for the crimes against the civilian population of Srebrenica occurring at Potocari is most appropriately determined under Article 7(1) by considering whether he participated [···] in a joint criminal enterprise to forcibly "cleanse" the Srebrenica enclave of its Muslim population. [···]

647. The evidence also satisfies the three-pronged test established by the jurisprudence for General Krsti to incur command responsibility under Article 7(3) for the participation of Drina Corps personnel in the killing campaign. [···]

652. Although the elements of Article 7(3) have thus been fulfilled, the Trial Chamber will not enter a conviction to that effect because in its view General

Krstic's responsibility for the participation of his troops in the killings is sufficiently expressed in a finding of guilt under Article 7(1). [⋯]

☑ 해   설

이 사건에서 재판부가 고민한 부분은 문제가 된 사실관계의 확인과 입증이었다. 이 사건의 핵심 쟁점 중 하나는 Srebrenica에서 세르비아계 민병대에 의해 보스니아 회교도에 대한 집단살해가 발생했을 당시, Krstic이 Drina Corp 부대의 사령관 직책에 있었는지 여부였다. 세르비아 대통령이 서명한 공식 문서에는 Krstic가 집단살해 발생 이후 사령관에 취임했고 그 이전에는 Zivanovic 장군이 사령관 직책을 수행한 것으로 기록되어 있었기 때문이다. 그러나 ICTY는 광범위한 정황증거 및 증언에 기초해 Krstic이 집단살해 발생 직전부터 '사실상' Drina Corp 부대의 사령관 직책을 수행하였음을 확인했다. 그리고 이를 통해 동인에 대해 집단살해 참여 및 하급자 제지 실패를 이유로 개인적 형사책임을 인정했다. 결국 ICTY는 단순히 서류상으로 누가 지휘관으로 기록되어 있었는지가 아니라 과연 누가 실제 지휘관으로 활동했는지 여부에 초점을 맞추었다. 한편, ICTY는 증거로 제시된 Krstic의 개인적 성향으로 보아 독자적으로 이러한 집단살해를 계획하거나 직접 지시할 것으로 판단되지는 않음을 인정했다. 그러나 자신의 관할구역내에서 집단살해가 진행 중이라는 사실은 충분히 인지할 만한 상황임에도 이를 묵인한 것은 ICTY 규정 제4조상 집단살해를 구성하기 위한 행위(*actus reus*) 및 의도(*mens rea*) 요건을 모두 충족하는 것으로 보았다. 즉, 단순한 수동적 묵인의 경우에도 집단살해의 범죄구성 요건을 충족할 수 있음을 확인한 것은 이 범죄의 적용범위를 확대시킬 수 있는 법적 기반을 구축한 것으로 볼 수 있다.

재판부의 판결은 소위 "공동범죄집단(Joint Criminal Enterprise: JCE)" 개념에 기초하고 있다. 보스니아 회교도에 대한 집단살해 자행 가능성을 충분히 인지하면서도 특별한 조치를 취하지 않고 주어진 자신의 역할을 수행함으로써 Krstic는 집단살해의 구체적 의도(genocidal intent)를 갖고 JCE에 참여했다는 것이다.

　　재판부는 집단살해에 대해 유죄를 확정하고 Krstic에게 46년 형을 선고 했다. 그러나 상소심 재판부는 1심 재판부와 입장을 달리하며 Krstic가 집단 살해의 구체적 의도는 가지지 않았음을 확인하고 대신 집단살해에 대한 방 조혐의만을 인정하여 형량을 35년으로 낮추었다. 단지 예측가능성이라는 추 상적 이유만으로 집단살해를 직접 범한 것으로 보기는 힘들다는 것이다. JCE 개념은 집단살해에 대한 효과적 처벌을 위한 중요한 개념이나, 한편으로 이 개념이 지나치게 확장되서는 안 된다는 점을 상소심 재판부는 고려한 것 으로 보인다. Krstic에 대한 감형은 보스니아 회교도들에 대해 일부 안전조치 를 취한 점에 대한 정상을 참작한 것이다. 형이 최종 확정된 Krstic는 2004년 영국으로 이송되어 수감되었다. 이후 2010년 5월 Krstic은 교도소 내에서 동 료 죄수들에게 공격을 받아 심각한 부상을 입었다. 이들은 이슬람교 신자들 로 같은 교도소에 복역 중인 Krstic를 응징하기 위해 살해를 공모한 뒤 공격 했다고 자백했다. Krstic은 이 공격으로 큰 부상을 입었고, 치료 후 2014년 3 월 보다 안전을 확보할 수 있는 폴란드 Piotrkow Trybunalski에 있는 교도소 내의 독방으로 이송되어 2020년 7월 현재까지 복역 중이다. Krstic은 35년 징역형을 선고받은바, 그는 폴란드의 교도소에서 2039년까지 복역을 할 것 으로 예상된다.

　　한편 상급자의 제7조 1항상 자기 책임과 동조 3항상 상급자 책임이 경 합하는 경우, 후자가 전자에 포함되는 개념으로 보아 제7조 1항만 적용되는 것으로 결정한 ICTY의 판결은 다소 의문의 여지가 있다. 제7조 1항의 자기 책임과 3항의 상급자 책임은 성격이 다른 형사법상 개인책임을 각각 규정한 것으로 볼 수 있기 때문이다. 요컨대 전자는 자신의 행위에 대한 스스로의 형사책임을, 반면에 후자는 하급자의 행위에 대해 상급자가 자신의 직책에 기초하여 형사책임을 부담하는 상황에 적용된다. 개인이 형사책임을 부담하 는 근거가 상이한 두 범죄를 연관성이 있다는 이유만으로(하급자의 행위를 통 해(through his subordinates)) 반드시 하나가 다른 하나에 부속하는 것으로 결 정할 수 있는지는 불분명하다. 중복적 책임원칙 확인을 통해 집단살해 범죄 에 대한 국제사회의 억지력 강화라는 형사정책적 측면에서도 양자 공히 소 추 및 처벌이 가능한 것으로 해석하는 것이 적절할 수도 있을 것이다.

➡ 참고문헌 ─────────────────────────────────────

- A. Zahar, Commentary on the judgment of the ICTY Appeals Chamber in the case of Prosecutor v. Radislav Krstic, Annotated Leading Cases of International Criminal Tribunals, Vol. 19(2004), p. 629.
- M. Drumbl, Case Notes, Prosecutor v. Radislav Krstic: ICTY Authenticates Genocide at Srebrenica and Convicts for Aiding and Abetting, Melbourne Journal of International Law, Vol. 5(2004).
- K. G. Southwick, Srebrenica as Genocide? The Krstic Decision and the Language of the Unspeakable, Yale Human Rights & Development Law Journal Vol. 8(2005), p. 188.

3. Jean-Paul Akayesu 시장에 대한 처벌(1998)
— 정치지도자의 개별적 형사책임

The Prosecutor v. Jean-Paul Akayesu, Trial Chamber I,
ICTR-96-4-T(1998).

☑ 사　안

1994년 4월 아프리카 중부에 위치한 르완다에서는 오랜 민족간 갈등과
반목으로 인해 대규모 집단살해사건이 발생했다. 이 집단살해사건은 3개월
이란 짧은 기간 동안 80만 명에 이르는 피해자가 발생하여 국제사회는 그
잔학성과 비인간성에 충격을 받았다. 이러한 르완다 사건의 책임자를 형사처
벌하기 위해 UN 안전보장이사회는 1993년 11월 ICTR을 탄자니아에 설치했
다. Jean-Paul Akayesu에 대한 재판은 ICTR에서 최초로 행해진 재판이다.
Akayesu는 후투족 출신의 정치지도자로서 1994년 당시 르완다 내 Gitarama
州 Taba市의 시장으로 재직 중이었다. Akayesu는 이 기간 동안 2,000여 명
의 투치족 살해 및 인권유린 행위에 직·간접적으로 관여해 집단살해죄, 인
도에 반한 죄 및 1949년 제네바 협정 공동 제3조를 위반한 혐의로 ICTR 검
사에 의해 기소되어 재판에 회부되었다.

☑ 쟁　점

⑴ 집단살해를 선동·조장하는 발언을 행한 정치인에 대해 집단살해죄
를 근거로 한 형사처벌의 가능 여부.

⑵ 이러한 처벌은 그러한 선동·조장 발언의 결과로 인해 집단살해가
반드시 발생할 것을 전제조건으로 하는지 여부.

☑ 판　결

(1) 집단살해에 직접 참여하지 않고 집단살해를 선동·조장하는 발언을 행한 정치인에 대하여도 그러한 선동·조장을 위한 구체적 의도(specific intent)가 존재하는 경우 집단살해죄를 근거로 처벌할 수 있다.

(2) 이러한 처벌은 선동·조장 발언의 결과 집단살해가 반드시 발생할 것을 전제조건으로 하지 않으며 결과와 상관 없이 그 행위 자체에 대해 처벌이 가능하다.

판 결 문

315. Paragraph 14 of the Indictment reads as follows: "The morning of April 19, 1994, following the murder of Sylvére Karera, Jean Paul Akayesu led a meeting in Gishyeshye sector at which he sanctioned the death of Sylvére Karera and urged the population to eliminate accomplices of the RPF, which was understood by those present to mean Tutsi. Over 100 people were present at the meeting. The killing of Tutsi in Taba began shortly after the meeting." […]

362. Finally, relying on substantial evidence which was not essentially called into question by the Defence, and as it was confirmed by the Accused, the Chamber is satisfied beyond a reasonable doubt that there was a causal link between the statement of the Accused at the 19 April 1994 gathering and the ensuing widespread killings in Taba. […]

549. Under count 4, the Prosecutor charges Akayesu with direct and public incitement to commit genocide, a crime punishable under Article 2(3)(c) of the Statute[of the ICTR].

550. Perhaps the most famous conviction for incitement to commit crimes of international dimension was that of Julius Streicher by the Nuremberg Tribunal for the virulently anti-Semitic articles which he had published in his weekly newspaper *Der Stürmer*. The Nuremberg Tribunal found that: "Streicher's incitement to murder and extermination, at the time when Jews in the East were being killed under the most horrible conditions, clearly constitutes persecution on political and racial grounds in connection with War Crimes, as defined by the Charter, and constitutes a Crime against Humanity".

551. At the time the Convention on Genocide was adopted, the delegates agreed to expressly spell out direct and public incitement to commit genocide as a specific crime, in particular, because of its critical role in the planning of a genocide, with the delegate from the USSR stating in this regard that, "It was impossible that hundreds of thousands of people should commit so many crimes unless they had been incited to do so and unless the crimes had been premeditated and carefully organized. [⋯]

554. Under the Statute[of the ICTR] direct and public incitement is expressly defined as a specific crime, punishable as such, by virtue of Article 2(3)(c). With respect to such a crime, the Chamber deems it appropriate to first define the three terms: incitement, direct and public. [⋯]

559. In light of the foregoing, it can be noted in the final analysis that whatever the legal system, direct and public incitement must be defined for the purposes of interpreting Article 2(3)(c), as directly provoking the perpetrator(s) to commit genocide, whether through speeches, shouting or threats uttered in public places or at public gatherings, or through the sale or dissemination, offer for sale or display of written material or printed matter in public places or at public gatherings, or through the public display of placards or posters, or through any other means of audiovisual communication. [⋯]

562. [⋯] In the opinion of the Chamber, the fact that such acts are in themselves particularly dangerous because of the high risk they carry for society, even if they fail to produce results, warrants that they be punished as an exceptional measure. The Chamber holds that genocide clearly falls within the category of crimes so serious that direct and public incitement to commit such a crime must be punished as such, even where such incitement failed to produce the result expected by the perpetrator. [⋯]

672. Count 4 deals with the allegations described in paragraphs 14 and 15 of the Indictment, relating, essentially, to the speeches that Akayesu reportedly made at a meeting held in Gishyeshye on 19 April 1994. The Prosecutor alleges that, through his speeches, Akayesu committed the crime of direct and public incitement to commit genocide, a crime punishable under Article 2(3)(c) of the Statute.

673. The Trial Chamber made the following factual findings on the events described in paragraphs 14 and 15 of the Indictment. The Chamber is satisfied beyond a reasonable doubt that:

(i) Akayesu, in the early hours of 19 April 1994, joined a crowd of over 100

people which had gathered around the body of a young member of the Interahamwe in Gishyeshye.

(ⅱ) He seized that opportunity to address the people and, owing, particularly,
to his functions as bourgmestre and his authority over the population, he led the
gathering and the proceedings.

(ⅲ) It has been established that Akayesu then clearly urged the population to
unite in order to eliminate what he termed the sole enemy: the accomplices of the
Inkotanyi.

(ⅳ) On the basis of consistent testimonies heard throughout the proceedings
and the evidence of Dr. Ruzindana, appearing as expert witness on linguistic
matters, the Chamber is satisfied beyond a reasonable doubt that the population
understood Akayesu's call as one to kill the Tutsi. [⋯]

(ⅴ) During the said meeting, Akayesu received from the Interahamwe
documents which included lists of names, and read from the lists to the crowd by
stating, in particular, that the names were those of RPF accomplices.

(ⅵ) Akayesu testified that the lists contained, especially, the name of Ephrem
Karangwa, whom he named specifically, while being fully aware of the consequences
of doing so. Indeed, he admitted before the Chamber that, at the time of the events
alleged in the Indictment, to label anyone in public as an accomplice of the RPF
would put such a person in danger.

(ⅶ) The Chamber is of the opinion that there is a causal relationship between
Akayesu's speeches at the gathering of 19 April 1994 and the ensuing widespread
massacres of Tutsi in Taba.

674. From the foregoing, the Chamber is satisfied beyond a reasonable doubt
that, by the above-mentioned speeches made in public and in a public place,
Akayesu had the intent to directly create a particular state of mind in his audience
necessary to lead to the destruction of the Tutsi group, as such. Accordingly, the
Chamber finds that the said acts constitute the crime of direct and public incitement to commit genocide, as defined above.

675. In addition, the Chamber finds that the direct and public incitement to
commit genocide as engaged in by Akayesu, was indeed successful and did lead to
the destruction of a great number of Tutsi in the commune of Taba. [⋯]

☑ 해　　설

이 판결은 정치인의 정치적 선동 발언 자체가 집단살해죄에 해당할 수 있음을 인정하고 그 구성요건을 제시한 점에서 그 의의를 찾을 수 있다. 통상 집단살해죄라고 하면 직접 무기를 사용해 집단살해에 참여하는 경우를 먼저 상정하게 된다. 그러나 이러한 직접적 참여 외에도 이러한 행위늘 소상 내지 지원하는 정치적 발언을 행하는 정치인도 동일하게 집단살해죄를 범할 수 있음을 이 판결은 보여주고 있다. 특히 집단살해죄 성립에 요구되는 "구체적 의도(specific intent)"가 여기서는 정치적 선동의 대상이 된 청중들이 그러한 발언에 영향을 받아 집단살해죄를 범할 것을 동 정치인이 "인식"하는 것으로 충족된다고 이 판결은 설명한다. 또한 "직접적(direct)," "공중(public)," 및 "선동(incitement)"이라는 용어의 법적 · 사전적 의미를 각각 분석해 집단살해죄의 의미를 보다 명확히 한 것도 이 판결의 기여라고 할 수 있다. 나아가 ICTR은 집단살해죄는 궁극적인 성공 또는 실패 여부와 상관없이 "그 자체로서(as such)" 처벌이 가능한 범죄임을 거듭 확인함으로써 동 범죄의 독자성을 강조하고 있다. 그러나 한편으로 이 사건에서 ICTR은 그러한 선동 발언의 결과 집단살해가 궁극적으로 발생한 것을 선동발언 범죄의 확인에 중요한 고려 요소 중 하나로 여전히 평가하고 있음을 알 수 있다. 이러한 점을 감안하면 결국 의도된 집단살해의 발생 또는 미발생이 선동발언 자체에 대한 처벌에 있어서도 결국 상당한 연관성을 보유하고 있음을 간접적으로는 인정하는 것으로 판단된다. 결론적으로 이 판결의 두 판시를 결합하면 실제 집단살해 발생과 상관 없이 이를 조장할 목적으로 정치인이 선동 발언을 하는 경우 그 자체로서 이미 집단살해죄가 성립된다는 것이다.

한편 Akayesu는 종신형을 선고받고 2001년 12월 말리로 이송되어 수감되었으며 2020년 7월 현재 복역 중이다. 르완다 집단학살사건 이후 25년이 지난 현재 종족갈등은 상당 부분 종식되었으며, 르완다는 안정을 되찾고 경제적 발전을 도모하고 있다. 가장 최근에 있었던 2018년 국회의원 선거에서는 여성이 64%의 의석을 차지하고, 야당도 선전하는 등 정치적으로도 점차 안정된 모습을 보이고 있다.

➠ 참고문헌 ─────────────────────────────

- 오미영, 국제인도법상 강간 개념에 관한 소고, 인도법논총 27권(2007), p. 49.
- H. Trouille, How far has the International Criminal Tribunal for Rwanda really come since Akayesu in the prosecution and investigation of sexual offences committed against women?, International Criminal Law Review, Vol. 13(2013), p. 747.
- B. H. Oxman & D. M. Amann, Prosecutor v. Akayesu. Case ICTR—96—4—T, American Journal of International Law Vol. 93(1999), pp. 195.

4. 프랑스-지부티 형사사법공조사건(2008)
— 형사사법공소조약에 따른 수사자료의 요청

Certain Questions of Mutual Assistance in Criminal
Matters.
Djibouti v. France, 2008 ICJ Reports 177.

☑ 사 안

1995년 10월 19일 아프리카 소국인 지부티의 사법부에 기술고문으로 파견되어 일하던 프랑스인 Bernard Borrel 판사의 사체가 지부티에서 발견되었다. 지부티 검찰은 Borrel 판사의 사망원인 규명을 위한 조사를 진행했고 2003년 12월 7일 자살로 결론지으며 조사를 종결했다.

한편 프랑스에서도 Borrel 판사의 사망과 관련된 형사 및 민사재판 절차가 1995년 12월 7일 Toulouse 소재 1심 법원에서 개시되었다. 프랑스 내 재판절차 진행과정에서 Borrel 판사의 자살로 결론을 내린 지부티 검찰의 조사결과에 상당한 의문이 제기되었으며 이에 따라 프랑스 수사판사는 정확한 사실관계 확인을 위해 지부티 사건 현장을 방문했다. 나아가 수사판사는 프랑스 정부를 통해 프랑스와 지부티간 1986년 체결된 형사사법공조조약에1) 따라 지부티에 대한 수사기록 협조요청서(letters rogatory)를 1998년 10월과 2000년 2월 두 차례에 걸쳐 각각 전달했다. 이러한 조사과정을 통해 지부티 정보당국이 Borrel 판사 살해에 관여했다는 증거가 수집되었다. 특히 프랑스 정보부가 수집한 비밀자료 등은 Guelleh 지부티 대통령 등 당시 지부티 고

---

1) The Convention on Mutual Assistance in Criminal Matters between the Djiboutian Government and the French Government, of 27 September 1986. 원래 형사사법공조조약은 조약(treaty)이라는 용어를 사용하는 것이 일반적이나 이 형사사법공조조약은 불어를 사용하는 두 국가간 조약으로 불어를 정본으로 convention이라는 이름으로 체결되었고 이에 따라 ICJ 판결 영문본도 convention을 사용하고 있다. 이 책에서는 형사사법공조조약이 조약이라는 용어를 사용하는 일반적인 관례에 따라 원문의 convention을 "조약"으로 번역했다.

위 관리들이 Borrel 판사 살해 사건에 직접 연루되었음을 시사했다.

　이러한 상황에서 2004년 5월 지부티 사법당국 역시 Borrel 사건을 재수사하기로 결정했다. 지부티 사법당국은 프랑스 사법당국이 그간 축적한 조사기록을 양국간 형사사법공조조약에 따라 자국에 넘겨 줄 것을 요청했다. 프랑스 사법당국은 지부티의 자료 요청이 프랑스 정보부의 비밀자료 등에 대한 출처를 확인해 추가 증거 수집을 방해하기 위한 것으로 이해하고 이 요청을 거부했다. 이에 대한 법적 근거로 프랑스는 양국간 형사사법공조조약 제2조에 따르면 자료 제공이 주권, 안전, 공공질서 또는 다른 본질적 이익을 침해할 가능성이 있는 경우 협조를 거부할 수 있음을 들었다. 지부티는 프랑스의 자료제공 거부가 "최대한 광범위한 협조(widest assistance)"를 규정한 형사사법공조조약 제1조 위반임을 주장했다. 또한 프랑스가 자료제공 거부에 관해 상세한 설명을 제시하지 않은 점은 이 조약 제17조를 위반한다고 주장했다. 이러한 이유로 지부티가 2006년 1월 9일 프랑스를 ICJ에 제소하자 프랑스는 ICJ 규칙(Rules of the Court) 제38조 5항에 따라 이 사건에 국한하여 법원 관할권을 수락했다.

　☑ 쟁　　점

　⑴ 피요청국 담당 관리(프랑스 판사)가 형사사법공조조약에 기해 요청된 자료가 국익을 침해할 비밀정보를 포함하고 있어 조약 상대방에 제공할 수 없다고 결정할 권한을 보유하는지 여부.

　⑵ 요청자료 제공 거부시 상세한 설명을 제공할 의무와 자료제공 거부를 허용하는 조항이 별도의 법적 요건과 의무를 부과하는지 여부. 즉, 거부에 대한 상세한 설명을 제공하지 않으면 자료제공 거부 근거 조항을 원용할 수 없는지 여부.

　☑ 판　　결

　⑴ 국익 침해 여부에 대한 판단은 체약당사국 외무부 등 정부 부처뿐 아니라 국내법상 정당한 권한을 부여받은 피요청국 담당 관리(이 사건에서는 담당판사) 역시 이에 대한 결정 권한을 보유한다.

(2) 요청자료 제공 거부시 상세한 설명을 제시할 의무와 자료제공 거부를 허용하는 조항은 각각 별도의 법적 요건과 의무를 부과한다. 따라서 자료 제공 거부에 대한 상세한 설명을 제공하지 않았더라도 이는 설명 제시 의무에 대한 위반을 구성할 따름이며 별도로 존재하는 자료제공 거부 근거 조항의 원용을 저해하지는 않는다.

판 결 문

116. According to Djibouti, the obligation to execute the international letter rogatory is laid down in Article 1 of the 1986 Convention, which provides that :

"The two States undertake to afford each other, in accordance with the provisions of this Convention, the widest measure of mutual assistance in proceedings in respect of offences the punishment of which, at the time of the request for assistance, falls within the jurisdiction of the judicial authorities of the requesting State."

The Applicant contends that this creates reciprocity in commitments and an obligation to execute the international letter rogatory. [⋯]

120. The Court will now turn to examining the obligation to execute the international letter rogatory set out in Article 1 of the 1986 Convention and, according to Djibouti, elaborated in Article 3, paragraph 1, of the Convention, in the following terms:

"The requested State shall execute in accordance with its law any letters rogatory relating to a criminal matter and addressed to it by the judicial authorities of the requesting State for the purpose of procuring evidence or transmitting articles to be produced in evidence, records or documents."

121. Djibouti argues that the wording of this Article confirms that the requested State is required to execute the international letter rogatory, since it contains an "obligation of result." The Applicant adds that, while the provision does state that execution must take place "in accordance with [the] law" of the requested State, this must be interpreted as simply an indication of the procedure to be followed in performing this "obligation of result," not a means for shirking it. In this regard, Djibouti contends that France may not invoke its internal law to escape its obligation to execute the international letter rogatory and, in support of this contention, relies on Article 27 of the Vienna Convention on the Law of Treaties

[···]

131. At first, Djibouti noted in its Memorial that France cannot rely on the provisions of Article 2 (*c*) of the Convention of 1986. In the first place, according to it, it would seem highly debatable whether an investigating judge alone is in a position to assess whether the fundamental interests of a State could be damaged by execution of an international letter rogatory. Djibouti considers that this type of assessment, concerning a possible risk to the sovereignty, security, *ordre public* or other essential interests of a State, must by its nature lie with the highest organs of that State [···].

132. Concerning the reasons of the refusal mentioned in the *soit-transmis*, Djibouti maintains that no *détournement* of French law could result from the declassified documents being transmitted to a foreign authority (and not merely to the French judge), when the parties to the judicial investigation opened in France have access to the file and the declassified documents in question would not appear likely to compromise the essential interests of France. Moreover, Djibouti disputes that its request can be countered by the assertion that it is impossible to hand over even a part of the file. It contends in this respect that the few pages which have been declassified and included in the record cannot have "permeated the entire file."

133. [···] Djibouti also emphasizes that France, in the letter from its Ambassador in Djibouti to the Djiboutian Minister for Foreign Affairs of 6 June 2005, omitted to provide any reason whatsoever for its "unilateral" refusal of mutual assistance, in violation of Article 17 of the Convention of 1986. [···]

145. The Court begins its examination of Article 2 of the 1986 Convention by observing that, while it is correct, as France claims, that the terms of Article 2 provide a State to which a request for assistance has been made with a very considerable discretion, this exercise of discretion is still subject to the obligation of good faith codified in Article 26 of the 1969 Vienna Convention on the Law of Treaties. [···] This requires it to be shown that the reasons for refusal to execute the letter rogatory fell within those allowed for in Article 2. Further, the Convention requires (in Art. 3) that the decision not to execute the letter must have been taken by those with the authority so to decide under the law of the requested State. [···].

146. The Court is unable to accept the contention of Djibouti that, under French law, matters relating to security and *ordre public* could not fall for determination by the judiciary alone. The Court is aware that the Ministry of Justice had at a certain time been very active in dealing with such issues. However, where ultimate authority lay in respect of the response to a letter rogatory was settled by the *Chambre de l'instruction* of the Paris Court of Appeal in its judgment of 19 October 2006. It held that the application in one way or another of Article 2 of the 1986 Convention to a request made by a State is a matter solely for the investigating judge (who will have available information from relevant government departments). The Court of Appeal further determined that such a decision by an investigating judge is a decision in law, and not an advice to the executive. It is not for this Court to do other than accept the findings of the Paris Court of Appeal on this point.

147. As to whether the decision of the competent authority was made in good faith, and falls within the scope of Article 2 of the 1986 Convention, the Court recalls that Judge Clément's *soit-transmis* of 8 February 2005 states the grounds for her decision to refuse the request for mutual assistance, explaining why transmission of the file was considered to be "contrary to the essential interests of France," in that the file contained declassified "defence secret" documents, together with information and witness statements in respect of another case in progress. [⋯]

148. It is not evident from this *soit-transmis* why Judge Clément found that it was not possible to transmit part of the file, even with some documents removed or blackened out, as suggested by Djibouti during the oral proceedings. It was only through the written and oral pleadings of France that the Court has been informed that the intelligence service documents and information permeated the entire file. However, the Court finds that those reasons that were given by Judge Clément do fall within the scope of Article 2 (*c*) of the 1986 Convention.

149. The Court now turns to Djibouti's claim that France has violated Article 17 of the 1986 Convention. Article 17 provides that "[r]easons shall be given for any refusal of mutual assistance."

150. The Court cannot accept that, as France contends, there was no violation of Article 17, as Djibouti in any event knew that Article 2 (*c*) was being invoked. [⋯]

152. As no reasons were given in the letter of 6 June 2005, the Court concludes that France failed to comply with its obligation under Article 17 of the 1986 Convention. The Court observes that even if it had been persuaded of the transmission of the letter of 31 May 2005, the bare reference it was said to contain to Article 2 (*c*) would not have sufficed to meet the obligation of France under Article 17. Some brief further explanation was called for. This is not only a matter of courtesy. It also allows the requested State to substantiate its good faith in refusing the request. [⋯].

153. Having found that France's reliance on Article 2 (*c*) was for reasons that fell under that provision, but that it has not complied with its obligation under Article 17, the Court now considers whether, as Djibouti has contended, a violation of Article 17 precludes a reliance on Article 2 (*c*) that might otherwise be available. The Court recalls that France maintained that Articles 2 and 17 impose distinct and unrelated obligations, and claimed in particular that they are removed from each other in the text of the Convention. [⋯]

154. That Articles 2 and 17 are in a sense linked is undeniable. Article 2 refers to possible exceptions to the granting of mutual assistance and Article 17 to the duty to give reasons for the invocation of such exceptions in refusing mutual assistance. [⋯]

156. The Court observes that Articles 2 and 17 are located in different sections of the 1986 Convention. [⋯] At the same time, Articles 2 and 17 provide for distinct obligations, and the terms of the Convention do not suggest that recourse to Article 2 is dependent upon compliance with Article 17. Further, had it been so intended by the Parties, this would have been expressly stipulated in the Convention. The Court thus finds that, in spite of the non-respect by France of Article 17, the latter was entitled to rely upon Article 2 (*c*) and that, consequently, Article 1 of the Convention has not been breached. [⋯]

203. The Court has found a violation by France of its obligation under Article 17 of the 1986 Convention. As regards possible remedies for such a violation, the Court will not order the publication of the reasons underlying the decision, as specified in the *soit-transmis* of Judge Clément, to refuse the request for mutual assistance, these having in the meantime passed into the public domain.

204. The Court determines that its finding that France has violated its obligation to Djibouti under Article 17 constitutes appropriate satisfaction. [⋯]

☑ 해　설

이 판결은 ICJ가 형사사법공조조약의 이행과 관련하여 심리한 유일한 사건이다. 특히 최근 범죄인인도조약과 형사사법공조조약의 체결이 전세계적으로 확산되고 있어 이들 조약의 이행과 관련한 분쟁이 발생할 가능성도 점차 대두하는 실정이다. 2020년 7월 현재 우리나라는 미국을 비롯한 30

여 개의 국가와 각각 범죄인인도조약과 형사사법공조조약을 체결하고 있다.

ICJ는 이 분쟁에서 국가의 주요 이익에 대한 침해 여부 판단은 해당국의 광범위한 재량이 적용되는 영역이라는 점을 거듭 확인했다. 그러한 맥락에서 국익 침해 판단 역시 해당국의 법령에 따라 결정되어야 함을 확인했다. 해당국의 법령이 특정인에 대해 주요 국익 침해 여부를 판단하도록 권한을 부여하고 있다면, 이에 대해 타국이 이견을 제시할 수 없다는 것이다. 이 문제는 오로지 해당국의 국내 법령에 따라 결정되어야 함을 ICJ는 확인하고 있다. 최근 국가안보 예외를 원용하는 사례들이 통상분쟁 및 투자분쟁에서도 심심찮게 원용되고 있는 상황에서 국가안보를 포함한 주요 국익 침해 상황에 대한 해당 여부를 결국 누가 판단하는지가 핵심 쟁점으로 대두하고 있다. 이 판결에서 나타난 ICJ 입장은 결국 이러한 문제에 대한 최종 결정은 해당국에 기본적으로 위임되어 있다는 것으로 최근 대두되는 문제에 대해 시사점을 제시하고 있다.

한편, 범죄인인도조약과 형사사법공조조약은 인도 여부 또는 자료 제공 여부를 결정함에 있어 인도 또는 제공 사유가 있음에도 불구하고 다른 정당한 이유가 있는 경우 이를 거부할 수 있는 조항들을 다수 포함하고 있다. 범죄인인도조약의 자국민불인도, 정치범불인도 원칙이나, 범죄인인도조약 및 형사사법공조조약에 포함되는 이중범죄성(double criminality) 미충족을 이유로 한 거부가 그러한 사례이다. 이러한 거부 사유가 적용되는 경우 조약에 특별한 규정이 존재하지 않는 한 피요청국의 거부는 그 자체로 타당하며 거부와 관련된 절차적 요건에 흠결이 있다고 하여 그러한 거부 자체의 타당성이 문제되지는 않는다는 점을 ICJ는 밝히고 있다. 즉, 이 문제와 관련하여 절차적 요건의 흠결이 실체적 요건의 흠결로 반드시 이어지지는 않는다는 점을 확인하고 있는 것이다. 절차적 요건의 흠결은 그 자체로 별도로 따져 볼 문제라는 것이다.

한편, 이러한 절차적 위반에 대한 구제수단은 상당히 경미하다. 이 판정에서 ICJ는 패소국인 프랑스가 승소국인 지부티를 위해 이행해야 할 별다른 구제조치는 필요없으며 프랑스에 대한 패소판정 자체가 "만족(satisfaction)"에 해당한다고 결정했다. 이러한 만족을 통해 프랑스는 패소국으로서 국가책임이 해제된다는 입장을 ICJ는 취하고 있다. 국가의 위신을 중시하는 국제사회의 특성에 비추어 때로는 "만족"이 주요한 책임해제 수단임을 이 판결은 보여주고 있다.

이 판결은 국가안보를 이유로 한 정보 제공 거부를 다룬 사건이라는 점에서 최근 국가안보 예외조항이 다양한 맥락에서 원용되는 상황에서 그 함의가 재조명되고 있다. 이 사건의 쟁점이 된 양국 형사사법공조조약 제2조는 "요청의 이행이 주권, 안보, 공공질서 또는 본질적 이익을 침해할 우려가 있는 경우 요청을 거절할 수 있다"고 규정한다. ICJ는 프랑스가 요청된 자료의 제공을 거부한 것은 국가안보 예외를 규정한 위 제2조에 포섭된다고 판단했으나, 프랑스가 거부의 근거를 제시하지 않음으로써 설명의무를 규정하는 이 조약 제17조를 위반한 것으로 결정했다. 그 근거를 개략적으로라도 언급하였으면 제17조를 충족하였을 가능성이 높을 것으로 보인다. 특히 상당수의 조약은 이러한 별도의 설명의무를 규정하고 있다는 점에서 국가안보를 언급하며 정보 제공을 거부하는 결정이 사실상 광범위하게 용인될 가능성을 이 판결은 시사하고 있다.

➡ **참고문헌** ─────────────────────────────

- 이재민, 국가안보 예외의 사각지대: '정보제공 거부' 조항의 의미와 문제점, 국제법학회논총 제65권(2020), p. 125.
- R. Briese & S. Schill, Djibouti v France: Self – judging Clauses Before the International Court of Justice, Melbourne Journal of International Law Vol. 10 Issue 1(2009).
- G. P. Buzzini, Lights and Shadows of Immunities and Inviolability of State Officials in International Law: Some Comments on the Djibouti v. France Case, Leiden Journal of International Law Vol. 22(2009), p. 45.

5. ICC 아프가니스탄 전범 조사 개시(2020)
— ICC 검찰관의 권한

Situation in the Islamic Republic of Afghanistan
ICC Appeals Chamber No. ICC-02/17 OA4.

☑ 사   안

2017년 11월 20일 국제형사재판소(International Criminal Court: ICC) 검찰부(Prosecutor)는 중요한 결정을 내렸다. 2001년 미국 9/11 테러 이후 발발한 아프가니스탄에서의 전쟁과 관련한 전쟁범죄에 대한 수사를 시도하기로 한 것이다. 먼저 이러한 수사를 개시할 수 있도록 허가해 달라는 신청을 ICC 전심재판부(Pre-Trial Chamber)에 제출했다. 주로 미국의 전쟁수행 행위가 수사 대상이 될 것을 우려한 미국은 이에 대해 크게 반발하며 다각도로 ICC 압박에 나섰다. 2019년 3월 15일 폼페이오 미국 국무장관은 ICC 및 그 구성원들에 대한 미국 입국비자 취소와 개별적 경제제재 등을 언급했고, 이후 2019년 4월 5일 미국 국무부는 실제로 ICC 검찰부를 이끄는 파투 벤수다 검찰관의 미국 입국비자를 취소했다. 2019년 4월 12일, 1년 반의 검토끝에 ICC 전심재판부는 검찰부의 아프가니스탄 관련 수사 개시를 불허하는 결정을 내렸다. 전심재판부는 불허의 이유로 ICC가 과연 성공적으로 수사를 할 수 있을지 여부에 대해 확신이 서지 않는다는 점을 들었다. 논리적으로 명확하지 않은 이러한 전심재판부의 결정에 대해 국제적 비난이 고조되었다. 지금까지 ICC가 주로 아프리카 국가들과 관련된 수사와 기소에 적극적이었던 상황을 감안하면 이 불허 결정이 결국 미국의 고강도 압박을 고려한 정치적인 판단의 결과인 것이 아닌가 하고 생각해볼 여지가 충분하였기 때문이다. ICC 입장에서도 전방위 압박을 가하는 미국의 입장을 고려하지 않을 수 없었을 것이다.

전심재판부의 결정에 대해 ICC 검찰부는 상소하였다. 2020년 3월 5일 ICC 상소심 재판부는 전심재판부의 결정을 번복하여 검찰부의 아프가니스탄 전쟁 관련 전쟁범죄 수사 개시를 허가하는 결정을 내렸다. 여러 관련 요건을 검토하니 수사 개시를 위한 기본 요건을 모두 충족했다는 것이다. 전심재판부와 반대의 결론을 도출한 것이다. 이 결정 이후 미국 정부와 ICC의 갈등은 점차 고조되고 있다. 수사 진행 방향과 결과에 따라 앞으로 상당한 파장이 초래될 수 있을 것이다. 2020년 7월 현재 미국은 ICC에 대한 압박과 비난을 지속하고 있다.

☑ 쟁   점

(1) ICC 전심재판부가 검찰관의 수사 개시 여부를 판단함에 있어 "정의의 이익(interest of justice)"에 근거하여 판단할 권한이 있는지 여부.

(2) 검찰관의 수사는 아프가니스탄 영토 내에서 체포 구금된 자에 대해 고문이 이루어진 경우에만 허용되는지 여부.

☑ 결   정

(1) ICC 전심재판부가 검찰관의 수사 개시 여부를 판단함에 있어 "정의의 이익"에 근거하여 판단할 권한은 없으며 이는 오로지 검찰관이 판단할 사항이다.

(2) 아프가니스탄뿐 아니라 여타 국가에서 체포 구금된 자에 대하여 고문이 이루어진 경우도 검찰관의 수사 범위에 포함된다.

판 결 문

(1) 수사 개시 여부 결정 시 전심재판부가 '정의의 이익'을 평가할 권한이 있는지 여부

3. Pursuant to article 15 of the Statute, the Prosecutor may initiate an investigation propio motu (on her own motion), without having received a referral from a State Party to the Rome Statute or the Security Council of the United Nations. However, in such a case, the investigation must be authorised by a pre-trial chamber. The present appeal concerns a situation where the Prosecutor's request for authorisation was rejected on the ground that an investigation would not serve the interests of justice.

4. On 20 November 2017, the Prosecutor filed a request for authorisation of an investigation into crimes allegedly committed in the Islamic Republic of Afghanistan (hereinafter: 'Afghanistan') since 1 May 2003, as well as related crimes allegedly committed in other States Parties since 1 July 2002 (the 'Request'). The Request involved: (i) the Taliban and affiliated groups for crimes against humanity and war crimes; (ii) the Afghan National Security Forces for war crimes; and (iii) the armed forces of the United States of America (the 'United States') and its Central Intelligence Agency (the 'CIA') for war crimes.

5. On 12 April 2019, Pre-Trial Chamber II (the 'Pre-Trial Chamber') decided to reject the Prosecutor's Request and not to authorise an investigation by the Prosecutor into the situation in Afghanistan (hereinafter: 'Impugned Decision'). Pursuant to article 15(4) of the Statute, the Pre-Trial Chamber was required to determine whether there was a reasonable basis to proceed with an investigation, and whether the case appeared to fall within the jurisdiction of the Court, in deciding whether to authorise the commencement of the investigation. In the Impugned Decision, the Pre-Trial Chamber concluded that, 'notwithstanding the fact that all the relevant requirements are met as regards both jurisdiction and admissibility, an investigation into the situation in Afghanistan would not serve the interests of justice'.

19. Under her first ground of appeal, the Prosecutor argues that the Pre-Trial Chamber erred by seeking to make a positive determination that the initiation of an investigation into the situation in Afghanistan was in the interests of justice.

28. If a situation is referred by a State Party or the Security Council, article 53(1) of the Statute places, in principle, an obligation on the Prosecutor to open an investigation, by providing that '[t]he Prosecutor shall [⋯] initiate an investigation unless he or she determines that there is no reasonable basis to proceed under this Statute'. The Prosecutor is obliged to evaluate the seriousness of the information received and may seek additional information for this purpose. In deciding whether to initiate an investigation, article 53(1) obliges the Prosecutor to consider three factors: (i) whether there is a reasonable basis to believe that a crime within the jurisdiction of the Court has been or is being committed; (ii) whether the case is or would be admissible; and (iii) whether, '[t]aking into account the gravity of the crime and the interests of victims, there are nonetheless substantial reasons to believe that an investigation would not serve the interests of justice'.

29. Article 53(1) of the Statute thus reflects an expectation that the Prosecutor will proceed to investigate referred situations, while allowing the Prosecutor not to proceed in the limited circumstances set out in article 53(1)(a) to (c) of the Statute. If the Prosecutor decides not to initiate an investigation under article 53(1) of the Statute, her decision is subject to certain notification requirements. Article 53(3) of the Statute envisages judicial control over the Prosecutor's decision not to investigate and aims at ensuring that the Prosecutor complies with her duty to investigate referred situations.

30. In contrast, article 15 of the Statute, titled 'Prosecutor', sets out the procedure for the triggering of an investigation by the Prosecutor proprio motu, that is, on her own motion when a situation has not been referred to her. Article 15 recognises the discretionary nature of this power, providing in paragraph 1 that 'the Prosecutor may initiate investigations proprio motu' (emphasis added). In this context, it is for the Prosecutor to determine whether there is a reasonable basis to initiate an investigation proprio motu. If the Prosecutor concludes that there is no reasonable basis to proceed (a scenario not arising in this appeal), article 15(6) of the Statute requires her to inform those who provided the information of her conclusion. They may provide additional information to the Prosecutor who may reconsider the matter; however, the legal framework does not envisage judicial review of the Prosecutor's conclusion.

31. In the view of the Appeals Chamber, this is consistent with the discretionary nature of the power accorded to the Prosecutor under article 15 of the Statute. Indeed, it would be contrary to the very concept to suggest that a duty to investigate could be imposed by the pre-trial chamber in the absence of a request for authorisation of an investigation by the Prosecutor. The Appeals Chamber notes, in this regard, that a proposal to allow for notification to the pre-trial chamber and judicial review of decisions of the Prosecutor not to request authorisation of an investigation under article 15(6) of the Statute was rejected by the drafters. Indeed, the right vested in all States Parties and in the Security Council to refer situations would provide the appropriate remedy in such circumstance.

32. Therefore, under the procedure set out in article 15 of the Statute, the pre-trial chamber has a role in respect of the Prosecutor's exercise of discretionary power only if she determines that there is a basis to initiate an investigation.54 If the Prosecutor wishes to investigate a situation in the absence of a referral, the pre-trial chamber's authorisation is required, in accordance with article 15(4) of the Statute. If authorisation is granted, the Prosecutor may initiate an investigation directly. She is not required to determine for a second time under article 53(1) of the Statute that there is a reasonable basis to proceed with an investigation. On the basis of the foregoing, the Appeals Chamber considers that the content and placement of articles 15 and 53(1) of the Statute make it clear that these are separate provisions addressing the initiation of an investigation by the Prosecutor in two distinct contexts. Article 15 of the Statute governs the initiation of a proprio motu investigation, while article 53(1) concerns situations which are referred to the Prosecutor by a State Party or the Security Council.

37. In light of the above, the Appeals Chamber considers that the 'interests of justice' factor set out in article 53(1)(c) of the Statute, while part of the Prosecutor's consideration under article 15(3) of the Statute as per rule 48 of the Rules, is not part of the pre-trial chamber's decision under article 15(4) of the Statute.

41. The Appeals Chamber considers that the drafting history supports its view that the pre-trial chamber's determination under article 15(4) should not incorporate issues of admissibility. In this regard, it notes that, during the Rome Conference, a provision was deleted from draft article 15 that would have expressly required the pre-trial chamber to take issues of admissibility into account in determining whether to authorise an investigation. Similarly, a proposal during the drafting of the Rules to incorporate admissibility and jurisdictional challenges into the authorization procedure was rejected by the drafters, inter alia, due to concerns that it would exceed the oversight role of the pre-trial chamber under article 15 and that it would not be feasible to resolve these issues at such an early stage of proceedings.

45. The Appeals Chamber concludes that a plain reading of the relevant legal provisions in their context suggests that the pre-trial chamber under article 15(4) of the Statute is only required to assess the information contained in the Prosecutor's request to determine whether there is a reasonable factual basis to proceed with an investigation, in the sense of whether crimes have been committed, and whether the potential case(s) arising from such investigation would appear to fall within the Court's jurisdiction. In this regard, the Appeals Chamber notes that the process under paragraphs 3-5 of article 15 is not a review of the Prosecutor's determination. Rather the Prosecutor seeks the pre-trial chamber's authorisation to proceed and that authorisation should be based on the application by the pre-trial chamber of the separate factors specified in paragraph 4, to the Prosecutor's application. Thus the pre-trial chamber is required to reach its own determination under article 15(4) of the Statute as to whether there is a reasonable basis to proceed with an investigation. It is not called to review the Prosecutor's analysis of the factors under article 53(1)(a) to (c) of the Statute. 46. Based on the foregoing, the Appeals Chamber finds that the Pre-Trial Chamber erred in deciding that 'an investigation into the situation in Afghanistan at this stage would not serve the interests of justice'. It finds that the Pre-Trial Chamber's decision under article 15(4) of the Statute should have addressed only whether there is a reasonable factual basis for the Prosecutor to proceed with an investigation, in the sense of whether crimes have been committed, and whether the potential case(s) arising from such investigation would appear to fall within the Court's jurisdiction.

(2) 피해자가 아프가니스탄 영토 내에서 체포·구금된 경우에만 수사가 적용되는지 여부

62. In relation to the Afghanistan situation, the Appeals Chamber notes that the Prosecutor presented information regarding the alleged large scale commission of multiple crimes against humanity and war crimes by various armed groups and actors involved in the conflict, which began prior to the entry into force of the Rome Statute on 17 July 2002 and continues to the present day. This information was accepted by the Pre-Trial Chamber as providing a reasonable basis to believe that the alleged events occurred and that they may constitute crimes within the jurisdiction of the Court. Given the scope of the information presented by the Prosecutor and accepted by the Pre-Trial Chamber, the Appeals Chamber considers that the requirements of article 15(4) of the Statute would be met by granting the authorisation in the terms requested by the Prosecutor, which sufficiently defines the parameters of the situation.

63. The Appeals Chamber considers that the alternative proposed by the Pre-Trial Chamber—that investigation of incidents not closely related to those authorised would be possible if they were the subject of a new request for authorisation under article 15—is unworkable in practice in the context of an investigation into large-scale crimes of the type proposed by the Prosecutor [⋯].

64. In view of foregoing, the Appeals Chamber finds that the Pre-Trial Chamber erred in finding that the scope of any authorisation granted would be limited to the incidents mentioned in the Request and those closely linked thereto.

65. In the Request, the Prosecutor provided information relating to alleged war crimes amounting to serious violations of article 3 common to the four Geneva Conventions ('Common Article 3') of torture and cruel treatment, outrages upon personal dignity, and rape and other forms of sexual violence, committed as part of a policy, by members of the CIA in a number of detention facilities in Afghanistan, as well as in detention facilities located on the territory of other States Parties. The Prosecutor presented information relating to individuals who were allegedly mistreated by the CIA as part of this program. Some of these individuals were allegedly captured outside Afghanistan; at least one individual was captured on the territory of Afghanistan, while the location of capture of the remaining individual was unclear. In all instances, the mistreatment was alleged to have taken place on the territory of States Parties.

66. The Prosecutor described the CIA detention program as 'global in nature' and indicated that it 'included persons with no direct connection to the conflict in Afghanistan, such as persons detained in connection with other armed conflicts or otherwise suspected of planning attacks against the United States'. However, for the purpose of the Request, the Prosecutor referred only to crimes allegedly committed on the territory of States Parties against individuals that she considered to have a nexus to the armed conflict in Afghanistan. The Prosecutor specified that she had included alleged crimes committed against individuals who were suspected by the CIA to be members of the Taliban and/or Al Qaeda, or of cooperating with those groups, or having 'links with or information about Al-Qaeda "core" or "central" group, allegedly responsible for the 11 September 2001 attacks'. She submitted that the 'detainees were interrogated for their (actual or perceived) knowledge of Taliban and Al Qaeda operations and planned attacks, locations of Taliban and Al Qaeda leaders or training camps, and other intelligence information about each organisation'. Conversely, she indicated that she had excluded the reported mis-treatment of persons who were 'allegedly linked to other "franchise" Al Qaeda groups or other terrorist organisations'.

71. In the Impugned Decision, the Pre-Trial Chamber found that the alleged incidents which the Prosecutor attributed to the CIA fell outside the Court's jurisdiction 'since these are said to have occurred against persons captured elsewhere than Afghanistan'. The Pre-Trial Chamber considered that the acts in question lacked the nexus with an internal armed conflict required to trigger the application of international humanitarian law. The Pre-Trial Chamber noted that the 'two requirements "in the context of" and "associated with" are clearly not in the alternative but cumulative'. The Pre-Trial Chamber supported its view by reference to the chapeau of Common Article 3, stating that '[b]oth the wording and the spirit of common article 3 to the Geneva Conventions are univocal in confining its territorial scope within the borders of the State where the hostilities are actually occurring'.

72. For the reasons that follow, the Appeals Chamber considers that the Pre-Trial Chamber's approach was incorrect. Common Article 3 reads, in full, as follows: In the case of armed conflict not of an international character occurring in the territory of one of the High Contracting Parties, each Party to the conflict shall be bound to apply, as a minimum, the following provisions: (1) Persons taking no active part in the hostilities, including members of armed forces who have laid down their arms and those placed hors de combat by sickness, wounds, detention, or any other cause, shall in all circumstances be treated humanely, without any adverse distinction founded on race, colour, religion or faith, sex, birth or wealth, or any other similar criteria. To this end, the following acts are and shall remain prohibited at any time and in any place whatsoever with respect to the above-mentioned persons: (a) violence to life and person, in particular murder of all kinds, mutilation, cruel treatment and torture; (b) taking of hostages; (c) outrages upon personal dignity, in particular humiliating and degrading treatment; (d) the passing of sentences and the carrying out of executions without previous judgment pronounced by a regularly constituted court, affording all the judicial guarantees which are recognized as indispensable by civilized peoples. (2) The wounded and sick shall be collected and cared for. An impartial humanitarian body, such as the International Committee of the Red Cross, may offer its services to the Parties to the conflict. The Parties to the conflict should further endeavour to bring into force, by means of special agreements, all or part of the other provisions of the present Convention. The application of the preceding provisions shall not affect the legal status of the Parties to the conflict.

73. While it is true that the chapeau of Common Article 3 refers to an 'armed conflict not of an international character occurring in the territory of one of the High Contracting Parties', this phrase does not have the function ascribed to it by the Pre-Trial Chamber, namely to limit the applicability of the provision to the State on the territory of which the armed conflict occurs. Rather, in the view of the Appeals Chamber, it simply describes the circumstances under which Common

Article 3 applies: there must be an armed conflict not of an international character in one of the States Parties to the Geneva Convention. As highlighted by the amicus curiae submission of Professor Rona, this view finds support in the position of the International Committee of the Red Cross (the 'ICRC'), which suggests that this phrase does not have the effect of restricting the application of Common Article 3 to the territory of the State in which the armed conflict occurs, but rather was aimed at ensuring that the provision would bind only those States that had ratified the Geneva Conventions. The ICRC indicates that this phrase 'has lost its importance in practice' as any armed conflict not of an international character 'cannot but take place on the territory of one of the Parties to the Convention' given the universal ratification of the Geneva Conventions. Indeed, all States relevant to the allegations in question—Afghanistan, Poland, Romania and Lithuania, as well as the United States—are parties to the four Geneva Conventions.

76. Thus, in the view of the Appeals Chamber, it is incorrect to assume that, merely because the alleged capture of the victim did not take place in Afghanistan and the alleged criminal act also occurred outside Afghanistan, the conduct cannot possibly have taken place in the context of, and have been associated with, the armed conflict in that State. Rather, a careful analysis of the circumstances of each case will need to be carried out to establish whether there is a sufficient nexus. The place of capture of the alleged victim may be a relevant factor for this analysis, but it does not settle the matter. In sum, the Appeals Chamber considers that the Pre-Trial Chamber's finding regarding the nexus requirement was incorrect. There is no reason to limit the Prosecutor's investigation in the manner envisaged by the Pre-Trial Chamber.

☑ 해   설

1998년 7월 이탈리아 로마에서 채택된 ICC 설립을 위한 로마규정(Rome Statute)은 2002년 7월 발효하였다. 이로써 국제사회를 향한 네 가지 국제범죄 — 집단살해(genocide), 인도에 반한 죄, 전쟁범죄 및 침략범죄 — 를 범한 개인을 처벌하기 위한 상설법원이 처음으로 도입되었다. 2020년 7월 현재 전세계 123개국이 로마규정에 가입하였다. 우리나라는 2000년 3월 로마규정에 서명하고 2002년 3월 국회 비준을 거쳐 가입하였다.

미국은 로마규정에 서명은 하였으나 가입하지 않고 있다. 전 세계 여러

곳에서 군사활동을 수행하는 미군과 이와 관련된 미 정부관료들에 대한 ICC
의 관할권 행사 가능성을 우려한 탓이다. 그런데 미국의 고민은 스스로 로마
규정에 가입하지 않더라도 이 문제가 완전하게 해결되지 않는다는 데 있다.
미국의 가입 여부와 상관없이 ICC가 관할권을 행사할 수 있는 길이 열려 있
기 때문이다. 실제 로마규정은 제12조 2항에서 "자국 영토 내에서 범죄가 발
생한 국가(the State on the territory of which the conduct in question occurred)"
또는 "범죄 혐의자가 자국 국적자인 국가(the State of which the person accused
of the crime is a national)"가 로마규정 당사국이면 ICC가 관할권을 행사할 수
있다고 규정하고 있다. 예를 들어 현재 미국은 로마규정에 가입하지 않았으
나 아프가니스탄이 가입하였으므로 아프가니스탄에서의 미군 관련 범죄에
대해 관할권을 갖는다. 바로 이에 따라 이번에 ICC 검찰관이 수사를 개시한
것이다.

2020년 3월 5일 ICC 상소심 재판부의 수사 허가 결정은 이러한 미국의
우려를 현실화하는 계기가 되었다. 이미 2016년 ICC는 보고서를 통해 아프
가니스탄 전쟁 와중에 CIA 주도로 비밀 구금 장소에서 인권 유린 행위가 발
생하였음을 언급한 바 있다. ICC 상소심 재판부도 2020년 3월 5일 결정에서
아프가니스탄에서 전쟁범죄가 발생하였다고 볼 근거가 충분하다는 점을 들
어 검찰부의 수사 개시를 허가하였다.

물론 ICC 검찰부의 수사는 단지 미군이나 미국 요원만을 대상으로 하는
것은 아니며 탈레반을 포함한 아프가니스탄 전쟁의 주요 교전 당사자를 망
라하고 있다. 그러나 그 수사의 방점이 결국 미군과 미국 요원으로 향할 가
능성이 높다는 점에서 미국은 그간 전방위 압박 작전으로 ICC 수사에 반대
하여 왔다.

2020년 3월 5일 수사 허가 결정이 내려진 이후 미국 정부는 이 결정을
지속적으로 비난하고 있다. 트럼프 대통령은 2020년 6월 11일 ICC 및 그 구
성원에 대한 제재를 승인하는 행정명령에 서명하였다. 이에 따라 미국 정부
는 2020년 9월 2일 파투 벤수다 ICC 검찰관과 파키소 모초초코 ICC 사법권
보상·협력 위원장에 대해 이들의 미국 내 자산동결과 여행금지 조치를 취하
였다. 업무 속성상 UN 본부가 있는 뉴욕으로의 출장이 빈번한 이들에 대해

미국 입국 금지 조치를 내린 것은 이들의 업무 수행에 상당한 지장을 초래할 것이다. 특히 국제기구 임직원의 미국 내 자산을 동결하고 입국을 불허하는 등 개인적인 차원의 압박과 제재는 주목할 만하다. 국제기구 임직원이 해당 협정 규정에 따라 권한을 행사한 것에 대해 특정 국가가 자국의 이해관계에 반한다는 이유로 그 임직원을 직접 제재할 수 있는지 의문이다. EU를 비롯한 여러 국가들이 미국의 이러한 움직임을 비판하고 있으나 미국의 제재는 지속될 전망이다.

미국의 일방주의적 조치에 대한 국제사회의 비난이 이어지고 있으나 동시에 ICC 내부의 불협화음도 국제사회의 우려를 자아내고 있다. 2018년 4월 ICC의 일부 재판관들은 ICC를 상대로 자신들의 처우와 근무조건 개선을 요구하는 소송을 제네바 소재 '국제노동기구 행정재판소(ILO Administrative Tribunal)'에 제기했다. ICC에 근무하는 일반 직원이 아닌 재판관들이 ICC를 상대로 소송을 제기하였다는 점에서 상당히 이례적이다. 구체적인 사실관계는 아직 충분히 알려지지 않았으나 ICC 내부의 지난 수년간 이러한 일련의 움직임들이 그 위상에 상당한 타격을 가지고 온 것도 사실이다. 설립 18년 만에 ICC는 심각한 내부적·외부적 위기에 직면하고 있다. 이들 위기를 어떻게 극복하는지 여부에 따라 ICC의 미래가 결정될 것이다.

➡ 참고문헌 ─────────────────────────────

- 김상걸, 아프간 전쟁에 대한 ICC 수사개시의 국제정치적 함의, 국가안보전략연구원 이슈브리프 통권 188호(2020)
- Contemporary Practice of the US, The Trump Administration Revokes the ICC Prosecutor's US Visa Shortly Before the ICC Pre-Trial Chamber Declines to Authorize an Investigation into War Crimes in Afghanistan, American Journal of International Law Vol. 113(2019), p. 625.
- J. N. Stefanelli, ICC Authorizes Investigation into Afghanistan, International Law in Brief, American Society of International Law(2020. 3. 5일자).
- J. Trahan, The Significance of the ICC Appeals Chamber's Ruling in the Afghanistan Situation, Opinio Juris(2020. 3. 10일자).

제17장
국제경제법

1. 한국산 반도체 상계관세 부과(2005)
─ 간접 보조금의 의미

United States-Countervailing Duty Investigation on Dynamic Random Access Memory Semiconductors(DRAMS) from Korea.
Korea. v. United States, Report of the Appellate Body, WT/DS296/AB/R(2005).

☑ 사   안

급격한 시장 상황 악화로 재정난에 처한 한국의 하이닉스 반도체를 위해 다수의 한국 금융기관은 수 차례에 걸쳐 대규모의 채무재조정(debt restructuring)을 실시해 회사의 회생을 도모했다. 미국 상무부는 곧이어 상계관세 조사를 실시해 이러한 채무재조정 조치가 금융기관의 자발적 선택이 아닌, 한국 정부의 압력을 통해 실시된 위장된 보조금 지급 조치임을 결정했다. 미국 상무부는 이에 따라 하이닉스 반도체가 미국으로 수출하는 DRAM 반도체에 대해 44%에 달하는 고율의 상계관세를 부과하기에 이르렀다. 이에 대해 한국 정부는 미국의 상계관세 부과조치가 WTO 보조금협정 위반임을 주장하여 WTO 분쟁해결기구에 제소했고 WTO 패널과 상소기구가 각각 심리를 실시했다. 그간 대부분 보조금 관련 소송은 정부의 직접적인 자금 제공과 관련된 소위 직접 보조금 사건이었음에 반해 본 소송은 정부가 우회적으로 특정 기업에 대한 지원을 유도하였는가에 관한 소위 간접 보조금 사건이라는 점에서 국제적으로 상당한 관심을 초래했다.

☑ 쟁   점

(1) 정부에 의한 재정적 기여의 한 형태로 보조금협정 제1.1(a)(1)(VI)조

가 규정하고 있는 "위임 및 지시"의 구체적 의미.

(2) "위임 및 지시" 입증에 있어 상계관세 조사 피조사국(현 제소국) 정부 정책의 전체적 맥락을 보여주는 것으로도 충분한지 여부.

(3) "위임 및 지시"를 통한 간접 보조금 확인에 있어 간접증거 또는 정황증거의 활용 범위 또는 증거 능력.

☑ 판　결

(1) 간접 보조금에 효과적으로 대처하기 위해 보조금협정상 "위임 및 지시"의 범위를 지나치게 좁게 해석해서는 안 되며 현실을 적절히 반영한 해석이 필요하다. 즉, 이에 관해 적용될 적절한 기준은 일국 정부가 보조금 지급의 효과를 달성하기 위해 특정 민간주체에 대해 명령을 발했는가 하는 정도의 높은 기준이 아니라 단지 그 민간주체에 책임을 부여하거나 또는 민간주체에 대해 정부의 권한을 행사했는지 여부이다.

(2) "위임 및 지시" 협의에 따라 조사를 실시하는 상계관세 조사당국은 문제가 된 개별 조치별로 검토를 실시할 의무는 없으며 관련된 조치를 전체적으로 파악하여 보조금 해당 여부를 판단하는 것도 보조금협정상 허용된다.

(3) 간접 보조금은 그 성격상 간접 및 정황증거가 광범위하게 활용될 수 있다.

판 결 문

107. Article 1.1(a)(1) makes clear that a "financial contribution" by a government or public body is an essential component of a "subsidy" under the *SCM Agreement*. No product may be found to be subsidized under Article 1.1(a)(1), nor may it be countervailed, in the absence of a financial contribution. Furthermore, situations involving exclusively private conduct—that is, conduct that is not in some way attributable to a government or public body—cannot constitute a "financial contribution" for purposes of determining the existence of a subsidy under the *SCM Agreement*.

108. Paragraphs (i) through (iv) of Article 1.1(a)(1) set forth the situations where there is a financial contribution by a government or public body. The situations listed in paragraphs (i) through (iii) refer to a financial contribution that is provided *directly* by the government through the direct transfer of funds, the foregoing of revenue, the provision of goods or services, or the purchase of goods. By virtue of paragraph (iv), a financial contribution may also be provided *indirectly* by a government where it "makes payments to a funding mechanism," or, as alleged in this case, where a government "entrusts or directs a private body to carry out one or more of the type of functions illustrated in (i) to (iii) [⋯] which would normally be vested in the government and the practice, in no real sense, differs from practices normally followed by governments." [⋯]

109. With this in mind, we turn to examine the meanings of the terms "entrusts" and "directs" in Article 1.1(a)(1)(iv). We recall that the Panel stated that it "agree[d] with the *US-Export Restraints* panel that '[i]t follows from the ordinary meanings of the two words "entrust" and "direct" that the action of the government must contain a notion of delegation (in the case of entrustment) or command(in the case of direction).'" In so doing, the Panel effectively replaced the terms "entrusts" and "directs" with two other terms, "delegation" and "command," whose scope it did not define, and went no further in clarifying the meaning of any of these terms. [⋯].

110. The term "entrusts" connotes the action of giving responsibility to someone for a task or an object. [⋯] Delegation is usually achieved by formal means, but delegation also could be informal. Moreover, there may be other means, be they formal or informal, that governments could employ for the same purpose. Therefore, an interpretation of the term "entrusts" that is limited to acts of "delegation" is too narrow.

111. As for the term "directs," we note that some of the definitions—such as "give authoritative instructions to" and "order (a person) *to do*"—suggest that the person or entity that "directs" has authority over the person or entity that is directed. [⋯] A "command" (the word used by the Panel) is certainly one way in which a government can exercise authority over a private body in the sense foreseen by Article 1.1(a)(1)(iv), but governments are likely to have other means at their disposal to exercise authority over a private body. [⋯] Thus, an interpretation of the term "directs" that is limited to acts of "command" is also too narrow. [⋯]

114. It follows, therefore, that not all government acts necessarily amount to entrustment or direction. We note that both the United States and Korea agree that "mere policy pronouncements" by a government would not, by themselves, constitute entrustment or direction for purposes of Article 1.1(a)(1)(ⅳ). [⋯] Thus, government "entrustment" or "direction" cannot be inadvertent or a mere by-product of governmental regulation. This is consistent with the Appellate Body's statement in *US-Softwood Lumber* IV that "not all government measures capable of conferring benefits would necessarily fall within Article 1.1(a)"; otherwise paragraphs (ⅰ) through (ⅳ) of Article 1.1(a) would not be necessary "because all government measures conferring benefits, *per se*, would be subsidies."

115. Furthermore, such an interpretation is consistent with the object and purpose of the *SCM Agreement*, which reflects a delicate balance between the Members that sought to impose more disciplines on the use of subsidies and those that sought to impose more disciplines on the application of countervailing measures. Indeed, the Appellate Body has said that the object and purpose of the *SCM Agreement* is "to strengthen and improve GATT disciplines relating to the use of both subsidies and countervailing measures, while, recognizing at the same time, the right of Members to impose such measures under certain conditions". This balance must be borne in mind in interpreting paragraph (ⅳ). [⋯]

116. In sum, we are of the view that, pursuant to paragraph (ⅳ), "entrustment" occurs where a government gives responsibility to a private body, and "direction" refers to situations where the government exercises its authority over a private body. In both instances, the government uses a private body as proxy to effectuate one of the types of financial contributions listed in paragraphs (ⅰ) through (ⅲ). It may be difficult to identify precisely, in the abstract, the types of government actions that constitute entrustment or direction and those that do not. The particular label used to describe the governmental action is not necessarily dispositive. Indeed, as Korea acknowledges, in some circumstances, "guidance" by a government can constitute direction. In most cases, one would expect entrustment or direction of a private body to involve some form of threat or inducement, which could, in turn, serve as evidence of entrustment or direction. The determination of entrustment or direction will hinge on the particular facts of the case. [⋯]

146. We find that the Panel erred, however, in the *manner* in which it reviewed the individual pieces of evidence. We note, first, that the Panel often appeared to examine whether each piece of evidence, viewed *in isolation*, demonstrated entrustment or direction. [⋯].

150. In our view, having accepted an investigating authority's approach, a panel normally should examine the probative value of a piece of evidence in a similar manner to that followed by the investigating authority. Moreover, if, as here, an investigating authority relies on individual pieces of circumstantial evidence viewed together as support for a finding of entrustment or direction, a panel reviewing such a determination normally should consider that evidence in its totality, rather than individually, in order to assess its probative value with respect to the agency's determination. Indeed, requiring that each piece of circumstantial evidence, on its own, establish entrustment or direction effectively precludes an agency from finding entrustment or direction on the basis of circumstantial evidence. [⋯].

151. Furthermore, in order to examine the evidence in the light of the investigating authority's methodology, a panel's analysis usually should seek to review the agency's decision on its own terms, in particular, by identifying the inference drawn by the *agency* from the evidence, and then by considering whether the evidence could sustain that inference. [⋯].

158. In sum, we are of the view that, in analyzing the USDOC[1]'s evidence under Article 1.1(a)(1)(iv), the Panel assessed the relevance of many individual pieces of evidence by examining whether *each* of them was sufficient to establish entrustment or direction. In so doing, the Panel failed to appreciate the circumstantial nature of the USDOC's evidence and to consider the relevance of that evidence for the particular inferences the USDOC sought to draw. This error, in turn, contributed to various findings of the Panel dismissing or discounting individual pieces of evidence relied on by the USDOC. Furthermore, in its "global" examination of the evidence, the Panel failed to consider that pieces of evidence, especially circumstantial evidence, might become more significant when viewed in their totality. For these reasons, we *find* that the Panel *erred* in failing to examine the USDOC's evidence in its totality, and requiring, instead, that individual pieces of evidence, in and of themselves, establish entrustment or direction by the GOK of Hynix's creditors. [⋯]

☑ 해　설

간접 보조금 문제가 처음으로 다루어진 이 사건은 이후 보조금협정 법리 발전에 상당한 영향을 미쳤다. WTO 회원국 정부들이 점점 다양하고 우회적인 방법으로 보조금을 제공하고자 노력하는 현실을 감안하면 간접 보조

---

1) United States Department of Commerce: 미국 상무부.

금에 대한 적절한 규제가 필요하고 이를 위해 조사당국의 조사 권한을 가급적 광범위하게 보장하는 것이 필요하다는 상소기구 결정의 취지는 기본적으로 타당하다. 그렇지 않을 경우 많은 국가들이 위장된 조치 및 방법을 통해 자국의 주요 기업에 대한 사실상의 보조금 지급을 도모하는 것을 적절히 규제할 수 없을 것이기 때문이다. 그러나 한편으로 불법 보조금 규제 노력이 타국의 정당한 경제정책 집행 및 운용을 불법 보조금 지급조치로 간주하고 이에 대해 제재조치를 취하는 부당한 결과를 초래해서도 안 될 것이다. 현 보조금협정에서 간접 보조금을 적절히 규제하기 위해서는 이러한 상충하는 양 이익간 적절한 균형을 유지하는 것이 필요하다. 상소기구의 이 사건에서의 판정은 이러한 문제에 대해 본격적인 검토를 실시하고 이에 관해 새로운 법적 기준을 제시한다는 점에서 기본적 의의를 찾을 수 있다. 즉, 보조금협정상 극히 추상적으로 규정된 "위임 및 지시"의 구체적 요건이 무엇인지, 나아가 WTO 회원국의 정당한 시장 개입과 불법적인 보조금 지급의 경계선이 무엇인지에 관해 기본적인 지침을 제공해 주고자 시도했다는 점에서 이 결정의 의의를 찾을 수 있을 것이다. 그러나 상소기구의 결정이 일부 사안에 관해서 기존 법리 및 이 사건 패널 결정 내용을 더욱 발전시킨 측면도 있는 반면, 일부 사안에 관해서는 다소 미흡한 분석으로 오히려 향후 혼선을 초래할 가능성을 열어 둔 것은 우려되는 부분이다. 특히, 조사당국의 권한 강화에 지나치게 치중하여 보조금협정의 기본 이념인 조사당국과 보조금 조사 대상국간의 적절한 이해관계의 균형을 사실상 무력화시킨 것이 아닌가 하는 비판도 가능할 것이다. 대표적인 사례로 들 수 있는 것이 증거채택 및 증거력 평가에 있어 조사당국의 광범위한 재량을 인정하고 이에 대하여 기본적으로 WTO 패널이 수용하도록 선언하고 있는 부분이다. 이러한 보조금 협정 해석이 DSU 제11조상 패널이 부담하는 "사안의 객관적 평가(objective assessment of a matter before it)" 원칙과 양립할 수 있을지 의문이다.

이 분쟁에서 상소기구가 미국의 상계관세 부과조치의 보조금 협정 합치성에 대한 평가를 사실상 유보함에 따라 미국은 한국산 반도체에 대한 상계관세 부과조치를 일몰재심 전까지인 2008년 8월까지 5년간 부과했다. 이 시점에서 미국 국내기업이 일몰재심 신청을 포기함에 따라 상계관세 부과조치는 자동 종료되었다. 연례재심 진행으로 인해 실제 모든 절차가 종료된 것은 2011년 2월의 일이다.

한편 이 분쟁에서 쟁점이 된 간접 보조금 문제는 2015년부터 격화된 미·중간 무역분쟁에서 본격적으로 제기된 바 있다. 가령 미국은 중국 정부가 다양한 산업지원 정책을 통해 수출증대를 도모하고 있음을 주장하며 중국산 수입품에 대해 추가관세를 부과했고, 이에 대해 중국도 미국산 상품에 대해 추가관세를 부과하는 등 양국의 무역분쟁은 파국으로 치닫는 양상을 보였다. 2020년 1월 15일 미중 양국은 1단계 무역합의안에 서명하며, 일단 갈등을 봉합하는 모습을 보였으나 2020년 3월부터 코로나 바이러스 사태의 국제적 확산 책임을 두고 다시 양국의 대립은 격화되고 있다.

또한 간접보조금 문제는 미국과 유럽연합 간 2005년부터 지금까지 지속되고 있는 대형 민간항공기(Large Civil Aircraft) 분쟁[2]에서도 다양한 맥락으로 제기되었다. 15년째 여러 단계를 오가며 이어지는 WTO 패널 및 상소기구 절차에서 양측은 서로 상대방이 각각 보잉사와 에어버스사를 위해 광범위한 직접 보조금 교부와 함께 다양한 형태의 '보이지 않는' 간접 보조금을 제공하였다고 주장했다. 항공기 제작 공장 주변에 대한 고속도로 건설, 민관합동 연구 프로젝트 진행, 채무재조정 주선, 특허 공유 등 다양한 방식이 이 과정에서 검토되었다. 이러한 간접 보조금도 대부분 보조금 협정에 저촉되는 "보조금"으로 판단되었다. 결국 양측이 모두 승소하고 동시에 모두 패소하는 상황이 되어 서로 상대방에 대한 보복권한을 획득했다. 2020년 현재 양국 무역 협상이 난항에 빠질 때마다 양측은 서로 상대방에 대한 보복권한 행사를 위협하고 있다.

➡ **참고문헌**

- 이환규, WTO 보조금 관련 주요 분쟁사례 이해, 국제경제법연구 제6권(2008), p. 157.
- D. Ahn, Korea in the GATT/WTO Dispute Settlement System: Legal Battle

---

2) Appellate Body Report, *European Communities and Certain Members States—Measures Affecting Trade in Large Civil Aircraft*, WT/DS316/AB/R.

for Economic Development, Journal of International Economic Law Vol. 6(2003), p. 597.

- R. Becroft, The Standard of Review Strikes Back: The US－Korea Drams Appeal, Journal of International Economic Law Vol. 9(2006), p. 207.
- J. Lee, State Responsibility and Government－Affiliated Entities in International Economic Law The Danger of Blurring the Chinese Wall between 'State Organ' and 'Non－State Organ' as Designed in the ILC Draft Articles, Journal of World Trade Vol. 49(2015), p. 117.

2. 미국 제로잉 제도(2007)
— 반덤핑 협정상 "공정한 비교"

United States-Measures Relating to Zeroing and Sunset
Reviews.
Japan v. the United States, Report of the Appellate Body,
WT/DS322/AB/R(2007).

☑ 사　　안

　　미국 정부(상무부)는 반덤핑 조사시 덤핑 마진율을 계산함에 있어 소위
제로잉(Zeroing)이라는 계산 방법을 전통적으로 사용해 왔다. 이 계산 방법은
덤핑 마진율 계산시 미국 상무부가 자신들에게 유리한 숫자만을 취하고 수
출업자에게 유리한 숫자는 무시하는 것을 골자로 한다. 즉, 수출가격과 정상
가격(국내 내수시장 가격)을 비교하는 덤핑 마진율 산정에서 정상가격이 수출
가격보다 높은 경우는(덤핑이 존재하는 경우) 이를 덤핑 계산에 그대로 반영하
고 반대로 수출가격이 정상가격보다 높은 경우는(즉, 덤핑이 존재하지 않는 경
우) 이를 덤핑 계산에 반영하지 않고 대신 해당 수치를 "0"으로 환산해 (즉,
마치 존재하지 않는 것으로 간주하여) 최종 덤핑 마진을 계산하는 것이다. 이 경
우 선별적 계산의 특성으로 인해 조사대상 기간 전체로 보면 덤핑이 발생하
지 않은 경우에도 마치 덤핑이 존재하는 것으로 결정이 되고, 또 덤핑이 존
재하는 것으로 결정된 경우에도 마진율이 인위적으로 증가하는 등 심각한
왜곡현상이 발생한다. 많은 국가들이 이러한 계산 방법은 공정한 비교(Fair
Comparison) 원칙을 언급한 WTO 반덤핑협정에 위반됨을 지적하며 WTO 분
쟁해결기구에 제소했고 WTO 패널 및 상소기구도 판정에서 그 위법성을 지
속적으로 확인해 왔다. 그러나 미국은 이러한 판정이 나올 때마다 해당 분쟁
에 국한하여 최소한의 범위 내에서만 자신들의 제로잉 계산 방법을 조금씩

수정하는 전략으로 대응해 왔다. 2005년 일본이 미국에 대해 제기한 이 분쟁은 이러한 일련의 제로잉 분쟁의 연장선상에서 제기되었다. 여기에서는 반덤핑 원심조사, 연례재심, 일몰재심 등 제로잉을 채용하는 일체의 반덤핑 조사 절차가 그 분쟁 대상에 포함되었다.

☑ 쟁   점

(1) 미국 상무부의 제로잉 계산 방법은 "제도 자체에 대한(as such)"제소를 위한 정부의 조치(measure)를 구성하는지 여부.

(2) 제로잉 계산 방법은 반덤핑 마진 계산이 실시되는 모든 절차에서 반덤핑협정 위반을 구성하는지 여부.

(3) 제로잉과 같은 구체적 덤핑 마진 산정 방법에 대해 반덤핑협정은 구체적 규범을 제시하지 않기에 각 회원국 조사당국이 이에 대해 재량권을 보유하는지 여부.

☑ 판   결

(1) 미국 상무부의 제로잉 계산 방법은 비록 법령에 명시되진 않았으나 계산방법이 컴퓨터 프로그램으로 작성되어 모든 반덤핑 마진산정에 자동적으로 적용되는 관행으로 "제도 자체에 대한"제소를 위한 정부의 조치를 구성한다.

(2) 제로잉 계산 방법은 반덤핑 마진이 산출되는 모든 절차에서 금지된다. 즉, 반덤핑 원심조사뿐 아니라 연례재심 및 일몰재심에서도 제로잉 계산 방법이 채택될 경우, 반덤핑협정 관련 조항을 위반한다.

(3) 구체적 덤핑 마진 산정에 대해 반덤핑협정이 이를 규정하고 있지 않은 경우라도 그 작업은 반덤핑협정의 내용과 합치되는 방법으로 진행되어야 하며 이에 위반되는 회원국 조사당국의 재량권 행사는 인정되지 아니한다.

99. The Panel found that, by maintaining "model zeroing procedures" when calculating margins of dumping on the basis of W-W comparisons in original investigations, the United States acted inconsistently with Article 2.4.2 of the *Anti-Dumping Agreement*. The United States does not appeal this finding of the Panel. [⋯]

114. Thus, it is evident from the design and architecture of the *Anti-Dumping Agreement* that: (a) the concepts of "dumping" and "margins of dumping" pertain to a "product" and to an exporter or foreign producer; (b) "dumping" and "dumping margins" must be determined in respect of each known exporter or foreign producer examined; (c) anti-dumping duties can be levied only if dumped imports cause or threaten to cause material injury to the domestic industry producing like products; and (d) anti-dumping duties can be levied only in an amount not exceeding the margin of dumping established for each exporter or foreign producer. These concepts are interlinked. They do not vary with the methodologies followed for a determination made under the various provisions of the *Anti-Dumping Agreement*. [⋯]

120. [⋯] The Appellate Body found that, in aggregating the results of transaction-specific comparisons, "an investigating authority must consider the results of all of the comparisons and may not disregard the results of comparisons in which export prices are above normal value." The Appellate Body concluded, therefore, that zeroing, as applied in the determination made on the basis of the T-T comparison[1] methodology at issue in that case, was inconsistent with Article 2.4.2 of the *Anti-Dumping Agreement*. [⋯]

135. We disagree with the assumption underlying the Panel's reasoning. The emphasis in the second sentence of Article 2.4.2 is on a "pattern," namely a "pattern of export prices which differs significantly among different purchasers, regions or time periods." The prices of transactions that fall within this *pattern* must be found to differ significantly from other export prices. We therefore read the phrase "individual export transactions" in that sentence as referring to the transactions that fall within the relevant pricing pattern. This universe of export transactions would necessarily be more limited than the universe of export transactions to which the symmetrical comparison methodologies in the first

---

1) T−T comparison: 개별 수출가격과 개별 정상가격을 각각 비교하는 방법.

sentence of Article 2.4.2 would apply. In order to unmask targeted dumping, an investigating authority may limit the application of the W-T comparison[2] methodology to the prices of export transactions falling within the relevant pattern. [⋯]

137. In the light of our analysis of Article 2.4.2 of the *Anti-Dumping Agreement*, we conclude that, in establishing "margins of dumping" under the T-T comparison methodology, an investigating authority must aggregate the results of all the transaction-specific comparisons and cannot disregard the results of comparisons in which export prices are above normal value.

138. Accordingly, we reverse the Panel's finding, in paragraphs 7.143 and 7.259(a) of the Panel Report, that the United States does not act inconsistently with Article 2.4.2 of the *Anti-Dumping Agreement* by maintaining zeroing procedures when calculating margins of dumping on the basis of T-T comparisons in original investigations, and find, instead, that the United States acts inconsistently with that provision. [⋯]

147. Accordingly, we reverse the Panel's finding, in paragraphs 7.161 and 7.259(a) of the Panel Report, that the United States does not act inconsistently with Article 2.4 of the *Anti-Dumping Agreement* by maintaining zeroing procedures when calculating margins of dumping on the basis of T-T comparisons in original investigations, and find, instead, that the United States acts inconsistently with that provision. [⋯]

157. Next, we examine the Panel's reasoning relating to Article 9.4(ii) of the *Anti-Dumping Agreement*, which deals with the calculation of the liability for payment of anti-dumping duties on the basis of a so-called "prospective normal value." [⋯]

161. The Panel stated that, in a prospective normal value system, "liability for payment of anti-dumping duties is incurred only to the extent that prices of individual export transactions are below normal value." Therefore, Article 9.4(ii) "confirms that the concept of dumping can apply on a transaction-specific basis to prices of individual export transactions below the normal value." The Panel also stated that "[i]f in a prospective normal value system individual export transactions at prices less than normal value can attract liability for payment of anti-dumping duties, without regard to whether or not prices of other export transactions exceed normal value," there is no reason why duties may not be similarly assessed under the United States' retrospective duty assessment system.

---

2) W－T comparison: 개별 수출가격과 가중평균 정상가격을 비교하는 방법.

162. We are unable to agree. Under any system of duty collection, the margin of dumping established in accordance with Article 2 operates as a ceiling for the amount of anti-dumping duties that could be collected in respect of the sales made by an exporter. To the extent that duties are paid by an importer, it is open to that importer to claim a refund if such a ceiling is exceeded. Similarly, under its retrospective system of duty collection, the United States is free to assess duty liability on a transaction-specific basis, but the total amount of anti-dumping duties that are levied must not exceed the exporters' or foreign producers' margins of dumping. [⋯]

164. The Panel's reasoning, which we rejected380, relates to periodic reviews under Article 9.3, as well as to new shipper reviews under Article 9.5. On appeal, Japan notes in this regard that the Panel "gave no separate interpretive consideration" to the latter types of reviews. [⋯]

166. In the light of these considerations, we reverse the Panel's finding, in paragraphs 7.222 and 7.259(b) of the Panel Report, that the United States does not act inconsistently with Articles 9.3 and 9.5 of the *Anti-Dumping Agreement* and Article VI:2 of the GATT 1994 by maintaining zeroing procedures in periodic reviews and new shipper reviews, and find, instead, that the United States acts inconsistently with these provisions.

167. We turn next to examine whether zeroing in periodic reviews and new shipper reviews is, as such, inconsistent with the "fair comparison" requirement in Article 2.4 of the *Anti-Dumping Agreement*.

168. If anti-dumping duties are assessed on the basis of a methodology involving comparisons between the export price and the normal value in a manner which results in anti-dumping duties being collected from importers in excess of the amount of the margin of dumping of the exporter or foreign producer, then this methodology cannot be viewed as involving a "fair comparison" within the meaning of the first sentence of Article 2.4. This is so because such an assessment would result in duty collection from importers in excess of the margin of dumping established in accordance with Article 2, as we have explained previously.

169. Accordingly, we reverse the Panel's finding, in paragraphs 7.219 and 7.259(b) of the Panel Report, that zeroing in the context of periodic reviews and new shipper reviews is not, as such, inconsistent with Article 2.4 of the *Anti-Dumping Agreement*, and find, instead, that zeroing, is, as such, inconsistent with that provision. [⋯]

184. In the present case, the Panel found, as a matter of fact, that, in its likelihood-of-dumping determination, the USDOC relied "on margins of dumping established in prior proceedings." The Panel further found that these margins were calculated during periodic reviews "on the basis of simple zeroing."

185. We have previously concluded that zeroing, as it relates to periodic reviews, is inconsistent, as such, with Article 2.4 and Article 9.3. As the likelihood-of-dumping determinations in the sunset reviews at issue in this appeal relied on margins of dumping calculated inconsistently with the *Anti-Dumping Agreement*, they are inconsistent with Article 11.3 of that Agreement. For these reasons, we reverse the Panel's finding, in paragraphs 7.257 and 7.259(e) of the Panel Report, that the United States acted consistently with Articles 2 and 11 of the *Anti-Dumping Agreement* by relying on margins of dumping calculated in previous proceedings in the sunset reviews at issue in this case, and find, instead, that the United States acted inconsistently with Article 11.3 of the *Anti-Dumping Agreement*. […]

☑ 해   설

제로잉 분쟁은 미국으로 수출하는 우리 수출업체에도 직접적인 영향을 미치는 사안이므로 그간 우리나라도 일련의 제로잉 관련 분쟁에 지속적으로 제3자 참여를 했을 뿐 아니라 2009년 11월에는 미국을 WTO 패널에 제소하기도 했다. 여기에 수록한 일본이 제기한 제로잉 분쟁은 이러한 일련의 제로잉 분쟁 중 중요한 위치를 차지하고 있다. WTO 상소기구는 원심조사뿐 아니라 연례재심 및 일몰재심에서도 제로잉 계산 방법의 사용은 그 "적용사례 (as applied)" 뿐 아니라 그 "제도 자체로도(as such)" 반덤핑협정 위반임을 확인했다는 데 그 의의가 있다. 제로잉 계산 방법에 대한 이러한 근본적인 위법성의 확인은 향후 진행된 제로잉 분쟁에서 이 제도의 위법성이 지속적으로 확인되는 기초를 마련했다고 볼 수 있다. 즉, 이 판정에 힘입어 반덤핑 조사절차에서 자의적 마진계산의 대표적 사례로 인식되어 반덤핑협정에 대한 불신 형성에 기여해 온 제로잉 계산방식에 대한 법리적 문제점이 최종적으로 정리되었다고 볼 수 있다. 제로잉 분쟁에서 계속 패소하게 된 미국은 패소 판정을 이행하고자 2006년 12월 새로운 상무성 규정을 도입하여 2007년 2월 9일 자로 원심조사에서의 제로잉 적용을 공식적으로 철폐하기에 이

르렀다. 일본과의 본건 제로잉 분쟁에서 패소하게 됨에 따라 (그리고 유럽연합
과의 제로잉 분쟁에서 연이어 패소함에 따라) 미국은 연례재심 및 일몰재심에서도
제로잉 제도를 철폐해야 하는 의무를 부담하게 되었다. 그 결과 미국은 2007
년 말까지 "합리적 이행기간(reasonable period of time for implementation)"을
부여받고 미흡하나마 나름대로 이행조치를 실시했다. 본건 승소국인 일본과
또 다른 제로잉 분쟁 승소국인 유럽연합의 보복이 2009년 임박하게 되자 미
국은 곤혹스러운 처지에 몰리게 되었다. 국내 시장이 큰 이들 두 국가가 미
국 상품에 대한 보복에 나선다면 미국에도 상당한 타격이 우려되었기 때문
이다. 이에 미국은 판정 이행계획을 이들 국가들에 설명하여 보복조치의 단
행을 연기시켜 줄 것을 요청하기에 이르렀다. 결국 2012년 4월 미국 상무부
는 이후 개시되는 반덤핑 조사와 일몰재심에서 제로잉을 사용하지 않고
WTO 협정에 합치하는 계산방식을 사용하겠다고 발표하였고 이에 2012년 6
월 및 8월 유럽연합과 일본은 각각 보복 요청을 철회하였다.

　　한편 위에서도 언급한 바와 같이 우리나라도 우리나라 철강제품에 대한
반덤핑 원심조사에서 적용된 제로잉 제도에 대해 WTO 반덤핑 협정 위반을
이유로 2009년 11월 미국을 제소했고 2011년 12월 승소판정을 받았다. 원심
조사에서의 제로잉 적용은 이미 미국이 국내제도를 개정하여 그 적용을 포
기했으므로 특별한 문제 없이 우리나라가 승소하게 되었으며 미국도 판정을
이행했다. 미국이 원심조사에서의 제로잉 조치를 철폐했지만 그 효과는
2007년 2월 9일부터 시행되는 반덤핑 조사부터 적용되며 우리나라(철강제품
반덤핑 조사)와 같이 과거(1996년)에 실시된 반덤핑 조사에서 적용된 제로잉
제도의 철폐를 위해서는 각 회원국이 개별적으로 WTO에 제소를 하여야만
구제를 받을 수 있다. 한편 우리나라는 미국의 연례재심 제로잉 제도 철폐가
계속 지연되자 2011년 4월 우리 철강제품에 대한 반덤핑 연례재심 및 일몰
재심에서의 제로잉 조치 적용에 대해 미국을 제소했고 2016년 3월(DS420) 우
리나라의 승소로 종결되었다. 이후 2012년에는 미국 상무부는 한국산 세탁
기에 대하여 반덤핑 조사를 진행하며 소위 "표적덤핑" 판정을 내리고 여전
히 기존의 제로잉 조치를 다시 적용했다. 이 조치에 대해 우리나라는 2013년
8월 WTO에 제소했다(DS464). 2016년 3월 패널 판정에서 우리측 입장이 지

지되었고 2016년 9월 상소심에서 최종 확정되었다. 미국의 지속적인 이행거
부로 우리나라는 2019년 2월 미국에 대한 보복권한을 획득하였다. 그러나
여러 가지 이유로 2020년 7월 현재까지 우리나라는 실체 보복소지에 나서지
는 않았다.

➡ 참고문헌 ─────────────────────────────────

- R. P. Alford, Reflections on Us—Zeroing: A Study in Judicial Overreaching by the WTO Appellate Body, Columbia Journal of Transnational Law Vol. 45(2006), p. 196.
- A. O. Canizares, Is Charming Betsy Losing Her Charm—Interpreting U.S. Statutes Consistently with International Trade Agreements and the Chevron Doctrine, Emory International Law Review Vol. 20(2006), p. 591.
- J. W. Spaulding, Do International Fences Really Make Good Neighbors— The Zeroing Conflict between Antidumping Law and International Obligations, New England Law Review Vol. 41(2007), p. 379.
- D. Ahn & P. Messerlin, United States? Anti—Dumping Measures on Certain Shrimp and Diamond Sawblades from China: Never Ending Zeroing in the WTO?, World Trade Review Vol. 13, No. 2(2014), pp. 267－279.

3. 미국 인터넷 사행성 산업 제한조치(2005)
— 서비스 교역의 규제

United States-Measures Affecting the Cross-Border Supply
of Gambling and Betting Services.
Antigua and Barbuda v. United States, Report of the
Appellate Body, WT/DS285/AB/R(2005).

☑ 사　　안

　카리브해에 위치한 인구 9만 6천명의 소국인 안티구아 바뷰다는 과거에
영국 식민지였다가, 1981년 11월 독립한 영연방 국가이다. 관광산업과 미국
시장에 대한 인터넷 서버 유치 산업이 이 나라의 주요 수입원을 이룬다. 안
티구아 바뷰다는 미국 소비자를 대상으로 하는 인터넷 서비스 제공자를 자
국에 유치하여 주요 산업으로 발전시켜 왔다. 다양한 범위의 서비스를 온라
인으로 제공하는 이러한 서비스 제공자 중 일부는 온라인 사행성 게임 및
도박 서비스를 제공하고 있었다. 한편 온라인 사행성 게임이 청소년에 대해
초래하는 문제점을 인식한 미국 주 정부 및 연방 정부는 이러한 온라인 서
비스 제공을 금지하기에 이르렀다. 이러한 미국의 금지 조치로 직접적인 피
해를 입게 된 안티구아 바뷰다는 인터넷 도박 등 사행성 온라인 서비스 제
공을 금지한 미국 연방법 및 주법 그리고 일련의 법원의 판결 등이 서비스
교역에 관한 일반협정(GATS)을 위반하였음을 이유로 2003년 WTO 분쟁해결
절차에 미국을 제소하였다. 안티구아 바뷰다 주장의 핵심은 미국이 1995년
WTO에 제출한 서비스교역 양허표에는 인터넷 사행성 산업도 외국 서비스
제공자에게 개방하는 내용이 포함되어 있으나, 추후에 이러한 서비스를 전면
금지함으로써 미국은 양허표상 약속을 위반했으며 이는 결국 GATS를 위반
한다는 것이다. 이에 대해 미국은 인터넷 사행성 산업은 최초 미국의 양허표

에 포함된 바가 없으며, 설사 포함되었더라도 이러한 조치가 도입된 배경이 청소년의 보호에 있으므로 그 목적의 정당성이 협정 위반을 정당화시켜 준 다는 입장을 견지했다.

☑ 쟁   점

(1) 인터넷 사행성 서비스 제공이 미국의 서비스 교역 양허표에 포함되어 있었는지 여부. 구체적으로 미국이 국경간 공급(Cross-Border Supply) 서비스 제공형태에 대해 완전한 시장접근 및 내국민 대우를 약속한 "기타 여가활동 및 서비스" 부분에 인터넷 사행성 산업 서비스가 포함되는지 여부.

(2) 미국의 인터넷 사행성 서비스에 대한 국경간 공급 금지 조치는 대상 서비스에 대한 "완전한 금지"이고 시장접근에 대한 명백한 제한을 가한 조치로서 GATS에 대한 위반을 구성하는지 여부.

(3) 미국의 제한 조치가 GATS 제14조상 공중도덕의 보호 또는 공공질서의 유지를 위해 필요한 조치에 해당하는지 여부. 또한 미국의 동 조치가 일반적 예외를 규정한 GATS 제14조 '모두조항(chapeau)'에 나열된 요건을 충족하는지 여부.

☑ 판   결

(1) 인터넷 사행성 산업은 그 통상적 의미(ordinary meaning)를 따를 경우 미국이 외국 서비스 공급자에 대해 구체적으로 양허에서 제외한 "스포츠 (sporting)" 산업에 포함된다고 볼 수 없으므로 동 산업은 미국이 외국 서비스 공급자에 대해 양허한 서비스 산업 중 하나로 간주되어야 한다.

(2) 미국의 인터넷 사행성 서비스 제한 조치는 국경간 공급자 수를 사실상 "0"으로 규정하므로 GATS 제16조에서 규정하는 수량 제한에 포함되며 따라서 미국은 시장접근에 관한 동 규정을 위반했다.

(3) 그러나 미국의 동 조치는 GATS 제14조상의 공중도덕의 보호 또는 공공질서의 유지를 위해 필요한 조치에 해당한다. 또한 제소국인 안티구아 바부다는 미국이 합리적으로 선택 가능했다고 볼 수 있는 대안 조치를 제시하는 데 실패했으므로 이러한 미국 연방법 및 주법이 "필요성" 요건을 충족

한다는 점을 미국이 입증하였다. 그러나 미국은 문제의 금지 조치에도 불구하고 미국 국내 업자가 제공하는 일부 인터넷 사행성 서비스는 계속 허용하고 있고 이는 '모두조항'이 규정하는 "자의적이거나 정당화될 수 없는 차별을 구성하지 않는 방식으로"라는 요건을 충족하지 못하여, 결국 미국의 조치는 예외조항으로 정당화되지 않는다.

판 결 문

212. We have already determined that the Panel committed certain errors in interpreting the United States' Schedule. Nevertheless, we have determined that a proper interpretation according to the principles codified in Articles 31 and 32 of the *Vienna Convention* leads to the same result that the Panel reached, namely, that subsector 10.D of the United States' GATS Schedule includes a specific commitment with respect to gambling and betting services. In the light of this finding, we need not decide whether the Panel erred in its treatment of the USITC Document.

213. Based on our reasoning above, we reject the United States' argument that, by excluding "sporting" services from the scope of its commitment in subsector 10.D, the United States excluded gambling and betting services from the scope of that commitment. Accordingly, we *uphold*, albeit for different reasons, the Panel's finding, in paragraph 7.2(a) of the Panel Report, that:

> ... the United States' Schedule under the GATS includes specific commitments on gambling and betting services under subsector […]

238. For the above reasons, we are of the view that limitations amounting to a zero quota are quantitative limitations and fall within the scope of Article XVI: 2(a).

239. As we have not been asked to revisit the other elements of the Panel's reasoning on this issue — in particular its findings regarding limitations on market access in respect of part of a committed sector, and limitations on one or more means of cross-border delivery for a committed service — we therefore, *uphold* the Panel's finding that:

> [a prohibition on one, several or all means of delivery cross-border] is a "limitation on the number of service suppliers in the form of numerical quotas" within the meaning of Article XVI : 2(a) because it totally prevents the use by service suppliers of one, several or all means of delivery that are

included in mode 1. [⋯]

251. In this case, the measures at issue, by prohibiting the supply of services in respect of which a market access commitment has been taken, amount to a "zero quota" on service operations or output with respect to such services. As such, they fall within the scope of Article XVI : 2(c).

252. For all of these reasons, we uphold the Panel's finding, in paragraph 6.355 of the Panel Report, that a measure prohibiting the supply of certain services where specific commitments have been undertaken is a limitation:

> ... within the meaning of Article XVI : 2(c) because it totally prevents the services operations and/or service output through one or more or all means of delivery that are included in mode 1. In other words, such a ban results in a "zero quota" on one or more or all means of delivery include in mode 1. [⋯]

296. In its analysis under Article XVI(a), the Panel found that "the term 'public morals' denotes standards of right and wrong conduct maintained by or on behalf of a community or nation." The Panel further found that the definition of the term "order", read in conjunction with footnote 5 of the GATS, "suggests that 'public order' refers to the preservation of the fundamental interests of a society, as reflected in public policy and law." The Panel then referred to Congressional reports and testimony establishing that "the government of the United States consider[s] [that the Wire Act, the Travel Act, and the Illegal Gambling Business Act] were adopted to address concerns such as those pertaining to money laundering, organized crime, fraud, underage gambling and pathological gambling." On this basis, the Panel found that the three federal statutes are "measures that are designed to 'protect public morals' and/or 'to maintain public order' within the meaning of Article XVI(a)."

297. Antigua contests this finding on a rather limited ground, namely that the Panel failed to determine whether the concerns identified by the United States satisfy the standard set out in footnote 5 to Article XVI(a) of the GATS, which reads:

> [t]he public order exception may be invoked only where a genuine and sufficiently serious threat is posed to one of the fundamental interests of society.

298. We see no basis to conclude that the Panel failed to assess whether the standard set out in footnote 5 had been satisfied. As Antigua acknowledges, the Panel expressly referred to footnote 5 in a way that demonstrated that it understood the requirement therein to be part of the meaning given to the term "public order." Although "no further mention" was made in the Panel Report of footnote 5 or of its text, this alone does not establish that the Panel failed to assess whether the interests served by the three federal statutes satisfy the footnote's criteria. Having defined "public order" to include the standard in footnote 5, and then applied that definition to the facts before it to conclude that the measures "are designed to 'protect public morals' and/or 'to maintain public order'," the Panel was not required, in addition, to make a separate, explicit determination that the standard of footnote 5 had been met.

299. We therefore *uphold* the Panel's finding, in paragraph 6.487 of the Panel Report, that "the concerns which the Wire Act, the Travel Act and the Illegal Gambling Business Act seek to address fall within the scope of 'public morals' and/or 'public order' under Article XVI(a)." [⋯]

370. Our findings under Article XIV lead us to modify the overall conclusions of the Panel in paragraph 7.2(d) of the Panel Report. The Panel found that the United States failed to justify its measures as "necessary" under paragraph (a) of Article XIV, and that it also failed to establish that those measures satisfy the requirements of the chapeau.

371. We have found instead that those measures satisfy the "necessity" requirement. We have also upheld, but only in part, the Panel's finding under the chapeau. We explained that the only inconsistency that the Panel could have found with the requirements of the chapeau stems from the fact that the United States did not demonstrate that the prohibition embodied in the measures at issue applies to both foreign *and* domestic suppliers of remote gambling services, notwithstanding the IHA—which, according to the Panel, "does appear, on its face, to permit" *domestic* service suppliers to supply remote betting services for horse racing. In other words, the United States did not establish that the IHA does not alter the scope of application of the challenged measures, particularly vis-à-vis domestic suppliers of a specific type of remote gambling services. In this respect, we wish to clarify that the Panel did not, and we do not, make a finding as to whether the IHA does, in fact, permit domestic suppliers to provide certain remote betting services that would otherwise be prohibited by the Wire Act, the Travel Act, and/or the IGBA.

372. Therefore, we *modify* the Panel's conclusion in paragraph 7.2(d) of the Panel Report. We *find*, instead, that the United States has demonstrated that the

Wire Act, the Travel Act, and the IGBA fall within the scope of paragraph (a) of Article XIV, but that it has not shown, in the light of the IHA, that the prohibitions embodied in these measures are applied to both foreign and domestic service suppliers of remote betting services for horse racing. For this reason alone, we *find* that the United States has not established that these measures satisfy the requirements of the chapeau. Here, too, we uphold the Panel, but only in part. [⋯]

☑ 해   설

이 사건은 안티구아 바뷰다가 자국보다 국력과 경제력이 막강히 큰 미국을 상대로 WTO 분쟁해결기구에 소송을 제기하여 일부 승소 판정을 이끌어냈다는 점에서 상당한 주목을 끌었다. 이 판정의 핵심 쟁점 중 하나였던 인터넷 사행성 산업의 미국 서비스 교역 양허표 포함 여부에 관한 패널 및 상소기구의 논리 전개를 보면 국제통상법의 세부적인 측면에서도 협정에 규정된 용어의 통상적 의미가 얼마나 중요한 역할을 수행하는지를 상징적으로 보여주고 있다. 상소기구는 영어 단어 "sporting"이 미국이 주장하는 바와 같이 인터넷 사행성 산업을 포함할 수 있는지에 관해 심도 있는 분석을 하여 결국 미국의 주장을 통상적 의미에 배치되는 것으로 기각했다. 일국의 서비스 교역 양허표에는 방대한 내용이 포함되는 현실을 감안하면 각각의 항목에 대해 정확한 용어와 문법의 사용이 항상 쉽지만은 않을 것이다. 만약 미국의 주장이 사실이라면 미국은 양허표 제출시 단어의 의미 검토에 좀 더 신중을 기울였어야만 했을 것이다. 또한 미국이 시장접근 약속이 이루어진 부문에서 서비스 공급자의 수를 0으로 제한한 행위는 GATS 제16조 2항 (a)호상의 수량 제한에 포함되어 동 조항을 위반하는 것으로 상소기구가 결정한 것도 주목을 요한다. 교역의 전면 금지도 쿼터를 도입한 것과 유사한 것으로 판단하고 있기 때문이다. 한편, 상소기구는 미국 연방법이 GATS 제14조 (a)호상 '공중도덕' 보호와 '공공질서' 유지를 위해 고안되었고 또 제14조 모두조항에서 요구하는 필요성 요건도 충족한다고 결정했다. 이 과정에서 제소국인 안티구아 바뷰다가 미국이 선택할 수 있었던 합리적 대안을 제시하지 못했으므로 미국의 조치가 필요한 것으로 간주되어야 한다고 결정한 부분은 그 타당성에 다소 의문이 제기된다. 제14조에 따른 정당화를 주장하는 국가가 피제소국인 미국이므로 제14조의 요건도 그 사실을 주장하는 당사자인 미국이 입증책임을 부담하는 것이 입증책임 분배에 관한 일반적 원칙에 보다 부합할 것이기 때문이다. 입증책임 문제가 WTO 분쟁의 승패를 좌우하는 주요 변수라는 점을 감안하면 향후 이에 대한 보다 면밀한 검토가 필요하다고 할 것이다.

　이 분쟁 패소 이후 미국은 필요한 입법 조치를 실시하지 않았다. 그 결과 승소국인 안티구아 바뷰다는 2100만불에 이르는 보복권한을 획득 후 보복 조치를 실시하기에 이르렀다. 특히 안티구아 바뷰다는 자국의 시장 규모가 미미하여 본건 분쟁과 동일한 영역인 서비스 영역에서의 보복만으로는 효과가 미약함을 언급하며 무역관련지적재산권협정(TRIPS 협정)이 규율하는 영역을 통한 보복을 승인해 줄 것을 WTO 분쟁해결기구(DSB)에 요청했다. 이를 '교차보복(cross-retaliation)'이라고 한다. WTO 분쟁해결기구가 이를 승인함에 따라 안티구아 바뷰다는 자국 내 미국인 및 미국기업의 지식재산권을 보호하지 않는 것으로 보복을 단행했으며 그 결과 미국은 타협책을 모색하기에 이르렀다. 이 분쟁에서의 패소는 일련의 제로잉 분쟁에서의 패소와 함께 WTO 분쟁해결절차에 대한 미국 국내의 반감을 더욱 증폭시키는 계기가 되었다.

➡ 참고문헌 ────────────────────────────────

- 이진규, '서비스무역에 관한 일반협정'상 외국서비스의 시장접근에 대한 국내규제의 구분: 'US-gambling 사건' 판정에 대한 분석을 중심으로, 한양법학 제43권(2013), p. 299.
- 안덕근, 이효영, WTO 분쟁해결제도에서의 교차보복: 제도상 문제점 및 적용사례 분석, 통상법률 제92권, 법무부(2010), p. 11.
- F. Ortino, Treaty Interpretation and the WTO Appellate Body Report in US-Gambling: A Critique, Journal of International Economic Law Vol. 9(2006), p. 117.
- P. Delimatsis, Determining the Necessity of Domestic Regulations in Services, European Journal of International Law Vol. 19(2008), p. 365.
- S. Jackson, Small states and compliance bargaining in the WTO: an analysis

of the Antigua—US Gambling Services Case, Cambridge Review of International Affairs Vol. 25(2012), p. 367.

- C. Bissett, All Bets Are off(Line): Antigua's Trouble in Virtual Paradise, University of Miami Inter—American Law Review Vol. 35(2004), p. 367.
- M. Grunfeld, Don't Bet on the United States's Internet Gambling Laws: The Tension Between Internet Gambling Legislation and WTO Commitments, 2007 Columbia Business Law Review, p. 439(2007).
- J. D. Thayer, The Trade of Cross—Border Gambling and Betting: The WTO Dispute Between Antigua and the United States, 2004 Duke Law & Technology Review, p. 13(2004).

4. 중국 지식재산권 분쟁(2009)
— 미중분쟁의 시작

China-Measures Affecting the Protection and Enforcement
of Intellectual Property Rights.
The United States v. China, Report of the Panel,
WT/DS362/R (2009).

☑ 사   안

중국 시장에서 외국 위조상품 판매가 성행하는 현실에 대해 여러 나라
가 우려를 표명하여 온 지 오래이다. 특히 미국은 중국에서의 자국민 및 자
국기업의 지식재산권 침해에 대해 오랫동안 문제를 제기해 왔다. 여타 국가
에 비해 미국의 피해가 특히 두드러졌기 때문이다. 미국의 불만은 중국 정부
가 지식재산권의 침해 상황을 인지하고도 적절하고 효과적인 처벌조치 및
법령집행 조치를 취하지 않는다는 데 있었다. 특히 미국은 중국 형법이 지식
재산권 침해사범에 대해 판매 금액이 일정 금액에 미달하는 경우 처벌을 원
천적으로 면제하는 제도가 지식재산권 침해를 더욱 부추긴다는 견해를 갖고
있었다. 지식재산권 보호 문제를 규율하는 WTO 무역관련지식재산권협정
(TRIPS 협정)은 제41조와 제61조에서 각 회원국이 행정, 민사, 형사 절차를 도
입하여 지식재산권 침해에 대해 효과적으로 대응할 의무를 구체적으로 부여
한다. 오랜 기간 동안 문제 제기에도 중국에서의 사정에 특별한 개선의 기미
가 보이지 않자 미국은 마침내 2007년 중국을 TRIPS 협정 위반을 이유로
WTO에 제소하기에 이르렀다. 여러 나라가 중국의 지식재산권 보호제도에
관해 이해관계를 보유하고 있었으므로 우리나라를 비롯한 많은 나라가 이
분쟁에 제3자 참여를 하게 되었다.

☑ 쟁   점

(1) WTO 회원국의 형사사법제도에 대한 문제 제기에는 보다 엄격한 입증책임이 요구되는지 여부.

(2) 지식재산권 침해 상품 판매를 통해 50,000 위안 이상의 판매액을 기록하는 경우에만 처벌하도록 하는 중국 형법은 "상업적 규모(on a commercial scale)"로 행해지는 침해행위를 처벌하도록 규정하는 TRIPS 협정 제61조에 대한 위반을 구성하는지 여부.

☑ 판   결

(1) WTO 회원국은 입법, 행정, 사법의 모든 측면에서 WTO 협정 의무를 이행할 의무를 부담하며 피제소국의 형사사법제도에 대한 문제가 제기된다고 하여 제소국이 일반의 경우보다 엄격한 입증책임을 부담하는 것은 아니다.

(2) 50,000 위안 미만의 지식재산권 판매 행위에 대한 처벌을 제도적으로 배제하는 중국 형법은 "상업적 규모(on a commercial scale)"로 행해지는 모든 형태의 침해행위를 처벌하도록 규정하는 TRIPS 협정 제61조를 위반하는지 여부에 대해 제소국은 입증책임을 완수하지 못하였다.

판 결 문

2.2 The United States claims that China has not provided for criminal procedures and penalties to be applied in cases of wilful trademark counterfeiting or copyright piracy on a commercial scale that fail to meet certain thresholds. […]

7.399 Article 213 of the Criminal Law may be translated as follows:

"Whoever, without permission from the owner of a registered trademark, uses a trademark which is identical with the registered trademark on the same kind of commodities shall, if *the circumstances are serious*, be sentenced to fixed-term imprisonment of not more than three years or criminal detention and shall also, or shall only, be fined; if the circumstances are especially serious, the offender shall be sentenced to fixed-term imprisonment of not less than three years but not more than seven years and shall also be fined." [···]

7.400 Article 1 of Judicial Interpretation No. 19 [2004] interprets the phrase "the circumstances are serious" in Article 213 of the Criminal Law and may be translated as follows:

> "Whoever, without permission from the owner of a registered trademark, uses a trademark which is identical with the registered trademark on the same kind of commodities, in any of the following circumstances which shall be deemed as 'the circumstances are serious' under Article 213 of the Criminal Law, shall be sentenced to fixed-term imprisonment of not more than three years or criminal detention for the crime of counterfeiting registered trademark, and shall also, or shall only, be fined:
>
> (1) *the illegal business operation volume* of not less than 50,000 Yuan or the *amount of illegal gains* of not less than 30,000 Yuan;
>
> (2) in the case of counterfeiting two or more registered trademarks, the *illegal business operation volume* of not less than 30,000 Yuan or the *amount of illegal gains* of not less than 20,000 Yuan;
>
> (3) other serious circumstances." [···]

7.425 China informs the Panel that it employs thresholds across a range of commercial crimes, reflecting the significance of various illegal acts for overall public and economic order and China's prioritization of criminal enforcement, prosecution and judicial resources. China submits that the criminal thresholds for counterfeiting and piracy are reasonable and appropriate in the context of this legal structure and the other laws on commercial crimes.

7.426 The United States responds that what China chooses to do with its domestic non-IPR criminal thresholds has no bearing on the Panel's assessment of whether China meets its international obligations under the first sentence of Article 61 of the TRIPS Agreement. [···]

7.497 China argues that the United States bears "a significantly higher burden [of proof] than it would normally encounter" because this claim concerns criminal law matters. China argues that the Panel should treat sovereign jurisdiction over police powers as a powerful default norm, departure from which can be authorized only in light of explicit and unequivocal consent of State parties. China later clarified that it was not referring to a factual burden of proof but rather to the inability of the United States to provide the evidence to support its legal interpretation of Article 61 of the TRIPS Agreement. China also argues for the application of the "interpretative canon" of *in dubio mitius* which, it submits, has a particular justification in the realm of criminal law.

7.498 The United States responds that the fact that Article 61 of the TRIPS Agreement touches on criminal law does not change the provisions of Article 3.2 of the DSU or the customary rules of treaty interpretation reflected in the Vienna Convention on the Law of Treaties ("Vienna Convention"). In this dispute, the meaning of "commercial scale" is reached through the general rule of interpretation in Article 31 of the Vienna Convention. There is no "doubt" which is a precondition of reliance on the concept of *in dubio mitius*. [⋯]

7.501 The Panel acknowledges the sensitive nature of criminal matters and attendant concerns regarding sovereignty. These concerns may be expected to find reflection in the text and scope of treaty obligations regarding such matters as negotiated by States and other Members. Section 5 of Part III of the TRIPS Agreement, dedicated to criminal procedures and remedies, is considerably briefer and less detailed than the other Sections on enforcement in Part III. Brief as it is, the text of Section 5 also contains significant limitations and flexibilities. The customary rules of treaty interpretation oblige the treaty interpreter to take these limitations and flexibilities into account in interpreting the relevant provision.

7.502 This claim is brought under the first sentence of Article 61 of the TRIPS Agreement. Article 61 constitutes the whole of Section 5 of Part III of that Agreement and provides as follows:

> "[⋯] Members shall provide for criminal procedures and penalties to be applied at least in cases of wilful trademark counterfeiting or copyright piracy on a commercial scale. Remedies available shall include imprisonment and/or monetary fines sufficient to provide a deterrent, consistently with the level of penalties applied for crimes of a corresponding gravity. In appropriate cases, remedies available shall also include the seizure, forfeiture and destruction of the infringing goods and of any materials and implements the predominant use of which has been in the commission of the offence. Members may provide for criminal procedures and penalties to be applied in other cases of infringement of intellectual property rights, in particular where they are committed wilfully and on a commercial scale."

7.503 The *first* sentence of this Article uses the word "shall," indicating that it is mandatory. This stands in contrast to the *fourth* sentence, which addresses the same issue with respect to other cases of infringement of intellectual property rights but uses the word "may," indicating that it is permissive. Unlike the *third* sentence, the first sentence contains no language such as "in appropriate cases" which might expressly introduce some margin of discretion. The terms of the first sentence of Article 61, read in context, impose an obligation. [⋯]

7.516 The terms of the obligation in the first sentence of Article 61 of the TRIPS Agreement are that Members shall "provide for criminal procedures and penalties to be applied." That obligation applies to "wilful trademark counterfeiting or copyright piracy on a commercial scale." Within that scope, there are no exceptions. The obligation applies to *all* acts of wilful trademark counterfeiting or copyright piracy on a commercial scale.

7.517 The Panel recalls its conclusion at paragraph 7.479 above that, in China, acts of trademark and copyright infringement falling below the applicable thresholds are not subject to criminal procedures and penalties. The issue that arises is whether any of those acts of infringement constitute "wilful trademark counterfeiting or copyright piracy on a commercial scale" within the meaning of the first sentence of Article 61. This requires the Panel to consider the interpretation of that phrase. [⋯]

7.524 The fourth limitation in the first sentence of Article 61 is indicated by the phrase "on a commercial scale" that follows the words "trademark counterfeiting or copyright piracy." This phrase, like the word "wilful," appears to qualify both "trademark counterfeiting" and "copyright piracy." The limitation to cases on a commercial scale, like the limitation to cases of wilfulness, stands in contrast to all other specific obligations on enforcement in Part Ⅲ of the TRIPS Agreement.

7.525 The principal interpretative point in dispute is the meaning of the phrase "on a commercial scale." This phrase functions in context as a qualifier, indicating that wilful trademark counterfeiting or copyright piracy is included in the scope of the obligation provided that it also satisfies the condition of being "on a commercial scale." Accordingly, certain acts of wilful trademark counterfeiting or copyright piracy are excluded from the scope of the first sentence of Article 61.

7.526 Despite the fact that trademark counterfeiting and copyright piracy infringe the rights of right holders, and despite the fact that they can be grave, the two qualifications of wilfulness and "on a commercial scale" indicate that Article 61 does not require Members to provide for criminal procedures and penalties to be applied to such counterfeiting and piracy *per se* unless they satisfy certain additional criteria. This is highlighted by the fourth sentence of Article 61, which allows Members to provide for criminal procedures and penalties to be applied in other cases of infringement, "in particular" where they are committed wilfully and on a commercial scale. This indicates that the negotiators considered cases of wilful infringement on a commercial scale to represent a subset of cases of infringement, comprising the graver cases. This is useful context for interpreting the first sentence of Article 61, even though it does not refer to "infringement" in general, because the first sentence refers to both "counterfeiting" and "piracy" and wilfulness and commercial scale, evidently to limit the cases of infringement in different ways. Therefore, the text of Article 61 indicates that it must not be assumed that the nature of counterfeiting and piracy *per se* is such that Members are obliged to provide for the application of *criminal* procedures and penalties. [⋯]

7.577 The Panel recalls its view at paragraph 7.545 above and, in light of the evidence considered above, finds that a "commercial scale" is the magnitude or extent of typical or usual commercial activity. Therefore, counterfeiting or piracy "on a commercial scale" refers to counterfeiting or piracy carried on at the magnitude or extent of typical or usual commercial activity with respect to a given product in a given market. The magnitude or extent of typical or usual commercial activity with respect to a given product in a given market forms a benchmark by which to assess the obligation in the first sentence of Article 61. It follows that what constitutes a commercial scale for counterfeiting or piracy of a particular product in a particular market will depend on the magnitude or extent that is typical or usual with respect to such a product in such a market, which may be small or large. The magnitude or extent of typical or usual commercial activity relates, in the longer term, to profitability.

7.578 The Panel observes that what is typical or usual in commerce is a flexible concept. The immediate context in the second sentence of Article 61, which is closely related to the first, refers to the similarly flexible concepts of "deterrent" and "corresponding gravity." Neither these terms nor "commercial scale" are precise but all depend on circumstances, which vary according to the differing forms of commerce and of counterfeiting and piracy to which these obligations apply. [⋯]

7.609 The Panel has reviewed the measures and agrees that, on their face, they do exclude certain commercial activity from criminal procedures and penalties. For example, some of the criminal thresholds are set in terms that refer expressly to commercial activity, such as "illegal business operation volume," which is defined in terms of "manufacture, storage, transportation, or sales" of infringing products, and "illegal gains" which is defined in terms of profit. However, based solely on the measures on their face, the Panel cannot distinguish between acts that, in China's marketplace, are on a commercial *scale*, and those that are not. […]

7.611 The Panel has noted the United States' repeated assertions that certain amounts constitute counterfeiting or piracy on a commercial scale. The most recurrent example concerns 499 copyright infringing "copies," although it is not related to the same product in all examples or, sometimes, to any product. The only facts in these examples are amounts equal to, or slightly less than, those in the measures themselves. Those amounts, in combination with the monetary thresholds and the factors used in the thresholds, demonstrate the class of acts for which China does not provide criminal procedures and penalties to be applied. Those numbers and factors do not, in themselves, demonstrate what constitutes a commercial scale for any product or in any market in China. […]

7.617 The Panel finds that, even if these sources were suitable for the purpose of demonstration of contested facts in this proceeding, the information that was provided was too little and too random to demonstrate a level that constitutes a commercial scale for any product in China. […]

7.623 The Panel notes that the question whether retail sales of infringing product take place below the thresholds is not dispositive of the claim, as the first sentence of Article 61 does not require Members to provide for criminal procedures and penalties to be applied to all such cases. Further, the CCA Report sets out for each raid "total units seized (DVD, CD, VCD)." For some raids, the total units seized were as few as five. Therefore, while the aggregate number of seizures below China's thresholds may or may not be "significant," the seizure data does not permit any deduction as to the scale of operations of the individual raided retail outlets. The total units seized in many cases may be only part of, or even incidental to, a commercial operation. The seizure data illustrates the scale of infringing stock on hand (as it is intended to do) but it does not show the scale of the individual retail businesses or what constitutes a commercial scale for those products in that market. […]

7.626 The Panel notes that these calculations are percentages of an average and may be relevant to establishing what is a typical or usual level of commercial activity in a general sense. However, the statistics are highly aggregated and do not refer to any particular products, according to which the benchmark of "a commercial scale" necessarily varies. Moreover, the statistics regarding individual operation households engaged in retail do not address the basic question of whether retail sales by individual operation households are typical or usual in China. Therefore, the Panel does not consider that these statistics are sufficient for it to form a view as to whether the illegal business operation volume thresholds capture all trademark counterfeiting or copyright piracy on a commercial scale in China. [⋯]

7.632 For the above reasons, the Panel finds that the United States has not made a prima facie case with respect to the first limb of its claim under the first sentence of Article 61 of the TRIPS Agreement. [⋯]

☑ 해   설

미국과 중국간 진행된 이 분쟁은 미중 갈등의 단초를 보여준 분쟁으로서, 우리에게도 중요한 의미를 가지는 분쟁이다. 중국 시장에서의 지식재산권 보호 문제는 미국뿐 아니라 우리나라 기업에게도 발등에 떨어진 불이라고 볼 수 있기 때문이다. 중국 지식재산권 보호 제도의 현황과 문제점이 이 분쟁을 통해 상당히 심도있게 논의되었으며 중국 정부의 입장이 상세하게 개진된 분쟁이기도 하다. 이 분쟁에서 결국 제소국인 미국이 승소했으나 정작 중요한 쟁점이었던 일정 가액에 미치지 못하는 규모로 이루어지는 위조상품 판매에 대한 중국 형법상 처벌 면제 조항에 대해서는 사실상 중국의 입장이 지지되었다. 중국의 이러한 처벌 면제 조항이 상업적 규모(commercial scale)로 이루어지는 위조상품 판매는 항상 처벌하도록 규정하고 있는 TRIPS 협정 제61조상 의무를 위반하도록 운용된다는 점을 제소국인 미국이 입증하지 못했다는 것이 그 표면상 이유이다. 그러나 이러한 판정의 기저에는 형사사법절차에 대해 각 WTO 회원국의 주권과 재량의 범위를 최대한 인정하고자 하는 고려가 반영되었다고 볼 수 있을 것이다. 사실 이 분쟁 패널 절차에서 중국은 회원국 형사사법절차 및 제도에 대해서는 WTO 패널이 존중해야 할 의무가 있으며, 이러한 절차와 제도는 특히 대표적인 국내문제로서 통상협정을 다루는 WTO가 개입할 수 있는 문제가 아님을 강조했다. 미국은 그 반대 입장을 개진했음은 물론이다. WTO 패널은 이 곤란한 질문에 대해 구체적인 판정을 내리는 것은 회피했으며 대신 미국이 입증책임을 완수하지 못했다는 결정으로 사실상 중국의 입장을 지지하는 결론을 도출했다.

이 분쟁은 국제분쟁해결절차에서 국내법이 어떤 지위를 차지하는지 잘 보여준다. 각국의 국내법은 하나의 사실(fact)로서 그 자체가 하나의 정부 조치(measure)를 구성하고, 이에 대해 국제분쟁을 담당하는 판정부가 "구속력을 갖는 법(governing law)"을 적용하여 그에 대한 위반 여부를 판단한다. 이 사건에서 문제가 된 중국의 다양한 법령은 중국 정부의 조치이고 이에 대해 적용되는 구속력을 갖는 법은 WTO TRIPs 협정이다. 2018년부터 WTO 분쟁해결절차 개혁을 주장하는 미국이 상소기구는 회원국의 법률을 심사하지 못하도록 규정하자는 주장을 내세우며 그 근거로 국내법은 사실문제이니 법률문제만을 다루는 상소심에서 배제되어야 한다는 주장을 내세우고 있다. 국제법원에서 국내법 자체는 사실문제이나 이에 대한 법적 평가는 법률문제라는 점을 의도적으로 간과하며 상소기구의 위상을 낮추기 위한 노력의 일환으로 비판을 받고 있다. 이러한 입장은 이 분쟁에서 중국에 대해 제시하였던 미국 자신의 주장과도 배치되는 내용으로 볼 수 있다.

한편 이 분쟁은 최근 진행되는 중국 관련 분쟁에서 제기되는 제반 문제를 여실히 보여주고 있다. 바로 중국의 경우 국내 법령과 제도가 복잡하고 중앙정부와 지방정부를 아우르는 여러 단계에 걸쳐 있어 제소국이 충분한 자료와 증거를 확보하고 제출하는 데 한계가 있다. WTO DSU 제6.2조는 제소국이 반드시 준수하여야 할 의무로 패널 설치요청서 제출시 제소 대상인 조치의 사실관계와 이러한 사실관계에 적용되는 WTO 협정 규정을 구체적으로 나열할 것을 요구하고 있다. 중국의 경우 법령과 제도가 워낙 복잡하여 적지 않은 경우 최초 제소 시에는 어떠한 법령이 문제가 되는지 모두 파악이 되지 않는 경우가 빈번하다. 이 경우 제소국은 문제의 조치를 총괄적으로만 기술하거나 관련 법령과 제도를 일부만 제시하는 고육지책을 쓰고 있다. 중국은 이러한 제소국의 패널 설치요청서는 DSU 제6.2조 위반임을 주장하며 패널 관할권 미비를 이유로 한 선결적 항변(preliminary objection)을 제기하는 것이 흔히 목도되는 상황이다. 국제통상 체제의 새로운 강자로 등장한 중국과 관련된 분쟁은 그 내용뿐 아니라 절차적 측면에서도 새로운 과제를 제시하고 있다.

▶ 참고문헌 ────────────────────────────────

- H. G. Ruse – Khan, China – Intellectual Property Rights: Implications for the TRIPS – Plus Border Measures, Journal of World Intellectual Property Vol. 13(2010), p. 620.
- R. Creemers, The Effects of WTO Case DS362 on Audiovisual Media Piracy in China, European Intellectual Property Review Vol. 31(2009), p. 569.
- R. Brewster, The Surprising Benefits to Developing Countries of Linking International Trade and Intellectual Property, Chicago Journal of International Law Vol. 12(2011), p. 1.

5. 미국 원산지 표시제도(2012)
― 내국민 대우의 외연

United States ― Certain Country of Origin Labelling
(COOL) Requirements.
Canada, Mexico v. the United States, Report of the
Appellate Body, WT/DS384, 386/AB/R(2012).

☑ 사　　안

이 분쟁은 2008년 미국 정부가 도입한 육류에 대한 원산지 표시제도
(Country of Origin Labelling: COOL)를 다루고 있다. 이 분쟁 제소국인 캐나다
와 멕시코는 이 육류 원산지 표시제도로 인해 자국산 육류가 미국 시장에서
미국산 육류에 비해 차별적 대우를 받았다고 주장했다. 이 원산지 표시제도
는 돼지고기, 소고기 등 육류상품에 대해 가축 생육국, 도축국, 포장국명을
각각 해당 상품의 외부포장에 의무적으로 표시하도록 했다. 이 규정은 외국
산 육류이든 미국산 육류이든 가리지 않고 동일하게 적용되었다. 즉, 외관상
으로 이 제도는 미국 국내 상품과 외국 상품을 차별하지 않는다. 그런데 이
제도를 실제 시장상황에 적용하여 보니 생육, 도축, 포장 중 한 가지라도 미
국이 아닌 다른 국가에서 이루어졌을 경우 원산지 표시제도의 요건을 이행
하는 데 적지 않은 비용이 소요되었다. 각각의 국명 표기의 정확성을 담보하
기 위해 입증자료를 보관해야 하고 그 위반시 행정제재가 따랐기 때문이다.
특히 미국 내 도축업자들은 이 표시요건을 정확하게 이행하기 위해서는 이
전과 달리 자국산 소와 외국산 소를 구별하여 도축하고 구별하여 포장을 해
야 하는 실질적인 어려움에 직면하였다. 이러한 이유로 미국 도축업자들은
가급적 외국산 돼지, 소를 도축하기보다는 미국산 돼지, 소를 도축하여 판매
하는 것을 점차 선호하기에 이르렀다. 그 결과 외국산 돼지, 소 등과 이들로

부터 산출된 육류제품은 미국산 동종상품보다 미국 시장에서의 경쟁력이 떨어지게 되었다. 특히 인접국으로서 미국 시장에 상당한 이해관계를 갖고 있던 캐나다와 멕시코는 이러한 미국의 제도는 국내산 상품과 수입 상품간 차별을 초래하는 것으로 내국민 대우 위반 문제를 초래한다고 주장했다. 이들은 미국의 조치가 TBT 협정 제2.1조와 제2.2조를 각각 위반한다는 입장이었다. 이 분쟁 패널은 제소국의 입장을 지지했다. 아래는 상소기구의 판정문을 정리한 것이다.

☑ 쟁   점

(1) 미국 원산지 표시제도의 내국민 대우 원칙 위반 여부(TBT 협정 제2조 1항).

(2) 원산지 표시제도가 무역에 불필요한 장애를 초래하는지 여부(TBT 협정 제2조 2항).

☑ 판   결

(1) 미국의 원산지 표시제도는 내국민대우 원칙의 위반이다. 국내상품과 외국상품간 외관상 공평한 대우에도 불구하고 실제 시장에서의 경쟁조건이 외국상품에 대해 불리하게 변경되었으며, 이는 비차별 의무를 규정하고 있는 TBT 협정 제2조 1항 위반이다.

(2) 문제된 조치가 필요 이상으로 무역제한적인지 여부는 이를 판단하기 위한 사실관계가 불충분하므로 판단을 유보한다.

판 결 문

287. The United States is correct to point out that, as the Panel found, the COOL measure does not legally compel market participants to choose between processing either exclusively domestic or exclusively imported livestock. However, the Panel also found that the design of the COOL measure and its operation within the US market meant that segregation of livestock was "a practical way to ensure [compliance]." In examining the various possible methods of compliance with the COOL measure, the Panel found that the less costly methods would include an "absolute form of segregation," whereby producers choose to process either exclusively domestic or exclusively imported livestock. Given the particular circumstances of the US livestock market—including the fact that "[l]ivestock imports have been and remain small compared to overall US livestock production and demand, and US livestock demand cannot be fulfilled with exclusively foreign livestock"—the Panel concluded that the least costly way of complying with the COOL measure is to rely exclusively on domestic livestock. The Panel then relied on this finding, together with its finding that the costs of compliance cannot fully be passed on to consumers, to find that the COOL measure creates an incentive for US market participants to process exclusively domestic livestock and reduces the competitive opportunities of imported livestock as compared to domestic livestock.

288. In our view, the circumstances of these disputes are similar to those in Korea—Various Measures on Beef. In that case, Korea established a "dual retail system" that required small retailers to sell either exclusively domestic beef or exclusively imported beef. The Appellate Body held that "the treatment accorded to imported beef, as a consequence of the dual retail system established for beef by Korean law and regulation, is less favourable than the treatment given to like domestic beef." The Appellate Body did not find a detrimental impact on imported beef due only to "[t]he legal necessity of making a choice" that the measure itself imposed. Rather, it held that the adoption of a measure requiring such a choice to be made had the "direct practical effect," in that market, of denying competitive opportunities to imports. Such an effect was not "solely the result of private entrepreneurs acting on their own calculations of comparative costs and benefits," but was the result of the governmental intervention that affected the conditions of competition for beef in Korea. [···] Thus, the findings in Korea—Various Measures on Beef are consistent with, and support the proposition that, whenever the operation of a measure in the market creates incentives for private actors systematically to make choices in ways that benefit domestic products to the detriment of like imported products, then such a measure may be found to treat imported products less favourably.

289. We furthermore agree with Canada and Mexico that the Panel's findings indicate that the COOL measure itself, as applied in the US livestock and meat market, creates an incentive for US producers to segregate livestock according to origin, in particular by processing exclusively US-origin livestock. [···]

293. Although the Panel's legal approach to assessing detrimental impact was correct, the Panel ended its analysis under Article 2.1 of the TBT Agreement there.

The Panel seems to have considered its finding that the COOL measure alters the conditions of competition to the detriment of imported livestock to be dispositive, and to lead, without more, to a finding of violation of the national treatment obligation in Article 2.1. In this sense, the Panel's legal analysis under Article 2.1 is incomplete. The Panel should have continued its examination and determined whether the circumstances of this case indicate that the detrimental impact stems exclusively from a legitimate regulatory distinction, or whether the COOL measure lacks even-handedness. [···] Therefore, we consider it appropriate to review the Panel's findings as they relate to the design, architecture, revealing structure, operation, and application of the COOL measure in order to determine whether we can reach a conclusion in this respect.

342. We start by considering the recordkeeping and verification requirements imposed by the COOL measure, which the Panel found to be the source of the incentive for US producers to process exclusively domestic livestock. [···]

346. Taking account of the overall architecture of the COOL measure and the way in which it operates and is applied, we consider the detail and accuracy of the origin information that upstream producers are required to track and transmit to be significantly greater than the origin information that retailers of muscle cuts of beef and pork are required to convey to their customers. That is, the labels prescribed by the COOL measure reflect origin information in significantly less detail than the information regarding the countries in which the livestock were born, raised, and slaughtered, which upstream producers and processors are required to be able to identify in their records and transmit to their customers. [···]

347. For all of these reasons, the informational requirements imposed on upstream producers under the COOL measure are disproportionate as compared to the level of information communicated to consumers through the mandatory retail labels. [···] Therefore, we consider the manner in which the COOL measure seeks to provide information to consumers on origin, through the regulatory distinctions described above, to be arbitrary, and the disproportionate burden imposed on upstream producers and processors to be unjustifiable.

348. We emphasize that this lack of correspondence between the recordkeeping and verification requirements, on the one hand, and the limited consumer information conveyed through the retail labelling requirements and exemptions therefrom, on the other hand, is of central importance to our overall analysis under Article 2.1 of the *TBT Agreement*. [···]

349. In sum, our examination of the COOL measure under Article 2.1 reveals that its recordkeeping and verification requirements impose a disproportionate burden on upstream producers and processors, because the level of information conveyed to consumers through the mandatory labelling requirements is far less detailed and accurate than the information required to be tracked and transmitted by these producers and processors. [⋯] Given that the least costly way of complying with these requirements is to rely exclusively on domestic livestock, the COOL measure creates an incentive for US producers to use exclusively domestic livestock and thus has a detrimental impact on the competitive opportunities of imported livestock. Furthermore, the recordkeeping and verification requirements imposed on upstream producers and processors cannot be explained by the need to convey to consumers information regarding the countries where livestock were born, raised, and slaughtered, because the detailed information required to be tracked and transmitted by those producers is not necessarily conveyed to consumers through the labels prescribed under the COOL measure. [⋯] Based on these findings, we consider that the regulatory distinctions imposed by the COOL measure amount to arbitrary and unjustifiable discrimination against imported livestock, such that they cannot be said to be applied in an even-handed manner. Accordingly, we find that the detrimental impact on imported livestock does not stem exclusively from a legitimate regulatory distinction but, instead, reflects discrimination in violation of Article 2.1 of the *TBT Agreement*. [⋯]

461. [⋯][I]n US - Tuna II (Mexico)[,] the Appellate Body clarified that an analysis under Article 2.2 involves an assessment of a number of factors, and that one such factor is whether a technical regulation "fulfils" an objective. The Appellate Body explained that this factor is concerned with the degree of contribution that the technical regulation makes towards the achievement of the legitimate objective, and that a panel must seek to ascertain to what degree, or if at all, the challenged technical regulation, as written and applied, actually contributes to the legitimate objective pursued by the Member. The degree of achievement of a particular objective may be discerned from the design, structure, and operation of the technical regulation, as well as from evidence relating to the application of the measure. [⋯]

466. Despite this overall finding, a number of findings and observations made by the Panel in the course of its analysis belie this conclusion and suggest that the COOL measure does contribute to the objective of providing information to consumers on the countries in which the livestock from which meat is derived were born, raised, and slaughtered. [···]

468. We have stated above that a panel's assessment of whether a measure fulfils its objective is concerned primarily with the actual contribution made by the measure towards achieving its objective. Thus, a panel's assessment should focus on ascertaining the degree of contribution achieved by the measure, rather than on answering the questions of whether the measure fulfils the objective completely or satisfies some minimum level of fulfilment of that objective. [···]

469. [···] The Appellate Body has found, and the participants do not contest, that the burden of proof with respect to such alternative measures is on the complainants. Accordingly, we agree with the United States that, by finding the COOL measure to be inconsistent with Article 2.2 of the TBT Agreement without examining the proposed alternative measures, the Panel erred by relieving Mexico and Canada of this part of their burden of proof.

470. We have reversed the Panel's finding that the COOL measure is inconsistent with Article 2.2 of the TBT Agreement because it does not fulfil the objective of providing consumer information on origin. Therefore, the condition that triggers Canada's and Mexico's requests for completion of the legal analysis under this provision has been met. Accordingly, we proceed to consider whether we can rule on the complainants' claims that the COOL measure is inconsistent with Article 2.2 because it is more trade restrictive than necessary to fulfil a legitimate objective. To the extent possible, we shall seek to complete the legal analysis in order to foster resolution of these disputes. However, we can do so only to the extent that "the factual findings of the panel and the undisputed facts in the panel record provide ··· a sufficient basis" for our analysis. [···]

478. The Panel did not make findings regarding the risks that non-fulfilment of the objective pursued by the United States through the COOL measure would create. The Panel did, however, cast doubt on the probative value of evidence presented by the United States in order to show that consumers want information on the countries of birth, raising, and slaughter of livestock from which meat is derived. [···]

479. Overall, in our view, the Panel's factual findings suggest that the COOL measure makes some contribution to the objective of providing consumers with information on origin; that it has a considerable degree of traderestrictiveness; and that the consequences that may arise from non-fulfilment of the objective would not be particularly grave. We stress, however, that we lack clear and precise Panel findings with regard to these factors, and, in particular, findings that would enable us to identify the degree of contribution made by the COOL measure to the United States' objective. [⋯]

490. [⋯] With regard to Mexico's argument that the United States already imposes a trace-back system on all Mexican cattle for sanitary and phytosanitary purposes, the Panel made no findings, and there are no undisputed facts on the record regarding how this trace-back scheme for Mexican cattle operates, or whether it would already satisfy the requirements of a trace-back regime imposed for labelling purposes. Therefore, we are not in a position to reach a conclusion as to how the trade-restrictiveness of a trace-back system would compare to the status quo.

491. Overall, due to the absence of relevant factual findings by the Panel, and of sufficient undisputed facts on the record, we are unable to complete the legal analysis under Article 2.2 of the TBT Agreement and determine whether the COOL measure is more trade restrictive than necessary to fulfil its legitimate objective. [⋯]

☑ 해 설

이 분쟁은 여러모로 1997년 우리나라의 쇠고기 구분판매제도를 다룬 Korea − Beef 분쟁1)과 유사하다. 해당 분쟁에서 한우쇠고기와 수입쇠고기를 선택하여 하나만 판매하도록 요구하는 한국의 구분판매제도가 GATT 협정 제3조의 내국민 대우 원칙을 위반하는 것으로 판정되었다. 구분판매제도가 판매상으로 하여금 한우쇠고기와 수입쇠고기 중 하나를 자율적으로 선택하도록 하여 중립적이고 비차별적인 외양을 띠고 있음에도 불구하고, 실제 한국 시장의 특별한 사정이 판매상들이 주로 한우쇠고기를 선택하도록 한다는 것이다. 이러한 시장에서의 경쟁조건의 구조적 차별이 내국민 대우 위반 판정의 주요한 동인이었다. 미국의 육류 원산지 표시제도를 다루고 있는 이 사건 패널 및 상소기구는 이 미국 조치가 한국의 쇠고기 구분판매제도와 유사한 효과를 갖는 것으로 판단했다. 즉, 미국의 원산지 표시제도가 유통과정에서 기록보관(recordkeeping)을 요구하고 인증요건(verification requirements)을

---

1) Appellate Body Report, *Korea−Measures Affecting Imports of Fresh, Chilled and Frozen Beef*, WT/DS161/AB/R, WT/DS169/AB/R(2001).

부과함으로써 미국 내 육류 도축업자와 가공업자들로 하여금 그러한 부담으로부터 자유로울 수 있는 선택을 유도했다는 것이다. 요컨대 이들은 "온전히(exclusively)" 미국산인 가축과 육류를 사용할 유인을 제공했다. 이는 시장에서 경쟁관계에 있는 수입 가축과 육류에 대한 구조적인 차별의 효과를 초래하는 것이다. 특히 이 분쟁에서 상소기구는 내국민 대우 위반 관련 패널 판정을 지지했으나 패널이 간과한 부분에 대한 분석과 판단을 추가했다. 이러한 차별적 효과가 "전적으로 정당한 규제를 목적으로 하는 차이에 기인한 것(stems exclusively from a legitimate regulatory distinction)"인지를 추가로 판단해야 한다는 것이다. 만약 차별적 효과가 전적으로 그러하다면 시장에서의 차별적 효과는 TBT 협정 제2.1조에 따라 용인된다는 것이다. 이 분석에서 상소기구는 생산 및 가공단계에서 부과되는 부담과 실제 구매단계에서 소비자들에게 전달되는 정보간 서로 균형이 맞지 않는다는 점을 확인했다. 이러한 불균형성을 감안하면 외국 상품에 대한 차별적인 "유해한 영향(detrimental impact)"이 전적으로 정당한 규제를 목적으로 하는 차이에서 기인한 것으로 볼 수 없다고 상소기구는 확인했다. 결국 제2.1조를 위반하는 차별적 조치라는 점에서 상소기구는 동일한 결론을 도출했다.

다만 무역에 덜 제한적인 조치를 취하도록 요구하는 TBT 협정 제2.2조를 위반하는지 여부에 대해 상소기구는 심리를 종결할 수 없었다. 패널 심리 과정에서 이 문제에 관한 사실축적이 충분히 이루어지지 않아 상소기구의 판단에 제약이 발생했기 때문이다. 상소기구는 사실심리를 할 수 없고 오로지 주어진 사실관계를 기초로 법률심리를 하는 것에 국한되므로 이러한 심리 불가 상황은 종종 발생하고 있다. 어차피 제2.1조 위반이 확인되었으므로 협정 위반의 조치인 것이 확인되기는 했으나 또 다른 주요한 조항인 제2.2조 위반 여부가 제대로 검토될 수 없었다는 점은 아쉬움이 남기도 한다.

한편 미국은 WTO 판정을 이행하고자 이후 문제의 육류 원산지 표시제도를 수정했다. 그러나 캐나다와 멕시코는 이러한 이행 조치가 여전히 TBT 협정 제2.1조와 제2.2조 위반이라며 2013년 8월 DSU 21.5조에 따라 '이행분쟁' 패널 설치를 요청하였다. 2014년과 2015년에 걸쳐 진행된 이행분쟁에서 상소기구는 미국의 수정된 조치가 여전히 차별적이라고 판단했고, 그에 따라

2015년 12월 캐나다와 멕시코는 WTO 분쟁해결기구로부터 보복조치를 승인 받았다. 결국 2016년 1월 미국은 쇠고기와 돼지고기에 대해 반드시 육류원 산지 표시제도를 강제하도록 한 자국 규정을 개정하여, 이를 포장 및 판매업 체의 자율적인 선택에 맡긴바, 보복조치는 피할 수 있게 되었다. 정부가 특 정한 제도를 도입하고 이에 대해 소비자들이 스스로의 기호에 따라 반응하 는 경우 원래 정부의 의도와 상관없이 차별적 효과가 발생하는 상황을 그 정부는 어떻게 사전에 인지하고 통제할 수 있는가? 이 분쟁은 이에 대한 근 본적인 의문을 제기하고 있다. 지금 상소기구의 판정은 이러한 경우까지도 해당 정부의 법적 책임을 묻고 있다.

➦ 참고문헌

- 고민영, 육류 상품에 대한 미국의 원산지 라벨링 조치를 둘러싼 국제통상법적 쟁점: TBT 협정 제2.1조 및 제2.2조를 중심으로, 국제경제법연구 Vol. 10, No. 2, 한국국제경제법학회(2012), pp. 167–193.
- P. Liu, WTO Dispute: United States—Certain Country of Origin Labelling (COOL) Requirements (Complaint by Canada), 14 Asper Rev. Int'l Bus. & Trade L. 223 (2014).
- C. P. Bown & R. Brewster, US–COOL Retaliation: The WTO's Article 22.6 Arbitration, World Trade Review Vol. 16(2017), p. 371.

6. 유럽 물개관련 상품 수입제한(2013)
— 정당한 정책과 내국민 대우

European Communities[1] — Measures Prohibiting the
Importation and Marketing of Seal Products.
Canada, Norway v. EC, Report of the Appellate Body,
WT/DS400, 401/AB/R(2013).

☑ 사   안

바다표범 사냥이 잔혹한 방식으로 이루어진다는 점은 국제사회의 주요
한 관심사항이었다. 특히 동물 애호가 그룹들은 이러한 사냥방식을 비판하며
바다표범으로 제작된 상품에 대한 보이콧을 선도하였다. 이러한 분위기를 반
영하여 유럽연합은 2009년 새로운 조치를 도입하여 잔혹한 사냥방식으로 포
획되는 바다표범 관련 제품의 수입과 판매에 일정한 요건을 부과했다. 다만
이 새로운 조치는 그린란드 섬 등 북극 인근지역에 거주하는 이누이트(Inuit)
족 및 토착부족(Indigenous Communities)이 생존을 위해 전통적인 방식으로 사
냥한 바다표범으로 만들어진 상품과 해양자원의 지속적인 관리를 위하여 사
냥한 바다표범으로 만들어진 상품에 대해서는 예외를 인정했다. 이 조치는
표면적으로는 외국산 상품과 국내산 상품을 차별하는 조항은 도입하고 있지
않다. 이 조치가 도입되자 가장 직접적으로 타격을 받은 국가는 상업적 목적
으로 바다표범을 사냥하는 캐나다와 노르웨이였다. 이들은 유럽연합의 바다
표범 관련 상품 수입 및 판매제한이 표면상으로는 원산지와 무관하게 적용
되고 있으니 결과적으로 자국산 상품의 판매 및 수입에 비차별적 효과를 초

---

1) 이 분쟁 발생 당시는 리스본 조약이 발효되기 전이었으므로 유럽공동체(European Communities)가 분쟁의 당사국이었으나, 리스본 조약 발효로 WTO에서 그 명칭이 유럽연합으로
변경된 이후 패널과 상소기구 판정이 내려짐에 따라 각 판정문 본문에는 유럽연합으로 명시되
어 있다.

래하고 있음을 주장하며 유럽연합을 WTO에 제소했다. 이 분쟁에서 패널 및 상소기구는 GATT 협정 제3조의 내국민 대우 위반이 발생했는지 여부를 검토했다. 아래 사안은 상소기구 판정에 관한 것이다.

☑ 쟁   점

(1) 문제의 수입 및 판매제한조치는 기술규정에 해당하는지 여부.

(2) 해당 조치는 GATT협정 제1조 1항의 최혜국 대우 원칙을 위반하는지 여부.

(3) 해당 조치는 GATT협정 제3조 4항의 내국민 대우 원칙을 위반하는지 여부.

(4) 해당 조치는 GATT협정 제20조 (a)항에 따라 정당화될 수 있는지 여부.

☑ 판   결

(1) 해당 조치는 유럽연합 시장에서 바다표범 상품을 판매하기 위한 조건으로 상품 그 자체의 특성(product characteristics)을 규제하는 것이 아니며 따라서 TBT협정 부속서 I의 1항에 정의된 기술규정에 해당하지 않는다.

(2) 해당 조치는 GATT협정 제1조 1항 상 최혜국 대우 원칙을 위반한다. 그린란드에 부여되었던 것과 동일한 시장접근 혜택(market access advantage)이 즉시 그리고 무조건적으로(immediately and unconditionally) 캐나다와 노르웨이산 바다표범 상품에 부여되지 않았기 때문이다.

(3) 유럽연합은 내국민 대우 원칙 위반이라는 패널의 판단에 대해 상소하지 않았다. TBT협정 제2조 1항 비차별의무(non-discrimination obligations)의 법적 기준이 GATT협정 제3조 4항에 동일하게 적용되는 것은 아니기 때문이다.

(4) 문제된 조치는 GATT협정 제20조 (a)항의 공중도덕(public morals) 보호에 필요한 조치에 해당하는 것으로 볼 수 있다. 그러나 이 조치는 비합리적이고 자의적인 차별을 내포하여 제20조의 '모두조항(chapeau)'요건을 충족하지 못했다.

판 결 문

5.58. [⋯] Instead, it establishes the conditions for placing seal products on the EU market based on criteria relating to the identity of the hunter or the type or purpose of the hunt from which the product is derived. We view this as the main feature of the measure. That being so, we do not consider that the measure as a whole lays down product characteristics. [⋯]

5.59. In the light of the above, we reverse the Panel's findings, in paragraphs 7.111 and 7.112 of the Panel Reports, that the EU Seal Regime lays down product characteristics. The Panel's conclusion that the EU Seal Regime constitutes a "technical regulation" relied on its intermediate finding that the EU Seal Regime lays down product characteristics. Accordingly, having reversed this finding by the Panel, we also reverse the Panel's findings in paragraphs 7.125 and 8.2(a) of the Panel Reports that the EU Seal Regime constitutes a "technical regulation" within the meaning of Annex 1.1 to the TBT Agreement.

5.60. [⋯] Indeed, as the Appellate Body has emphasized, a determination of whether a measure constitutes a technical regulation "must be made in the light of the characteristics of the measure at issue and the circumstances of the case." [⋯]

5.95. We note that, in these disputes, the Panel concluded that the measure at issue, although origin-neutral on its face, is de facto inconsistent with Article I : 1. The Panel found that, while virtually all Greenlandic seal products are likely to qualify under the IC exception for access to the EU market, the vast majority of seal products from Canada and Norway do not meet the IC requirements for access to the EU market. Thus, the Panel found that, "in terms of its design, structure, and expected operation," the measure at issue detrimentally affects the conditions of competition for Canadian and Norwegian seal products as compared to seal products originating in Greenland. Based on these findings, the Panel considered, correctly in our view, that the measure at issue is inconsistent with Article I : 1 because it does not, "immediately and unconditionally," extend the same market access advantage to Canadian and Norwegian seal products that it accords to seal products originating from Greenland. [⋯]

5.114. It is well established that the general principle expressed in Article III : 1—that internal measures should not be applied to afford protection to domestic production—informs the rest of Article III, including Article III : 4. This general principle, however, informs the other paragraphs of Article III in different ways, depending on the textual connection between Article Ⅲ:1 and the other paragraphs of Article Ⅲ. Thus, the interpretative direction that Article Ⅲ:1 provides to the other paragraphs of Article Ⅲ must respect, and in no way diminish, the meaning of the words actually used in those other paragraphs. [⋯]

5.116. As noted above, the term "treatment no less favourable" in Article Ⅲ:4 requires effective equality of opportunities for imported products to compete with like domestic products. Thus, Article Ⅲ:4 permits regulatory distinctions to be drawn between products, provided that such distinctions do not modify the conditions of competition between imported and like domestic products. [⋯]

5.123. We observe that the GATT 1994, the TBT Agreement and the other covered agreements are integral parts of the Marrakesh Agreement Establishing the World Trade Organization (WTO Agreement). Thus, the provisions of the WTO covered agreements should be interpreted in a coherent and consistent manner, giving meaning to all applicable provisions harmoniously. This principle applies to the relationship between the TBT Agreement and the GATT 1994, [⋯]

5.124. The Appellate Body has observed that the TBT Agreement does not contain a general exceptions clause similar to Article XX of the GATT 1994. This does not mean, however, that Members do not have a right to regulate under the TBT Agreement. Instead, the sixth recital of the preamble of the TBT Agreement suggests that a Member's right to regulate should not be constrained if the measures taken are necessary to fulfil certain legitimate policy objectives, and provided that they are not applied in a manner that would constitute a means of arbitrary or unjustifiable discrimination or a disguised restriction on international trade, and are otherwise in accordance with the provisions of the Agreement. As the Appellate Body has explained, it is the specific context of Article 2.1 of the TBT Agreement— which includes Annex 1.1; Article 2.2; and the second, fifth, and sixth recitals of the preamble—that supports a reading that Article 2.1 does not operate to prohibit a priori any restriction on international trade.

5.125. By contrast, as noted by the Panel, the obligations assumed by Members to respect the non-discrimination disciplines under Articles Ⅰ:1 and Ⅲ:4 of the GATT 1994 are balanced by a Member's right to regulate in a manner consistent with the requirements of the separate general exceptions clause of Article XX and its chapeau. In our view, the fact that, under the GATT 1994, a Member's right to regulate is accommodated under Article XX, weighs heavily against an interpretation of Articles Ⅰ:1 and Ⅲ:4 that requires an examination of whether the detrimental impact of a measure on competitive opportunities for like imported products stems exclusively from a legitimate regulatory distinction. In the light of the immediate contextual differences between the TBT Agreement and the GATT 1994, we do not consider that the legal standard for the non-discrimination obligation under Article 2.1 of the TBT Agreement applies equally to claims under Articles I : 1 and III : 4 of the GATT 1994. [⋯]

5.129. Finally, we note that our interpretation of the legal standards under Articles I : 1 and III : 4 of the GATT 1994, and Article 2.1 of the TBT Agreement, is based on the text of those provisions, as understood in their context, and in the light of the object and purpose of the agreements in which they appear, as is our mandate. If there is a perceived imbalance in the existing rights and obligations under the TBT Agreement and the GATT 1994, the authority rests with the Members of the WTO to address that imbalance.

5.130. In the light of the foregoing considerations, we uphold the Panel's finding, at paragraph 7.586 of its Reports, that the legal standard for the non-discrimination obligations under Article 2.1 of the TBT Agreement does not apply equally to claims under Articles I : 1 and III : 4 of the GATT 1994. [⋯]

5.144. As noted above, the Panel sought first to identify the objective of the EU Seal Regime when assessing the claims under Article 2.2 of the TBT Agreement. The Panel subsequently relied on that assessment in its analysis under Article XX of the GATT 1994. [⋯]

5.166. The Appellate Body has consistently recognized that panels enjoy a margin of discretion in their assessment of the facts. This margin includes the discretion of the panel to decide which evidence it chooses to utilize in making its findings, and to determine how much weight to attach to the various items of evidence placed before it by the parties to the case. A panel does not commit error simply because it declines to accord to the evidence the weight that one of the parties believes should be accorded to it. Although the Panel could have provided more reasoning to support its findings, we do not think that any shortcomings in the Panel's analysis of the expected operation of the EU Seal Regime are so serious as to amount to a failure to make an objective assessment of the matter before it. [⋯]

5.167. For the reasons stated above, we reject Norway's contentions that the Panel erred in its characterization of the objective of the EU Seal Regime, and that the Panel failed to comply with its duties under Article 11 of the DSU in its assessment of the evidence regarding the objective of the EU Seal Regime. Having reviewed the Panel's findings and the participants' arguments on appeal, we consider that the principal objective of the EU Seal Regime is to address EU public moral concerns regarding seal welfare, while accommodating IC and other interests so as to mitigate the impact of the measure on those interests. [⋯]

5.289. The foregoing discussion has entailed an extensive assessment of the Panel's analysis of whether the EU Seal Regime is necessary to protect public morals within the meaning of Article XX(a) of the GATT 1994. [⋯] We further consider that the Panel did not err in concluding that, although the alternative measure was less trade restrictive than the EU Seal Regime, it was not reasonably available given inter alia the inherent animal welfare risks and challenges found to exist in seal hunting. Overall, in the light of the specific circumstances of this case, and the particular nature of the measure at issue, we have endorsed the Panel's analysis of the EU Seal Regime under Article XX(a) of the GATT 1994.

5.290. Accordingly, having rejected the claims on appeal by Canada and Norway as they relate to Article XX(a), we uphold the Panel's finding at paragraph 7.639 of its Reports that "the EU Seal Regime is provisionally deemed necessary within the meaning of Article XX(a) of the GATT 1994." [⋯]

5.291. Having upheld the Panel's finding that the EU Seal Regime is "necessary to protect public morals" within the meaning of Article XX(a) of the GATT 1994, we now turn to review the Panel's analysis as it pertains to the chapeau of Article XX of the GATT 1994. [⋯]

5.338. In sum, we have identified several features of the EU Seal Regime that indicate that the regime is applied in a manner that constitutes a means of arbitrary or unjustifiable discrimination between countries where the same conditions prevail, in particular with respect to the IC exception. First, we found that the European Union did not show that the manner in which the EU Seal Regime treats seal products derived from IC hunts as compared to seal products derived from "commercial" hunts can be reconciled with the objective of addressing EU public moral concerns regarding seal welfare. Second, we found considerable ambiguity in the "subsistence" and "partial use" criteria of the IC exception. Given the ambiguity of these criteria and the broad discretion that the recognized bodies consequently enjoy in applying them, seal products derived from what should in fact be properly characterized as "commercial" hunts could potentially enter the EU market under the IC exception. We did not consider that the European Union has sufficiently explained how such instances can be prevented in the application of the IC exception. Finally, we were not persuaded that the European Union has made "comparable efforts" to facilitate the access of the Canadian Inuit to the IC exception as it did with respect to the Greenlandic Inuit. We also noted that setting up a "recognized body" that fulfils all the requirements of Article 6 of the Implementing Regulation may entail significant burdens in some instances.

5.339. For these reasons, we find that the European Union has not demonstrated that the EU Seal Regime, in particular with respect to the IC exception, is designed and applied in a manner that meets the requirements of the chapeau of Article XX of the GATT 1994. It follows that the European Union has not justified the EU Seal Regime under Article XX(a) of the GATT 1994. [⋯]

☑ 해   설

이 분쟁은 내국민 대우와 관련하여 2012－2013년간 다루어진 여러 분쟁에서 확인된 법리를 최종적으로 확인, 정리하고 있다는 데에서 그 의의를 찾을 수 있다. 특히 TBT 협정상 의무와 GATT 협정상 의무의 상호 관계를 정리하고, 나아가 TBT 협정 제2조와 GATT XX조간 관계를 체계화함으로써 두 협정이 어떻게 적용되는지에 대하여 보다 분명한 가이드라인을 제시하고 있다. 요컨대 두 협정은 서로 밀접히 연관되어 있지만 각각 별도의 의무를 부과하므로 하나의 협정에서 발전된 법리가 그대로 다른 협정의 해석에 적용될 수는 없다는 것이다. 모두 WTO 설립협정의 큰 우산아래 있으므로 양 부속협정간 조화로운 해석이 필요한 것은 타당하나, 그렇다고 하여 양 협정이 부과하는 의무가 동일한 것은 아니라는 것이다. 이러한 인식에 기초하여 이 분쟁에서 상소기구는 내국민 대우 및 최혜국 대우 원칙의 범위도 GATT 협정과 TBT 협정이 서로 상이하다는 점을 확인하였다. GATT 제I조와 제III조가 각각 최혜국 대우와 내국민 대우 원칙을 규정하고 있고 TBT 협정 제2.1조가 이를 합하여 비차별 원칙을 규정하고 있으나 그 해석이 동일할 수는 없다는 것이다. 바로 GATT 협정의 경우 별도로 제XX조에서 일반적 예외가 규정되어 있으나 TBT 협정은 그러한 예외가 부재하고 단지 제2.1조와 제2.2조에서 정당한 정책목표를 반영하기 위한 기제가 비차별 의무와 동시에 병기되어 있기 때문이다. 이러한 판단에 기초하여 TBT 협정 제2조의 법리와 해석으로 GATT 제I조와 제III조를 해석하고자 시도했던 유럽연합의 입장이 기각되었다.

이 분쟁은 GATT 제XX조의 일반적 예외 요건의 충족이 어려운 작업이라는 점을 거듭 보여주고 있다. 브라질의 유럽연합산 재생타이어 수입제한조치를 다룬 Brazil—Retreaded Tyres,[2] 그리고 미국의 안티구아 바뷰다 인터넷 사행산업 차단조치와 관련한 U.S.—Gambling 사건[3]에서도 GATT 제XX와 GATS 제XIV조가 규정하고 있는 일반적 예외가 검토되며 그 엄격한 요건이 확인된 바 있다. 이 분쟁에서도 유럽연합의 조치가 일단 공중도덕을 보호하기 위해 필요한 조치라는 기본적인 요건은 충족했다 그러나 동일하거나 유사한 상황을 차별적으로 대우함으로써 "자의적이고 정당화되기 힘든(arbitrary and unjustifiable)" 조치에 해당하여 이 조 모두조항의 요건을 충족하는데 실패했다. 아무리 정당한 정책목표를 추구하더라도 일부 지역이나 상황을 국내 정치적·경제적 이유로 예외로 남겨두게 되면 결국 일반적 예외조항을 충족하기 힘들다는 점을 이 판정은 잘 보여주고 있다.

➡ 참고문헌

- 조희경, Case note : EC Seals : A Review of the Decision of the Appellate Body, 서울법학 Vol. 22, No. 3, 서울시립대학교 법학연구소(2015. 2), pp. 515–553.
- C. J. Ekuzibdim, European Communities—Measures Prohibiting the Importation and Marketing of Seal Products, 11 Manchester J. Int'l Econ. L. 312 (2014).
- L. Nielsen, Systemic Implications of the EU—Seal Products Case, 8 Asian J. WTO & Int'l Health L & Pol'y 41 (2013).
- T. Perisin, Is the EU Seal Products Regulation a Sealed Deal: EU and WTO Challenges, 62 Int'l & Comp. L. Q. 373 (2013).

---

2) Appellate Body Report, *Brazil—Measures Affecting Imports of Retteaded Tyres*, WT/DS332/AB/R(2007).

3) Appellate Body Report, *United States—Measures Affecting the Cross—Bordes Supply of Gambling and Betting Services*, WT/DS285/AB/R(2005).

7. 인도네시아 제지 분쟁(2005)
— 조사과정의 절차적 정당성 보장

Korea — Anti-Dumping Duties on Imports of Certain Paper from Indonesia.
Indonesia v. Korea, Panel Report, WT/DS312/R(2005)[1]

☑ 사 안

이 분쟁은 우리나라가 WTO에 제소당한 대표적인 사안 중 하나이다. 우리나라가 인도네시아산 인쇄용지에 반덤핑 관세를 부과하자 인도네시아는 WTO 반덤핑협정 위반을 주장하며 우리나라를 WTO에 제소했다.

2002년 국내 제지업체 5개사는 산업자원부(현 산업통상자원부) 무역위원회(Korea Trade Commission)에 인도네시아산 인쇄용지에 대한 반덤핑 조사를 신청했다. 조사 대상 기업은 인도네시아의 3개 수출업체(Indah Kiat, Pindo Deli 및 Tjiwi Kimia)였다. 1년 여에 걸친 반덤핑 조사 결과 무역위원회는 이들 인도네시아산 인쇄용지의 덤핑수입으로 인해 국내 제지산업에 "실질적 피해(material injury)"가 발생했다고 판정했다. 조사 진행 과정에서 인도네시아 3개 수출기업의 인도네시아 내수시장 판매를 담당하는 대행업체의 협조 거부로 무역위원회는 반덤핑협정 제6조 8항에 따라 "이용가능한 사실(facts available)" 기준을 적용했다. 이 조항은 조사과정에서 대상 기업이나 이해관계자가 협조를 거부하는 경우 조사당국이 자신이 필요한 정보를 다른 방식으로 획득하여 사용할 수 있다는 내용을 규정하고 있다. 이에 따라 무역위원회는 당시 재정경제부(현 기획재정부)에 인도네시아 3사에 대해 각각 8.22%의 반덤핑 관세 부과를 건의했고, 재정경제부는 이를 부과했다. 우리 법제상 관

---

1) 이 분쟁은 양측 모두 항소하지 않아 패널 판정이 최종 판정으로 확정되었다.

세 부과 권한은 기획재정부에 있어 무역위원회는 반덤핑 조사 이후 관세 부과를 기획재정부에 건의하고, 기획재정부가 관세 부과 여부에 대한 최종 결정을 내리게 된다.

인도네시아 3개 수출기업이 별개 법인이었음에도 불구하고 동일한 반덤핑 관세가 부과된 이유는 무역위원회가 이들을 사실상 단일의 수출자(single exporter)로 취급했기 때문이다. 인도네시아 3개 기업이 모두 인도네시아 재벌인 Sinar Mas Group 소속이라는 것이 중요한 논거였다. 이 반덤핑 관세는 2003년 11월 7일부터 2006년 11월 6일까지 3년간 부과되었다. 인도네시아는 2004년 4월 우리나라를 WTO 패널에 제소했다.

☑ **쟁   점**

(1) 이용가능한 사실(facts available) 기준 적용의 정당성 여부.

(2) 3개 별도 법인을 동일한 수출자로 취급한 결정의 타당성 여부.

(3) 서면이 아닌 구두 통지의 협정 요건 충족 여부.

☑ **판   정**

(1) 한국 무역위원회가 인도네시아 수출기업인 Indah Kiat와 Pindo Deli의 정상가격(인도네시아 국내시장 가격) 산정시 인도네시아 국내판매자료를 배제하고 "이용가능한 사실"을 적용한 것은 요청된 정보가 합리적 기간 내에 (within a reasonable period of time) 제출되지 않았기 때문으로 이는 반덤핑협정 제6조 8항 및 부속서 Ⅱ 제3조에 합치한다. 그러나 또 다른 기업인 Tjiwi Kimia의 덤핑마진 산정시 무역위원회는 "이용가능한 사실"을 적용하며 2차 자료(secondary source)를 원용했으나 그 자료에 대한 신뢰도 검증을 실시하지 않아 이 협정 제6조 8항을 위반했다.

(2) 반덤핑협정 제6조 10항과 제9조 5항을 동시에 해석하면 '모든 경우에' 개별 법인에 개별 덤핑 마진을 산정해야 하는 것으로 해석되지는 않고, 이 문제는 개별 사안별로 여러 사정을 종합적으로 감안하여 판단해야 할 문제이다. 따라서 3개 수출기업을 단일의 수출자로 취급한 무역위원회의 판정은 반덤핑협정에 합치한다.

(3) 반덤핑협정 제6조 7항은 현장실사 결과에 대한 통지의 형식까지 규정하고 있지는 않아 반드시 서면 통지를 요구하는 것으로 볼 수는 없다. 다만 이 조항 상 통지의 목적은 해당 결과를 당사자에게 알림으로써 조사과정에서 방어권을 보장하기 위한 것이므로 구두 통지 시에도 현장실사의 모든 측면에 관한 적절한 정보가 포함되어야 한다. 한국 무역위원회의 구두 통지는 이를 충족하지 못하여 이 조항을 위반했다.

판 결 문

(1) 이용 가능한 사실(facts available) 기준 적용의 정당성 여부

7.43 Article 6.8 of the Agreement stipulates that failure to provide necessary information within a reasonable period may allow the IA[2] to resort to facts available. In our view, the decision as to whether or not a given piece of information constitutes "necessary information" within the meaning of Article 6.8 has to be made in light of the specific circumstances of each investigation, not in the abstract. [⋯].

7.44 We note that in this investigation, the KTC[3] based its normal value determinations on CMI's[4] sales of the subject product to independent buyers, rather than Indah Kiat's and Pindo Deli's sales to CMI. Therefore, information pertaining to CMI's sales played a critical role with respect to the KTC's normal value determinations. [⋯] It follows that the KTC could legitimately consider as necessary information about CMI's selling activities, including its costs associated with the domestic sales of the subject product. [⋯].

7.55 We therefore conclude that in the investigation at issue, the Sinar Mas Group's submission of CMI's financial statements on 10 April 2003 was not made within a reasonable period as set out in Article 6.8 of the Agreement and that the KTC was entitled to disregard CMI's financial statements and resort to facts available. Furthermore, we note that Sinar Mas Group's post-verification submission was limited to CMI's financial statements, which were submitted for the specific purpose of demonstrating CMI's SG&A and financial expenses. The Group never attempted to submit other accounting records which, as we have found above, were

---

2) WTO 회원국 조사당국 (Investigating Authority): 편집자 주.
3) 한국 무역위원회 (Korea Trade Commission): 편집자 주.
4) 인도네시아의 국내 판매 대행업체인 Cakrawala Mega Indah 사: 편집자 주

also sought by the KTC during verification and not submitted by the Group. Obviously, therefore, these accounting records were not submitted within a reasonable period either.

7.56 It follows that the KTC did not act inconsistently with Article 6.8 in resorting to facts available with respect to Indah Kiat and Pindo Deli.

7.119 [⋯] Tjiwi Kimia intentionally chose not to submit information in response to the KTC's questionnaire. In its preliminary dumping determinations, the KTC treated the three Sinar Mas Group companies separately. In its final determinations, however, it treated them as a single exporter and assigned to them one single margin of dumping. In its final margin calculations, the KTC first calculated individual normal values and export prices for each company and then weighted them in order to come up with a final normal value and export price figure. These final figures were then used to calculate the final (single) margin of dumping. In this process, normal value and export price figures for Tjiwi Kimia were obtained from the information submitted by the applicants in the application.

7.123 Turning to the investigation at issue, we note that in the process of calculating the single margin of dumping for the three Sinar Mas Group companies, the KTC based Tjiwi Kimia's normal value and export price on the information submitted by the applicants in the application. Korea does not dispute this fact. However, parties' views diverge regarding whether or not that information was later on corroborated by the KTC against information from other independent sources. [⋯] Korea asserts that in the investigation at issue, there was no need to corroborate the normal value and export price data obtained from the application because these data came from independent and reliable sources such as the Korean government customs statistics ("KOTIS") and the Korea Trade-Investment Promotion Agency ("KOTRA"). [⋯].

7.124 We consider the obligations set forth under Article 5.3 and paragraph 7 of Annex II to be different. Firstly, these two sets of obligations apply at different stages of an investigation: Article 5.3 concerns the quality of the evidence that would justify the initiation of an investigation whereas paragraph 7 of Annex II has to do with the evidence on which the IA's final determination may be based. Secondly, the standards of these two obligations are different. The standard under Article 5.3 is that evidence be "adequate and accurate" so as to justify initiation whereas paragraph 7 of Annex II requires that information from secondary sources be compared against that from other independent sources. [⋯] We therefore disagree with Korea's contention that in certain cases, the fulfilment of the obligation under Article 5.3 may also suffice to meet the requirements of paragraph 7 of Annex Ⅱ.

7.125 [⋯] [T]he KTC was under the obligation to take the procedural step under paragraph 7 of Annex Ⅱ, to confirm the reliability of that information for purposes of its determinations in the investigation. [⋯].

7.126 [⋯] We are left in a position where there is evidence on the record that demonstrates that the KTC did corroborate export price information from the data of KOTIS, but no evidence as to whether or not the same was done with respect to the normal value. It is for a party asserting a fact to provide proof thereof. We therefore consider that Korea has not established as a matter of fact that the KTC compare the normal value figure for Tjiwi Kimia against other independent sources. It follows that Korea has not rebutted the *prima facie* case made by Indonesia in this regard. We therefore conclude that the KTC acted inconsistently with Article 6.8 of the Agreement and paragraph 7 of Annex II by failing to fulfil its obligation to corroborate information obtained from secondary sources for purposes of calculating Tjiwi Kimia's dumping margin against other independent sources at its disposal.

(2) 3개 별도 법인을 동일한 수출자로 취급한 결정의 타당성 여부

7.157 The claim at issue concerns the first sentence of Article 6.10. The issue here is whether, and if so under what circumstances, Article 6.10 permits an IA to treat separate legal entities, which export the subject product to the importing Member and which are in certain ways related to one another, as a single exporter and to determine an individual margin of dumping for that exporter. We note that Article 6.10 mentions "exporters" and "producers" of the subject product and requires that an individual margin be calculated for each of them. It does not, however, define these two words. [⋯].

7.158 Turning to the context of Article 6.10, we find important guidance in Article 9.5 of the Agreement. Article 9.5 reads in pertinent parts:

> "If a product is subject to anti-dumping duties in an importing Member, the authorities shall promptly carry out a review for the purpose of determining individual margins of dumping for any exporters or producers in the exporting country in question who have not exported the product to the

importing Member during the period of investigation, provided that these exporters or producers can show that they are not related to any of the exporters or producers in the exporting country who are subject to the anti-dumping duties on the product ... " (emphasis added)

7.159 Article 9.5 requires that the IA determine individual margins for exporters and producers who did not export during the POI. Article 9.5 further provides, however, that the IA is not required to calculate an individual dumping margin for a newcomer who is related to an exporter subject to an existing anti-dumping duty. [···] The logic of Article 9.5 would appear to be that to allow related companies to obtain individual rates could undermine the efficiency of the existing duties. [···] Article 9.5 as context strongly suggests that the term "exporter" in Article 6.10 should not be read in a way to require an individual margin of dumping for each independent legal entity under all circumstances.

7.161 Thus, we consider that, when read in context, Article 6.10 does not necessarily preclude treating distinct legal entities as a single exporter or producer for purposes of dumping determinations in anti-dumping investigations. Having said that, however, we do not consider that Article 6.10 provide the IA with unlimited discretion to do so. While Article 6.10 does not by its terms require that each separate legal entity be treated as a single "exporter" or "producer", neither does it allow a Member to treat distinct legal entities as a single exporter or producer without justification. Whether or not the circumstances of a given investigation justify such treatment must be determined on the basis of the record of that investigation. In our view, in order to properly treat multiple companies as a single exporter or producer in the context of its dumping determinations in an investigation, the IA has to determine that these companies are in a relationship close enough to support that treatment.

7.163 With these considerations in mind, we now turn to the facts before the KTC in this investigation. We note that, in its preliminary determination, the KTC rejected the domestic industry's request that the three Sinar Mas Group companies be treated as a single exporter and that a single margin of dumping be assigned to them. At the final stage of the investigation, however, the KTC did treat them as a single exporter or producer and assigned a single margin to them. The KTC explained the reasons for its decision in its Final Dumping Report, [···]

7.165 We consider the commonality of management among these three companies, coupled with the fact that they were all owned by the same parent company, to be indications of a close legal and commercial relationship between these three companies. Given these similarities, one might, in our view, expect that commercial decisions for the three companies could be made in substantial part by the same closely interlocked group of individuals, and the management of all three companies could ultimately be answerable to their majority shareholder Ekapersada. […].

7.166 In addition to these factors specifically referred to by the KTC in the above-quoted part of the Final Dumping Report, the record also shows that CMI acted practically as the sole channel through which all three companies made their domestic sales in Indonesia. […]

7.168 […], the fact that the three Sinar Mas Group companies made almost all their domestic sales through CMI, coupled with the commonality regarding shareholdings and management and the existence of cross-sales of the subject product among the three companies, is an adequate basis for the KTC's decision to treat the three Sinar Mas Group companies as a single exporter or producer. We therefore reject Indonesia's claim that Korea acted inconsistently with Article 6.10 of the Agreement.

(3) 서면이 아닌 구두 통지의 협정 요건 충족 여부

7.188 Next, we shall address Korea's allegation that certain documents sent by the KTC also informed the Sinar Mas Group of the verification results. In this context, we shall first address the issue of whether or not Article 6.7 requires that the disclosure regarding the verification results be made in a written format. Since Indonesia submits that an oral disclosure would not satisfy Article 6.7, we understand Indonesia to argue that a written disclosure is necessary. Korea disagrees with Indonesia in this regard. […] We note that when they intended that written format be used with respect to certain communications in the course of an anti-dumping investigation, drafters stated it clearly in the Agreement. […] These examples support our interpretation that Article 6.7 does not require that disclosure be a written disclosure. As long as it can be proved that the substantive requirements of that provision have been fulfilled, the format of the disclosure would not matter.

7.189 We now turn to the contents of the documents mentioned by Korea to examine whether they informed the Sinar Mas Group of the verification results. […].

7.191 We note that these reports clearly disclose that the respondent Indonesian exporters failed to provide CMI's financial statements during verification and that the KTC therefore based their normal values on facts available. However, the reports contain no clarification with respect to the other aspects of the verification and hence do not add much to the content of the oral briefing that took place on 4 April 2003.

7.192 On the basis of the above explanations, it becomes factually clear that the contents of the disclosure regarding verification made through the oral briefing during the April 4 meeting and the KTC's reports issued following the verification were limited to the fact that the Sinar Mas Group failed to submit CMI's financial statements during verification and that the KTC decided to use facts available with respect to Indah Kiat and Pindo Deli. The issue is whether or not this limited disclosure was enough to satisfy the requirements of Article 6.7. […].

7.193 On the basis of these considerations, we find that in this case the KTC's disclosure of the verification results vis-à-vis the Sinar Mas Group fell short of meeting this standard. It did not inform the two Sinar Mas Group companies of the verification results in a manner that would allow them to properly prepare their case for the rest of the investigation. We therefore conclude that the KTC acted inconsistently with Article 6.7 of the Agreement in this regard.

☑ 해   설

이 분쟁은 우리나라가 WTO 분쟁해결절차에서 패소한 대표적인 사안이다. 실질적으로 우리나라의 패소 사항이 경미하여 우리나라도 그 결과에 대체로 만족했던 분쟁이다. 또한 판정 내용도 상대적으로 명확하여 우리나라도 인도네시아도 상소하지 않았다. 그런데 8개월에 걸친 WTO 패널 판정의 "이행기간(Reasonable Period of Time)" 동안 한국이 판정을 제대로 이행하지 않았다는 이유로 인도네시아가 우리나라를 다시 WTO 패널에 제소하여 승소함으로써, WTO 분쟁해결기구(Dispute Settlement Body: DSB)가 우리나라에 대한 인도네시아의 보복을 허용하기에 이르렀다. 최초 판정에서 KTC 조사과정에서 문제로 지적된 부분은 경미한 절차적인 사항으로 우리나라가 이행기간 내에 필요한 조치를 취할 수 있었으나 그 처리가 늦어져 추후 분쟁과 보복절차로 이어지게 되었다. 이 분쟁은 경미한 절차적 하자에 대한 판정도 신속

히 이행하여 추가 분쟁의 가능성을 사전에 차단하는 것이 중요하다는 점을
잘 보여주고 있다. 우리나라로서는 승소에 가까운 판정을 이끌어 냈으나 그
관리를 소홀히 하여 어려운 상황에 저리게 된 것이다.

특히 이 분쟁은 반덤핑 조사 과정에서 외국 수출업체와 이해관계자들에
게 충분한 설명을 제공하고 의견개진의 기회를 부여해야 하는 절차적 정당
성이 자세히 논의된 사안이기도 하다. 절차적 정당성은 반덤핑 협정 제6조를
관통하는 원칙이고, 반덤핑 조사와 유사한 상계관세 조사 및 세이프가드 조
사에서도 동일하게 강조되고 있다. 최종 판정과 상관없이 거기에 이르는 절
차가 중요하다는 내용이다. 사실 이 분쟁에서도 최종 판정 자체에 대해서는
우리 무역위원회의 입장이 지지되었기에 결과에는 문제가 없으나 이에 이르
는 과정에 일부 경미한 문제가 있었다는 것이 패널 판정의 주된 내용이다.
절차적 정당성의 확보는 결국 각각의 조사에 그만큼 많은 인력과 자원의 투
입을 요구하는 것으로 앞으로 여러 나라의 무역구제 조사에 있어 중요한 숙
제이기도 하다.

한편 이 분쟁에서 인도네시아를 대리하여 패널절차를 진행한 법률대리
인은 WTO가 개도국의 분쟁해결절차 참여를 지원하기 위해 설립한 "WTO
법률 자문센터(Advisory Center for WTO Law: ACWL)"이다. 이 센터는 적은 비
용으로 개도국들의 패널 및 상소기구 절차 참여를 지원하고 법률자문을 진
행한다. 개도국의 AWCL에 대한 의존도가 높아지고 그 성과도 적지 않아 그
역할을 확대하자는 요구가 지속적으로 제기되고 있으나 선진국들은 이에 대
해 소극적인 반응을 보이고 있다. 이 문제는 지금 WTO 개혁 과제 중 하나
로 개도국들이 강하게 요구하는 이슈이기도 하다. 미국, EU 등 선진국들은
개도국에 대한 분쟁해결절차 관련 지원을 강화하더라도 중국, 인도, 브라질
등 경제적으로는 개도국이나 법률 역량 면에서는 그렇다고 보기 어려운 국
가들은 제외해야 한다는 입장을 강하게 제시하고 있다.

한편 이 분쟁에서 인도네시아는 WTO DSB로부터 보복 권한을 부여받
았으나 우리나라와의 경제·외교관계 등을 고려하여 실제 보복조치를 취하
지는 않았고, 그 과정에서 우리 반덤핑 관세 부과 조치가 종료됨에 따라 분
쟁은 자연스럽게 해결되었다. 큰 규모의 국내시장을 가진 선진국과 달리 필

요한 물품만 선별적으로 수입하는 개도국은 수입상품에 대한 관세 인상을 통해 보복을 구현한다는 아이디어 자체가 제대로 작동하기 힘들 수 있음을 이 분쟁은 잘 보여준다. 지금과 같은 '시장 연동형' 보복 제도는 결국 선진국에는 유리하나 개도국에는 불리한 제도로 협정에 명백히 저촉되는 조치를 남발하는 선택을 조장하는 원인 중 하나이다. 이는 현재 WTO 체제가 안고 있는 근본적인 한계 중 하나로 볼 수 있다.

➥ 참고문헌 ────────────────────────────

- 공수진, WTO '한국－인도네시아산 특정 종이 수입에 대한 반덤핑관세' 사건, 국제경제법연구 제3권(2005), p. 151.
- H. Qureshi & N. Hur, Korea's Responses in WTO Disputes and Trade Policy Reviews: A Perspective of Non－State Actors, KLRI Journal of Law and Legislation Vol. 3(2013) p. 105.
- D. Ahn, Legal Development of WTO Trade Remedy Practices in East Asia, International Economic Law and Governance: Essay in Honour of Mitsuo Matsushita Chapter 30(2015), p. 515.
- M. Matsushita, Some International and Domestic Antidumping Issues, Asian Journal of WTO and International Health Law and Policy(2010), p. 249.
- Y, Lu, Exploring Aggerssive Legalism: Is Now a Good Time to Promote this Approach in Greater Asia?, Asian Journal of Law and Economics Vol. 6(2015), p. 85

8. White Industries 사건(2011)
— 법원의 부작위와 조약 위반

White Industries Australia Limited v. The Republic of India.
UNCITRAL 투자분쟁(호주-인도 BIT)(2011년 11월 30일).

☑ 사　　안

이 사건은 호주 투자자가 인도 정부를 제소한 국제투자분쟁이다. 호주 철광석 수출기업인 White Industries사는 인도 내 사업 파트너인 인도 국영 기업 Coal India사와 인도 내 탄광 개발과 설비 공급을 핵심으로 하는 계약을 체결했다. 그런데 탄광 개발을 진행하던 중 White Industries사와 Coal India사 간 계약 조건 미이행 여부를 둘러싼 분쟁이 발생했다. 계약 체결 당시 합의된 바에 따라 White Industries사는 1999년 파리 소재 국제상업회의소(International Chamber of Commerce: ICC)에 Coal India사를 상대로 한 상사중재를 신청했고, 2002년 승소 판정을 받았다. White Industries사는 1958년 뉴욕협약에 따라 이 중재판정을 인도에서 집행하고자 인도 법원에 집행 신청을 했으나, 여러 심급의 인도 법원에서 그 절차가 지연되었다. 하급심을 거쳐 White Industries사는 2004년 인도 대법원에 상고했으나 2010년까지 최종판결이 내려지지 않자, White Industries사는 그 방향을 바꾸어 호주-인도 간 체결된 투자협정(Bilateral Investment Treaty: BIT)에 따른 국제투자분쟁해결(Investor-State Dispute Settlement: ISDS) 절차를 신청했다. 이 BIT는 양국간 1999년 2월 체결되었다. 상사중재 분쟁이 투자중재 분쟁으로, 계약상 분쟁이 조약상 분쟁으로 변화한 것이다.

이 투자분쟁에서 White Industries사의 핵심 주장은 인도 대법원의 중재판정 집행 판결의 과도한 지연(inordinate delay)은 양국 BIT에 규정된 공정하

고 공평한 대우, 수용 및 최혜국대우 등 주요 조항에 대한 위반에 해당한다
는 것이다. 특히 분쟁의 대상이 된 조치가 일반적인 투자분쟁의 대상인 행정
부의 처분조치가 아니라 사법부의 심리 지연이라는 점에서 여러 관심을 촉
발했다. 특히 이 문제는 사법주권 문제와 협정상 의무의 이행이 만나는 내용
이라는 점에서 중요한 함의를 내포하고 있다.

☑ 쟁   점

(1) White Industries가 투자협정상 '투자자'의 요건을 충족하는지 여부.

(2) ICC 중재판정도 투자협정이 규정하는 외국인의 '투자'에 해당하는지
여부.

(3) 인도 법원이 중재판정 취소의 소를 진행한 방식이 BIT를 위반하는지
여부.

☑ 판   정

(1) 상사중재 판정의 집행을 구하는 White Industries는 양국간 BIT에 명
시된 바에 따라 금전에 대한 권리(right to money)를 가진 '투자자'에 해당한다.

(2) ICC 상사중재판정 자체는 독립적인 투자가 아니나 그 내용이 최초
투자의 권리와 의무를 구체화하는 한도에서는 그러한 투자의 일부를 구성하
는 것으로 볼 수 있고 BIT 적용대상인 투자에 해당한다.

(3) 인도 법원의 심리 절차 지연은 호주－인도 BIT 제4조 2항(최혜국 대
우)에 의해 편입된 인도－쿠웨이트 BIT 제4조 5항이 규정하는 "효과적인 권
리보장 수단(effective means of asserting claims and enforcing rights)" 제공 의무
를 위반한다.

판 결 문

(1) White Industries가 '투자자'의 요건을 충족하는지 여부

7.2.1 Article 1 of the BIT provides that an "investor" may be a "company" or
a natural person (where the latter must be either a citizen or permanent resident).
It further defines a "company" as including any corporation that is "incorporated,

constituted, set up or duly organised" under the laws of a Contracting Party.

7.2.2 Although India does not dispute that White is a company incorporated in Australia, it argues that it is not an "investor" for the purposes of the BIT based on its assertion that White has not made an "investment" under the BIT.

7.2.3 Under these circumstances, there being no denial of White's claim to be an "investor" in India, both limbs of India's defence in this respect will be disposed of should the Tribunal find that White has made an "investment".

7.3.1 The definition of "investment" in the BIT is set out in broad terms. Article 1 of the BIT defines "investment" as follows:

"investment means every kind of asset, including intellectual property rights, invested by an investor of one Contracting Party in the territory of the other Contracting Party in accordance with the laws and investment policies of that Contracting Party, and in particular, though not exclusively, includes:

(i) moveable and immovable property as well as other rights such as mortgages, liens, or pledges;

(ii) shares, stocks, bonds and debentures and any other form of participation in a company;

(iii) right to money or to any performance having a financial value, contractual or otherwise;

(iv) business concessions and any other rights required to conduct economic activity and having economic value conferred by law or under a contract, including rights to search for, extract and utilise oil and other minerals;

(v) activities associated with investments, such as the organisation and operation of business facilities, the acquisition, exercise and disposition of property rights including intellectual property rights." (emphasis added)

7.3.2 The correct approach to be adopted by the Tribunal in assessing whether an "investment" has been made is to consider the plain and ordinary meaning of the words used in the BIT in their context and in the light of its object and purpose and to determine whether the matters relied on by White satisfy the definition employed in the BIT.

7.3.3 India's principal arguments against White having made an "investment" are based on the writings of Zachary Douglas, who sets out what he considers to be an appropriate general test of what constitutes an "investment". This test is said to be applicable in all investment treaty claims—regardless of whether they are brought under the ICSID Convention, the UNCITRAL or any other rules of arbitration.

7.3.4 For Douglas, it is essential than an "investment" have certain legal and economic characteristics. These are described in his "Rules" 22 and 23, which provide:

> "Rule 22: the legal materialization of an investment is the acquisition of a bundle of rights in property that has the characteristics of one or more of the categories of an investment defined by the applicable investment treaty where such property is situated in the territory of the host State or is recognised by the rules of the host State's private international law to be situated in the host State or is created by the municipal law of the host State.
>
> Rule 23: the economic materialization of an investment requires the commitment of resources to the economy of the host State by the Claimant entailing the assumption of risk in the expectation of commercial return."

7.3.5 Douglas's requisite legal characteristics are derived from the non-exhaustive examples of an "asset" that constitutes "investments" in investment treaties. This forms the basis of Rule 22, which generalises the requirement as the acquisition of property rights in the host State.

7.3.6 The requisite economic characteristics are derived from what is described as the common economic concept of foreign direct investment. In Rule 23, they are "codified" as the transfer of resources into the economy of the State and the assumption of risk in the expectation of commercial return.

7.3.7 India further relies on Douglas's proposition that, where a claimant relies upon a contract to establish an investment pursuant to Rule 22 and 23:

> "the Tribunal should differentiate between rights *in personam* as between the Contracting Parties and rights *in rem* that are memorialised by the contract. The rights *in personam* do not generally qualify as an investment independently of the rights *in rem*."

7.3.8 The difficulty with India's position on this point is that the BIT simply does not provide that, in order to be a covered investment, the investment must be a right "in rem", or must have Douglas's economic characteristics. Indeed, the BIT expressly includes in its definition of an "investment" what can only be in personam rights, namely: the "right to money or to any performance having a financial value, contractual or otherwise". And this is precisely what White had under the Contract: a "right to money" from Coal India for the performance of its obligations under the Contract.

(2) ICC 상사중재판정도 '투자'에 해당하는지 여부

7.6.1 White's position as to whether the Award constitutes an "investment" has been argued somewhat inconsistently. In paragraph 1.106 of its Memorial, it asserts that the Award is an "investment" because it constitutes a "right to money or to any performance having a financial value, contractual or otherwise" as provided by Article 1(c)(iii) of the BIT.

7.6.2 However, in paragraph 1.107 of the Memorial it is stated that "White Industries does not, however, allege that its rights under the Award represent an investment in itself, but rather that the Award, is part of the original investment."

7.6.3 The Tribunal concludes that this latter statement more accurately describes the status of the Award.

7.6.4 The *Saipem* tribunal reached a similar conclusion when it held that:

> "The rights embodied in the ICC Award were not created by the Award but arise out of the Contracts. The ICC Award crystallized the parties' rights and obligations under the original contract."

7.6.5 Similar reasoning was employed by the tribunals in *Mondev, Chevron, and Frontier Petroleum Services*. In those decisions, the tribunals characterised arbitral awards as "continuing" an investment under a contract.

7.6.6 India has cited the recent decision in *GEA Group Aktiengesellschaft v Ukraine* (ICSID Case No. ARB/08/16), Award, 31 March 2011 in support of its argument that White's rights pursuant to the Award are not a covered investment for the purposes of the BIT.

7.6.7 However, the Tribunal notes that the statement made at paragraph 161 of the *GEA* Award, ("the ICC Award—in and of itself—cannot constitute an 'investment'. Properly analysed it's a legal instrument which provides for the disposition of rights and obligations arising out of the Settlement Agreement and Repayment Agreement (neither of which was itself an 'investment'...)") was *obiter dicta* in light of the tribunal's finding that neither the Settlement Agreement nor the Repayment Agreement were "investments" for the purposes of the Germany-Ukraine BIT.

7.6.8 The Tribunal considers that the conclusion expressed by the *GEA Tribunal* represents an incorrect departure from the developing jurisprudence on the treatment of arbitral awards to the effect that awards made by tribunals arising out of disputes concerning "investments" made by "investors" under BITs represent a continuation or transformation of the original investment.

7.6.9 The tribunal in the Chevron Jurisdiction Award concluded:

"Once an investment is established, it continues to exist and be protected until its ultimate disposal 'has been completed.'"

7.6.10 Accordingly, the Tribunal concludes that rights under the Award constitute part of White's original investment (i.e., being a crystalisation of its rights under the Contract) and, as such, are subject to such protection as is afforded to investments by the BIT.

(3) 인도 법원의 심리지연이 BIT 위반에 해당하는지 여부

11.4.1 White argued its case (for breach of the effective means standard) on the basis of overall delay experienced to date from the beginning of the set aside and enforcement proceedings, both of which commenced in September 2002. It did not seek to analyse the two proceedings separately in connection with an assessment of "effective means".

11.4.2 In the set aside proceedings, even though Coal India was the applicant, White can properly be described as having been "asserting claims" that the Indian courts lacked set aside jurisdiction on the facts before them. In the enforcement proceedings, however, White, as the applicant was acting to "enforce [its] rights" in connection with the Award. That being the case, India was under an obligation to ensure it had "effective means" to deal with its interests in each of the two proceedings.

11.4.16 The question of whether White's claims in the set aside proceedings (i.e. that the Calcutta High Court lacked jurisdiction to entertain Coal India's application to set aside the award) were subject to indefinite or undue delay is, however, another matter entirely.

11.4.17 In his opening, when discussing the delay White has faced in the Supreme Court, Mr Landau said that it was extraordinary that it had not made a further application for expedition after the hearing of 16 January 2008, or not made an appointment with the Chief Justice of India to complain about the pace of proceedings. To the Tribunal's mind, these steps were not required.

11.4.18 Having already applied for and obtained an order for expedited hearings in 2006 and 2007, White appears to have done everything that could reasonably be expected of it to have the Supreme Court deal with its appeal in a timely manner. Mr Bonnell made the point in his closing speech, with which the Tribunal agrees, that there was no effective course open to White to seek to expedite the appeal further. He noted that:

> "It has already been granted the right to an early appeal. That happened, comically, five and a half years ago. The matter sits in the court's weekly list, which is where expedited appeals go."

11.4.19 In these circumstances, and even though we have decided that the nine years of proceedings in the set aside application do not amount to a denial of justice, the Tribunal has no difficulty in concluding the Indian judicial system's inability to deal with White's jurisdictional claim in over nine years, and the Supreme Court's inability to hear White's jurisdictional appeal for over five years amounts to undue delay and constitutes a breach of India's voluntarily assumed obligation of providing White with "effective means" of asserting claims and enforcing rights.

11.4.20 Accordingly, India is in breach of Article 4(2) of the BIT.

☑ 해   설

ISDS 절차로 흔히 약칭되는 국제투자분쟁 사건은 2020년 7월 현재 1,000건을 넘어설 정도로 지속적인 증가 추세를 보이고 있다. 이러한 급증 추세는 각국의 우려를 초래하여 2015년부터 국제사회에서 다양한 맥락과 경로를 통해 ISDS 제도 개선 논의가 진행되고 있으며, 특히 UNCITRAL, OECD 및 ICSID에서 이에 대한 논의가 활발하게 진행되고 있다. 이 분쟁은 인도 정부가 외국인 투자자에 의해 최초로 ISDS 절차에 제소당한 사건이다. 인도는 그간 70개국이 넘는 국가와 BIT를 체결했으며, 광대한 투자시장을 가진 주요 투자유치국이라는 점을 고려하면 2010년에 최초의 분쟁이 제기된 것은 이례적이라고 할 수 있다. 결국 이 분쟁에서 인도 정부가 패소했는데, 이로 인해 인도 내에서 ISDS 절차에 대한 비판적인 시각과 기존의 BIT 체결 전략 및 방식에 대한 재검토를 요구하는 목소리가 커지게 되었다. 최근 국제사회의 ISDS 개선 논의에서 인도가 적극적인 입장을 개진하는 배경에는 이 사건의 경험이 주효했다.

사건 내용 자체는 인도 정부가 BIT 위반 문제를 피해나가기 쉽지 않다. 대법원에서의 재판지연 자체가 인도 대법원의 그간 관례를 감안하더라도 전례없이 지연되었기 때문이다. 따라서 재판 지연은 때로는 불가피하며 사안의 복잡성으로 인해 그러하다는 인도 정부의 주장이 ISDS 중재 판정부에 의해 받아들여지지 않았다. 재판부는 의도적인 재판 지연으로 판단하였고 이러한 의도적인 지연이 외국인 투자자인 White Industries가 가지는 양국 BIT상 권리를 침해하였다고 판단했다. 한편 이 판정 내용은 장기간에 걸친 지연이 있었더라도 만약 그러한 지연에 대한 기본적인 설명이 제공됐다면 BIT 위반에는 이르지 않았을 것임을 시사하고 있다. 이 판정은 각국 사법부의 판단과 결정을 존중해야 할 필요성을 지속적으로 언급하며 지극히 예외적인 경우에 한해 사법부의 조치가 BIT 위반으로 이어질 수 있음을 언급하고 있다. 사법부는 행정부와 그 성격을 달리한다는 점을 전제하고 사법부의 조치가 — 판결이든 판결의 거부이든 — 투자협정상 정부 조치로 간주되기 위해서는 일반적인 상식에 명백히 반할 정도의 충격적인 위반이 필요하다는 점을 전제한 것이다. 요컨대 사법부의 조치도 투자협정의 대상이 될 수는 있지만 여기에는 상당히 높은 요건이 부과된다는 것이다. 최근 법원의 조치가 여러 맥락에서 투자협정 위반 문제로 이어지는 상황이 늘어나고 있어 이 판정은 그 법적 요건을 설명하는 데 중요한 지침을 제시하고 있다. 결국 이 분쟁을 담당한 ISDS 판정부는 인도 법원의 조치가 인도 국내법에 따르더라도 지극히 이례적이라고 판단한 것이다.

한편 이 분쟁에서 제기된 또 다른 쟁점은 Coal India(인도 석탄공사)를 인도 정부로 볼 수 있는지 여부이다. 만약 그렇다면 Coal India의 결정은 인도 정부의 조치로 간주되고, 그 조치가 호주 – 인도 BIT에 위반하는지 여부를 검토할 수 있는 가능성이 열리게 된다. 이 문제를 다룬 ISDS 판정부는 Coal India는 인도 정부가 지분을 소유하는 국영기업이나 그 사실만으로 이 기업이 인도 정부로 자동적으로 간주되지는 않는다고 결정했다. 그리고 이에 따라 Coal India의 여러 결정은 인도 정부의 조치가 아니며 따라서 이 부분은 BIT 적용대상에서 배제되고 오로지 인도 법원의 지연 내지 부작위 문제만 남게 된 것이다.

생각건대 ISDS 판정부의 이러한 결정은 타당하다. 이 판정부는 인도 정부의 지분소유에도 불구하고 구체적인 사건에서 인도 정부가 권한을 행사한 경우에만 정부기관으로 간주할 수 있다는 입장을 밝혀 기존의 ICJ 판결 및

WTO 상소기구의 입장과 동일한 취지의 결정을 도출했다. 특히 이 과정에서 석탄의 생산과 판매는 정부가 일반적으로 수행하는 기능이 아니라는 점도 Coal India의 성격을 정부기관으로 파악하지 않은 중요한 근거가 되었다. 가령 화폐를 찍어내는 중앙은행이나 정부자금을 운용하는 국영은행과는 구별된다는 것이다. 국영기업의 범위와 외연을 어떻게 이해할 것인지의 문제는 지금 국제사회의 주요한 현안 중 하나이다. 이 문제는 현재 진행되는 통상협정 협상과 미중 분쟁의 핵심쟁점이다. 동일한 문제가 투자협정과 투자분쟁에서도 제기되는 것이다. 우리나라 역시 이 문제와 밀접하게 관련되어 있다.

➡ 참고문헌

- 이재민, 조약상 의무 이행과 사법부 — 대법원 강제동원 판결에 대한 한일 투자협정의 적용 가능성, 서울국제법연구원 제20권 제2호(2013), p. 73.
- P. Nacimiento & S. Lange, White Industries Australia Limited v The Republic of India, ICSID Review — Foreign Investment Law Journal Vol. 27(2012), p. 274.
- P. Ranjan & P. Anand, The 2016 Model Indian Bilateral Investment Treaty: A Critical Deconstruction, Northwestern Journal of International Law & Business Vol. 38(2017), p. 1.
- A. Kawharu & L. Nottage, The Curious Case of ISDS Arbitration involving Australia and New Zealand, University of Western Australia Law Review Vol. 44(2018), p. 32.
- P. Ranjan, India and Bilateral Investment Treaties — Refusal, Acceptance, Backlash, Oxford University Press(2019).

9. 러시아 영토 통과 제한(2019)
― 국가안보 예외의 의미와 적용범위

Russia - Measures Concerning Traffic in Transit
Ukraine v. Russia, Panel Report, WT/DS512/R(2019)

☑ 사 안

1991년 우크라이나가 러시아로부터 독립한 이래 크림반도는 양국간 긴장의 상징이 되었다. 원래 크림반도는 러시아 통치 하에 있던 지역이었으나 1954년 구 소련 체제 하에서 행정구역 조정 차원에서 우크라이나로 편입된 이후 그대로 우크라이나와 함께 독립했기 때문이다. 이 지역 갈등이 고조되자 크림 자치 공화국 주민의 대다수를 차지하는 러시아계 주민들은 2014년 3월 16일, 우크라이나의 러시아 귀속 여부에 대해 주민투표를 실시했다. 그 결과 95%에 가까운 찬성으로 크림반도의 러시아 복귀를 결정했다. 이에 따라 크림 자치 공화국은 러시아와 합병 조약을 체결하고 러시아로 귀속되었다.

2017년 1월 우크라이나는 러시아의 크림반도 병합과 우크라이나 사태 개입을 이유로 러시아를 ICJ에 제소했다.[1] 이와 동시에 우크라이나는 러시아를 WTO 분쟁해결절차에도 회부했다. 우크라이나 상품을 운송하는 기차와 차량의 러시아 영토 통과를 러시아가 차단했기 때문이다. 사실 우크라이나는 카자흐스탄, 우즈베키스탄 등 중앙아시아 국가들과 교역량이 상당하였고 이들은 대부분 철도를 이용해 러시아 영토를 통과하는 방식으로 교역이 이루어져왔으나 러시아가 이제 이 길을 차단한 것이다. 우크라이나는 러시아의 이러한 제한조치가 "통과통행의 자유(Freedom of Transit)"를 규정하는 GATT

---

1) International Court of Justice, Application of the International Convention for the Suppression of the Financing of Terrorism and of the International Convention on the Elimination of All Forms of Racial Discrimination (Ukraine v. Russian Federation) (2017).

제V조에 위반한다고 주장했다. 이에 대해 러시아는 제V조 위반 문제에 대해 항변하지 않고 자국의 조치가 GATT 제XXI조가 규정하는 "국가안보 예외 (Security Exceptions)"에 따라 정당화된다고 주장했다. 특히 러시아는 이 조항이 자기 판단(self-judging) 문구를 포함하기에 패널의 심리 자체가 불가능하다는 입장을 제시했다. 그리고 자국의 조치는 "핵심 안보이익(essential security interest)"을 보호하기 위해 GATT 제XXI조 (b)항 (ii)호에 따라 전시상황에서 취해진 조치로 정당화됨을 강조했다.

☑ 쟁 점

(1) GATT 제XXI조 국가안보 예외에 포함된 자기 판단 문구가 패널 심리를 불가능하게 하는지 여부.

(2) 러시아의 자국 영토 통과 제한조치는 전시 또는 기타 국제관계의 긴급상황에서 취해진 조치인지 여부.

(3) 러시아의 자국 영토 통과 제한조치는 핵심 안보이익을 보호하기 위한 조치인지 여부.

☑ 판 정

(1) GATT 제XXI조 요건 충족 여부는 자기 판단 문구에도 불구하고 WTO 패널과 상소기구가 판단하며, 다만 패널과 상소기구는 심리 과정에서 해당국의 판단을 가급적 존중해야 한다.

(2) 우크라이나 주변 상황 및 국제기구의 논의 등을 종합하면 이 조치가 취해지던 시점에 이 지역에서 전쟁 또는 국제관계의 긴급한 상황이 존재했다.

(3) 러시아의 조치는 GATT 제XXI조 (b)항 (ii)호에 따라 전시상태에 핵심 안보이익을 보호하기 위해 취해진 것으로 정당화된다.

판 결 문

(1) 자기 판단 조항의 의미

7.62. Paragraph (b) of Article XXI includes an introductory part (chapeau), which qualifies action that a Member may not be prevented from taking as that "which [the Member] considers necessary for the protection of its essential security interests".

7.67. As previously noted, the words of the chapeau of Article XXI(b) are followed by the three enumerated subparagraphs, which are relative clauses qualifying the sentence in the chapeau, separated from each other by semicolons. They provide that the action referred to in the chapeau must be:

> i "relating to fissionable materials or the materials from which they are derived";
>
> ii "relating to the traffic in arms, ammunition and implements of war and to such traffic in other goods and materials as is carried on directly or indirectly for the purpose of supplying a military establishment";
>
> iii "taken in time of war or other emergency in international relations".

7.70. The phrase "taken in time of" in subparagraph (iii) describes the connection between the action and the events of war or other emergency in international relations in that subparagraph. The Panel understands this phrase to require that the action be taken *during* the war or other emergency in international relations. This chronological concurrence is also an objective fact, amenable to objective determination.

7.101. The Panel concludes that the adjectival clause "which it considers" in the chapeau of Article XXI(b) does not extend to the determination of the circumstances in each subparagraph. Rather, for action to fall within the scope of Article XXI(b), it must objectively be found to meet the requirements in one of the enumerated subparagraphs of that provision.

7.102. It follows from the Panel's interpretation of Article XXI(b), as vesting in panels the power to review whether the requirements of the enumerated subparagraphs are met, rather than leaving it to the unfettered discretion of the invoking Member, that Article XXI(b)(iii) of the GATT 1994 is not totally "self-judging" in the manner asserted by Russia.

7.103. Consequently, Russia's argument that the Panel lacks jurisdiction to review Russia's invocation of Article XXI(b)(iii) must fail. The Panel's interpretation of Article XXI(b)(iii) also means that it rejects the United States' argument that Russia's invocation of Article XXI(b)(iii) is "on-justiciable", to the extent that this argument also relies on the alleged totally "self-judging" nature of the provision.

7.104. Russia's invocation of Article XXI(b)(iii) being within the Panel's terms of reference under Article XXIII of the GATT 1994, as further elaborated and modified by the DSU, the Panel finds that it has jurisdiction to determine whether the requirements of Article XXI(b)(iii) of the GATT 1994 are satisfied.

(2) 전시 또는 기타 국제관계의 긴급 상황에서 취해진 조치인지 여부

7.119. Accordingly, Russia has identified the situation that it considers to be an emergency in international relations by reference to the following factors: (a) the time-period in which it arose and continues to exist, (b) that the situation involves Ukraine, (c) that it affects the security of Russia's border with Ukraine in various ways, (d) that it has resulted in other countries imposing sanctions against Russia, and (e) that the situation in question is publicly known. The Panel regards this as sufficient, in the particular circumstances of this dispute, to clearly identify the situation to which Russia is referring, and which it argues is an emergency in international relations.

7.120. Therefore, the Panel must determine whether this situation between Ukraine and Russia that has existed since 2014 constitutes an emergency in international relations within the meaning of subparagraph (iii) of Article XXI(b).

7.121. The Panel notes that it is not relevant to this determination which actor or actors bear international responsibility for the existence of this situation to which Russia refers. Nor is it necessary for the Panel to characterize the situation between Russia and Ukraine under international law in general.

7.122. There is evidence before the Panel that, at least as of March 2014, and continuing at least until the end of 2016, relations between Ukraine and Russia had deteriorated to such a degree that they were a matter of concern to the international community. By December 2016, the situation between Ukraine and Russia was recognized by the UN General Assembly as involving armed conflict.204 Further evidence of the gravity of the situation is the fact that, since 2014, a number of countries have imposed sanctions against Russia in connection with this situation.

7.123. Consequently, the Panel is satisfied that the situation between Ukraine and Russia since 2014 constitutes an emergency in international relations, within the meaning of subparagraph (iii) of Article XXI(b) of the GATT 1994.

7.124. It thus remains for the Panel to determine whether the measures taken by Russia with respect to Ukraine were "taken in time of" the emergency in international relations. In this regard, the Panel notes that the 2016 Belarus Transit Requirements were introduced by Russia on 1 January 2016, the 2016 Transit Bans on Non-Zero Duty and Resolution No. 778 Goods were introduced on 1 July 2016, and the 2014 Belarus-Russia Border Bans on Transit of Resolution No. 778 Goods were introduced by Russia in November 2014. All of the measures were therefore introduced during the emergency in international relations and thus were "taken in time of" such emergency for purposes of subparagraph (iii).

7.125. On the basis of the foregoing considerations, the Panel concludes that each of the measures at issue was "taken in time of" an emergency in international relations, within the meaning of subparagraph (iii) of Article XXI(b) of the GATT 1994.

(3) 핵심 안보이익을 보호하기 위한 조치에 해당하는지 여부

7.129. Russia argues that the adjectival clause means that both the deter-mination of a Member's essential security interests, and the determination of the necessity of the action taken for the protection of those interests, is left entirely to the discretion of the invoking Member. Several of the third parties also consider that Members have wide discretion to identify for themselves their essential security interests. Ukraine argues that, while all Members have the right to determine their own level of protection of essential security interests, that does not mean that a Member may unilaterally define what are essential security interests. According to Ukraine, it is for panels, rather than for Members, to interpret the term "essential security interests", which forms part of the WTO covered agreements, in accordance with customary rules of interpretation of public international law. Consistent with its interpretation of Article XXI(b)(iii), Ukraine argues that Russia has failed to identify the essential security interests that are threatened by the 2014 emergency, and has not explained or demonstrated the connection between the measures and its essential security interests. While Russia also argued that, pursuant to Article XXI(a) of the GATT 1994, it cannot be required to further explain its actions, beyond what it has declared in its first written submission and opening statement at the first meeting of the Panel, Ukraine considers that Russia cannot invoke Article XXI(a) of the GATT 1994 to evade its burden of proof under Article XXI(b)(iii).

7.130. "Essential security interests", which is evidently a narrower concept than "security interests", may generally be understood to refer to those interests relating to the quintessential functions of the state, namely, the protection of its territory and its population from external threats, and the maintenance of law and public order internally.

7.131. The specific interests that are considered directly relevant to the protection of a state from such external or internal threats will depend on the particular situation and perceptions of the state in question, and can be expected to vary with changing circumstances. For these reasons, it is left, in general, to every Member to define what it considers to be its essential security interests.

7.132. However, this does not mean that a Member is free to elevate any concern to that of an "essential security interest". Rather, the discretion of a Member to designate particular concerns as "essential security interests" is limited by its obligation to interpret and apply Article XXI(b)(iii) of the GATT 1994 in good faith. The Panel recalls that the obligation of good faith is a general principle of law and a principle of general international law which underlies all treaties, as codified in Article 31(1) ("[a] treaty shall be interpreted in good faith …") and Article 26 ("[e]very treaty … must be performed [by the parties] in good faith") of the Vienna Convention.

7.133. The obligation of good faith requires that Members not use the exceptions in Article XXI as a means to circumvent their obligations under the GATT 1994. A glaring example of this would be where a Member sought to release itself from the structure of "reciprocal and mutually advantageous arrangements" that constitutes the multilateral trading system simply by re-labelling trade interests that it had agreed to protect and promote within the system, as "essential security interests", falling outside the reach of that system.

7.134. It is therefore incumbent on the invoking Member to articulate the essential security interests said to arise from the emergency in international relations sufficiently enough to demonstrate their veracity.

7.135. What qualifies as a sufficient level of articulation will depend on the emergency in international relations at issue. In particular, the Panel considers that the less characteristic is the "emergency in international relations" invoked by the Member, i.e. the further it is removed from armed conflict, or a situation of breakdown of law and public order (whether in the invoking Member or in its immediate surroundings), the less obvious are the defence or military interests, or maintenance of law and public order interests, that can be generally expected to arise. In such cases, a Member would need to articulate its essential security interests with greater specificity than would be required when the emergency in international relations involved, for example, armed conflict.

7.136. In the case at hand, the emergency in international relations is very close to the "hard core" of war or armed conflict. While Russia has not explicitly articulated the essential security interests that it considers the measures at issue are necessary to protect, it did refer to certain characteristics of the 2014 emergency that concern the security of the Ukraine-Russia border.

7.137. Given the character of the 2014 emergency, as one that has been recognized by the UN General Assembly as involving armed conflict, and which affects the security of the border with an adjacent country and exhibits the other features identified by Russia, the essential security interests that thereby arise for Russia cannot be considered obscure or indeterminate. Despite its allusiveness, Russia's articulation of its essential security interests is minimally satisfactory in these circumstances. Moreover, there is nothing in Russia's expression of those interests to suggest that Russia invokes Article XXI(b)(iii) simply as a means to circumvent its obligations under the GATT 1994.

7.138. The obligation of good faith, […], applies not only to the Member's definition of the essential security interests said to arise from the particular emergency in international relations, but also, and most importantly, to their connection with the measures at issue. Thus, as concerns the application of Article XXI(b)(iii), this obligation is crystallized in demanding that the measures at issue meet a minimum requirement of plausibility in relation to the proffered essential security interests, i.e. that they are not implausible as measures protective of these interests.

7.139. The Panel must therefore review whether the measures are so remote from, or unrelated to, the 2014 emergency that it is implausible that Russia implemented the measures for the protection of its essential security interests arising out of the emergency.

7.145. In these circumstances, the measures at issue cannot be regarded as being so remote from, or unrelated to, the 2014 emergency, that it is implausible that Russia implemented the measures for the protection of its essential security interests arising out of that emergency. This conclusion is not undermined by evidence on the record that the general instability of the Ukraine-Russia border did not prevent some bilateral trade from taking place along parts of the border.

7.146. This being so, it is for Russia to determine the "necessity" of the measures for the protection of its essential security interests. This conclusion follows by logical necessity if the adjectival clause "which it considers" is to be given legal effect

7.148. The Panel finds that Russia has satisfied the conditions of the chapeau of Article XXI(b) of the GATT 1994.

7.149. Accordingly, the Panel finds that Russia has met the requirements for invoking Article XXI(b)(iii) of the GATT 1994 in relation to the measures at issue, and therefore the measures are covered by Article XXI(b)(iii) of the GATT 1994.

☑ 해　　설

최근 통상협정과 투자협정에 포함된 국가안보 예외(security exceptions) 조항은 새로운 조명을 받고 있다. 그러나 이 조항에 대한 그간의 분쟁 사례가 희소하여 법리 발전은 미미했다. 이 분쟁은 GATT 제XXI조에 포함된 국가안보 예외를 WTO 패널이 최초로 검토한 사안이라는 점에서 그 의의를 찾을 수 있다. 다만 이 분쟁은 양국간 교전상태의 존재라는 객관적 사실이 분명하여 제XXI조의 적용이 상대적으로 용이하였던 것으로 평가할 수 있다. 이에 이르지 않지만 최근 국가안보 예외 맥락에서 검토되는 다양한 분쟁 — 가령 미국의 국가안보를 이유로 한 일련의 수입제한 조치 및 일본의 한국에 대한 수출제한 조치 등 — 은 어떻게 평가될 것인지 아직은 불분명한 부분이 많이 남아 있다. 특히 미중 분쟁이 격화되며 서로 국가안보 측면에서 기존의 협정상 의무 이행을 재검토하는 단계로 진행하며 이 조항에 대한 활용 내지 남용 가능성은 더욱 높아지고 있다.

이 분쟁에서 WTO 패널은 국가안보 예외의 적용과 관련하여 가장 중요한 원칙 중 하나로 조치시행국의 선의(善意: good faith)를 내세웠다. 보다 구체적으로 이 문제는 결국 국가안보 예외를 원용하는 국가가 자신의 조치에 대해 그 "근거를 충분히 제시할 수 있는지(sufficiently demonstrate the veracity)" 여부와 직결된다.[2] 핵심 안보이익이 광범위한 영역을 대상으로 하고 그 판단에 있어 해당국의 독자적인 판단을 존중하여야 하지만 이를 근거없이 확

---

2) See *ibid.*, para. 7.134.

장하여 원용하는 것은 ― 즉 악의를 깔고 있는 기술적인 원용은 ― 허용될 수 없다는 것이다. 이는 결국 국가안보 예외도 안보상 이익보호와 자유교역이라는 상충하는 가치의 균형점을 찾는 작업이라는 생각에서 출발하고 있다. 다만 그 균형점이 다른 예외조항에 비해 더욱 원용국에 유리한 쪽으로 기울어져 있는 것으로 이해할 수 있을 것이다. 어쨌든 앞으로 이 조항 적용 여부를 따짐에 있어 문제의 조치를 왜 취하였는지에 대한 그 본질과 숨겨진 배경을 확인하는 것이 중요하다고 하겠다.

또한 이 분쟁 패널은 "핵심 안보이익(essential security interest)"이 무엇인지에 대해서도 중요한 언급을 했다. 바로 "외부로부터의 영토 및 국민의 보호, 그리고 국내적으로 법률과 공공질서의 유지라는 국가의 본질적 기능에 관련되는 이익"이라는 것이다.[3] 그리고 이는 단순한 "안보이익(security interests)"보다는 좁은 개념이라고 설명했다.[4] 이 언급은 "핵심 안보이익"이 여러 영역에 걸쳐 여러 방식으로 관련될 수 있음을 시사한다. 영토와 국민의 보호 그리고 법률과 질서의 유지는 여러 영역을 그 대상으로 할 수 있기 때문이다. 이 사건에서 우크라이나와 러시아 양국이 모두 상소하지 않아 패널 판정이 최종 판정으로 확정되었다.

➡ 참고문헌 ───────────

- 김보연, 국가안보 예외조항의 '자기판단' 범위 ― 국제법상 의미와 WTO협정에의 적용, 국제경제법연구 제17권 제2호(2019), p. 181.
- 배성호, A Study on the WTO Security Exceptions: Focusing on Russia ― Measures Concerning Traffic in Transit, 통상정보연구 제22권 제1호(2020), p. 191.
- T. Voon, Can International Trade Law Recover? The Security Exception in WTO Law: Entering a New Era, American Journal of International Law Vol. 113(2019), p. 45.
- D. Boklan & A. Bahri, The First WTO's Ruling on National Security Exception: Balancing Interests or Opening Pandora's Box?, World Trade

───────────

3) *Russia ― Traffic in Transit* Panel Report, *supra* note 13, para. 7.130.
4) *See Ibid.*

Review Vol. 19(2020), p. 123.

• T. L. Prazeres, Trade and National Security: Rising Risks for the WTO, World Trade Review Vol. 19(2020), p. 137.

• S. M. Blanco & A. Pehl, National Security Exceptions in International Trade and Investment Agreements — Justiciability and Standards of Review, Springer(2020).

• I. Bogdanova, Adjudication of the GATT security clause: to be or not to be, this is the question, World Trade Institute Working Paper No. 01/2019, University of Bern, Switzerland(2019).

제18장
─ ─ ─ ─ ─
분쟁의 평화적 해결

1. 인터한델 사건(1959)
— 국내적 구제 완료 원칙

Interhandel Case(Preliminary Objection).
Switzerland v. United States of America, 1959 ICJ Reports 6.

☑ 사   안

미국은 1942년 대 적성국 교역법(Trading with the Enemy Act)에 근거해 자국내 General Aniline and Film Company(GAF)의 자산을 압류했다. 이 회사의 대 주주는 스위스 회사인 인터한델이었지만, 실제 이 회사는 독일회사인 IG Farben의 통제하에 있다고 판단했기 때문이다. 이후 1946년 미국·영국·프랑스와 스위스는 워싱턴 협정을 체결해 스위스 내 독일재산의 조사와 청산 절차에 합의했다. 그런데 인터한델사의 성격에 대하여는 쉽게 합의가 이루어지지 않았다. 최종적으로 스위스 당국은 인터한델사가 독일 회사와 관계가 없다고 판단하고 자국 내 이 회사의 자산 동결을 취소하기로 결정했다. 그리고 미국에 대하여도 몰수된 이 회사 자산의 반환을 요청했다. 미국이 스위스 정부의 요청을 거부하자 인터한델사는 1948년 미국 법원에 이 사건을 제소했다.

재판과정에서 미국 연방법원은 인터한델사에 심리에 필요한 일정한 서류의 제출을 명했으나, 그중 일부 서류는 스위스 정부가 이미 압류를 명령한 상태라 제출할 수 없었다. 미국 연방지방법원은 스위스 정부의 이러한 조치를 부적절한 개입으로 판단해 3개월 내에 문제의 서류를 제출하지 않으면 인터한델사의 청구를 기각한다고 결정했다.[1] 이 같은 판단은 연방고등법원과 연방대법원에 의해서도 유지되었다.[2] 그러나 스위스 정부의 거부로 인터

---

1) 111 Fed. Sup. 435(1953).
2) 225 F.2d 532(1955) & 350 U.S. 937(1956).

한델사는 서류를 제출하지 못했고, 결국 연방지방법원은 인터한델사의 청구를 기각했다. 미국 국무부는 워싱톤 주재 스위스 공사에 이 사건이 기각되었음을 통지했다. 인터한델사는 이 판결에 상소했는데, 그 사이 스위스 정부는 1957년 10월 2일 이 사건을 ICJ에 제소했다. 그러나 그로부터 12일 후인 10월 14일 미국 연방대법원은 이송영장(writ of *certiorari*)을 발부해 이 사건의 심리재개가 가능해졌다. 이어 1958년 6월 연방대법원은 항소심에서의 인터한델의 패소판결을 번복하고, 사건을 지방법원으로 되돌려 보냈다.

ICJ의 소송에서 미국은 4가지 선결적 항변을 제기했으며, 그 중 하나가 이 사건에 대하여는 아직 국내적 구제가 완료되지 않았다는 주장이었다.

☑ 쟁   점
국내적 구제 완료 원칙의 적용.

☑ 판   결
국내 사법절차에서 재심절차가 진행되고 있다면 국내적 구제 완료 원칙을 준수했다고 보기 어렵다.

판 결 문

(p. 26-) The Third Preliminary Objection seeks a finding that "there is no jurisdiction in this Court to hear or determine the matters raised by the Swiss Application and Memorial, for the reason that Interhandel, whose case Switzerland is espousing, has not exhausted the local remedies available to it in the United States courts."

Although framed as an objection to the jurisdiction of the Court, this Objection must be regarded as directed against the admissibility of the Application of the Swiss Government. Indeed, by its nature it is to be regarded as a plea which would become devoid of object if the requirement of the prior exhaustion of local remedies were fulfilled.

The Court has indicated in what conditions the Swiss Government, basing itself on the idea that Interhandel's suit had been finally rejected in the United

States courts, considered itself entitled to institute proceedings by its Application of October 2nd, 1957. However, the decision given by the Supreme Court of the United States on October 14th, 1957, on the application of Interhandel made on August 6th, 1957, granted a writ of *certiorari* and readmitted Interhandel into the suit. The judgment of that Court on June 16th, 1958, reversed the judgment of the Court of Appeals dismissing Interhandel's suit and remanded the case to the District Court. It was thenceforth open to Interhandel to avail itself again of the remedies available to it under the Trading with the Enemy Act, and to seek the restitution of its shares by proceedings in the United States courts. Its suit is still pending in the United States courts. The Court must have regard to the situation thus created.

The rule that local remedies must be exhausted before international proceedings may be instituted is a well-established rule of customary international law; the rule has been generally observed in cases in which a State has adopted the cause of its national whose rights are claimed to have been disregarded in another State in violation of international law. Before resort may be had to an international court in such a situation, it has been considered necessary that the State where the violation occurred should have an opportunity to redress it by its own means, within the framework of its own domestic legal system. A *fortiori*[3] the rule must be observed when domestic proceedings are pending, as in the case of Interhandel, and when the two actions, that of the Swiss company in the United States courts and that of the Swiss Government in this Court, in its principal Submission, are designed to obtain the same result: the restitution of the assets of Interhandel vested in the United States.

☑ 해   설

이 사건에서 재판소는 4가지 사항에 대해 판단을 요청받았다. 본문에서 설명된 국내구제 완료 원칙 이외에 재판소가 다룬 3가지 문제는 다음과 같다. 첫째 당해 분쟁은 미국이 국제사법재판소의 관할권을 수락하기 이전에 발생했고, 둘째 선택조항이 미국에 대해서 구속력을 갖기 이전에 분쟁이 발생했으며, 셋째 이 사건의 내용은 미국의 국내 관할사항에 속하므로 국제사법재판소는 관할권이 없다는 주장이었다.

---

3) with stronger reason — 저자 주.

이에 대해서 국제사법재판소는 먼저 첫 번째 문제에 대해서는 당해 분쟁이 1946년 8월 26일 미국의 선택조항 수락이 발효한 이후인 1947년 1월 11일 미국 국무부에 대한 스위스의 요청이 거절된 때에 발생한 것으로 볼 수 있다고 판단했다. 두 번째 문제에 대해서는 스위스의 선택조항 수락 선언은 분쟁 발생 이후인 1948년 7월 28일부터 발효되었고 동 선택조항에는 스위스 수락선언 이후에 발생한 분쟁에 대해서만 재판소 관할권을 인정한다는 것이 포함되어 있지 않다고 하더라도(미국의 경우에는 미국의 선택조항 수락 선언 이후에 발생한 분쟁에 대해서만 재판소 관할권을 인정하고 있다) 이것이 상호주의 원칙에 의해서 재판소의 관할권을 배제하는 것은 아니라고 판단했다. 세 번째 문제에 대해서 재판소는 당해 분쟁은 충분히 국제적 성격을 갖고 있다고 판단했다.

본문에서 소개된 국내적 구제 완료 원칙과 관련하여서는 당해 분쟁이 미국 법원 내에서 계쟁 중이고, 국내적 구제 완료 원칙은 국제법상 확고히 확립된 원칙이라는 점을 확인했다. 이렇게 국내적 구제 미완료에 기한 미국의 선결적 항변이 받아들여짐에 따라서 재판소는 더 이상 사건 본안에 대한 심의를 진행하지 아니했다.

한편 1963년 12월 미국과 스위스는 이 사건처리에 관하여 합의를 했다. 이에 1964년 4월에는 미국 법원에서의 심리도 최종적으로 중단되었다. 합의의 내용은 압류된 주식의 89%를 매각하여 그 대금을 양측이 절반씩 갖고, 나머지 11%는 미국에 귀속한다는 것이었다.

➡ 참고문헌 ─────────────────────────────

• 이한기, 인터한델 사건, (서울대) 법학 제6권 제1호(1964), p. 120.
• T. Moon, The Incidence of the Rule of Exhaustion of Local Remedies, BYIL Vol. 35(1960), p. 83.
• K. R. Simmonds, The Interhandel Case, ICLQ Vol. 10(1961), p. 495.

2. 평화조약 해석에 관한 사건(1950)
— 분쟁해결에 관한 조약 규정의 해석

Interpretation of Peace Treaties with Bulgaria, Hungary
and Romania.
Advisory Opinion, 1950 ICJ Reports 65: 1950 ICJ Reports 221
(second Phase).

☑ 사   안

제2차 대전 후인 1947년 연합국과 체결한 평화조약에서 불가리아, 헝가리, 루마니아는 사상과 표현의 자유, 언론출판의 자유, 종교예배의 자유, 정치적 의견의 자유, 집회의 자유 등을 포함한 인권과 기본적 자유를 보장하기 위하여 필요한 모든 조치를 취할 것을 약속했다. 1947년 말 미국과 영국은 이러한 약속이 준수되지 않고 있다고 비난했으나, 소련은 이에 동의하지 않았다. 위 평화조약에는 조약의 해석과 적용에 관하여 분쟁이 발생하는 경우, 1차적으로 협의를 통하여 해결하고, 이를 통하여 해결되지 않는 분쟁은 3인으로 구성된 위원회에서 해결하도록 규정하고 있었다. 3인의 위원은 양 분쟁 당사국이 각 1인씩 추천하고, 제3의 위원은 양 분쟁 당사국들이 합의하여 구성하도록 규정했다. 다만 제3의 위원에 대한 합의가 이루어지지 않는 경우에는 유엔 사무총장이 이를 임명하도록 규정했다. 미국과 영국은 평화조약의 이행문제를 위원회에 회부하려고 했으나, 불가리아·헝가리 및 루마니아 등은 자국측 위원의 임명부터 거부했다. 1949년 10월 유엔 총회는 이 평화조약의 해석과 관련하여 다음과 같은 쟁점에 대한 ICJ의 권고적 의견을 구하기로 결의했다. ICJ는 다음 질문을 2단계로 나누어 답했다.

☑ 쟁 점

(1) 불가리아, 헝가리 및 루마니아 정부는 위원회 구성을 위하여 지국측 위원을 임명할 의무가 있는가?

(2) 일방 분쟁 당사국이 의무를 위반하고 자국측 위원을 임명하지 않을 경우, 유엔 사무총장은 제3의 위원을 임명할 수 있는가?

(3) 일반 분쟁 당사국과 유엔 사무총장이 임명한 위원만으로 분쟁을 해결할 권한이 있는 위원회를 구성할 수 있는가?

☑ 판 결

(1) 분쟁 당사국은 평화조약의 분쟁 해결조항에 따라서 위원회를 구성하는 경우 자국측 위원을 임명할 의무가 있다.

(2) 그렇지만 분쟁 당사국이 위원 임명 의무를 해태하는 경우 유엔 사무총장이 세 번째 위원을 임명할 수는 없다.

판 결 문

(p. 75-)[1] In these circumstances,[2] it becomes necessary to take up Question II, which is as follows:

'Are the Governments of Bulgaria, Hungary and Romania obligated to carry out the provisions of the articles referred to in Question I, including the provisions for the appointment of their representatives to the Treaty Commissions?'

[…]

The real meaning of Question II, in the opinion of the Court, is this: In view of the disputes which have arisen and which have so far not been settled, are Bulgaria, Hungary and Romania obligated to carry out, respectively, the provisions of Article 36 of the Treaty with Bulgaria, Article 40 of the Treaty with Hungary,

---

[1] ICJ Reports 1950, p. 75-.

[2] 질문 I에 대한 답에서 ICJ는 평화조약에 관한 분쟁이 존재한다고 인정했다.

and Article 38 of the Treaty with Romania?

The articles for the settlement of disputes provide that any dispute which is not settled by direct diplomatic negotiations shall be referred to the Three Heads of Mission. If not resolved by them within a period of two months, the dispute shall, unless the parties to the dispute agree upon another means of settlement, be referred at the request of either party to the dispute to a Commission composed of one representative of each party and a third member, to be selected in accordance with the relevant articles of the Treaties.

The diplomatic documents presented to the Court show that the United Kingdom and the United States of America on the one hand, and Bulgaria, Hungary and Romania on the other, have not succeeded in settling their disputes by direct negotiations. They further show that these disputes were not resolved by the Heads of Mission within the prescribed period of two months. It is a fact that the parties to the disputes have not agreed upon any other means of settlement. It is also a fact that the United Kingdom and the United States of America, after the expiry of the prescribed period, requested that the disputes should be settled by the Commissions mentioned in the Treaties.

This situation led the General Assembly to put Question II so as to obtain guidance for its future action.

The Court finds that all the conditions required for the commencement of the stage of the settlement of disputes by the Commissions have been fulfilled.

In view of the fact that the Treaties provide that any dispute shall be referred to a Commission at the request of either party', it follows that either party is obligated, at the request of the other party, to co-operate in constituting the Commission, in particular by appointing its representative. Otherwise the method of settlement by Commissions provided for in the Treaties would completely fail in its purpose.

The reply to Question II, as interpreted above, must therefore be in the affirmative. [⋯]

(p. 227-)[3] The question at issue is whether the provision empowering the Secretary-General to appoint the third member of the Commission applies to the present case, in which one of the parties refuses to appoint its own representative to the Commission.

It has been contended that the term "third member" is used here simply to

---

3) ICJ Reports 1950, p. 227-.

distinguish the neutral member from the two Commissioners appointed by the parties without implying that the third member can be appointed only when the two national Commissioners have already been appointed, and that therefore the mere fact of the failure of the parties, within the stipulated period, to select the third member by mutual agreement satisfies the condition required for the appointment of the latter by the Secretary-General.

The Court considers that the text of the Treaties does not admit of this interpretation. While the text in its literal sense does not completely exclude the possibility of the appointment of the third member before the appointment of both national Commissioners it is nevertheless true that according to the natural and ordinary meaning of the terms it was intended that the appointment of both the national Commissioners should precede that of the third member. This clearly results from the sequence of the events contemplated by the article: appointment of a national Commissioner by each party selection of a third member by mutual agreement of the parties failing such agreement within a month, his appointment by the Secretary-General. Moreover, this is the normal order followed in the practice of arbitration, and in the absence of any express provision to the contrary there is no reason to suppose that the parties wished to depart from it.

The Secretary-General's power to appoint a third member is derived solely from the agreement of the parties as expressed in the disputes clause of the Treaties; by its very nature such a clause must be strictly construed and can be applied only in the case expressly provided for therein. The case envisaged in the Treaties is exclusively that of the failure of the parties to agree upon the selection of a third member and by no means the much more serious case of a complete refusal of co-operation by one of them, taking the form of refusing to appoint its own Commissioner. The power conferred upon the Secretary-General to help the parties out of the difficulty of agreeing upon a third member cannot be extended to the situation which now exists.

Reference has been made for the purpose of justifying the reversal of the normal order of appointment, to the possible advantage that might result, in certain circumstances, from the appointment of a third member before the appointment by the parties of their respective commissioners. Such a change in the normal sequence could only be justified if it were shown by the attitude of the parties that they desired such a reversal in order to facilitate the constitution of the Commissions in accordance with the terms of the Treaties. But such is not the present case. The

Governments of Bulgana, Hungary and Romania have from the beginning denied the very existence of a dispute, and have absolutely refused to take part, in any mannes whatever, in the procedure provided for in the disputes clauses of the Treaties. Even after the Court had given its Advisory Opinion of March 3oth, 1950, which declared that these three Governments were bound to carry out the provisions of the Peace Treaties for the settlement of disputes, particularly the obligation to appoint their own Commissioners, these Governments have continued to adopt a purely negative attitude.

In these circumstances, the appointment of a third member by the Secretary-General, instead of bringing about the constitution of a three member Commission such as the Treaties provide for, would result only in the constitution of a two-member Commission. A Commission consisting of two members is not the kind of commission for which the Treaties have provided. The opposition of the Commissioner of the only party represented could prevent a Commission so constituted from reaching any decision whatever. Such a Commission could only decide by unanimity, whereas the dispute clause provides that "the decision of the majority of the members of the Commission shall be the decision of the Commission and shall be accepted by the parties as definitive and binding". Nor would the decisions of a Commission of two members, one of whom is appointed by one party only, have the same degree of moral authority as those of a threemember Commission. In every respect, the result would be contrary to the letter as well as the spirit of the Treaties.

In short, the Secretary-General would be authozised to proceed to the appointment of a third member only if it were possible to constitute a Commission in conformity with the provisions of the Treaties. In the present case, the refusal by the Governments of Bulgaria, Hungary and Romania to appoint their own Commissioners has made the constitution of such a Commission impossible and has deprived the appointment of the third member by the Secretary-General of every purpose.

As the Court has declared in its Opinion of March 30th, 1950, the Governments of Bulgaria, Hungary and Romania are under an obligation to appoint their representatives to the Treaty Commissions, and it is clear that refusal to fulfil a treaty obligation involves international responsibility. Nevertheless, such a refusal cannot alter the conditions contemplated in the Treaties for the exercise by the Secretary-General of his power of appointment.

These conditions are not present in this case, and their absence is not made good by the fact that it is due to the breach of a treaty obligation. The failure of machinery for settling disputes by reason of the practical impossibility of creating the Commission provided for in the Treaties is one thing international responsibility is another. The breach of a treaty obligation cannot be remedied by creating a Commission which is not the kind of Commission contemplated by the Treaties. It is the duty of the Court to interpret the Treaties, not to revise them.

The principle of interpretation expressed in the maxim : *Ut res magis valeat quam pereat*,[4] often referred to as the rule of effectiveness, cannot justify the Court in attributing to the provisions for the settlement of disputes in the Peace Treaties a meaning which, as stated above, would be contrary to their letter and spirit.

It has been pointed out that an arbitration commission may make a valid decision although the original number of its members, as fixed by the arbitration agreement, is later reduced by such circumstances as the withdrawal of one of the commissioners. These cases presuppose the initial validity of a commission, con-stituted in conformity with the will of the parties as expressed in the arbitration agreement, whereas the appointment of the third member by the Secretary-General in circumstances other than those contemplated in the Treaties raises precisely the question of the initial validity of the constitution of the Commission. In law, the two situations are clearly distinct and it is impossible to argue from one to the other.

Finally, it has been alleged that a negative answer by the Court to Question III would seriously jeopardize the future of the large number of arbitration clauses which have been drafted on the same model as that which appears in the Peace Treaties with Bulgaria, Hungary and Romania. The ineffectiveness in the present case of the clauses dealing with the settlement of disputes does not permit such a generalization. An examination of the practice of arbitration shows that, whereas the draftsmen of arbitration conventions have very often taken care to provide for the consequences of the inability of the parties to agree on the appointment of a third member, they have, apart from exceptional cases, refrained from anticipating a refusal by a party to appoint its own commissioner. The few Treaties containing express provisions for such a refusal indicate that the States which adopted this course felt the impossibility of remedying this situation simply by way of inter-pretation. In fact, the risk of such a possibility of a refusal is a small one, because

---

4) It is better for a thing to have effect than to be void. 무효보다는 효과가 있는 것이 낫다.

normally each party has a direct interest in the appointment of its commissioner and must in any case be presumed to observe its treaty obligations. That this was not so in the present case does not justify the Court in exceeding its judicial function on the pretext of remedying a default for the occurrence of which the Treaties have made no provision.

☑ 해   설

1947년 평화조약의 해석과 이행을 위한 혼성위원회 구성과 관련하여 국제사법재판소는 1950년 3월 30일과 1950년 7월 18일 두 차례에 걸쳐서 권고적 의견을 제시했다. 당시 유엔 총회는 다음 4개 사항에 대해서 국제사법재판소에 권고적 의견을 구했다.

1. 평화조약상 분쟁해결에 대한 조항에 따른 분쟁이 존재하는지 여부가 외교문서의 교환에 의해서 나타나는지 여부
2. 불가리아 등 3개국이 위원회 구성 시 자신들을 대표하는 위원을 임명할 의무가 있는지 여부
3. 만일 이들이 위원 임명 의무를 이행하지 않는 경우 유엔 사무총장이 세 번째 위원을 임명할 수 있는지 여부
4. 만일 한 당사국 측에서 임명한 위원과 유엔사무총장이 임명한 위원만 있는 경우 위원회가 해당 분쟁을 해결할 수 있는 권한이 있는지 여부

첫 번째 권고적 의견은 처음 2개의 문제에 대해서 판단을 했는데 첫 번째 이슈에 대해서는 특정 평화조약상 의무 이행 여부에 대해서 양측 간의 이견이 있으므로 분쟁이 존재한다고 확인했다. 그리고 두 번째 문제에 대해서는 평화조약의 이행을 위해서 명백히 양측은 각각의 위원을 임명할 의무가 있다는 것이 이들의 애당초 의사이고, 따라서 불가리아 등 3개국은 위원회 구성시 자신들을 대표하는 위원을 임명할 의무가 있다고 확인했다.

그 후 문제의 3개국이 재판소에 의해서 주어진 30일 내에 자국 측 위원을 임명하지 않자 재판소는 나머지 2개의 문제에 대해서 권고적 의견을 내

었다. 이에 따라서 세 번째 문제에 대해서 재판소는 유엔 사무총장이 세 번째 위원을 임명할 수 있는 권한은 오로지 양 측이 먼저 각각의 위원을 임명한 후에만 가능하기 때문에 유엔 사무총장은 세 번째 위원을 임명할 수 없다고 판단했으며, 이에 따라서 네 번째 문제는 다뤄지지 않았다.

　　이러한 국제사법재판소의 권고적 의견의 결과에도 불구하고 관련 국가에 대해 유엔에 의한 어떠한 조치로 이어지지는 않았다. 유엔 총회는 단지 1950년 11월 3일 3개국을 비난하는 결정을 채택했을 뿐이다. 그러나 국제사법재판소의 권고적 의견은 이후 중재합의나 중재재판소 구성을 위한 문구 작성에 변화를 가져왔다. 즉 1957년 「분쟁의 평화적 해결에 관한 유럽협약」(European Convention for the Peaceful Settlement of Disputes 1957)에서 볼 수 있듯 위원회 구성이 잘 합의되지 않는 경우에는 제3자에 의해서 위원임명이 가능할 수 있도록 문구를 미리 넣음으로써 본 건과 같은 바람직하지 못한 결과를 피하려 했다.

▶ 참고문헌 ────────────────────────────────

• K. S. Carlston, Interpretation of Peace Treaties with Bulgaria, Hungary and Romania, AJIL Vol. 44(1950), p. 734.

3. 노르웨이 공채 사건(1957)
― 선택조항 유보의 상호주의적 적용

Certain Norwegian Loans.
France v. Norway, 1957 ICJ Reports 9.

☑ 사   안

　　1885년부터 1909년 사이 노르웨이 정부와 노르웨이 은행은 프랑스를 비롯한 외국 시장에서 많은 공채를 발행했다. 제1차 대전의 발발로 노르웨이 은행권의 금태환은 정지되었다. 이후 금태환이 재개되었다가 정지되는 일이 몇번 반복되다가 1931년 이후에는 태환 정지가 계속되었다. 노르웨이는 1923년 크론화로 표시된 금전채무를 금으로 지불하기로 한 채무라도, 명목 금가치를 기준으로 한 노르웨이 화폐로의 지불을 채권자가 거부한다면 금태환 의무가 적용되지 않는 기간 중에는 채무 지불을 연기할 수 있다는 법률을 제정했다. 1925년 프랑스 정부는 노르웨이의 이 같은 일방적 조치를 외국 채권자에게 강요할 수 없다고 주장했다. 프랑스 정부는 각 공채증서에는 금 시세에 따른 상환규정이 포함되어 있다고 주장했다. 이후 양국간에는 장기간의 교섭이 계속되었으나 합의를 볼 수 없었다. 결국 1955년 프랑스는 이 문제를 ICJ에 제소했다.

　　양국 정부는 일정한 유보 하에 ICJ 규정 제36조 2항 선택조항을 수락하고 있었다. 그 중 프랑스의 유보에는 "이 선언은 프랑스 정부가 이해하는 바와 같이 본질적으로 국내관할에 속하는 사항에 관한 분쟁에는 적용하지 않는다"는 내용이 포함되어 있었다(이른바 자동유보). 프랑스의 본건 제소에 대하여 노르웨이 정부는 4개의 선결적 항변을 제기했다. 그 중 첫 번째 항변은 이 문제는 노르웨이의 국내법상의 문제에 불과하므로 재판소의 관할에 속하지 아니하며, 보충적으로 프랑스의 위 유보를 이용하여 이 분쟁은 노르웨이가 이해하는 한 국내문제이므로 재판소의 관할권이 성립하지 않는다는 주장이었다.

☑ 쟁　점

ICJ 강제관할권에 관한 선택조항에 관하여 상대국이 한 유보 내용을 상호주의에 의해서 원용가능한지 여부.

☑ 판　결

상호주의 원칙에 따라서 프랑스의 국내문제에 관한 유보를 노르웨이도 원용할 수 있으며, 따라서 ICJ는 이 사건에 관한 관할권이 없다.

판 결 문

(p. 23-) In the Preliminary Objections filed by the Norwegian Government it is stated:

'The Norwegian Government did not insert any such reservation in its own Declaration. But it has the right to rely upon the restrictions placed by France upon her own undertakings.

Convinced that the dispute which has been brought before the Court by the Application of July 6th, 1955, is within the domestic jurisdiction, the Norwegian Government considers itself fully entitled to rely on this right. Accordingly, it requests the Court to decline, on grounds that it lacks jurisdiction, the function which the French Government would have it assume.'

In considering this ground of the Objection the Court notes in the first place that the present case has been brought before it on the basis of Article 36, paragraph 2, of the Statute and of the corresponding Declarations of acceptance of compulsory jurisdiction; that in the present case the jurisdiction of the Court depends upon the Declarations made by the Parties in accordance with Article 36, paragraph 2, of the Statute on condition of reciprocity; and that, since two unilateral declarations are involved, such jurisdiction is conferred upon the Court only to the extent to which the Declarations coincide in conferring it. A comparison between the two Declarations shows that the French Declaration accepts the Court's jurisdiction within narrower limits than the Norwegian Declaration; consequently, the common will of the Parties, which is the basis of the Court's jurisdiction, exists within these narrower limits indicated by the French reservation. [⋯]

France has limited her acceptance of the compulsory jurisdiction of the Court by excluding beforehand disputes 'relating to matters which are essentially within the national jurisdiction as understood by the Government of the French Republic'. In accordance with the condition of reciprocity to which acceptance of the compulsory jurisdiction is made subject in both Declarations and which is provided for in Article 36, paragraph 3, of the Statute, Norway, equally with France, is entitled to except from the compulsory jurisdiction of the Court disputes understood by Norway to be essentially within its national jurisdiction.

In its Observations and Submissions on the Preliminary Objections raised by the Norwegian Government, the French Government points to what it regards as a contradiction in the attitude of Norway:

> 'Between France and Norway, there exists a treaty which makes the payment of any contractual debt a question of international law. In this connection the two States cannot therefore speak of domestic jurisdiction.'

The treaty here referred to is the Second Hague Convention of 1907 respecting the limitation of the employment of force for the recovery of contract debts. The French Government invokes it principally against the first ground of the first Objection and as such it does not fall for consideration here; but the passage quoted from the Observations and Submissions purports to show also that the second ground of the first Objection is not valid since both Parties are signatories of the Second Hague Convention of 1907. This calls for but brief observations by the Court.

The purpose of the Convention in question is that indicated in its title, that is to say 'the Limitation of the Employment of Force for the Recovery of Contract Debts'. The aim of this Convention is not to introduce compulsory arbitration in the limited field to which it relates. The only obligation imposed by the Convention is that an intervening Power must not have recourse to force before it has tried arbitration. The Court can find no reason why the fact that the two Parties are signatories of the Second Hague Convention of 1907 should deprive Norway of the right to invoke the reservation in the French Declaration. [⋯]

As already shown, the Application of the French Government is based clearly and precisely on the Norwegian and French Declarations under Article 36, paragraph 2, of the Statute. In these circumstances the Court would not be justified in seeking a basis for its jurisdiction different from that which the French Government itself set out in its Application and by reference to which the case has been presented by both Parties to the Court.

From one point of view it might be said that the second ground of the first Objection, namely the ground based on the reservation in the French Declaration, is merely subsidiary in character. It is true that the first ground of the first Preliminary Objection relies upon the proposition that the Court lacks jurisdiction because the dispute falls to be dealt with under the municipal law of Norway. But Norway has also relied upon the second ground of its first Preliminary Objection. Norway requests the Court 'to decline, on grounds that it lacks jurisdiction, the function which the French Government would have it assume'. It is clear that this request is based on both grounds, the character of the dispute and the French reservation. In the opinion of the Court, the second ground cannot be regarded as subsidiary, in the sense that Norway would invoke the French reservation only in the event of the first ground of its Objection being held to be legally unfounded. The Court's competence is challenged on both grounds and the Court is free to base its decision on the ground which in its judgment is more direct and conclusive.

Not only did the Norwegian Government invoke the French reservation, but it maintained this second ground of its first Objection throughout and at no time did it abandon it. [⋯]

The Court does not consider that it should examine whether the French reservation is consistent with the undertaking of a legal obligation and is compatible with Article 36, paragraph 6, of the Statute which provides:

> "In the event of a dispute as to whether the Court has jurisdiction, the matter shall be settled by the decision of the Court."

The validity of the reservation has not been questioned by the Parties. It is clear that France fully maintains its Declaration, including the reservation, and that Norway relies upon the reservation.

In consequence the Court has before it a provision which both Parties to the dispute regard as constituting an expression of their common will relating to the competence of the Court. The Court does not therefore consider that it is called upon to enter into an examination of the reservation in the light of considerations which are not presented by the issues in the proceedings. The Court, without prejudging the question, gives effect to the reservation as it stands and as the Parties recognize it.

The Court considers that the Norwegian Government is entitled, by virtue of the condition of reciprocity, to invoke the reservation contained in the French Declaration of March 1st, 1949; that this reservation excludes from the jurisdiction of the Court the dispute which has been referred to it by the Application of the French Government; that consequently the Court is without jurisdiction to entertain the Application.

☑ 해   설

ICJ의 강제관할권을 인정하는 선택조항은 이를 수락한 국가에 대해서만 효력이 있다. 선택조항 수락시에는 적지 않은 유보가 첨부되고 있다. 이 경우 국제법상 상호주의 원칙에 따라 강제관할권의 수락 선언시 행한 유보는 상대국도 원용할 수 있다. 이는 강제관할권 수락 선언에 포함된 당사국의 모든 유보를 서로 원용할 수 있게 되는 결과를 가져오게 된다. 이러한 원칙에 따라 노르웨이는 프랑스가 행한 수락선언에 포함된 유보를 원용하여 ICJ가 관할권이 없다고 주장했고, 재판소는 이를 확인했다.

한편 ICJ의 출범 이래 선택조항 수락시의 이른바 자동유보의 유효성에 관하여 논란이 제기되어 왔었다. 자동유보란 국내문제는 ICJ의 관할에 포함되지 않으며, 무엇이 국내문제인지는 자국이 판단하겠다는 유보이다. 이에 따르면 ICJ 규정 제36조 2항의 선택조항을 수락한 국가라도 제기된 문제가 국내문제라고 선언하기만 하면 자동적으로 재판소의 관할권이 부인당하게 된다. 이는 과거 미국과 프랑스 등 많은 국가가 활용했던 유보이며, 아직도 상당수의 국가가 이러한 유보를 유지하고 있다.

그런데 ICJ 규정 제36조 6항은 관할권의 존부에 관해 다툼이 있을 경우 이 문제는 재판소가 결정한다고 규정하고 있으므로, 이른바 자동유보는 이 조항에 저촉되어 무효라는 주장이 계속되어 왔다. 만약 자동유보가 무효라면 그 같은 조건에서 선택조항을 수락한 국가의 지위는 어떻게 되는가? 무효인 자동유보 없이 선택조항을 수락한 것으로 해석해야 하는가? 아니면 선택조항 수락 자체를 무효로 하여야 하는가? 이 사건에서 ICJ는 자동유보의 법적 효력을 판단할 수도 있었으나, 재판부는 프랑스와 노르웨이 양 당사국이 모두 이의를 제기하지 않는다는 이유에서 이 문제를 다루지 않기로 했다. 한편 Lauterpacht 판사는 소수의견에서 프랑스의 자동유보는 ICJ 규정 제36조 6항 위반으로 무효이고, 이 유보는 프랑스의 본질적인 입장을 구성하므로 결국 자동유보가 무효라면 프랑스의 선택조항 수락 자체를 무효로 보아야 한다고 해석했다.

➡ 참고문헌 ─────────────────────────────────

- G. R. Delaume, Jurisdiction of Courts and International Loans, American Journal of Comparative Law Vol. 6(1957), p. 189.
- R. Y. Jennings, Recent Cases on "Automatic" Reservations to the Optional Clause, ICLQ Vol. 7(1958), p. 349.

4. 동티모르 사건(1995)
― 제3국에 영향을 미칠 판결의 진행

Case concerning East Timor.
Portugal v. Australia. 1995 ICJ Reports 90.

☑ 사   안

티모르 섬의 동반부는 16세기 포르투갈의 식민지가 되었으며, 서반부는 과거 네덜란드의 식민지였다가 이후 인도네시아의 일부로 되었다. 포르투갈이 자국내 정치적 혼란으로 지배력이 약화되자, 동티모르에서는 독립운동이 시작되었다. 1975년 동티모르는 독립을 선언했으나, 곧바로 내전에 휩싸였다. 그러자 인도네시아 군이 동티모르를 침략하여 점령하고 이를 자국의 27번째 주로 만들었다. 유엔 안전보장이사회는 인도네시아의 침략을 비난하며, 포르투갈을 동티모르의 명목상 시정권자로 인정했다. 이 사건은 그러한 와중에 발생했다.

1989년 호주와 인도네시아는 동티모르 부근의 대륙붕을 개발하는 협정을 체결했다. 포르투갈은 이 협정이 동티모르의 자결권과 이에 대한 합법적 시정국인 자신의 권리를 침해한다고 주장하며 호주를 ICJ에 제소했다. 포르투갈과 호주는 선택조항을 수락하고 있었기 때문에 ICJ의 관할권이 성립할 수 있었다. 그러나 인도네시아는 선택조항을 수락하지 않고 있었기 때문에 제소할 수 없었다. 이 사건은 내용상 인도네시아와 밀접한 관계가 있을 수밖에 없는데, 인도네시아의 참여 없이도 이 소송을 진행할 수 있는가가 문제되었다.

☑ 쟁　점

ICJ는 소송에 참여하지 않는 제3국의 권리에 영향을 미칠 분쟁에 대하여 관할권을 행사할 수 있는가?

☑ 판　결

재판소는 당사국의 동의가 있어야만 관할권을 행사할 수 있으므로, 만약 재판이 제3국의 권리의무에 직접적인 영향을 미칠 경우 재판소는 관할권을 행사할 수 없다.

판　결　문

26. The Court recalls in this respect that one of the fundamental principles of its Statute is that it cannot decide a dispute between States without the consent of those States to its jurisdiction. This principle was reaffirmed in the Judgment given by the Court in the case concerning Monetary Gold Removed from Rome in 1943 and confirmed in several of its subsequent decisions [⋯].

27. The Court notes that Portugal's claim that, in entering into the 1989 Treaty with Indonesia, Australia violated the obligation to respect Portugal's status as administering Power and that of East Timor as a non-self-governing territory, is based on the assertion that Portugal alone, in its capacity as administering Power, had the power to enter into the Treaty on behalf of East Timor; that Australia disregarded this exclusive power, and, in so doing, violated its obligations to respect the status of Portugal and that of East Timor.

The Court also observes that Australia, for its part, rejects Portugal's claim to the exclusive power to conclude treaties on behalf of East Timor, and the very fact that it entered into the 1989 Treaty with Indonesia shows that it considered that Indonesia had that power. Australia in substance argues that even if Portugal had retained that power, on whatever basis, after withdrawing from East Timor, the possibility existed that the power could later pass to another State under general international law, and that it did so pass to Indonesia; Australia affirms moreover that, if the power in question did pass to Indonesia, it was acting in conformity with international law in entering into the 1989 Treaty with that State, and could not have violated any of the obligations Portugal attributes to it. Thus, for Australia, the fundamental question in the present case is ultimately whether, in 1989, the power to conclude a treaty on behalf of East Timor in relation to its continental shelf lay with Portugal or with Indonesia.

28. The Court has carefully considered the argument advanced by Portugal which seeks to separate Australia's behaviour from that of Indonesia. However, in the view of the Court, Australia's behaviour cannot be assessed without first entering into the question why it is that Indonesia could not lawfully have concluded the 1989 Treaty, while Portugal allegedly could have done so; the very subject-matter of the Court's decision would necessarily be a determination whether, having regard to the circumstances in which Indonesia entered and remained in East Timor, it could or could not have acquired the power to enter into treaties on behalf of East Timor relating to the resources of its continental shelf. The Court could not make such a determination in the absence of the consent of Indonesia.

29. However, Portugal puts forward an additional argument aiming to show that the principle formulated by the Court in the case concerning Monetary Gold Removed from Rome in 1943 is not applicable in the present case. It maintains, in effect, that the rights which Australia allegedly breached were rights *erga omnes* and that accordingly Portugal could require it, individually, to respect them regardless of whether or not another State had conducted itself in a similarly unlawful manner.

In the Court's view, Portugal's assertion that the right of peoples to self-determination, as it evolved from the Charter and from United Nations practice, has an *erga omnes* character, is irreproachable. The principle of self-determination of peoples has been recognized by the United Nations Charter and in the jurisprudence of the Court([⋯]); it is one of the essential principles of contemporary international law.

However, the Court considers that the *erga omnes* character of a norm and the rule of consent to jurisdiction are two different things. Whatever the nature of the obligations invoked, the Court could not rule on the lawfulness of the conduct of a State when its judgment would imply an evaluation of the lawfulness of the conduct of another State which is not a party to the case. Where this is so, the Court cannot act, even if the right in question is a right *erga omnes*. [⋯]

33. It follows from this that the Court would necessarily have to rule upon the lawfulness of Indonesia's conduct as a prerequisite for deciding on Portugal's contention that Australia violated its obligation to respect Portugal's status as administering Power, East Timor's status as a nonself-governing territory and the right of the people of the Territory to self-determination and to permanent sovereignty over its wealth and natural resources

34. [···] However, in this case, the effects of the judgment requested by Portugal would amount to a determination that Indonesia's entry into and continued presence in East Timor are unlawful and that, as a consequence, it does not have the treaty-making power in matters relating to the continental shelf resources of East Timor. Indonesia's rights and obligations would thus constitute the very subject-matter of such a judgment made in the absence of that State's consent. Such a judgment would run directly counter to the "well-established principle of international law embodied in the Court's Statute, namely, that the Court can only exercise jurisdiction over a State with its consent"(*Monetary Gold Removed from Rome in 1943, Judgment, I.C.J. Reports 1954*, p. 32).

35. The Court concludes that it cannot, in this case, exercise the jurisdiction [···].

☑ 해   설

ICJ의 관할권은 분쟁 당사국의 동의에 기초한다. 따라서 만약 제소된 분쟁에 대한 판결이 현재의 당사국 외 제3국의 권리 · 의무를 대상으로 하는 경우 해당 국가의 동의 없이 ICJ는 사건을 심리할 수 없다. 이 같은 법리는 일찍이 The Monetary Gold Removed from Rome in 1943(Preliminary Question) (1954 ICJ Reports 19)에서 부각되어 흔히 Monetary Gold 원칙이라고도 부른다. 다만 판결의 결과 제3국의 법익이 단지 영향을 받을 수 있다는 이유만으로는 ICJ가 재판진행을 거부하지 않는다. 즉 제3국의 법적 책임에 대한 판단이 재판을 진행하기 위한 전제조건인 경우에만 이 원칙이 적용된다.

이 사건에서 포르투갈은 호주가 대세적 의무인 민족자결권을 위반하여 대륙붕개발협정을 체결했으므로, 자신은 호주에 대해 이를 존중하라는 요구를 할 수 있다고 주장했다. 그러나 재판부는 민족자결권의 존중이 대세적 의무임에는 이의가 없으나, 대세적 의무를 위반했다고 하여 관할권 행사에 대한 당사국 동의의 원칙이 무시될 수 있는 것은 아니라고 판단했다.

인도네시아는 동티모르의 독립운동을 강압적으로 탄압했으나, 무자비한 탄압으로 동티모르는 국제적인 동정을 받았다. 1999년 유엔과 인도네시아는 동티모르에서 주민투표를 실시해 정치적 향방을 결정하기로 합의했다. 선거 결과는 독립을 원하는 것으로 나타났고, 유엔은 1999년 10월부터 평화유지군을 파견해 독립을 후원했다. 동티모르에서는 2002년 독립 정부가 출범했다.

➡ **참고문헌** ————————————————————————————————

- 이성덕, 동티모르 사건의 경과 및 배경, (홍익대) 법학연구 4집(2002).
- 박배근, 동티모르 사건(국제판례연구 2집, 2001), p. 1.
- C. Chinkin, ICJ: Recent Cases, ICLQ Vol. 45(1996), p. 712.
- P. F. Bekker, International Decisions, AJIL Vol. 90(1996), p. 94.

5. ICJ 재판사건 소송참가(2011)

Territorial and Maritime Dispute.
Nicaragua v. Colombia(Application for permission to
Intervene by Honduras), 2011 ICJ Reports 420.

☑ 사   안

2001년 12월 니카라과는 콜롬비아를 상대로 서부 캐리비아해 지역의 영토 및 해양경계에 관한 분쟁을 ICJ에 제소했다. 이 소송에 대해서는 온두라스를 포함한 여러 인접국이 관심을 가지며, 재판소 규칙 제53조 1항에 근거한 소송서류 사본을 요청했다. 이어 온두라스는 2010년 6월 재판소 규정 제62조에 따른 소송참가를 신청했다. 즉 니카라과와 콜롬비아의 해양경계에 관한 주장을 감안할 때, 온두라스는 재판의 결과에 따라 자국의 법적 권리와 이익이 영향을 받게 된다고 주장했다. 이 때 온두라스는 1차적으로 소송 당사자로서의 참가를 요청하며, 수락된다면 판결의 구속력을 수락하겠다는 의사를 표명했다. 이어 당사자 참가가 수락되지 않는다면 비당사자 참가라도 허락해 달라고 요청했다. 이에 대해 니카라과는 온두라스의 소송참가 신청이 재판소 규정과 규칙에 합당하지 않다며 기각을 요청한 반면, 콜롬비아는 비당사자 참가에는 반대하지 않으며 당사자 참가의 문제는 재판소가 결정할 문제라는 입장을 표시했다. 한편 이 사건에 대해서는 해양경계 부분에 한하여 코스타리카도 2010년 2월 비당사자 소송참가 신청을 했었다.[1]

---

1) Territorial and Maritime Dispute, Nicaragua v. Colombia(Application by Costa Rica for Permission to Intervene), 2011 ICJ Reports 348.

☑ 쟁 점

소송참가의 종류와 요건.

☑ 판 결

⑴ 계류 중인 소송에 법률적 이해관계를 갖는 국가는 소송참가를 신청할 수 있다.

⑵ 당사자 참가를 위해서는 원 소송 당사국과 소송 참가국 간에 ICJ 관할권이 성립될 수 있어야 하며, 소송 참가국은 본안 판결의 구속력을 받는다.

⑶ 비당사자 참가를 위해 원 소송 당사국과 소송 참가국 간에 ICJ 관할권이 성립될 필요가 없으며, 소송 참가국은 본안 판결의 구속력을 받지 않는다.

판 결 문

22. Honduras is seeking permission to intervene as a party in the case before the Court in order to achieve a final settlement of the dispute between itself and Nicaragua, including the determination of the tripoint with Colombia, and, in the alternative, as a non-party, in order to inform the Court of its interests of a legal nature which may be affected by the decision the Court is to render in the case between Nicaragua and Colombia, and to protect those interests. [···]

27. The Court observes that neither Article 62 of the Statute nor Article 81 of the Rules of Court specifies the capacity in which a State may seek to intervene. However, in its Judgment of 13 September 1990 on Nicaragua's Application for permission to intervene in the case concerning Land, Island and Maritime Frontier Dispute(El Salvador/Honduras), the Chamber of the Court considered the status of a State seeking to intervene and accepted that a State may be permitted to intervene under Article 62 of the Statute either as a nonparty or as a party: [···]

28. In the opinion of the Court, the status of intervener as a party requires, in any event, the existence of a basis of jurisdiction as between the States concerned, the validity of which is established by the Court at the time when it permits intervention. However, even though Article 81 of the Rules of Court provides that the application must specify any basis of jurisdiction claimed to exist as between the State seeking to intervene and the parties to the main case, such a basis of jurisdiction is not a condition for intervention as a non-party.

29. If it is permitted by the Court to become a party to the proceedings, the intervening State may ask for rights of its own to be recognized by the Court in its future decision, which would be binding for that State in respect of those aspects for which intervention was granted, pursuant to Article 59 of the Statute. *A contrario*, as the Chamber of the Court formed to deal with the case concerning the Land, Island and Maritime Frontier Dispute(El Salvador/Honduras) has pointed out, a State permitted to intervene in the proceedings as a non-party "does not acquire the rights, or become subject to the obligations, which attach to the status of a party, under the Statute and Rules of Court, or the general principles of procedural law"(*Application to Intervene, Judgment, I.C.J. Reports 1990*, p. 136, para. 102).

30. The fact remains that, whatever the capacity in which a State is seeking to intervene, it must fulfil the condition laid down by Article 62 of the Statute and demonstrate that it has an interest of a legal nature which may be affected by the future decision of the Court. Since Article 62 of the Statute and Article 81 of the Rules of Court provide the legal framework for a request to intervene and define its constituent elements, those elements are essential, whatever the capacity in which a State is seeking to intervene; that State is required in all cases to establish its interest of a legal nature which may be affected by the decision in the main case, and the precise object of the requested intervention.

☑ 해   설

ICJ에서 진행 중인 사건의 결정에 의해 영향을 받을 수 있는 제3국은 소송참가(intervention)를 할 수 있다. 소송참가에는 사건의 결정에 의해 영향 받는 법률적 이해관계(interest of legal nature)가 있는 국가가 신청하는 경우(제62조)와 다자조약의 해석이 문제가 되는 경우 조약의 다른 당사국이 참가하는 경우가 있다(제63조). 전자는 재판소의 허가결정이 있어야 참가할 수 있으나, 후자의 경우 신청국이 권리로서 참가할 수 있다. ICJ 규정 제63조에 의한 소송참가는 그 요건과 효과가 비교적 분명하게 규정되어 있으므로 이의 적용에 관한 논란이 적은 편이다. 그러나 제62조에 의한 소송참가는 참가 요건도 추상적이고, 이의 허용 여부에 있어서 재판소가 상당한 재량을 행사할 수 있다. 소송참가의 필요성은 신청국이 입증해야 한다.

과거 ICJ는 제62조에 의한 소송참가를 허용하는 데 극히 신중한 태도를 보이며 소송참가를 거의 허가하지 않았다가 PCIJ 설립 이래 근 70년만인 1990년 ICJ는 엘살바도르/온두라스 국경분쟁 사건에서 니카라과에게 비당사자 참가(non-Party intervener)를 처음으로 허용했다.[2] 비당사자 참가라는 개념은 ICJ 규정이나 규칙에 직접 규정된 내용이 아니며, ICJ가 이 판결을 통해 처음으로 제시한 것이다. 이 판결에서 ICJ는 "비당사자 참가"의 기본 개념을 다음과 같이 설명했다. 즉 비당사자 참가란 계류 중인 소송에 법률적 성질의 이해관계를 갖는 국가가 소송의 당사국은 아닌 자격에서 소송참가를 하는 것이다. 해당 사건의 당사국이 되는 것은 아니므로 기존의 소송 당사국들과 소송참가국 사이에 별도로 ICJ의 재판관할권이 성립될 근거는 필요 없다.[3] 소송에서 당사국으로서의 권리·의무를 갖지 못하며, 판결도 소송참가국에게 구속력을 갖지 않는다.[4] 이는 곧 소송참가국 역시 판결의 결과를 원 소송당사국들에게 법적 권리로 요구할 수 없음을 의미한다. 해당 판결문의 내용은 아래와 같다.

> **99.** [⋯] It is therefore clear that a State which is allowed to intervene in a case, does not, by reason only of being an intervener, become also a party to the case. It is true, conversely, that, provided that there be the necessary consent by the parties to the case, the intervener is not prevented by reason of that status from itself becoming a party to the case. That the competence given to the Court in Article 62 of the Statute is not extendable to making an intervener a party to the case unless the parties to the case have consented to the change [⋯]
>
> **100.** It thus follows also from the juridical nature and from the purposes of intervention that the existence of a valid link of jurisdiction between the would-be intervener and the parties is not a requirement for the success of the application. On the contrary, the procedure of intervention is to ensure that a State with possibly affected interests may be permitted to intervene even

---

2) Land, Island and Maritime Frontier Dispute(Application to Intervene by Nicaragua), El Salvador/Honduras, 1990 ICJ Reports 92.
3) 같은 판결, paras. 100-101.
4) 같은 판결, para. 102.

though there is no jurisdictional link and it therefore cannot become a party. […]

　　102. […] In the first place, as has been explained above, the intervening State does not become party to the proceedings, and does not acquire the rights, or become subject to the obligations, which attach to the status of a party, under the Statute and Rules of Court, or the general principles of procedural law.

한편 본 사건에서 온두라스는 1차적으로 당사자 참가를 신청했다. 이제까지 ICJ가 당사자 참가를 인정한 예는 없었다. 이 판결에서 ICJ는 처음으로 당사자 참가의 의미를 분석했다. 즉 당사자 참가(Party intervener)는 소송참가를 하는 제3국이 사건의 당사국이 되는 경우이다. 따라서 당사자 참가를 하는 경우 원 소송 당사국과 소송참가국간에 ICJ 재판관할권 성립의 근거가 필요하다.5) 당사자 참가국은 소송과정에서 본안사건 당사국과 동일한 권한을 행사할 수 있으며, 본안 판결의 구속력을 받는다.6) 당사자 참가국은 소송과정에서 본안과 관련되는 범위 내에서 적극적으로 자신의 청구를 제기할 수 있다.

그러나 이 사건의 판결에서는 온두라스의 당사자 참가는 물론 비당사자 참가 신청도 기각했다. 온두라스가 소송참가에 필요한 법률적 이해관계를 제시하지 못했다고 판단했다. 또한 코스타리카의 비당사자 소송참가 신청 역시 기각 당했다.

▶ 참고문헌

- 최지현, 국제사법재판소 규정 제62조 소송참가의 현재와 미래: 해양 경계획정 소송을 중심으로, 국제법학회논총 58권 3호(2013), p. 231.

---

5) 본 항목 판결, para. 28; 전계주 1 판결, para. 39.
6) 본 항목 판결, para. 29.

6. LaGrand 사건(2001)
— 잠정조치의 구속력

LaGrand.
Germany v. U.S.A., 2001 ICJ Reports 46.

☑ 사 안

ICJ 소송에서 청구취지의 대상인 권리가 급박하고도 회복 불가능한 위험상태에 놓여 있어 당사자의 권리를 보호하기 위해 필요하다고 인정되면 종국판결 이전에도 재판소가 잠정조치(provisional measure)를 취할 수 있다(제41조). 독일인인 LaGrand 형제는 1982년 미국에서 살인 및 은행강도 혐의로 체포되어 그중 1명에 대해서는 1999년 사형이 집행되었다.

「영사관계에 관한 비엔나 협약」 제36조 1항에 따르면 이들은 체포 직후 본국 영사의 조력을 받을 수 있음을 지체 없이 고지받았어야 했으나, 미국 관헌은 1998년에야 뒤늦게 이 사실을 통지했다. 독일은 미국이 이 사건을 처리함에 있어서 비엔나 협약을 위반했다고 주장하며 ICJ에 제소했다. 독일은 미국이 영사접견권을 알려주지 않음으로써 협약 당사국인 독일의 권리를 침해했을 뿐 아니라, LaGrand 형제의 권리를 침해했고, 결국 이들에 대한 독일의 외교적 보호권도 침해했다고 주장했다.

ICJ는 일단 미국에 대하여 Walter LaGrand에 대한 사형집행을 중지하라는 잠정조치 명령을 내렸다. 미국 정부는 ICJ의 결정을 사형 집행권을 가진 애리조나 주지사에 전달했으나, 한편으로는 ICJ의 잠정조치가 구속력을 갖지 않는다는 입장을 갖고 있었다. 애리조나주는 ICJ의 잠정조치에도 불구하고 LaGrand에 대한 사형을 집행했다. 이 소송에서는 ICJ의 잠정조치가 미국에 대해 구속력이 있는가가 다투어졌다.

☑ 쟁   점

ICJ 재판절차 중 잠정조치의 구속력 여부.

☑ 판   결

ICJ의 잠정조치는 재판 당사국에게 구속력을 갖는다.

판 결 문

99. The dispute which exists between the Parties with regard to this point essentially concerns the interpretation of Article 41, which is worded in identical terms in the Statute of each Court. [⋯] The Court will therefore now proceed to the interpretation of Article 41 of the Statute. It will do so in accordance with customary international law, reflected in Article 31 of the 1969 Vienna Convention on the Law of Treaties. [⋯]

100. The French text of Article 41 reads as follows:

"1. La Cour a le pouvoir d'indiquer, si elle estime que les circonstances l'exigent, quelles mesures conservatoires du droit de chacun doivent être prises á titre provisoire.

2. En attendant l'arrêt définitif, l'indication de ces mesures est immédiatement notifiée aux parties et au Conseil de sécurité." [⋯]

In this text, the terms "indiquer" and "l'indication" may be deemed to be neutral as to the mandatory character of the measure concerned; by contrast the words "doivent être prises" have an imperative character.

For its part, the English version of Article 41 reads as follows:

"1. The Court shall have the power to indicate, if it considers that circumstances so require, any provisional measures which ought to be taken to preserve the respective rights of either party.

2. Pending the final decision, notice of the measures suggested shall forthwith be given to the parties and to the Security Council." [⋯]

According to the United States, the use in the English version of "indicate" instead of "order," of "ought" instead of "must" or "shall," and of "suggested" instead of "ordered," is to be understood as implying that decisions under Article 41 lack mandatory effect. It might however be argued, having regard to the fact that in

1920 the French text was the original version, that such terms as "indicate" and "ought" have a meaning equivalent to "order" and "must" or "shall."

101. [⋯] In cases of divergence between the equally authentic versions of the Statute, neither it nor the Charter indicates how to proceed. In the absence of agreement between the parties in this respect, it is appropriate to refer to paragraph 4 of Article 33 of the Vienna Convention on the Law of Treaties, which in the view of the Court again reflects customary international law. This provision reads "when a comparison of the authentic texts discloses a difference of meaning which the application of Articles 31 and 32 does not remove, the meaning which best reconciles the texts, having regard to the object and purpose of the treaty, shall be adopted."

The Court will therefore now consider the object and purpose of the Statute together with the context of Article 41.

102. The object and purpose of the Statute is to enable the Court to fulfil the functions provided for therein, and, in particular, the basic function of judicial settlement of international disputes by binding decisions in accordance with Article 59 of the Statute. The context in which Article 41 has to be seen within the Statute is to prevent the Court from being hampered in the exercise of its functions because the respective rights of the parties to a dispute before the Court are not preserved. It follows from the object and purpose of the Statute, as well as from the terms of Article 41 when read in their context, that the power to indicate provisional measures entails that such measures should be binding, inasmuch as the power in question is based on the necessity, when the circumstances call for it, to safeguard, and to avoid prejudice to, the rights of the parties as determined by the final judgment of the Court. The contention that provisional measures indicated under Article 41 might not be binding would be contrary to the object and purpose of that Article. [⋯]

104. Given the conclusions reached by the Court above in interpreting the text of Article 41 of the Statute in the light of its object and purpose, it does not consider it necessary to resort to the preparatory work in order to determine the meaning of that Article. The Court would nevertheless point out that the preparatory work of the Statute does not preclude the conclusion that orders under Article 41 have binding force. [⋯][1]

---

1) 이어서 재판부는 PCIJ가 이 규정 조항을 채택할 때의 경과를 살펴보아도 잠정조치의 구속력을 부인하려는 의미가 아니었음을 설명했다.

109. In short, it is clear that none of the sources of interpretation referred to in the relevant Articles of the Vienna Convention on the Law of Treaties, including the preparatory work, contradict the conclusions drawn from the terms of Article 41 read in their context and in the light of the object and purpose of the Statute. Thus, the Court has reached the conclusion that orders on provisional measures under Article 41 have binding effect.

☑ 해 설

잠정조치는 재판의 어느 단계에서도 신청할 수 있으며, 신청이 있으면 재판소는 이를 우선적으로 처리한다.2) 잠정조치가 내려지면 이는 안보리로 통보된다. 성격상 잠정조치는 원고국이 신청하는 경우가 많을 것이나, 피고국도 신청할 수 있으며, 당사국의 신청 없이 재판소 스스로가 잠정조치를 취할 수도 있다(규칙 제75조 1항). 이 사건에서도 ICJ는 독일의 잠정조치 신청이 있자 사안의 급박성을 감안해 피소국인 미국의 견해 청취 없이 바로 규칙 제75조 1항에 근거하여 직권으로 잠정조치를 내렸다.

잠정조치가 법적 구속력을 갖느냐는 PCIJ 이래 논란의 대상이었다. 재판소가 잠정조치를 단지 제시(indicate, suggest)한다고 규정되어 있다는 점에서 구속력을 인정할 수 없다는 주장도 있었다. LaGrand 사건은 잠정조치의 구속력 여부가 문제되었던 첫 번째 사건이었다. 이 사건에서 ICJ는 처음으로 잠정조치의 구속력을 확인했고, 이후 ICJ는 같은 입장을 유지하고 있다.

과거에 비해 ICJ는 잠정조치의 부여 요건을 완화시키는 경향을 보이고 있다. 그러나 ICJ는 잠정조치를 직접 강제할 능력이 없기 때문에 이의 현실적 실효성에 의문이 제기되는 것도 부인할 수 없다. 한편 ICJ가 잠정조치를 내린 이후 사건의 본안 판결에서 이와 반대되는 결정을 내린 경우는 극히 예외적이며, 대부분의 사건에서 잠정조치의 내용이 본안판결에서도 지지를 받았다.

---

2) ICJ 규정에서는 provisional measure라고 표현하고 있으나, 규칙에서는 interim protection이라는 표현도 사용되고 있다. 가보전조치라고도 번역된다.

▶▶ 참고문헌 ─────────────────────────────────

- 최지현, 국제사법재판소의 잠정조치에 관한 연구, 국제법평론 2010년 Ⅱ호, p. 183.
- 최지현, 국제사법재판소 잠정조치 명령의 이행강제, 국제법학회논총 제56권 제2호(2011), p. 185.

7. 차고스 군도 분쟁(2019)
― 권고적 의견 부여의 기준

Legal Consequences of the Separation of the Chagos Archipelago from Mauritius in 1965.
Advisory Opinion, 2019 ICJ Reports.

☑ 사   안

인도양에 위치한 차고스 군도는 과거 모리셔스 소속으로 영국의 지배를 받다가 1968년 모리셔스 독립 직전 행정적으로 분리되어 이후에도 영국령으로 존속했다. 1980년대 들어 모리셔스는 차고스 군도의 영유권을 주장하기 시작했다. 영국이 2010년 차고스 군도 주변 수역을 해양보호구역으로 설정하자, 모리셔스는 이곳이 자신의 주권에 속하는 지역이므로 해양보호구역 설정에는 자국의 동의가 필요하다고 주장했다. 특히 영국은 차고스 군도의 연안국이 아니므로 해양보호구역을 설정할 권리가 없다고 주장하며, 이 사건을 유엔 해양법협약상 중재재판에 회부했다. 중재재판부는 영국의 해양보호구역 선언이 해양법협약 위반이라고 판정했다.

모리셔스의 주장을 계기로 유엔 총회는 2017년 6월 ① 차고스 군도가 분리된 다음 모리셔스가 독립했다면 모리셔스의 탈식민과정이 완수되었는가 ② 영국의 차고스 군도 지배로 인한 국제법상 결과는 무엇인가라는 질문으로 ICJ에 권고적 의견을 요청하는 결의를 채택했다.

이 사건의 본질은 차고스 군도의 영유권 다툼이다. 영국은 이 분쟁이 자신과 모리셔스 양자간에 해결될 문제이며, 특히 분쟁 당사국의 동의 없이 사건을 ICJ에 회부하는 결과가 된다며 권고적 의견 부여에 반대했다. 이에 대한 판단과정에서 ICJ의 권고적 부여 기준이 검토되었다.

☑ 쟁 점

ICJ의 권고적 의견 부여 여부의 판단기준.

☑ 판 결

ICJ의 권고적 의견 부여는 유엔 활동에 참여를 의미하며 "긴요한 이유 (compelling reasons)"가 없는 한 거부되지 말아야 한다.

판 결 문

63. The fact that the Court has jurisdiction does not mean, however, that it is obliged to exercise it:

> "The Court has recalled many times in the past that Article 65, paragraph 1, of its Statute, which provides that 'The Court may give an advisory opinion ...', should be interpreted to mean that the Court has a discretionary power to decline to give an advisory opinion even if the conditions of jurisdiction are met." [⋯]

64. The discretion whether or not to respond to a request for an advisory opinion exists so as to protect the integrity of the Court's judicial function as the principal judicial organ of the United Nations [⋯].

65. The Court is, nevertheless, mindful of the fact that its answer to a request for an advisory opinion "represents its participation in the activities of the Organization, and, in principle, should not be refused" [⋯]. Thus, the consistent jurisprudence of the Court is that only "compelling reasons" may lead the Court to refuse its opinion in response to a request falling within its jurisdiction [⋯].

66. The Court must satisfy itself as to the propriety of the exercise of its judicial function in the present proceedings. It will therefore give careful consideration as to whether there are compelling reasons for it to decline to respond to the request from the General Assembly.

67. Some participants in the present proceedings have argued that there are "compelling reasons" for the Court to exercise its discretion to decline to give the advisory opinion requested. Among the reasons raised by these participants are that, first, advisory proceedings are not suitable for determination of complex and disputed factual issues; secondly, the Court's response would not assist the General Assembly in the performance of its functions, thirdly, it would be inappropriate for the Court to re-examine a question already settled by the Arbitral Tribunal constituted under Annex VII of UNCLOS in the Arbitration regarding the Chagos Marine Protected Area; and fourthly, the questions asked in the present proceedings relate to a pending bilateral dispute between two States which have not consented to the settlement of that dispute by the Court.

68. The Court will now turn to the examination of these arguments.

1. Whether advisory proceedings are suitable for determination of complex and disputed factual issues

69. It has been argued by some participants that the questions raise complex and disputed factual issues which are not suitable for determination in advisory proceedings. Those participants have contended that in these proceedings the Court does not have sufficient information and evidence to arrive at a conclusion on the complex and disputed questions of fact before it. […]

71. The Court recalls that in its Advisory Opinion on Western Sahara when it was faced with the same argument, it concluded that what was decisive was whether it had

> "sufficient information and evidence to enable it to arrive at a judicial conclusion upon any disputed questions of fact the determination of which is necessary for it to give an opinion in conditions compatible with its judicial character" (*I.C.J. Reports 1975*, pp. 28-29, para. 46). […][1]

74. The Court is therefore satisfied that there is in the present proceedings sufficient information on the facts before it for the Court to give the requested opinion. Accordingly, the Court cannot decline to answer the questions put to it.

2. Whether the Court's response would assist the General Assembly in the performance of its functions

75. It has been argued by some participants that the advisory opinion requested would not assist the General Assembly in the proper exercise of its functions. These participants have maintained that the General Assembly has not been actively engaged in the decolonization of Mauritius since 1968. […]

76. The Court considers that it is not for the Court itself to determine the

---

1) 이어 재판부는 각종 출처로부터 이미 수많은 자료를 수집했음을 지적하고 — 필자 주.

usefulness of its response to the requesting organ. Rather, it should be left to the requesting organ, the General Assembly, to determine "whether it needs the opinion for the proper performance of its functions" […] The Court observed that:

> "it is not for the Court itself to purport to decide whether or not an advisory opinion is needed by the Assembly for the performance of its functions. The General Assembly has the right to decide for itself on the usefulness of an opinion in the light of its own needs." (*I.C.J. Reports 1996 (I)*, p. 237, para. 16.) […]

78. It follows that in the present proceedings the Court cannot decline to answer the questions posed to it by the General Assembly in resolution 71/292 on the ground that its opinion would not assist the General Assembly in the performance of its functions.

3. Whether it would be appropriate for the Court to re-examine a question allegedly settled by the Arbitral Tribunal constituted under UNCLOS Annex VII in the Arbitration regarding the Chagos Marine Protected Area

79. Certain participants have argued that an advisory opinion by the Court would reopen the findings of the Arbitral Tribunal in the Arbitration regarding the Chagos Marine Protected Area that are binding on Mauritius and the United Kingdom. […]

81. The Court recalls that its opinion "is given not to States, but to the organ which is entitled to request it" […] The Court observes that the principle of *res judicata* does not preclude it from rendering an advisory opinion. When answering a question submitted for an opinion, the Court will consider any relevant judicial or arbitral decision. In any event, the Court further notes that the issues that were determined by the Arbitral Tribunal in the Arbitration regarding the Chagos Marine Protected Area ([…]) are not the same as those that are before the Court in these proceedings.

82. It follows from the foregoing that the Court cannot decline to answer the questions on this ground.

4. Whether the questions asked relate to a pending dispute between two States, which have not consented to its settlement by the Court

83. Some participants have argued that there is a bilateral dispute between Mauritius and the United Kingdom regarding sovereignty over the Chagos Archipelago and that this dispute is at the core of the advisory proceedings.

According to those participants, to determine the issues in the present proceedings, the Court would be required to arrive at conclusions on certain key points such as the effect of the 1965 Lancaster House agreement. Certain participants have contended that the dispute over sovereignty, which arose in the 1980s in bilateral relations, is the "real dispute" that motivates the request. These participants have further contended that Mauritius' claims in the *Arbitration regarding the Chagos Marine Protected Area* revealed the existence of a bilateral territorial dispute between that State and the United Kingdom. Therefore, to render an advisory opinion would contravene "the principle that a State is not obliged to allow its disputes to be submitted to judicial settlement without its consent" (*Western Sahara, Advisory Opinion, I.C.J. Reports 1975*, pp. 24-25, paras. 32-33; *Interpretation of Peace Treaties with Bulgaria, Hungary and Romania, First Phase, Advisory Opinion, I.C.J. Reports 1950*, p. 71). [⋯]

85. The Court recalls that there would be a compelling reason for it to decline to give an advisory opinion when such a reply "would have the effect of circumventing the principle that a State is not obliged to allow its disputes to be submitted to judicial settlement without its consent" (*Western Sahara, Advisory Opinion, I.C.J. Reports 1975*, p. 25, para. 33).

86. The Court notes that the questions put to it by the General Assembly relate to the decolonization of Mauritius. The General Assembly has not sought the Court's opinion to resolve a territorial dispute between two States. Rather, the purpose of the request is for the General Assembly to receive the Court's assistance so that it may be guided in the discharge of its functions relating to the decolonization of Mauritius. The Court has emphasized that it may be in the interest of the General Assembly to seek an advisory opinion which it deems of assistance in carrying out its functions in regard to decolonization: [⋯]

87. The Court observes that the General Assembly has a long and consistent record in seeking to bring colonialism to an end. From the earliest days of the United Nations, the General Assembly has played an active role in matters of decolonization. [⋯]

88. The Court therefore concludes that the opinion has been requested on the matter of decolonization which is of particular concern to the United Nations. The issues raised by the request are located in the broader frame of reference of decolonization, including the General Assembly's role therein, from which those issues are inseparable [⋯].

90. In these circumstances, the Court does not consider that to give the opinion requested would have the effect of circumventing the principle of consent by a State to the judicial settlement of its dispute with another State. The Court therefore cannot, in the exercise of its discretion, decline to give the opinion on that ground.

91. In light of the foregoing, the Court concludes that there are no compelling reasons for it to decline to give the opinion requested by the General Assembly.

☑ **해　　설**

인도양에 위치한 차고스 군도는 처음에는 네덜란드령, 이후 프랑스의 식민지로 개척되었다. 모리셔스와 차고스는 약 2,200km 떨어져 있다. 1814년 프랑스가 모리셔스를 영국으로 할양에 합의하면서 차고스 군도도 이의 일부로 함께 영국령이 되었다. 영국은 차고스 군도를 모리셔스의 속령 형태로 지배했다. 영국은 모리셔스의 독립이 논의 중이던 1965년 차고스 군도를 모리셔스로부터 분리해 영국 인도양 영토(British Indian Ocean Territory)로 지정하고, 1966년 그 중 디에고 가르시아 섬을 미국에 임대해 군사기지를 세우도록 허용했다. 현재 임대계약은 2036년까지이다. 영국은 모리셔스의 독립을 논의하던 1965년 런던회의에서 차고스의 분리를 수용하지 않으면 독립을 인정하지 않겠다고 협박했다고 한다. 독립 논의과정에서 영국은 차고스 군도의 군사시설 이용의 필요성이 소멸되면 차고스 군도를 모리셔스에게 반환하기로 약속했다. 모리셔스는 1968년 독립했다. 차고스 분리 과정에서 주민의 강제이주가 있었는데, 영국과 모리셔스는 1982년 보상협정을 타결하고 차고스와 관련된 모든 청구권은 "완전하고 최종적으로" 해결된 것으로 합의했다.

2017년 유엔 총회에 의한 권고적 의견이 요청되자 특히 영국을 중심으로 이 사건은 권고적 의견이 부여되기에 적합하지 않으므로 ICJ가 의견 부여를 거부해야 된다는 주장이 제기되었다.

권고적 의견의 부여는 ICJ의 재량사항이다. 종전부터 ICJ는 자신이 유엔 주요 기관의 하나로 권고적 의견의 부여는 유엔 활동에의 참여를 의미하므로, 긴요한 이유가 없는 한 권고적 의견의 부여는 거부되지 말아야 한다는 입장을 정리하고 있었다. 심리과정에서는 이 사건의 경우 의견이 부여되지 말아야 할 긴요한 이유가 있는지 여부가 검토되었다. 즉 ① 이 문제는 복잡하고 논란이 많은 쟁점을 제기하고 있어서 권고적 의견을 통한 결정이 부적합하다. ② 권고적 의견 부여가 총회의 적절한 기능 수행에 도움이 되지 않는다. ③ 이미 구속력 있는 중재판정이 내려진 사건을 다시 재개하는 결과가 된다. ④ 이 사건의 본질은 영유권 분쟁으로, 이에 대한 권고적 의견의 부여는 분쟁의 당사국인 영국의 동의 없이 사건을 사법절차에 회부하는 결과가 된다는 등의 주장이 전개되었다. 재판부는 위 판결문에서와 같이 이러한 사항을 일일이 검토한 결과 어느 하나도 권고적 의견 부여를 거부해야 할 긴요한 이유는 되지 않는다고 판단했다.

이어 ICJ는 영국이 모리셔스로부터 차고스 군도를 위법하게 분리해 새로운 식민지로 편입시킨 결과 모리셔스의 탈식민 과정은 합법적으로 완수되지 않았으며, 영국은 차고스 군도의 지배를 조속히 종료시켜야 한다는 의견을 제시했다. 유엔 총회는 ICJ의 이 권고적 의견을 환영하며 차고스 군도가 모리셔스의 일부임을 확인하며, 영국이 6개월 이내에 차고스 군도로부터 떠날 것을 요구하는 결의를 채택했다(결의 73/295호, 2019. 5. 22).

➡ 참고문헌 ─────────────────────────────

• 황준식, 국제사법재판소(ICJ)의 권고적 의견과 동의(consent)의 원칙 ─ 차고스(Chagos) 군도 사건에서 제출된 서면의견을 중심으로, 국제법학회논총 제63권 제4호(2018), p. 309.
• 정경수, 미완의 비식민화 잔여물의 탈식민적 청산 ─ 차고스 군도에 관한 권고적 의견을 중심으로, 국제법평론 2019년 ─ Ⅲ(2019), p. 101.

제19장

국제사회의 평화와 안전보장

1. 니카라과 사건(1986)
― 무력행사와 집단적 자위권

Case Concerning the Military and Paramilitary Activities In
and Against Nicaragua(Merits).
Nicaragua v. United States of America, 1986 ICJ Reports 14.

☑ 사   안

1979년 중미의 니카라과에서 실시된 총선에서 50년간 독재를 실시해 온 Somoza 정권이 무너지고 좌익 정권이 출범했다. Daniel Ortega가 이끄는 좌익 산디니스타 당은 그간 친미 노선을 표방한 우익 정권을 대체하여 새로운 정부를 구성했다. 새로이 니카라과 대통령에 취임한 Ortega는 이후 지속적인 반미 노선을 걷게 되어 미국과 마찰이 발생했다. 인접지역인 중미에 반미 정권이 출범한 점과 향후 이 지역에서 좌익 정권 확산의 신호탄이 될 수 있음을 미국은 우려했다. 이에 따라 당시 미국 레이건 행정부는 산디니스타 정부를 전복하고자 니카라과 내 우익 무장세력인 콘트라 반군을 지원하기 시작했다. 동 지원에는 무기의 제공, 군사고문단 파견 등이 포함되었다. 미국이 직접 니카라과 내 군사활동을 수행한 것은 아니나 미국의 군사적 지원을 통해 콘트라 반군이 산디니스타 정부를 전복하고자 다양한 작전을 전개하는 것은 공지의 사실이었다. 미국은 이러한 지원을 통해 중미에서의 반미정권 확산을 차단하고 자국 이익을 수호하고자 했다. 미국의 콘트라 반군에 대한 군사적 지원이 지속적으로 강화되자 1984년 니카라과는 이러한 미국의 일련의 활동이 니카라과에 대한 무력침공을 구성한다고 주장하며 ICJ에 제소했다.

☑ 쟁   점

(1) 콘트라 반군에 대한 미국의 군사지원 활동이 UN 헌상 제2소 4항 및 관습국제법이 금지하는 타국에 대한 무력공격에 해당하는지 여부.

(2) 미국의 콘트라 반군 군사지원 활동이 UN 헌장 제51조상 자위권 행사에 해당하여 정당화되는지 여부.

☑ 판   결

(1) 니카라과 정부를 전복하기 위한 목적으로 시행된 군사고문단 파견, 무기제공 등을 포함하는 미국의 콘트라 반군 지원활동은 UN 헌장 제2조 4항 및 관습국제법이 금지하는 니카라과에 대한 무력공격을 구성한다.

(2) 제반 상황을 고려할 경우, 미국에 대한 니카라과의 무력 공격이 임박했다고 판단할 근거가 없으므로 미국의 자위권 행사 주장은 정당화되지 않는다.

판 결 문

122. The Court concludes that in 1983 an agency of the United States Government supplied to the FDN a manual on psychological guerrilla warfare which, while expressly discouraging indiscriminate violence against civilians, considered the possible necessity of shooting civilians who were attempting to leave a town; and advised the "neutralization" for propaganda purposes of local judges, officials or notables after the semblance of trial in the presence of the population. The text supplied to the contras also advised the use of professional criminals to perform unspecified "jobs," and the use of provocation at mass demonstrations to produce violence on the part of the authorities so as to make "martyrs." [···]

165. In view of the assertion by the United States that it has acted in exercise of the right of collective self-defence for the protection of El Salvador, Honduras and Costa Rica, the Court has also to consider the evidence available on the question whether those States, or any of them, made a request for such protection. In its Counter-Memorial on jurisdiction and admissibility, the United States informed the Court that "El Salvador, Honduras, and Costa Rica have each sought outside assistance, principally from the United States, in their self-defense against Nicaragua's aggression. Pursuant to the inherent right of individual and collective self-defense, and in accordance with the terms of the Inter-American Treaty of Reciprocal Assistance, the United States has responded to these requests." No indication has however been given of the dates on which such requests for assistance were made. [⋯]

188. The Court thus finds that both Parties take the view that the principles as to the use of force incorporated in the UN Charter correspond, in essentials, to those found in customary international law. The Parties thus both take the view that the fundamental principle in this area is expressed in the terms employed in Article 2, paragraph 4, of the UN Charter. They therefore accept a treaty-law obligation to refrain in their international relations from the threat or use of force against the territorial integrity or political independence of any State, or in any other manner inconsistent with the purposes of the UN. The Court has however to be satisfied that there exists in customary international law an *opinio juris* as to the binding character of such abstention. This opinio juris may, though with all due caution, be deduced from, *inter alia*, the attitude of the Parties and the attitude of States towards certain General Assembly resolutions, and particularly resolution 2625(XXV) entitled "Declaration on Principles of International Law concerning Friendly Relations and Cooperation among States in accordance with the Charter of the UN." [⋯] The principle of non-use of force, for example, may thus be regarded as a principle of customary international law, not as such conditioned by provisions relating to collective security, or to the facilities or armed contingents to be provided under Article 43 of the Charter. It would therefore seem apparent that the attitude referred to expresses an *opinio juris* respecting such rule (or set of rules), to be thenceforth treated separately from the provisions, especially those of an institutional kind, to which it is subject on the treaty-law plane of the Charter. [⋯]

193. The general rule prohibiting force allows for certain exceptions. In view of the arguments advanced by the United States to justify the acts of which it is accused by Nicaragua, the Court must express a view on the content of the right of self-defence, and more particularly the right of collective self-defence. First, with regard to the existence of this right, it notes that in the language of Article 51 of the UN Charter, the inherent right (or "droit naturel") which any State possesses in the event of an armed attack, covers both collective and individual self-defence. Thus, the Charter itself testifies to the existence of the right of collective self-defence

in customary international law. Moreover, just as the wording of certain General Assembly declarations adopted by States demonstrates their recognition of the principle of the prohibition of force as definitely a matter of customary international law, some of the wording in those declarations operates similarly in respect of the right of self-defence (both collective and individual). Thus, in the declaration quoted above on the Principles of International Law concerning Friendly Relations and Co-operation among States in accordance with the Charter of the UN, the reference to the prohibition of force is followed by a paragraph stating that: "nothing in the foregoing paragraphs shall be construed as enlarging or diminishing in any way the scope of the provisions of the Charter concerning cases in which the use of force is lawful." This resolution demonstrates that the States represented in the General Assembly regard the exception to the prohibition of force constituted by the right of individual or collective self-defence as already a matter of customary international law.

194. With regard to the characteristics governing the right of self-defence, since the Parties consider the existence of this right to be established as a matter of customary international law, they have concentrated on the conditions governing its use. In view of the circumstances in which the dispute has arisen, reliance is placed by the Parties only on the right of self-defence in the case of an armed attack which has already occurred, and the issue of the lawfulness of a response to the imminent threat of armed attack has not been raised. Accordingly the Court expresses no view on that issue. The Parties also agree in holding that whether the response to the attack is lawful depends on observance of the criteria of the necessity and the proportionality of the measures taken in self-defence. Since the existence of the right of collective self-defence is established in customary international law, the Court must define the specific conditions which may have to be met for its exercise, in addition to the conditions of necessity and proportionality to which the Parties have referred. [···]

201. To justify certain activities involving the use of force, the United States has relied solely on the exercise of its right of collective self-defence. However the Court, having regard particularly to the non-participation of the United States in the merits phase, considers that it should enquire whether customary international law, applicable to the present dispute, may contain other rules which may exclude the unlawfulness of such activities. It does not, however, see any need to reopen the question of the conditions governing the exercise of the right of individual self-defence, which have already been examined in connection with collective self-defence. On the other hand, the Court must enquire whether there is any justification for the activities in question, to be found not in the right of collective self-defence against an armed attack, but in the right to take counter-measures in response to conduct of Nicaragua which is not alleged to constitute an armed attack. It will examine this point in connection with an analysis of the principle of non-intervention in customary international law. [⋯]

211. [⋯] In the view of the Court, under international law in force today-whether customary international law or that of the UN system-States do not have a right of "collective" armed response to acts which do not constitute an "armed attack." Furthermore, the Court has to recall that the United States itself is relying on the "inherent right of self-defence"[⋯], but apparently does not claim that any such right exists as would, in respect of intervention, operate in the same way as the right of collective self-defence in respect of an armed attack. [⋯]

232. The exercise of the right of collective self-defence presupposes that an armed attack has occurred; and it is evident that it is the victim State, being the most directly aware of that fact, which is likely to draw general attention to its plight. It is also evident that if the victim State wishes another State to come to its help in the exercise of the right of collective self-defence, it will normally make an express request to that effect. Thus in the present instance, the Court is entitled to take account, in judging the asserted justification of the exercise of collective self-defence by the United States, of the actual conduct of El Salvador, Honduras and Costa Rica at the relevant time, as indicative of a belief by the State in question that it was the victim of an armed attack by Nicaragua, and of the making of a request by the victim State to the United States for help in the exercise of collective self-defence.

233. The Court has seen no evidence that the conduct of those States was consistent with such a situation, either at the time when the United States first embarked on the activities which were allegedly justified by self-defence, or indeed for a long period subsequently. [⋯]

242. The Court therefore finds that the support given by the United States, up to the end of September 1984, to the military and paramilitary activities of the contras in Nicaragua, by financial support, training, supply of weapons, intelligence and logistic support, constitutes a clear breach of the principle of nonintervention. [⋯]

☑ 해   설

이 판결의 의의는 UN 헌장 제2조 4항의 '타국에 대한 무력행사 금지 원칙'과 이에 대한 예외를 구성하는 제51조의 '자위권 행사'의 법적 의미를 체계적으로 정리했다는 점이다. 특히, 이 판결에서 집단적 자위권 행사를 위한 선결 요건을 설시한 것은 그 의미가 크다고 할 수 있다. 즉, 미국이 주장하는 집단적 자위권 행사가 인정되기 위해서는 피침략국인 미국의 동맹국에 대한 니카라과의 명백한 무력행사가 선행되어야 하고 단지 추상적인 위협의 존재만으로는 불충분하다는 것이다. 이는 군사적 동맹체제를 통해 집단적 자위권 행사가 남용되지 않도록 구체적인 제한을 가한 것으로 타당한 입장이라고 볼 수 있다. 따라서 동맹국에 대한 군사적 위협 내지 침략이 현실화되거나 임박한 경우에 한해 집단적 자위권이 원용될 수 있을 것이다. 일본의 헌법 개정을 통한 집단적 자위권 행사 움직임과 관련한 논의에서도 이 사건에서의 ICJ 법리는 심도 있게 검토되고 있다. 그 핵심적 요건으로는 동맹국에 대한 피침략국의 구체적인 지원요청이 선행돼야 한다는 것이다.

한편 이 판결은 관습국제법과 관련해서도 중요한 내용을 포함한다. 관습국제법의 형성시 필요한 객관적 요소로서 "일관된 국가관행(consistent and uniform usage)"은 유사 상황에서 모든 국가의 획일적인 행위를 요구하는 것이 아니라 전체적으로 일반적인 국가관행을 의미한다는 것이다. 따라서 국제사회에서 100% 획일적인 국가관행이 존재하지 않더라도 압도적인 다수의 증거를 통해 그러한 관행의 존재가 지지된다면 그 요건은 충족된 것으로 보아야 한다는 것이다. 이 역시 관습국제법 창설의 현실을 적절히 반영한 타당한 결론이라고 하겠다.

원래 이 사건에서 니카라과의 제소 움직임을 파악한 미국은 제소를 불과 며칠 앞두고 ICJ 규정 제36조 2항상 선택조항에 대한 철회의사를 ICJ에 통보했다. 이를 근거로 미국은 이 사건에 대해 ICJ가 관할권이 없음을 주장했다. 그러나 ICJ는 제소직전 미국의 이러한 선택조항 철회는 신의성실 원칙에 어긋난 것으로 간주하고 미국의 관할권 부재 주장을 배척하며 본안 심리를 진행했다.

　　한편 ICJ는 니카라과가 입은 손해에 대해 미국이 배상해야 한다고 판시했고, 이 판결에 따라 니카라과는 미국에 손해배상을 요구했다. 그러나 미국은 ICJ 판결의 이행을 지속적으로 거부했다. 니카라과의 배상요구가 계속되던 중 1990년 2월 실시된 니카라과 대선에서 친미·보수세력을 대표하는 Chamorro가 대통령으로 당선됐다. Chamorro 정권은 미국으로부터 상당한 규모의 원조금을 받는 대가로 1991년 ICJ 판결에 따른 손해배상 요구를 철회하기로 합의함으로써 이 사건은 종결됐다. ICJ 판결의 집행은 UN헌장 제94조 2항에 따라 안전보장이사회가 보장하지만 안전보장이사회 표결과정에서 거부권을 보유한 상임이사국이 ICJ 절차의 패소국인 경우 사실상 판결의 집행이 곤란함을 이 사례는 보여준다.

➠ 참고문헌 ─────────────────────────────────

• I. R. Cohn, Nicaragua V. United States: Pre−Seisin Reciprocity and the Race to The Hague, Ohio State Law Journal Vol. 46(1985), p. 699.

• L. D. Hole, Towards a Test of the International Character of an Armed Conflict: Nicaragua and Tadic, Syracuse Journal of International Law and Commerce Vol. 32(2005), p. 269.

• P. S. Reichler, Holding America to Its Own Best Standards: Abe Chayes and Nicaragua in the World Court, Harvard International Law Journal Vol. 42(2001), p. 15.

• M. Kohen, The Principle of Non−Intervention 25 Years after the Nicaragua Judgment, Leiden Journal of International Law Vol. 25, No. 1(2012), pp. 157−164.

• 이영준, ICJ 판례상 나타난 미국의 니카라과에 대한 군사적 활동사건: 재판관할권을 중심으로, 국제법학회논총 제40권(1995), p. 197.

2. 이란 석유생산 시설물 공격 사건(2003)
─ 무력행사 금지 원칙

Case Concerning Oil Platforms(Merits).
Islamic Republic of Iran v. United States of America,
2003 ICJ Reports 161.

☑ 사 안

1987년 이란이 미국적 유조선을 공격한 것에 대한 보복으로 미국은 이란의 연안 석유 생산시설을 공격했다. 또한 1988년 미국 군함이 이란이 부설한 기뢰에 의해 손상을 입자 미국은 곧바로 이란 석유시설에 대한 공격을 감행했다. 미국은 이란이 기뢰와 미사일로 미국 및 중립국 선박을 공격함으로써 양국이 1955년 체결한 영사우호조약(1955 Treaty of Amity, Economic Relations and Consular Rights)을 위반했다고 주장했다. 특히 미국은 체약국간 통항의 자유를 규정한 이 조약 규정을 이란이 위반했으며, 미국의 무력사용은 이 조약에서 인정하는 자위권 행사로 정당화됨을 주장했다. 이에 대해 이란은 미국 및 중립국 선박에 대한 공격행위가 자국이 아닌 이라크의 행위이며 따라서 미국의 무력행사가 오히려 이 조약의 위반임을 주장했다. 이에 대해 이란은 미국의 무력행사는 이 조약 제10조상 항행의 자유 및 제20조상 무력행사 금지 원칙을 위반하며 이로 인해 이란이 입은 피해에 대해 미국은 손해배상책임을 부담한다고 주장했다. 양국간 분쟁이 해결되지 않자 1992년 이란은 ICJ에 미국을 제소했다. 이란이 미국을 제소한 근거는 침략전쟁 금지를 규정한 UN헌장 등이 아닌, 1955년 영사우호조약이었다. 미국이 자국의 對이란 무력공격 자체를 부인하지는 않았으므로 양국간 분쟁의 핵심은 미국의 공격행위가 이 조약을 위반하는 무력행사에 해당하는지 여부였다.

☑ 쟁   점

(1) 미국의 對이란 석유생산시설물 공격행위가 국제법(미-이란 영사우호조약)을 위반하는 무력행사에 해당하는지 여부.

(2) 미국의 공격행위가 미-이란 영사우호조약상 자위권 행사의 요건을 충족하여 정당화가 가능한지 여부.

(3) 이란 석유생산시설에 대한 미국의 무력행사는 미-이란 영사우호조약상 항행의 자유조항에 대한 위반에 해당하는지 여부.

☑ 판   결

(1) 해군전투기를 동원한 미국의 이란 석유생산 시설물 공격은 미-이란 영사우호조약을 위반하는 이란에 대한 무력행사에 해당한다.

(2) 미국에 대한 이란의 공격이 임박했다고 판단할 만한 객관적 증거가 부재하므로 미국의 공격행위는 이 조약상 자위권 행사 요건을 충족하지 아니한다.

(3) 이 사건 이전에도 해당 해역에서 이란의 국제교역은 이미 상당한 제한을 받고 있었으므로 미국의 무력행사가 국제교역상 장애를 초래했다고 보기 힘들다. 따라서 미국의 공격행위는 항행의 자유를 규정한 미-이란 영사우호조약을 위반하지 아니한다.

판 결 문

21. The task of the Court in the present proceedings is to determine whether or not there have been breaches of the 1955 Treaty, and if it finds that such is the case, to draw the appropriate consequences according to the submissions of the Parties. The Court is seised both of a claim by Iran alleging breaches by the United States, and of a counter-claim by the United States alleging breaches by Iran. Its jurisdiction to entertain both the claim and the counter-claim is asserted to be based upon Article XXI, paragraph 2, of the 1955 Treaty. [⋯]

26. These attacks by United States forces on the Iranian oil platforms are claimed by Iran to constitute breaches of the 1955 Treaty; and the attacks on the

Sea Isle City and the *USS Samuel B. Roberts* were invoked in support of the United States' claim to act in self-defence. The counter-claim of the United States is however not limited to those attacks; according to the United States, Iran was in breach of its obligations under Article X, paragraph 1, of the 1955 Treaty, "In attacking vessels in the Gulf with mines and missiles and otherwise engaging in military actions that were dangerous and detrimental to commerce and navigation between the territories of the United States and the Islamic Republic of Iran". [···]

43. The Court will thus examine first the application of Article XX, paragraph 1 (d), of the 1955 Treaty, which in the circumstances of this case, as explained above, involves the principle of the prohibition in international law of the use of force, and the qualification to it constituted by the right of self-defence. On the basis of that provision, a party to the Treaty may be justified in taking certain measures which it considers to be "necessary" for the protection of its essential security interests. [···]

49. In its Counter-Memorial, the United States linked its previous invocation of the right of self-defence with the application of Article XX, paragraph 1 (d), of the 1955 Treaty. It argued that Iranian actions during the relevant period con-stituted a threat to essential security interests of the United States, inasmuch as the flow of maritime commerce in the Persian Gulf was threatened by Iran's repeated attacks on neutral vessels; that the lives of United States nationals were put at risk. [···]

50. [···] To justify its choice of the platforms as target, the United States asserted that they had "engaged in a variety of actions directed against United States flag and other non-belligerent vessels and aircraft". Iran has denied any responsibility for (in particular) the attack on the *Sea Isle City*, and has claimed that the platforms had no military purpose, and were not engaged in any military activity. [···]

59. There is a conflict of evidence between the Parties as to the characteristics of the Silkworm missile, in particular its maximum range, and whether or not when fired it always follows a straight-line course. [···] There is however no direct evidence at all of the type of missile that struck the *Sea Isle City*; the evidence as to the nature of other missiles fired at Kuwaiti territory at this period is suggestive, but no more. In considering whether the United States has discharged the burden of proof that Iranian forces fired the missile that struck the *Sea Isle City*, the Court must take note of this deficiency in the evidence available. [···]

61. In short, the Court has examined with great care the evidence and arguments presented on each side, and finds that the evidence indicative of Iranian responsibility for the attack on the *Sea Isle City* is not sufficient to support the contentions of the United States. [⋯]

71. [⋯] The main evidence that the mine struck by the *USS Samuel B. Roberts* was laid by Iran was the discovery of moored mines in the same area, bearing serial numbers matching other Iranian mines, in particular those found aboard the vessel Iran Ajr. This evidence is highly suggestive, but not conclusive.

72. [⋯] The Court does not exclude the possibility that the mining of a single military vessel might be sufficient to bring into play the "inherent right of self-defence"; but in view of all the circumstances, including the inconclusiveness of the evidence of Iran's responsibility for the mining of the *USS Samuel B. Roberts*, the Court is unable to hold that the attacks on the Salman and Nasr platforms have been shown to have been justifiably made in response to an "armed attack" on the United States by Iran, in the form of the mining of the *USS Samuel B. Roberts*. [⋯]

74. In its decision in the case concerning *Military and Paramilitary Activities in and against Nicaragua*, the Court endorsed the shared view of the parties to that case that in customary law "whether the response to the [armed] attack is lawful depends on observance of the criteria of the necessity and the proportionality of the measures taken in self-defence." [⋯] One aspect of these criteria is the nature of the target of the force used avowedly in self-defence. [⋯] In the present proceedings, the United States has continued to maintain that they were such, and has presented evidence directed to showing that the platforms collected and reported intelligence concerning passing vessels, acted as a military communication link coordinating Iranian naval forces and served as actual staging bases to launch helicopter and small boat attacks on neutral commercial shipping. [⋯]

75. [⋯] Iran asserts further that reports and testimony referred to by the United States are mostly non-specific about the use of the platforms as staging bases to launch attacks, and that the equipment at its disposal could be used from mainland and offshore islands, without any need to have recourse to the platforms.

76. The Court is not sufficiently convinced that the evidence available supports the contentions of the United States as to the significance of the military presence and activity on the Reshadat oil platforms; and it notes that no such evidence is offered in respect of the Salman and Nasr complexes. However, even accepting those contentions, for the purposes of discussion, the Court is unable to hold that the attacks made on the platforms could have been justified as acts of self-defence. [···] In the case both of the attack on the *Sea Isle City* and the mining of the *USS Samuel B. Roberts*, the Court is not satisfied that the attacks on the platforms were necessary to respond to these incidents. In this connection, the Court notes that there is no evidence that the United States complained to Iran of the military activities of the platforms, in the same way as it complained repeatedly of minelaying and attacks on neutral shipping, which does not suggest that the targeting of the platforms was seen as a necessary act. [···].

77. As to the requirement of proportionality, the attack of 19 October 1987 might, had the Court found that it was necessary in response to the *Sea Isle City* incident as an armed attack committed by Iran, have been considered proportionate. In the case of the attacks of 18 April 1988, however, they were conceived and executed as part of a more extensive operation entitled "Operation Praying Mantis."[1] [···] As a response to the mining, by an unidentified agency, of a single United States warship, which was severely damaged but not sunk, and without loss of life, neither "Operation Praying Mantis" as a whole, nor even that part of it that destroyed the Salman and Nasr platforms, can be regarded, in the circumstances of this case, as a proportionate use of force in self-defence.

78. The Court thus concludes from the foregoing that the actions carried out by United States forces against Iranian oil installations on 19 October 1987 and 18 April 1988 cannot be justified, under Article XX, paragraph 1 (d), of the 1955 Treaty, as being measures necessary to protect the essential security interests of the United States, since those actions constituted recourse to armed force not qualifying, under international law on the question, as acts of self-defence, and thus did not fall within the category of measures contemplated, upon its correct interpretation, by that provision of the Treaty. [···]

98. The Court thus concludes, with regard to the attack of 19 October 1987 on the Reshadat platforms, that there was at the time of those attacks no commerce between the territories of Iran and the United States in respect of oil produced by those platforms and the Resalat platforms, inasmuch as the platforms were under repair and inoperative; and that the attacks cannot therefore be said to have infringed the freedom of commerce in oil between the territories of the High Contracting Parties protected by ArticleX, paragraph 1, of the 1955 Treaty, particularly taking into account the date of entry into force of the embargo effected

---

1) 미국의 이란 석유생산시설물 공격 작전명.

by Executive Order 12613.[2] The Court notes further that, at the time of the attacks of 18 April 1988 on the Salman and Nasr platforms, all commerce in crude oil between the territories of Iran and the United States had been suspended by that Executive Order, so that those attacks also cannot be said to have-infringed the rights of Iran under Article X, paragraph 1, of the 1955 Treaty.

99. The Court is therefore unable to uphold the submissions of Iran, that in carrying out those attacks the United States breached its obligations to Iran under Article X, paragraph 1, of the 1955 Treaty. In view of this conclusion, the Iranian claim for reparation cannot be upheld. [···]

119. Having disposed of all objections of Iran to its jurisdiction over the counter-claim, and to the admissibility thereof, the Court has now to consider the counter-claim on its merits. To succeed on its counter-claim, the United States must show that:

(a) its freedom of commerce or freedom of navigation between the territories of the High Contracting Parties to the 1955 Treaty was impaired; and that

(b) the acts which allegedly impaired one or both of those freedoms are attributable to Iran.

The Court would recall that Article X, paragraph 1, of the 1955 Treaty does not protect, as between the Parties, freedom of commerce or freedom of navigation in general. As already noted above[···], the provision of that paragraph contains an important territorial limitation. In order to enjoy the protection provided by that text, the commerce or the navigation is to be *between the territories* of the United States and Iran. The United States bears the burden of proof that the vessels which were attacked were engaged in commerce or navigation between the territories of the United States and Iran. [···]

121. None of the vessels described by the United States as being damaged by Iran's alleged attacks was engaged in commerce or navigation "between the territories of the two High Contracting Parties." Therefore, the Court concludes that there has been no breach of Article X, paragraph 1, of the 1955 Treaty in any of the specific incidents involving these ships referred to in the United States pleadings. [···]

124. The Court has thus found that the counter-claim of the United States concerning breach by Iran of its obligations to the United States under Article X, paragraph 1, of the 1955 Treaty [···] must be rejected; there is therefore no need

---

2) 미국 대통령의 對이란 교역 제한 행정명령.

for it to consider, under this head, the contested issues of attribution of those incidents to Iran. In view of the foregoing, the United States claim for reparation cannot be upheld. [⋯]

☑ 해   설

이 판결에서 ICJ는 무력행사 금지 및 자위권 행사와 관련된 원칙을 UN헌장이 아닌 1955년 체결된 미－이란 영사우호조약의 범위 내에 국한하여 판단했다. UN헌장 이외의 일반 조약을 통해 침략전쟁 금지 및 자위권 행사 등을 검토한 것은 눈에 띄는 대목이다. ICJ의 심리 범위는 이 조약 내로 국한되어 있지만 이 조약 관련 조항의 의미를 해석하는 데 있어 ICJ는 관습국제법을 원용했다. 즉, 이 조약 범위 내에서 미국의 군사행동을 평가함에 있어 ICJ는 Nicaragua 사건3)에서 확인된 자위권 행사를 위한 관습국제법상 원칙(가령, 필요성의 원칙, 비례성의 원칙)을 인용했다. 이를 통해 ICJ는 미국의 주장이 이러한 요건을 충족하지 못함을 확인하고 있다.

다만, 항행의 자유와 관련하여 ICJ가 지나치게 형식적인 접근법을 채택한 듯한 모습도 보인다. 이란 및 미국에 의한 무력공격의 위법성을 항행의 자유에 관해 규정한 1955년 영사우호조약의 제10조에만 기초하여 평가하다 보니 제시된 무력공격이 상업적 거래에 결정적 영향을 미쳤다는 증거가 없다는 이유로 이 조항 위반이라고 볼 수 없다는 기계적인 결정을 내린 것으로 보인다. 즉, 미국에 의해 피격된 이란석유생산시설의 생산량이 사건 당시 미미하고 또 이미 미국의 교역 규제 대상 품목에 포함되어 있었으므로 항행의 자유에 영향을 미칠 수 없었다는 것이 판결의 주된 논리였다. 생각건대, 설사 생산량이 미미하고 이미 다른 형태의 규제조치에 직면하였더라도 무력공격은 그 자체로서 항행의 자유를 침해할 가능성이 없지 않다는 점을 감안하면 ICJ의 결정은 지나친 형식 논리에 치우친 것으로 보인다. 규모가 미미하더라도 최소한 기존에 존재하던 교역상 내지 항행상의 자유를 더욱 위축시키는 결과는 있었을 것이기 때문이다. 또한 이러한 공격은 더욱 확장될 가능성도 있는 교역을 장래적으로 제한하는 효과도 있을 것이다. 아마도 ICJ는

---

3) Military and Paramilitary Activities in and against Nicaragua(Nicaragua v. United States of America), Merits, Judgment, ICJ Reports 1986, p. 14.

이란이 이러한 주장을 전개하는 근본취지는 항행의 자유가 아닌 무력행사 부분임을 인식하고 전자에 관한 이란의 주장을 배척하기 위한 법적 근거를 제시하고자 노력한 것으로 보인다.

한편 미－이란 양국간 군사적 긴장은 이란 핵개발이 본격화된 2000년대 중반에 다시 고조된 바 있다. 2011년 11월 국제원자력기구(IAEA)가 이란의 핵 개발 의혹을 지적한 보고서를 채택한 이후 국제사회가 이란에 대한 경제 제재의 수위를 높였기 때문이다. 2011년 12월 이란은 자국 영공을 침범했다는 이유로 미국의 무인 정찰기를 격추시킨 바 있다. 이란산 원유 수송의 핵심통로인 호르무즈 해협에서 양국 해군력은 장기간 대치하기도 했다. 2015년 11월 제네바에서 이란과 미국이 이란 핵문제에 관한 합의에 도달하여 이러한 군사적 긴장은 해소되는 듯했으나, 2018년 5월 미국 트럼프 행정부는 이 합의에서 탈퇴하며 이란에 대한 경제제재를 다시 부과하여 양국 간 갈등은 다시 재연되었다. 독일, 프랑스 등 유럽국가들은 미국의 이러한 탈퇴결정을 강력히 비난했다. 이같은 미국의 대이란 경제제재 조치에 대해 이란은 미국을 두 번에 걸쳐 ICJ에 제소하여 2020년 7월 현재 이 사건들은 계류 중이다.

➡ 참고문헌 ───

- M. Koehler, Two Nations, A Treaty, and the World Court an Analysis of United States－Iranian Relations Under the Treaty of Amity before the ICJ, Wisconsin International Law Journal Vol. 18(2000), p. 287.
- W. H. Taft, Self－Defense and the Oil Platforms Decision, Yale Journal of International Law Vol. 29(2004), p. 295.
- S. M. Young, Destruction of Property (On an International Scale): The Recent Oil Platforms Case and the ICJ's Inconsistent Commentary on the Use of Force by the United States, North Carolina Journal of International Law and Commercial Regulation Vol. 30(2004), p. 335.
- J. A. Green, The Oil Platforms Case: An Error in Judgment?, Journal of Conflict & Security Law Vol. 9(2004), p. 357.

3. 핵무기의 위협 및 사용(1996)
― 핵무기 위협 및 사용의 국제법상 허용 여부

Legality of the Threat or Use of Nuclear Weapons.
Advisory Opinion, 1996 ICJ Reports 226.

☑ 사   안

대량살상 및 무차별살상을 초래하는 핵무기의 본질적 속성으로 인해 그 사용이 국제법 위반을 초래한다는 주장은 오래 전부터 제기되었다. 1990년대에 동서 냉전 체제가 붕괴되고 평화 무드가 조성되자 이러한 주장은 새로운 힘을 얻었다. 특히 국제평화를 주장하는 NGO를 중심으로 핵무기 사용의 위법성을 주장하는 분위기가 국제사회에서 확산되었다. 이러한 분위기의 구체적 발로로 몇몇 국제기구가 이 문제에 대해 직접 관여했다. 이에 따라 1993년과 1994년, 세계보건기구(WHO)와 UN 총회는 각각 권고적 의견을 ICJ에 요청했다. 먼저 WHO는 "환경 및 인류 건강에 대한 핵무기의 심각한 위협을 고려할 때 전쟁 및 무력충돌 과정에서 핵무기의 사용은 WHO 설립헌장을 비롯한 국제법에 대한 위반을 구성하는지" 여부에 대해, ICJ에 권고적 의견을 요청했다. 그리고 이듬해 UN 총회는 "핵무기의 사용 및 위협은 어떤 경우에도 국제법이 허용하는지" 여부에 대해 권고적 의견을 요청했다. 이 요청에 대해 ICJ는 WHO의 요청은 WHO 설립헌장의 범위를 벗어나는 월권행위(ultra vires)로 결정하여 권고적 의견 신청을 각하했으나, UN 총회의 요청에 대해서는 권고적 의견을 부여했다. ICJ에 따르면 WHO는 국제사회의 보건 증진을 위해 설립된 국제기구이므로 국제평화와 안전보장과 직접 연관되는 핵무기 사용 관련 문제에 대해서는 WHO 설립헌장상 권한이 없기에 WHO는 이에 관한 권고적 의견도 요청할 수 없다는 것이었다. 이 책의 권고적 의견은 UN 총회의 요청에 대해 부여된 것이다.

☑ 쟁   점

핵무기의 위협과 사용, 특히 무력분쟁에 있어 핵무기의 위협과 사용을 금지하는 국제법 원칙의 존재 여부.

☑ 판   결

무력분쟁에서 특정 형태의 무기의 사용을 금지하는 조약이 존재하지만 이런 조약이 핵무기에도 적용된다고 볼 근거는 없다. 또한 핵무기 사용을 금지하는 내용의 관습국제법 존재 여부와 관련하여 그러한 취지의 법적 확신이 국제사회에 존재한다고 볼 수 없으므로 이에 관한 관습국제법 역시 존재하지 아니한다. 다만 핵무기는 무기의 일종으로 그 사용이 전시에 적용되는 기존의 국제인도법에 위반될 가능성은 존재한다.

판 결 문

36. In consequence, in order correctly to apply to the present case the Charter law on the use of force and the law applicable in armed conflict, in particular humanitarian law, it is imperative for the Court to take account of the unique characteristics of nuclear weapons, and in particular their destructive capacity, their capacity to cause untold human suffering, and their ability to cause damage to generations to come.

37. The Court will now address the question of the legality or illegality of recourse to nuclear weapons in the light of the provisions of the Charter relating to the threat or use of force.

38. The Charter contains several provisions relating to the threat and use of force. [⋯]

39. These provisions do not refer to specific weapons. They apply to any use of force, regardless of the weapons employed. The Charter neither expressly prohibits, nor permits, the use of any specific weapon, including nuclear weapons. A weapon that is already unlawful *per se*, whether by treaty or custom, does not become lawful by reason of its being used for a legitimate purpose under the

Charter. [···]

41. The submission of the exercise of the right of self-defence to the conditions of necessity and proportionality is a rule of customary international law. As the Court stated in the case concerning *Military and Paramilitary Activities in and against Nicaragua* (*Nicaragua v. United States of America*): there is a "specific rule whereby self-defence would warrant only measures which are proportional to the armed attack and necessary to respond to it, a rule well established in customary international law." [···] This dual condition applies equally to Article 51 of the Charter, whatever the means of force employed.

42. The proportionality principle may thus not in itself exclude the use of nuclear weapons in self-defence in all circumstances. But at the same time, a use of force that is proportionate under the law of self-defence, must, in order to be lawful, also meet the requirements of the law applicable in armed conflict which comprise in particular the principles and rules of humanitarian law. [···]

55. The Court will observe that the Regulations annexed to the Hague Convention IV do not define what is to be understood by "poison or poisoned weapons" and that different interpretations exist on the issue. Nor does the 1925 Protocol specify the meaning to be given to the term "analogous materials or devices". The terms have been understood, in the practice of States, in their ordinary sense as covering weapons whose prime, or even exclusive, effect is to poison or asphyxiate. This practice is clear, and the parties to those instruments have not treated them as referring to nuclear weapons.

56. In view of this. it does not seem to the Court that the use of nuclear weapons can be regarded as specifically prohibited on the basis of the above-mentioned provisions of the Second Hague Declaration of 1899, the Regulations annexed to the Hague Convention IV of 1907 or the 1925 Protocol [···]

70. The Court notes that General Assembly resolutions, even if they are not binding, may sometimes have normative value. They can, in certain circumstances, provide evidence important for establishing the existence of a rule or the emergence of an *opinio juris*. To establish whether this is true of a given General Assembly resolution, it is necessary to look at its content and the conditions of its adoption; it is also necessary to see whether an *opinio juris* exists as to its normative character. Or a series of resolutions may show the gradual evolution of the *opinio juris* required for the establishment of a new rule.

71. Examined in their totality, the General Assembly resolutions put before the

Court declare that the use of nuclear weapons would be "a direct violation of the Charter of the UN"; and in certain formulations that such use "should be prohibited." The focus of these resolutions has sometimes shifted to diverse related matters; however, several of the resolutions under consideration in the present case have been adopted with substantial numbers of negative votes and abstentions; thus, although those resolutions are a clear sign of deep concern regarding the problem of nuclear weapons, they still fall short of establishing the existence of an *opinio juris* on the illegality of the use of such weapons. [···]

74. The Court not having found a conventional rule of general scope, nor a customary rule specifically proscribing the threat or use of nuclear weapons *per se*, it will now deal with the question whether recourse to nuclear weapons must be considered as illegal in the light of the principles and rules of international humanitarian law applicable in armed conflict and of the law of neutrality. [···]

79. It is undoubtedly because a great many rules of humanitarian law applicable in armed conflict are so fundamental to the respect of the human person and "elementary considerations of humanity" as the Court put it in its Judgment of 9 April 1949 in the *Corfu Channel* case [···] that the Hague and Geneva Conventions have enjoyed a broad accession. Further these fundamental rules are to be observed by all States whether or not they have ratified the conventions that contain them, because they constitute intransgressible principles of international customary law. [···]

82. The extensive codification of humanitarian law and the extent of the accession to the resultant treaties, as well as the fact that the denunciation clauses that existed in the codification instruments have never been used, have provided the international community with a corpus of treaty rules the great majority of which had already become customary and which reflected the most universally recognized humanitarian principles. These rules indicate the normal conduct and behaviour expected of States. [···]

85. Turning now to the applicability of the principles and rules of humanitarian law to a possible threat or use of nuclear weapons, the Court notes that doubts in this respect have sometimes been voiced on the ground that these principles and rules had evolved prior to the invention of nuclear weapons and that the Conferences of Geneva of 1949 and 1974-1977 which respectively adopted the four Geneva Conventions of 1949 and the two Additional Protocols thereto did not deal with nuclear weapons specifically. Such views, however, are only held by a small minority. In the view of the vast majority of States as well as writers there can be no doubt as to the applicability of humanitarian law to nuclear weapons.

86. The Court shares that view. Indeed, nuclear weapons were invented after most of the principles and rules of humanitarian law applicable in armed conflict had already come into existence; the Conferences of 1949 and 1974-1977 left these weapons aside, and there is a qualitative as well as quantitative difference between nuclear weapons and all conventional arms. However, it cannot be concluded from this that the established principles and rules of humanitarian law applicable in armed conflict did not apply to nuclear weapons. Such a conclusion would be incompatible with the intrinsically humanitarian character of the legal principles in question which permeates the entire law of armed conflict and applies to all forms of warfare and to all kinds of weapons, those of the past, those of the present and those of the future. [⋯]

95. Nor can the Court make a determination on the validity of the view that the recourse to nuclear weapons would be illegal in any circumstance owing to their inherent and total incompatibility with the law applicable in armed conflict. Certainly, as the Court has already indicated, the principles and rules of law applicable in armed conflict-at the heart of which is the overriding consideration of humanity-make the conduct of armed hostilities subject to a number of strict requirements. Thus, methods and means of warfare, which would preclude any distinction between civilian and military targets, or which would result in unnecessary suffering to combatants, are prohibited. In view of the unique characteristics of nuclear weapons, to which the Court has referred above, the use of such weapons in fact seems scarcely reconcilable with respect for such requirements. [⋯]

97. Accordingly, in view of the present state of international law viewed as a whole, as examined above by the Court, and of the elements of fact at its disposal, the Court is led to observe that it cannot reach a definitive conclusion as to the legality or illegality of the use of nuclear weapons by a State in an extreme circumstance of self-defence, in which its very survival would be at stake. [⋯]

  ☑ 해　설

　본 건은 정치적으로 민감한 사안인 만큼 ICJ는 이 사건에서 상당히 조심스러운 의견을 제시하는 것으로 보인다. ICJ는 기본적으로 현재 국제법 원칙이 핵무기의 위협 및 사용을 금지하는 내용을 포함하고 있지는 않음을 확인하고 있다. 그 다음 기존 국제법 법리에 기초하여 핵무기 위법성 여부를 제한적으로 평가했다. 즉, 핵무기의 위협 및 사용이 국제법에 위반되는지에 대한 문제를 직접 다루기보다는 무력분쟁시 특정 형태의 무기사용금지에 관한 기존 조약이 핵무기에도 적용되는지 여부에 국한하여 검토하는 데 그치고 있다. 이러한 검토에 기초하여 기존의 조약이 핵무기에도 적용된다고 볼 근거가 없다고 결정했다. 이미 금지된 무기류와 비교하여 유례 없이 압도적 파괴력을 보유한 핵무기를 금지하는 조약은 정작 부재한다는 점을 확인하고 있다. 마찬가지로 핵무기 사용을 금지하는 내용의 관습국제법도 아직 존재하지 않음을 밝히고 있다. 다만 핵무기 사용은 전시에 적용되는 국제인도법에 위반될 가능성은 존재한다고 결정하여 역시 이 문제를 기존의 전시 국제인도법에 국한하여 검토하고 있다. 이 역시 핵무기 위협과 사용에 연관되는 문제에 대한 별도의 검토를 했다기보다는 일반적인 무기에 적용되는 기존 법리에 기초하여 의견을 제시한 것으로 평가할 수 있다. 이러한 보수적 성향의 판결을 내린 배경은 아마도 이 문제가 초래할 정치·외교적 파급효과를 고려했기 때문일 것이다. 한편, 세계보건문제를 총괄하는 WHO가 정치·외교적으로 민감한 핵무기사용과 관련한 권고적 의견을 신청한 것을 각하한 ICJ의 결정 역시 음미할 만하다. 국가와 달리 오직 설립헌장의 목적이 규정한 범위 내에서만 국제법적 법인격을 보유하는 국제기구의 특성 및 한계를 잘 보여주기 때문이다.

➡ **참고문헌** ─────────────────────────────

- 박배근, 핵무기 사용의 합법성에 대한 ICJ의 권고적 의견, 국제법평론 통권 8호 (1997), p. 119.
- 최태현, 핵무기 사용의 합법성 여부에 관한 권고적 의견에 관한 비판적 고찰, 국제법평론 통권 16호(2002), p. 57.
- S. M. Howley, Legality of the Threat or Use of Nuclear Weapons, New York International Law Review Vol. 10(1997), p. 237.
- L. Doswald−Beck, International Humanitarian Law and the Advisory Opinion of the International Court of Justice on the Legality of the Threat or Use of Nuclear Weapons, International Review of the Red Cross Vol. 37(1997) p. 35.

4. 유엔 일부 경비 부담 문제(1962)
— UN평화유지활동의 법적 근거

Certain Expenses of the United Nations.
Advisory Opinion, 1962 ICJ Reports 151.

☑ 사   안

1956년 수에즈 운하(UNEF) 및 1960년 콩고(ONUC)에서 UN평화유지활동이 각각 실시되었다. 이에 대해 소련과 프랑스가 UN헌장 위반 문제를 제기하며 이 활동에 소요된 경비 부담을 거부함에 따라 UN 총회는 1961년 12월 ICJ에 권고적 의견을 요청했다. 소련과 프랑스의 주장은 UN평화유지활동은 헌장상 명문 규정이 없는 활동으로 이에 대해 총회가 UN 회원국에 경비 부담을 요청할 수 없다는 것이다. UN헌장에 평화유지활동에 관한 명문 규정이 존재했다면 쉽게 해결될 문제였으나 그러한 조항이 부재함에 따라 회원국간 이견이 발생한 것이다. 따라서 이 문제 해결을 위해서는 헌장에 명문 규정이 부재하는 UN평화유지활동의 헌장 적합성 문제가 먼저 해결되어야만 했다. 만약 UN평화유지활동이 헌장에 규정된 총회의 권한에 포함된 것으로 해석되면 이는 헌장 제17조 2항이 규정하는 "UN의 경비(expenses of the Organization)"에 해당되기에 회원국들은 자신의 분담 비율에 따라 그 경비를 분담해야 한다. 반대로 만약 그러한 활동이 총회의 권한에 속하지 않는다면 이는 일종의 월권행위(ultra vires)로서 이에 대해 회원국의 경비 분담을 요청할 수는 없을 것이다.

☑ 쟁   점

(1) UN헌장상 명시적 근거가 부재한 평화유지활동의 UN헌장 합치 여부.

(2) UN 총회가 평화유지활동에 관한 조치를 회원국에 권고할 수 있는지 여부.

(3) UN평화유지활동 경비가 회원국이 분담 책임을 부담하는 헌장 제17조 2항상 UN 경비에 해당하는지 여부.

☑ 판　결

(1) UN평화유지활동은 비록 헌장상 명문의 규정은 부재하나 국제평화와 안전의 달성이라는 UN헌장 목적 달성을 위해 필요한 조치이므로 헌장에 합치한다.

(2) UN 안전보장이사회의 국제평화와 안전보장에 관한 권한은 배타적이 아니라 일차적일 뿐이다. 또한 총회의 권한을 광범위하게 규정한 헌장 제10, 11, 14조의 취지에 비추어 총회는 평화유지활동에 관해 회원국에 권고할 권한도 보유한다.

(3) UN평화유지활동의 경비는 헌장상 정당한 활동을 수행하는 과정에서 발생한 경비로서 헌장 제17조 2항상 UN의 경비에 해당되며 이에 대해 회원국은 분담 책임을 부담한다.

판 결 문

(p. 156-) The question on which the Court is asked to give its opinion is whether certain expenditures which were authorized by the General Assembly to cover the costs of the United Nations operations in the Congo (hereinafter referred to as ONUC) and of the operations of the United Nations Emergency Force in the Middle East (hereinafter referred to as UNEF), "constitute 'expenses of the Organization' within the meaning of Article 17, paragraph 2, of the Charter of the United Nations." [⋯]

(p. 160-) It is a consistent practice of the General Assembly to include in the annual budget resolutions, provision for expenses relating to the maintenance of international peace and security. Annually, since 1947, the General Assembly has made anticipatory provision for "unforeseen and extraordinary expenses" arising in relation to the "maintenance of peace and security." [⋯]

(p. 163-) The responsibility conferred [to the Security Council under Article 24] is "primary," not exclusive. [···]

The Charter makes it abundantly clear, however, that the General Assembly is also to be concerned with international peace and security. Article 14 authorizes the General Assembly to "recommend measures for the peaceful adjustment of any situation, regardless of origin, which it deems likely to impair the general welfare or friendly relations among nations, including situations resulting from a violation of the provisions of the present Charter setting forth the purposes and principles of the United Nations." [···]

(p. 168-) The primary place ascribed to international peace and security is natural, since the fulfilment of the other purposes will be dependent upon the attainment of that basic condition. These purposes are broad indeed, but neither they nor the powers conferred to effectuate them are unlimited. Save as they have entrusted the Organization with the attainment of these common ends, the Member States retain their freedom of action. But when the Organization takes action which warrants the assertion that it was appropriate for the fulfilment of one of the stated purposes of the United Nations, the presumption is that such action is not *ultra vires* the Organization.

If it is agreed that the action in question is within the scope of the functions of the Organization but it is alleged that it has been initiated or carried out in a manner not in conformity with the division of functions among the several organs which the Charter prescribes, one moves to the internal plane, to the internal structure of the Organization. If the action was taken by the wrong organ, it was irregular as a matter of that internal structure, but this would not necessarily mean that the expense incurred was not an expense of the Organization. Both national and international law contemplate cases in which the body corporate or politic may be bound, as to third parties, by an *ultra vires* act of an agent. [···]

(p. 175-) The Court concludes that, from year to year, the expenses of UNEF have been treated by the General Assembly as expenses of the Organization within the meaning of Article 17, paragraph 2, of the Charter. [···]

(p. 178-) The conclusion to be drawn from these paragraphs is that the General Assembly has twice decided that even though certain expenses are "extraordinary" and "essentially different" from those under the "regular budget," they are none the less "expenses of the Organization" to be apportioned in accordance with the power granted to the General Assembly by Article 17, paragraph 2. [⋯]

(p. 179-) At the outset of this opinion, the Court pointed out that the text of Article 17, paragraph 2, of the Charter could lead to the simple conclusion that "the expenses of the Organization" are the amounts paid out to defray the costs of carrying out the purposes of the Organization. It was further indicated that the Court would examine the resolutions authorizing the expenditures referred to in the request for the advisory opinion in order to ascertain whether they were incurred with that end in view. The Court has made such an examination and finds that they were so incurred. The Court has also analyzed the principal arguments which have been advanced against the conclusion that the expenditures in question should be considered as "expenses of the Organization within the meaning of Article 17, paragraph 2, of the Charter of the United Nations," and has found that these arguments are unfounded. Consequently, the Court arrives at the conclusion that the question submitted to it in General Assembly resolution 1731 (XVI) must be answered in the affirmative. [⋯]

☑ 해 설

현재에도 전세계 곳곳에서 활발하게 진행되는 UN평화유지활동의 UN헌장상 근거가 명확하게 정리되었다는 점에서 이 권고적 의견의 의의를 찾을 수 있다. 이 사안에서 평화유지활동의 헌장상 근거와 그 경비의 UN 경비 해당 여부가 직접적 쟁점이었다. 그러나 ICJ가 여기에서 설시한 바는 이 문제에 국한되지 않고 국제기구의 활동과 관련되는 다른 분야에 대하여도 다양한 시사점을 제공하고 있다. 요컨대, 헌장상 명문 규정이 부재하더라도 헌장 목적 달성을 위해 취하는 구체적 조치는 기본적으로 월권행위에 해당하지 않는다는 점이 이 권고적 의견으로 다시 확인되었다. 이에 따라 묵시적 권한 (implied power) 이론을 확인한 1949년의 유엔 근무중 입은 손해배상에 관한 권고적 의견[1]과 함께 이 권고적 의견은 이후 UN을 비롯한 여타 국제기구의 활동 영역 확대에 중요한 법적 근거를 제공했다. 물론 앞서 살펴본 핵무기 사용의 위법성 사건에서 보는 바와 같이 이러한 국제기구 활동의 외연은 존재한다. 또한 UN안전보장이사회의 국제평화와 안전의 유지에 관한 권한은

---

1) Certain expenses of the United Nations(Article 17, Paragraph 2 of the Chartes), Advisory Opinion of 20 July 1962: ICJ Reports 1962, p. 151.

배타적 권한이 아님을 확인함에 따라 이 문제에 관해 여타 UN 기관이 고유
이 역할을 수행할 가능성이 있음을 지적하고 있는 점 역시 주목할 만하다.
ICJ에 의한 UN안전보장이사회 설치 및 결의에 대한 사법심사의 가능성을 주
장하는 학자들의 의견도 이 권고적 의견의 취지에 상당 부분 기초하고 있음
은 바로 이러한 이유이다.

현재 UN은 정규예산(regular budget)과는 다른 특별계정(special account)을
설치하여 별도의 예산으로 평화유지활동을 운영하고 있으며, 회원국들은 자
신의 분담비율에 따라 그 경비를 분담하고 있다. 평화유지활동 경비로 1948
년부터 2010년 6월까지 약 690억 달러가 지출되었으며, 2019년 7월 1일부터
2020년 6월 30일까지 1년의 기간동안 평화유지활동 예산으로 65억 1천만 달
러가 편성되어 있다. 참고로 2020년 7월 현재 UN은 전 세계에서 13개의 평
화유지활동을 수행하고 있다.

이와 같은 유엔의 평화유지활동과 관련하여 전반적으로는 분쟁을 겪은
국가들의 평화와 안정의 회복을 위한 가장 효과적인 도구로서 기능을 한다
는 평가를 받고 있으며, 이에 따라 유엔 총회에서도 넓은 지지를 받으며 평
화유지활동은 지속적으로 그 범위를 확대하고 있다. 하지만 평화유지활동 과
정에서 평화유지군에 의해 발생하는 각종 범죄 등으로 인해 동 활동에 대한
우려 또한 동시에 제기되고 있다.

➡ 참고문헌 ─────────────────────────────

• 전순신, 어떤 종류의 유엔경비(헌장 제17조 2항), 동아법학 제19권(1995), p.
  219.
• A. Orakhelashvili, The Legal Basis of the UN Peace−Keeping Operations,
  Virginia Journal of International Law Vol. 43(2003), p. 485.
• L. B. Sohn, Panel II: Global Attitudes on the Role of the United Nations in
  the Maintenance and Restoration of Peace, Georgia Journal of International
  & Comparative Law Vol. 26, No. 1(2014).
• L. Gross, Expenses of the United Nations for Peace−Keeping Operations:
  The Advisory Opinion of the International Court of Justice, International
  Organization Vol. 17(1963), p. 1.

5. 팔레스타인 점령지역에서 이스라엘의 장벽 건설 사건(2004)
—국내 테러 위협에 대한 자위권 행사 허용 여부

Legal Consequences of the Construction of a Wall in the Occupied Palestine Territory.
Advisory Opinion, 2004 ICJ Reports 136.

☑ 사　　안

이 사건은 이스라엘과 팔레스타인간 오래된 분쟁을 다룬다. 2002년 자살폭탄 공격과 테러행위가 증가하자 이스라엘은 팔레스타인과 이스라엘 사이에 소위 "안보장벽(Security Fence)"을 건설했다. 원래 이 장벽은 팔레스타인 자치정부가 자리잡고 있는 요르단강 서안지구(West Bank)의 16%에 해당하는 지역을 격리할 계획이었으나 추후 7%로 조정되었다. 안보장벽의 대부분은 철제 그물망으로 건설되었으나 일부 지역에서는 두꺼운 콘크리트 장벽이 설치되었다. 여기에는 전자감응장치가 부설되고 접근을 차단하기 위해 4미터에 달하는 웅덩이가 장벽 주변에 구축되었다. 이에 따라 서안지구에 거주하는 팔레스타인 주민들은 안보장벽 외부에 있는 자신들의 농장 및 여타 마을과의 접촉이 차단되었다. 이 장벽 건설 후 이스라엘 내 테러행위는 상당 부분 감소했으며 이를 근거로 이스라엘은 안보장벽 설치의 필요성을 주장했다. 그러나 이스라엘이 건설한 장벽에 대한 국제사회의 비난이 증가하자 유엔 총회는 2003년 12월 8일 유엔 총회결의를 통해 이스라엘의 안보장벽이 국제법에 합치하는지 여부에 관해 ICJ의 권고적 의견을 구하기로 결정했다.

☑ **쟁 점**

⑴ 1949년 제네바 협정, 유엔 총회 결의, 유엔 안보리 결의 등에 나타난 국제법의 원칙에 비추어 이스라엘이 팔레스타인 점령지역 내에 건설한 안보장벽의 법적 성격.

⑵ 이스라엘의 안보장벽 건설은 정당한 자위권의 행사에 해당하는지 여부.

⑶ 안보장벽 설치가 국제법 위반에 해당한다면 그로 인해 초래되는 법적 결과.

☑ **판 결**

⑴ 팔레스타인 점령지역 내에 건설한 안보장벽은 이 지역의 인위적 분리를 고착화시키고 재산권 행사 등을 제약하여 팔레스타인 주민들의 민족자결권 및 국제인권법이 보장하는 기본적 인권의 침해이다

⑵ 유엔 헌장 제51조상 자위권의 행사는 다른 '국가'가 자국에 대해 무력공격을 행한 경우 인정되나 이스라엘은 자국에 대한 공격의 주체를 다른 국가라고 주장하지는 않았다. 이스라엘이 주장한 위협은 외부가 아닌, 이스라엘이 통제권을 행사하는 점령지역 내에서 발생한 것이므로, 이스라엘의 장벽 설치는 제51조가 규정하는 자위권에 의해 정당화되지 않는다.

⑶ 이스라엘은 장벽 건설을 중단하고 이미 건설된 장벽은 철거해야 하며, 장벽 건설 관련 국내법령을 개폐해야 한다. 아울러 이스라엘은 장벽 건설로 피해를 입은 자연인 및 법인에 대하여 손해배상을 해야 한다. 여타 국가들은 장벽 건설로 인해 초래된 불법적인 상황을 인정하거나 그러한 설치를 지원해서는 아니 된다.

판 결 문

14. The Court will thus first address the question whether it possesses jurisdiction to give the advisory opinion requested by the General Assembly on 8 December 2003. The competence of the Court in this regard is based on Article 65, paragraph 1, of its Statute, according to which the Court "may give an advisory opinion on any legal question at the request of whatever body may be authorized by or in accordance with the Charter of the United Nations to make such a request." [⋯]

80. The report of the Secretary-General States that "The Government of Israel has since 1996 considered plans to halt infiltration into Israel from the central and northern West Bank ..." (para. 4). According to that report, a plan of this type was approved for the first time by the Israeli Cabinet in July 2001. Then, on 14 April 2002, the Cabinet adopted a decision for the construction of works, forming what Israel describes as a "security fence," 80 kilometers in length, in three areas of the West Bank. The project was taken a stage further when, on 23 June 2002, the Israeli Cabinet approved the first phase of the construction of a "continuous fence" in the West Bank (including East Jerusalem). [⋯] Furthermore, on 1 October 2003, the Israeli Cabinet approved a full route, which, according to the report of the Secretary-General, "will form one continuous line stretching 720 kilometers along the West Bank." A map showing completed and planned sections was posted on the Israeli Ministry of Defence website on 23 October 2003. According to the particulars provided on that map, a continuous section (Phase C) encompassing a number of large settlements will link the north-western end of the "security fence" built around Jerusalem with the southern point of Phase A construction at Elkana. According to the same map, the "security fence" will run for 115kilometers from the Har Gilo settlement near Jerusalem to the Carmel settlement south-east of Hebron (Phase D). [⋯]

82. According to the description in the report and the Written Statement of the Secretary-General, the works planned or completed have resulted or will result in a complex consisting essentially of:

> (1) a fence with electronic sensors;
> (2) a ditch (up to 4 :meters deep);
> (3) a two-lane asphalt patrol road;
> (4) a trace road (a strip of sand smoothed to detect footprints) running parallel to the fence;
> (5) a stack of six coils of barbed wire marking the perimeter of the complex. [⋯]

87. The Court first recalls that, pursuant to Article 2, paragraph 4, of the United Nations Charter:

> "All Members shall refrain in their international relations from the threat

or use of force against the territorial integrity or political independence of any State, or in any other manner inconsistent with the Purposes of the United Nations." [⋯]

88. The Court also notes that the principle of self-determination of peoples has been enshrined in the United Nations Charter and reaffirmed by the General Assembly in resolution 2625 (XXV) cited above, pursuant to which "Every State has the duty to refrain from any forcible action which deprives peoples referred to [in that resolution] ⋯ of their right to self-determination." [⋯]

121. Whilst the Court notes the assurance given by Israel that the construction of the wall does not amount to annexation and that the wall is of a temporary nature, it nevertheless cannot remain indifferent to certain fears expressed to it that the route of the wall will prejudge the future frontier between Israel and Palestine, and the fear that Israel may integrate the settlements and their means of access. The Court considers that the construction of the wall and its associated régime create a "fait accompli" on the ground that could well become permanent, in which case, and notwithstanding the formal characterization of the wall by Israel, it would be tantamount to *de facto* annexation. [⋯]

132. From the information submitted to the Court, particularly the report of the Secretary-General, it appears that the construction of the wall has led to the destruction or requisition of properties under conditions which contravene the requirements of Articles 46 and 52 of the Hague Regulations of 1907 and of Article 53 of the Fourth Geneva Convention.

133. That construction, the establishment of a closed area between the Green Line and the wall itself and the creation of enclaves have moreover imposed substantial restrictions on the freedom of movement of the inhabitants of the Occupied Palestinian Territory. [⋯]

134. To sum up, the Court is of the opinion that the construction of the wall and its associated régime impede the liberty of movement of the inhabitants of the Occupied Palestinian Territory [⋯] as guaranteed under Article 12, paragraph 1, of the International Covenant on Civil and Political Rights. They also impede the exercise by the persons concerned of the right to work, to health, to education and to an adequate standard of living as proclaimed in the International Covenant on Economic, Social and Cultural Rights and in the United Nations Convention on the Rights of the Child. Lastly, the construction of the wall and its associated régime, by contributing to the demographic changes referred to in paragraphs 122 and 133 above, contravene Article 49, paragraph 6, of the Fourth Geneva Convention and the Security Council resolutions cited in paragraph 120 above. [⋯]

138. The Court has thus concluded that the construction of the wall constitutes action not in conformity with various international legal obligations incumbent upon Israel. However, Annex I to the report of the Secretary-General states that, according to Israel: "the construction of the Barrier is consistent with Article 51 of the Charter of the United Nations, its inherent right to self-defence and Security Council resolutions 1368 (2001) and 1373 (2001)". More specifically, Israel's Permanent Representative to the United Nations asserted in the General Assembly on 20 October 2003 that "the fence is a measure wholly consistent with the right of States to self-defence enshrined in Article 51 of the Charter." [⋯]

139. Under the terms of Article 51 of the Charter of the United Nations:

"Nothing in the present Charter shall impair the inherent right of individual or collective self-defence if an armed attack occurs against a Member of the United Nations, until the Security Council has taken measures necessary to maintain international peace and security."

Article 51 of the Charter thus recognizes the existence of an inherent right of self-defence in the case of armed attack by one State against another State. However, Israel does not claim that the attacks against it are imputable to a foreign State. The Court also notes that Israel exercises control in the Occupied Palestinian Territory and that, as Israel itself states, the threat which it regards as justifying the construction of the wall originates within, and not outside, that territory. The situation is thus different from that contemplated by Security Council resolutions 1368 (2001) and 1373 (2001), and therefore Israel could not in any event invoke those resolutions in support of its claim to be exercising a right of self-defence. Consequently, the Court concludes that Article 51 of the Charter has no relevance in this case.

140. The Court has, however. considered whether Israel could rely on a state of necessity, which would preclude the wrongfulness of the construction of the wall. In this regard the Court is bound to note that some of the conventions at issue in the present instance include qualifying clauses of the rights guaranteed or provisions for derogation. [⋯] In the light of the material before it, the Court is not convinced that the construction of the wall along the route chosen was the only means to safeguard the interests of Israel against the peril which it has invoked as justification for that construction. [⋯]

142. In conclusion, the Court considers that Israel cannot rely on a right of self-defence or on a state of necessity in order to preclude the wrongfulness of the construction of the wall resulting from the considerations mentioned in paragraphs 122 and 137 above. The Court accordingly finds that the construction of the wall, and its associated régime, are contrary to international law. [···]

145. As regards the legal consequences for Israel, it was contended that Israel has, first, a legal obligation to bring the illegal situation to an end by ceasing forthwith the construction of the wall in the Occupied Palestinian Territory, and to give appropriate assurances and guarantees of non-repetition. It was argued that, secondly, Israel is under a legal obligation to make reparation for the damage arising from its unlawful conduct. It was submitted that such reparation should first of all take the form of restitution, namely demolition of those portions of the wall constructed in the Occupied Palestinian Territory and annulment of the legal acts associated with its construction and the restoration of property requisitioned or expropriated for that purpose; reparation should also include appropriate compensation for individuals whose homes or agricultural holdings have been destroyed. [···]

146. As regards the legal consequences for States other than Israel, it was contended before the Court that all States are under an obligation not to recognize the illegal situation arising from the construction of the wall, not to render aid or assistance in maintaining that situation and to co-operate with a view to putting an end to the alleged violations and to ensuring that reparation will be made therefor. [···]

☑ 해   설

이 권고적 의견은 팔레스타인 지역에 건설한 장벽과 관련하여 이스라엘에 대한 대내외 압력을 더욱 가중시켰으며 결국 문제의 장벽이 상당 부분 철거되도록 유도했다. ICJ는 이 권고적 의견에서 팔레스타인 주민들에 대한 인권 침해 문제를 상당 부분 다루고 있으나, 국제평화와 안전보장과 관련해서도 주목할 만한 법리를 제시하고 있다. 안보장벽 설치에 대해 이스라엘은 이를 유엔 헌장 제51조상 자위권 행사의 일환인 것으로 설명했다. 계속되는 테러리스트 공격 등으로 인해 자국민의 안전을 확보하고자 장벽 설치가 불가피했다는 것이다. 그러나 이러한 자위권 주장은 원칙적으로 ICJ에 의해 배척되었다. ICJ는 이스라엘의 자위권 행사를 부인하며 두 가지 근거를 제시했다.

먼저, 헌장 제51조상 자위권은 오로지 일국이 타국에 의해 군사적 공격을 받는 경우에 원용할 수 있으나 이스라엘의 경우에는 타국으로부터의 공격은 없었다는 점이다. 이스라엘이 여러 가지 대내외 위협에 직면하고 있었다는 점은 객관적 사실이나 그렇다고 하여 이스라엘에 대한 외국으로부터의 공격이 존재했다고 볼 수는 없다는 것이다. 이러한 위협은 일반적인 안보상 또는 치안상 위협이라고 볼 수는 있을 것이나 이에 대해 타국으로부터의 군사적 위협에 적용되는 자위권 행사를 원용할 수는 없다는 점을 ICJ는 확인했다. 두 번째로는 팔레스타인 지역에 대해 이스라엘이 통제권을 이미 행사하므로 이 지역은 자위권 행사의 대상이 되지 않는다는 것이다. 이미 자국이 통제권을 행사하는 지역에 대해 자위권을 행사하는 것은 모순이라는 것이다. 통제권을 행사하므로 외국으로부터의 군사적 위협이 부재한다는 점을 법원은 거듭 확인하고 자위권 행사를 부인한 것이다. 요컨대 국내 또는 자신이 관할권을 행사하는 지역 내에서의 형사사법 조치에 대해 자위권 발동을 원용하는 것은 허용되지 않는다는 것이다. 논란의 여지는 있을 수 있으나, 일단 두 근거 모두 유엔 헌장 제51조의 의미를 충실히 해석한 것으로 판단된다.

그러나 한편으로 최근 탈레반 및 이슬람 국가(Islamic State: IS) 사례에서 보는 바와 같이 국가 이외의 주체에 의한 무력 위협이 점차 심각하게 대두하는 상황이다. 이러한 현실에 직면하여 자위권 행사를 오로지 외국으로부터의 군사적 위협에만 국한하여 해석하는 입장이 앞으로도 타당할지 여부는 면밀하게 검토할 필요가 있다. 전통적 방식의 국가 대 국가간 충돌이 아닌 여러 지역에 산재하는 비국가적 실체에 의한, 또는 이들에 대한 대규모 전쟁이 이라크, 아프가니스탄, 시리아 등에서 전개되어 온 점을 감안하면 때로는 비국가적 실체의 무력공격이 국가의 무력공격에 버금가는 상황도 충분히 발생할 수 있다. 이 경우 자위권 행사를 부인한다면 현실과 유리된 법리 해석으로 비판받을 소지가 있을 것이다. 나아가 특정 지역이 전체적으로 특정 국가의 통제하에 있는 경우에도 이러한 비국가적 주체에 의한 군사적 위협은 실질적으로 제기될 수 있다는 측면도 고려할 필요가 있다. 그렇다면 이 권고적 의견에서 제시된 법리가 최근 급변하는 국제상황에 포괄적으로 대처할 수 있는 원칙을 담고 있는지 다시 한번 생각해 볼 여지가 있을 것이다.

이 권고적 의견은 팔레스타인 주민에 대한 이스라엘의 조치라는 점에서 현재 세계 여러 곳에서 진행되고 있는 탈레반 및 IS와의 전쟁과는 상이한 측면이 있다. 팔레스타인 지역 맥락에서는 이스라엘의 자위권 행사 주장이 타당하지 않다고 결정한 ICJ의 권고적 의견은 설득력이 있다. 그러나 그 논리가 자위권 행사를 전통적인 방식으로만 국한하는 내용으로 이해된다면 다양한 새로운 형태의 위협에 대한 국가의 합법적 방어수단 모색을 저해하는 효과가 발생할 수도 있을 것이다.

➡ 참고문헌 ─────────────────────────────

- 나인균, '점령된 팔레스타인영역에서 건설된 장벽의 법적 결과'에 관한 ICJ 권고적 의견, 성균관법학 Vol. 22, No. 3(2010).
- 오인미, 팔레스타인 점령지역에서 이스라엘의 장벽 건설에 관한 ICJ 권고적 의견에 대한 고찰, 충남대학교 법학연구 제15권(2004).
- M. Burgis, Discourses of Division: Law, Politics and the ICJ Advisory Opinion on the Legal Consequences of the Construction of a Wall in the Occupied Palestinian Territory, Chinese Journal of International Law(2008).
- A. Orakhelashvili, Legal Consequences of the Construction of a Wall in the Occupied Palestinian Territory: Opinion and Reaction, Journal of Conflict & Security Law(2006).
- Fr. R. J. Araujo, S.J., Implementation of the ICJ Advisory Opinion ─ Legal Consequences of the Construction of a Wall in the Occupied Palestinian Territory: Fences [Do Not] Make Good Neighbors, Boston University International Law Journal(2004).
- R. Kahan, Building a Protective Wall Around Terrorisms ─ How the International Court of Justice's Ruling in The Legal Consequences of the Construction of a Wall in the Occupied Palestinian Territory Made the World Safer for Terrorists and More Dangerous for Member States of the United Nations, Fordham International Law Journal Vol. 28(2004).

6. 로커비 사건(1998)
― 유엔 헌장상 안전보장이사회와 ICJ의 권한

Questions of Interpretation and Application of the 1971
Montreal Convention arising from the Aerial Incident at
Lockerbie(Libyan Arab Jamahiriya v. United Kingdom),
Preliminary Objections, Judgment, ICJ Reports 1998, p. 9.

☑ 사 안

1988년 12월 21일 미국 팬암사의 여객기가 스코틀랜드 Lockerbie 마을 상공에서 공중 폭발하여 259명의 탑승객과 지상에 있던 11명의 주민이 사망하는 사건이 발생했다. 미국과 영국 사법당국의 조사 결과 이 항공기 테러가 리비아 정보요원의 소행인 것으로 확인되자, 미국과 영국은 1971년 몬트리올 협약에 따라 해당 정보요원 2인에 대한 범죄인 인도를 리비아 정부에 요청했다. 이에 대해 리비아는 자국민 불인도 원칙을 내세우며 이들의 인도를 거부했다. 미국과 영국은 이 사건을 유엔 안전보장이사회에 회부하여 안보리 결의 제748호(1992)와 제883호(1993)를 채택하고 범죄인 인도를 거부한 리비아에 대해 강력한 경제제재를 실시했다.

한편 리비아는 1971년 몬트리올 협약 제9조에 따라 이 분쟁을 다룰 관할권이 ICJ에게 있음에도 불구하고 미국과 영국이 이 조항을 준수하지 않고 유엔 안전보장이사회에 회부했음을 들어 양국을 ICJ에 제소했다. 미국과 영국은 선결적 항변을 통해 이 사건은 이미 안전보장이사회가 담당하는 사안으로 이에 대해 ICJ가 관할권을 행사할 수 없다고 주장했다. 또한 양국은 설사 ICJ가 이 사건에 대해 관할권이 있더라도 안전보장이사회 결의 제748호와 제883호로 인해 리비아의 청구를 본안 판결을 할 소의 이익이 없으므로, ICJ가 이 제소에 대해 본안심리를 해서는 안 된다고 주장했다. 결국 동일한 사건에 대해 미국과 영국은 안전보장이사회로, 리비아는 ICJ로 각각 별도의 절차를 진행한 것이다. 유엔 체제의 핵심을 이루는 두 기구의 권한 충돌을 어떻게 이해할 것인지에 대해 국제사회의 관심이 집중되있다.

☑ 쟁   점

(1) 유엔 안전보장이사회가 담당하고 있는 사건에 대해 ICJ가 관할권을 행사할 수 있는지 여부.

(2) 관할권 존부와 별도로 안전보장이사회가 이미 담당하는 이 사건에 대해 ICJ의 본안심리를 인정하기 위한 소의 이익(admissibility)이 있는지 여부.

☑ 판   결

(1) 안전보장이사회가 유엔 헌장에 규정된 권한을 행사하고 있더라도 ICJ는 유엔의 주요 사법기관으로 스스로의 관할권을 행사할 수 있다.

(2) 안전보장이사회 논의 및 결의 채택 여부와 상관없이 이 사건에 대해 ICJ의 본안심리를 위한 소의 이익을 인정할 수 있다.

판 결 문

18. Libya submits that the Court has jurisdiction on the basis of Article 14, paragraph 1, of the Montreal Convention, which provides that:

"Any dispute between two or more Contracting States concerning the interpretation or application of this Convention which cannot be settled through negotiation, shall, at the request of one of them, be submitted to arbitration. If within six months of the date of the request for arbitration the Parties are unable to agree on the organization of the arbitration, any one of those Parties may refer the dispute to the International Court of Justice by request in conformity with the Statute of the Court."

19. The Parties agree that the Montreal Convention is in force between them and that it was already in force both at the time of the destruction of the Pan Am aircraft over Lockerbie, on 21 December 1988, and at the time of filing of the Application, on 3 March 1992 [⋯].

23. In its Application and Memorial, Libya maintained that the Montreal

Convention was the only instrument applicable to the destruction of the Pan Am aircraft over Lockerbie [···].

29. In view of the positions put forward by the Parties, the Court finds that there exists between them not only a dispute of a general nature, as defined in paragraph 25 above, but also a specific dispute which concerns the interpretation and application of Article 7—read in conjunction with Article 1, Article 5, Article 6 and Article 8—of the Montreal Convention and which, in accordance with Article 14, paragraph 1, of the Convention, falls to be decided by the Court.

35. The United Kingdom maintains that it is not for the Court, on the basis of Article 14, paragraph 1, of the Montreal Convention, to decide on the lawfulness of actions which are in any event in conformity with international law, and which were instituted by the Respondent to secure the surrender of the two alleged offenders. It concludes from this that the Court lacks jurisdiction over the submissions presented on this point by Libya.

36. The Court cannot uphold the line of argument thus formulated. Indeed, it is for the Court to decide, on the basis of Article 14, paragraph 1, of the Montreal Convention, on the lawfulness of the actions criticized by Libya, in so far as those actions would be at variance with the provisions of the Montreal Convention.

37. In the present case, the United Kingdom has contended, however, that even if the Montreal Convention did confer on Libya the rights it claims, they could not be exercised in this case because they were superseded by Security Council resolutions 748 (1992) and 883 (1993) which, by virtue of Articles 25 and 103 of the United Nations Charter, have priority over all rights and obligations arising out of the Montreal Convention. The Respondent has also argued that, because of the adoption of those resolutions, the only dispute which existed from that point on was between Libya and the Security Council; this, clearly, would not be a dispute falling within the terms of Article 14, paragraph 1, of the Montreal Convention and thus not one which the Court could entertain.

38. The Court cannot uphold this line of argument. Security Council resolutions 748 (1992) and 883 (1993) were in fact adopted after the filing of the Application on 3 March 1992. In accordance with its established jurisprudence, if the Court had jurisdiction on that date, it continues to do so; the subsequent coming into existence of the above-mentioned resolutions cannot affect its jurisdiction once established [···].

39. In the light of the foregoing, the Court concludes that the objection to jurisdiction raised by the United Kingdom on the basis of the alleged absence of a dispute between the Parties concerning the interpretation or application of the Montreal Convention must be rejected, and that the Court has jurisdiction to hear the disputes between Libya and the United Kingdom as to the interpretation or application of the provisions of that Convention.

40. The Court will now proceed to consider the objection of the United Kingdom that the Libyan Application is not admissible.

41. [⋯] According to the United Kingdom, those resolutions require the surrender of the two suspects by Libya to the United Kingdom or the United States for trial, and this determination by the Security Council is binding on Libya irrespective of any rights it may have under the Montreal Convention. On this basis, the United Kingdom maintains that

> "the relief which Libya seeks from the Court under the Montreal Convention is not open to it, and that the Court should therefore exercise its power to declare the Libyan Application inadmissible". [⋯]

44. In the view of the Court, this last submission of Libya must be upheld. The date, 3 March 1992, on which Libya filed its Application, is in fact the only relevant date for determining the admissibility of the Application. Security Council resolutions 748 (1992) and 883 (1993) cannot be taken into consideration in this regard since they were adopted at a later date. As to Security Council resolution 731 (1992), adopted before the filing of the Application, it could not form a legal impediment to the admissibility of the latter because it was a mere recommendation without binding effect, as was recognized moreover by the United Kingdom itself. Consequently, Libya's Application cannot be held inadmissible on these grounds.

45. In the light of the foregoing, the Court concludes that the objection to admissibility derived by the United Kingdom from Security Council resolutions 748 (1992) and 883 (1993) must be rejected, and that Libya's Application is admissible.

42. [⋯] Libya also observes that the arguments of the United Kingdom based on the provisions of the Charter raise problems which do not possess an exclusively preliminary character, but appertain to the merits of the dispute. It argues in particular that the question of the effect of the Security Council resolutions is not of an exclusively preliminary character, inasmuch as the resolutions under consideration are relied upon by the United Kingdom in order to overcome the application of the Montreal Convention, and since Libya is justified in disputing that these resolutions are opposable to it.

43. Libya furthermore draws the Court's attention to the principle that "The critical date for determining the admissibility of an application is the date on which it is filed" [···] It points out in this connection that its Application was filed on 3 March 1992; that Security Council resolutions 748 (1992) and 883 (1993) were adopted on 31 March 1992 and 11 November 1993, respectively; and that resolution 731 (1992) of 21 January 1992 was not adopted under Chapter VI1 of the United Nations Charter and was only a mere recommendation. Consequently, Libya argues, its Application is admissible in any event.

44. In the view of the Court, this last submission of Libya must be upheld.[···]

45. In the light of the foregoing, the Court concludes that the objection to admissibility derived by the United Kingdom from Security Council resolutions 748 (1992) and 883 (1993) must be rejected, and that Libya's Application is admissible.

50. [···] However, by requesting such a decision, the United Kingdom is requesting, in reality, at least two others which the decision not to proceed to judgment on the merits would necessarily postulate: on the one hand a decision establishing that the rights claimed by Libya under the Montreal Convention are incompatible with its obligations under the Security Council resolutions; and, on the other hand, a decision that those obligations prevail over those rights by virtue of Articles 25 and 103 of the Charter. [···] the United Kingdom Government thus implicitly acknowledged that the objection raised and the merits of the case were "closely interconnected" [···] If the Court were to rule on that objection, it would therefore inevitably be ruling on the merits [···]

51. Having established its jurisdiction and concluded that the Application is admissible, the Court will be able to consider this objection when it reaches the merits of the case.

☑ 해   설

이 사건은 유엔 내에서 ICJ와 안전보장이사회간의 구조적인 문제를 검토하고 있다. 유엔의 주요 사법기관(principal judicial organ)으로서 ICJ의 위상과1) 유엔의 최고 의사결정기구로서 안전보장이사회의 권한2)이 충돌하는 문제를 어떻게 다룰 것인지가 이 분쟁의 핵심이기 때문이다. 이 분쟁이 선결적 항변 절차임을 감안하여 ICJ는 영국과 미국의 주장은 오히려 본안에서 필연

---

1) UN 헌장 제92조 참조.
2) UN헌장 제24조 제1항 및 제25조 참조.

적으로 다루어질 두 가지 쟁점과 관련된다고 보았다. 즉, 1971년 몬트리올 협약상의 권리가 안전보장이사회 결의에 따른 의무와 양립할 수 있는지 여부와, 그러한 의무가 헌장 제25조와 제103소에 따리 1971년 몬트리올 협약 상 권리에 우선하는지 여부가 그것이다. 전자는 안전보장이사회 결의의 해석을, 그리고 후자는 헌장 제25조 및 제103조의 해석을 수반하게 된다. 이들 문제는 본안에서 다루어야 할 사항으로 선결적 항변에서 결정할 것은 아니라는 것이다. 이 두 쟁점은 결국 ICJ가 안전보장이사회 결의의 합법성을 심사하는 문제와 직결된다. 유엔 체제의 거버넌스 맥락에서 상당히 중요한 문제가 아닐 수 없다. 그러나 ICJ가 그러한 심사 권한을 행사할 수 있는지 여부에 관한 판단은 이후 소가 취하됨으로써 후일로 미루어졌다.

1988년 Lockerbie 사건 발생 이후 리비아의 책임 소재가 확인된 1990년 초반부터 미국/영국은 유엔 안전보장이사회를 통해 리비아에 대한 강력한 제재를 실시하여 사건의 진상 규명과 관련자 처벌을 리비아에 요구했다. 이에 대해 리비아는 유엔 안전보장이사회를 통한 상임이사국 2개국의 횡포와 주권침해라는 주장으로 맞섰다. 오랜 대립 끝에 양측은 1999년 4월 합의에 이르렀다. 용의자로 지목된 리비아 국적자 2인을 네덜란드로 인도하기로 한 것이다. 이에 따라 2000년 네덜란드에서 사고발생지인 스코틀랜드법에 따른 형사재판이 이루어졌다. 네덜란드 내 미군 기지(Camp Zeist)에서 스코틀랜드 법관들로 구성된 재판부가 스코틀랜드법을 적용하는 특별 형사재판을 진행했다. 2001년 종결된 형사재판 결과 리비아 정보요원인 Al-Megrahi에 대한 유죄판결이 내려졌다. 또한 2002년 리비아는 자국에 대한 경제제재 해제 조건으로 270명의 유가족에게 1천만불씩 지급하기로 합의했다.

한편 국가간 합의 절차와 별도로 사망한 일부 탑승객의 유가족들은 리비아를 상대로 미국 연방법원에서 손해배상 청구소송을 시작했다.3) 원래 리비아는 미국의 주권면제법(Foreign Sovereign Immunity Act of 1975)상 주권면제를 향유하는 주권국가이나, 원고인 유족들은 이 법에 포함된 국가지원 테러리즘 예외조항(28 U.S.C. § 1605(a)(7))을 원용하여 본 건에서는 주권면제의 보호가 리비아에 적용되지 않는다고 주장하며 손해배상 청구소송을 제기한

---

3) Hurst v. Socialist People's Libyan Arab Jamahiriya, 474 F. Supp. 2d 19 (D.D.C. 2007).

것이다. 특히 유족들은 2001년 네덜란드에서 진행된 형사재판에서 Al-Megrahi에 대한 유죄판결이 내려졌으므로 핵심 쟁점에 대한 그 판결의 기판력으로 인해(issue preclusion) 미국 법원 심리에서도 그대로 받아들여져야 한다고 주장했다.

이 사건을 담당한 미국 워싱턴 D.C. 연방지방법원은 (1) 문제의 쟁점이 외국 법원에서 실제로 구체적으로 다툼이 있고 이에 대해 해당 외국 법원이 구체적으로 판결했으며, (2) 미국 법원에서 이러한 외국 법원의 판결을 수용하는 것이 불공정(unfair)한 상황을 초래하지 아니하며, (3) 해당 외국에서 "완전하고 공정한 재판(full and fair trial)"이 진행되었고, 나아가 (4) 그러한 외국 재판과 판결의 승인 및 집행이 미국의 공공정책(public policy)에 위반되지 않으면 해당 외국 판결을 미국 법원에서 승인하여 집행해야 한다는 기본원칙을 본 사안에 적용했다. 또한 DC 연방지방법원은 피고 Al-Megrahi의 재판이 84일간 진행되었고 231명의 증인이 출석하여 그 중 132명에 대해 교차심문이 진행되는 등 상당히 심도있게 진행되었다는 점에 주목했다. 이러한 심도깊은 심리에 기초하여 피고에 대한 유죄판결이 내려졌으며, 해당 형사재판의 상소법원도 피고의 상소를 장문의 판결로 기각했다는 점에 역시 주목했다.

따라서 이러한 점을 고려할 때 DC 지방법원은 네덜란드에서 진행된 형사재판에서 확정된 사실을 미국 법원 심리에서 그대로 수용해도 미국 국내법상 문제될 것이 없다는 결정을 내렸다. 이에 따라 DC 지방법원은 피해 탑승객의 사망에 Al-Megrahi가 법적 책임이 있다는 결론을 도출했다.

➡ **참고문헌** ─────────────────────────────────

- 박현석, UN헌장상 강제조치와 국제재판의 관계: Lockerbie 사건(1988-98), 국제법학회논총 제43권 제2호(1998), p. 97.
- 나인균, 국제연합(UN)에서의 '법의 지배' 원리: 로커비사건과 관련하여, 국제법학회논총 제50권 제1호(2005), p. 57.
- K. Skubiszewski, "The International Court of Justice and the Security Council", in V. Lowe & M. Fitzmaurice (ed.), Fifty Years of the International

Court of Justice, Cambridge University Press(1996), pp. 615－619.

• V. Gowlland－Debbas, The Relationship between the International Court of Justice and the Security Council In the Light of the Lockerbie Case, American Journal of International Law Vol. 88(1994), p. 643.

• P. H. Koojimans, "The ICJ: Where Does It Stand?" in A. S. Muller, D. Raič & J. M. Thuránszky (ed.), The International Court of Justice: Its Future Role After Fifty Years, Martinus Nijhoff Publishers(1997), pp. 416－417.

• F. Beveridge & M. D. Evans, The Lockerbie Cases, International and Comparative Law Quarterly Vol. 48(1999), p. 658.

• M. Plachta, The Lockerbie Case: The Role of the Security Council in Enforcing the Principle Aut Dedere Aut Judicare, European Journal of International Law Vol. 12(2001), p. 125.

제20장

남북한 관계

☑ 사 안

현행 헌법 제3조는 대한민국의 영토를 한반도와 그 부속도서로 규정하
고 있는 한편, 제4조는 대한민국이 평화적 통일을 지향한다고 규정하고 있
다. 남북한이 주권국가만이 회원국이 될 수 있는 유엔에 동시 가입을 하였
고, 남북기본합의서도 채택한 마당에 북한의 법적 지위는 여전히 반국가단체
인가?

☑ 쟁 점

평화통일을 지향하는 현행 헌법하에서 북한의 법적 지위.

☑ 판 결

북한은 조국의 평화적 통일을 위한 대화와 협력의 동반자이나 동시에
적화통일노선을 고수하면서 우리의 자유민주주의 체제를 전복하고자 획책하
는 반국가단체이다.

판 결 문

1991. 9. 17. 대한민국과 북한이 유엔에 동시 가입하였고, 같은 해 12.
13. 이른바 남북 고위급회담에서 남북기본합의서가 채택되었으며, 2000. 6.

15. 남북정상회담이 개최되고 남북공동선언문이 발표된 이후 남북이산가족 상봉행사를 비롯하여 남·북한 사이에 정치·경제·사회·문화·학술·스포츠 등 각계 각층에서 활발한 교류와 협력이 이루어져 왔음은 상고이유에서 지적하는 바와 같고, 이러한 일련의 남북관계의 발전은 우리 헌법 전문과 헌법 제4조, 제66조 3항, 제92조 등에 나타난 평화통일 정책의 국가목표 수립과 그 수행이라는 범위 안에서 헌법적 근거를 가진다.

그러나 북한이 조선민주주의인민공화국이라는 이름으로 유엔에 가입하였다는 사실만으로는 유엔이라는 국제기구에 가입한 다른 가맹국에 대해서 당연히 상호간에 국가승인이 있었다고 볼 수는 없다는 것이 국제정치상 관례이자 국제법상 통설적인 입장이다. 그리고 기존의 남북합의서, 남북정상회담, 남북공동선언문 등과 현재 진행되고 있는 남북회담과 경제협력 등의 현상들만으로 북한을 국제법과 국내법적으로 독립한 국가로 취급할 수 없다. 남·북한 사이의 법률관계는 우리의 헌법과 법률에 따라 판단해야 하며, 북한을 정치·경제·법률·군사·문화 등 모든 영역에서 우리와 대등한 별개의 독립된 국가로 볼 수 없다. 남·북한의 관계는 일정한 범위 안에서 "국가간의 관계가 아닌 통일을 지향하는 과정에서 잠정적으로 형성되는 특수 관계"(남북관계 발전에 관한 법률 제3조 1항 참조)로서, 남·북한은 자주·평화·민주의 원칙에 입각하여 남북공동번영과 한반도의 평화통일을 추구하는 방향으로(같은 법 제2조 1항 참조) 발전하여 나아가도록 상호 노력하여야 하고, 우리나라의 법률도 그러한 정신과 취지에 맞게 해석·적용하지 않으면 안 된다.

무릇 우리 헌법이 전문과 제4조, 제5조에서 천명한 국제평화주의와 평화통일의 원칙은 자유민주주의적 기본질서라는 우리 헌법의 대전제를 해치지 않는 것을 전제로 하는 것이다. 그런데 북한은 현시점에서도 우리 헌법의 기본원리와 서로 조화될 수 없으며 적대적이기도 한 그들의 사회주의 헌법과 그 헌법까지도 영도하는 조선로동당규약을 통하여 북한의 최종 목적이 주체사상화와 공산주의 사회를 건설하는 데에 있다는 것과 이러한 적화통일의 목표를 위하여 이른바 남한의 사회 민주화와 반외세 투쟁을 적극 지원하는 정책을 명문으로 선언하고 그에 따른 정책들을 수행하면서 이에 대하여 변경을 가할 징후를 보이고 있지 않다. 그러므로 북한이 남북관계의 발전에 따라 더 이상 우리의 자유민주주의 체제에 위협이 되지 않는다는 명백한 변화를 보이고 그에 따라 법률이 정비되지 않는 한, 국가의 안전을 위태롭게 하는 반국가활동을 규제함으로써 국가의 안전과 국민의 생존 및 자유를 확보함을 목적으로 하는 국가보안법이 헌법에 위반되는 법률이라거나 그 규범력을 상실하였다고 볼 수는 없고, 나아가 국가보안법의 규정을 그 법률의 목적에 비추어 합리적으로 해석하는 한 국가보안법이 정하는 각 범죄의 구성요건의 개념이 애매모호하고 광범위하여 죄형법정주의의 본질적 내용을 침해하는 것이라고 볼 수도 없다. 양심의 자유, 언론·출판의 자유 등은 우리 헌법이 보장하는 기본적인 권리이기는 하지만 아무런 제한이 없는 것은 아니며, 헌법 제37조 2항에 의하여 국가의 안전보장, 질서유지 또는 공공복리를 위하여 필요한 경우에는 그 자유와 권리의 본질적인 내용을 침해하지 아니하는 범위 내에서 제한할 수 있는 것이므로, 국가보안법의 입법목적과 적용한계를 위와 같이 자유와 권리의 본질적인 내용을 침해하지 아니하는 한도 내에서 이를 제한하는 데에 있는 것으로 해석하는 한 헌법에 위반된다고 볼 수 없다.

따라서 종래 대법원이 국가보안법과 북한에 대하여 표명하여 온 견해 즉, 북한은 조국의 평화적 통일을 위한 대화와 협력의 동반자이나 동시에 남·북한 관계의 변화에도 불구하고, 적화통일노선을 고수하면서 우리의 자유민주주의 체제를 전복하고자 획책하는 반국가단체라는 성격도 아울러 가지고 있고, 반국가단체 등을 규율하는 국가보안법의 규범력이 상실되었다고 볼 수는 없다고 하여 온 판시(대법원 1992년 8월 14일 선고, 92도1211 판결; 대법원 1999년 12월 28일 선고, 99도4027 판결; 대법원 2003년 5월 13일 선고, 2003도604 판결; 대법원 2003년 9월 23일 선고, 2001도4328 판결 등)는 현시점에서도 그대로 유지되어야 할 것이다.

☑ 해   설

제헌 이래 우리 헌법은 "대한민국의 영토는 한반도와 그 부속도서로 한다"(현행 헌법 제3조)는 조항을 두고 있다. 이를 근거로 법원은 북한지역도 대한민국 영토의 일부이며, 대한민국 법률의 적용대상이라는 입장에 일관하여 왔다.

"我憲法 제4조(현행 헌법 제3조 — 편자수)에 의하면 […] 북한이 我國 領土임은 다언을 요치 아니한다 할 것이니 법률론으로는 국가보안법이 동 지역내에서 행한 행위에도 적용된다 할 것이요, 다만 사실상으로 만 적용할 수 없는 형편에 처하여 있다 할 것인바, 만일 이 형편이 제거되고 사실상 적용할 수 있는 가능상태에 이르렀다면 적용함이 당연하다 할 것"(대법원 1957년 9월 20일 선고, 4290형상228 판결).

"헌법 제3조는 "대한민국의 영토는 한반도와 그 부속도서로 한다" 고 규정하고 있어 법리상 이 지역에서는 대한민국의 주권과 부딪치는 어떠한 국가단체도 인정할 수가 없는 것이므로(당원 1961년 9월 28일 선고, 4292형상48 판결 참조), 비록 북한이 국제사회에서 하나의 주권국가로 존속하고 있고, 우리정부가 북한 당국자의 명칭을 쓰면서 정상회담 등을 제의하였다 하여 북한이 대한민국의 영토고권을 침해하는 반국가단체가 아니라고 단정할 수 없으며"(대법원 1990년 9월 25일 선고, 90도1451 판결).

1987년 개정 헌법은 영토 조항 다음 제4조에서 "대한민국은 통일을 지향하며, 자유민주적 기본 질서에 입각한 평화적 통일정책을 수립하고 이를 추진한다"고 규정했고, 1980년대 말부터 남북교류가 차츰 가시화되기 시작했다. 이는 국내법제에도 반영되어 "군사분계선 이남지역과 그 이북지역간의 상호교류와 협력을 촉진하기"(제1조) 위해 1990년 8월 「남북교류협력에 관한 법률」이 제정되었다. 이어 1991년 9월 남북한은 UN에 동시 가입을 했고, 1991년 12월 남북한은 「남북 사이의 화해와 불가침 및 교류협정에 관한 합의서」(남북 기본합의서)를 채택해 1992년 2월 19일 발효시켰다. 남북기본합의서를 통해 양측은 "남과 북은 서로 상대방의 체제를 인정하고 존중"하고(제1조), "남과 북은 상대방의 내부문제에 간섭하지 아니한다"(제2조)고 약속했다. 비록 전문에서 "쌍방 사이의 관계가 나라와 나라 사이의 관계가 아닌 통일을 지향하는 과정에서 잠정적으로 형성되는 특수관계"라고 설명하고 있으나,

기본합의서의 내용은 남북한이 서로 상대를 국가적 실체로 인정한 셈이었다. 그렇다면 북한을 계속 "반국가단체"로 간주해야 하는가에 관해 이의가 제기되었다.

헌법재판소에서는 주로 국가보안법의 합헌성 판단과정에서 북한의 법적 지위에 관한 문제가 취급되었다. 변화된 시대상황에 맞추어 헌법재판소 1993. 7. 29. 선고, 92헌바48 결정부터는 북한이 "조국의 평화적 통일을 위한 대화와 협력의 동반자임과 동시에 대남적화노선을 고수하면서 우리 자유민주체제의 전복을 획책하고 있는 반국가단체라는 성격도 함께 갖고" 있다며 북한의 법적 성격을 이중적으로 판단하기 시작한 이래, 현재까지 이를 유지하고 있다.

대법원은 헌법재판소보다는 다소 늦은 1999. 7. 23. 99두3690 판결에서 처음으로 북한이 "조국의 평화적 통일을 위한 대화와 협력의 동반자임과 동시에 대남적화노선을 고수하면서 우리 자유민주체제의 전복을 획책하고 있는 반국가단체의 성격도 아울러 가지고 있음은 부인할 수 없는 현실"이라는 인식을 표시한 이래, 현재까지 유지되고 있다.

현재 헌법재판소와 대법원 공히 북한의 기본적 법적 지위를 동반자 겸 반국가단체라는 2중적 성격으로 파악하고 있지만, 아직도 반국가단체에 방점이 찍혀 있다고 볼 수 있다. 북한이 남북통일을 위한 협력의 대상이요 동반자임에도 불구하고 여전히 국가안보에 위협이 되는 반국가단체로 규정하고 있기 때문이다.

➠ 참고문헌 ───────────────────────────

- 제성호, 국가보안법상 반국가단체의 개념과 범위: 대법원 판례를 중심으로, 법조 2010년 8월호, p. 5.
- 제성호, 북한의 법적 지위 재검토: 국내법(헌법) 및 국제법적 측면의 종합적 이해를 위하여, 법조 2011년 4월호, p. 37.
- 이효원, 남북한 관계에 대한 판례분석: 국가보안법의 최근 변화 동향과 남북교류협력에 관한 판례를 중심으로, (서울대) 법학 52권 3호(2011), p. 1.

대법원 2006년 5월 11일 선고, 2005도798 판결.
판례공보 제252호(2006. 6. 15.), p. 1089.

☑ 사　안

이 사건의 피고는 주한 미군속으로 교통사고를 일으켰다. 주한미군지위협정 합의의사록에는 "평화시(in peacetime)"에는 이 같은 사건에 대해 미군당국이 형사재판권을 갖지 않는다고 규정해, 이는 한국 법원의 관할에 속함을 확인하고 있다. 그렇다면 한국의 정전상태를 "평화시"로 해석하는가라는 문제가 대두되었다.

☑ 쟁　점

한국의 정전상태는 평화시로 해석되는가?

☑ 판　결

한국의 정전상태는 평화시에 해당한다.

판 결 문

"협정 제22조 제1항 (가)는 "합중국 군 당국은 합중국 군대의 구성원, 군속 및 그들의 가족에 대하여 합중국 법령이 부여한 모든 형사재판권 및 징계권을 대한민국 안에서 행사할 권리를 가진다."고 하고, 위 조항에 관한 합의의사록에서는 "합중국 법률의 현 상태에서 합중국 군 당국은 평화시에는 군속 및 가족에 대하여 유효한 형사재판권을 가지지 아니한다. 추후의 입법, 헌법 개정 또는 합중국 관계당국에 의한 결정의 결과로서 합중국 군사재판권의 범위가 변경된다면, 합중국 정부는 외교경로를 통하여 대한민국 정부에 통보하여야 한다."고 정하고 있다. 위 조항들은 1967. 2. 9. 협정 발효 당시의 한반도의 평시(平時)상태 즉, 1953. 7. 27. 발효된 한국 군사정전에 관한 협정에 따른 정전(停戰)상태에서의 한반도의 평상시에는 미합중국 군 당국의 군사재판권이 군속 및 그 가족에 미치지 못한다는 것을 의미하는 것이다. 이에 대하여 한반도의 비상상태 발생시 즉, 대한민국이 계엄령을 선포하는 경우(협정 제22조 제1항에 관한 합의의사록 및 양해사항)나 대한민국과 미합중국 간의 상호방위조약 제2조가 적용되는 적대행위가 발생하는 경우(협정 제22조 제11항)에 대하여는, 협정에서 별도의 조항을 마련하여 대한민국의 형사재판권 행사가 즉시 정지되고 합중국 군 당국이 합중국 군대의 군속 및 가족에 대하여 전속적 형사재판권을 행사할 권리를 가진다고 정하고 있다.

위 조항들을 종합하면, 한반도의 평시상태에서 미합중국 군 당국은 미합중국 군대의 군속에 대하여 형사재판권을 가지지 않으므로 미합중국 군대의 군속이 범한 범죄에 대하여 대한민국의 형사재판권과 미합중국 군 당국의 형사재판권이 경합하는 문제는 발생할 여지가 없고, 대한민국은 협정 제22조 제1항 (나)에 따라 미합중국 군대의 군속이 대한민국 영역 안에서 저지른 범죄로서 대한민국 법령에 의하여 처벌할 수 있는 범죄에 대한 형사재판권을 바로 행사할 수 있는 것이다."

☑ 해　　설

6.25 전쟁은 1953년 7월 27일 정전협정의 성립으로 전투가 종료되었다. 일반적으로 휴전협정은 전투를 제한적 기간 동안 정지시키는 효과만 있으며 전쟁을 법적으로 종료시키지는 않는다고 해석되고 있다. 한반도의 경우 1953년 정전협정 이후 근 70십년간 휴전상태가 계속되고 있는데, 적어도 법적으로 한국은 여전히 전쟁상태에 있는가? 법적으로 전쟁상태라면 정부는 계엄령 선포 등 막대한 긴급권을 행사할 수 있다.

대법원은 1957년 1월 11일 선고, 4290재신1 결정에서

　　"휴전 협정 후 교전상태가 종식되고 사회질서가 회복되었으므로 평
시라고 운위하나 동란 이후 아(我)정부가 전쟁의 종료를 선명한 사실이
없음은 물론 교통관계가 전연 두절되었을 뿐 아니디 휴전협정은 전투의
일시적 정지에 불과하며 계엄해제가 있고 국내치안의 일시적 평온을 벌
었다 할지라도 이것만으로는 전시상태가 종료되었다 할 수 없고 현하
국가적 위험상태가 의연 계속 중임은 전술 한 바와 같다 할 것이니"

라며 휴전상태인 당시를 평시(平時)로 해석하지 않았다.[1]

　　그러나 휴전 중인 한국이 전시(戰時)라는 법원의 판단은 더 이상 나오지
않았다. 본건과 같은 사안의 처리에 있어서 휴전협정 상태인 한국은 평시로
해석되었다(서울지방법원 2004년 1월 9일 선고, 2001고단3598 판결 참조). 본 판결
역시 이러한 기조의 일환이다.

➡ **참고문헌** ──────────────────────────────

• 박이규, 한반도 평시 상태의 미군 군속에 대한 형사재판권, 대법원 판례해설 제
　62호(2006), p. 495.

──────────────

1) 정인섭, 한국법원에서의 국제법판례(박영사, 2018), p. 153 이하 수록.

3. 개별법상 북한의 법적 지위(2005)

헌법재판소 2005년 6월 30일 선고, 2003헌바114 결정.
헌법재판소판례집 제17권 1집(2005), 879쪽 이하.

☑ **사 안**

이 사건은 2000년 남북 정상회담과 관련하여 발생한 것이다. 청구인은 남북정상회담 준비에 관여한 핵심관료로서 회담 성사를 위해 북한과의 경제 협력사업이라는 명목하에 상당액의 미화를 국내법상의 절차를 밟지 않고 북한측으로 송금되도록 조치했다. 후일 특별검사에 의해 외국환관리법 위반 등으로 기소되자, 북한인을 비거주자, 즉 대한민국 영토에 거주하지 않는 자로 보는 것은 헌법 제3조 영토조항에 위반되어 무효라고 주장했다. 판단과정에 북한지역과 북한인의 법적 지위에 관한 설시가 포함되었다.

☑ **쟁 점**

외국환거래상 북한의 법적 지위.

☑ **판 결**

남북한 특수관계를 고려할 때 북한은 외국에 준하는 지역으로 규정될 수도 있다. 다만 본 사건은 남북교류협력에 관한 법률이라는 특별법이 적용될 대상이므로 북한인이 외국환거래법상의 거주자인지 여부는 논의의 필요가 없다.

결 정 문

(3) "거주자 또는 비거수사" 부분에 대한 판단

(가) '거주자 및 비거주자'의 개념은 외국환거래법 전반에 걸쳐 사용되고 있는 외국환관리의 기본적인 개념이다. 즉, 외국환관리의 원리는 거주자와 비거주자간의 채권·채무 관계를 규제하는 것인바, 거주자와 비거주자를 구분하는 거주성(居住性) 개념은 국적과는 관계없이 일정 기간을 거주하고 있거나 거주할 의사를 가지고 있고 경제적으로 밀착되어 있는 지역을 기준으로 한다. 즉, 외국 국적을 가진 사람이 대한민국에 경제이익의 중심을 두고 있는 경우에는 외국인이라고 하여도 거주자로 취급되므로, 거주성의 개념이 국적과 논리 필연적인 관계에 있는 것은 아니다.

법은 거주자 개념의 중요성을 감안하여 거주자와 비거주자의 개념을 정의하고 있다. 즉, 제3조 1항 12호의 규정에 의하면 "거주자"라 함은 대한민국 안에 주소 또는 거소를 둔 개인과 대한민국 안에 주된 사무소를 둔 법인을 말하고, 동 조항 제13호의 규정에 의하면 "비거주자"라 함은 거주자 외의 개인 및 법인을 말하는데, 다만 비거주자의 대한민국 안의 지점·출장소 기타의 사무소는 법률상 대리권의 유무에 불구하고 거주자로 본다.

이와 같은 거주자 개념 정의는 앞에서 본 거주성의 기본적인 원리에 따른 것이고, 이들 조항에 포함된 단어들은 대부분 법률용어로서 서술적인 개념을 사용하고 있어 그 의미에 혼동을 초래할 정도로 불명확한 것은 없다고 할 것이므로, 죄형법정주의가 요구하는 명확성의 원칙에 위배되는 것이라고 할 수 없다.

(나) 한편, 우리 헌법이 "대한민국의 영토는 한반도와 그 부속도서로 한다"는 영토조항(제3조)을 두고 있는 이상 대한민국의 헌법은 북한지역을 포함한 한반도 전체에 그 효력이 미치고 따라서 북한지역은 당연히 대한민국의 영토가 되므로, 북한을 법 소정의 "외국"으로, 북한의 주민 또는 법인 등을 "비거주자"로 바로 인정하기는 어렵지만, 개별 법률의 적용 내지 준용에 있어서는 남북한의 특수관계적 성격을 고려하여 북한지역을 외국에 준하는 지역으로, 북한주민 등을 외국인에 준하는 지위에 있는 자로 규정할 수 있다

고 할 것이다(대법원 2004년 11월 12일 선고, 2004도4044 판결 참조).

1988. 7. 7. 남북한간의 화해를 위한 6개항의 대북한 제의인 이른바 "7. 7. 선언"이 발표된 후 그 동안 원칙적으로 금지되었던 북한주민과의 접촉, 왕래 및 교류 등을 허용·지원하고, 우리 국민들의 북한 방문 및 남북한 왕래·교류에 대한 요구를 적절히 수용하기 위한 법률적 후속조치로서 남북교류협력에관한법률(이하 '남북교류법'이라 한다)이 1990. 8. 1. 법률 제4239호로 제정되었다. 남북교류법은 군사분계선 이남지역(남한)과 그 이북지역(북한)간의 상호교류와 협력을 촉진하기 위하여 필요한 사항을 규정함을 목적으로 하고 있으며(제1조), 남북교류와 협력을 목적으로 하는 행위에 관하여는 다른 법률에 우선하여 동법을 적용하도록 규정하고 있는(제3조) 점에 비추어 보면 동법은 평화적 통일과 남북교류를 위한 기본법으로서의 성격을 갖고 있다(헌재 2000. 7. 20. 98헌바63, 판례집 12-2, 52, 61 참조).

남북교류법 제26조 3항은 남한과 북한간의 투자, 물품의 반출·반입 기타 경제에 관한 협력사업 및 이에 수반되는 거래에 대하여는 대통령령이 정하는 바에 의하여 외국환거래법 등을 준용하고, 같은 조 제4항은 제3항의 규정에 의하여 다른 법률을 준용함에 있어서는 대통령령으로 그에 대한 특례를 정할 수 있다고 규정하고 있다. 그리고 동법시행령 제50조 6항에서는 동법 제26조 4항의 규정에 의한 특례는 관계 행정기관의 장이 협의회의 의결을 거쳐 고시한다고 규정하고 있으며, 그에 따라 외국환거래법 소정의 거주자 등이 북한에 투자를 목적으로 수행하는 행위 또는 거래에 관하여 외국환거래법을 준용함에 있어 그 특례를 정할 목적으로 1995. 6. 28. 재정경제원 고시 1995-23호로 '대북투자 등에 관한 외국환관리지침'이 제정되었다.

위 규정들을 종합하여 보면, 남한과 북한의 주민(법인, 단체 포함) 사이의 투자 기타 경제에 관한 협력사업 및 이에 수반되는 거래에 대하여는 우선적으로 남북교류법과 동법시행령 및 위 외국환관리지침이 적용되며, 관련 범위 내에서 외국환거래법이 준용된다. 즉, '남한과 북한의 주민'이라는 행위 주체 사이에 '투자 기타 경제에 관한 협력사업'이라는 행위를 할 경우에는 남북교류법이 다른 법률보다 우선적으로 적용되고, 필요한 범위 내에서 외국환거래법 등이 준용되는 것이다.

그 결과 당해 사건과 같이 남한과 북한 주민 사이의 외국환 거래에 대하여는 법 제15조 3항에 규정되어 있는 "거주자 또는 비거주자" 부분, 즉 대한민국 안에 주소를 둔 개인 또는 법인인지 여부가 문제되는 것이 아니라, 남북교류법 제26조 3항의 "남한과 북한,"즉 군사분계선 이남지역과 그 이북지역의 주민인지 여부가 문제되는 것이다. 즉, 외국환거래의 일방 당사자가 북한의 주민일 경우 그는 이 사건 법률조항의 '거주자' 또는 '비거주자'가 아니라 남북교류법의 '북한의 주민'에 해당하는 것이다. 그러므로, 당해 사건에서 아태위원회가 법 제15조 3항에서 말하는 '거주자'나 '비거주자'에 해당하는지 또는 남북교류법상 '북한의 주민'에 해당하는지 여부는 위에서 본 바와 같은 법률해석의 문제에 불과한 것이고, 헌법 제3조의 영토조항과는 관련이 없는 것이다.

☑ 해 설

헌법 제3조 영토조항에 근거하여 규범적으로는 북한지역을 외국이 아닌 대한민국 영토의 일부로 간주하는 경우도 많지만, 이러한 처리가 비현실적이어서 북한을 외국으로 북한인을 외국인으로 취급하여야 할 경우도 많다. 본 결정에도 후자의 가능성에 관한 일반적 설시가 포함되어 있다. 북한을 외국으로 전제하는 대표적 사례로는 간첩죄 적용상 북한을 적국으로 취급하는 경우를 들 수 있다(대법원 1958년 9월 26일 선고, 4291형사352 판결; 대법원 1982년 11월 23일 선고, 82도2201 판결; 대법원 1983년 3월 22일 선고, 82도3036 판결 등).[1]

---

1) 정인섭, 한국법원에서의 국제법 판례(박영사, 2018), p. 149 이하 참조.

4. 북한 주민의 국적(2016)

대법원 2016년 1월 28일 선고, 2011두24675 판결.
판례공보 2016년(상), 358쪽 이하.

☑ 사   안

「대일항쟁기 강제동원 피해조사 및 국외강제동원 희생자 등 지원에 관한 특별법」은 1938년 4월 1일부터 1945년 8월 15일 사이에 일제에 의하여 군인·군무원 또는 노무자 등으로 국외로 강제동원되어 그 기간 중 또는 국내로 돌아오는 과정에서 사망하거나 행방불명된 사람 또는 대통령령으로 정하는 부상으로 장해를 입은 국외강제동원 희생자 또는 그 유족에게 일정한 위로금 등을 지원하도록 규정하고 있다(제2조, 제4조). 다만 지원 제외대상의 하나로 '대한민국의 국적을 갖고 있지 아니한 사람'(제7조 제4호)이 규정되어 있다. 이 소송 원고의 형은 1943년 일제에 의해 노무자로 동원되었다가, 종전 후 북한으로 귀환해 북한에 거주하다 사망했다. 원고는 6.25 전쟁 당시 남한으로 월남했다. 일제강점하강제동원피해진상규명위원회는 원고의 형을 일제강점하 강제동원 피해자로 결정했다. 이에 원고는 위법에 따른 위로금 지급을 신청했으나, 행정 당국은 형이 북한적자로서 대한민국 국적을 갖고 있지 아니한 사람에 해당한다는 이유로 지급을 거절했다.

☑ 쟁   점

북한적자는 "대한민국 국적을 갖지 아니한 사람"인가?

☑ 판   결

북한적자 역시 대한민국 국적을 가진 자에 해당한다.

판 결 문

"1. […] 강제동원조사법은 1965년에 체결된 「대한민국과 일본국 간의 재산 및 청구권에 관한 문제의 해결과 경제협력에 관한 협정」과 관련하여 국가가 태평양전쟁 전후 국외강제동원 희생자와 그 유족 등에게 인도적 차원에서 위로금 등을 지원함으로써 이들의 고통을 치유하고 국민화합에 기여함을 목적으로 제정된 것으로서, […] ② 우리 헌법이 대한민국의 영토는 한반도와 그 부속도서로 한다는 영토조항을 두고 있는 이상 대한민국 헌법은 북한 지역을 포함한 한반도 전체에 그 효력이 미치는 것이므로 북한 지역도 당연히 대한민국의 영토가 되고, 북한주민 역시 일반적으로 대한민국 국민에 포함된다고 보아야 하는 점, ③ 강제동원조사법은 위로금 지원 제외대상을 '대한민국 국적을 갖지 아니한 사람'으로 정하고 있을 뿐, 북한주민을 그 지원 대상에서 제외하는 명시적인 규정을 두고 있지 않은 점, ④ 일제에 의한 강제동원으로 인한 피해를 입은 사람 등의 고통을 치유하고자 하는 위법의 입법 목적에 비추어 그 적용 범위를 남북 분단과 6·25 등으로 그 의사와 무관하게 북한정권의 사실상 지배 아래 놓이게 된 군사분계선 이북 지역의 주민 또는 그의 유족을 배제하는 방향으로 축소 해석할 이유가 있다고 볼 수 없는 점 등을 종합하여 보면, 북한주민은 강제동원조사법상 위로금 지급 제외대상인 '대한민국 국적을 갖지 아니한 사람'에 해당하지 않는다고 보는 것이 타당하다.

2. 원심은 제1심판결 이유를 인용하여, 망인이 1943. 5. 1. 일제에 의해 일본지역에 노무자로 강제동원되었다가 1945년 이후 북한 지역으로 돌아온 후 6·25 당시 북한 지역에 남게 된 사실을 인정한 다음, 대한민국 헌법 제정 당시 시행 중이던 남조선과도정부법률 제11호 국적에 관한 임시조례 제2조 제1호, 제2호는 조선인을 부친으로 하여 출생한 자는 조선의 국적을 가지는 것으로 규정하고 있고, 제헌헌법은 제3조에서 대한민국의 국민이 되는 요건을 법률로써 정한다고 규정하면서 제100조에서 현행 법령은 이 헌법에 저촉되지 아니하는 한 효력을 가진다고 규정하고 있으므로, 제헌헌법 공포 당시 조선인을 부모로 하여 출생하는 등의 요건을 갖추어 위 임시조례의 규정

에 따라 조선국적을 취득한 사람은 1948. 7. 17. 제헌헌법의 공포와 동시에 대한민국 국적을 취득하였다고 할 것이고, 설령 망인이 북한법의 규정에 따라 북한국적을 취득하였다고 하더라도 북한 지역 역시 대한민국의 영토에 속하는 한반도의 일부를 이루는 것이어서 대한민국의 주권이 미치므로 그러한 사정은 망인이 대한민국 국적을 취득하고 이를 유지하는 데 영향을 미칠 수 없다는 이유로, 망인이 이 사건 특별법상 위로금 지급 제외대상인 '대한민국의 국적을 갖지 아니한 사람'에 해당함을 전제로 한 이 사건 처분이 위법하다고 판단하였다.

앞서 본 법리에 비추어 보면 원심의 이러한 판단은 정당하고, 거기에 강제동원조사법상의 위로금 지원 제외대상 등의 해석에 관한 법리를 오해한 위법이 없다."

☑ 해 설

이 판결 이전에도 북한적자면 국내에서는 당연히 대한민국 국민으로 인정한 판례로는 대법원 1994년 8월 26일 선고, 94누3223 판결; 대법원 1996년 11월 12일 선고, 96누1221 판결 등이 있다.

대법원 1990년 9월 28일 선고, 89누6396 판결.
대법원 판례집 제38권 3집(특별)(1990), 161쪽 이하.

☑ 사   안

이 사건 원고는 납북 및 월북된 작가의 작품을 국내에서 출판하려고 하였다. 단 이들 납월북 작가나 그들의 유족으로부터 저작권 사용동의는 받은 바 없었다. 과거 한국정부는 납북 또는 월북 작가의 작품을 국내에서 출판 판매하는 것을 금하고 있었는데, 원고는 정부의 납월북 작가 작품 출판금지처분이 무효라고 주장했다. 재판과정에서는 납월북 작가의 저작물에 대하여도 대한민국 저작권법이 적용되는가 여부도 쟁점의 하나로 제기되었다. 대법원은 납월북 작가 또는 상속인으로부터 저작물 이용권을 허락받지 않은 원고는 이 같은 소송을 제기할 자격 자체가 없다고 판단했다.

☑ 쟁   점

북한지역 거주자의 저작물에 대한 대한민국 저작권법의 적용 여부.

☑ 판   결

대한민국 저작권법은 북한지역에도 적용된다.

판 결 문

저작권법의 규정들(제36조 제1항, 제41조, 제42조, 제47조 제1항)에 의하면 저작자의 저작물을 복제, 배포, 발행하고자 하는 자는 저작자로부터 저작재산권의 일부 또는 전부를 양수하거나 그의 저작물 이용허락을 받아야 하고, 상당한 노력을 기울였어도 공표된 저작물의 저작재산권자나 그의 거소를 알수 없어 그 저작물의 이용허락을 받을 수 없는 경우에는 대통령령이 정하는 바에 의하여 문화부장관(정부조직법 1989. 12. 30. 법률 제4183호 부칙 제6조)의 승인을 얻고 문화부장관이 소정의 보상금기준에 의하여 정한 보상금을 공탁하고 이를 이용할 수 있다고 되어 있으며, 이러한 저작재산권은 특별한 경우를 제외하고는 저작자가 생존하는 동안과 사망 후 50년간 존속한다고 규정하고 있다. 그리고 이 법규정의 효력은 대한민국 헌법 제3조에 의하여 여전히 대한민국의 주권범위 내에 있는 북한지역에도 미치는 것이다. 원심판결 목록기재 저작자들은 모두 6·25 사변 전후에 납북되거나 월북한 문인들로서, 그들이 저작한 위 목록기재 작품들을 발행하려면 아직 그 저작재산권의 존속기간이 만료되지 아니하였음이 역수상 명백한 만큼, 동인들이나 그 상속인들로부터 저작재산권의 양수 또는 저작물이용허락을 받거나 문화부장관의 승인을 얻었음을 인정할 자료가 없는 이 사건에 있어서 원고는 이 사건 처분의 부존재확인을 구할 법률상 지위에 있는 자라고 할 수 없다 할 것이고, 헌법상 국민에게 부여된 출판의 자유로부터도 확인을 구할 법률상의 지위가 부여된다고는 볼 수 없다 할 것이므로 이 사건 처분의 부존재확인을 구하는 원고의 예비적 청구에 관한 소 역시 원고적격이 없어 부적법하다 할 것이고, […] 그렇다면 원고의 이 사건 주위적 청구 및 예비적 청구인 이 사건무효 내지 부존재확인을 구하는 청구에 관한 소는 모두 부적법하여 각하하여야 할 것인바, 원심판결은 이와 결론이 같아 원심판결의 위와 같은 법리오해의 위법이 판결의 결과에 영향을 미친 바 되지 못하므로 결국 상고논지는 모두 이유 없음에 돌아간다 할 것이다.

☑ 해 설

북한 주민의 저작물도 대한민국 저작권법의 보호대상이 된다는 여타의 판례로는 서울민사지방법원 1989년 7월 26일 선고, 89카13692 판결; 서울지방법원 1996년 9월 12일 선고, 96노3819 판결; 서울고등법원 2006년 3월 29일 선고, 2004나14033 판결 등이 있다.

➡ 참고문헌 ─────────────────────────────────

• 강병근, 남한에서의 북한저삭물 보호, 국제판례연구 1집(1999), p. 164.
• 박성호, 북한저작물의 현행 저작권법상 이용방법, 인권과 정의 183호(1991년 11월), p. 61.
• 이은정, 남북교류와 지적 재산권의 보호, 남북교류와 관련한 법적 문제점: 특수 사법제도연구위원회 제6 · 7차 회의 결과보고(법원행정처, 2002), p. 107.
• 김영기, 북한저작물 보호를 위한 준거법 결정을 둘러싼 우리나라 판례의 비판적 고찰: 북한의 베른협약 가입에 따른 논의를 포함하여, 법조 2012년 4월호, p. 243.
• 이종석, 북한 저작물의 법적 보호, (대구판례연구회) 재판과 판례 11집(2002), p. 323.
• 김형진, 북한 저작물의 출판권 문제: 서울고등법원 2004나 14033 손해배상, 저작권문화 제142호(2006).

판례색인

한국판례

사항색인

공저자약력

정인섭
서울대학교 법과대학 및 동대학원 졸업(법학박사)
국가인권위원회 인권위원 역임(2004 – 2007)
대한국제법학회 회장 역임(2009)
인권법학회 회장(2015 – 2017)
현: 서울대학교 법학전문대학원 명예교수

주요저서
재일교포의 법적 지위(서울대학교출판부, 1996)
국제인권규약과 개인통보제도(사람생각, 2000)
신국제법강의(제10판)(박영사, 2020)
에센스 국제조약집(개정4판)(박영사, 2020)
생활 속의 국제법 읽기(일조각, 2012)
조약법강의(박영사, 2016)
신국제법입문(제3판)(박영사, 2019)
한국법원에서의 국제법판례(박영사, 2018)
국제법 시험 25년(박영사, 2020)
국제법 학업 이력서(박영사, 2020)
Korean Questions in the United Nations(Seoul National University Press, 2002) 외.

이재민
서울대학교 법과대학 및 동대학원 졸업(법학박사)
미국 Georgetown University Law Center(LL.M.), Boston College Law School 졸업(Juris Doctor)
한양대학교 법과대학/법학전문대학원 조교수, 부교수, 교수(2004 – 2013)
한국국제경제법학회장(2020)
현: 서울대학교 법학전문대학원 교수

주요저서 및 논문
WTO 보조금 협정상 "위임 및 지시" 보조금의 법적 의미(경인문화사, 2008)
신통상법 및 통상정책(2인 공저, 박영사, 2012)
금융위기 극복을 위한 정부 및 기업의 조치와 국제통상법(박영사, 2016) 외.

정서용
서울대학교 법과대학 법학사, 법학석사 및 박사과정 수료
영국 런던정경대학교(LSE) 국제관계학 석사(Diploma)
미국 스탠포드대학교 법학석사(JSM), 법학박사(JSD)
대통령직속 녹색성장위원회 민간위원 역임
바젤협약 이행준수위원회 위원(부의장) 역임
서울국제법연구원 기후환경법정책센터 센터장
현: 고려대학교 국제학부 교수

주요저서 및 논문
동북아시아 환경협력: 황해와 황사(아산재단연구총서, 집문당, 2005)
글로벌 기후변화 거버넌스와 국제법(박영사, 2011) 외.

신국제법판례 120선

초판발행	2020년 10월 30일
지은이	정인섭·이재민·정서용
펴낸이	안종만·안상준
편 집	김선민
기획/마케팅	조성호
표지디자인	조아라
제 작	우인도·고철민·조영환
펴낸곳	(주) **박영사**
	서울특별시 금천구 가산디지털2로 53, 210호(가산동, 한라시그마밸리)
	등록 1959. 3. 11. 제300-1959-1호(倫)
전 화	02)733-6771
f a x	02)736-4818
e-mail	pys@pybook.co.kr
homepage	www.pybook.co.kr
ISBN	979-11-303-3670-1 93360

정 가	42,000원